D0064064

ZAGAT
2017

New York City
Restaurants

EDITOR
Emily Rothschild

PRODUCTION EDITOR
Aynsley Karps

DESIGNER
Thea Kluge Carter

COORDINATOR
Larry Cohn

Published and distributed by
Zagat Survey, LLC
76 Ninth Avenue, New York, NY 10011
feedback@zagat.com
www.zagat.com

ABOUT ZAGAT

In 1979, we asked friends to rate and review restaurants purely for fun. The term "user-generated content" had yet to be coined. That hobby grew into Zagat; 38 years later, we have a loyal network of avid restaurant reviewers. Along the way, we evolved from being a print publisher to a digital content provider. You can find us on our new iPhone app, zagat.com and across the Google products you use every day.

The reviews in this guide are based on feedback from in-the-know diners. The ratings reflect the average scores submitted for each establishment, while the text is based on quotes from diners, curated by expert Zagat editors. Ratings and reviews have been updated throughout this edition based on our most recent results. Phone numbers, addresses and other factual data were correct to the best of our knowledge when published in this guide.

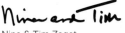

Nina & Tim Zagat

ACKNOWLEDGMENTS

First and foremost, we thank the thousands of people who contributed ratings and reviews — they are the real authors of this guide. We also thank Daniel Balgley, Erinn Blicher, Sarina Bloodgood, Shandana Durrani, Caley Goldblatt, Karen Hudes, Katharine Hylton, Francis Lewis, Lacey Muszynski, Bernard Onken, Jason Orlovich, Kayla Parent, Catherine Quayle, Emily Saladino, Elaine Simpson, Veronika Taylor and Anna Zappia, as well as the following members of our staff: Reni Chin, Carol Diuguid, Kelly Dobkin, Randi Gollin, Justin Hartung, Tiffany Herklots, Alex Horowitz, Ryutaro Ishikane, Miranda Levenstein, Polina Paley, Albry Smither, Amanda Spurlock, Nika Vagner, Art Yagci and Kyle Zolner.

JOIN IN

To improve our guides, we solicit your comments — positive or negative; it's vital that we hear your opinions. Just contact us at **feedback@zagat.com**.

© 2016 Zagat Survey, LLC
ISBN-13: 978-1-60478-796-2
ISBN-10: 1-60478-796-1
Printed in the United States of America

CONTENTS

QUICK GUIDES

RESTAURANT DIRECTORY

INDEXES

Special features

NYC AT A GLANCE

NEWS

It's been a big year for Zagat. In addition to debuting a snazzy new logo, we've simplified our ratings system, moving from a scale of 0–30 points to 1.0–5.0 points (see the legend on the inside cover). We still provide separate ratings for Food, Decor and Service. And our expertly curated reviews still highlight opinions from avid diners (now bolded). We trust they'll continue to help you discover the best dining experiences. Bon appétit!

KEY STATS

2,171
RESTAURANTS

102
NEW RESTAURANTS

51
NEW BRANCHES
OF EXISTING PLACES

126
NEIGHBORHOODS
COVERED

98
CUISINES COVERED

BIG WINNERS

TOP FOOD
LE BERNARDIN

TOP DECOR
ASIATE

TOP SERVICE
LE BERNARDIN

TOP NEWCOMER
KINGSLEY

MOST POPULAR
LE BERNARDIN

BOROUGH CHAMPS

🅱️ **CHEF'S TABLE AT BROOKLYN FARE**

🆀 **TRATTORIA L'INCONTRO**

🆁 **ROBERTO'S**

🆂 **TRATTORIA ROMANA**

TOP FOODS

BAGELS
ABSOLUTE BAGELS

COFFEE
LA COLOMBE

DIM SUM
PACIFICANA

DONUTS
PETER PAN DONUT

DUMPLINGS
KUNG FU RAMEN

ICE CREAM
AMPLE HILLS CREAMERY

LOBSTER ROLL
PEARL OYSTER BAR

PIZZA
JULIANA'S

RAMEN
MU RAMEN

SANDWICHES
ALIDORO

TACOS
LOS TACOS

TRENDS

BIG TRENDS

PIZZA AND PASTA RESURGENCE If there was any doubt that low-carb hysteria is o-v-e-r, this year settled it. In a matter of months, pasta- and pizza-centric places like **Emmy Squared**, **La Sirena**, **Lilia** and **Pasquale Jones** opened and became immediate hot spots.

POKE HITS NYC Poke, Hawaii's answer to sushi, also had a big moment with the arrival of popular stops like **Chikarashi**, **Sons of Thunder** and **Wisefish Poke**. Sweetcatch Poke from the **Kang Ho Dong Baekjeong** team is also on the way.

THE VEGGIE BURGER CRAZE CONTINUES Ignited by Daniel Humm (**NoMad Bar**) and Brooks Headley (**Superiority Burger**) over the past few years, the unexpected rise of the humble veggie burger continues, as evidenced by the lines at **by Chloe** and **Momofuku Nishi**, where David Chang debuted his 'impossible burger.'

FOOD HALLS KEEP COMING Building on last year's crop (**City Kitchen**, **Le District**, **UrbanSpace Vanderbilt**), a glut of new arrivals including **The Great Northern Food Hall**, **Union Fare**, **The Pennsy** and **TurnStyle** continued the trend, and there are plenty more on the horizon.

Here's a look at how New Yorkers feel about some of these trends:

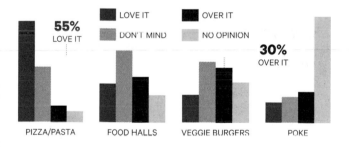

OTHER TRENDS

NO TIPPING POLICIES GAINED IN POPULARITY Many newcomers including **Agern**, **Faun**, **Freek's Mill**, **Pasquale Jones** and **Teisui** joined a growing number of established favorites like **Dirt Candy**, **Huertas**, **Eleven Madison Park** and Danny Meyer restaurants (**The Modern**, **Maialino**) in raising prices to eliminate tipping.

INDIAN FOOD HEATS UP Indian Accent, **Paowalla**, **Pondicheri** and **Tapestry** were among the buzzy places to lift NYC's Indian dining scene.

DISH DÉJÀ VU Kale salad, pricey roast chicken and lobster mac 'n' cheese led the field of ubiquitous dishes diners said they were tired of seeing.

KEY NEWCOMERS

MIDTOWN / MURRAY HILL

AGERN | Sophisticated Scandinavian fare in Grand Central

HER NAME IS HAN | Hot spot for homestyle Korean cooking

INDIAN ACCENT | High-end Indian tasting menus

MOMOSAN | Ramen from *Iron Chef* Masaharu Morimoto

CHELSEA / MEATPACKING / FLATIRON

HIGH STREET ON HUDSON | Bakery/American restaurant from Philly

GUNTER SEEGER | European prix fixe dining

LA SIRENA | Splashy Italian from Mario Batali

LE COQ RICO | Refined chicken-focused bistro

MOMOFUKU NISHI | David Chang's latest for Asian fusion

EAST VILLAGE / LES

DINNERTABLE | Tiny, hidden spot for creative American dinners

KINGSLEY | Market-driven French-American cooking

LE TURTLE | Modern French bistro with hip accents

LUCKY BEE | Seasonal Southeast Asian street food

GREENWICH VILLAGE / SOHO / NOLITA

CAFE ALTRO PARADISO | Italian follow-up to Estela

LE COUCOU | Classic French cooking in an elegant setting

MIMI | Polished French fare in cozy, candlelit digs

NIX | Ambitious vegetarian dining from John Fraser

PAOWALLA | Goa-inspired Indian food via Floyd Cardoz

PASQUALE JONES | Charlie Bird sib for pizza and Italian fare

SUSHI ZO | High-end branch of an LA sushi restaurant

BROOKLYN

EMMY SQUARED | Detroit-style pizza from the Emily team

LILIA | Instant hit for Italian fare by Missy Robbins

LLAMA INN | Buzzy Peruvian joint with a big bar

OLMSTED | Farm-to-table hot spot with an urban garden

SAUVAGE | Oysters, American fare and cocktails

PROJECTS ON TAP

ABCV | Jean-Georges' much-delayed vegan/vegetarian restaurant

AUGUSTINE | French bistro from Keith McNally in the Financial District's Beekman Hotel

CUT BY WOLFGANG PUCK | Upscale steakhouse chain in Downtown's Four Seasons Hotel and Wolfgang Puck's first-ever NYC restaurant

FOWLER & WELLS | Modern American dining from Tom Colicchio in the Beekman Hotel

HWA YUAN | Grand revival of a classic Chinese restaurant in its original Chinatown digs

LEUCA | Andrew Carmellini does coastal-inspired Italian cuisine in Williamsburg's William Vale Hotel

UNION SQUARE CAFE | Danny Meyer's iconic New American reopens farther north in a new space

WHITE GOLD | Part butcher shop, part steakhouse on the UWS from April Bloomfield

*For more information on hot openings and to rate and review restaurants, visit **zagat.com**.*

For info on even more hot openings and to see what's new in your 'hood, download the new Zagat app for iPhone. Check it out at zagat.com/app

MOST POPULAR

1	**LE BERNARDIN** | Fr./Seafood	**26**	**KEENS STEAKHOUSE** | Steak
2	**GRAMERCY TAVERN** | Amer.	**27**	**WOLFGANG'S** | Steak
3	**PETER LUGER** | Steak	**28**	**SHAKE SHACK** | Burgers
4	**GOTHAM B&G** | American	**29**	**2ND AVE DELI** | Deli/Kosher
5	**BOULEY** | French	**30**	**THE MODERN** | Amer./French
6	**JEAN-GEORGES** | French	**31**	**BAR BOULUD** | French
7	**DANIEL** | French	**32**	**BOULUD SUD*** | Med.
8	**ATLANTIC GRILL** | Seafood	**33**	**ROSA MEXICANO** | Mexican
9	**MAREA** | Italian/Seafood	**34**	**CARMINE'S** | Italian
10	**CAPITAL GRILLE** | Steak	**35**	**AQUAGRILL** | Seafood
11	**ELEVEN MADISON** | American	**36**	**5 NAPKIN BURGER** | Burgers
12	**KATZ'S DELICATESSEN** | Deli	**37**	**MILOS** | Greek/Seafood
13	**BALTHAZAR** | French	**38**	**PER SE** | American/French
14	**DEL POSTO*** | Italian	**39**	**LINCOLN** | Italian
15	**BABBO** | Italian	**40**	**BLUE WATER GRILL** | Seafood
16	**CAFÉ BOULUD** | French	**41**	**FELIDIA** | Italian
17	**21 CLUB** | American	**42**	**GRAND CENT. OYSTER** | Seafood
18	**LA GRENOUILLE** | French	**43**	**AUREOLE** | American
19	**BECCO** | Italian	**44**	**GABRIEL KREUTHER** | French
20	**IL MULINO** | Italian	**45**	**CAFE LUXEMBOURG** | French
21	**JEAN-GEORGES' NOUG.** | Fr.	**46**	**EATALY** | Food Hall/Italian
22	**ABC KITCHEN** | American	**47**	**FIG & OLIVE** | Med.
23	**DEL FRISCO'S** | Steak	**48**	**THE SMITH** | American
24	**THE PALM** | Steak	**49**	**SMITH & WOLLENSKY** | Steak
25	**NOBU** | Japanese	**50**	**LE CIRQUE** | French

Lists exclude places with low votes, unless otherwise indicated

* Indicates a tie with restaurant above

WINNERS

TOP FOOD

4.9 **LE BERNARDIN** | Fr./Seafood
4.9 **BOULEY** | French
4.8 **JEAN-GEORGES** | French
4.8 **DANIEL** | French
4.8 **GOTHAM B&G** | Amer.
4.8 **PETER LUGER** | Steak
4.8 **GABRIEL KREUTHER** | French
4.8 **TOCQUEVILLE** | Amer./French
4.8 **GRAMERCY TAVERN** | Amer.
4.8 **SUSHI YASUDA** | Japanese
4.7 **LA GRENOUILLE** | French
4.7 **ELEVEN MADISON PARK** | Amer.
4.7 **MAREA** | Ital./Seafood
4.7 **BLUE HILL** | American
4.7 **DEL POSTO** | Italian
4.7 **TANOREEN** | Med./Mideast.
4.7 **CAFÉ BOULUD** | French
4.7 **JEAN-GEORGES' NOUG.** | Fr.
4.7 **SCALINI FEDELI** | Italian
4.7 **SUSHI NAKAZAWA** | Japanese

4.7 **NOBU** | Japanese
4.7 **TRATTORIA L'INCONTRO** | It.
4.7 **DON PEPPE** | Italian
4.7 **ANNISA** | American
4.7 **MAS (FARMHOUSE)** | Amer.
4.7 **MILOS** | Greek/Seafood
4.7 **AMMA** | Indian
4.7 **AQUAGRILL** | Seafood
4.7 **L'ARTUSI** | Italian
4.7 **TAMARIND** | Indian
4.6 **THE MODERN** | Amer./French
4.6 **RIVER CAFÉ** | American
4.6 **BRUSHSTROKE** | Japanese
4.6 **PER SE** | Amer./French
4.6 **SEA FIRE GRILL** | Seafood
4.6 **DOVETAIL** | American
4.6 **BABBO** | Italian
4.6 **PEARL OYSTER** | New Eng./Sea.
4.6 **HOMETOWN** | BBQ
4.6 **SUSHI OF GARI** | Japanese

TOP DECOR

4.8 **ASIATE**
4.8 **DANIEL**
4.8 **LE BERNARDIN**
4.8 **BOULEY**
4.8 **LA GRENOUILLE**
4.8 **RIVER CAFÉ**
4.8 **ELEVEN MADISON PARK**
4.7 **PER SE**
4.7 **JEAN-GEORGES**
4.7 **RAINBOW ROOM**

4.7 **DEL POSTO**
4.7 **GABRIEL KREUTHER**
4.7 **GRAND TIER**
4.7 **RIVERPARK**
4.7 **ONE IF BY LAND, TWO IF BY SEA**
4.7 **TOCQUEVILLE**
4.7 **GOTHAM BAR & GRILL**
4.6 **VAUCLUSE**
4.6 **BUDDAKAN**
4.6 **LEOPARD AT DES ARTISTES**

TOP SERVICE

4.9 **LE BERNARDIN**
4.9 **BOULEY**
4.8 **DANIEL**
4.8 **JEAN-GEORGES**
4.8 **ELEVEN MADISON PARK**
4.7 **GOTHAM BAR & GRILL**
4.7 **GRAMERCY TAVERN**
4.7 **LA GRENOUILLE**
4.7 **GABRIEL KREUTHER**
4.7 **DEL POSTO**

4.7 **BLUE HILL**
4.7 **MAS (FARMHOUSE)**
4.7 **PER SE**
4.7 **SCALINI FEDELI**
4.7 **SUSHI NAKAZAWA**
4.6 **RIVER CAFÉ**
4.6 **THE SIMONE**
4.6 **TOCQUEVILLE**
4.6 **CAFÉ BOULUD**
4.6 **ASIATE**

TOP LISTS

TOPS BY CUISINE/SPECIALTY

AMERICAN
4.8 KINGSLEY
4.8 GOTHAM BAR & GRILL
4.8 TOCQUEVILLE
4.8 GRAMERCY TAVERN
4.7 UPHOLSTERY STORE
4.7 ELEVEN MADISON PARK
4.7 BLUE HILL
4.7 MOMOFUKU KO
4.7 ANNISA
4.7 MAS (FARMHOUSE)
4.7 BLANCA
4.7 MEADOWSWEET

ASIAN
4.6 ASIATE
4.4 BUDDAKAN
4.4 TALDE
4.4 ASIA DE CUBA
4.3 MOMOFUKU NISHI
4.3 NYONYA
4.3 MIMI CHENG'S DUMPLINGS
4.3 SALT & FAT

AUSTRIAN/GERMAN
4.6 WALLSÉ
4.5 ZUM STAMMTISCH
4.4 CAFE KATJA
4.3 BLAUE GANS
4.3 FREUD NYC
4.2 NURNBERGER BIERHAUS
4.2 CAFÉ FLEDERMAUS
4.2 EDI & THE WOLF

BAGELS
4.6 ABSOLUTE BAGELS
4.4 ESS-A-BAGEL
4.4 TOMPKINS SQUARE BAGELS
4.3 KOSSAR'S BAGELS & BIALYS
4.3 MURRAY'S BAGELS
4.3 SADELLE'S
4.3 BAGELWORKS

4.3 LEO'S BAGELS
4.2 ZUCKER'S BAGELS
4.1 BLACK SEED BAGELS

BAKERIES
4.7 LEVAIN BAKERY
4.6 BREADS BAKERY
4.5 MADONIA BROTHERS BAKERY
4.5 ARCADE BAKERY
4.5 ORWASHER'S BAKERY
4.5 FOUR & TWENTY BLACKBIRDS
4.5 DOMINIQUE ANSEL BAKERY
4.5 PANEANTICO

BARBECUE
4.6 HOMETOWN BBQ
4.5 FETTE SAU
4.3 BUTCHER BAR
4.3 MIGHTY QUINN'S BARBECUE
4.3 JOHN BROWN SMOKEHOUSE
4.2 DINOSAUR BAR-B-QUE
4.2 HILL COUNTRY
4.1 FLETCHER'S BBQ

BURGER JOINTS
4.4 BLACK IRON BURGER
4.4 SUPERIORITY BURGER
4.4 BURGER JOINT
4.3 AMSTERDAM BURGER CO.
4.2 CORNER BISTRO
4.2 BLACK TAP
4.2 BURGER & BARREL
4.1 BONNIE'S GRILL

CARIBBEAN/CUBAN
4.4 ALI'S ROTI
4.4 ASIA DE CUBA
4.3 VICTOR'S CAFE
4.3 CUBA
4.2 MALECON
4.1 MISS LILY'S
4.1 CAFÉ HABANA
4.1 HABANA OUTPOST

CHICKEN

4.3 PIO PIO
4.2 FUKU
4.2 BONCHON
4.1 HILL COUNTRY CHICKEN
4.1 BLUE RIBBON FRIED CHICKEN
4.0 COCO ROCO
4.0 KYOCHON CHICKEN
3.8 STREETBIRD

CHINESE

4.7 DECOY
4.5 PACIFICANA
4.5 WU LIANG YE
4.4 REDFARM
4.4 HAKKASAN
4.4 CAFE CHINA
4.4 SPICY & TASTY
4.4 LA CHINE

COFFEE

4.4 LA COLOMBE COFFEE
4.3 NINTH STREET ESPRESSO
4.3 BLUESTONE LANE
4.2 BLUE BOTTLE COFFEE
4.2 PICCOLO CAFE
4.1 BIRCH COFFEE
4.1 TOBY'S ESTATE COFFEE
4.1 JOE

DELIS

4.7 RUSS & DAUGHTERS
4.5 SHELSKY'S OF BROOKLYN
4.5 KATZ'S DELICATESSEN
4.5 BARNEY GREENGRASS
4.5 SABLE'S SMOKED FISH
4.4 HARRY & IDA'S
4.3 LIEBMAN'S DELICATESSEN
4.3 B & H DAIRY

DESSERT (see also Bakeries, Ice Cream, Donuts)

4.6 TWO LITTLE RED HENS
4.6 JACQUES TORRES
4.6 LADY M CAKE BOUTIQUE
4.5 PETER PAN DONUT
4.5 CHIKALICIOUS
4.5 COURT PASTRY SHOP
4.4 VENIERO'S PASTRY
4.4 CHOCOLATE ROOM

DIM SUM

4.5 PACIFICANA
4.4 REDFARM
4.4 HAKKASAN
4.3 ORIENTAL GARDEN
4.3 MÁ PÊCHE
4.1 NOM WAH TEA PARLOR
4.1 JING FONG
4.1 GOLDEN UNICORN

DONUTS

4.5 PETER PAN DONUT
4.5 ORWASHER'S BAKERY
4.4 DOUGH
4.3 DUN-WELL DOUGHNUTS
4.3 DOUGHNUT PLANT
4.2 THE DONUT PUB

DUMPLINGS

4.4 KUNG FU RAMEN
4.4 TALDE
4.3 SHANGHAI CAFE
4.3 MIMI CHENG'S DUMPLINGS
4.3 TASTY HAND-PULLED
4.2 THE BAO
4.2 DELUXE GREEN BO
4.2 JOE'S SHANGHAI

FOOD HALLS

4.3 EATALY
4.3 SMORGASBURG
4.2 URBANSPACE VANDERBILT
4.1 NEW WORLD MALL
4.1 GOTHAM WEST MARKET
4.1 HUDSON EATS
4.1 LE DISTRICT
4.1 PLAZA FOOD HALL

FRENCH

4.9 LE BERNARDIN
4.9 BOULEY
4.8 KINGSLEY
4.8 JEAN-GEORGES
4.8 DANIEL
4.8 CHEF'S TABLE / BROOKLYN
4.8 GABRIEL KREUTHER
4.8 TOCQUEVILLE

FRENCH BISTRO

4.6 WALLFLOWER
4.5 LE GIGOT
4.5 RAOUL'S
4.4 FRENCH LOUIE
4.4 DB BISTRO MODERNE
4.4 LA SIRÈNE
4.3 BAR BOULUD
4.3 LUCIEN

GLUTEN-FREE OPTIONS

4.7 DEL POSTO
4.5 RUBIROSA
4.5 DON ANTONIO
4.5 BETONY
4.4 CARACAS
4.4 ALTA
4.4 CANDLE 79
4.4 KESTE PIZZA

GREEK

4.7 MILOS
4.6 AVRA
4.5 PYLOS
4.5 TAVERNA KYCLADES
4.5 LOUKOUMI TAVERNA
4.5 ELIÁ
4.5 THALASSA
4.5 ELIAS CORNER

ICE CREAM

4.7 AMPLE HILLS CREAMERY
4.6 IL LABORATORIO
4.6 LEMON ICE KING OF CORONA

4.5 GROM
4.5 EDDIE'S SWEET SHOP
4.5 DAVEY'S ICE CREAM
4.5 CONES ICE CREAM ARTISANS
4.4 RALPH'S FAMOUS ITALIAN

INDIAN

4.7 INDIAN ACCENT
4.7 AMMA
4.7 TAMARIND
4.5 BABU JI
4.4 DAWAT
4.4 SARAVANAA BHAVAN
4.4 VATAN
4.4 TULSI

ITALIAN

4.7 MAREA
4.7 DEL POSTO
4.7 SCALINI FEDELI
4.7 ALIDORO
4.7 TRATTORIA L'INCONTRO
4.7 DON PEPPE
4.7 L'ARTUSI
4.6 ANTICA PESA
4.6 BABBO
4.6 LUPA
4.6 PICCOLA VENEZIA
4.6 AL DI LA

JAPANESE/SUSHI

4.8 SUSHI YASUDA
4.7 KYO YA
4.7 SUSHI NAKAZAWA
4.7 NOBU
4.7 SOTO
4.6 SASABUNE
4.6 TANOSHI SUSHI
4.6 BRUSHSTROKE / ICHIMURA
4.6 SUSHI OF GARI
4.6 BOHEMIAN
4.6 MORIMOTO
4.6 SUSHI SEKI

KOREAN

4.7 JUNGSIK
4.5 HANGAWI
4.5 DANJI
4.5 OIJI
4.4 KANG HO DONG
4.4 HANJAN
4.4 DON'S BOGAM BBQ
4.4 FRANCHIA

KOSHER

4.5 ORWASHER'S BAKERY
4.3 LIEBMAN'S DELICATESSEN
4.3 RESERVE CUT
4.3 BEN'S BEST
4.3 MILL BASIN DELI
4.2 PASTRAMI QUEEN
4.2 2ND AVE DELI
4.2 HUMMUS PLACE

LOBSTER ROLLS

4.6 PEARL OYSTER BAR
4.4 LOBSTER JOINT
4.4 GREENPOINT FISH
4.4 MARY'S FISH CAMP
4.3 LUKE'S LOBSTER
4.3 ED'S LOBSTER BAR
4.3 RED HOOK LOBSTER POUND
4.2 MERMAID INN

MEXICAN

4.7 LOS TACOS
4.5 TORTILLERIA NIXTAMAL
4.5 EMPELLÓN COCINA
4.5 CASA ENRIQUE
4.5 COSME
4.4 MESA COYOACAN
4.4 TOLOACHE
4.4 PAMPANO

MEDITERRANEAN

4.7 MEADOWSWEET
4.6 TAÏM
4.6 CONVIVIUM OSTERIA
4.6 ESTELA
4.5 LITTLE OWL
4.5 IL BUCO
4.5 BOULUD SUD
4.5 OLEA

MIDDLE EASTERN

4.7 TANOREEN
4.5 BAR BOLONAT
4.5 TABOON
4.5 ILILI
4.4 ALMAYASS
4.4 BALABOOSTA
4.4 MAMOUN'S
4.3 MIMI'S HUMMUS

NEWCOMERS

4.8 KINGSLEY
4.7 INDIAN ACCENT
4.6 LILIA
4.5 QUALITY EATS
4.5 LLAMA INN
4.5 HIGH STREET ON HUDSON
4.4 LE COQ RICO
4.4 CAFÉ ALTRO PARADISO

NOODLE SHOPS (see also Ramen)

4.5 SOBA TOTTO
4.4 KUNG FU RAMEN
4.3 SOBA-YA
4.3 OOTOYA
4.3 SOBA NIPPON
4.3 TASTY HAND-PULLED
4.3 GREAT NY NOODLE TOWN
4.2 XI'AN FAMOUS FOODS

PIZZA

4.7 JULIANA'S
4.7 EMILY
4.7 LUCALI
4.6 SAN MATTEO
4.6 ROBERTA'S
4.6 PAULIE GEE'S
4.6 DI FARA
4.5 RUBIROSA

RAMEN
4.5 MU RAMEN
4.5 IPPUDO
4.4 HIDE-CHAN
4.4 GANSO
4.3 CHUKO
4.3 JIN RAMEN
4.2 MEIJIN RAMEN
4.1 IVAN RAMEN

RAW BARS
4.6 PEARL OYSTER BAR
4.5 UPSTATE
4.5 MAISON PREMIERE
4.5 OCEANA
4.5 BLUE RIBBON SUSHI
4.4 ESCA
4.4 LURE FISHBAR

SANDWICHES (see also Delis)
4.7 ALIDORO
4.6 LEO'S LATTICINI
4.5 DEFONTE'S
4.5 IL BAMBINO
4.4 PORCHETTA
4.3 BANH MI SAIGON
4.3 PRESS 195
4.3 BRENNAN & CARR

SEAFOOD
4.9 LE BERNARDIN
4.7 MAREA
4.7 MILOS
4.7 AQUAGRILL
4.6 SEA FIRE GRILL
4.6 PEARL OYSTER BAR
4.6 AVRA
4.6 CULL & PISTOL

SOUTH AMERICAN
4.5 LLAMA INN
4.4 CHURRASCARIA PLATAFORMA
4.4 CARACAS AREPA BAR
4.4 EMPANADA MAMA
4.3 AREPAS CAFÉ
4.3 RAYMI

4.3 YERBA BUENA
4.3 PIO PIO

SOUTHERN/SOUL
4.4 ROOT & BONE
4.4 AMY RUTH'S
4.3 BOBWHITE
4.3 MELBA'S
4.3 EGG
4.3 PEACHES
4.3 PIES-N-THIGHS
4.3 SWEET CHICK

SPANISH/TAPAS
4.7 LA VARA
4.6 BESO
4.6 CASA MONO
4.5 HUERTAS
4.5 SALINAS
4.5 TORO
4.5 EL QUINTO PINO
4.4 SEVILLA

STEAKHOUSES
4.8 PETER LUGER
4.6 BENJAMIN STEAK HOUSE
4.6 PORTER HOUSE NEW YORK
4.5 KEENS STEAKHOUSE
4.5 QUALITY EATS
4.5 QUALITY MEATS
4.5 WOLFGANG'S
4.5 MANZO
4.5 OLD HOMESTEAD
4.5 ST. ANSELM
4.5 SPARKS STEAK HOUSE
4.5 PIETRO'S

TAQUERIAS
4.7 LOS TACOS
4.4 TOLOACHE
4.4 PAMPANO
4.3 LA ESQUINA
4.2 EL PASO
4.2 EMPELLÓN TAQUERIA
4.2 CALEXICO
4.2 EL TORO BLANCO

THAI

4.6 SRIPRAPHAI
4.5 AYADA
4.5 UNCLE BOONS
4.5 PURE THAI COOKHOUSE
4.4 POK POK NY
4.3 ROOM SERVICE
4.3 THAI MARKET
4.3 NGAM

TURKISH

4.6 TACI'S BEYTI
4.3 TURKISH KITCHEN
4.3 SIP SAK
4.2 BEYOGLU
4.2 BODRUM
4.2 USKUDAR
4.1 TURKUAZ
4.0 SAHARA

VEGETARIAN

4.6 TAÏM
4.5 AVANT GARDEN
4.5 HANGAWI
4.4 SARAVANAA BHAVAN
4.4 CANDLE 79
4.4 VATAN
4.3 BY CHLOE
4.3 B & H DAIRY

VIETNAMESE

4.4 BRICOLAGE
4.3 BANH MI SAIGON
4.3 INDOCHINE
4.2 OMAI
4.2 LE COLONIAL
4.2 NHA TRANG
4.2 VIETNAAM
4.1 PHO BANG

TOPS BY LOCATION - MANHATTAN

BATTERY PARK CITY

4.5 BLUE RIBBON SUSHI
4.5 NORTH END GRILL
4.3 MIGHTY QUINN'S BARBECUE
4.3 FRANÇOIS PAYARD BAKERY
4.2 NUM PANG
4.1 BLACK SEED BAGELS
4.1 HARRY'S ITALIAN
4.1 HUDSON EATS

CHELSEA

4.7 DEL POSTO
4.7 LOS TACOS
4.6 MORIMOTO
4.6 SUSHI SEKI
4.6 CULL & PISTOL
4.5 SALINAS
4.5 SCARPETTA
4.5 OLD HOMESTEAD

THE BOWERY

4.4 BAR PRIMI
4.3 SAXON & PAROLE
4.3 PEARL & ASH
4.3 GEMMA
4.3 REBELLE
4.3 VANDAL
4.3 GREAT NY NOODLE TOWN
4.2 DBGB

CHINATOWN

4.3 ORIENTAL GARDEN
4.3 TASTY HAND-PULLED
4.3 GREAT NY NOODLE TOWN
4.3 PEKING DUCK HOUSE
4.2 DELUXE GREEN BO
4.2 JOE'S SHANGHAI
4.2 XI'AN FAMOUS FOODS
4.2 BIG WONG

EAST 40S

4.8 SUSHI YASUDA
4.6 SEA FIRE GRILL
4.6 BENJAMIN STEAK HOUSE
4.6 AVRA
4.5 IL POSTINO
4.5 WOLFGANG'S STEAKHOUSE
4.5 HATSUHANA
4.5 SPARKS STEAK HOUSE

EAST 50S

4.7 LA GRENOUILLE
4.7 AMMA
4.6 FELIDIA
4.5 LE PERIGORD
4.5 AQUAVIT
4.5 SAN PIETRO
4.5 WOLFGANG'S STEAKHOUSE
4.5 CAVIAR RUSSE

EAST 60S

4.8 DANIEL
4.6 SUSHI SEKI
4.6 IL MULINO UPTOWN
4.4 JOJO
4.4 TIELLA
4.4 VAUCLUSE
4.4 SCALINATELLA
4.4 PRIMOLA

EAST 70S

4.7 CAFÉ BOULUD
4.6 SASABUNE
4.6 TANOSHI SUSHI
4.6 SUSHI OF GARI
4.5 ORWASHER'S BAKERY
4.5 SABLE'S SMOKED FISH
4.4 CAMPAGNOLA
4.4 CARAVAGGIO

EAST 80S

4.6 THE SIMONE
4.6 SAN MATTEO
4.5 ELIO'S
4.5 POKE

4.4 ERMINIA
4.4 SISTINA
4.4 FLEX MUSSELS
4.4 RISTORANTE MORINI

EAST 90S/EAST HARLEM

4.5 NICK'S
4.5 RUSS & DAUGHTERS
4.4 TABLE D'HÔTE
4.4 SFOGLIA
4.3 EARL'S BEER & CHEESE
4.3 PAOLA'S
4.3 RAO'S
4.3 PIO PIO

EAST VILLAGE

4.8 KINGSLEY
4.7 KYO YA
4.7 MOMOFUKU KO
4.6 PRUNE
4.6 DEGUSTATION
4.6 KANOYAMA
4.6 GRAFFITI
4.5 PYLOS

FINANCIAL DISTRICT

4.4 THE CAPITAL GRILLE
4.4 DELMONICO'S
4.4 ADRIENNE'S PIZZABAR
4.4 MORTON'S
4.3 LUKE'S LOBSTER
4.3 RESERVE CUT
4.3 HARRY'S CAFE & STEAK
4.3 CIPRIANI CLUB 55

FLATIRON/UNION SQUARE

4.8 TOCQUEVILLE
4.8 GRAMERCY TAVERN
4.7 ELEVEN MADISON PARK
4.6 BREADS BAKERY
4.6 15 EAST
4.5 CRAFT
4.5 ABC KITCHEN
4.5 MANZO

GRAMERCY PARK
4.6 MAIALINO
4.6 CASA MONO
4.5 NOVITÁ
4.5 POSTO
4.5 BLT PRIME
4.4 YAMA
4.3 MIMI'S HUMMUS
4.3 MOLLY'S

GREENWICH VILLAGE
4.8 GOTHAM BAR & GRILL
4.7 BLUE HILL
4.6 BABBO
4.6 LUPA
4.6 SHUKO
4.6 IL MULINO
4.5 TOMOE SUSHI
4.5 NETA

HARLEM
4.4 AMY RUTH'S
4.4 THE CECIL
4.3 MELBA'S
4.2 PONTY BISTRO
4.2 RED ROOSTER
4.1 LIDO
4.1 CHEZ LUCIENNE
3.9 HARLEM SHAKE

LITTLE ITALY
4.4 PELLEGRINO'S
4.4 ANGELO'S OF MULBERRY
4.3 BANH MI SAIGON
4.3 NYONYA
4.3 SHANGHAI CAFE
4.3 IL CORTILE
4.3 FERRARA
4.1 DA NICO

LOWER EAST SIDE
4.6 CONTRA
4.5 KATZ'S DELICATESSEN
4.5 THE BOIL
4.5 BLUE RIBBON SUSHI IZAKAYA
4.5 CLINTON ST. BAKING CO.
4.5 STANTON SOCIAL
4.5 RUSS & DAUGHTERS CAFE
4.4 WILDAIR

MEATPACKING
4.5 VALBELLA
4.5 HIGH STREET ON HUDSON
4.4 UNTITLED
4.3 CATCH
4.2 SANTINA
4.2 STK
4.2 FIG & OLIVE
4.1 STANDARD GRILL

MURRAY HILL
4.7 ALIDORO
4.6 O YA
4.6 TEMPURA MATSUI
4.5 HANGAWI
4.5 WOLFGANG'S
4.5 MARCONY
4.5 RIVERPARK
4.5 NICK'S

NOHO
4.6 BOHEMIAN
4.5 IL BUCO
4.5 BOND ST
4.5 IL BUCO ALIMENTARI
4.5 GATO
4.3 SAXON & PAROLE
4.3 LAFAYETTE
4.3 THE SMILE

NOLITA
4.6 EMILIO'S BALLATO
4.6 ESTELA
4.5 MUSKET ROOM
4.5 RUBIROSA
4.5 CHEFS CLUB
4.5 LOMBARDI'S
4.5 UNCLE BOONS
4.5 PEASANT

NOMAD

4.6 THE NOMAD
4.5 ILILI
4.4 BEN & JACK'S STEAK HOUSE
4.4 MARTA
4.4 SWEETGREEN
4.4 THE NOMAD BAR
4.3 THE BRESLIN
4.2 JOHN DORY OYSTER BAR

PARK AVENUE SOUTH

4.4 UPLAND
4.4 PARK AVENUE
4.4 MORTON'S
4.2 LITTLE BEET TABLE
4.2 HILLSTONE
4.1 BARBOUNIA
4.1 FLORIAN
4.0 HARU

SOHO

4.7 ALIDORO
4.7 AQUAGRILL
4.5 OSTERIA MORINI
4.5 DOMINIQUE ANSEL BAKERY
4.5 BLUE RIBBON SUSHI
4.5 RAOUL'S
4.4 AURORA
4.4 DAVID BURKE KITCHEN

TRIBECA

4.9 BOULEY
4.7 SCALINI FEDELI
4.7 NOBU
4.7 JUNGSIK
4.7 TAMARIND
4.6 BRUSHSTROKE/ICHIMURA
4.6 ATERA
4.6 SUSHI OF GARI

WEST 30S

4.6 AI FIORI
4.5 KEENS STEAKHOUSE
4.4 DELMONICO'S KITCHEN
4.3 TAVOLA

4.3 NEW WONJO
4.3 KRISTALBELLI
4.3 SNACK EOS
4.3 MERCATO

WEST 40S

4.8 GABRIEL KREUTHER
4.6 SUSHI OF GARI
4.6 SUSHI SEKI
4.6 AUREOLE
4.5 WOLFGANG'S
4.5 OCEANA
4.5 PRINT
4.5 SULLIVAN STREET BAKERY

WEST 50S

4.9 LE BERNARDIN
4.7 MAREA
4.7 INDIAN ACCENT
4.7 NOBU 57
4.7 MILOS
4.6 THE MODERN
4.6 PER SE
4.6 ASIATE

WEST 60S

4.8 JEAN-GEORGES
4.7 JEAN-GEORGES' NOUGATINE
4.6 BREADS BAKERY
4.5 BOULUD SUD
4.5 LINCOLN
4.3 BAR BOULUD
4.3 GABRIEL'S
4.3 LEOPARD AT DES ARTISTES

WEST 70S

4.7 LEVAIN BAKERY
4.6 DOVETAIL
4.6 GARI
4.4 REDFARM
4.4 SARAVANAA BHAVAN
4.4 SALUMERIA ROSI
4.3 TESSA
4.3 LINCOLN SQUARE STEAK

WEST 80S

4.5 BARNEY GREENGRASS
4.4 MOMOYA
4.4 CELESTE
4.3 LUKE'S LOBSTER
4.3 MILLING ROOM
4.3 CRAVE FISHBAR
4.3 PIZZERIA SIRENETTA
4.3 BUSTAN

WEST 90S & UP

4.6 ABSOLUTE BAGELS
4.5 GENNARO
4.4 PISTICCI
4.3 AWADH

4.3 AWASH
4.3 THAI MARKET
4.3 MANHATTAN VALLEY
4.3 AMSTERDAM BURGER CO.

WEST VILLAGE

4.7 UPHOLSTERY STORE
4.7 DECOY
4.7 SUSHI NAKAZAWA
4.7 SOTO
4.7 ANNISA
4.7 MAS (FARMHOUSE)
4.7 L'ARTUSI
4.6 PEARL OYSTER BAR

TOPS BY LOCATION - BROOKLYN

BAY RIDGE

4.7 TANOREEN
4.6 ELIÁ
4.5 TUSCANY GRILL
4.5 PANEANTICO
4.4 GINO'S
4.4 AREO
4.4 CHADWICK'S
4.3 DAVID'S BRISKET HOUSE

BOERUM HILL/COBBLE HILL

4.7 LA VARA
4.6 BATTERSBY
4.6 HIBINO
4.5 KI SUSHI
4.5 SHELSKY'S OF BROOKLYN
4.4 FRENCH LOUIE
4.4 RUCOLA
4.3 AWASH

BROOKLYN HEIGHTS/DUMBO

4.7 JULIANA'S
4.6 RIVER CAFÉ
4.5 ALMONDINE BAKERY
4.5 COLONIE

4.5 HENRY'S END
4.5 LUZZO'S
4.4 NOODLE PUDDING
4.4 FORNINO

CARROLL GARDENS

4.7 LUCALI
4.6 BUTTERMILK CHANNEL
4.5 DOVER
4.4 FRAGOLE
4.4 FRANKIES SPUNTINO
4.3 PRIME MEATS
4.2 MARCO POLO
4.1 ZAYTOONS

CROWN HEIGHTS / PROSPECT HEIGHTS

4.4 BAR CORVO
4.4 JAMES
4.4 ALI'S ROTI
4.3 AITA
4.3 CHUKO
4.3 MIGHTY QUINN'S BARBECUE
4.1 MORGANS BBQ
4.1 ZAYTOONS

FORT GREENE/CLINTON HILL

4.7 EMILY
4.5 OLEA
4.5 SPEEDY ROMEO
4.4 LOCANDA VINI & OLII
4.3 AITA
4.2 CAFFE E VINO
4.2 MADIBA
4.1 HABANA OUTPOST

GREENPOINT

4.6 PAULIE GEE'S
4.4 LOBSTER JOINT
4.4 FORNINO
4.4 GREENPOINT FISH
4.3 SCALINO
4.3 FIVE LEAVES
4.2 XI'AN FAMOUS FOODS
4.2 CALEXICO

PARK SLOPE

4.6 CONVIVIUM OSTERIA
4.6 AL DI LA
4.6 ROSE WATER
4.5 STONE PARK CAFÉ
4.4 TALDE
4.4 BRICOLAGE
4.4 BLUE RIBBON BROOKLYN
4.3 LUKE'S LOBSTER

WILLIAMSBURG

4.8 PETER LUGER STEAK HOUSE
4.7 MEADOWSWEET
4.6 ANTICA PESA
4.6 LILIA
4.6 TRAIF
4.6 SEMILLA
4.6 ZENKICHI
4.5 MAISON PREMIERE

BROOKLYN: OTHER AREAS

4.8 CHEF'S TABLE | Downtown Bklyn
4.7 BLANCA | Bushwick
4.6 HOMETOWN BBQ | Red Hook
4.6 ROBERTA'S | Bushwick
4.6 TACI'S BEYTI | Sheepshead Bay
4.6 DI FARA | Midwood
4.5 DEFONTE'S | Red Hook
4.5 RUNNER & STONE | Gowanus

TOPS BY LOCATION - OTHER BOROUGHS

BRONX

4.5 ROBERTO'S
4.4 ARTIE'S
4.4 ENZO'S
4.4 ALI'S ROTI
4.4 DOMINICK'S
4.3 PATRICIA'S
4.3 ZERO OTTO NOVE
4.3 TRA DI NOI

QUEENS: ASTORIA

4.7 TRATTORIA L'INCONTRO
4.6 PICCOLA VENEZIA
4.5 TAVERNA KYCLADES
4.5 LOUKOUMI TAVERNA
4.5 ELIAS CORNER
4.5 IL BAMBINO
4.4 BAHARI ESTIATORIO
4.4 VESTA

QUEENS: FLUSHING

4.4 SPICY & TASTY
4.2 JOE'S SHANGHAI
4.2 XI'AN FAMOUS FOODS
4.2 SZECHUAN GOURMET
4.2 KUM GANG SAN
4.1 NEW WORLD MALL
4.1 DUMPLING GALAXY
4.1 PHO BANG

QUEENS: LONG ISLAND CITY

4.6 HIBINO
4.5 MU RAMEN
4.5 CASA ENRIQUE
4.5 MAIELLA
4.4 IL FALCO
4.4 MANETTA'S
4.3 MANDUCATIS
4.3 LIC MARKET

QUEENS: OTHER AREAS

4.7 **DON PEPPE** | South Ozone Park
4.6 **LEO'S LATTICINI** | Corona
4.6 **SRIPRAPHAI** | Woodside
4.5 **TORTILLERIA NIXT.** | Corona
4.5 **AYADA** | Elmhurst
4.5 **PARK SIDE** | Corona
4.5 **NICK'S** | Forest Hills
4.5 **ZUM STAMMTISCH** | Glendale

STATEN ISLAND

4.6 TRATTORIA ROMANA
4.6 BESO
4.5 DEFONTE'S
4.5 BOCELLI
4.5 DENINO'S PIZZERIA
4.5 CAROL'S CAFE
4.4 BRIOSO
4.4 ENOTECA MARIA

BEST BETS

DESTINATIONS

BARCLAYS CENTER
CONVIVIUM OSTERIA
GANSO YAKI
HABANA OUTPOST
MIRIAM
MORGANS BBQ
NO. 7
ROSE'S ∇
SHAKE SHACK
SMOKE JOINT
SUSHI GANSO

BROOKLYN BRIDGE PARK (NORTH)
ATRIUM DUMBO
GRAN ELECTRICA
GRIMALDI'S
HENRY'S END
JACK THE HORSE
JULIANA'S
LUKE'S LOBSTER
NOODLE PUDDING
NO. 7 SUB
SHAKE SHACK

BROOKLYN BRIDGE PARK (SOUTH)
AMPLE HILLS
BEASTS & BOTTLES
CHIPSHOP
COLONIE
FORNINO
FRIEND OF A FARMER
HANCO'S
LUZZO'S
POK POK NY
SMORGASBURG

GRAND CENTRAL
AGERN
AMMOS
CAFE CENTRO
CAPITAL GRILLE
GREAT NORTHERN FOOD HALL

LA FONDA DEL SOL
MICHAEL JORDAN'S
OYSTER BAR
PERA
SUSHI YASUDA
URBANSPACE VANDERBILT

HIGH LINE / WHITNEY MUSEUM
(GANSEVOORT ST.)
BARBUTO
BUBBY'S
CAFE GITANE
CATCH
DOS CAMINOS
FIG & OLIVE
HIGH STREET ON HUDSON
SANTINA
STANDARD GRILL
UNTITLED

HIGH LINE (23RD ST. EXIT)
CO.
COOKSHOP
EL QUINTO PINO
OMAI
RED CAT
SALINAS
TIA POL
TIPSY PARSON
TRESTLE ON TENTH
TXIKITO

JURY DUTY (MANHATTAN)
BLAUE GANS
EXCELLENT DUMPLING
GREAT NY NOODLE TOWN
LANDMARC
NHA TRANG
THE ODEON
PEKING DUCK HOUSE
TAKAHACHI
XI'AN FAMOUS FOODS
ZUCKER'S BAGELS

JURY DUTY (BROOKLYN)
BAREBURGER
FRENCH LOUIE
GANSO
HANCO'S
HILL COUNTRY
JOYA
JUNIOR'S
MILE END
QUEEN
SHAKE SHACK

MADISON SQUARE GARDEN
DAVID BURKE FABRICK
DELMONICO'S KITCHEN
FRANKIE & JOHNNIE'S
GAONNURI
KEENS
L'AMICO
LUPULO
NICK & STEF'S
PARKER & QUINN
THE PENNSY

METROPOLITAN MUSEUM
CAFÉ BOULUD
CAFÉ SABARSKY
E.A.T.
GIOVANNI VENTICINQUE
GRAZIE
KAPPO MASA ▽
THE MARK
RISTORANTE MORINI
SANT AMBROEUS
SERAFINA

MOMA
BENOIT
CHINA GRILL
FOGO DE CHÃO
LA BONNE SOUPE
MÁ PÊCHE
MICHAEL'S
THE MODERN
OBICÀ MOZZARELLA BAR
PIZZARTE
21 CLUB

MUSEUM OF NATURAL HISTORY
CALLE OCHO
DOVETAIL
ISABELLA'S
LUKE'S LOBSTER
NICE MATIN
PATSY'S PIZZERIA
SARABETH'S
SHAKE SHACK
SPRING NATURAL KITCHEN
SUSHI OF GARI

9/11 MEMORIAL
AMADA
BEAUBOURG
EATALY
EL VEZ
HARRY'S ITALIAN
HUDSON EATS
LE DISTRICT
NORTH END GRILL
P.J. CLARKE'S
SHAKE SHACK

ROCKEFELLER CENTER
ALDO SOHM WINE BAR
BOUCHON BAKERY
BRASSERIE RUHLMANN
DEL FRISCO'S GRILLE
FOGO DE CHÃO
LIMANI
NYY STEAK
OCEANA
SEA GRILL
WU LIANG YE

THEATER DISTRICT DELUXE
AUREOLE
CHARLIE PALMER AT THE KNICK
DB BISTRO MODERNE
ESCA
GABRIEL KREUTHER
HUNT & FISH CLUB
LAMBS CLUB
STK
STRIP HOUSE
WOLFGANG'S

THEATER DISTRICT FAMILY-FRIENDLY

BAREBURGER
BECCO
CARMINE'S
CITY KITCHEN
5 NAPKIN BURGER
JOHN'S PIZZERIA
JUNIOR'S
SHAKE SHACK
TONY'S DI NAPOLI
VIRGIL'S

THEATER DISTRICT OLD-SCHOOL

BARBETTA
CHEZ JOSEPHINE
CHEZ NAPOLEON
FRANKIE & JOHNNIE'S
ORSO
PATSY'S
SARDI'S
JOE ALLEN
LANDMARK TAVERN
LE RIVAGE

OCCASIONS & SITUATIONS

ANNIVERSARY-WORTHY

DEL POSTO
GABRIEL KREUTHER
GRAMERCY TAVERN
THE HOUSE
IL BUCO
LE BERNARDIN
LE COUCOU
RAINBOW ROOM
RIVER CAFÉ
SHUKO

BAR SCENES

ARLINGTON CLUB
THE BRESLIN
THE CLOCKTOWER
GATO
HUNT & FISH CLUB
MARGAUX
MINETTA TAVERN
THE NOMAD
RED ROOSTER
UPLAND

BEER STANDOUTS

BERG'N
BIRRERIA
CAFE D'ALSACE
CANNIBAL
DBGB

ELEVEN MADISON PARK
GRAMERCY TAVERN
JACOB'S PICKLES
LUKSUS ∇
QUEENS KICKSHAW

BREAKFAST

BALTHAZAR
BUVETTE
COOKSHOP
EGG
IL BUCO ALIMENTARI
LAFAYETTE
LA PECORA BIANCA
LITTLE PARK
NORMA'S
THE ODEON

BRIDAL/BABY SHOWERS

ALICE'S TEA CUP
ANASSA
BEAUTY & ESSEX
BOBO
KINGS' CARRIAGE HOUSE
LADURÉE
LADY MENDL'S
MARI VANNA
PALM COURT
SARABETH'S

BRUNCH (DOWNTOWN)
ABC KITCHEN
CLINTON ST. BAKING CO.
ESTELA
FREEMANS
JACK'S WIFE FREDA
LOCANDA VERDE
PRUNE
RUSS & DAUGHTERS
SADELLE'S
THE SMILE

BRUNCH (MIDTOWN)
DB BISTRO MODERNE
44 & X
LAVO
LE COQ RICO
MÁ PÊCHE
PENELOPE
RAINBOW ROOM
SALVATION TACO
THE SMITH
UPLAND

BRUNCH (UPTOWN)
BARNEY GREENGRASS
CAFE D'ALSACE
CAFE LUXEMBOURG
THE CECIL
EAST POLE
JACOB'S PICKLES
NICE MATIN
PENROSE
RISTORANTE MORINI
THE SMITH

BRUNCH (BROOKLYN)
AITA
BUTTERMILK CHANNEL
COLONIE
DELAWARE & HUDSON
EGG
FIVE LEAVES
FRANKIES SPUNTINO
FRENCH LOUIE
ROBERTA'S
ROSE WATER
STONE PARK CAFÉ

BUSINESS DINING
(FINANCIAL DISTRICT)
BEAUBOURG
BOBBY VAN'S
CAPITAL GRILLE
CIPRIANI
DELMONICO'S
HARRY'S CAFE
MARKJOSEPH STEAKHOUSE
MORTON'S
NORTH END GRILL
P.J. CLARKE'S ON THE HUDSON

BUSINESS DINING (MIDTOWN)
CASA LEVER
DEL FRISCO'S
GABRIEL KREUTHER
JEAN-GEORGES
LE BERNARDIN
LE CIRQUE
MAREA
MICHAEL'S
QUALITY MEATS
21 CLUB

BYO
AZURI CAFE ▽
GAZALA'S PLACE
KUMA INN ▽
LUCALI
PHOENIX GARDEN
POKE
QUEENS COMFORT
TACI'S BEYTI
TARTINE
ZAYTOONS | Crl. Gdns./Clinton Hill

CHILD-FRIENDLY
ALICE'S TEA CUP
BROOKLYN FARMACY
BUBBY'S
COWGIRL
FARM ON ADDERLEY
HUGO & SONS
L&B SPUMONI
NINJA
OTTO
SERENDIPITY 3

CHILDREN'S MENUS
BLUE RIBBON BROOKLYN
BLUE SMOKE
BUTTERMILK CHANNEL
DBGB
DINOSAUR BAR-B-QUE
HAN DYNASTY
ISABELLA'S
KEFI
LANDMARC
ROSA MEXICANO

COCKTAIL STARS
ATERA
BAR GOTO
CAFÉ MEDI
DEAD RABBIT
DECOY
GRAND ARMY ▽
NOMAD BAR
OLEANDERS
SANTINA
SAUVAGE

DESIGN STANDOUTS
THE CLOCKTOWER
GABRIEL KREUTHER
LAFAYETTE
LE COUCOU
LIMANI
MAISON PREMIERE
MAREA
NOMAD BAR
POLO BAR
VAUCLUSE

GROUP DINING
AMADA
BEAUTY & ESSEX
BUDDAKAN
DECOY
KANG HO DONG BAEKJEONG
MISSION CHINESE
ROSA MEXICANO
TAO
TORO
UNION FARE
VANDAL

HAPPY HOURS
BKW BY BROOKLYN WINERY
BURGER & LOBSTER
THE CLAM
FONDA
KEENS
MAIALINO
MERMAID INN
MOMOFUKU NISHI
RED ROOSTER
RYE

HOT DATES
CHARLIE BIRD
L'ARTUSI
LA SIRENA
LE COUCOU
LILIA
MIMI
OLMSTED
PASQUALE JONES ▽
WILDAIR
ZENKICHI

OLD NY VIBE
BAMONTE'S
BARNEY GREENGRASS
IL MULINO
KEENS
MINETTA TAVERN
MORGAN DINING ROOM
OLD HOMESTEAD
PETER LUGER
21 CLUB
WAVERLY INN

PATIOS/GARDENS
AURORA | Williamsburg
BARBETTA
BRASSERIE RUHLMANN
BRYANT PARK GRILL
CATCH
LADURÉE | SoHo
SALINAS
SANTINA
TAVERN ON THE GREEN
UNTITLED

SOCIALITE CENTRAL
AMARANTH
BEAUTIQUE
BLACK BARN
ELIO'S
HUNT & FISH CLUB
LE BILBOQUET
LEOPARD AT DES ARTISTES
POLO BAR
RISTORANTE MORINI
SANT AMBROEUS

THANKSGIVING
BENOIT BISTRO
BLUE HILL
BRESLIN
COOKSHOP
GRAMERCY TAVERN
MAS (FARMHOUSE)
ONE IF BY LAND
TAVERN ON THE GREEN
21 CLUB
WAVERLY INN

24/7
BCD TOFU HOUSE | W 30s
CAFETERIA
COPPELIA
GRAY'S PAPAYA
KANG SUH
KUNJIP
L'EXPRESS
NEW WONJO
SARGE'S DELI
VESELKA

VIEWS
ASIATE
GAONNURI
MICHAEL JORDAN'S
THE MODERN
PER SE
RIVERPARK
ROBERT
SEA GRILL
STELLA 34
THE VIEW

WATERSIDE
BATTERY GARDENS
BEAUBOURG
BOATHOUSE
BROOKLYN CRAB
MAIELLA
PIER A HARBOR HOUSE
RIVER CAFÉ
RIVERPARK
SHI
WATER CLUB

WINE BARS
ALDO SOHM
BAR JAMÓN
CASELLULA
CORKBUZZ
DESNUDA ▽
D.O.C. WINE BAR ▽
EL QUINTO PINO
THE FOUR HORSEMEN ▽
IL BUCO ALIMENTARI
UPHOLSTERY STORE

WINE: CONNOISSEUR PICKS
BABBO
BÂTARD
CHARLIE BIRD
DANIEL
ELEVEN MADISON PARK
GABRIEL KREUTHER
JEAN-GEORGES
LE BERNARDIN
PEARL & ASH
21 CLUB

WINE: UNUSUAL LISTS
BIRDS & BUBBLES
CASA MONO
ESTELA
THE FOUR HORSEMEN ▽
MOMOFUKU KO
M. WELLS STEAKHOUSE
O YA
RACINES
REBELLE
WILDAIR

BEST BANGS FOR THE BUCK

FULL-MEAL BARGAINS

4.7 JULIANA'S	4.5 DON ANTONIO
4.7 EMILY	4.5 PACIFICANA
4.7 LUCALI	4.5 LUZZO'S
4.6 HOMETOWN BBQ	4.5 LOMBARDI'S
4.6 SRIPRAPHAI	4.5 BARNEY GREENGRASS
4.6 SAN MATTEO	4.5 POSTO
4.6 ROBERTA'S	4.5 ELIAS CORNER
4.6 TACI'S BEYTI	4.5 WU LIANG YE
4.6 CHAIWALI	4.5 NICK'S
4.6 MOMOSAN RAMEN & SAKE	4.5 CLINTON ST. BAKING CO.
4.6 PAULIE GEE'S	4.5 PURE THAI COOKHOUSE
4.6 PIZZA MOTO	4.5 THE LOBSTER PLACE
4.6 HIBINO	4.5 RIBALTA
4.5 KATZ'S DELICATESSEN	4.5 MOMOFUKU NOODLE BAR
4.5 RUBIROSA	4.5 BUN-KER VIETNAMESE
4.5 MU RAMEN	4.5 RUSS & DAUGHTERS CAFE
4.5 OLEA	4.4 JUN-MEN
4.5 WHEATED	4.4 GINO'S
4.5 FETTE SAU	4.4 RUNNER & STONE
4.5 IPPUDO	4.4 NORMA'S

CHEAP QUICK BITES

4.7 ALIDORO	4.5 ARCADE BAKERY
4.7 LOS TACOS	4.5 TORTILLERIA NIXTAMAL
4.6 AREPA LADY	4.5 AYADA
4.6 GENUINE SUPERETTE	4.5 JOE'S PIZZA
4.6 TAÏM	4.5 SULLIVAN STREET BAKERY
4.6 LEO'S LATTICINI	4.5 DENINO'S PIZZA
4.6 BREADS BAKERY	4.5 IL BAMBINO
4.6 ABSOLUTE BAGELS	4.5 TOTONNO'S PIZZERIA
4.6 UNTAMED SANDWICHES	4.4 BEST PIZZA
4.6 DI FARA	4.4 HARRY & IDA'S
4.5 SHELSKY'S OF BROOKLYN	4.4 PORCHETTA
4.5 DEFONTE'S	4.4 ESS-A-BAGEL
4.5 ALMONDINE BAKERY	

BY CUISINE

FRENCH
4.2 CAFE LULUC
4.2 ÉPICERIE BOULUD
4.2 TARTINE
4.1 AU ZA'ATAR
4.1 BAR TABAC

SEAFOOD
4.5 ELIAS CORNER
4.5 THE LOBSTER PLACE
4.4 GREENPOINT FISH
4.4 LOBSTER JOINT
4.3 LUKE'S LOBSTER

SOMETHING DIFFERENT
4.6 CHAIWALI
4.5 TORTILLERIA NIXTAMAL
4.3 LOLO'S SEAFOOD SHACK ▽
4.3 ODA HOUSE ▽
4.3 DUCKS EATERY

SUSHI
4.6 HIBINO
4.2 YUKA
4.1 KO SUSHI
4.1 KOUZAN
4.1 TENZAN

BY DESTINATION

COLUMBUS CIRCLE
4.3 KASHKAVAL GARDEN
4.3 BOUCHON BAKERY
4.0 EL CENTRO
3.9 BAREBURGER
4.2 FUKU+

MADISON SQUARE GARDEN
4.4 LARB UBOL
4.2 KATI ROLL COMPANY
4.2 BCD TOFU HOUSE
4.2 FRIEDMAN'S
3.9 THE PENNSY

MUSEUM MILE
4.5 RUSS & DAUGHTERS CAFE
4.3 BLUESTONE LANE
4.2 EL PASO
4.0 SHAKE SHACK
4.0 SARABETH'S

THEATER DISTRICT
4.5 WU LIANG YE
4.4 KUNG FU RAMEN
4.3 LUKE'S LOBSTER
4.3 OOTOYA
4.3 JOHN'S PIZZERIA

BY SPECIAL FEATURE

BUZZING SCENE (MANHATTAN)
4.6 MOMOSAN RAMEN & SAKE
4.5 KIKI'S
4.5 MOMOFUKU NOODLE BAR
4.1 MISS LILY'S
4.1 YUCA BAR

CHEAP DATE (MANHATTAN)
4.4 ADORO LEI
4.4 MURRAY'S CHEESE BAR
4.3 MALATESTA TRATTORIA
4.3 THE SMILE
3.9 LA LANTERNA DI VITTORIO ▽

BUZZING SCENE (BROOKLYN)
4.6 HOMETOWN BBQ
4.6 ROBERTA'S
4.4 SARAGHINA
4.3 GRAN ELECTRICA
4.3 CAFE MOGADOR

CHEAP DATE (BROOKLYN)
4.7 EMILY
4.5 OLEA
4.4 ESME
4.3 CHUKO
3.9 BERG'N

NOTABLE PRIX FIXES

LUNCH

$19	OBICÀ MOZZARELLA BAR
$20.16	JUE LAN CLUB
$25	ILILI
$25	JUNOON
$25	MURRAY'S CHEESE BAR
$29	MILOS
$29	OSTERIA MORINI
$29	PERRY ST
$29	REMI
$29	VANDAL
$32	BAR BOULUD
$33	FELIDIA
$34	THE NOMAD
$36	ASIATE
$38	AUREOLE
$38	GOTHAM BAR & GRILL
$38	JEAN-GEORGES' NOUG.
$42	BETONY
$42	21 CLUB
$45	BRUSHSTROKE
$49	DEL POSTO
$52	MAREA
$56	LA GRENOUILLE
$59	BOULEY
$65	GRAMERCY TAVERN
$85	LE BERNARDIN

DINNER

$25	BECCO
$36	ATOBOY
$58	BÂTARD
$58	DELAWARE & HUDSON
$62	BABU JI
$75	BATTERSBY
$75	INDIAN ACCENT
$85	DEGUSTATION
$85	SEMILLA
$88	LA CHINE
$98	GRAMERCY TAVERN
$120	AGERN
$120	SUSHI NAKAZAWA
$125	GABRIEL KREUTHER
$135	SHUKO
$147	LE BERNARDIN
$148	GUNTER SEEGER
$160	SUSHI ZO
$185	O YA
$190	JUNGSIK
$195	MOMOFUKU KO
$215	ASKA
$275	ATERA
$325	PER SE
$329	CHEF'S TABLE / BROOKLYN
$595	MASA

RESTAURANT DIRECTORY

ABC COCINA | Pan-Latin   4.4   4.3   4.2 $$$
Flatiron | ABC Carpet & Home | 38 E. 19th St. (bet. B'way & Park Ave. S.)
212-677-2233 | www.abccocinanyc.com

"**Complex flavors**" elevate the "**imaginative**" tapas at Jean-Georges Vongerichten's "**high-energy**" Pan-Latin standout in ABC Carpet & Home, where the "**beautiful**" (if "**noisy**") setting is the backdrop for a "**cool scene**"; reservations remain "**hard to get**", but walk-ins can always pass the wait time "**downing delicious drinks**" at the bar.

ABC KITCHEN | American   4.5   4.4   4.3 $$$
Flatiron | ABC Carpet & Home | 35 E. 18th St. (bet. B'way & Park Ave. S.)
212-475-5829 | www.abckitchennyc.com

Jean-Georges Vongerichten's "**hip**" Flatiron "**winner**" "**still delivers**" with "**original**", "**all-around delicious**" American cooking ordered from a "**sophisticated**" farm-to-table menu; a "**stylish**", "**airy**" space further justifies the "**spendy**" tabs – and the "**challenge to get a reservation.**"

ABIGAEL'S | American/Kosher   4.0   3.6   3.9 $$$
West 30s | 1407 Broadway (bet. 38th & 39th Sts.)
212-575-1407 | www.abigaels.com

A menu spanning "**short ribs to sushi**" gives kosher cuisine an "**upscale**" global gloss at this "**solid**" Garment District New American; "**bland**" atmospherics detract, but it remains a "**staple**" for observant folks.

ABRAÇO ESPRESSO | Coffee   ▽ 4.6   3.3   4.0 $
East Village | 81 E 7th St. (bet. 1st & 2nd Aves.)
no phone | www.abraconyc.com

They have "**espresso down proper**" at this East Village "**standout**", where the "**cool**" baristas offer "**top-notch coffee**" (drips included) and nibbles like the "**tantalizing**" olive-oil cake; after a move across the street, it has a larger space with seats, but given the "**cult following**", you should still expect a line.

ABSOLUTE BAGELS | Bagels   4.6   2.7   3.7 $
West 100s | 2788 Broadway (bet. 107th & 108th Sts.)
212-932-2052 | www.absolutebagels.com

"**Old-fashioned**" bagels have "**just the right texture**" ("**crunchy on the outside, soft inside**") at this Columbia-area storefront, a "**benchmark for rivals**" turning out "**piping hot**" rounds available with "**tons**" of spreads or just "**perfect by themselves**"; just expect "**zero atmosphere**" and "**crazy-long**" weekend lines.

ABURIYA KINNOSUKE | Japanese   4.5   3.9   4.1 $$$
East 40s | 213 E. 45th St. (bet. 2nd & 3rd Aves.)
212-867-5454 | www.aburiyakinnosuke.com

A "**true izakaya experience**" awaits at this East Midtown Japanese, where the "**fantastic**" non-sushi menu highlights "**traditional**" robata grill specialties; the style might be "**relaxed**", but that doesn't rule out "**hefty**" tabs – though there's always the "**cost-effective lunch special.**"

ABV | American   3.9   3.6   3.9 $$
East 90s | 1504 Lexington Ave. (97th St.)
212-722-8959 | www.abvny.com

"**Something different**" for Carnegie Hill, this "**with-it**" wine bar matches "**interesting**" American nibbles with an "**eclectic**" list of wines and at

"**approachable**" prices; the space may be "**no-frills**" but it has "**lots of energy**" and even a touch of "**downtown**" "**swagger.**"

ACAPPELLA | Italian	4.4	4.2	4.4	$$$

TriBeCa \| 1 Hudson St. (Chambers St.)
212-240-0163 \| www.acapellarestaurant.com

Dining is "**an event**" at this "**old-world**" TriBeCa Northern Italian renowned for "**delicious**" food, "*Godfather* opulent" decor and "**warm**" staffers who "**treat you like gold**"; "**try not to faint when you get the check**" or you'll miss out on the complimentary grappa.

ACME \| French/Italian 4.2 4.0 4.0 $$$

NoHo \| 9 Great Jones St. (Lafayette St.)
212-203-2121 \| www.acmenyc.com

This "**transformed**" NoHo bistro's latest iteration is a "**pleasant surprise**" offering "**tasty**" upmarket French-Italian dishes and "**sophisticated**" cocktails, downed by a "**lively**", "**trendy**" crowd; with its downstairs lounge and "**party**" vibe, it "**fits the neighborhood to a T.**"

ACQUA AT PECK SLIP \| Italian 4.1 3.8 4.0 $$

South Street Seaport \| 21 Peck Slip (Water St.)
212-349-4433 \| www.acquarestaurantnyc.com

"**Away from the touristy Seaport places**", this "**simple**", rustic Italian is praised for its housemade pastas and "**interesting**" selection of boutique wines; despite "**reasonable**" prices, "**attentive**" service and "**lovely**" outdoor seating on a cobblestone street, there's "**never a long wait**" here.

ADORO LEI \| Italian ▽ 4.4 4.3 4.3 $$

Hudson Square \| 287 Hudson St. (bet. Dominick & Spring Sts.)
646-666-5096 \| www.adorolei.com

Offering "**a menu built to share**", this "**cool**" Hudson Square Italian turns out "**excellent**" wood-oven pizzas in "**classic and New Age**" varieties along with "**fancy bar food**" to accompany the "**delicious cocktails**"; a "**chic, comfy**" space manned by "**dedicated**" staffers completes the "**memorable**" picture.

ADRIENNE'S PIZZABAR \| Pizza 4.4 3.6 3.9 $$

Financial District \| 54 Stone St. (Old Slip)
212-248-3838 \| www.adriennespizzabarnyc.com

Brace yourself for "**lunchtime madness**" when "**Wall Street suits**" and "**casual passersby**" descend on this FiDi pizzeria for its "**outstanding**" thin-crust pies; "**adequate**" service and "**nonexistent decor**" are part of the package, making it best enjoyed at an alfresco seat on "**picturesque Stone Street.**"

NEW AGERN \| Scandinavian — — — $$$$

East 40s \| Grand Central \| 89 E. 42nd St. (Vanderbilt Ave.)
646-568-4018 \| www.agernrestaurant.com

Inside Grand Central Terminal, this airy Scandinavian arrival from Claus Meyer (co-founder of Copenhagen's Noma) showcases locally farmed and foraged ingredients with its dishes offered on two tasting menus (one centered on vegetables) or à la carte; natural woods, charcoal banquettes and central counter seating distinguish the space.

AGNANTI \| Greek 4.3 3.5 3.9 $$

Astoria \| 19-06 Ditmars Blvd. (19th St.) \| Queens
718-545-4554 \| www.agnantimeze.com

A "**notch above the typical Astorian**", this "**tried-and-true**" Hellenic taverna rolls out "**delicious**", "**reasonably priced**" meals that conjure up the "**Greek isles**"; the decor is on the "**forgettable**" side, so regulars request seats on the "**wonderful**" sidewalk patio next to Astoria Park.

| **AGORA TAVERNA** | Greek | 3.9 | 3.7 | 3.8 | $$ |

Forest Hills | 70-09 Austin St. (70th Ave.) | Queens
718-793-7300 | www.agorataverna.com

"**They know how to grill fish**" at this Forest Hills taverna, whose "**varied menu**" ups the local ante for "**traditional Greek dishes**"; it can get "**noisy**", but it's "**amiable**" if you're "**not in the mood to go to Astoria**" and if you score a seat outside.

| **AI FIORI** | Italian | 4.6 | 4.6 | 4.5 | $$$$ |

West 30s | Langham Place Fifth Avenue Hotel | 400 Fifth Ave. (bet. 36th & 37th Sts.)
212-613-8660 | www.aifiorinyc.com

A "**Michael White triumph**" on the second floor of the Langham Place Fifth Avenue Hotel, this "**classy**" Italian delivers Riviera-inspired dishes, including "**sublime**" pastas, via a "**polished, unobtrusive**" crew; the "**glamorous**" setting feels "**so magical**", you almost don't mind the "**astronomical**" tab, especially if it's a "**special occasion.**"

| **AITA** | Italian | 4.3 | 4.3 | 4.1 | $$ |

Clinton Hill | 132 Greene Ave. (Waverly Ave.) | Brooklyn | 718-576-3584
Crown Heights | 798 Franklin Ave. (bet. Lincoln Pl. & Service Rd.) | Brooklyn | 917-966-2670
www.aitarestaurant.com

These "**homey**" trattorias produce "**excellent**" pasta-centric Italian fare highlighting ingredients "**straight from the farmer's market**"; while the "**intimate**" Clinton Hill original is a "**neighborhood favorite**" and the newer Crown Heights locale is a "**good entry to the scene**", both are favored for their "**must-try**" brunch.

| **AKDENIZ** | Turkish | 4.0 | 3.3 | 3.8 | $$ |

West 40s | 19 W. 46th St. (bet. 5th & 6th Aves.)
212-575-2307 | www.akdenizturkishusa.com

It's all about "**value**" at this Midtown Turk offering a "**can't-be-beat**" dinner prix fixe that's a showstopper for theatergoers; the "**tiny**", "**unmemorable**" setting can feel a bit "**claustrophobic**", but the grub's "**solid**" and the service "**accommodating.**"

| **A LA TURKA** | Turkish | 4.0 | 3.5 | 3.9 | $$ |

East 70s | 1417 Second Ave. (74th St.)
212-744-2424 | www.alaturkarestaurant.com

A "**reliable neighborhood place**", this Upper Eastsider "**always delivers**" ("**just like the mailman**") with "**solid**" Turkish fare and live music several nights a week; when it's "**crowded**" the "**pleasant**" service can be "**lacking**", and the space could use a "**makeover**", but "**totally reasonable**" tabs save the day.

| **ALBERTO** | Italian | 4.3 | 3.9 | 4.2 | $$ |

Forest Hills | 98-31 Metropolitan Ave. (bet. 69th & 70th Aves.) | Queens
718-268-7860 | www.albertorestaurant.com

A "**Forest Hills find**", this "**marvelously old-fashioned**" Italian remains a "**steady**" neighborhood "**institution**" (since '73) thanks to "**well-prepared** classics" and a "**staff and owners who greet you like family**"; indeed, the "**high prices**" and "**romantic**", fireplace-equipped room suggest "**special occasion.**"

AL BUSTAN | Lebanese   4.2   4.0   4.1 $$$
East 50s | 319 E. 53rd St. (bet. 1st & 2nd Aves.)
212-759-5933 | www.albustanny.com

"**Hidden**" on an East Midtown side street, this upscale double-decker delivers "**succulent**" Lebanese classics in a "**modern**", chandeliered room; although the "**big space**" is "**rarely busy**" at the dinner hour, at least it's "**comfortable**" and you can "**hear yourself speak.**"

ALCALA RESTAURANT | Spanish   4.1   3.5   4.1 $$$
East 40s | 246 E. 44th St. (2nd Ave.)
212-370-1866 | www.alcalarestaurant.com

For a taste of "**Spain in Manhattan**", this "**fixture**" near the U.N. fits the bill, offering a "**variety**"-filled menu highlighted by "**well-made**" tapas; "**welcoming**" service and "**cozy**" confines are other reasons it's a "**nice neighborhood place.**"

ALDEA | Mediterranean   4.5   4.2   4.4 $$$
Flatiron | 31 W. 17th St. (bet. 5th & 6th Aves.)
212-675-7223 | www.aldearestaurant.com

George Mendes' "**superb, creative twists**" on Mediterranean cuisine come in "**chic**", "**grown-up**" confines at this Flatiron "**gem**", where sitting at the kitchen-facing counter makes for a "**really fun**" meal; "**attentive**" service is another plus, so while "**expensive**", it's a "**true dining pleasure**".

AL DI LA | Italian   4.6   3.9   4.3 $$$
Park Slope | 248 Fifth Ave. (Carroll St.) | Brooklyn
718-783-4565 | www.aldilatrattoria.com

"**Not much changes**" yet it "**always feels special**" at this Park Slope "**classic**" that earns "**Brooklynite love**" with its "**superb**" Venetian fare, "**decent prices**" and "**lively**", "**warm**" vibe; yes, the "**no-rez policy**" and inevitable "**wait**" are a "**drag**", but getting into the "**wine bar annex**" is "**easier**" – or there's always a "**more civilized**", rarely crowded lunch.

ALDO SOHM WINE BAR | French   4.0   4.3   4.4 $$
West 50s | 151 W. 51st St. (bet. 6th & 7th Aves.)
212-554-1143 | www.aldosohmwinebar.com

Le Bernardin's master sommelier, Aldo Sohm, brings "**vaunted wine expertise**" to his nearby Midtown namesake, where "**wonderful**" vintages complement light lunches and "**original**", French-informed small plates at dinner; with a "**well-versed**" staff manning the "**smart-casual**" space (think "**upscale living room**"), it's "**buzzy**" and "**reasonably priced**" – although "**not cheap.**"

AL FORNO PIZZERIA | Pizza   4.0   3.3   3.9 $$
East 70s | 1484 Second Ave. (bet. 77th & 78th Sts.)
212-249-5103 | www.alfornopizzeria77.com

This "**no-frills**" Yorkville "**standby**" churns out "**quality**" brick-oven pizzas on the "**quick**" for low dough; "**typical**" Italian pastas and salads are also on offer, but given "**lots of kids**" and little atmosphere, delivery may be the way to go.

	FOOD	DECOR	SERVICE	COST

ALFREDO 100 | Italian   4.0   4.0   4.0 $$
East 50s | 7 E. 54th St. (bet. 5th & 6th Aves.)
212-688-1999 | www.alfredo100.com

Spun off from an Italy-based original, this Midtowner provides "**generous portions**" of "**pretty good**" Roman cooking (including the trademark fettuccini) via a "**cordial staff**"; with Al Hirschfeld prints lining the "**spacious**" room, it caters to corporate sorts with the lire to settle "**expensive**" tabs.

ALI BABA | Turkish   4.0   3.5   3.7 $$
East 40s | 862 Second Ave. (46th St.)
212-888-8622 | www.alibabasterrace.com

The "**solid menu**" offers "**ample choices**" for "**any size appetite**" at this East Midtown Turk, a "**fairly priced**" standby that rolls out the magic carpet to "**lots of U.N. types**" at lunch; a "**relaxed**" roof terrace easily trumps the "**nothing-special**" downstairs.

ALICE'S TEA CUP | Teahouse   3.9   4.0   3.9 $$
East 60s | 156 E. 64th St. (Lexington Ave.) | 212-486-9200
East 80s | 220 E. 81st St. (bet. 2nd & 3rd Aves.) | 212-734-4832
West 70s | 102 W. 73rd St. (bet. Amsterdam & Columbus Aves.) |
212-799-3006
www.alicesteacup.com

"**Heaven for little girls (and big ones too)**", these "**darling**" tearooms with "**whimsical**" *Alice in Wonderland* decor serve a "**staggering**" selection of brewed pots and "**scrumptious**" scones with an actual side of "**fairy dust**"; not even "**long lines**", "**rushed**" service or "**cramped**" quarters can break the "**enchanting**" spell.

ALIDORO | Italian/Sandwiches   4.7   3.4   3.7 $
Murray Hill | 18 E. 39th St. (bet. 5th & Madison Aves.) | 646-692-4330
NEW **NoHo** | Bowery Mkt. | 348 Bowery St. (Great Jones St.) | no phone
SoHo | 105 Sullivan St. (bet. Prince & Spring Sts.) | 212-334-5179
www.alidoronyc.com

"**Fresh, crispy**" bread plus "**so many choices**" of "**high-quality**" meats and cheeses add up to "**heavenly**", "**humongous**" panini at these "**primo**" Italian sandwich shops (with a Bowery Market stand); just brace for "**long lines**" at lunchtime, "**grumpy**" counter service and a cash-only policy, not to mention limited seating ("**take it to go and enjoy**").

ALI'S ROTI | Caribbean   4.4   3.2   3.7 $
Wakefield | 4220 White Plains Rd. (E. 233rd St.) | Bronx | 718-655-2178
Bedford-Stuyvesant | 1267 Fulton St. (Arlington Pl.) | Brooklyn | 718-783-0316
Crown Heights | 337 Utica Ave. (Carroll St.) | Brooklyn | no phone

"**Mouthwatering**" rotis made with "**fresh dough**" and meaty fillings ("**ask for them spicy**") bring the "**Trini flavor**" to NYC at these low-cost Trinidadians; despite "**no-frills**" setups and sparse seating, expect a "**line of loyal customers**" at prime times.

ALLSWELL | American   ∇ 4.1   3.8   3.9 $$
Williamsburg | 124 Bedford Ave. (10th St.) | Brooklyn
347-799-2743 | www.allswellnyc.tumblr.com

"**Very Brooklyn**", this rustic Williamsburg pub serves up a "**rotating menu**" of "**flavorful**" American grub with "**complex**" farm-to-table ingredients; occupying "**cozy, ski-chalet**" quarters with an "**appropriately hipsterized**" staff and clientele, it's especially "**popular at brunch.**"

	FOOD	DECOR	SERVICE	COST

ALMA | Mexican   4.0   3.9   3.9 $$

Columbia Street Waterfront District | 187 Columbia St., 2nd fl. (Degraw St.) | Brooklyn
718-643-5400 | www.almarestaurant.com

"**Mind-altering**" Manhattan skyline views from a rooftop are the bait at this Columbia Street Waterfront District Mexican where the chow is as "**solid**" as the margaritas are "**strong**"; an "**off-the-beaten-path**" address "**not close to public transportation**" makes "**walking shoes**" the footwear of choice.

ALMAYASS | Armenian/Lebanese   4.4   4.4   4.4 $$

Flatiron | 24 E. 21st St. (bet. B'way & Park Ave. S.)
212-473-3100 | www.almayassnyc.com

An offshoot of the Beirut original, this Flatiron "**surprise**" offers a "**wide**" selection of "**mouthwatering**" Lebanese-Armenian fare with "**standout**" servers to "**guide you through the menu**"; the "**comfortable**" space's "**familial atmosphere**" is "**good for groups**" aiming to "**order a variety and share.**"

ALMOND | French   3.9   3.9   3.9 $$$

Flatiron | 12 E. 22nd St. (bet. B'way & Park Ave. S.)
212-228-7557 | www.almondnyc.com

The cousin of a "**Hamptons old-timer**", this "**dependable**" Flatiron "**drop-in**" serves "**updated takes on French bistro favorites**" in "**roomy**", "**rustic**" surrounds; "**loud but livable**", it's "**good for groups**" and kids, and is also a "**favorite**" for brunch.

ALMONDINE BAKERY | French   4.5   3.7   3.9 $

Dumbo | 85 Water St. (Main St.) | Brooklyn
718-797-5026 | www.almondinebakery.com

It "**feels like Paris**" at this "**authentically French**" Dumbo cafe where the "**delicious baked goods**" include "**excellent**" croissants and some of the "**best baguettes in Brooklyn**"; the "**small**" brick-walled space also has a few tables – ideal for sampling from the "**nice variety**" of soups, salads and quiches.

ALOBAR | American   ∇ 3.9   3.8   4.0 $$

Long Island City | 46-42 Vernon Blvd. (47th Ave.) | Queens
718-752-6000 | www.alobarnyc.com

An "**intelligent**" take on "**farm-to-table**" cuisine showcased in rustic-chic accommodations sets this LIC American abuzz with locals; the "**solid**" offerings can make for spendy tabs, but the consensus is it's "**cool and bold**" for the 'hood.

AL SEABU | Malaysian   —   —   — $

Park Slope | 383 Fifth Ave. (6th St.) | Brooklyn
718-369-0309 | www.alseabu.com

Seafood-focused Malaysian fare, including a "**spicy**" dish or two, is what you'll find at this Park Slope storefront; small and cheery, the "**nothing-fancy**" digs are warmed by exposed brick and wood bench seating.

ALTA | Mediterranean   4.4   4.2   4.2 $$

Greenwich Village | 64 W. 10th St. (bet. 5th & 6th Aves.)
212-505-7777 | www.altarestaurant.com

Small plates are "**full of big flavors**" at this Village Med, which stays "**on its game**" serving "**premier**" tapas and "**awesome sangria**" in "**warm**" bi-level surroundings helmed by a "**welcoming**" crew; prices are "**fair**", but they can still "**add up**", as with the "**super-fun**" $485 "**everything-on-the-menu**" deal.

	FOOD	DECOR	SERVICE	COST

ALTESI RISTORANTE | Italian   4.1   4.1   4.1 $$$
East 60s | 26 E. 64th St. (Madison Ave.)
212-759-8900 | www.altesinyc.com

"**Chic yet warm**", this all-day Italian in an UES brownstone takes diners "**to the Amalfi Coast**" with its "**quite good**" plates served by a "**lovely**" staff; the "**contemporary**" setting includes a "**gem**" of a back garden, and "**pricey**" tariffs just come with the territory.

NEW **AMADA** | Spanish   —   —   — $$$
Battery Park City | Brookfield Pl. | 250 Vesey St. (North End Ave.)
212-542-8947 | www.amadarestaurant.com

A spin-off of chef Jose Garces' Philadelphia tapas spot, this Battery Park City arrival focuses on Andalusian cooking, with both small plates and tasting menus; its sprawling setting with an open kitchen has tiled floors, toffee-toned banquettes and a bar pouring Spanish wines, sherries and gin and tonics.

AMALI | Mediterranean   4.3   4.0   4.2 $$$
East 60s | 115 E. 60th St. (Park Ave.)
212-339-8363 | www.amalinyc.com

"**Classic Mediterranean flavors**" with "**farm-to-table**" sensibilities are an "**inspired**" mix at this Periyali sib tucked away near Bloomie's, which also "**surprises**" Midtowners with a "**biodynamic wine list**"; "**warm**" service and rustically "**stylish**" decor help justify the "**high**" price tag.

AMARANTH | Mediterranean   4.2   3.9   4.0 $$$
East 60s | 21 E. 62nd St. (bet. 5th & Madison Aves.)
212-980-6700 | www.amaranthrestaurant.com

Aka "**air-kissing central**", this "**buzzy**" Madison Avenue–area Med is the kind of place where the "**better-than-average**" food is accompanied by even better "**people-watching**"; service is generally "**attentive**" (especially if you've got a "**European title**"), and "**expensive**" pricing is part of the deal.

AMARONE | Italian   4.1   3.5   4.1 $$
West 40s | 686 Ninth Ave. (47th St.)
212-245-6060 | www.amaroneristorantenyc.com

A "**perfect choice**" pre-theater, this Hell's Kitchen trattoria delivers "**solid**" Italian fare via "**convivial**" staffers sure to "**get you out in time**" for the show; "**modest**" digs mean it's "**nothing fancy**", but that just makes it a "**go-to staple**" kind of place.

AMAZING 66 | Chinese   4.1   3.1   3.6 $$
Chinatown | 66 Mott St. (bet. Bayard & Canal Sts.)
212-334-0099 | www.amazing66.com

"**Genuine**" Cantonese cooking comes at "**reasonable prices**" at this Chinatown storefront where the encyclopedic menu includes "**some real gems**" for "**adventurous**" eaters and the lunch specials are "**unbelievable**"; just know that service is "**quick**" ("**don't expect to linger**") and the decor "**pretty much nonexistent.**"

AMERICAN CUT | Steak   4.4   4.3   4.3 $$$$
NEW **East 50s** | 109 E. 56th St. (bet. Lexington & Park Aves.) | 212-388-5277
TriBeCa | 363 Greenwich St. (bet. Franklin & Harrison Sts.) | 212-226-4736
www.americancutsteakhouse.com

"**A cut above your typical steakhouse**", these "**swanky**" meateries deliver "**regal**" chops that "**melt like butter**"; with "**sophisticated**", "**loungey**" settings and **"pro"** staffers adept at tableside tasks (such as mixing **"fabulous"** cocktails), they're sure to **"impress"** – as are the **"Wall Street"** prices.

| **AMMA** | Indian | 4.7 | 3.9 | 4.3 | $$$ |

East 50s | 246 E. 51st St. (bet. 2nd & 3rd Aves.)
212-644-8330 | www.ammanyc.com

It's **"not your usual"** Indian lineup at this **"exceptional"** East Midtowner, where a **"warm"** staff serves **"beautifully spiced"** multiregional plates, plus tasting menus that are a **"revelation"** for vegetarians and omnivores alike; the **"homey"** yet **"sophisticated"** space can get **"cramped"**, but it's **"perfect for conversation."**

| **AMMOS** | Greek/Seafood | 4.2 | 4.1 | 4.0 | $$$ |

East 40s | 52 Vanderbilt Ave. (bet. 44th & 45th Sts.)
212-922-9999 | www.ammosnewyork.com

This **"business standard"** near Grand Central turns out **"flavorful"** Greek fare in a **"pretty"** white-tablecloth setting with an **"active"** (read: **"noisy"**) bar scene; seating can be **"tight"**, and tabs trend **"high"**, especially if you go with the **"excellent"** whole fish option.

| **AMOR CUBANO** | Cuban | ∇ 4.3 | 3.9 | 4.0 | $$ |

East Harlem | 2018 Third Ave. (111th St.)
212-996-1220 | www.amorcubanonyc.com

Giving Miami a run for its money, this **"hopping"** East Harlem Cuban plates **"muy bueno"** chow right out of **"pre-Castro Havana"**, paired with **"amazing"** mojitos; live music via a **"loud band"** adds **"authenticity"** and adds to the **"time warp"** experience.

| **AMORINA** | Italian/Pizza | ∇ 4.3 | 3.4 | 4.0 | $$ |

Prospect Heights | 624 Vanderbilt Ave. (Prospect Pl.) | Brooklyn
718-230-3030 | www.amorinapizza.com

When in the mood for **"delicious"** Roman-style pizzas and pastas at moderate prices, locals turn to this Prospect Heights Italian; even though it can be **"literally crawling"** with **"toddlers"**, the **"small"**, red-checkered-tablecloth setting exudes a **"homey"** vibe and is overseen by a **"hard-working"** staff.

| **AMORINO** | Ice Cream | 4.4 | 3.8 | 3.9 | $ |

Chelsea | 162 Eighth Ave. (18th St.) | 212-255-6471
Greenwich Village | 60 University Pl. (bet. 10th & 11th Sts.) | 212-253-5599
West 40s | 721 Eighth Ave. (45th St.) | 212-445-0101
NEW **West 70s** | 414 Amsterdam Ave. (80th St.) | 646-918-7501
www.amorino.com

Some of the most **"delicious"** gelato **"outside of Italy"** can be found at these outposts of a European chain offering **"bold"** flavors in **"flower-shaped"** scoops plus **"divine"** macaron sandwiches too; since you can get **"as many flavors as you'd like"**, the kinda **"hefty"** prices are easier to take.

| **AMPLE HILLS CREAMERY** | Ice Cream | 4.7 | 3.7 | 4.2 | $ |

West 40s | 600 11th Ave. (bet. 44th & 45th Sts.) | 212-582-9354
Gowanus | 305 Nevins St. (Union St.) | Brooklyn | 347-725-4061
Prospect Heights | 623 Vanderbilt Ave. (St. Marks Ave.) | Brooklyn |
347-240-3926
www.amplehills.com

Every **"creamy, dreamy"** scoop is a **"revelation"** at these **"hip"** ice cream parlors where the **"endlessly creative"** flavors (e.g. the **"sensational"** Salted

Crack Caramel) are housemade; "**long lines**" mean some "**grab a pint and flee**", though Gowanus' "**cool**" roof deck is a "**must**" in summer.

AMSTERDAM BURGER COMPANY | Burgers   4.3   3.3   3.6 $

West 90s | 654 Amsterdam Ave. (92nd St.)
212-362-0700 | www.amsterdamburger.com

Those seeking a "**quality**" kosher burger praise the "**enormous, juicy, perfectly seasoned**" patties at this UWSider; "**prompt**" service is another plus, and while the "**ambiance leaves a lot to be desired**", the place is still often "**packed.**"

AMY RUTH'S | Soul Food   4.4   3.2   3.9 $$

Harlem | 113 W. 116th St. (bet. Lenox & 7th Aves.)
212-280-8779 | www.amyruths.com

Those jonesing for a taste of "**classic Harlem**" head to this low-budget soul food "**stalwart**" for "**hearty**" cooking highlighted by "**amazing**" chicken and waffles; regulars "**ignore the decor**" and "**spotty**" service, and get there early "**before the tourist buses arrive.**"

AMY'S BREAD | Bakery   4.4   3.3   3.8 $

Chelsea | Chelsea Mkt. | 75 Ninth Ave. (bet. 15th & 16th Sts.) | 212-462-4338
West 40s | 672 Ninth Ave. (bet. 46th & 47th Sts.) | 212-977-2670
West Village | 250 Bleecker St. (Leroy St.) | 212-675-7802
Sunnyside | 4809 34th St. (48th Ave.) | Queens | 212-462-2038
www.amysbread.com

"**Sublime**", "**crusty loaves**" star at these "**scrumptious**" bakery/cafes, which are "**popular**" stops for "**coffee and carbs in the morning**" and "**healthy, affordable lunches**" of "**tasty**" sandwiches and salads; "**there's always a line**" and the few tables are "**precious**", so for many "**takeout works best.**"

ANASSA TAVERNA | Greek   4.1   3.8   3.9 $$$

East 60s | 200 E. 60th St (3rd Ave.)
212-371-5200 | www.anassataverna.com

A "**lively**" Avra sibling "**convenient to Bloomie's**", this UES Greek "**hits the spot**" with a lineup of seafood and other staples that's "**pretty solid**" if "**a little pricey**"; the "**casual**", split-level setting emits "**feel-good vibes**", though at peak hours it can be "**quite noisy.**"

ANDANADA 141 | Spanish   4.1   4.0   4.0 $$$

West 60s | 141 W. 69th St. (bet. B'way & Columbus Ave.)
646-692-8762 | www.andanada141.com

This "**lovely**" Upper Westsider serves tapas and other Spanish classics "**done with modern flair**" in "**sleek**", graffiti-mural-adorned digs; the vibe is "**lively but allows for conversation**", and its location is tailor-made for the "**pre–Lincoln Center**" set.

AÑEJO | Mexican   3.9   3.9   3.9 $$

TriBeCa | 301 Church St. (Walker St.) | 212-920-6270 | www.anejotribeca.com
West 40s | 668 10th Ave. (47th St.) | 212-920-4770 | www.anejonyc.com

"**Interesting**" Mexican small plates are perfect for "**trying a multitude of items**" at these "**hip**" cantinas where an "**excellent**" tequila lineup and "**inventive**" combinations make for "**fabulous**" cocktails; if the digs get "**noisy**" you can take refuge on the sidewalk patios or at Abajo, TriBeCa's downstairs speakeasy.

	FOOD	DECOR	SERVICE	COST

ANGELICA KITCHEN | Vegan/Vegetarian   4.2   3.5   4.0 $$
East Village | 300 E. 12th St. (2nd Ave.)
212-228-2909 | www.angelicakitchen.com

A longtime vegan "**standard-bearer**", this "**go-with-the-flow**" East Village
mainstay is a "**wholesome**" destination for "**your-body-as-a-temple**"
dining at a "**reasonable**" cost; though the decor is "**spartan**" and the service
"**loose**", there's "**always a line for a table**" (no reservations), and it now
serves beer and wine.

ANGELINA'S | Italian   4.1   4.4   4.1 $$$
Tottenville | 399 Ellis St. (Arthur Kill Rd.) | Staten Island
718-227-2900 | www.angelinasristorante.com

Set in a "**stunning**" tri-level mansion on the water, this "**fine-dining**"
destination in Tottenville pairs upscale Italian cuisine with "**choreographed**"
service; though the "**average**" fare is "**expensive**" for SI and the crowd a bit
"**Jersey Shore**", most say it's a bona fide "**special-occasion**" hub.

ANGELO'S OF MULBERRY STREET | Italian   4.4   3.6   4.1 $$
Little Italy | 146 Mulberry St. (bet. Grand & Hester Sts.)
212-966-1277 | www.angelosofmulberryst.com

It doesn't get more "**old school**" than this circa-1902 Little Italy "**favorite**" that
stays popular thanks to "**consistently delicious**" Neapolitan cooking and
"**attentive**" service; maybe the "**stereotypical**" decor could use "**a little
touching up**", but otherwise fans "**feel the love**" – "**maybe the tourists know
something**" after all.

ANGUS CLUB STEAKHOUSE | Steak   4.4   4.2   4.4 $$$
East 50s | 135 E. 55th St. (Lexington Ave.)
212-588-1585 | www.angusclubsteakhouse.com

You can "**cut the meat with your fork**" at this Midtown East chophouse
pairing "**excellent**" dry-aged Angus beef (natch) with "**properly done**" sides
and "**exceptional**" wines; "**attentive**" servers preside over the "**lovely**" bi-level
setting where it's "**calm**" enough to "**enjoy conversation.**"

ANNABEL | Italian/Pizza   4.1   4.0   3.9 $$
West 50s | 809 Ninth Ave. (bet. 53rd & 54th Sts.)
212-245-2209 | www.annabelnyc.com

"**Lively**" crowds, "**delicious**" wood-fired pizzas and reliable service all "**come
together**" at this "**cozy**" Hell's Kitchen Italian, which also serves "**inventive**"
cocktails and loads of craft beers; "**reasonable**" prices suit it just as well to
pre- and post-theater meals as to brunch.

ANN & TONY'S | Italian   3.8   3.3   3.7 $$
Arthur Avenue/Belmont | 2407 Arthur Ave. (bet. 187th & 188th Sts.) | Bronx
718-933-1469 | www.annandtonysonline.com

Talk about "**classic**" – this circa-1927 "**Arthur Avenue mainstay**" remains a
steady "**favorite**" thanks to its "**healthy portions**" of "**old-fashioned**", if "**basic**",
Italiana served by a "**welcoming**" crew; "**reasonable**" prices mean most
overlook "**decor from the '70s.**"

ANNISA | American   4.7   4.3   4.6 $$$$
West Village | 13 Barrow St. (bet. 7th Ave. S. & W. 4th St.)
212-741-6699 | www.annisarestaurant.com

Chef Anita Lo's "**subtle fusion**" of American cuisine with "**Asian influences**" results in culinary "**marvels**" at this "**elegant**" West Village "**food temple**"; the "**unobtrusive**" pro service and "**calm**", "**ultra-sophisticated**" modern setting further ensure a "**special evening.**"

ANTICA PESA | Italian   4.6   4.4   4.4 $$$
Williamsburg | 115 Berry St. (bet. 7th & 8th Sts.) | Brooklyn
347-763-2635 | www.anticapesa.com

It might be "**fancy for the 'burg**", but this "**suave**" Williamsburg sibling to a Rome original has built a following for its "**delicious**" Italian classics (including "**exquisite**" housemade pastas) and "**serious**" wine list, presented by a "**charming**" staff; there's also a "**lively**" fireplace-furnished lounge within its "**sleek**", "**lovely**" dome-lit space.

ANTONUCCI CAFE | Italian   4.4   3.7   4.1 $$
East 80s | 170 E. 81st St. (bet. Lexington & 3rd Aves.)
212-570-5100

In a "**neighborhood filled with Italian restaurants**", this "**nice-and-easy**" UES trattoria holds its own with "**consistently good**" fare highlighted by especially "**excellent pastas**"; seating is "**tight**" and tabs "**pricey for every day**", but "**warm**" vibes and "**unhurried**" service help compensate.

A.O.C. L'AILE OU LA CUISSE | French   4.1   3.9   3.9 $$
West Village | 314 Bleecker St. (Grove St.)
212-675-9463 | www.aocnyc.com

"**You just might be in Paris**" at this "**Frenchy French**" West Village bistro, supplier of "**unfussy but tasty**" staples at "**not haute**" prices in a "**throwback**" setting with a "**sweet petite garden**"; the "**everyday**" style means sometimes "**sloppy**" service, but for a Gallic "**hankering**" it'll do "**in a pinch.**"

AQUAGRILL | Seafood   4.7   4.0   4.4 $$$
SoHo | 210 Spring St. (6th Ave.)
212-274-0505 | www.aquagrill.com

A "**mainstay**" for "**consistently excellent**" seafood, this SoHo "**institution**" offers "**perfectly cooked**" fish and "**super-fresh**" oysters, plus a "**fabulous**" brunch; if the "**low-key**" dining room is "**showing its age**", service remains "**seamless**" and the seasonal patio is a "**delight.**"

AQUAVIT | Scandinavian   4.5   4.4   4.5 $$$$
East 50s | 65 E. 55th St. (bet. Madison & Park Aves.)
212-307-7311 | www.aquavit.org

After more than 25 years, this "**elegant, but low-key**" Midtown "**fixture**" is still "**pushing the envelope**", turning out "**innovative**" Scandinavian tasting menus of the "**highest level**"; the "**sleek**" space is matched by "**top-notch**" service, and while prices are "**steep**", sampling from its "**huge**" aquavit selection will have you thinking "**you're dining in Denmark.**"

ARCADE BAKERY | Bakery/French   4.5   3.6   4.1 $$
TriBeCa | 220 Church St. (bet. Thomas & Worth Sts.)
212-227-7895 | www.arcadebakery.com

"**You've stumbled upon a secret**" when you find this "**lovely**" French bakery "**tucked away**" in the lobby of a TriBeCa office building where it offers "**exceptional**" breads ("**especially the laminated baguette**"), "**delicious**" croissants and "**tasty**" lunch options; "**minimal**" seating leads most to take out.

	FOOD	DECOR	SERVICE	COST

AREO | Italian   4.4   3.7   4.1 $$$

Bay Ridge | 8424 Third Ave. (bet. 84th & 85th Sts.) | Brooklyn
718-238-0079

"Fuhgeddaboudit" – this "**busy**" Bay Ridge "**staple**" continues to "**stand the test of time**" as a supplier of "**wonderful**" Italiana and "**old-world**" service; assuming "**you can handle the noise**", its "**lively scene**" and "**local color**" are an all-around "**hoot.**"

AREPA LADY | S American   ∇ 4.6   3.3   4.2 $

Elmhurst | 77-02 Roosevelt Ave. (enter on 77th St.) | Queens
347-730-6124

After plying her "**fabulous**" mozzarella-stuffed corn cakes from an "**insanely popular**" cart, Maria Cano is now doing her thing at this "**small**" Elmhurst storefront where fans say "**the lady's still got it**"; the digs "**aren't much to look at**", but with "**friendly**" service and "**reasonable**" prices, "**who cares?**"

AREPAS CAFÉ | Venezuelan   4.3   3.3   3.9 $$

Astoria | 33-07 36th Ave. (bet 33rd & 34th Sts.) | Queens | 718-937-3835

AREPAS GRILL | Venezuelan

Astoria | 21-19 Broadway (bet. 21st & 23rd Sts.) | Queens | 718-355-9686

"**Flavors straight out of Caracas**" are stuffed into "**fluffy**", affordable arepas at these "**something-different**" Astoria Venezuelans; the bite-size Cafe original sports a "**diner atmosphere**" that suggests "**takeout**", but the Grill offshoot is roomier, with a broader menu that includes Caribbean and Med dishes.

ARETSKY'S PATROON | American   4.3   4.3   4.4 $$$$

East 40s | 160 E. 46th St. (bet. Lexington & 3rd Aves.)
212-883-7373 | www.aretskyspatroon.com

Ken Aretsky's "**polished**" East Midtown "**business**" "**oasis**" remains a place to "**impress clients**" with "**well-prepared**" American fare and "**first-class service**" in "**men's club**" digs done up with "**classic photos**"; "**especially nice**" are the private rooms and roof bar, but just "**watch out for those prices.**"

ARLINGTON CLUB | Steak   4.1   4.2   4.1 $$$

East 70s | 1032 Lexington Ave. (bet. 73rd & 74th Sts.)
212-249-5700 | www.arlingtonclubny.com

A "**steady**" UES choice, this "**upscale**" steakhouse supplies "**pricey**" cuts alongside modern American fare in a "**busy**" setting sporting a "**vaulted ceiling**" and hardwood aplenty; the "**over-the-top**" scene is popular with locals "**of a certain age**" who've "**removed their wedding rings**" at the "**cougarville**" bar.

ARMANI RISTORANTE | Italian   4.3   4.4   4.3 $$$$

East 50s | 717 Fifth Ave., 3rd fl. (56th St.)
212-207-1902 | www.armaniristorante.com

"**A terrific find**" say "**fashionistas**" of this "**suave**" and "**sleek**" Italian "**charmer**" in Giorgio Armani's Midtown flagship, where the "**creative**" fare is prepared with the "**surest hand**"; while the "**trendy**" lunch crowd makes way for "**quiet**", "**pleasant**" dinners, tabs stay "**expensive.**"

ARNO | Italian   4.2   3.7   4.2 $$$

West 30s | 141 W. 38th St. (B'way)
212-944-7420 | www.arnoristorante.com

A "**go-to place**" in Midtown's Garment District, this "**old-fashioned**" Northern Italian is targeted to the "**garmento**" business-lunch trade; the "**down-to-**

earth" cooking is "**reliable**" and the service "**friendly**", but the decor seems a bit "**plain**" given the tabs.

ARTICHOKE BASILLE'S PIZZA | Pizza   4.1   3.0   3.5 $

Chelsea | 114 10th Ave. (17th St.) | 212-792-9200
East Village | 328 E. 14th St. (bet. 1st & 2nd Aves.) | 212-228-2004
Greenwich Village | 111 MacDougal St. (bet. Bleecker & 3rd Sts.) | 646-278-6100
Park Slope | 59 Fifth Ave. (St Marks Ave) | Brooklyn | 347-763-1975
Astoria | 22-56 31st St. (bet. Ditmars Blvd. & 23rd Ave.) | Queens | 718-215-8100
www.artichokepizza.com

"**Messy but delicious**", the "**monster**" namesake slices topped with "**gooey**", "**creamy**" artichoke dip are a "**force to be reckoned with**" at this "**popular**" pizzeria mini-chain; it's "**no-frills**" and a popular pick when "**late-night munchies**" hit, so expect "**long lines even in the early morning hours.**"

ARTIE'S | Seafood/Steak   4.4   3.7   4.1 $$$

City Island | 394 City Island Ave. (Ditmars St.) | Bronx
718-885-9885 | www.artiesofcityisland.com

"**Actual City Island residents**" eat at this "**been-there-forever**" surf 'n' turfer offering an "**always good**" "**retro**" Italian-accented menu; true, it's "**not on the water**", but "**unhurried**" service and fair pricing keep locals "**happy as clams.**"

ARTISANAL | French   4.2   4.0   3.9 $$$

Murray Hill | 2 Park Ave. (bet. 32nd & 33rd Sts.)
212-725-8585 | www.artisanalbistro.com

It's all about the "**heavenly**" cheese at this "**classic**" Midtown "**standby**" where a "**crazy variety**" (including "**unbeatable**" fondues) is offered alongside "**tasty**" French brasserie dishes in a "**soaring**" Parisian-style space; "**high prices**", "**spotty service**" and "**noisy**" conditions to one side, most say it's still "*très bien*."

ARTURO'S PIZZERIA | Pizza   4.2   3.5   3.8 $$

Greenwich Village | 106 W. Houston St. (Thompson St.)
212-677-3820 | www.arturoscoaloven.com

"**Old Greenwich Village**" endures at this 1957-vintage pizzeria where a "**slice of the past**" comes via "**delicious, no-nonsense**" pies "**straight out of the coal oven**"; a live jazz combo and an "**unpretentious**" mood compensate for decor that's somewhere between "**faded**" and "**dingy.**"

A SALT & BATTERY | British   4.2   3.2   3.9 $$

West Village | 112 Greenwich Ave. (bet. 12th & 13th Sts.)
212-691-2713 | www.asaltandbattery.com

This West Village "**hole-in-the-wall**" does a "**jolly good**" rendition of British fish 'n' chips for an "**affordable**" sum; other "**anti–health food**" grub like deep-fried candy bars fill out the "**greasy**" bill, but since there's "**no decor**" and seating's just a "**few stools**", most get the goods to go.

ASIA DE CUBA | Asian/Cuban   4.4   4.3   4.2 $$$

Greenwich Village | 415 Lafayette St. (4th St.)
212-726-7755 | www.asiadecuba.com

"**Still sexy after *Sex and the City***", this Greenwich Village revival of the former Morgans Hotel hot spot serves "**fantastic**" Asian-Cuban fusion fare and "**excellent**" cocktails in "**cool**" digs; it's a "**little pricey**", but the "**fun**" vibe is "**perfect**" for a group.

	FOOD	DECOR	SERVICE	COST

ASIATE | American/Asian 　　　　　4.6　4.8　4.6　$$$$

West 50s | Mandarin Oriental Hotel | 80 Columbus Circle, 35th fl. (B'way)
212-805-8881 | www.mandarinoriental.com

"**Elegant, calm**" surroundings and "**spectacular views**" over Central Park
make an "**incomparable**" backdrop for the "**exquisite**" New American cuisine
at this "**special-occasion**" go-to "**atop the Mandarin Oriental**"; the prices are
equally "**out of this world**" (dinner is prix fixe–only), but "**stellar**" service helps
take the sting out – and the 'express' lunch is a "**steal.**"

NEW ASKA | Scandinavian 　　　　　　—　—　—　$$$$

Williamsburg | 47 S. Fifth St. (bet. Kent & Wythe Aves.) | Brooklyn
929-337-6792 | www.askanyc.com

At this modern Scandinavian in Williamsburg, chef-owner Fredrik Berselius'
cuisine draws from local farms and touches on the unfamiliar; tasting
menu–format dinners in the petite dining room are by reservation only and
can last for hours, but there's also a more casual garden and below-ground
bar offering small plates, wines and cocktails.

ASTOR ROOM | American 　　　　　　3.9　4.3　4.1　$$

Astoria | 34-12 36th St. (bet. 35th & 36th Aves.) | Queens
718-255-1947 | www.astorroom.com

It "**feels like the 1920s**" at this "**throwback**" spot inside Kaufman Astoria
Studios, supplying American eats to "**TV and movie**" industry types;
"**speakeasy**" looks, a "**great bar**" mixing "**vintage**" drinks and frequent
"**live jazz**" complete the "**old-school**" vibe.

ATERA | American 　　　　　　　4.6　4.7　4.7　$$$$

TriBeCa | 77 Worth St. (bet. B'way & Church St.)
212-226-1444 | www.ateranyc.com

"**Creativity at its peak**" is in evidence at this tasting menu–only TriBeCa
"**delight**", where a "**fun-loving**" staff delivers chef Ronny Emborg's
"**phenomenal**" New American cuisine to diners seated at a kitchen-facing
counter; the "**unforgettable**" experience is "**as high as high-end gets**" ($235
for 18 courses, tip included), but to most it's "**worth every dollar**" – assuming
"**you can secure a reservation.**"

ATLANTIC GRILL | Seafood 　　　　　4.3　4.0　4.1　$$$

East 70s | 1341 Third Ave. (bet. 76th & 77th Sts.) | 212-988-9200
West 60s | 49 W. 64th St. (bet. B'way & CPW) | 212-787-4663
www.atlanticgrill.com

"**Still going strong**" after many years, these "**steady**" "**local favorites**" reel
'em in with "**creatively prepared**" fish, "**extravagant raw towers**" and
"**surprisingly good**" sushi; sure, they can "**get crowded**" at prime times,
but the "**comfortable ambiance**" wins over most, ditto the "**divine**" brunch
(an "**amazing deal**").

NEW ATOBOY | Korean 　　　　　　—　—　—　$$

NoMad | 43 E. 28th St. (Park Ave. S.)
646-476-7217 | www.atoboynyc.com

Sharing is the way to go at this NoMad Korean helmed by a Jungsik alum,
where the affordable tasting menu provides a choice of small banchan
dishes and rice. The understated space has mottled walls and rustic
light-wood tables.

	FOOD	DECOR	SERVICE	COST

ATRIUM DUMBO | French   4.0   4.0   4.1 $$
Dumbo | 15 Main St. (bet. Plymouth & Water Sts.) | Brooklyn
718-858-1095 | www.atriumdumbo.com

An "**airy, modernist-rustic**" space and "**locavore**" fare "**with flair**" have locals declaring this "*très* chic" French-influenced New American "**so completely Dumbo**", especially with its "**lively**" downstairs bar and outdoor seating; despite "**hit or miss**" results and somewhat "**high**" prices, fans like that it's "**blessedly close**" to St. Ann's Warehouse.

AUREOLE | American   4.6   4.4   4.5 $$$$
West 40s | 135 W. 42nd St. (bet. B'way & 6th Ave.)
212-319-1660 | www.charliepalmer.com

An "**oasis of calm**" in Times Square, Charlie Palmer's "**classy**" flagship "**sets the bar**" with "**exquisite**" New American fare "**presented like art**" by a staff "**with finesse**"; the "**beautiful**", "**modern**" dining room is a natural for "**special occasions**" and while dinner tabs are "**over-the-top**", lunch is a relative "**bargain.**"

AURORA | Italian   4.4   4.2   4.3 $$$
SoHo | 510 Broome St. (bet. Thompson St. & W. B'way) | 212-334-9020 | www.aurorasoho.com
Williamsburg | 70 Grand St. (Wythe Ave.) | Brooklyn | 718-388-5100 | www.aurorabk.com

Whether for a "**romantic**" evening or meal "**with your pals**", these "**fairly priced**" Italians do the trick, supplying "**well-executed**" fare in "**cozy**" digs that "**bring out the charm of Tuscany**"; the "**cheerful vibes**" get an extra lift from a "**beautiful**" garden area at the Williamsburg original.

AUTRE KYO YA | French/Japanese   ▽ 4.4   4.1   4.4 $$$
East Village | 10 Stuyvesant St. (9th St.)
212-598-0454 | www.autrekyoya.com

Melding Japanese cuisine with French techniques, this Kyo Ya East Village offshoot is "**growing up to become a star of its own**" thanks to a "**delicious**" menu that's high-end yet less expensive than the kaiseki-based original; the minimalist, wood-centric space also provides a brief raw-bar selection and sophisticated cocktails.

AU ZA'ATAR | French/Mideastern   4.1   3.4   3.8 $$
East Village | 188 Ave. A (12th St.)
212-254-5660 | www.auzaatar.com

"**A French slant**" animates the "**flavorful**" Middle Eastern eats at this all-day East Villager, where the "**deep menu**" includes Lebanese meze with "**many vegetarian options**"; "**homey**" digs with "**wood everywhere**" keep the focus on the food, which leaves the majority "**satisfied.**"

AVANT GARDEN | Vegan   4.5   4.0   4.3 $$
East Village | 130 E. Seventh St. (Ave. A)
646-922-7948 | www.avantgardennyc.com

Turning "**preconceived notions of vegan food on their head**", this "**cozy**" East Villager crafts plant-based small plates that are "**exquisite for the eye and palate**", served up in "**rustic**" digs with a kitchen-facing bar; the check "**can add up fast**", but to most the "**provocative**" experience is "**worth the extra cash.**"

	FOOD	DECOR	SERVICE	COST

A VOCE | Italian — 4.3 — 4.3 — 4.3 — $$$

Flatiron | 41 Madison Ave. (26th St.) |
212-545-8555 | www.avocerestaurant.com

"**Reliable for both business and pleasure**", this Flatiron contemporary Italian is known for "**marvelous**" pastas and other artful dishes matched with a "**top-notch**" wine selection and served by "**pros**"; with "**eye-pleasing**" decor rounding out "**the whole package**" for "**elegant**" dining, most don't mind if it's "**a bit pricey.**"

AVRA | Greek/Seafood — 4.6 — 4.2 — 4.1 — $$$

East 40s | 141 E. 48th St. (bet. Lexington & 3rd Aves.) | 212-759-8550

NEW **AVRA MADISON** | Greek/Seafood

East 60s | 14 E. 60th St. (bet. 5th & Madison Aves.) | 212-937-0100
www.avrany.com

A "**mainstay**" for East Midtown "**suits**", this "**buzzing**" "**upscale taverna**" (with an UES sequel) beckons with "**unforgettable**" grilled fish and other "**terrific Greek seafood**" dispatched by a "**helpful**" team; the by-the-pound selections trend quite "**expensive**", though the "**tight**", "**loud**" quarters can be sidestepped by snagging a "**great**" outdoor table.

AWADH | Indian — 4.3 — 3.9 — 4.0 — $$

West 90s | 2588 Broadway (98th St.)
646-861-3604 | www.awadhnyc.com

"**A far cry**" from your average Indian eatery, this "**contemporary**" UWS duplex showcases "**high-end**" Awadhi cuisine "**innovatively prepared**" with "**complex**" flavors; service ranges from "**prompt**" to "**spotty**", but it's still hailed as a "**gem**" whose "**flair**" is "**no longer a secret.**"

AWASH | Ethiopian — 4.3 — 3.4 — 3.9 — $$

East Village | 338 E. Sixth St. (bet. 1st & 2nd Aves.) | 212-982-9589
West 100s | 947 Amsterdam Ave. (bet. 106th & 107th Sts.) | 212-961-1416
Cobble Hill | 242 Court St. (bet. Baltic & Kane Sts.) | Brooklyn | 718-243-2151
www.awashny.com

"**Different experience**" seekers tout these "**unsung**", utensil-free Ethiopians where "**savory deliciousness**" comes in the form of stews scooped up with "**terrific**" injera flatbread; "**somewhat vague**" service and "**unassuming**" settings come with the territory, but at least you'll walk out awash with cash.

AYADA | Thai — 4.5 — 3.2 — 3.8 — $$

Elmhurst | 77-08 Woodside Ave. (bet. 77th & 78th Sts.) | Queens
718-424-0844 | www.ayadathaiwoodside.com

"**Spicy means spicy**" at this "**friendly**" Elmhurst Thai whose "**uncompromising**" dishes pack "**powerful flavors**" and come at a "**fair price**"; the "**humble**" storefront space gets "**crowded**" with "**lines out the door**" at prime times, but a recent expansion has added a bit of elbow room.

AZURI CAFE | Israeli/Kosher — ∇ 4.4 — 2.8 — 3.2 — $$

West 50s | 465 W. 51st St. (bet. 9th & 10th Aves.)
212-262-2920 | www.azuricafe.com

Falafel "**from heaven**" and other "**cheap**", "**delicious**" Israeli eats offset the "**dumpy**" decor at this Hell's Kitchen "**hole-in-the-wall**"; just "**don't expect a warm welcome**" – the "**short-tempered**" owner is the neighborhood's "**favorite curmudgeon.**"

	FOOD	DECOR	SERVICE	COST

BABA'S PIEROGIES | E European ▽ 4.4 3.6 4.0 $

Gowanus | 295 Third Ave. (Carroll St.) | Brooklyn
718-222-0777 | www.babasbk.com

Inspired by "**bubby's**" recipes, this Gowanus Eastern European turns out "**delicious**" pierogi, with both "**classic**" fillings (cheese, potato) and modern variations (jalapeño, bacon-cheese), plus soups, salads and sandwiches; its "**humble**" counter-service space features a few light-wood tables.

BABBO | Italian 4.6 4.3 4.5 $$$$

Greenwich Village | 110 Waverly Pl. (bet. MacDougal St. & 6th Ave.)
212-777-0303 | www.babbonyc.com

"**Still a bastion of fine Italian dining**", this Village "**star**" in the Batali-Bastianich firmament continues to "**impress**" with "**phenomenal**" pastas and other "**exceptional**" dishes delivered by a "**polished**" team in "**warm**" (if "**boisterous**") carriage house digs; yes, it's "**a pain to get a table**" and tabs run "**high**", but to most the "**always-spot-on**" experience is "**well worth it.**"

BABU JI | Indian 4.5 3.8 4.2 $$

East Village | 175 Ave. B (11th St.)
212-951-1082 | www.babujinyc.com

"**Full of excellent surprises**", this "**hoppin'**" Australian import in the East Village features "**transformative**" modern takes on Indian staples – including an "**incredible**" tasting menu – chased with suds from the self-serve beer fridge; since it's "**so popular**", the "**only con**" is the "**crammed space**" and inevitable "**waits.**"

BACARO | Italian ▽ 4.2 4.4 4.2 $$$

Lower East Side | 136 Division St. (bet. Ludlow & Orchard Sts.)
212-941-5060 | www.bacaronyc.com

There's a "**sultry**", "**wine-cellar vibe**" in play at this "**gorgeous**" LES basement offering "**delicious**" Venetian small plates (and particularly "**wonderful**" pastas) to a crowd of "**hipsters, artists and the Uptowners who love them**"; "**flickering candles**" keep things seriously "**romantic**", so it's "**perfect for a date.**"

BACCHUS | French 4.1 3.9 4.2 $$

Downtown Brooklyn | 409 Atlantic Ave. (bet. Bond & Nevins Sts.) | Brooklyn
718-852-1572 | www.bacchusbistro.com

"**Classic French bistro**" fare draws fans to this "**charming little**" Downtown Brooklyn wine bar/eatery; "**reasonable**" rates, "**no pretension**" and a "**beautiful**" back garden lend "**lazy-day**" appeal, plus it's a "**hop and a skip**" from BAM.

BACI & ABBRACCI | Italian ▽ 4.3 4.0 4.3 $$

Williamsburg | 204 Grand St. (Driggs Ave.) | Brooklyn
718-599-6599 | www.baciny.com

There's lots of neighborhood love for the "**delicious**" Italian "**basics**" served at this "**modern**" Williamsburg joint; "**value**" tabs, "**friendly**" staffers and a "**lovely**" garden are other reasons it's a "**charming**" pick.

BAGATELLE | French 4.0 4.3 4.0 $$$

Meatpacking District | 1 Little W. 12th St. (9th Ave.)
212-488-2110 | www.bagatellenyc.com

"**Hot and cool at the same time**", this Meatpacking "**bacchanal**" bolsters its splurgy but "**better-than-average**" French fare with an exuberant "**funday mentality"; its infamous "**party brunch**" featuring "**expensive champagne**", "**throbbing Euro house**" sounds and "**dancing on the tables**" is "**not for the faint of heart**" (or wallet).

		FOOD	DECOR	SERVICE	COST
BAGELWORKS	Bagels	4.3	2.6	3.8	$

East 60s | 1229 First Ave. (bet. 65th & 66th Sts.)
212-744-6444 | www.bagelworks.nyc

"**Fresh**" bagels "**made the old-fashioned way**" generate "**lines out the door**" at this UES neighborhood deli with spreads, salads and sandwiches that also "**please**"; there's "**no place to sit**" in the "**bare-bones**" space, but "**efficient**" service makes it "**easy**" to grab and go.

		FOOD	DECOR	SERVICE	COST
BAHARI ESTIATORIO	Greek	4.4	3.5	4.0	$$

Astoria | 31-14 Broadway (32nd St.) | Queens
718-204-8968 | www.bahariestiatorio.com

"**Excellent**" Hellenic "**home cooking**" served "**with a smile**" explains why this Astoria "**neighborhood**" joint is usually "**packed**"; the spare storefront space may be "**a little tight**", but given the "**authentic**" eats and "**bargain prices**", no one minds.

		FOOD	DECOR	SERVICE	COST
BAKED	Bakery	4.4	3.7	4.0	$

TriBeCa | 279 Church St. (White St.) | 212-775-0345
Red Hook | 359 Van Brunt St. (Dikeman St.) | Brooklyn | 718-222-0345
www.bakednyc.com

"**Everything is divine**" at these American-style bakery/cafes that are "**sweet-tooth heaven**" for "**guilty treats**" like layer cakes, signature 'brookstore' (a cookie-brownie hybrid), whoopie pies and bars "**galore**"; fans say it's "**nice to hang out**" in their "**comfortable**" spaces over coffee, breakfast pastries and "**light lunch fare.**"

			FOOD	DECOR	SERVICE	COST
BAKERI	Bakery/European	▽	4.3	4.2	3.9	$

Greenpoint | 105 Freeman St. (Franklin St.) | Brooklyn | 718-349-1542
Williamsburg | 150 Wythe Ave. (8th St.) | Brooklyn | 718-388-8037
www.bakeribrooklyn.com

These "**cute**" bakery/cafes specialize in breads, "**devilish pastries and delights**" and other German-Scandinavian baked goods, including a "**delicious**" orange brioche roll; although "**service can be harried**", regulars say the "**very Brooklyn-French**" decor is an ideal backdrop for "**sitting in the front window seats with a good book for a while.**"

		FOOD	DECOR	SERVICE	COST
BALABOOSTA	Mediterranean/Mideastern	4.4	3.9	4.1	$$$

NoLita | 214 Mulberry St. (Spring St.)
212-966-7366 | www.balaboostanyc.com

Applying "**artful flair**" to Med-Mideastern "**comfort**" classics, the Taïm team spins a "**gourmet experience**" at this NoLita "**favorite**"; the space is "**cute**" but "**always packed**", so you may gain acquaintance with your "**neighbor's elbow**", but that's easy to overlook given such "**warm welcomes**" and "**reasonable**" prices.

		FOOD	DECOR	SERVICE	COST
BALADE	Lebanese	4.2	3.8	4.1	$$

East Village | 208 First Ave. (bet. 12th & 13th Sts.)
212-529-6868 | www.baladerestaurants.com

"**Hidden away**" in the East Village, this "**traditional**" Lebanese is lauded for "**mouthwatering**" meals (the "**meze are a must**") at "**reasonable prices**"; with a "**friendly**" staff manning the "**low-key**" quarters, "**addicted**" followers keep "**coming back.**"

	FOOD	DECOR	SERVICE	COST

BALTHAZAR | French — 4.4 4.3 4.1 $$$
SoHo | 80 Spring St. (Crosby St.)
212-965-1414 | www.balthazarny.com

Keith McNally's "**legendary**" SoHo brasserie "**still delivers the goods**" with its "**magnifique**" French fare ("**blissful**" breakfast, "**oh such wonderful**" breads) and atmosphere straight out of "**Belle Époque Paris**"; it's "**always buzzing**" with "**locals and tourists alike**", plus a "**celebrity or two**", meaning the "**tight quarters**" can be a "**madhouse**" – but that's part of what makes it "**a New York classic.**"

BALVANERA | Argentinean — ▽ 4.5 4.0 4.4 $$$
Lower East Side | 152 Stanton St. (Suffolk St.)
212-533-3348 | www.balvaneranyc.com

The first solo offering from chef Fernando Navas (a vet of Nobu and Spain's elBulli), this LES "**rising star**" offers "**top-notch**" Argentinean cuisine, including grass-fed steaks, in a "**romantic**" whitewashed space with a small bar; service "**that makes you feel like family**" completes the all-around "**warm**" experience.

BAMONTE'S | Italian — 4.3 3.9 4.3 $$
Williamsburg | 32 Withers St. (bet. Lorimer St. & Union Ave.) | Brooklyn
718-384-8831

"**Red sauce is king**" at this "**long-established**" (since 1900) Williamsburg Italian, which remains "**the ultimate old-school Brooklyn**" joint for "**belly-bustin'**" standards "**like grandma made**"; the "**time warp**" backdrop's "**not fancy**", but the "**tuxedoed waiters**" and assorted "**characters**" (e.g. "**wise guys**") are "**wildly entertaining.**"

B & H DAIRY | Deli/Vegetarian — 4.3 2.9 4.1 $
East Village | 127 Second Ave. (bet. 7th St. & St. Marks Pl.)
212-505-8065

This "**hole-in-the-wall**" East Village "**patch of history**" has been filling bellies with veggie borscht-and-blintz fare (aka kosher "**Jewish soul food**") since the 1940s; talk about kickin' it "**old school**" – the "**diner**" ambiance "**hasn't changed since your grandpa ate there**" way back when.

BANH MI SAIGON | Sandwiches/Vietnamese — 4.3 2.7 3.3 $
Little Italy | 198 Grand St. (bet. Mott & Mulberry Sts.)
212-941-1541 | www.banhmisaigonnyc.com

"**Super-delicious**" Vietnamese sandwiches with "**airy-yet-crusty**" French bread and "**flavorful**" pork are the eponymous specialty at this cash-only Little Italy storefront; "**dirt-cheap prices**" make it "**popular with the lunch crowd**", though spare seating at "**countertops with stools**" encourages takeout.

BANN | Korean — 4.2 4.0 4.0 $$$
West 50s | 350 W. 50th St. (bet. 8th & 9th Aves.)
212-582-4446 | www.bannrestaurant.com

"**Classy**" Korean barbecue is no oxymoron at this Theater District "**change of pace**" where the smokeless tabletop grills and "**modern**" setting impress fans; maybe the tabs skew "**upscale**", but the food's "**exciting**", the service "**caring**" and the overall experience "**satisfying.**"

	FOOD	DECOR	SERVICE	COST

THE BAO | Chinese   4.2   3.5   3.8 $

East Village | 13 St. Marks Pl. (bet. 2nd & 3rd Aves.)
212-388-9238

"Not-to-be-missed" signature soup dumplings lead the multiregional menu at this East Village Chinese, also appreciated for its "unbeatable" prices; the modest digs get "packed" and "loud", but the "delicious" grub "more than makes up for all of that."

BAOHAUS | Taiwanese   4.1   2.9   3.3 $

East Village | 238 E. 14th St. (bet. 2nd & 3rd Aves.)
646-669-8889 | www.baohausnyc.com

The "savory" Taiwanese steamed buns are "tasty and surprisingly filling" at Eddie Huang's East Villager, whose "fast-food vibe" gets a boost from "blaring hip-hop music"; despite "teenage" service and "no decor to speak of", "cheap" checks keep its "college" crowd content.

BAR AMERICAIN | American   4.3   4.3   4.2 $$$

West 50s | 152 W. 52nd St. (bet. 6th & 7th Aves.)
212-265-9700 | www.baramericain.com

Bobby Flay "doesn't disappoint" at this Midtown New American offering "inventive" yet "accessible" cuisine in "big, open" surrounds complete with a "slick" (if "noisy") bar; though you'll pay a "premium", "prompt service" and a "convenient location" make it "perfect for pre-theater."

NEW **BARANO** | Italian   —   —   — $$$

Williamsburg | Bridgeview Towers | 26 Broadway (Kent Ave.) | Brooklyn
347-987-4500 | www.baranobk.com

Wood-fired pizzas, housemade pastas and three kinds of house mozzarella come out of the open kitchen at this South Side Williamsburg Italian, situated near the waterfront; along with warm woods, its space features stylized red-and-white banquettes and a bar pouring Italian wines and beers.

BARBETTA | Italian   4.1   4.3   4.2 $$$

West 40s | 321 W. 46th St. (bet. 8th & 9th Aves.)
212-246-9171 | www.barbettarestaurant.com

Dating to 1906, this Theater District "grande dame" turns back the clock with "polite waiters" setting down "well-prepared" Northern Italian dishes in a "lovely old" setting that includes a "beautiful", "vacation"-like back garden; just be aware that this "throwback to a different time" has distinctly up-to-date pricing.

BAR BOLONAT | Israeli/Mideastern   4.5   4.0   4.2 $$

West Village | 611 Hudson St. (W. 12th St.)
212-390-1545 | www.barbolonatny.com

Chef Einat Admony (Balaboosta, Taïm) takes Israeli cuisine to "new levels" at this West Village "standout", where her "inspired" dishes "showcase the Middle East's best flavors"; "tiny" digs and "not-so-tiny" prices are offset by "helpful" service and an "upscale" yet "relaxed" vibe.

BAR BOULUD | French   4.3   4.0   4.2 $$$

West 60s | 1900 Broadway (bet. 63rd & 64th Sts.)
212-595-0303 | www.barboulud.com

An "interesting" part of Daniel Boulud's "empire", this "civilized" bistro opposite Lincoln Center is known for "beautifully presented" French fare, "as-good-as-it-gets" charcuterie and "interesting" wines; the casually "**elegant**" space is joined by "**swell**" sidewalk tables for prime people-watching.

| **BARBOUNIA** | Mediterranean | 4.1 | 4.1 | 3.9 | $$$ |

Flatiron | 250 Park Ave. S. (20th St.)
212-995-0242 | www.barbounia.com

"**Stylish**" and "**upbeat**", this "**cacophonous**" Flatiron Med lures "**see-and-be-seen**" "**Gen-X**" types with a "**tasty**", "**something-for-everyone**" menu (and one "**crazy brunch**"); the "**beautiful**", "**airy**" setting – replete with vaulted ceilings – also hosts a "**great bar scene.** "

| **BARBUTO** | Italian | 4.6 | 4.0 | 4.2 | $$$ |

West Village | 775 Washington St. (bet. Jane & W. 12th Sts.)
212-924-9700 | www.barbutonyc.com

The "**rewards**" are many at Jonathan Waxman's West Village Italian, from the "**simple**" yet "**delicious**" menu starring his "**legendary**" roast chicken to the "**vibrant**" garage/urban setting; the "**scene-oriented**" crowd's "**punishing**" acoustics are eased in warm weather "**when the doors are up.**"

| **BAR CENTRALE** | American | 3.9 | 4.0 | 4.2 | $$ |

West 40s | 324 W. 46th St. (bet. 8th & 9th Aves.)
212-581-3130 | www.barcentralenyc.com

"**Hidden**" in a second-floor address on Restaurant Row, this semi-"secret" bar/lounge is a "**relaxing**" post-show clubhouse for theater insiders, random "**Broadway stars**" and their entourages; just be aware that the "**tasty**" American bites and "**throwback**" sips run "**expensive**" and that reservations are a must – if you can get them.

| **BAR CORVO** | Italian | 4.4 | 3.8 | 4.1 | $$ |

Prospect Heights | 791 Washington Ave. (bet. Lincoln & St Johns Pls.) | Brooklyn
718-230-0940 | www.barcorvo.com

A "**real winner**", this Prospect Heights Al Di La "**offspring**" fields a "**well-curated menu**" of "**delicious**" Italian dishes in "**cozy**" quarters run by an "**attentive**" team; "**reasonable**" prices ensure it "**does fill up**", though a patio helps stretch the space.

| **BAREBURGER** | Burgers | 3.9 | 3.4 | 3.7 | $ |

Chelsea | 153 Eighth Ave. (bet. 17th & 18th Sts.) | 212-414-2273
East 70s | 1370 First Ave. (73rd St.) | 212-510-8559
East 80s | 1681 First Ave. (87th St.) | 212-390-1344
East Village | 85 Second Ave. (5th St.) | 212-510-8610
Financial District | 155 William St. (Ann St.) | 646-657-0388
Greenwich Village | 535 Laguardia Pl. (bet. 3rd St. & Washington Square Vill.) | 212-477-8125
Murray Hill | 514 Third Ave. (bet. 34th & 35th Sts.) | 212-679-2273
West 40s | 366 W. 46th St. (9th Ave.) | 212-673-2273
West 50s | 313 W. 57th St. (8th Ave.) | 212-685-2273
West 90s | 795 Columbus Ave. (bet. 97th & 100th Sts.) | 646-398-7177
Cobble Hill | 149 Court St. (Pacific St.) | Brooklyn | 347-529-6673
Park Slope | 170 Seventh Ave. (bet. 1st St. & Garfield Pl.) | Brooklyn | 718-768-2273
Astoria | 33-21 31st Ave. (34th St.) | Queens | 718-777-7011
Astoria | 23-01 31st St. (23rd Ave.) | Queens | 718-204-7167

continued

Long Island City | 48-19 Vernon Blvd. (49th Ave.) | Queens | 718-937-2273
www.bareburger.com

A "**relatively guilt-free**" option for "**getting your nom on**", this "**wholesome**" burger chain "**stands out**" with organic, natural patties (beef, veggie or "**outside-of-the-box**" game meats) "**personalized**" with a "**plethora of toppings**"; the "**green**" pedigree costs a "**few extra bucks**", but that barely dents its "**popularity.**"

BAR EOLO | Italian   4.2   3.6   3.8 $$

Chelsea | 190 Seventh Ave. (bet. 21st & 22nd Sts.)
646-225-6606 | www.eolonewyork.com

There's "**intelligent life in the kitchen**" of this Sicilian "**contender**" offering "**off-the-beaten-recipe-path**" dishes paired with "**exceptional wines**"; the "**nondescript**" trattoria setting may be at odds with the "**Chelsea prices**", perhaps why there are "**no struggles to get a table.**"

BAR GOTO | Japanese   ▽ 4.4   3.9   4.4 $$$

Lower East Side | 245 Eldridge St. (Houston St.)
212-475-4411 | www.bargoto.com

A Tokyo native and Pegu Club vet is behind this "**lovely**" LES bar offering "**divine**" Japanese-inspired cocktails and "**delicious**" izakaya bites, including okonomiyaki pancakes that are "**a true revolution starter**"; fans can also leave the "**small but lovely**" surrounds without having spent a fortune.

BAR JAMÓN | Spanish   ▽ 4.5   4.1   4.3 $$

Gramercy Park | 125 E. 17th St. (Irving Pl.)
212-253-2773 | www.casamononyc.com

Mario Batali's "**convivial**" Gramercy tapas bar–cum–"holding pen" for his 'round-the-corner Casa Mono puts out "**top-of-the-line**" Spanish small plates paired with an "**extensive**" wine list; it's a "**light squeeze**" and the tabs are "**not cheap**", but most don't mind given the "**sexy-time**" mood.

BARNEY GREENGRASS | Deli   4.5   3.0   3.7 $$

West 80s | 541 Amsterdam Ave. (bet. 86th & 87th Sts.)
212-724-4707 | www.barneygreengrass.com

An "**essential**" UWS "**institution**", this circa-1908 "**temple to smoked fish**" "**still reigns**" with its "**fabulous fresh bagels**", "**silky**" nova and other "**quintessential**" Jewish deli fare; on weekends service turns more "**brusque**" and the "**cramped**" space gets "**chaotic**", but "**so what?**" – it's "**part of the charm.**"

BARN JOO | Korean   4.1   4.0   3.9 $$

Flatiron | 893 Broadway (bet. 19th & 20th Sts.)
646-398-9663 | www.barnjoo.com
West 30s | 34 W. 35th St. (bet. 5th & 6th Aves.)
212-564-4430 | www.barnjoo35.com

Korean fare takes an "**interesting twist**" at these "**barn-esque**" gastropubs, which match "**inventive fusion**" plates with "**legit**" cocktails in sprawling, wood-lined surrounds; while "**not exactly authentic**", they're "**reasonably priced**" and can be a "**lively**" scene.

BAROSA | Italian   4.2   3.9   4.1 $$

Rego Park | 62-29 Woodhaven Blvd. (62nd Rd.) | Queens
718-424-1455 | www.barosas.com

"**Tasty**" red-sauce fare "**like mom used to make**" is available for a "**good price" at this "**neighborhood favorite**" Rego Park Italian; its "**upscale**" ambitions are apparent in the "**polite**" service, while "**fantastic specials**" seal the deal.

BAR PITTI | Italian   4.4   3.5   3.8 $$

Greenwich Village | 268 Sixth Ave. (bet. Bleecker & Houston Sts.)
212-982-3300

Home to "**many a celeb sighting**", this "**jet-set**" Village Italian is best known for its "**excellent people-watching**" from indoor/outdoor tables, even if the "**easygoing**" fare is pretty "**delicious**" as well; no reservations, no plastic, "**no discernible decor**" and "**far-from-friendly**" service don't faze its "**paparazzi**"-ready patrons.

BAR PLEIADES | American   4.2   4.5   4.3 $

East 70s | Surrey Hotel | 20 E. 76th St. (Madison Ave.)
212-772-2600 | www.barpleiades.com

"**It doesn't get any sexier**" than this "**grown-up**" UES lounge in the Surrey Hotel, an "**elegant**", art deco "**oasis**" serving "**inspired**" cocktails and "**delicious**" New American snacks by Daniel Boulud (whose Café Boulud adjoins); it's "**expensive**" for sure, but the "**sophisticated crowd**" barely notices.

BAR PRIMI | Italian   4.4   4.1   4.1 $$

East Village | 325 Bowery (2nd St.)
212-220-9100 | www.barprimi.com

Fans swear the "**undeniably fresh**" pastas are "**worth going off Paleo**" for at Andrew Carmellini's "**lively**" Bowery Italian; the "**rustic**" double-decker space hosts a "**cool scene**" but "**without a pretentious crowd**", and "**fair pricing**" is another plus.

BARRIO CHINO | Mexican   ∇ 4.3   3.5   3.9 $$

Lower East Side | 253 Broome St. (bet. Ludlow & Orchard Sts.)
212-228-6710 | www.barriochinonyc.com

"**It doesn't look like much**", but this "**microscopic**" LES cantina is still "**something of a scene**" after more than a decade, serving "**flavorful**" Mexican fare and a "**lay-you-out-flat**" tequila list; its "**highly affordable**" price point doesn't hurt either.

BAR SARDINE | American   4.3   4.1   4.1 $$

West Village | 183 W. 10th St. (bet. 7th Ave. S. & W. 4th St.)
646-360-3705 | www.barsardinenyc.com

Gabe Stulman (Perla) pairs "**sophisticated**" cocktails with "**upscale**" American bar fare, including a "**fantastic**" burger at this "**charming**" West Village hang; it's "**small**" and fills up fast ("**go early**"), but the format is perfect for a "**drinks date that turns into dinner.**"

BAR TABAC | French   4.1   3.8   4.0 $$

Cobble Hill | 128 Smith St. (Dean St.) | Brooklyn
718-923-0918 | www.bartabacny.com

A "**Parisian bistro transplanted**" to Cobble Hill, this "**hip**" Gallic eatery has plenty of "**good energy**", especially during its "**tasty**" brunch; "**tight**" seating and occasionally "**lackadaisical**" service aside, it's a neighborhood "**favorite**" and late-night "**staple.**"

	FOOD	DECOR	SERVICE	COST

BAR TANO | Italian   ▽ 4.3   3.9   4.3 $$

Gowanus | 457 Third Ave. (9th St.) | Brooklyn
718-499-3400 | www.bartano.com

"Pastas and pizzas are the strong suit" of this Gowanus Italian, a
"neighborhood staple" that's convenient for a pre–Bell House bite or drink; its
"classic" Brooklyn bistro digs (pressed-tin ceiling, long zinc bar) get
"mobbed" at prime times, but the "friendly" staff keeps pace.

BASSO56 | Italian   4.1   3.7   4.3 $$$

West 50s | 234 W. 56th St. (bet. B'way & 8th Ave.)
212-265-2610 | www.basso56.com

A "warm welcome awaits" at this "reliable" Carnegie Hall "resource" in
Midtown, featuring a "nicely-put-together" Italian menu with "modern flair";
though "small" and "nothing fancy", the space rates "homey", and prices are
"reasonable for the quality."

BASTA PASTA | Italian   4.2   3.6   4.0 $$

Flatiron | 37 W. 17th St. (bet. 5th & 6th Aves.)
212-366-0888 | www.bastapastanyc.com

"Japanese-style Italian food" begs the question "where else but NY?" – and
this "unusual" Flatiron "change of pace" comes through with "interesting"
dishes led by a signature "pasta tossed in a Parmesan wheel"; if the decor's
getting "dated", the "hospitable" service is fine as is.

BÂTARD | American   4.5   4.2   4.4 $$$

TriBeCa | 239 W. Broadway (bet. Walker & White Sts.)
212-219-2777 | www.batardtribeca.com

"Choose your own adventure" at Drew Nieporent's "refined" TriBeCa
"experience", where "praiseworthy" European-influenced New American fare
comes in a "whimsical", customizable tasting menu format, matched with an
"off-the-hook", "mostly French" wine list; factor in "gracious" service, and
fans say the "high-end" tab is almost "reasonable" "considering the quality."

BATTERSBY | American   4.6   3.9   4.5 $$$

Boerum Hill | 255 Smith St. (bet. Degraw & Douglass Sts.) | Brooklyn
718-852-8321 | www.battersbybrooklyn.com

"Endlessly inventive" flavor combinations make for "inspired" New American
meals at this "outstanding" Smith Street "shoebox"; "friendly" service helps
distract from the "elbow-to-elbow" setup, but since reservations are only
taken for the "memorable" tasting menu, "be prepared to wait."

BATTERY GARDENS | American/Continental   4.0   4.2   4.0 $$$

Financial District | SW corner of Battery Park (State St.)
212-809-5508 | www.batterygardens.com

The "harbor is at your feet" at this "shoreline" Financial District bastion
where the "peerless" views of the harbor and Lady Liberty are matched with
"better-than-expected" American-Continental fare; tabs skew high, but for
the most "priceless" experience, go for "outdoor cocktails at sunset."

BAYOU | Cajun   4.3   4.1   4.2 $$

Rosebank | 1072 Bay St. (bet. Chestnut & St. Marys Aves.) | Staten Island
718-273-4383 | www.bayounyc.com

"Ragin' Cajun" cooking and "real Southern hospitality" come to Staten Island
via this Rosebank "favorite" where the "tasty" cooking is as "true" to N'Awlins

as the "**Big Easy**" decor; "**affordable**" tabs and "**designated-driver-recommended**" drinks ratchet up the "**festive**" vibrations.

BAZ BAGEL | Bagels/Jewish   ∇ 4.1   3.9   3.8 $

Little Italy | 181 Grand St. (bet. Baxter & Mulberry Sts.)
212-335-0609 | www.bazbagel.com

"**Delicious**" hand-rolled bagels and "**all the toppings**" (lox, whitefish, schmear) are the focus of this Little Italy daytime cafe from Barney Greengrass and Rubirosa alums; classic Jewish staples round out the menu, and it's all on offer in a narrow space with a "**kitschy dinerlike**" vibe.

BCD TOFU HOUSE | Korean   4.2   3.5   3.6 $$

West 30s | 5 W. 32nd St. (bet. B'way & 5th Ave.) | 212-967-1900
Bayside | 220-05 Northern Blvd. (220th St.) | Queens | 718-224-8889
www.bcdtofu.com

Signature tofu soups come "**spicy to your heart's content**" at these "**no-frills**" Korean joints, links in an LA-based chain where the "**flavorful**" eats come at "**reasonable**" prices; despite "**abrupt**" service, they're "**usually packed**", even "**late-night**" at the 24/7 K-town location.

NEW   **BEASTS & BOTTLES** | Chicken   —   —   — $$

Brooklyn Heights | 151 Atlantic Ave. (bet. Clinton & Henry Sts.) | Brooklyn
718-855-3158 | www.beastsandbottles.com

Out of this Brooklyn Heights poultry specialist's open kitchen, the rotisserie chickens (of select breeds and farms) come in just a few styles; the other focus here is wine, with a list strong on unusual French finds – no surprise given that it's from the owners of Atrium DUMBO, one of whom is a master sommelier.

BEATRICE INN | American   4.1   4.2   4.0 $$$

West Village | 285 W. 12th St. (bet. 4th & Hudson Sts.)
917-566-7400 | www.thebeatriceinn.com

This "**grown-up**" destination inhabits a storied West Village basement, where the New American fare is considered "**good**" enough, but it's the cocktails and clubby "**mystique**" that people "**love**"; it's equally suited "**for a group of friends or date night**", though plan on "**upscale**" pricing.

BEAUBOURG | French   3.9   4.0   3.8 $$$

Battery Park City | Brookfield Place | 230 Vesey St. (West St.)
212-981-8589 | www.ledistrict.com

Set in Battery Park's Le District food hall, this roomy "**fine French option**" specializes in "**classic bistro food**", including raw-bar items; maybe it's "**expensive for what it is**", but to most the seasonal terrace and its "**stunning**" Hudson River views make it "**worth a trip.**"

BEAUTIQUE | American/French   3.9   4.1   3.7 $$$

West 50s | 8 W. 58th St. (bet. 5th & 6th Aves.)
212-753-1200 | www.beautiquedining.com

This "**stylish underground boîte**" neighboring Midtown's Paris Theatre is a "**sexy, upscale**" enclave where the French-influenced American fare is "**unexpectedly good**", though the premium pricing is less of a surprise; "**nothing special**" to a few, it's still an "**it**" place for "**beautiful**" people who stay for "**late nights**" in the back lounge.

	FOOD	DECOR	SERVICE	COST

BEAUTY & ESSEX | American — 4.2 — 4.6 — 4.0 — $$$

Lower East Side | 146 Essex St. (bet. Rivington & Stanton Sts.)
212-614-0146 | www.beautyandessex.com

Behind an "**extra-cool**" hidden entrance in a pawn shop, this "**vibrant**" LES resto-lounge draws a "**glam crowd**" to "**splurge**" on "**imaginative**" New American bites in a bi-level space that "**truly is a beauty**"; if you "**don't mind a bit of shameless trendiness**" (free champagne in the ladies' room is a "**nice touch**"), it "**does impress.**"

BECCO | Italian — 4.2 — 3.8 — 4.1 — $$$

West 40s | 355 W. 46th St. (bet. 8th & 9th Aves.)
212-397-7597 | www.becco-nyc.com

This "**festive**" Restaurant Row "**staple**" from Joe and Lidia Bastianich "**still Beccons**" with "**rustic**" Italian cooking – including a "**can't-miss**" all-you-can-eat pasta deal – and an "**unbelievable**" $29 wine list, "**no matter how crowded**" it is, "**efficient**" servers still "**get you to the show on time.**"

BECCOFINO | Italian — 4.3 — 3.6 — 4.0 — $$

Riverdale | 5704 Mosholu Ave. (bet. Fieldston Rd. & Spencer Ave.) | Bronx
718-432-2604 | www.beccofinorestaurant.com

Pretty "**happening**" for Riverdale, this "**traditional**" Italian offers "**Manhattan-quality**" red-sauce cooking at Bronx prices; "**somewhat crowded and dark**" environs are boosted by a "**neighborly atmosphere**", but no reservations mean you must "**come early or be prepared to wait.**"

NEW **BEDFORD & CO.** | American — ▽ 4.1 — 4.1 — 4.2 — $$$

East 40s | The Renwick | 118 E. 40th St. (Lexington Ave.)
212-634-4040 | www.bedfordandco.com

John DeLucie (of now-closed Crown and Lion) is behind this bi-level American inside Midtown's Renwick hotel, emphasizing wood-grilled meats, seafood and vegetables from local farms; the space has a sleek look with midcentury-modern furnishings and a marble bar.

BEEHIVE OVEN BISCUIT CAFE | Southern — ▽ 4.3 — 4.0 — 4.5 — $

Williamsburg | 182 S. Second St. (Driggs Ave.) | Brooklyn
347-987-4960 | www.beehiveoven.com

"**Sumptuous**" biscuits join all-day breakfast and other "**inventive**" takes on Southern comfort food at this affordable South Williamsburg shop where everyone "**makes you feel like family**", there's also beer, wine and housemade lemonade, but the "**cozy living room**" setup's "**a little small so get there early.**"

BELLA BLU | Italian — 4.1 — 3.7 — 4.0 — $$

East 70s | 967 Lexington Ave. (bet. 70th & 71st Sts.)
212-988-4624 | www.baraondany.com

"**Well-to-do**" Upper Eastsiders "**get happy**" at this "**popular**" Italian where a "**solicitous**" team presents a "**high-quality**" menu led by "**fantastic**" pizzas; granted, it's "**pricey**" and the seating's "**cheek-by-jowl**", but a "**convivial**" vibe saves the day.

BELLA VIA | Italian — 3.8 — 3.5 — 3.9 — $$

Long Island City | 47-46 Vernon Blvd. (48th Ave.) | Queens
718-361-7510 | www.bellaviarestaurant.com

"**Funky**" Long Island City is home to this "**reliable**" Italian known for its pastas and coal-fired pizzas at prices that "**won't break the bank**"; set in a big-windowed storefront with a sidewalk patio, it features "**simple**" decor that contributes to its "**pleasant**" mien.

BEN & JACK'S STEAK HOUSE | Steak   4.4   4.1   4.5 $$$
NoMad | 255 Fifth Ave. (bet. 28th & 29th Sts.)
212-532-7600 | www.benandjackssteakhouse.com

"**Perfect for a guys' night out**", this "**throwback**" NoMad chophouse stays "**true to form**" with "**substantial**", "**butter-tender**" steaks served "**like a well-oiled machine**"; while "**not cheap**", it earns a "**thumbs-up**" as a "**dependable**" pick.

BENARES | Indian   4.0   3.6   3.9 $$
TriBeCa | 45 Murray St. (bet. B'way & Church St.) | 212-766-4900
West 50s | 240 W. 56th St. (bet. B'way & 8th Ave.) | 212-397-0707
www.benaresnyc.com

The "**flavorful**" Indian menu includes dishes "**not often found**" at these "**upscale**" venues where the wide-ranging choices ("**veggie-friendly**" options are a focus) are presented in "**comfortable**", modern surrounds; the Midtown branch's buffet lunch "**steal**" is matched by a prix fixe option in TriBeCa.

BENCHMARK | American/Steak   4.2   4.1   4.1 $$$
Park Slope | 339 Second St. (bet. 4th & 5th Aves.) | Brooklyn
718-965-7040 | www.benchmarkrestaurant.com

Nestled in an "**intimate**" carriage house, this "**somewhat overlooked**" Park Slope steakhouse offers "**quality**" cuts as well as "**quite good**" American accompaniments; fans admire its "**calm**" mood and midrange tabs, while a "**lovely patio**" allows it to "**double in size**" in good weather.

BENJAMIN STEAK HOUSE | Steak   4.6   4.2   4.5 $$$
East 40s | Dylan Hotel | 52 E. 41st St. (bet. Madison & Park Aves.)
212-297-9177 | www.benjaminsteakhouse.com

You can "**eat like a man**" at this "**first-class**" chop shop in the Dylan Hotel, supplying "**perfectly prepared**" beef and "**top-shelf**" service in "**clubby**" quarters with a "**soaring ceiling**" and "**massive fireplace**"; it's certainly "**not cheap**", but then again this "**sublime experience**" is always "**memorable.**"

BENOIT BISTRO | French   4.2   4.2   4.2 $$$
West 50s | 60 W. 55th St. (bet. 5th & 6th Aves.)
646-943-7373 | www.benoitny.com

"**Bringing France across the pond**", Alain Ducasse's "**likable**" Midtown bistro stays "**on target**" serving a "**très bien**" mix of Gallic classics and updated plates in "**attractive**" revamped quarters with a spiffy pearl-white look and a "**Parisian feel**"; prices may skew "**high**", but its many fans deem it "**a keeper.**"

BEN'S BEST | Deli/Kosher   4.3   3.0   3.8 $$
Rego Park | 96-40 Queens Blvd. (bet. 63rd Dr. & 64th Rd.) | Queens
718-897-1700 | www.bensbest.com

For an "**authentic artery-clogging experience**", look no further than this circa-1945 Rego Park Jewish deli known for "**old-time**" kosher fare "**and lots of it**"; the "**oy!**" decor is "**just what you'd expect**", but "**Queens prices**" and "**OK service**" compensate.

	FOOD	DECOR	SERVICE	COST

BEN'S KOSHER DELI | Deli/Kosher   4.0   3.3   3.7 $$

West 30s | 209 W. 38th St. (bet. 7th & 8th Aves.) | 212-398-2367
Bayside | 211-37 26th Ave. (Bell Blvd.) | Queens | 212-398-2367
www.bensdeli.net

These "**retro**" delis cater to the "**masses**" with "**colossal**" sandwiches and other kosher staples; sure, some protest the "**pedestrian**" eats, "**so-so**" service and "**tired**" "**Miami Beach decor**", but they're "**accessible**" enough in a pinch.

BERG'N | Food Hall   3.9   3.8   3.6 $$

Crown Heights | 899 Bergen St. (bet. Classon & Franklin Aves.) | Brooklyn
718-857-2337 | www.bergn.com

"**Super Brooklynized fun**" is on tap at this all-day Crown Heights beer hall from the Smorgasburg crew, offering a "**large**" list of microbrews, as well as cocktails and "**interesting**" grub from an "**eclectic**" array of vendors; though not for the "**hipster**"-averse, the "**industrial**" digs and "**long picnic tables**" work for a "**boozy weekend afternoon.**"

BESO | Spanish   4.6   4.2   4.3 $$

St. George | 11 Schuyler St. (Richmond Terr.) | Staten Island
718-816-8162 | www.besonyc.com

This "**intimate**" St. George Spaniard "**right across from the ferry**" supplies "**superb**" tapas and "**some of the best sangria in town**" in a brick-walled space that exudes a "**Village dining feel**"; tabs are also "**affordable**", but "**come early**" since reservations are only for five or more.

BEST PIZZA | Pizza   ▽ 4.4   3.2   3.7 $

Williamsburg | 33 Havemeyer St. (bet. 7th & 8th Sts.) | Brooklyn
718-599-2210

Though it "**looks like your typical corner pizza shop**", this Williamsburg joint "**doesn't shirk**" from its "**bold**" name, turning out "**delicious**" brick-oven pies ("**absolutely get the white slice**") plus a handful of Italian subs; the "**small, crowded**" space with paper-plate decor does the job for "**a quick bite.**"

BETONY | American   4.5   4.4   4.4 $$$

West 50s | 41 W. 57th St. (bet. 5th & 6th Aves.)
212-465-2400 | www.betony-nyc.com

You're in for a "**fancy**" "**foodie experience**" at this Midtown New American where "**impressive**" and "**complex**" tasting menus are paired with "**carefully crafted**" cocktails; a "**polished**" staff watches over the "**civilized**" bi-level space – just "**bring your expense account**" as bills run "**high.**"

BEYOGLU | Turkish   4.2   3.6   3.8 $$

East 80s | 1431 Third Ave. (81st St.)
212-650-0850

A "**lively crowd**" descends on this UES Turkish "**standby**" to graze on "**irresistible meze**" at an "**oh-so-reasonable**" cost; it can be "**rushed**", "**cramped**" and "**loud**", but the upstairs room is "**quieter**" and come summer the sidewalk seats are a "**big draw.**"

BIG GAY ICE CREAM SHOP | Ice Cream   4.2   3.4   3.9 $

East Village | 125 E. Seventh St. (bet. Ave. A & 1st Ave.) | 212-533-9333
West Village | 61 Grove St. (7th Ave. S.) | 212-414-0222
www.biggayicecream.com

The name's as "**hard to resist**" as the "**heavenly**" licks at these soft-serve ice cream parlors, famed for creating "**cool**" cones with "**campy**" handles (e.g. the "**life-changing**" Salty Pimp); most agree the "**long lines**" are a "**small price to pay**" for the "**sweet finish.**"

	FOOD	DECOR	SERVICE	COST

BIG WONG | Chinese — 4.2 2.6 3.2 $

Chinatown | 67 Mott St. (bet. Bayard & Canal Sts.)
212-964-0540 | www.bigwongking.com

Known for roast meats and "**excellent congee**", this cash-only "**Chinatown favorite**" is ever "**reliable**" for "**real**" Cantonese grub; it's also known for "**bustling**" crowds, "**revolving-door**" service and "**zero decor**", but given the "**outstanding value**", "**who cares?**"

BILLY'S BAKERY | Bakery — 4.3 3.5 3.9 $

Chelsea | 184 Ninth Ave. (bet. 21st & 22nd Sts.) | 212-647-9956
TriBeCa | 75 Franklin St. (bet. B'way & Church St.) | 212-647-9958
West 50s | Plaza Food Hall | 1 W. 59th St. (bet. 5th & 6th Aves.) | 212-371-1133 |
www.billysbakerynyc.com

"**Cupcake heaven**", these bakeshops offer the "**real thing**" in a variety of flavors plus other "**delicious**" sweets like "**old-fashioned**" layer cakes, mini cheesecakes and brownies "**to kill for**"; the "**charming**" Chelsea and TriBeCa locales are also "**great for a cup of coffee.**"

BIRCH COFFEE | Coffee — 4.1 3.7 3.9 $

East 60s | 134½ E. 62nd St. (Lexington Ave.) | 212-686-1444
NEW **Financial District** | 8 Spruce St. (William St.) | 212-686-1444
Murray Hill | 432 Third Ave. (30th St.) | 212-686-1444
NoMad | 21 E. 27th St. (Madison Ave.) | 212-686-1444
West 90s | 750 Columbus Ave. (bet. 96th & 97th Sts.) | 212-665-1444
West Village | 56 Seventh Ave. (bet. 13th & 14th Sts.) | 212-686-1444
Long Island City | 40-35 23rd St. (bet. 40th & 41st Aves.) | Queens |
212-686-1444
www.birchcoffee.com

They sure "**know their coffee**" at this rapidly growing Manhattan-based chain where "**personable**" baristas pour "**strong and flavorful**" brews made from thoughtfully sourced beans; snacks like pastries are "**excellent**" too, and the "**relaxed**" vibe is just right for a "**leisurely afternoon.**"

BIRDS & BUBBLES | Southern — 4.2 3.7 4.0 $$

Lower East Side | 100 Forsyth St. (bet. Broome & Grand Sts.)
646-368-9240 | www.birdsandbubbles.com

The "**name says it all**" at this "**hip**" LES Southerner where "**tender**" fried chicken and other "**elevated**" comfort fare pairs with a "**thoughtful**" champagne list; an "**adorable patio**" gives the "**small**", brick-walled quarters some breathing room when things feel "**tight.**"

BIRRERIA | Italian — 4.2 4.1 3.8 $$

Flatiron | Eataly | 200 Fifth Ave. (bet. 23rd & 24th Sts.)
212-937-8910 | www.eataly.com

"**Hard to beat on a nice summer**" day, this "**cool**" hangout atop Eataly is an all-year, retractable-roofed "**experience**" that changes theme (always Italy-focused) and menu seasonally, though an "**excellent**" selection of cask ales is a constant; the place is "**hopping**" from lunch till late, so "**to actually gain access, go early**" or make a reservation.

	FOOD	DECOR	SERVICE	COST

BISTANGO | Italian   4.0   3.7   4.1 $$
East 50s | 145 E. 50th St. (bet. Lexington & 3rd Aves.) | 212-888-4121
Murray Hill | 415 Third Ave. (29th St.) | 212-725-8484
www.bistangonyc.com

With a "**plethora**" of "**classic**" Italian dishes prepared gluten-free (if requested), these neighborhood standbys deliver "**goodness that all can enjoy**"; "**reasonable**" pricing and "**warm**" service (with a "**sweetheart**" host at the Murray Hill original) come with the territory.

BISTRO CHAT NOIR | French   4.0   3.8   4.1 $$$
East 60s | 22 E. 66th St. (bet. 5th & Madison Aves.)
212-794-2428 | www.bistrochatnoir.com

A "**low-key fave**" in a "**chic**" address off Madison Avenue, this Gallic Eastsider caters to "**fashionable**" folk with "**Parisian intimacy**" and "**quite good**" French bistro fare dispensed in a "**snug**" setting; tabs are "**expensive**", but a "**fantastic**" owner and "**convivial staff**" keep customers satisfied.

BISTRO LES AMIS | French   4.3   4.0   4.3 $$
SoHo | 180 Spring St. (Thompson St.)
212-226-8645 | www.bistrolesamis.com

Bringing a soupçon of the "**Left Bank**" to SoHo, this seasoned French bistro lures fans with its "**comforting**" cooking vs. cost ratio; OK, there's "**no scene**" going on, but sidewalk seats provide prime people-watching and the "**charmant**" staff lives up to the promise of its name.

NEW BKW BY BROOKLYN WINERY | American   —   —   — $$$
Crown Heights | 747 Franklin Ave. (Sterling Pl.) | Brooklyn
718-399-1700 | www.bkwnyc.com

This Crown Heights spin-off of Brooklyn Winery serves a New American menu to accompany house vintages produced both in Williamsburg and in the micro-winery on-site. Blue tiles accent the wood and brick barroom upfront, while an airy dining room in back is brightened by a skylight.

BLACK ANT | Mexican   4.0   3.7   3.8 $$
East Village | 60 Second Ave. (bet. 3rd & 4th Sts.)
212-598-0300 | www.blackantnyc.com

"**Be prepared for the unexpected**" at this East Village Mexican whose "**innovative**" menu showcases actual ants (and grasshoppers too), plus "**amazing**" agave-based cocktails, though some find it "**more gimmicky than delicious**", a "**lively crowd**" still has plenty of "**fiesta fun**" in the "**dark**" "**lounge**"-like surrounds.

BLACK BARN | American   4.1   4.3   4.1 $$$
NoMad | 19 E. 26th St. (bet. 5th & Madison Aves.)
212-265-5959 | www.blackbarnrestaurant.com

A "**cool**", three-level space with an appropriately "**rustic barn feel**" sets the stage for "**inventive**" farm-to-table fare at this "**enjoyable**" NoMad American, where "**creative drinks**" fuel a "**vibrant bar scene**"; tabs run "**expensive**" but "**attentive**" service adds to the reasons it's "**worth repeat visits.**"

	FOOD	DECOR	SERVICE	COST

BLACK IRON BURGER | Burgers   4.4 3.6 4.1 $$
Chelsea | 333 Seventh Ave. (bet. 28th & 29th Sts.) | 646-666-0071
East Village | 540 E. Fifth St. (Ave. B) | 212-677-6067
West 30s | 245 W. 38th St. (bet. 7th & 8th Aves.) | 646-476-3116
www.blackironburger.com

"**Pretty damn good**" "**no-frills**" burgers paired with draft pints "**go down easy**" at these "**hole-in-the-wall**" pubs; though the "**earthy**" spaces are on the "**small**" side, the "**chill atmosphere**" and "**reasonable**" tabs make them perfect for "**an easy dinner.**"

BLACK SEED BAGELS | Bagels   4.1 3.3 3.6 $
Battery Park City | Hudson Eats | 200 Vesey St. (West St.) | 212-786-0402
NEW **East Village** | 176 First Ave. (11th St.) | 646-484-5718
NoLita | 170 Elizabeth St. (bet. Kenmare & Spring Sts.) | 212-730-1950
www.blackseedbagels.com

"**Flavorful**" Montreal-style bagels (hand-rolled and wood oven–baked "**with a honey twinge**") provide the base for "**solid**" housemade schmears and "**satisfying sandwiches**" at these shops from the Mile End team; if they're "**splurgey**", tell that to the "**bagel snobs**" forming "**crazy long**" weekend lines.

NEW **BLACKTAIL** | American   —   —   — $$$
Battery Park City | Pier A Harbor Hse. | 22 Battery Pl., 2nd fl. (Little West St.)
212-785-0153 | www.blacktailnyc.com

The Dead Rabbit team is behind this Battery Park City resto-bar on Pier A, which harks back to the expat life in Havana with its highballs, punches and sours, accompanied by seafood-focused American fare. The space includes a wood-panelled main bar and a 'lobby' area.

BLACK TAP | Burgers   4.2 3.6 3.8 $$
SoHo | 529 Broome St. (bet. Sullivan & Thompson Sts.) | 917-639-3089
West Village | 248 W. 14th St. (8th Ave.) | 212-675-7236
www.blacktapnyc.com

"**Creative**" craft burgers join an "**interesting**" lineup of beers at these "**friendly**" joints, though it's the "**Instagram-ready**" milkshakes "**spilling over**" with "**decadent**" toppings that garner "**insane**" lines; the "**tiny**" digs have "**minimal seating**", but still manage to pack in "**a lot of wow.**"

BLACK TREE | American   ▽ 4.3 4.1 4.1 $$
Lower East Side | 131 Orchard St. (bet. Delancey & Rivington Sts.) | 212-533-4684
Williamsburg | 261 Metropolitan Ave. (Driggs Ave.) | Brooklyn | 718-387-7611
www.blacktreenyc.com

"**High-end**" takes on American bar food is what you'll find at these "**small**" but "**aesthetically pleasing**" hangouts, where the farm-to-table menu highlights house-butchered meats alongside seasonal cocktails; the LES original majors in "**creative, delicious**" sandwiches while its Williamsburg spin-off adds multicourse tasting menus.

BLACK WHALE | American   4.0 4.0 3.9 $$
City Island | 279 City Island Ave. (Hawkins St.) | Bronx
718-885-3657 | www.theblackwhalefb.wix.com

The "**offbeat**" nautical decor conjures up "**Cape Cod in the Bronx**" at this "**cute**" City Island vet where the "**inexpensive**" New American menu includes some notably "**decadent desserts**"; fans find the "**terrific**" Sunday brunch and "**lovely**" back patio equally "**memorable.**"

	FOOD	DECOR	SERVICE	COST

BLANCA | American   4.7   4.1   4.5 $$$$
Bushwick | 261 Moore St. (Bogart St.) | Brooklyn
347-799-2807 | www.blancanyc.com

Set in a sleek, **"industrial yet intimate"** space behind Bushwick hit Roberta's, this **"culinary tour de force"** from Carlo Mirarchi presents a **"simply unreal"** New American tasting menu – 20-plus **"playful"** courses – at a 12-seat counter facing the kitchen; prepare for **"special-occasion pricing"** ($195 a pop, not including wine), but it's one for **"any serious eater's NYC list."**

BLAUE GANS | Austrian/German   4.3   3.9   4.1 $$$
TriBeCa | 139 Duane St. (B'way)
212-571-8880 | www.blauegans.com

"First-rate" Wiener schnitzel heads the list of **"hearty"** Austro-German dishes at Kurt Gutenbrunner's **"down-to-earth"** neighborhood TriBeCan, abetted by **"wonderful"** Teutonic brews; the **"artsy poster-clad"** room is **"simple"** but **"cool"**, while **"fair prices"** and **"pleasant"** staffers add to the **"gemütlich"** mood.

BLENHEIM | American   4.0   4.1   4.1 $$
West Village | 283 W. 12th St. (4th St.)
212-243-7073 | www.blenheimhill.com

"Innovation is key" at this West Village **"farm-to-table experience"**, where **"high ambitions"** often produce **"flavorful"** American dishes featuring ingredients from the namesake Catskills grange; the **"comfortable"** space has **"homey"** accents, and while it's **"a little pricey"**, there's **"always a welcome surprise on the menu."**

BLOSSOM | Vegan/Vegetarian   4.2   3.5   3.8 $$
Chelsea | 187 Ninth Ave. (bet. 21st & 22nd Sts.) | 212-627-1144
West 80s | 507 Columbus Ave. (bet. 84th & 85th Sts.) | 212-875-2600
West Village | 41 Carmine St. (bet. Bedford & Bleecker Sts.) | 646-438-9939
www.blossomnyc.com

BLOSSOM DU JOUR | Vegan/Vegetarian
Chelsea | 259 W. 23rd St. (bet. 7th & 8th Aves.) | 212-229-2595
West 40s | 617 Ninth Ave. (bet. 43rd & 44th Sts.) | 646-998-3535
West 80s | 449 Amsterdam Ave. (bet. 81st & 82nd Sts.) | 212-712-9822
www.blossomdujour.com

The food's **"completely vegan"** but **"you wouldn't know"** at these **"earthy"** organic **"havens"**, whose **"impressive"** fare makes healthy almost seem **"hedonistic"**; **"efficient"** service and **"relaxed"** surroundings add to the overall **"solid"** feel, while the du Jour outlets offer a **"quick"** fix to go.

BLT PRIME | Steak   4.5   4.3   4.3 $$$
Gramercy Park | 111 E. 22nd St. (bet. Lexington Ave. & Park Ave. S.)
212-995-8500 | www.bltprime.com

"Perfectly marbled" prime cuts and **"puffy"** popovers are the big draws at this Gramercy steakhouse whose bi-level **"modern"** space comes **"without the macho"**; **"well-made"** classic cocktails and **"friendly"** servers add further appeal – fans just **"wish it were cheaper."**

BLT STEAK | Steak   4.5   4.1   4.3 $$$$
East 50s | 106 E. 57th St. (bet. Lexington & Park Aves.)
212-752-7470 | www.bltsteak.com

It's the **"caveman experience"** gone **"chic"** at this **"busy"** East Midtown steakhouse, where the **"flavorful"**, **"perfectly done"** cuts and **"out-of-this-world"** signature popovers come in **"modern"**, decidedly **"not stuffy"** surrounds; "**attentive**" service and "**pricey**" tabs are other reasons it's a standby for the "**corporate lunch**" set.

BLUE BOTTLE COFFEE	Coffee	4.2	3.6	3.9	$

Chelsea | 450 W. 15th St. (10th Ave.) | 510-653-3394
Chelsea | The High Line | Enter on 16th St. & 10th Ave. | 510-653-3394
West 40s | Gotham West Mkt. | 600 11th Ave. (bet. 44th & 45th Sts.) | 510-653-3394
West 40s | 54 W. 40th St. (6th Ave.) | 510-653-3394
West 40s | 1 Rockefeller Plaza (bet. 48th & 49th Sts.) | 510-653-3394
Boerum Hill | 85 Dean St. (bet. Hoyt & Smith Sts.) | Brooklyn | 510-653-3394
Williamsburg | 160 Berry St. (bet. 4th & 5th Sts.) | Brooklyn | 718-387-4160
www.bluebottlecoffee.com

Every hipster's "**favorite way to start the day**", these Bay Area imports are known for their "**killer**" slow-drip coffee (including a "**showstopper**" New Orleans–style iced brew) and "**intense**", freshly roasted blends; "**knowledgeable baristas**" do the honors, but "**the line's often long**" – "**and deservedly so.**"

BLUE FIN	Seafood	4.2	4.0	4.0	$$$

West 40s | W Hotel Times Sq. | 1567 Broadway (47th St.) 212-918-1400 | www.bluefinnyc.com

"**Handy**" for pre-theater dining, this "**reliable**" Times Square "**staple**" offers "**tasty**" seafood and "**delicious**" sushi in a "**high-energy**" setting; it's not cheap, but prices are "**not-bad**" for the location, and "**courteous**" servers will get you "**out in time**" for the show.

BLUE HILL	American	4.7	4.4	4.7	$$$$

Greenwich Village | 75 Washington Pl. (bet. MacDougal St. & 6th Ave.) 212-539-1776 | www.bluehillfarm.com

A true "**farm-to-table pioneer**", Dan Barber's Village American "**does a magnificent job**" producing "**unbelievably fresh and flavorful**" American fare with "**thoroughly satisfying**" seasonal "**integrity**"; set in a "**lovely, calm**" room run by an "**especially caring**" staff, it "**isn't cheap**" but the performance is "**worth repeat visits.**"

BLUE RIBBON	American	4.4	3.8	4.2	$$$

SoHo | 97 Sullivan St. (Spring St.) | 212-274-0404

BLUE RIBBON AT BROOKLYN BOWL | American
Williamsburg | 61 Wythe Ave. (12th St.) | Brooklyn | 718-963-3369

BLUE RIBBON BAKERY | American
West Village | 35 Downing St. (Bedford St.) | 212-337-0404

BLUE RIBBON BROOKLYN | American
Park Slope | 280 Fifth Ave. (bet. 1st St. & Garfield Pl.) | Brooklyn | 718-840-0404
www.blueribbonrestaurants.com

The Bromberg brothers "**consistently get it right**" at these "**beloved**" New Americans where "**down-home**" cooking ("**wonderful**" matzo ball soup, "**ballin'**" fried chicken) make for "**comfort-food heaven**"; the original SoHo "**standby**" is a late-night "**haunt for off-duty chefs**", while the Bakery Kitchen has "**intoxicating**" smells of baking bread, and though they're not inexpensive, they remain "**perennial favorites.**"

BLUE RIBBON FRIED CHICKEN | Chicken   4.1   3.3   3.6 $

East Village | 28 E. First St. (2nd Ave.)
212-228-0404 | www.blueribbonfriedchicken.com

Offering over-the-counter access to the **"super-tasty"**, Southern-style fried chicken served at some of the Bromberg brothers' other restaurants, this **"functional"** East Villager sells its **"well-seasoned"** poultry by the piece along with shakes and sides, plus beer and wine; it's **a little pricey for fast food"**, but late hours mean it's a good option **"after your night out."**

BLUE RIBBON SUSHI | Japanese   4.5   4.0   4.1 $$$

Battery Park City | Hudson Eats | 230 Vesey St. (West St.) | 212-417-7000
SoHo | 119 Sullivan St. (bet. Prince & Spring Sts.) | 212-343-0404

BLUE RIBBON HI-BAR | Japanese

West 50s | 6 Columbus Hotel | 308 W. 58th St. (bet. 8th & 9th Aves.) |
212-397-0404

BLUE RIBBON SUSHI IZAKAYA | Japanese

Lower East Side | Sixty LES Hotel | 187 Orchard St. (bet. Houston & Stanton Sts.) | 212-466-0404
www.blueribbonrestaurants.com

"First-class" fish in **"creative and classic"** combos makes for **"dazzling"** sushi at these Japanese **"go-tos"** by the brothers Bromberg; you'll also find brasserie favorites (like **"surprisingly good fried chicken"**) at some locales, and while the SoHo original is more **"minimalist"** than the rest (minus the Hudson Eats counter), all will cost you a **"chunk of change."**

BLUE SMOKE | BBQ   4.1   3.7   4.0 $$$

Battery Park City | 255 Vesey St. (bet. North End Ave. & West St.) |
212-889-2005
Murray Hill | 116 E. 27th St. (bet. Lexington Ave. & Park Ave. S.) | 212-447-7733
www.bluesmoke.com

"Rib lovers rejoice" over **"solid"** 'cue delivered by a **"congenial"** crew at Danny Meyer's **"accessible and lively"** BBQ barns; OK, **"you ain't in Texas"**, but a **"well-curated"** bourbon list and **"terrific"** live sets at the Murray Hill original's Jazz Standard add incentive to **"return for seconds."**

BLUESTONE LANE | Australian/Coffee   4.3   3.7   3.8 $

Financial District | Continental Bank Building | 30 Broad St. (Exchange Pl.) |
646-684-3771
`NEW` **East 90s** | 2 E. 90th St. (5th Ave.) | 646-869-7812
`NEW` **Greenwich Village** | 51 Astor Pl. (8th St.) | 646-863-3197
`NEW` **West Village** | 30 Carmine St. (Bleecker St.) | 212-627-2763
West Village | 55 Greenwich Ave. (Perry St.) | 646-368-1988
`NEW` **Dumbo** | 55 Prospect St. (Adams St.) | Brooklyn | 347-202-0352
www.bluestonelaneny.com

Those looking **"for a true Australian coffee experience"** head to these Melbourne-style shops pouring **"terrific espresso"**, long blacks and **"proper flat whites"** paired with Down Under bites like **"amazing avocado smash"**, lamingtons and gluten-free options; weekends can mean **"packed"** conditions, but **"good-looking"**, **"happy"** staffers make up for it; P.S. a few locales offer table service.

	FOOD	DECOR	SERVICE	COST

BLUE WATER GRILL | Seafood   4.3   4.2   4.2 $$$

Union Square | 31 Union Sq. W. (16th St.)
212-675-9500 | www.bluewatergrillnyc.com

This "**time-tested**" Union Square "**oasis**" is still "**holding strong**" after a revamp, with a market menu of "**first-rate seafood**" served by "**engaging**" staffers in an "**impressive**" former bank with "**marble all around**" and a "**wonderful**" side terrace; it runs "**a bit expensive**", but the "**energetic**" regulars say it "**never fails**" "**for business or pleasure.**"

BLUJEEN | American   ▽ 4.1   3.5   3.7 $$

Harlem | 2143 Frederick Douglass Blvd. (bet. 115th & 116th Sts.)
212-256-1073 | www.blujeennyc.com

This spacious "**find**" on Harlem's Restaurant Row turns out "**down-home**" American comfort food with Southern "**flair**"; contemporary surrounds are warmed by homey touches, and a large bar pours craft beers and domestic wines.

NEW **BLU ON PARK** | Seafood/Steak   ▽ 4.3   4.3   4.2 $$$$

East 60s | 116 E. 60th St. (bet. Lexington & Park Aves.)
212-256-1929 | www.bluonpark.com

Inside a three-floor brownstone, this "**lovely, civilized**" Upper East Side "**surprise**" features steaks and seafood, enhanced by raw-bar selections; "**expensive**" tabs match the swanky space where a first-floor bar and lounge also offers a brief menu of small plates, accompanied by 1920s drinks highlighting house cocktails and champagne.

BOATHOUSE | American   3.9   4.6   3.8 $$$

Central Park | Central Park Lake, enter on E. 72nd St. (Park Dr. N.)
212-517-2233 | www.thecentralparkboathouse.com

It's all about the "**unbeatable location**" at this lakeside American, where "**the decor is Central Park**" and watching the rowboats drift by "**feels like being on vacation**"; the menu's "**not overly exciting**" and the service just "**so-so**", but for tourists and natives alike, this "**must-have**" NYC experience truly "**sells itself.**"

BOBBY VAN'S STEAKHOUSE | Steak   4.2   4.0   4.2 $$$$

East 40s | 230 Park Ave. (46th St.) | 212-867-5490
East 50s | 131 E. 54th St. (bet. Lexington & Park Aves.) | 212-207-8050
Financial District | 25 Broad St. (Exchange Pl.) | 212-344-8463
JFK Airport | JFK Airport, Terminal 8 | JFK Access Rd. (JFK Expy.) | Queens |
718-553-2100

BOBBY VAN'S STEAKHOUSE | Steak
& GRILL

West 40s | 120 W. 45th St. (bet. 6th & 7th Aves.) | 212-575-5623
West 50s | 135 W. 50th St. (bet. 6th & 7th Aves.) | 212-957-5050
www.bobbyvans.com

"**A staple**" for the business set, these "**solidly consistent**" steakhouses "**have the formula down**" with "**real pros**" serving "**hearty**" cuts in "**boys' club**" surroundings that include an "**old bank vault**" at the FiDi locale; a "**big bill**" is part of the "**predictable**" package.

BOBO | French   4.3   4.2   4.2 $$$

West Village | 181 W. 10th St. (7th Ave. S.)
212-488-2626 | www.bobonyc.com

At this West Village "**standby**", a "**professional**" staff delivers "**solid**" French cooking in a "**civilized**" townhouse space spanning an upstairs dining room, "**lively**" lower-level bar area and "**cute**" back garden; it's "**romantic**" enough for a date, but "**equally great**" for just "**meeting with friends.**"

BOBWHITE | Southern   4.3   3.4   4.0 $

East Village | 94 Ave. C (6th St.) | 212-228-2972
NEW **West Village** | 57 Seventh Ave. S. (Commerce St.) | 646-861-1743
www.bobwhitecounter.com

The "**fabulous**" fried chicken is "**what dreams are made of**" at these counter serves where "**classic Southern**" eats come courtesy of a "**friendly**" staff; the digs aren't much, but given the "**bargain**" prices, "**who cares?**"

BOCCA | Italian   4.4   4.0   4.3 $$

Flatiron | 39 E. 19th St. (bet. B'way & Park Ave. S.)
212-387-1200 | www.boccanyc.com

It "**feels like Rome**" at this "**enjoyable**" Cacio e Pepe sibling in the Flatiron known for its "**expert**" Italian cooking, "**appealing**" modern look and "**friendly**" service; regulars say "**pasta is the thing to eat**" here, notably its "**cool**" signature dish tossed tableside in a wheel of pecorino.

BOCELLI | Italian/Seafood   4.5   4.3   4.3 $$

Old Town | 1250 Hylan Blvd. (Parkinson Ave.) | Staten Island
718-420-6150 | www.bocellirest.com

This "**old-school**" Old Town Italian offers a "**top-notch**" menu that includes many "**well-prepared**" seafood specialties in an "**inviting**" white-tablecloth space with a Tuscan feel; the staff "**makes you feel like family**", and despite "**pricey**" tabs, it's often "**busy**", especially on weekends.

BODEGA NEGRA | Mexican   4.1   4.0   4.1 $$$

Chelsea | Dream Downtown Hotel | 355 W. 16th St. (bet. 8th & 9th Aves.)
212-229-2336 | www.bodeganegranyc.com

The "**fun and young**" tout this Serge Becker sequel to a buzzy London original, furnishing "**inventive**" Mexicana in rancho-style quarters inside Chelsea's Dream Downtown Hotel, there's "**people-watching**" aplenty, with "*muy delicioso*" margaritas to help make it "**a blast**" – though the front cafe is a mellower alternative.

BODRUM | Mediterranean/Turkish   4.2   3.6   4.0 $$

West 80s | 584 Amsterdam Ave. (bet. 88th & 89th Sts.)
212-799-2806 | www.bodrumnyc.com

"**Small and cozy**", this UWS neighborhood Med is the "**real deal**" for "**inexpensive**" dining on "**stellar**" Turkish meze and "**tasty thin-crust pizza**"; though service is "**speedy**", it's often "**crowded and cramped**", so insiders flee to the "**outside tables.**"

BOGOTA LATIN BISTRO | Pan-Latin   4.2   3.7   4.1 $$

Park Slope | 141 Fifth Ave. (St. Johns Pl.) | Brooklyn
718-230-3805 | www.bogotabistro.com

"**It's always a party**" at this "**hyper-popular**" Park Slope Pan-Latin, where the "**tasty**", "**Colombian-style**" eats and "**exotic drinks**" whisk you to "**Bogotá**"; "**decent prices**" and a "**friendly staff**" help keep the "**good times**" and "**noise level**" going strong.

BOHEMIAN | Japanese   4.6   4.4   4.5 $$$

NoHo | 57 Great Jones St. (bet. Bowery & Lafayette St.)
no phone

"**You'll need a reservation**" and a referral (there's "**no listed phone number**") to access this **"exclusive"** NoHo Japanese hidden **"behind a butcher shop"**, where the **"exceptional"** food and cocktails are presented by **"truly wonderful people"**; an **"intimate"**, denlike room is perfect for conversation, and while prices run **"steep"**, it will leave a **"lasting memory."**

THE BOIL | Seafood   4.5   3.4   4.0 $$

Lower East Side | 139 Chrystie St. (bet. Broome & Delancey Sts.)
212-925-8815 | www.theboilny.com

"Don't wear your best clothes" to this **"down-and-dirty"** cash-only LES seafood spot, where the **"super-messy"**, **"Louisiana-style"** shellfish boils come with **"addictive"** sauces plus wet naps and gloves; the **"busy"**, no-reservations setup often means **"long"** waits, but **"what fun it is"** in the end.

BONCHON | Chicken   4.2   3.2   3.5 $

Financial District | 104 John St. (Cliff St.) | 646-692-4660
Murray Hill | 325 Fifth Ave. (bet. 32nd & 33rd Sts.) | 212-686-8282
West 30s | 207 W. 38th St. (bet. 7th & 8th Aves.) | 212-221-3339
Astoria | 25-30 Broadway (29th St.) | Queens | 929-522-0171
Bayside | 45-37 Bell Blvd. (bet. 45th Dr. & 45th Rd.) | Queens | 718-225-1010
www.bonchon.com

"Habit-forming" is the verdict on the **"out-of-sight"** Korean fried chicken with **"crispy, parchmentlike skin"** sold at this international chain; since the birds are cooked to order, expect **"forever"** waits, not to mention **"slipshod"** service, **"no decor"** and just-**"decent"** prices.

BOND ST | Japanese   4.5   4.2   4.1 $$$

NoHo | 6 Bond St. (bet. B'way & Lafayette St.)
212-777-2500 | www.bondstrestaurant.com

"Awe-inspiring" sushi and other **"cut-above"** Japanese bites get a **"creative fusion spin"** at this still-**"hip"** NoHo veteran known for drawing the **"glitterati"** into its **"sexy"** dining room and **"fun"** downstairs lounge; yes, prices are **"steep"** and service can be just so-so, but fans say **"sit at the sushi bar"** and you **"won't be disappointed."**

BONNIE'S GRILL | Burgers   4.1   3.3   3.6 $$

Park Slope | 278 Fifth Ave. (bet. 1st St. & Garfield Pl.) | Brooklyn
718-369-9527 | www.bonniesgrill.com

Park Slopers refuel at this **"short-order joint"** offering **"damn-good burgers"** and other basics in **"classic diner"** digs; it's **"fun sitting at the counter"** and the grub's **"well priced"**, but since the dimensions are **"slim"**, **"good luck getting a seat on the weekend."**

BOQUERIA | Spanish   4.3   3.8   4.0 $$$

East 70s | 1460 Second Ave. (76th St.) | 212-343-2227
Flatiron | 53 W. 19th St. (bet. 5th & 6th Aves.) | 212-255-4160
SoHo | 171 Spring St. (bet. B'way & Thompson St.) | 212-343-4255
www.boquerianyc.com

"Graze your way" through **"top-class tapas"** at these **"happening"**, **"no-room-to-spare"** Spaniards with a **"transported-to-Barcelona"** feel; **"well-priced"** wines offset tabs that can **"add up pretty quickly"** – though groups of six or more can go for the **"value"** tasting menu that's a **"nonstop parade of fabulous"** little bites.

	FOOD	DECOR	SERVICE	COST

BOSIE TEA PARLOR | Teahouse 4.1 3.8 4.2 $$
West Village | 10 Morton St. (bet. Bleecker St. & 7th Ave. S.)
212-352-9900 | www.bosienyc.com

This "**quiet**" West Village teahouse offers "**exotic**" brews and "**delicate**" nibbles (including "**delish**" French macarons) in a "**quaint**" cafe setting; fans say this "**delightful oasis**" makes for a "**truly relaxing**" dining experience.

BOTTEGA | Italian 4.0 3.9 4.0 $$$
East 70s | 1331 Second Ave. (bet. 70th & 71st Sts.)
212-288-5282 | www.bottegany.com

A "**nice neighborhood place**", this UES trattoria turns out "**accessible**" Italian staples in a "**pleasant**" atmosphere; other pluses include a "**large, comfortable**" setting with a "**busy bar**" and "**terrific outdoor**" seating, as well as "**personable**" service.

NEW **BOTTLE & BINE** | American ▽ 4.3 4.1 4.4 $$$
East 50s | 1085 Second Ave. (57th St.)
212-888-7405 | www.bottleandbine.com

At this Midtown haunt, "**delicious**" New American fare is accompanied by a "**fabulous**" selection of cocktails, wines and craft beers (including taps of rare brews); a "**charming**" staff watches over the bi-level space, which features rich woods, leather banquettes and two bars.

BOUCHON BAKERY | American/French 4.3 3.7 3.8 $$
West 40s | Rockefeller Ctr. | 1 Rockefeller Plaza (bet. 48th & 49th Sts.) | 212-782-3890
West 50s | Time Warner Ctr. | 10 Columbus Circle, 3rd fl. (60th St. at B'way) | 212-823-9363
www.bouchonbakery.com

You can "**treat yourself**" to "**quality**" bites at Thomas Keller's French-inspired bakery/take-out counters, where the "**distinctive**" macarons, "**first-rate pastries**", "**mouthwatering breads**" and sandwiches are "**worth the guilt**"; they can be "**frenetic**" and "**costly**", but the Time Warner Center original's "**wonderful view**" of Columbus Circle is "**certainly an added value.**"

BOULEY | French 4.9 4.8 4.9 $$$$
TriBeCa | 163 Duane St. (bet. Hudson St. & W. B'way)
212-964-2525 | www.davidbouley.com

"**Maestro**" David Bouley delivers a "**truly refined experience**" at his "**blissful**" TriBeCa flagship, where French "**culinary wonders**" are served with "**true professionalism**" in an "**opulent**", jackets-required setting; it's a "**special-occasion sure thing**" at a "**hefty**" cost that's "**well worth the indulgence**", though the lunch tasting menu is "**such a deal.**"

BOULTON & WATT | American 4.0 3.9 3.8 $$
East Village | 5 Ave. A (1st St.)
646-490-6004 | www.boultonandwattnyc.com

Gastropub grub gets "**kicked up a couple of notches**" at this "**barlike**" East Village American offering updated comfort fare, "**inventive**" drinks (including "**must-try**" picklebacks) and an "**especially awesome**" brunch; "**fair prices**" help compensate for "**noisy**" conditions, so it's a "**safe bet**" for the "**young crowd.**"

	FOOD	DECOR	SERVICE	COST

BOULUD SUD | Mediterranean   4.5   4.3   4.4 $$$
West 60s | 20 W. 64th St. (bet. B'way & CPW)
212-595-1313 | www.bouludsud.com

A "**top choice near Lincoln Center**", Daniel Boulud's "**calm oasis**" continues to "**excel**" with "**beautifully prepared**" Mediterranean dishes served "**with aplomb**" in a "**civilized**" adult setting; there may be "**a bit of sticker shock**", but it "**never fails to deliver**" quality to "**justify the price.**"

NEW THE BOWERY MARKET | Food Hall   —   —   — $
NoHo | 348 Bowery (Great Jones St.)
no phone | www.thebowerymarket.com

A handful of all-season stands, housed behind rustic, shipping containerlike storefronts, populates this outdoor NoHo market. Sushi, Italian sandwiches, salads, juices and tacos from name-brand eateries such as Alidoro, Pulqueria and the Butcher's Daughter are represented, along with coffee and Mexican-leaning drinks.

BOWERY MEAT CO. | Steak   4.4   4.2   4.2 $$$
East Village | 9 E. First St. (Bowery)
212-460-5255 | www.bowerymeatcompany.com

The team behind Burger & Barrel and Lure "**bring innovation**" to this Italian-influenced East Village steakhouse, offering "**interesting**" choices (duck lasagna is a "**must**") and "**decadent**", "**top-cut**" chops; a retro '60s vibe gives the space an "**inviting**" feel, and while tabs are predictably "**pricey**", there are many reasons to "**return again and again.**"

BRASSERIE COGNAC | French   3.9   3.7   3.8 $$$
West 50s | 1740 Broadway (55th St.) | 212-757-3600 |
www.cognacrestaurant.com

BRASSERIE COGNAC EAST | French
East 70s | 963 Lexington Ave. (70th St.) | 212-249-5100 |
www.cognaceast.com

"**Homesick Parisians**" feel at home at these "**debonair**" brasseries where "**simple, tasty**" standards come at "**reasonable**" prices; the West 50s original is "**convenient to Carnegie Hall**" and City Center, but both locations are deemed "**attractive**" enough for a "**romantic**" tête-à-tête.

BRASSERIE 8½ | French   4.2   4.3   4.2 $$$
West 50s | 9 W. 57th St. (bet. 5th & 6th Aves.)
212-829-0812 | www.patinagroup.com

Make an "**entrance**" down a "**sweeping stairway**" at this subterranean Midtown brasserie that provides "**delicious**" French fare, prix fixe "**steals**" and "**cordial**" service in "**charming**", "**elegant**" environs with "**fine art on display**"; it's a "**haven**" for "**conversational dining**", albeit with a "**busy**" post-work bar scene.

BRASSERIE RUHLMANN | French   3.9   4.1   4.0 $$$
West 50s | Rockefeller Ctr. | 45 Rockefeller Plaza (bet. 50th & 51st Sts.)
212-974-2020 | www.brasserieruhlmann.com

"**Hobnob with the NBC crowd**" and others "**happily expensing their meals**" at Laurent Tourondel's "**heart-of-Rock-Center**" brasserie providing a "**sumptuous art deco**" setting for "**good**" (if "**not spectacular**") French cooking; the "**fascinating people-watching**" from its "**amazing**" patio supplies added "**fun.**"

NEW **BRASSERIE WITLOF** | Belgian   —   —   — $$

Williamsburg | 292 Bedford Ave (Grand St.) | Brooklyn
347-987-4305 | www.witlofnyc.com

A long-closed bank space on a Williamsburg corner hosts this Flemish brasserie offering hearty fare plus late-night dollar oysters. With its lofty, exposed-beam ceilings, high-design chandeliers and sidewalk seating, the setting feels decidedly grown-up for the neighborhood.

BREADS BAKERY | Bakery   4.6   3.4   3.9 $

Union Square | 18 E. 16th St. (bet. B'way & 5th Ave.) | 212-633-2253
NEW **West 60s** | 1890 Broadway (63rd St.) | 212-633-2253
www.breadsbakery.com

As its name suggests, you'll find "**unbeatable**" breads (100% rye, French sourdough, challah), but also "**unbelievably good**" babkas, "**delicious**" rugelach and more at these "**welcoming**" stops from Israeli baker Uri Scheft; the "**wide variety**" of snacks and sandwiches is also perfect for a "**quick bite on the run.**"

BRENNAN & CARR | Sandwiches   4.3   3.1   3.9 $$

Sheepshead Bay | 3432 Nostrand Ave. (Ave. U) | Brooklyn
718-646-9559

More than 75 years old, this cash-only Sheepshead Bay "**tradition**" still "**rocks**" thanks to "**outrageous**" double-dipped roast beef sandwiches "**drowned in au jus**"; it's something of a "**dive**" with "**table-mat menus**", but enthusiasts of "**old-fashioned goodness**" keep returning "**with the new generation in tow.**"

THE BRESLIN | British   4.3   4.0   4.1 $$$

NoMad | Ace Hotel | 16 W. 29th St. (bet. B'way & 5th Ave.)
212-679-1939 | www.thebreslin.com

"**Haute comfort food**" reigns at April Bloomfield and Ken Friedman's "**NY version of an English pub**" in the Ace Hotel, dishing up "**elevated**", "**unapologetically hearty**" fare (including a "**perfect**" lamb burger) to the "**hip throngs**"; despite a surplus of "**attitude**", most find it "**worth**" the "**steep**" bill.

BRICCO | Italian   4.0   3.7   4.1 $$$

West 50s | 304 W. 56th St. (bet. 8th & 9th Aves.)
212-245-7160 | www.bricconyc.com

This Midtown Italian hideaway is a "**steady**" source of "**consistently good**" pasta and wood-oven pizza delivered by the "**nicest staff**"; "**reasonable rates**" and "**warm**" atmospherics (check out the lipsticked kisses on the ceiling) buttress its "**reliable**" rep.

BRICK LANE CURRY HOUSE | Indian   4.1   3.6   3.8 $$

East 50s | 235 E. 53rd St. (bet. 2nd & 3rd Aves.) | 212-339-8353 |
www.bricklanetoo.com
East Village | 99 Second Ave. (6th St.) | 212-979-2900 |
www.bricklanecurryhouse.com

"**London-style curries**" come "**as hot (or meek)**" as you want at these "**reliable**" Indian joints where the "**well-done**" selections include a "**wicked**" phaal that's "**only for the bravest**"; there's "**not much**" decor, but "**copious**" portions and "**low prices**" keep fans "**happy.**"

BRICOLAGE | Vietnamese   4.4   3.9   4.2 $$

Park Slope | 162 Fifth Ave. (Degraw St.) | Brooklyn
718-230-1835 | www.bricolage.nyc

Alums from San Francisco's famed Slanted Door present an "**expert balance of flavors" via "**well-prepared**" modern Vietnamese fare at this "**serious foodie destination**" in Park Slope; while a "**beautiful**" back patio and a few "**creative cocktails**" help distract from "**cramped**" conditions, it's the food that has fans "**coming back.**"

BRINDLE ROOM	American	4.2	3.4	3.8	$$

East Village | 277 E. 10th St. (Ave. A)
212-529-9702 | www.brindleroom.com

It's all about the "**worth-a-trip**" burger at this compact but "**cozy**" East Villager that also features a "**small**" menu of "**inventive**", "**always changing**" American dishes; some complain about "**sitting on high stools**", but at least the service and pricing are "**accommodating.**"

BRIOSO	Italian	4.4	4.0	4.2	$$$

New Dorp | 174 New Dorp Ln. (9th St.) | Staten Island
718-667-1700 | www.briosoristorante.com

A "**vast**" menu of "**delectable**" Italian dishes (plus lots of nightly specials) arrives in a white-tablecloth setting at this "**rustic**" Staten Island standby; some find the "**festive**" atmosphere verges on "**noisy**", but others say the "**pro**" service helps justify the pricey tabs.

BRISKETTOWN	BBQ	∇ 4.3	3.2	3.8	$$

Williamsburg | 359 Bedford Ave. (bet. 4th & 5th Sts.) | Brooklyn
718-701-8909 | www.delaneybbq.com

Pitmaster Daniel Delaney is the mind behind this "**destination**" Williamsburg joint smoking "**melt-in-your-mouth**" BBQ – notably "**unequaled**" brisket – at "**great prices**"; a "**friendly**" counter crew and "**rustic, old-wood**" decor are also part of the package – just know it "**can be crazy**" at prime times, and when they run out of meat, it's closing time.

BROKEN SPOKE EATERY	Latin American	∇ 4.2	3.6	4.0	$

Murray Hill | 439 Third Ave. (bet. 30th & 31st Sts.)
212-889-6298 | www.brokenspokenyc.com

"**Delicious**" slow-roasted chicken, pork and a "**beast of the week**" are the focus at this Murray Hill Latin American also featuring "**surprising new tastes**" in the form of small bites and sides; what the "**cozy**" space "**lacks**" in atmosphere, it makes up for with "**fair prices.**"

BROOKLYN CRAB	Seafood	4.0	4.1	3.9	$$

Red Hook | 24 Reed St. (bet. Conover & Van Brunt Sts.) | Brooklyn
718-643-2722 | www.brooklyncrab.com

From the owners of Alma, this "**casual**" Red Hook triplex fields a "**solid**" menu of fish-shack classics and raw-bar snacks that taste even better given its "**to-die-for**" views of the harbor; additional perks like "**fun**" mini-golf and plenty of "**outdoor seats**" offset the "**ridiculous**" waits and "**slow**" service.

BROOKLYN FARMACY	Ice Cream	4.1	4.4	4.2	$

Carroll Gardens | 513 Henry St. (Sackett St.) | Brooklyn
718-522-6260 | www.brooklynfarmacy.blogspot.com

"**Nostalgia**" and seasonal ice cream flavors add up to "**a lot of fun**" at this Carroll Gardens homage to "**old-school soda shops**", where the sundaes, egg creams and such – plus "**simple, satisfying**" diner staples – are "**expertly**" dispensed by "**friendly**" staffers; housed in a "**beautiful**" restored apothecary, it's "**retro**" to the core.

	FOOD	DECOR	SERVICE	COST

BROOKLYN ICE CREAM FACTORY | Ice Cream   4.4   3.2   3.7 $

Dumbo | Brooklyn Bridge Park | Old Fulton St. (Water St.) | Brooklyn | 718-246-3963

Greenpoint | 97 Commercial St. (Manhattan Ave.) | Brooklyn | 718-349-2506
www.brooklynicecreamfactory.com

"**Creamy-dreamy**" ice cream comes in a "**limited**" but "**decadent**" variety at these "**old-time**" Brooklyn scoop shops; "**million-dollar**" skyline views at the pierside Dumbo original "**don't hurt**" when you're waiting out "**those summertime lines.**"

THE BROOKLYN STAR | Southern   ▽ 4.4   4.0   4.1 $$

Williamsburg | 593 Lorimer St. (Conselyea St.) | Brooklyn
718-599-9899 | www.thebrooklynstar.com

"**Come hungry**" to this "**excellent**" Williamsburg Southerner where "**interesting takes**" on "**good ol'**" American food are served up in "**plentiful**" portions; though it's "**perennially packed**" for brunch, the "**reasonable**" bills, "**jovial**" staff and "**homey**" vibe all add up to one "**lucky find.**"

BRUNO PIZZA | Italian   4.5   3.4   4.1 $$

East Village | 204 E. 13th St. (3rd Ave.)
212-598-3080 | www.brunopizzanyc.com

"**Packed since day one**", this "**hip**", "**energetic**" East Village Italian turns out pizzas "**kicked up a notch**" ("**impossibly light**" crusts made from house-milled flour, "**creative**" toppings), along with "**lovely**" small plates and pastas; if the setup is "**rather spartan**", service is "**warm**" – plus the moderate tabs are "**tip-included.**"

BRUSHSTROKE | Japanese   4.6   4.5   4.6 $$$$

TriBeCa | 30 Hudson St. (Duane St.) | 212-791-3771

ICHIMURA AT BRUSHSTROKE | Japanese

TriBeCa | 30 Hudson St. (Duane St.) | 212-791-3771
www.davidbouley.com

David Bouley and Osaka's Tsuji Culinary Institute present "**sublime**" kaiseki menus in an atmosphere of "**serene**" "**elegance**" at this "**splurge-worthy**" TriBeCa Japanese, where the "**picturesque plates**" (including "**melt-in-your-mouth**" sushi) are also offered à la carte; if you're really "**prepared to shell out**", try chef Eiji Ichimura's "**world-class**" omakase at his "**intimate**" 12-seat bar.

BRYANT PARK GRILL/CAFE | American   3.9   4.3   3.9 $$$

West 40s | 25 W. 40th St. (bet. 5th & 6th Aves.)
212-840-6500 | www.bryantparkgrillnyc.com

"**Primo**" Bryant Park scenery is the main "**selling point**" of these American eateries, where "**location, location, location**" trumps the "**pricey**" tabs and rather "**average**" food and service; the Grill's the more "**handsome**" of the pair with both indoor and outdoor seats, while the alfresco-only Cafe is more of a "**tourist magnet.**"

BUBBY'S | American   4.0   3.6   3.8 $$

TriBeCa | 120 Hudson St. (Moore St.) | 212-219-0666

BUBBY'S HIGH LINE | American

Meatpacking District | 71 Gansevoort St. (bet. Greenwich & Washington Sts.) | 212-206-6200

continued

www.bubbys.com

"**Put your diet aside**" for "**hearty portions of comfort classics**" at these "**down-to-earth**" Americans, home to "**breakfast all day**" and "**mayhem**" at brunch; the longtime TriBeCa original serves round-the-clock on weekends, while its Meatpacking sib is "**convenient to the High Line and the Whitney Museum**", making it a "**welcome stop**" for "**tourists.**"

BUDDAKAN | Asian   4.4   4.6   4.2 $$$$

Chelsea | 75 Ninth Ave. (bet. 15th & 16th Sts.)
212-989-6699 | www.buddakannyc.com

"**Stunning**" decor lends a "**dark, sexy**" backdrop to the "**trendy**" scene at Stephen Starr's Chelsea multilevel "**mega room**", a "**bigger-than-life experience**" where the "**energetic**" crowd is "**blown away**" by "**flavorful**" Asian dishes; just "**bring earplugs**" and sufficient funds to cover the "**splurge.**"

BUENOS AIRES | Argentinean/Steak   4.4   3.4   4.1 $$

East Village | 513 E. Sixth St. (bet. Aves. A & B)
212-228-2775 | www.buenosairesnyc.com

"**If you're in the mood for meat**", this East Village Argentine steakhouse offers "**mouthwatering**", chimichurri-slathered chops that you can "**cut with a fork**" and wash down with a "**great selection of Malbecs**"; forget the "**don't-judge-a-book-by-its-cover**" decor: "**super**" service and "**gentle**" tabs make this a "**keeper.**"

BUKHARA GRILL | Indian   4.3   3.6   4.0 $$

East 40s | 217 E. 49th St. (bet. 2nd & 3rd Aves.)
212-888-2839 | www.bukharany.com

They "**spice it up**" at this "**authentic**" North Indian near the U.N., where the cooking's "**a cut above**" and the service "**courteous**"; if it seems "**a bit pricey**" given the "**nothing-to-write-home-about**" digs, at least the lunch buffet is a "**terrific bargain.**"

BULL & BEAR | Steak   4.3   4.3   4.1 $$$$

East 40s | Waldorf-Astoria Hotel | 540 Lexington Ave. (bet. 49th & 50th Sts.)
212-872-1275 | www.bullandbearsteakhouse.com

"**Time travel**" to *Mad Men* days at this circa-1960 Waldorf-Astoria steakhouse where "**professional**" servers ply "*Wall Street Journal*" subscribers with "**quality**" cuts ("**strong**" cocktails gratify those on a "**liquid diet**"); it's a NYC "**tradition**", assuming one can "**bear what they charge.**"

BUN-KER VIETNAMESE | Vietnamese   ▽ 4.5   3.1   4.0 $$

Ridgewood | 46-63 Metropolitan Ave. (bet. Onderdonk & Woodward Aves.) | Queens
718-386-4282 | www.bunkervietnamese.com

A "**delicious adventure**" awaits at this way "**out-of-the-way**" Ridgewood Vietnamese, which renders "**high-quality**" street-food staples in a "**hipsterish**" "**hole-in-the-wall**" setting; since it won't cost a bundle many find it "**worth the Uber ride.**"

BURGER & BARREL | Burgers/Pub Food   4.2   3.8   3.9 $$

SoHo | 25 W. Houston St. (bet. Greene & Mercer Sts.)
212-334-7320 | www.burgerandbarrel.com

"**Trendy**" burgers, "**barrel beers**" and "**wine on tap**" collide in a "**high-energy**" setting at this **"happy"** SoHo gastropub from the Lure Fishbar folks; if it's **"loud"** and **"lighting's so low you can barely see your food"**, that suits the **"cool"** crowd.

	FOOD	DECOR	SERVICE	COST
BURGER & LOBSTER | American	4.1	3.7	4.0	$$

Flatiron | 39 W. 19th St. (bet. 5th & 6th Aves.)
646-833-7532 | www.burgerandlobster.com

"It's easy to decide what to eat" at this **"no-muss-no-fuss"** Flatiron American, a British import with a **"simple"** formula: a choice of lobster roll, steamed lobster or burger, **"all well prepared"** and a **"complete steal"**; staffers are **"upbeat"**, and the **"hangarlike"** setup is perfect for **"large groups."**

	FOOD	DECOR	SERVICE	COST
BURGER JOINT | Burgers	4.4	3.2	3.4	$

Greenwich Village | 33 W. Eighth St. (bet. 5th & 6th Aves.) | 212-432-1400
West 50s | Le Parker Meridien | 119 W. 56th St. (bet. 6th & 7th Aves.) | 212-708-7414
www.burgerjointny.com

The **"gold standard"** in burgers, these **"dives"** supply **"sublime"** patties with **"no gimmicks"** and **"minimal service"**; you'll need **"patience"** for the **"lines"** at the **"grungy"** original, **"concealed"** in the **"ritzy"** Parker Meridien, but the **"less crowded"** Village spin-off adds space and **"more alcohol choices."**

	FOOD	DECOR	SERVICE	COST
BURKE & WILLS | Australian	4.3	4.1	4.2	$$

West 70s | 226 W. 79th St. (B'way)
646-823-9251 | www.burkeandwillsny.com

At this UWS **"surprise"** you'll find **"beautifully done"** fare off an **"interesting"** Australian menu that's **"kangaroo inclusive"** (**"check out the 'roo burger"**); its white-tiled bar and **"greenhouse"**-like dining area are **"jovial"** places to hang, and there's also an upstairs speakeasy, Manhattan Cricket Club.

	FOOD	DECOR	SERVICE	COST
BUSTAN | Mediterranean	4.3	4.0	4.0	$$$

West 80s | 487 Amsterdam Ave. (bet. 83rd & 84th Sts.)
212-595-5050 | www.bustannyc.com

A neighborhood **"favorite"**, this **"warm"** Upper Westsider supplies **"shockingly good"** dishes from **"all around the Mediterranean"** (including **"fabulous flatbreads"**) via a **"welcoming"** staff; while the arty interior can be **"packed"** and **"noisy"**, the **"sweet garden"** is **"a real draw."**

	FOOD	DECOR	SERVICE	COST
BUTCHER BAR | BBQ	4.3	3.9	4.1	$$

Astoria | 37-08 30th Ave. (bet. 37th & 38th Sts.) | Queens
718-606-8140 | www.butcherbar.com

"Melt-in-your-mouth" BBQ (including burnt ends **"to die for"**) are the specialty of this Astoria smoke joint that sources local, organic meats and butchers them in-house; its **"roomy"**, **"welcoming"** space features plenty of **"reclaimed wood"** as well as a bar mixing Southern-accented cocktails.

	FOOD	DECOR	SERVICE	COST
BUTCHER'S DAUGHTER | Vegan	4.2	4.0	3.9	$$

NoLita | 19 Kenmare St. (Elizabeth St.) | 212-219-3434
NEW **West Village** | 581 Hudson St. (Bank St.) | 917-388-2132
www.thebutchersdaughter.com

A **"go-to"** for a **"fairly healthy"** bite, these **"sceney"** vegetarian cafes/juice bars provide **"delicious"** all-day fare (toasts, grain bowls, pizza) upgraded with **"interesting twists"**; the **"funky"**, **"cheerful"** spaces offer seating inside and out.

BUTTER | American   4.1   4.2   4.0 $$$

West 40s | Cassa Hotel | 70 W. 45th St. (bet. 5th & 6th Aves.)
212-253-2828 | www.butterrestaurant.com

This "**upscale**" Midtown New American from Alex Guarnaschelli offers "**creatively prepared**" dishes in a "**striking**" subterranean space; the "**bustling**" scene is "**cool**" for the area, even if it's a "**business**" crowd.

BUTTERMILK CHANNEL | American   4.6   4.1   4.4 $$

Carroll Gardens | 524 Court St. (Huntington St.) | Brooklyn
718-852-8490 | www.buttermilkchannelnyc.com

"**Still going strong**", this "**sunny**" Carroll Gardens "**stalwart**" supplies "**killer**" fried chicken and other "**excellent**" New American comfort food at the hands of a "**gracious**" crew; while often "**busy**", it's a "**madhouse**" at brunch when limited reservations make for "**long waits.**"

BUVETTE | French   4.4   4.1   4.0 $$$

West Village | 42 Grove St. (bet. Bedford & Bleecker Sts.)
212-255-3590 | www.ilovebuvette.com

At this "**charming**" West Villager, Jody Williams' "**sublime**" French small plates and "**thoughtful**" wine list will "**transport you to Europe**" – right down to the "**tiny tables**"; since it's "**postage-stamp-sized**" and doesn't take reservations, it can be "**difficult to snag a table**", but it's "**worth the wait – and the squeeze.**"

BY CHLOE | Vegan   4.3   3.8   3.7 $$

NEW **Flatiron** | 60 W. 22nd St. (6th Ave.) | no phone
Greenwich Village | 185 Bleecker St. (MacDougal St.) | no phone
www.bychefchloe.com

The "**innovative**" vegan grub ("**delish**" veggie burgers, "**supremely satisfying**" avocado toast) draws "**crazy long lines**" to these "**hip**" counter serves from cookbook author Chloe Coscarelli; once inside you'll also have to "**fight hoards**" of "**well-to-do millennials**" for a seat, but given the "**addictive**" fare, the effort is considered "**well worth it.**"

CABANA | Nuevo Latino   4.2   3.7   4.0 $$

East 60s | 1022 Third Ave. (bet. 60th & 61st Sts.) | 212-980-5678
Forest Hills | 107-10 70th Rd. (bet. Austin St. & Queens Blvd.) | Queens | 718-263-3600
www.cabanarestaurant.com

It "**always feels like a party**" at these "**casual**", "**colorful**" Nuevo Latinos where "**nicely spiced**" chow and "**rocket-fuel**" mojitos make for a "**happening**" vibe; the "**noise factor**" and "**erratic**" service may be sore points, but at least the tabs are "**reasonable.**"

CACIO E PEPE | Italian   4.2   3.5   4.1 $$

East Village | 182 Second Ave. (bet. 11th & 12th Sts.)
212-505-5931 | www.cacioepepe.com

The "**titular**" pasta served in a "**massive round**" of pecorino is the star of the "**traditional Roman**" menu at this "**sweet**" East Village Italian; "**pleasant**" service and "**fair prices**" keep things "**bustling**", so regulars take "**respite**" in the "**pretty**" back garden.

NEW **CAFÉ ALTRO PARADISO** | Italian   4.4   4.1   4.0 $$$

Hudson Square | 234 Spring St. (6th Ave.)
646-952-0828 | www.altroparadiso.com

"**Rock star**" chef Ignacio Mattos (Estela) puts "**his spin**" on Italian cuisine with "fresh ingredients and innovative flavor combinations" at this "fantastic new kid on the block" in Hudson Square; the "gorgeous" setting is "open, airy and high ceilinged", and tabs are high as well.

CAFÉ BOULUD | French   4.7   4.5   4.6 $$$$

East 70s | Surrey Hotel | 20 E. 76th St. (bet. 5th & Madison Aves.)
212-772-2600 | www.cafeboulud.com

A "timeless" Daniel Boulud "success story", this "classy" UES "mainstay" impresses with "invariably artful" French fare served by an "expert staff" in "subdued", "grown-up" surroundings; "1%ers" say the "high standards" are "worth every nickel", though the prix fixe lunch remains "a relative bargain."

CAFE CENTRO | French/Mediterranean   4.1   4.0   4.0 $$$

East 40s | MetLife Bldg. | 200 Park Ave. (45th St.)
212-818-1222 | www.patinagroup.com

An "escalator ride" from Grand Central, this "reliable" bistro offers "well-prepared" French-Med fare via an "efficient" crew in "comfortable" surrounds with an art deco bar and a sidewalk patio; at lunch it's "buzzing" with a "business crowd", but it "settles down" during the evening.

CAFE CHINA | Chinese   4.4   3.8   3.8 $$

Murray Hill | 13 E. 37th St. (bet. 5th & Madison Aves.)
212-213-2810 | www.cafechinanyc.com

Fans praise the "authentically spicy Sichuan" fare at this "novel" Murray Hill Chinese that offers "outstanding" specialties in a setting recalling a "circa-1930 Shanghai teahouse"; "moderate" prices make some amends for sometimes "spotty service."

CAFE CLOVER | American   4.1   4.1   4.0 $$$

West Village | 10 Downing St. (6th Ave.)
212-675-4350 | www.cafeclovernyc.com

Health-conscious fare in a "chic" setting is the "refreshing" spin at this West Village New American, where the "creatively prepared" locavore menu features "ultrafresh" vegetables; "inviting" vibes and seasonal cocktails help account for the "lively atmosphere."

CAFE CLUNY | American/French   4.2   4.0   4.0 $$$

West Village | 284 W. 12th St. (4th St.)
212-255-6900 | www.cafecluny.com

A "wonderful vibe" has evolved at this "quaint" West Village bistro, a bona fide "nabe fave" thanks to "appetizing" Franco-American cooking served in a "bright" space; since the weekend brunch can be a "free-for-all", regulars say "arrive early."

CAFÉ D'ALSACE | French   4.1   3.8   4.0 $$$

East 80s | 1695 Second Ave. (88th St.)
212-722-5133 | www.cafedalsace.com

This "unpretentious" Yorkville brasserie is a "bustling" standby for "stick-to-your-ribs" Alsatian fare paired with an epic beer menu that merits its own sommelier; given the "too-close" quarters and "high decibels", many opt to sit outside, weather permitting.

CAFE ESPANOL | Spanish   4.1   3.7   4.0 $$

Greenwich Village | 172 Bleecker St. (Sullivan St.)
212-505-0657 | www.cafeespanol.com

When you "don't want to spend much" on "traditional" Spanish fare, this "**been-there-forever**" Villager provides "**satisfying**" basics doled out in "**generous**", "**paella-for-days**" portions; sure, the space is "**tight**" and "**hokey**", but the sangria "**always calls you back.**"

CAFE EVERGREEN | Chinese   4.0   3.6   4.0 $$

East 70s | 1367 First Ave. (bet. 73rd & 74th Sts.)
212-744-3266 | www.cafeevergreenchinese.com

Upper Eastsiders who "**don't want to schlep to Chinatown**" depend on this "**reliable**" vet for "**tasty**" dim sum and other "**solid**" Chinese classics ferried by "**efficient**" servers; the decor gets mixed responses, but there's always "**speedy delivery.**"

CAFE FIORELLO | Italian   4.0   3.8   4.0 $$$

West 60s | 1900 Broadway (63rd St.)
212-595-5330 | www.cafefiorello.com

"**Convenience to Lincoln Center**" makes this Italian vet a "**swift**"-paced "**default**" for "**satisfying**" staples like its "**fresh antipasti bar**" and "**super-pizza**"; the interior gets "**ridiculously crowded**" and "**chaotic**" pre-performance, so "**don't forget the outdoor seating.**"

CAFE GITANE | French/Moroccan   4.0   3.8   3.8 $$

NoLita | 242 Mott St. (Prince St.) | 212-334-9552
West Village | Jane Hotel | 113 Jane St. (bet. Washington & West Sts.) |
212-255-4143
www.cafegitanenyc.com

A "**cool crowd**" packs into these "**hipster-chic**" French-Moroccans for "**delicious**" couscous and other "**satisfying**" dishes (including that "**famous**" avocado toast); the "**small**" NoLita original "**fills up fast**" while the Jane Hotel sequel is "**less crowded**", but both are "**great for brunch.**"

CAFÉ HABANA | Cuban/Mexican   4.1   3.4   3.6 $$

NoLita | 17 Prince St. (Elizabeth St.) | 212-625-2001 | www.cafehabana.com

HABANA OUTPOST | Cuban/Mexican

Fort Greene | 757 Fulton St. (Portland Ave.) | Brooklyn | 718-858-9500 |
www.habanaoutpost.com

HABANA TO GO | Cuban/Mexican

NoLita | 229 Elizabeth St. (Prince St.) | 212-625-2002 | www.cafehabana.com
Fort Greene | 690 Fulton St. (Portland Ave.) | Brooklyn | 718-858-9500 |
www.habanatogo.com

"**Must-have**" grilled corn, "**addicting**" Cuban sandwiches and "**strong**" margaritas are highlights on the "**tasty, affordable**" menu at these "**buzzy**" Cuban-Mexican kitchens with sister to-go outlets; the "**tiny**" "**dinerlike**" NoLita original is "**usually packed**" with a "**young**" crowd, while "**it's all about the garden**" at the seasonal, solar-powered Fort Greene outpost.

CAFÉ HENRI | French   4.0   3.4   3.6 $$

Long Island City | 10-10 50th Ave. (Vernon Blvd.) | Queens
718-383-9315 | www.henrinyc.com

This all-day "**slice of Paris**" in LIC supplies "**simple**" French bites ("**get the crêpes!**") at an agreeable "**quality-to-price ratio**"; it's also "**relaxed**" *jour et nuit* "**if you need a place to chat.**"

	FOOD	DECOR	SERVICE	COST

CAFE KATJA | Austrian — 4.4 3.9 4.1 $$

Lower East Side | 79 Orchard St. (bet. Broome & Grand Sts.)
212-219-9545 | www.cafekatja.com

"Genuine" Austrian "classics" like wursts and schnitzel are "produced with a deft hand" at this Lower Eastsider, a "local hot spot" run by a "hospitable" team; the "homey" quarters, "excellent beer selection" and "companionable clientele" all play a part in the "gemütlichkeit."

CAFE LALO | Coffee/Dessert — 4.0 4.0 3.5 $$

West 80s | 201 W. 83rd St. (Amsterdam Ave.)
212-496-6031 | www.cafelalo.com

Famously "featured in *You've Got Mail*", this veteran UWS "sweetery" is ever a "tempting" rendezvous for "decadent desserts"; despite "wall-to-wall" tourists and "can't-be-bothered" service, it still makes fans "fall in love with NYC all over again."

CAFE LOUP | French — 3.9 3.8 4.1 $$$

West Village | 105 W. 13th St. (6th Ave.)
212-255-4746 | www.cafeloupnyc.com

Long a West Village "neighborhood standby", this "timeless" bistro is a "grown-up" nexus for "fairly priced" French fare "like *grand-mère* used to make" dispatched by a "personable" crew; the room may need "updating", but fans attest it's "worth repeating", especially for "Sunday jazz brunch."

CAFE LULUC | French — 4.2 3.7 3.9 $$

Cobble Hill | 214 Smith St. (bet. Baltic & Butler Sts.) | Brooklyn
718-625-3815

An "easy way to feel Parisian", this cash-only Cobble Hill bistro offers "satisfying" French food served "sans attitude" at "Brooklyn prices"; just "be ready to wait" on weekends – it's a renowned "brunch destination", flipping some of the "world's best pancakes."

CAFE LUXEMBOURG | French — 4.2 3.9 4.2 $$$

West 70s | 200 W. 70th St. (bet. Amsterdam & West End Aves.)
212-873-7411 | www.cafeluxembourg.com

By "now a neighborhood landmark", this "perennial favorite" brings a "touch of glamour" to the UWS with its "arty", "adult" crowd, Parisian atmosphere and "jolly" mood; the "simple" French cooking is "delicious" enough, but the "stargazing" and "eavesdropping" are even better.

NEW **CAFÉ MEDI** | Mediterranean — — — $$$

Lower East Side | Hotel on Rivington | 107 Rivington St. (bet. Essex & Ludlow Sts.)
212-796-8040 | www.cafemedinyc.com

At this chic eatery in the Hotel on Rivington, coastal Mediterranean fare (including seafood and vegan dishes) is served in an airy, skylit space designed with hand-painted tiles. A crudo bar, outdoor seating and cocktails by Allen Katz of New York Distilling Company are further draws.

CAFE MOGADOR | Moroccan — 4.3 3.8 3.9 $$

East Village | 101 St. Marks Pl. (bet. Ave. A & 1st Ave.) | 212-677-2226
Williamsburg | 133 Wythe Ave. (bet. 7th & 8th Sts.) | Brooklyn | 718-486-9222
www.cafemogador.com

"Everything is delicious" at these "popular" Moroccan "standbys" that are especially known for their "unbeatable" brunches, "tight seating" and "long waits" are part of the deal, but "**gentle prices**" help, and Williamsburg's "**cute indoor garden**" is especially "**charming.**"

CAFE ORLIN	American	4.2	3.6	4.0	$$

East Village | 41 St. Marks Pl. (2nd Ave.)
212-777-1447 | www.cafeorlin.com

Something of a "**neighborhood institution**", this East Villager's "**satisfying**" American basics (with some Middle Eastern accents) are dished up in "**mellow**" confines; it's a "**brunch hot spot**", so "**get there early**" to avoid the line – and even earlier to snag a "**coveted**" outdoor seat.

CAFÉ SABARSKY	Austrian	4.2	4.5	4.0	$$$

East 80s | Neue Galerie | 1048 Fifth Ave. (86th St.) | 212-288-0665

CAFÉ FLEDERMAUS | Austrian

East 80s | Neue Galerie | 1048 Fifth Ave., downstairs (86th St.) | 212-288-0665
www.kg-ny.com

Kurt Gutenbrunner's "**civilized**" Neue Galerie cafes transport you to "**fin de siècle Vienna**" with "**exquisite pastries**" and "**vonderful**" Austrian savories dispensed in "**glorious**", "**old-worldy**" settings; Sabarsky is the "**prettier**" of the pair while Fledermaus is "**easier to get into**", but both are "**pretty expensive.**"

CAFETERIA	American	3.9	3.5	3.6	$$

Chelsea | 119 Seventh Ave. (17th St.)
212-414-1717 | www.cafeteriagroup.com

With a 24/7 open-door policy, this longtime Chelsea "**after-the-clubs**" spot serves "**dressed-up**" American comfort classics to a crowd that "**clearly expects to be watched**"; though it's lost the "**allure of years past**", it's reassuring to know that it's there when you feel like "**meatloaf and a Cosmopolitan at 3 AM.**"

CAFFE E VINO	Italian	4.2	3.4	4.0	$$

Fort Greene | 112 Dekalb Ave. (bet. Ashland Pl. & St. Felix Sts.) | Brooklyn
718-855-6222 | www.caffeevino.com

"**Delightful**", "**rustic**" Italian food is the thing at this "**tiny**" Fort Greene trattoria near BAM; the "**unpretentious**" setting (complete with "**requisite brick wall**") can be "**cramped**", but the "**attentive**" servers will "**get you out well-fed**" before curtain time.

CAFFE STORICO	Italian	3.9	4.1	3.9	$$$

West 70s | NY Historical Society | 170 CPW (77th St.)
212-485-9211 | www.caffestorico.com

"**A lovely little secret**", Stephen Starr's "**charming**" UWS Italian within the New-York Historical Society offers "**artful**" fare with Venetian leanings via "**courteous**" servers; "**ladies who lunch**" applaud a "**bright, sunny**" space that's "**tastefully decorated**" with china selected from the museum.

CALEXICO	Mexican	4.2	3.6	3.8	$

Columbia Street Waterfront District | 122 Union St. (bet. Columbia & Hicks Sts.) | Brooklyn | 718-488-8226 | www.calexiconyc.com
Greenpoint | 645 Manhattan Ave. (Bedford Ave.) | Brooklyn | 347-763-2129 |
www.calexiconyc.com
Park Slope | 278 Fifth Ave. (1st St.) | Brooklyn | 347-254-7644 |
www.calexico.net

Mexican food fans "**all abuzz**" over these "**rough-and-ready**" street-cart spin-offs call out their "**outstanding**", "**Cali-inspired**" tacos and burritos;

"fabulous prices" and "fast service" offset the "simple" "hole-in-the-wall" settings; P.S. "make sure to get the 'crack' sauce on anything you order."

CALLE OCHO | Nuevo Latino   4.1   4.0   4.1 $$

West 80s | Excelsior Hotel | 45 W. 81st St. (bet. Columbus Ave. & CPW) 212-873-5025 | www.calleochonyc.com

The "gourmet aspirations" are still "interesting" and the "fabulous mojitos" still flowing at this UWS Nuevo Latino vet situated in "attractive" Excelsior Hotel digs; weekends the "party" picks up during the "unlimited sangria brunch" (just "bring a designated driver").

CAMPAGNOLA | Italian   4.4   3.9   4.2 $$$

East 70s | 1382 First Ave. (74th St.) 212-861-1102 | www.campagnolany-hub.com

A "well-heeled crowd" ("mayors, models, moguls and mobsters") frequents this "clubby" UES veteran for "old-school excellence" in the form of "classic" Italian fare and white-tablecloth surroundings; sure, "regulars" may get "preferential" treatment and tabs run "steep", but you're also paying for the "scene."

CANDLE CAFE | Vegan/Vegetarian   4.3   3.7   4.1 $$

East 70s | 1307 Third Ave. (bet. 74th & 75th Sts.) | 212-472-0970

CANDLE CAFE WEST | Vegan/Vegetarian

West 80s | 2427 Broadway (bet. 89th & 90th Sts.) | 212-769-8900 www.candlecafe.com

Candle 79's crosstown cousins lure "Gwyneth Paltrow wannabes" with "intriguing" vegan eats "prepared with love"; though the low-key East Side locale is "cramped", things are more "upscale" if you head west – either way the cooking is "right-on" at both.

CANDLE 79 | Vegan/Vegetarian   4.4   4.0   4.2 $$$

East 70s | 154 E. 79th St. (bet. Lexington & 3rd Aves.) 212-537-7179 | www.candle79.com

"Tasting is believing" at this UES "phenom" that "sets the standard" for vegan "fine dining" with "distinctive", "quality-sourced" organic dishes and wines delivered by "enthusiastic" servers in "intimate" digs; a "pleasant departure from meaty fare", it's "so worth" the "premium price."

THE CANNIBAL | Belgian   4.4   3.8   4.2 $$$

Murray Hill | 113 E. 29th St. (bet. Lexington & Park Aves.) | 212-686-5480 **West 40s** | Gotham West Mkt. | 600 11th Ave. (bet. 44th & 45th Sts.) | 212-582-7947 www.thecannibalnyc.com

You can feed "your inner carnivore" at these joints where "fantastic", "meat-centric" Belgian gastropub fare pairs with a "phenomenal" beer list; the "so-small" Murray Hill original draws "endless crowds" for a "social" scene, while the Gotham West counter is pretty "lively" too.

THE CAPITAL GRILLE | Steak   4.4   4.3   4.4 $$$

East 40s | Chrysler Ctr. | 155 E. 42nd St. (bet. Lexington & 3rd Aves.) | 212-953-2000 **Financial District** | 120 Broadway (Pine St.) | 212-374-1811 **West 50s** | Time-Life Bldg. | 120 W. 51st St. (bet. 6th & 7th Aves.) | 212-246-0154 www.thecapitalgrille.com

"Power brokers seal deals" while others mark "special occasions" at these steakhouses known for "**top-notch**" beef "**prepared with care**" and "**impressive**" wines delivered by "**pro**" staffers in "**refined**", "**contemporary**" rooms; the Chrysler Center locale is particularly "**splendid**", but they're all a "**splurge.**"

NEW CAPRI | Italian — ▽ 4.3 — 3.7 — 4.1 — $$

Little Italy | 145 Mulberry St. (Grand St.)
212-625-2626 | www.caprinyc.com

"**Top-notch**" pastas, seafood and brick-oven pizzas lead the "**authentic**" Italian menu at this "**charming**" Little Italy place; tile and exposed brick lend the space a "**traditional**" feel that's right in step with the "**great value.**"

CARACAS AREPA BAR | Venezuelan — 4.4 — 3.5 — 3.8 — $

East Village | 93½ E. Seventh St. (bet. Ave. A & 1st Ave.) | 212-529-2314

CARACAS BROOKLYN | Venezuelan

Williamsburg | 291 Grand St. (bet. Havemeyer & Roebling Sts.) | Brooklyn | 718-218-6050

CARACAS ROCKAWAY | Venezuelan

Rockaway Park | 106-01 Shore Front Pkwy. (Beach 106th St.) | Queens | 718-474-1709

CARACAS TO GO | Venezuelan

East Village | 91 E. Seventh St. (1st Ave.) | 212-228-5062
www.caracasarepabar.com

Vending "**real-deal**" arepas with "**piping-hot**" fillings so "**addictive**" you'll "**want to try them all**", these "**cheerful**" Venezuelans "**hit the spot**" "**for little money**"; if the East Village "**shoebox**" is a bit "**squished**" (nearby To Go is "**great for takeaway**"), the patio-equipped Williamsburg site is "**more low-key**" and there's always "**watching the surf**" in Rockaway.

CARA MIA | Italian — 3.9 — 3.5 — 3.8 — $$

West 40s | 654 Ninth Ave. (bet. 45th & 46th Sts.)
212-262-6767 | www.caramianyc.com

"**Not fancy but plenty comfortable**", this "**red-sauce**" Italian is a Theater District "**standby**" for homemade pasta; granted, it's "**space-challenged**" and "**crazy busy**" pre-curtain, but at least you can mangia "**without paying an arm and a leg.**"

CARAVAGGIO | Italian — 4.4 — 4.4 — 4.4 — $$$$

East 70s | 23 E. 74th St. (bet. 5th & Madison Aves.)
212-288-1004 | www.caravaggioristorante.com

More than "**just dining out**", this "**refined**" UES Italian is a "**special-occasion**" nexus owing to its "**sophisticated**" cooking, "**flawless**" service and "**exquisite**" modern setting; "**money is no object**" for most of its "**mature**" fan base, though frugal folks find the prix fixe lunch quite "**enticing.**"

CARBONE | Italian — 4.5 — 4.2 — 4.3 — $$$$

Greenwich Village | 181 Thompson St. (bet. Bleecker & Houston Sts.)
212-254-3000 | www.carbonenewyork.com

"**Amazing twists**" on "**old-school**" Italian cooking (including "**life-changing**" rigatoni) make for a serious "**feast**" at this "**clubby**" Village "**destination**", where the "**classic**" decor, "**nattily dressed**" servers and "**throwback**" soundtrack will take you back to "**Little Italy of the '50s**"; the bill might "**set off the smoke alarm**" (beware the specials), but reservations still remain "**too hard to get.**"

	FOOD	DECOR	SERVICE	COST

NEW CARLA HALL'S | Southern — — — $
SOUTHERN KITCHEN

Columbia Street Waterfront District | 115 Columbia St. (Kane St.) | Brooklyn
718-855-4668 | www.carlahallsouthernkitchen.com

Spicy plates of Nashville hot chicken come with homey Southern sides at this
Columbia Street eatery by chef Carla Hall. It's a polished fast-casual setting
with communal tables and window counter seating, plus frozen drinks, tap
wines and Tennessee and Brooklyn beers at the ready.

THE CARLYLE RESTAURANT | French   4.2   4.6   4.4 $$$$
East 70s | Carlyle Hotel | 35 E. 76th St. (Madison Ave.)
212-570-7192 | www.thecarlyle.com

"Synonymous with class", this "old-world" room in the Carlyle Hotel holds
"fond memories" for a "blue-blood" fan base in thrall to its "refined" New
French fare, "royal-treatment" service and "Dorothy Draper"-esque digs;
plan to wear your "finest baubles" (jackets required for dinner), and be
prepared for "super-premium prices."

CARMINE'S | Italian   4.1   3.7   3.9 $$
West 40s | 200 W. 44th St. (bet. 7th & 8th Aves.) | 212-221-3800
West 90s | 2450 Broadway (bet. 90th & 91st Sts.) | 212-362-2200
www.carminesnyc.com

Built for "group feasting", these "boisterous", "fast-paced" Italians offer
"whirlwind experiences in family-style dining" via "large platters" of
"red-sauce" cooking with a "punch of garlic"; granted, the Times Square
outlet may be too "touristy" for some, but overall "you can't beat it for
taste and value."

CARNEGIE DELI | Deli   4.3   3.1   3.5 $$
West 50s | 854 Seventh Ave. (55th St.)
212-757-2245 | www.carnegiedeli.com

For "mile-high" pastrami on rye and a side of "attitude", "tourists" and
"regulars" alike hit this "quintessential" Midtown deli that's been supplying
"kosher-style" noshes since 1937; it's "cramped" and "frenzied" with "crusty"
service and prices as "overstuffed as the sandwiches", but that's all part of
the "real NY experience."

CAROL'S CAFE | Eclectic   4.5   4.1   4.3 $$$
Todt Hill | 1571 Richmond Rd. (bet. 4 Corners Rd. & Garretson Ave.) |
Staten Island
718-979-5600 | www.carolscafe.com

"Thoughtful", "Manhattan-quality" cooking via chef Carol Frazzetta is yours
at this "pretty" Eclectic standby in Staten Island's Todt Hill; maybe the tabs
run "a little high" for these parts, but "perfect-ending" desserts and weekly
"cooking lessons" sweeten the pot.

NEW CASA APICII | Italian   — — — $$$
Greenwich Village | 62 W. Ninth St. (6th Ave.)
212-353-8400 | www.casaapicii.com

Inside a lofty Village townhouse, this Italian specializes in seasonal plates,
pastas and fresh mozzarella, with tasting-menu options for both meat eaters
and vegetarians. Starburst chandeliers, leather banquettes and sleek velvet
chairs set the tone, while aperitifs encourage lingering at the marble bar.

CASA ENRIQUE | Mexican   4.5   3.7   4.1 $$

Long Island City | 5-48 49th Ave. (bet. 5th St. & Vernon Blvd.) | Queens
347-448-6040 | www.henrinyc.com

A "**fresh take on Mexican**", this LIC sib to Cafe Henri is a "**hidden**" local "**favorite**" for "**incredible**" regional cooking crafted with a "**complex**", Chiapas-style "**twist**" and "**served with a smile**" for "**reasonable**" pesos; the cantinalike quarters may seem "**sparse**", but "**it's not about the decor.**"

CASA LEVER | Italian   4.4   4.5   4.4 $$$

East 50s | Lever House | 390 Park Ave. (53rd St.)
212-888-2700 | www.casalever.com

A Midtown "**power lunch**" staple, this "**posh**" Milanese in the "**iconic**" Lever House is a modernist "**design gem**" whose "**drop-dead**" original Warhols nearly outshine the "**fantastic**" food; its "**busy bar scene**" extends out onto the courtyard in summer – but whatever the season, "**don't forget your Prada**" or the "**corporate card.**"

CASA MONO | Spanish   4.6   3.7   4.1 $$$

Gramercy Park | 52 Irving Pl. (17th St.)
212-253-2773 | www.casamononyc.com

You'll "**feel like you're in Spain**" at Mario Batali's "**tiny**" Gramercy hang where "**inventive**" Spanish tapas are complemented by a "**super-deep**" wine list; "**quickly escalating**" tabs and "**cheek-to-cheek**" seating are easily "**overwhelmed by the out-of-this world food.**"

CASA NONNA | Italian   4.3   4.2   4.3 $$

West 30s | 310 W. 38th St. (bet. 8th & 9th Aves.)
212-736-3000 | www.casanonna.com

A "**perfect place to unwind**" near the Javits Center, this Italian has its "**act together**" offering "**creative glosses**" on Roman-Tuscan standards served with "**quick**" "**professionalism**"; it's a "**wonderful surprise**" in a "**lacking**" area, with well-spaced tables allowing for "**private conversations.**"

CASCABEL TAQUERIA | Mexican   4.1   3.4   3.8 $$

East 80s | 1556 Second Ave. (81st St.) | 212-717-8226
West 100s | 2799 Broadway (108th St.) | 212-665-1500
www.cascabeltaqueria.com

"*Ay caramba*", these "**popular**" taquerias are about as "**legitimate**" as you'll find in these parts, slinging "**above-average**" tacos in "**funky**" quarters; "**bargain**" tabs and "**Downtown**" vibes keep them "**overwhelmingly busy**", so expect service that's "**cheerful**" but "**not very polished.**"

CASELLULA | American   4.4   3.8   4.1 $$

West 50s | 401 W. 52nd St. (bet. 9th & 10th Aves.)
212-247-8137 | www.casellula.com

"**Perfect for date nights**", this rustic Hell's Kitchen American offers a "**never-ending**" wine and cheese list nightly till 2 AM; the "**little sliver**" of a setting is "**cozy**" to some, "**tight**" to others, but the "**bustling**" mood speaks for itself.

CATA | Spanish   ∇ 4.3   4.0   4.1 $$

Lower East Side | 245 Bowery (bet. Rivington & Stanton Sts.)
212-505-2282 | www.catarestaurant.com

"**Taking tapas to the next level**", this "**low-key**" Bowery Spaniard from the

Alta crew offers both "**creative and traditional**" small plates in a "**relaxed**", brick-lined room outfitted with a dining counter and communal tables; regulars recommend "**working your way**" through its "**extensive gin-and-tonic selection.**"

CATCH | Seafood   4.3   4.3   3.9 $$$
Meatpacking District | 21 Ninth Ave. (bet. Little W. 12th & 13th Sts.)
212-392-5978 | www.emmgrp.com

"**Beautiful people**" and random "**Kardashians**" populate this "**trendy**" Meatpacking "**scene**" for "**very good**" seafood in a sprawling, "**pumping**" duplex with a rooftop lounge; "**expensive**" tabs aside, it's "**good for groups.**"

ÇA VA | French   4.0   3.9   4.0 $$$
West 40s | InterContinental Hotel Times Sq. | 310 W. 44th St. (bet. 8th & 9th Aves.)
212-803-4545 | www.cavatoddenglish.com

"**Above the norm**" for the Theater District, Todd English's "**civilized**" hotel brasserie delivers a "**varied**" menu of "**reliable**" French eats; despite somewhat "**steep**" tabs, the "**convenient**" locale makes it "**a good bet**" for a "leisurely" pre-show meal.

CAVIAR RUSSE | American   4.5   4.1   4.4 $$$$
East 50s | 538 Madison Ave., 2nd fl. (bet. 54th & 55th Sts.)
212-980-5908 | www.caviarrusse.com

The "**decadent experience**" at this Midtown New American "**conjures up tsars**" as patrons are "**pampered**" with "**exquisite caviar**" and crudo from "**knowledgeable**" staffers in "**deluxe**" digs suitable for an "**illicit affair**"; prices are predictably "**astronomical**", but big spenders urge "**Indulge in this when you can.**"

CEBU | Continental   4.2   3.8   4.0 $$
Bay Ridge | 8801 Third Ave. (88th St.) | Brooklyn
718-492-5095 | www.cebubrooklyn.com

A "**busy**" local "**staple**", this "**reasonably priced**" Continental brings a bit of "**Manhattan chic**" to Bay Ridge via an "**enjoyable**" menu, "**on-the-ball**" service and night-owl noshing; "**younger**" folks with "**fake tans**" keep the bar scene "**buzzing.**"

CECI-CELA | Bakery   4.4   3.2   3.6 $
Lower East Side | 14 Delancey St. (bet. Bowery & Chrystie St.) | 646-861-0374
NoLita | 55 Spring St. (bet. Lafayette & Mulberry St.) | 212-274-9179
www.cecicelanyc.com

"**Sinfully delicious Napoleons**", "**to-die-for**" éclairs, "**buttery croissants**" and other "**works of art**" provide "**a taste of Paris**" at these "**real-thing**" patisseries; the "**pipsqueak**" NoLita original is joined by a roomier offshoot on Delancey.

THE CECIL | African/American   4.4   4.3   4.2 $$
Harlem | 210 W. 118th St. (St. Nicholas Ave.)
212-866-1262 | www.thececilharlem.com

A "**happening**" place with an "**outstanding, inventive**" menu, this Harlem "**hit**" puts together "**foodie**"-approved Afro-Asian-American dishes highlighting "**flavor combinations that are hard to find elsewhere**"; "**noisy**" digs and "**Downtown**" prices aside, it's "**great for groups**" and also has an "**exceptionally good**" weekend brunch.

		FOOD	DECOR	SERVICE	COST

CELESTE | Italian — **4.4** **3.1** **3.7** **$$**

West 80s | 502 Amsterdam Ave. (bet. 84th & 85th Sts.)
212-874-4559 | www.celestenewyork.com

"**Down-home**" Neapolitan cooking, "**excellent**" wood-fired pizzas and "**standout**" cheese plates add up to a "*molto buono*" dining experience at this UWS "**gem**"; a "**cramped**" space, no reservations and no credit cards are part of the deal, "**but for the price you can get over it.**"

CELLINI | Italian — **4.2** **3.8** **4.1** **$$$**

East 50s | 65 E. 54th St. (bet. Madison & Park Aves.)
212-751-1555 | www.cellinirestaurant.com

A "**staple**" for "**entertaining clients**", this "**expense-account**" Midtowner draws a "**chatty lunch crowd**" with "**authentic**", "**sure-bet**" Italian standards served in a "**not-so-fancy**" setting; it's more subdued at dinner, but you can expect "**comfortable, grown-up**" dining at any hour.

'CESCA | Italian — **4.2** **4.1** **4.1** **$$$**

West 70s | 164 W. 75th St. (Amsterdam Ave.)
212-787-6300 | www.cescanyc.com

Those seeking "**civilized**" surrounds rely on this "**comfortable**" UWS "**standby**" for "**consistently solid**" Italian fare at "**slightly-above-average**" prices; the "**vibrant**" (if "**noisy**") front bar and "**accommodating**" staff have many returning to it "**like an old friend.**"

CHA AN | Japanese/Teahouse — **4.2** **4.1** **4.2** **$$**

East Village | 230 E. Ninth St. (bet. 2nd & 3rd Aves.)
212-228-8030 | www.chaanteahouse.com

A "**hideaway**" from East Village "**hustle and bustle**", this second-story Japanese "**sanctuary**" offers "**quality**" teas, "**delicate bites**" and "**inventive**" desserts; the "**tranquil vibes**" suit the "**traditional**" setting.

CHADWICK'S | American — **4.4** **4.0** **4.3** **$$**

Bay Ridge | 8822 Third Ave. (89th St.) | Brooklyn
718-833-9855 | www.chadwicksbrooklyn.com

A "**Bay Ridge anchor**" since '87, this "**stroll down memory lane**" supplies "**outstanding**" American fare dispatched by "**old-time waiters**" who "**treat you right**"; the decor may "**need a little uplift**", but the "**value**" is intact, notably its "**early-bird specials**" Monday–Thursday.

CHAIWALI | Indian — ▽ **4.6** **4.6** **4.1** **$$**

Harlem | 274 Lenox Ave. (124th St.)
646-688-5414 | www.chaiwali.com

"**Not your average Indian cafe**", this "**charming**" Harlem kitchen presents "**thoughtful**" dishes (including vegan and gluten-free options) in an art-filled space so "**magical**", you'll "**want their interior decorator**"; a "**beautiful**" garden and "**reasonable prices**" are other reasons to "**love**" it.

CHALK POINT KITCHEN | American — **4.2** **4.1** **4.0** **$$**

SoHo | 527 Broome St. (Thompson St.)
212-390-0327 | www.chalkpointkitchen.com

"**Fresh-from-the-farm**" ingredients yield "**flavorful**" cooking with "**tons**" of "**vegetable-centric**" options at this SoHo American; reclaimed wood and exposed brick lend the space "**rustic appeal**", and there's also a "**cool**" downstairs lounge, the Handy Liquor Bar.

	FOOD	DECOR	SERVICE	COST

CHARLIE BIRD | American   4.2   3.9   4.0 $$
SoHo | 5 King St. (6th Ave.)
212-235-7133 | www.charliebirdnyc.com

The "**scene buzzes**" at this SoHo "**destination**" for "**thinsters glamming it up**" over "**spot-on**" American fare with Italian "**twists**" and an "**incredible**" wine list; flaunting "**hip-hop inspiration**" with boom-box prints and "**loud beats in the background**", it's both "**accomplished**" and "**too cool for school.**"

CHARLIE PALMER AT THE KNICK | American   4.2   4.1   4.1 $$$
West 40s | Knickerbocker Hotel | 6 Times Sq. (bet. B'way & 42nd St.)
855-865-6425 | www.theknickerbocker.com

Charlie Palmer "**raises the bar**" in Times Square with this Knickerbocker Hotel dining room, serving "**impressive**" (if "**expensive**") American fare in soothing contemporary surrounds; add the adjacent lounge with a roving martini cart, and it's a natural "**for pre- or post-theater.**"

CHARLIE PALMER STEAK | Steak   4.4   4.2   4.4 $$$
East 50s | 3 E. 54th St. (5th Ave.)
646-559-8440 | www.charliepalmer.com

A "**classic**" menu starring "**high-quality**" steaks and "**step-above**" sides is the "**impressive**" draw at this Midtown outpost of Charlie Palmer's chophouse chain; "**expensive**" tabs are part of the deal, but so are "**attentive**" service and a "**classy**" modern setting.

CHAVELA'S | Mexican   ▽ 4.3   3.9   3.9 $$
Crown Heights | 736 Franklin Ave. (Sterling Pl.) | Brooklyn
718-622-3100 | www.chavelasnyc.com

This Crown Heights Mexican "**shines**" with "**fantastic**" cooking, "**quick**" service and prices that "**don't hurt**"; sure, "**there's always a wait**" to get in, but the reward – at least according to margarita fans – is a "**permanent smile on your face.**"

CHAZZ PALMINTERI | Italian   4.2   4.1   4.3 $$$
RISTORANTE ITALIANO
East 40s | 890 Second Ave. (bet. 47th & 48th Sts.)
212-355-5540 | www.chazzpalminterinyc.com

On the "**right night**" you might see "**Chazz holding court**" at this "**warm**" Midtown kitchen that has an "**old-school Italian feel**" with "**traditional**" cooking and "**attractive**" surrounds full of "**dark-wood elegance**"; "**welcoming**" service and an "**excellent**" prix fixe lunch menu are other reasons to go.

CHEF HO'S PEKING DUCK GRILL | Chinese   4.3   3.5   4.0 $$
East 80s | 1720 Second Ave. (bet. 89th & 90th Sts.)
212-348-9444 | www.chefho.com

"**After all these years**", this "**busy**" Yorkville "**stalwart**" still turns out "**excellent Peking duck**" ("**deserves four quacks!**") and other "**delicious**" Chinese standards; its "**small**" space is "**basic**" but overseen by a "**cheerful**" crew, so never mind if "**the prices are higher than Chinatown's.**"

CHEFS CLUB BY FOOD & WINE | American   4.5   4.6   4.5 $$$
NoLita | Puck Bldg. | 275 Mulberry St. (Jersey St.)
212-941-1100 | www.chefsclub.com

At this "**upscale but accessible**" NoLita American from *Food & Wine* magazine, a "**rotating cast**" of chefs work the open kitchen and the "**menu is** always changing" ("**love the concept**"); its "**dramatic**", "**beautiful**" loft space hosts a "**fun**", "**noisy**" scene, all overseen by an "**enthusiastic**" staff – just the formula for a "**festive**" night out.

CHEF'S TABLE AT | French/Japanese   4.8   4.3   4.7 $$$$
BROOKLYN FARE

Downtown Brooklyn | Brooklyn Fare | 200 Schermerhorn St.
(bet. Bond & Hoyt Sts.) | Brooklyn
718-243-0050 | www.brooklynfare.com

An "**off-the-charts**" gastronomic "**showcase**", chef Cesar Ramirez's 18-seat counter in an "**industrial**" Downtown Brooklyn kitchen presents "**exquisite**", Japanese-inspired French dishes via 15-plus-course tasting menus served with "**Swiss-watch**" form; if you're "**lucky enough**" to score a reservation (and manage the "**over-the-top**" set price), "**the phenomenal experience will stay with you for years**"; P.S. jackets required.

CHERCHE MIDI | French   4.2   4.1   4.1 $$

NoLita | 282 Bowery (Houston St.)
212-226-3055 | www.cherchemidiny.com

"**Take a quick trip to Paris**" courtesy of Keith McNally's upscale Bowery bistro, where a "**caring**" team delivers "**well-prepared**" French classics including "**must-try**" prime rib and an "**unbelievable**" burger; filled with "**flattering light**", the "**carefully distressed**" space is often "**bustling**" and perfect for "**people-watching.**"

[NEW] **CHERRY POINT** | American   —   —   — $$$

Greenpoint | 664 Manhattan Ave. (bet. Nassau & Norman Aves.) | Brooklyn
718-389-3828 | www.cherrypointnyc.com

Inside a refurbished 1930s butcher shop, this woodsy Greenpoint eatery by an alum of The Spotted Pig focuses on housemade charcuterie, American bistro dishes and seasonal sides and salads. There are also unique cocktails and boutique wines, some served by the glass and carafe.

CHERYL'S GLOBAL SOUL | Soul Food   ▽ 4.3   3.4   3.8 $$

Prospect Heights | 236 Underhill Ave. (Lincoln Pl.) | Brooklyn
347-529-2855 | www.cherylsglobalsoul.com

Soul food gets an "**inspired**" global spin at this "**welcoming**", moderately priced Prospect Heights nook from Food Network star Cheryl Smith; the "**flavorful**" options include all-day breakfast and weekend brunch, dished up in a small, "**colorful**" space with a "**nice**" back garden.

CHEZ JACQUELINE | French   4.0   3.8   4.1 $$

Greenwich Village | 72 MacDougal St. (bet. Bleecker & Houston Sts.)
212-505-0727 | www.chezjacquelinerestaurant.com

This "**unassuming**", "**been-there-forever**" Village bistro is home to "**satisfying**" French standards served by a "**charming**" staff that "**keeps the vin rouge flowing**"; even if you "**won't be surprised**" here, it has a "**winning way.**"

CHEZ JOSEPHINE | French   4.1   4.3   4.2 $$$

West 40s | 414 W. 42nd St. (bet. Dyer & 9th Aves.)
212-594-1925 | www.chezjosephine.com

They "**hit the right notes**" at this "**stalwart**" Theater District "**tribute to Josephine Baker**", an "**old-style Parisian**" joint featuring "**capable**" French bistro fare from a "**welcoming**" staff; colorful "**boudoir**" decor and a pianist "**tinkling the ivories**" boost the "**theatrical vibe.**"

	FOOD	DECOR	SERVICE	COST

CHEZ LUCIENNE | French — 4.1   3.7   3.9 $$

Harlem | 308 Lenox Ave. (bet. 125th & 126th Sts.)
212-289-5555 | www.chezlucienne.com

"**Parisian soul**" marks this French bistro on a happening stretch of Harlem's Lenox Avenue, where the midpriced Gallic grub makes for "**pleasing meals**"; it's a "**great alternative**" to Red Rooster next door, and sidewalk seats supply "**people-watching**" galore.

CHEZ NAPOLÉON | French — 4.1   3.4   4.0 $$$

West 50s | 365 W. 50th St. (bet. 8th & 9th Aves.)
212-265-6980 | www.cheznapoleon.com

"**Vérité**" could be the motto of this circa-1960 Theater District "**relic**" where an "**old-school**" crew dispatches "**time-stood-still**" French bistro classics à la escargot, frogs' legs and calf's brains; it's "**tiny**" and "**faded**", but you're "**there to eat, not sightsee.**"

CHEZ OSKAR | French — 4.0   3.9   4.0 $$

Bedford-Stuyvesant | 310 Malcolm X Blvd. (bet. Decatur & MacDougal Sts.) | Brooklyn
718-852-6250 | www.chezoskar.com

This "**very Brooklyn**" bistro continues to purvey "**enjoyable**" French plates enhanced by frequent "**live music**" in its new Bed-Stuy quarters; fans appreciate its "**lack of pretension**", not to mention the rather "**reasonable**" prices.

CHIKALICIOUS | Dessert — 4.5   3.4   3.9 $

East Village | 203 E. 10th St. (bet. 1st & 2nd Aves.) | 212-475-0929
East Village | 204 E. 10th St. (bet. 1st & 2nd Aves.) | 212-475-0929
www.chikalicious.com

A "**must**" for sweet tooths, this "**charming**" East Village dessert bar offers "**imaginative**" tasting menus "**prepared in front of your eyes**" and wine pairings too; there's "**always a line**" to get into the "**tiny**" space, but an across-the-street bakery provides "**creative**" treats to go.

NEW **CHIKARASHI** | Hawaiian/Seafood — — — — $

Little Italy | 227 Canal St. (bet. Baxter & Centre Sts.)
646-649-5963 | www.chikarashi.com

Japanese and other Asian flavors accent the chirashi-style Hawaiian poke bowls at this fast-casual Little Italy option from an ex Neta chef. A sleek wooden setting with counter seats boosts the appeal.

CHIMICHURRI GRILL | Argentinean/Steak — 4.4   3.8   4.2 $$$

West 40s | 609 Ninth Ave. (bet. 43rd & 44th Sts.)
212-586-8655 | www.chimichurrigrill.com

"**Well-cooked**" Argentine steaks topped with the namesake sauce "**wow**" carnivores at this "**tiny**" Hell's Kitchen hideout; "**efficient**" staffers and "**reasonable**" pricing make it a natural for "**pre-theater**" diners who only "**wish it had more tables.**"

CHINA BLUE | Chinese — 4.1   4.2   3.6 $$$

TriBeCa | 135 Watts St. (Washington St.)
212-431-0111 | www.chinabluenewyork.com

"**Unreal**" soup dumplings are a highlight at this "**expensive**" TriBeCa Chinese, offering "**well presented**" if "**not extraordinary**" Shanghainese cuisine in a "**beautiful**", Eastern art deco–inspired space; a few find the service lacking, but the "**unique**" atmosphere makes it "**fun for a group.**"

CHINA GRILL | Asian
4.2   4.1   4.0 $$$

West 50s | 60 W. 53rd St. (bet. 5th & 6th Aves.)
212-333-7788 | www.chinagrillmgt.com

Long a bastion of "**upmarket chic**", this Midtown "**powerhouse**" offers "**fancy takes**" on Asian cuisine served in "**dark**", airy digs with an "'**80s** *James Bond*" vibe; it's "**deafeningly loud**" and "**definitely not a bargain**", but "**business**" types still belly up for its "**fun bar scene.**"

CHIPSHOP | British
4.0   3.4   3.8 $$

Brooklyn Heights | 129 Atlantic Ave. (bet. Clinton & Henry Sts.) | Brooklyn
718-855-7775 | www.chipshopnyc.com

The "**fried goodness**" "**hits the spot**" at this Brooklyn Heights British pub and "**cardiac alert zone**", where Anglophiles scarf staples like "**scrumptious**" fish 'n' chips and deep-fried candy bars; set to a "**child-of-the-'80s**" soundtrack, it's a "**true English experience**" that "**can easily become habit-forming.**"

CHOBANI | Mediterranean
4.2   3.8   3.9 $

SoHo | 152 Prince St. (W. B'way)
646-998-3800 | www.chobani.com

You can "**get your yogurt fix**" at this "**cute**" SoHo cafe dishing out "**deliciously fresh, thick**" Greek yogurt with "**surprising**" sweet and savory toppings; there's also coffee and a handful of sandwiches too – just beware the "**tight**" space gets as "**crowded**" as a "**singles mixer.**"

CHOCOLATE ROOM | Dessert
4.4   3.9   4.0 $$

Cobble Hill | 269 Court St. (bet. Butler & Douglass Sts.) | Brooklyn |
718-246-2600
Park Slope | 51 Fifth Ave. (bet. Bergen St. & St. Marks Ave.) | Brooklyn |
718-783-2900
www.thechocolateroombrooklyn.com

"**Paradise**" for the "**chocolate lover**", these "**welcoming**" Brooklyn dessert cafes specialize in indulgences like sundaes, floats and "**life-changing**" cakes; there are also wine, bubbles and even cocoa-based stouts, so it's got all of the ingredients for a "**great date place.**"

CHOLA | Indian
4.3   3.6   3.9 $$$

East 50s | 232 E. 58th St. (bet. 2nd & 3rd Aves.)
212-688-4619 | www.cholamidtowneast.com

"**Spices abound**" at this "**authentic Indian**" on East 58th Street's subcontinental strip, supplying a "**wide-ranging**" roster of "**complex**" dishes; tariffs are "**moderate**", but for "**quality and selection**" the buffet lunch provides true "**value for the money.**"

CHOMP CHOMP | Singaporean
4.0   3.5   3.8 $$

West Village | 7 Cornelia St. (W. 4th St.)
212-929-2888 | www.chompchompnyc.com

Offering a "**classy**" riff on Singaporean street food, this "**friendly**" West Villager from Simpson Wong (of erstwhile Café Asean) turns out "**solid**" dishes with some "**surprising**" flavors; service can be "**spotty**" and the "**small**" space can be "**tightly packed**", but it works for a "**quick, inexpensive meal.**"

CHRISTOS STEAK HOUSE | Steak   4.4   3.9   4.1 $$$
Astoria | 41-08 23rd Ave. (41st St.) | Queens
718-777-8400 | www.christossteakhouse.com

"**Fabulous**" cuts of meat plus apps and sides with a "**Greek twist**" are "**cheerfully served**" at this Astoria "**neighborhood steakhouse**"; it's "**not cheap**" for these parts and the space "**could be fixed up**", but hey, the valet parking's a "**real winner.**"

CHUKO | Japanese/Noodle Shop   4.3   3.6   3.9 $$
Prospect Heights | 565 Vanderbilt Ave. (Dean St.) | Brooklyn
718-576-6701 | www.barchuko.com

Prospect Heights' "**ramen of choice**" comes with more elbow room now that this Prospect Heights Japanese "**favorite**" has moved up the block to roomier digs; it ladles out the same "**exceptional**" pork or vegetarian "**slurpers**" merging "**full-bodied**" broths and noodles with "**just the right chew**", but now takes credit cards too.

CHURRASCARIA | Brazilian/Steak   4.4   4.1   4.4 $$$
PLATAFORMA
West 40s | 316 W. 49th St. (bet. 8th & 9th Aves.)
212-245-0505 | www.churrascariaplataforma.com

Brace yourself for a "**food coma**" at this Theater District Brazilian rodizio, an all-you-can-eat "**extravaganza**" where "**skewer-bearing**" waiters bring on a "**nonstop**" barrage of "**cooked-to-perfection**" meats; it's "**kinda expensive**", so "**try not to fill up**" at the "**bountiful**" salad bar.

CIPRIANI | Italian   4.3   4.2   4.2 $$$$
East 40s | 110 E. 42nd St. (Park Ave.) | 212-247-7426
East 40s | 89 E. 42nd St. (Park Ave.) | 212-973-0999

CIPRIANI CLUB 55 | Italian
Financial District | 55 Wall St., 2nd fl. (William St.) | 212-699-4096

CIPRIANI DOWNTOWN | Italian
SoHo | 376 W. Broadway (bet. Broome & Spring Sts.) | 212-343-0999

CIPRIANI LE SPECIALITÀ | Italian
Murray Hill | 120 E. 42nd St. (bet. Lexington & Park Aves.) | 212-557-5088
www.cipriani.com

"**Air kisses**" abound at these "**posh**" Italians where "**pretty people**", "**billionaires**" and those wanting to "**feel powerful**" go for "**well-prepared**" Italian dishes at "**absurdly expensive**" tabs; all offer "**chic**" surrounds, including a columned terrace over Wall Street and a "**spectacular**" perch above Grand Central's concourse (with a take-out bakery/cafe across the street).

CITY BAKERY | Bakery   4.2   3.4   3.6 $
Flatiron | 3 W. 18th St. (bet. 5th & 6th Aves.)
212-366-1414 | www.thecitybakery.com

It's beloved for its "**ever-so-rich**" hot chocolate, "**one-of-a-kind**" pretzel croissants and "**scrumptious**" sweets, but this Flatiron bakery also wins favor with its "**wholesome**" salad and juice bars; maybe prices are "**out of whack**" given the "**mess-hall**" decor and "**unhelpful service**", but that doesn't faze the "**crazed**" lunch crowds.

	FOOD	DECOR	SERVICE	COST

CITY ISLAND LOBSTER HOUSE | Seafood   4.1   3.6   4.0 $$$

City Island | 691 Bridge St. (City Island Ave.) | Bronx
718-885-1459 | www.cilobsterhouse.com

Fans commend this "**basic**" City Island "**throwback**" as a "**fine and dandy**"
option for "**abundant**", satisfying seafood; sure, it offers "**not much decor**", but
alfresco dining "**overlooking Long Island Sound**" gives it "**staycation**" status.

CITY KITCHEN | Food Hall   4.0   3.5   3.7 $

West 40s | 700 Eighth Ave. (bet. 44th & 45th Sts.)
646-863-0901 | www.citykitchen.nyc

A "**welcome oasis**" in Times Square, this "**bright and open**" food hall
offers "**something for everyone**" with "**a plethora**" of vendors like Dough,
Luke's Lobster and ilili Box alongside counters for tacos, sushi, burgers
and more; add cafe seating for the "**hopping**" crowds, and perusers are
"**pleasantly surprised.**"

CITY LOBSTER & STEAK | Seafood/Steak   3.9   3.7   3.9 $$$

West 40s | 121 W. 49th St. (6th Ave.)
212-354-1717 | www.citylobster.com

For surf 'n' turf with "**no surprises**", this "**convenient**" harbor is a "**good
all-around**" performer in the "**touristy**" vicinity of Rock Center; some crab
about shelling out for "**standard**" eats, but then again the pre-theater prix
fixes are a "**best buy.**"

THE CLAM | Seafood   4.4   4.1   4.4 $$

West Village | 420 Hudson St. (St. Lukes Pl.)
212-242-7420 | www.theclamnyc.com

Yep, you'll find "**all things clam**" ("**pizza, sliders, chowder**") at this "**charming**"
West Village seafood spot where "**interesting**" preparations elevate classic
dishes to "**excellent**" levels; "**welcoming**" staffers and a "**grown-up**"
atmosphere make it a "**slam dunk**" for both a "**hot date**" or dinner with
"**your parents.**"

CLAUDETTE | French   4.2   4.3   4.1 $$$

Greenwich Village | 24 Fifth Ave. (9th St.)
212-868-2424 | www.claudettenyc.com

It's like "**stepping into a restaurant in Provence**" at this "**breezy**" Village
bistro, where a "**charming**" "**French country**" setting provides the backdrop
for "**delightful**" Provençal cuisine; "**dim lighting**" lends "**date**"-night appeal,
but the "**noise averse**" should "**go early.**"

CLEMENT RESTAURANT & BAR | American   4.6   4.6   4.6 $$

West 50s | Peninsula Hotel | 700 Fifth Ave. (55th St.)
212-903-3918 | www.peninsula.com

A "**civilized**" "**surprise**" in Midtown, this high-end New American "**gem**" set
on The Peninsula's mezzanine provides "**excellent**" food and "**impeccable**"
service in "**chic, modern**" surrounds overlooking Fifth Avenue; the
"**spaciously**" arranged layout makes it "**comfortable**" for "**conversation**" –
just be ready to "**pay for quality.**"

CLINTON ST. BAKING COMPANY | American   4.5   3.5   3.9 $

Lower East Side | 4 Clinton St. (bet. Houston & Stanton Sts.)
646-602-6263 | www.clintonstreetbaking.com

"**Bring War and Peace**" to pass the time in the brunch line at this LES bakery/
cafe, which repays "**daunting**" waits with homespun Americana "**made with

love" (especially those "**divine pancakes**"); a recent expansion may relieve the daytime crowds, though insiders hint "**dinner is just as good.**"

THE CLOCKTOWER | American   4.3   4.5   4.2 $$$
Flatiron | Edition Hotel | 5 Madison Ave., 2nd Fl. (24th St.)
212-413-4300 | www.theclocktowernyc.com

"**A bit of a scene**", this "**chic take on a supper club**" in the Flatiron's Edition Hotel serves "**flavorful**" New American cuisine with a "**British tilt**" in a "**gorgeous old-world space**" with an "**ultrahip**" billiards room; it's "**firing on all cylinders – and charging for it**", so some just stop in for the "**unbelievable**" cocktails.

CLUB A STEAK HOUSE | Steak   4.5   4.2   4.5 $$$
East 50s | 240 E. 58th St. (bet. 2nd & 3rd Aves.)
212-688-4190 | www.clubsteak.com

Set in the "**lesser known**" area near the Queensboro Bridge, this bi-level steakhouse draws locals with "**A-1**" chops, "**top-notch**" service and a fireplace-equipped setting; the "**relaxed**" mood comes in handy when it's time to pay the bill.

CO. | Pizza   4.2   3.6   3.8 $$
Chelsea | 230 Ninth Ave. (24th St.)
212-243-1105 | www.co-pane.com

"**Perfectly salted**" dough with "**immense flavor**" underpins the pies at this Chelsea pizzeria from the "**king of all crusts**", Jim Lahey, whose brick-oven beauties sport "**innovative**" toppings; though the space is "**cozy**" and "**fun**", the communal tables aren't for everyone – fortunately, a sidewalk patio provides a warm-weather alternative.

NEW **COCO & CRU** | Australian   —   —   — $$
Greenwich Village | 643 Broadway (Bleecker St.)
212-614-3170 | www.cocoandcru.com

This Aussie cafe in Greenwich Village focuses on breakfast and lunch bites – largely eggs, salads and grain-based bowls – with vibrant, healthful toppings and freshly pressed juices. Coffee (straight or boozy) and cocktails heighten the energy in the inviting space with tall windows and wooden tables.

COCO ROCO | Chicken/Peruvian   4.0   3.3   3.6 $$
Park Slope | 392 Fifth Ave. (bet. 6th & 7th Sts.) | Brooklyn
718-965-3376 | www.cocorocorestaurant.com

"**Juicy-crisp**" rotisserie chicken is the signature of this Park Slope Peruvian known for "**substantial portions**" of "**hearty**" grub that "**won't empty your wallet**", "**no atmosphere**" leads some to fly the coop via takeout or delivery.

COCORON | Japanese   ▽ 4.3   3.3   3.5 $$
Lower East Side | 61 Delancey St. (Allen St.) | 212-925-5220
NoLita | 37 Kenmare St. (Elizabeth St.) | 212-966-0800
www.cocoron-soba.com

For "**amazingly delicious**" soba "**done right**", fans command you "**go immediately**" to these tiny noodle shops set in "**unpretentious digs**" just like "**you'll find in Japan**"; while the staff is "**friendly**", be prepared "**for long waits at peak time**"; P.S. the NoLita outpost's next-door sib, Goemon Curry, focuses on Japanese curry.

	FOOD	DECOR	SERVICE	COST

COFFEE SHOP | American/Brazilian — 3.6 · 3.3 · 3.5 · $$
Union Square | 29 Union Sq. W. (16th St.)
212-243-7969 | www.thecoffeeshopnyc.com

Still "**happening**" after "**all these years**", this "**fun**", "**noisy**" 23-hour diner is a "**tried and true**" landing pad on Union Square, where "**old friends**", "**newbies**", "**club kids**" and others "**refuel**" with "**decent**" American-Brazilian fare; "**aspiring somethings**" provide "**so-so**" service within its "**lackluster**", "**deco**" digs, but the "**people-watching**" from its sidewalk tables is "**the best.**"

COLONIE | American — 4.5 · 4.2 · 4.2 · $$$
Brooklyn Heights | 127 Atlantic Ave. (bet. Clinton & Henry Sts.) | Brooklyn
718-855-7500 | www.colonienyc.com

"**Vibrant atmosphere meets inspired menu**" at this Brooklyn Heights New American, where a seasonal lineup of "**exceptional locavore**" dishes pairs with "**top-notch**" service in a space sporting a "**lush garden**" wall; it's an acknowledged "**keeper**", though the "**energetic**" crowds and "**tight**" quarters can make it "**hard to snag a table.**"

THE COMMODORE | Southern — ▽ 4.2 · 3.4 · 3.4 · $$
Williamsburg | 366 Metropolitan Ave. (Havemeyer St.) | Brooklyn
718-218-7632

It "**looks and acts like a dive bar**", but this Williamsburg standby houses "**some of the finest fried chicken and biscuits**" going, along with other "**revisited**" Southern fare and "**fabulous cocktails**"; its "'**70s den**" look-alike digs are predictably "**packed on weekends**", and the "**order-your-food-at-the-bar system isn't ideal**", but "**super-cheap**" tabs and an overall "**chill vibe**" go a long way.

COMMUNITY FOOD & JUICE | American — 4.1 · 3.6 · 3.7 · $$
Morningside Heights | 2893 Broadway (bet. 112th & 113th Sts.)
212-665-2800 | www.communityrestaurant.com

"**Beloved by its own community**", this "**buzzy**" Morningside Heights New American is a "**healthy**" haven in "**Columbialand**" for "**nourishing**" eats with "**locavore-ish**" leanings; exuding "**good vibes**" all day, it's "**wildly popular**" for brunch, when there's "**always a line.**"

CÓMODO | Latin American — ▽ 4.3 · 4.1 · 4.3 · $$
SoHo | 58 MacDougal St. (bet. Houston & King Sts.)
646-580-3866 | www.comodonyc.com

This "**sweet little**" SoHo "**gem**" is a candlelit, brick-lined "**date spot**" where "**gracious**" staffers serve "**unique**" Latin dishes drawn from Mexican, Spanish and South American recipes; the dimensions are "**tiny**", but regulars dig the "**intimate**" atmosphere.

CONES ICE CREAM ARTISANS | Ice Cream — 4.5 · 3.2 · 4.1 · $
West Village | 272 Bleecker St. (bet. Jones & Morton Sts.)
212-414-1795

The "**fab**" Argentinean-style scoops seem to have been created by an "**ice cream wizard**" at this simple West Village gelateria; alongside the traditional choices, you'll find loads of "**adventurous**" flavors (that "**amazing corn**") that'll "**keep your taste buds guessing.**"

CONGEE BOWERY | Chinese — 4.0 · 3.3 · 3.4 · $$
Lower East Side | 207 Bowery (bet. Rivington & Spring Sts.) | 212-766-2828 |
www.congeebowerynewyork.com

continued

CONGEE VILLAGE | Chinese

Lower East Side | 100 Allen St. (bet. Broome & Delancey Sts.) | 212-941-1818 | www.congeevillagerestaurants.com

"**All tastes can be satisfied**", including the "**adventurous**" at these LES "**standbys**" where the "**huge**" menu of "**yummy**" (if "**inconsistent**") Cantonese fare includes the "**tasty**" namesake porridge; "**crowded**", "**neon-bright**" surroundings and "**rushed**" service aren't hard to tolerate when tabs are this "**cheap.**"

CONTRA | American   4.6   3.9   4.2 $$$$

Lower East Side | 138 Orchard St. (bet. Delancey & Rivington Sts.) 212-466-4633 | www.contranyc.com

"**Inventiveness and originality**" are hallmarks of this LES American, where the nightly tasting menu showcases "**exciting**" dishes crafted from seasonal ingredients; the "**spare**" setting is "**totally unpretentious**", and though "**not cheap at all**", prices are considered "**fair for the quality.**"

CONVIVIUM OSTERIA | Mediterranean   4.6   4.3   4.4 $$$

Park Slope | 68 Fifth Ave. (bet. Bergen St. & St. Marks Ave.) | Brooklyn 718-857-1833 | www.convivium-osteria.com

"**Superb**" Mediterranean cooking and "**ambiance to burn**" define this Park Slope "**date-night**" nexus where the mood's "**intimate**" and service "**shines**"; a "**quality**" wine list, "**fantastic**" garden and "**particularly romantic**" cellar are bonuses, and if that's not enough, it's an "**easy walk to Barclays Center.**"

COOKSHOP | American   4.3   3.9   4.1 $$$

Chelsea | 156 10th Ave. (20th St.) 212-924-4440 | www.cookshopny.com

Always "**bustling**" with everyone from "**High Line–walkers**" to "**art collectors**", this Chelsea "**favorite**" keeps 'em coming back with "**farm-to-table**" American fare that's "**creatively prepared**" but "**not pretentious**", and delivered by a "**friendly, efficient**" crew; its "**pleasant**", "**open**" space "**can get noisy**", so many "**sit outside**" when possible.

COPPELIA | Diner/Pan-Latin   4.3   3.6   4.0 $$

Chelsea | 207 W. 14th St. (bet. 7th & 8th Aves.) 212-858-5001 | www.coppelianyc.com

An "**interesting**" spin on a Cuban diner, this "**hopping**" Chelsea luncheonette slings "**accomplished**" Pan-Latin comfort chow in "**colorful**" confines; the "**low tabs**", "**no-rush atmosphere**" and 24/7 open-door policy make it a hit with early risers and "**all-nighters**" alike.

NEW COPPER KETTLE KITCHEN | American   4.1   3.8   3.9 $$

East 70s | 1471 Second Ave. (bet. 76th & 77th Sts.) 212-744-1100 | www.copperkettlekitchen.com

"**Local, fresh ingredients**" yield "**interesting**" "**plates for sharing**" at this UES American bistro in the "**comfortably informal**" space that previously housed Spigolo; classic cocktails with a twist add a splash of adventure.

CORKBUZZ | Eclectic   4.0   3.9   4.2 $$$

Chelsea | Chelsea Mkt. | 75 Ninth Ave. (bet. 15th & 16th Sts.) | 646-237-4847 **Greenwich Village** | 13 E. 13th St. (bet. 5th Ave. & University Pl.) | 646-873-6071 www.corkbuzz.com

Like the name suggests, wine is "**the star**" at these "**lively**" enotecas, where "**inventive**" Eclectic nibbles provide "**thoughtful**" pairings for "**interesting**" pours dispensed by "**knowledgeable**" staffers (aka "**wine Jedis**"); the "**warm, relaxed**" atmosphere makes for a "**perfect date spot.**"

CORNELIA STREET CAFE | American   3.8   3.5   3.9 $$
West Village | 29 Cornelia St. (bet. Bleecker & W. 4th Sts.)
212-989-9319 | www.corneliastreetcafe.com

"**Old-school**" West Village dining thrives at this circa-1977 "**charmer**" with a "**yoga vibe**", offering "**perfectly acceptable**" New American fare and a "**cheap and cheerful**" brunch; although "**starting to show its age**", it gets "**bonus**" points for the "**cool**" performance space downstairs.

CORNER BISTRO | Burgers   4.2   3.1   3.5 $$
West Village | 331 W. Fourth St. (Jane St.) | 212-242-9502
Long Island City | 47-18 Vernon Blvd. (47th Rd.) | Queens | 718-606-6500
www.cornerbistrony.com

"**Memorable**", "**messy**" burgers dished out on paper plates in "**sticky booths**" make for classic "**slumming**" at this "**dingy**" Village perennial (with a slightly "**nicer**" LIC spin-off); "**cheap beer**", "**long waits**" and "**student crowds**" are all part of the timelessly "**cool**" experience, as are the late-night hours.

COSME | Mexican   4.5   4.1   4.2 $$
Flatiron | 35 E. 21st St. (bet. B'way & Park Ave. S.)
212-913-9659 | www.cosmenyc.com

"**Creative, brilliant**" contemporary Mexican cuisine from chef Enrique Olvera comes in "**chic**", "**modern**" quarters at this "**über-trendy**" Flatiron "**scene**"; you'll "**spend a bundle**" – assuming you score a "**hard-to-come-by**" reservation – and the "**quintessentially 'buzzy' room**" gets "**loud**", but most hardly notice after an "**original, delicious**" cocktail or two.

COTTA | Italian   4.1   3.8   4.0 $$
West 80s | 513 Columbus Ave. (bet. 84th & 85th Sts.)
212-873-8500 | www.cottanyc.com

"**Busy and lively**", this "**rustic**" UWS "**neighborhood**" Italian puts forth "**delicious**" pizza and tapas-style plates in a ground-floor wine bar or "**cozy**" mezzanine; it's "**perfect for a casual date**", with equally casual tabs to match.

COURT PASTRY SHOP | Dessert/Italian   4.5   3.3   4.1 $
Cobble Hill | 298 Court St. (Degraw St.) | Brooklyn
718-875-4820

"**Terrific**" cannoli, sfogliatelle and cheesecakes are just some of what's awaiting at this "**classic**" Sicilian pasticceria in Cobble Hill, "**one of the last bastions of the old neighborhood**"; it's a "**sweet tradition**" during the holidays, while in summer it's the place for "**delicious**" Italian ices.

NEW **COVINA** | American/Mediterranean   ∇ 4.4   4.0   4.3 $$$
Murray Hill | Park South Hotel | 127 E. 27th St. (bet. Lexington Ave. & Park Ave. S.)
212-204-0225 | www.covinanyc.com

The "**simple, refined**" Mediterranean-American menu featuring pasta, pizza and wood-grilled meats will "**please everyone in the group**" at this spot in Murray Hill's Park South Hotel; "**inviting**" with patterned banquettes, it operates as a cafe during the day for coffee and housemade pastries.

	FOOD	DECOR	SERVICE	COST

CRAFT | American   4.5   4.4   4.5 $$$
Flatiron | 43 E. 19th St. (bet. B'way & Park Ave. S.)
212-780-0880 | www.craftrestaurant.com

"**Still inventive, still exciting**", this "**grown-up**" Flatiron American from *Top Chef* star Tom Colicchio offers "**simply yet expertly prepared**" food that's "**perfect for group sharing**", served in "**warm, modern**" digs by a "**terrific**" team; though the "**one-percenter**" pricing suggests "**special occasions**", it's a "**worthy splurge**" at any time.

CRAFTBAR | American   4.2   4.0   4.1 $$$
Flatiron | 900 Broadway (20th St.)
212-461-4300 | www.craftrestaurantsinc.com

"**More affordable**" and thus "**more accessible**" than Tom Colicchio's Craft, this "**casually elegant**" Flatiron American plates "**quality**" fare in a "**dark**", "**relaxed**" setting patrolled by an "**attentive**" team; its "**young, noisy**" crowd labels it a "**go-to for weekend brunch.**"

CRAVE FISHBAR | Seafood   4.3   3.9   4.1 $$$
East 50s | 945 Second Ave. (bet. 50th & 51st Sts.) | 646-895-9585
NEW **West 80s** | 428 Amsterdam Ave. (bet. 80th & 81st Sts.) | 646-494-2750
www.cravefishbar.com

"**Popular**" neighborhood "**standouts**", these seafood spots specialize in "**fresh**" sustainable catch "**well prepared**" with "**interesting**" flavors; the "**modern**" digs host an "**energetic**" scene, especially during happy hour, when "**you've gotta love those dollar oysters.**"

CRIF DOGS | Hot Dogs   4.1   3.2   3.6 $
East Village | 113 St. Marks Pl. (bet. Ave. A & 1st Ave.) | 212-614-2728
Williamsburg | 555 Driggs Ave. (7th St.) | Brooklyn | 718-302-3200
www.crifdogs.com

"**Spunky**", "**deep-fried**" hot dogs are a "**guilty pleasure**" at these "**gritty**" joints famed for their "**fun toppings**" (like bacon, avocado and pineapple); they're a natural for "**cheap**", "**late-night munchies**", and the East Village original houses the famed "**speakeasy**" bar PDT, accessed through a phone booth.

CRISPO | Italian   4.3   3.9   4.1 $$$
West Village | 240 W. 14th St. (bet. 7th & 8th Aves.)
212-229-1818 | www.crisporestaurant.com

Fans are "**blown away**" by this "**favorite**" West Village trattoria purveying "**gratifying**" Northern Italiana led by a signature spaghetti carbonara that "**has no rivals**"; its "**popularity**" results in "**loud, cramped**" conditions, so insiders head for the "**all-seasons garden.**"

CUBA | Cuban   4.3   3.8   4.0 $$
Greenwich Village | 222 Thompson St. (bet. Bleecker & 3rd Sts.)
212-420-7878 | www.cubanyc.com

Everyone's "**Havana great time**" at this "**high-energy**" Village supplier of "**authentic**" Cuban standards and "**heavenly**" mojitos "**charmingly**" served in "**funky**" Latin digs; live bands, "**relatively affordable**" tabs and a "**cigar-rolling man**" lend the proceedings a "**vacation**" vibe.

CULL & PISTOL | Seafood   4.6   3.8   4.1 $$$
Chelsea | Chelsea Mkt. | 75 Ninth Ave. (bet. 15th & 16th Sts.)
646-568-1223 | www.cullandpistol.com

A "**welcome respite from the craziness of Chelsea Market**", this "**lively**"

Lobster Place offshoot offers the same "**amazingly fresh catches**" (including "**pristine**" oysters) turned into "**creative**", "**well-crafted**" dishes; the narrow space makes for "**sardine**"-like conditions, but the happy hour "**can't be beat.**"

CULTURE ESPRESSO | Coffee   ▽ 4.4 3.6 4.0 $

West 30s | 72 W. 38th St. (6th Ave.) | 212-302-0200

CULTURE 36 | Coffee

West 30s | 247 W. 36th St. (bet. 7th & 8th Aves.) | no phone
www.cultureespresso.com

These "**chill**" coffee bars are home to "**lovingly made**" espresso bevs, including "**excellent flat whites**", not to mention "**awesome**" baked treats; the goods are dispensed by a "**friendly**" crew of "**legit hipsters.**"

DA ANDREA | Italian   4.3 3.6 4.3 $$

Greenwich Village | 35 W. 13th St. (bet. 5th & 6th Aves.)
212-367-1979 | www.daandreanyc.com

"**Delicious**" housemade pastas and other Emilia-Romagna standards are a "**steal**" at this "**cozy**", "**unpretentious**" Villager; with "**warm**", "**friendly**" staffers keeping the vibe copacetic, it's no wonder "**neighborhood**" denizens come back "**time after time.**"

DAFNI GREEK TAVERNA | Greek   3.9 3.3 3.9 $$

West 40s | 325 W. 42nd St. (bet. 8th & 9th Aves.)
212-315-1010 | www.dafnitaverna.com

Set on a "**no-man's-land**" block opposite Port Authority, this "**genuine**" Greek comes across with "**satisfying**" fare like "**yia-yia used to make**"; "**convenience to the theater**", a short trip to Jersey and "**affordability**" are its trump cards, though the "**nothing-special**" decor needs work.

DAISY MAY'S BBQ | BBQ   4.1 2.7 3.4 $$

West 40s | 623 11th Ave. (46th St.)
212-977-1500 | www.daisymaysbbq.com

"**Fall-off-the-bone**" ribs and other "**darn-good**" BBQ allow patrons to "**get in touch with the caveman within**" at this Hell's Kitchen 'cue hut; despite "**cafeteria-style**" service, decor "**best left undescribed**" and a "**nearly-in-the–Hudson River**" address, fans feel "**lucky to have it.**"

DA NICO | Italian   4.1 3.8 4.1 $$$

Little Italy | 164 Mulberry St. (bet. Broome & Grand Sts.) | 212-343-1212
Tottenville | 7324 Amboy Rd. (bet. Sleight & Sprague Aves.) | Staten Island |
718-227-7200
www.danicoristorante.com

A "**Mulberry Street staple**" for more than 20 years, this "**traditional**" Italian and its Staten Island sequel roll out "**gargantuan**" portions of "**tasty**" fare; "**welcoming**" service and "**nominal**" prices (plus a "**beautiful**" back garden at the original) complete the overall "**comfortable**" picture.

DANIEL | French   4.8 4.8 4.8 $$$$

East 60s | 60 E. 65th St. (bet. Madison & Park Aves.)
212-288-0033 | www.danielnyc.com

A "**wow every time**", Daniel Boulud's "**luxurious**" UES "**icon**" "**sweeps you into another world**" with "**masterly**" New French fare and a "**rarefied atmosphere**" defined by "**magnificent**" decor, "**VIP**" service and a "**dressed-up**" clientele (jackets are required); granted, the prix fixe–only tabs are "**Himalayan**",

but "**you'll understand why**" – and the bar provides the "**same stellar**" quality à la carte.

DANJI | Korean   4.5   3.7   4.1 $$$
West 50s | 346 W. 52nd St. (bet. 8th & 9th Aves.)
212-586-2880 | www.danjinyc.com

"**Original**" and "**unfailingly delicious**", the "**modern**" Korean tapas at this "**bustling**" Midtown "**find**" will "**leave you satisfied**" thanks to "**intense**" flavors that "**surprise the palate**"; expect to "**wait**" for a seat in the "**small**", "**sparse**" setting, but "**fantastic**" drinks help pass the time.

DA NOI | Italian   4.2   3.8   4.1 $$$
East 40s | 214 E. 49th St. (bet. 2nd & 3rd Aves.) | 212-754-5710
Shore Acres | 138 Fingerboard Rd. (Tompkins Ave.) | Staten Island |
718-720-1650
Travis-Chelsea | 4358 Victory Blvd. (Crabbs Ln.) | Staten Island |
718-982-5040
www.danoinyc.com

"**Old-world**" "**red-sauce**" cooking "**like nonna's**" draws fans to these "**congenial**" Italians where "**generous portions**" turn somewhat "**pricey**" tabs into "**money well spent**"; the crowd's right out of a "**scene from *The Godfather***", and the Midtown locale adds a summer patio.

DANTE | Italian   ▽ 4.5   4.5   4.4 $$$
Greenwich Village | 79-81 MacDougal St. (bet. Bleecker & Houston Sts.)
212-982-5275 | www.dante-nyc.com

A "**revamp of a New York classic**", this update of a circa-1915 Greenwich Village cafe focuses on "**sophisticated**" Italian fare and "**amazing**" cocktails (including an entire Negroni menu); the original's "**old-school**" charm has been updated with whitewashed brick walls and a restored tin ceiling.

DARBAR | Indian   4.1   3.6   3.9 $$
East 40s | 152 E. 46th St. (bet. Lexington & 3rd Aves.) | 212-661-4500 |
www.darbarny.com

DARBAR GRILL | Indian
East 50s | 157 E. 55th St. (bet. Lexington & 3rd Aves.) | 212-751-4600 |
www.darbargrill.com

These East Midtown Indians offer a "**standard repertoire**" of "**well-prepared**" dishes served by a "**gracious**" team in "**comfortable**" (if a "**bit threadbare**") confines; even better, there's "**no sticker shock**", particularly at the "**can't-be-beat**" lunch buffet.

DA SILVANO | Italian   4.2   3.7   4.0 $$
Greenwich Village | 260 Sixth Ave. (bet. Bleecker & Houston Sts.)
212-982-2343 | www.dasilvano.com

The "**glitterati**" draw the "**paparazzi**" to this ever-"**trendy**" Villager where "**celeb-spotting**" is the "**main course**", though the Tuscan eats are almost as "**delicious**"; it costs "**wads of cash**" and the staff can be "**snooty**" to outsiders, so for best results, bring "**George Clooney**" – and get him to pick up the check.

DA TOMMASO | Italian   4.0   3.5   4.0 $$$
West 50s | 903 Eighth Ave. (bet. 53rd & 54th Sts.)
212-265-1890 | www.datommasonewyork.com

"**Not fancy but always good**", this enduring Midtown Italian turns out "**red-sauce**" classics in a "**1950s**" vintage room with "**hustling**" waiters and a "**neighborhood feel**"; "**reasonable**" prices add to the "**old-school charm**", and make it just about "**perfect**" for a pre-theater meal.

DA UMBERTO | Italian   4.5   4.0   4.3 $$$

Chelsea | 107 W. 17th St. (bet. 6th & 7th Aves.)
212-989-0303 | www.daumbertonyc.com

"**Still a classic**", this longtime Chelsea "**favorite**" rolls out "**serious**" Northern Italian cuisine with "**vibrant**" flavors in a "**simple**" space where the white-tablecloth "**elegance**" is matched by "**impeccable**" service; "**costly**" tabs aside, it fits the bill for a "**romantic**" or otherwise "**special**" occasion.

DAVEY'S ICE CREAM | Ice Cream   4.5   3.5   4.2 $

East Village | 137 First Ave. (bet. 9th St. & St. Marks Pl.)
212-228-8032
Williamsburg | 201 Bedford Ave. (bet. 5th & 6th Sts.) | Brooklyn |
718-388-3363
www.daveysicecream.com

With both the "**old standbys**" ("**incredible**" cookies and cream) and more "**interesting**" scoops, these parlors "**nail it**", offering "**creamy**" housemade ice cream that's a "**perfect balance of sweetness and strong flavor**"; the simple setups include minimal seating, but Brooklyn has a few outdoor tables.

DAVID BURKE FABRICK | American   4.2   4.1   4.2 $$$

West 30s | Archer Hotel | 47 W. 38th St. (bet. 5th & 6th Aves.)
212-302-3838 | www.davidburkefabrick.com

David Burke's trademark "**creativity**" is on display at this Midtown American in the Archer Hotel, where the "**bold**" fare focuses on "**wittily**" conceived share plates (e.g. "**candied bacon on a clothesline**"); "**solicitous**" staffers oversee a "**modern**" setting that's "**upscale yet relaxed**", while an attached lounge offers light fare and patio seats.

DAVID BURKE KITCHEN | American   4.4   4.2   4.2 $$$

SoHo | James Hotel | 23 Grand St., downstairs (6th Ave.)
212-201-9119 | www.davidburkekitchen.com

"**Fit for foodies**", this "**farm-to-fork**" option from David Burke matches "**inventive**" New Americana with "**on-point**" service and a "**semi-subterranean**" setting in SoHo's James Hotel; the "**charming**" rooftop bar, Garden, adds an extra dimension to the "**inviting**" package.

DAVID'S BRISKET HOUSE | Deli   4.3   2.9   3.8 $

Bay Ridge | 7721 Fifth Ave. (78th St.) | Brooklyn | 718-333-5662
Bedford-Stuyvesant | 533 Nostrand Ave. (Herkimer Pl.) | Brooklyn |
718-789-1155
www.davidsbriskethouseinc.com

Catering to Brooklynites with a "**big taste**" for "**lots of meat**", these delis turn out "**piled-high**" sandwiches stuffed with "**phenomenal**" pastrami, brisket and other classics; they're "**nothing special to look at**", but are "**one of the musts**" in the neighborhood.

DAWAT | Indian   4.4   3.9   4.3 $$$

East 50s | 210 E. 58th St. (bet. 2nd & 3rd Aves.)
212-355-7555 | www.dawatrestaurant.com

East Midtown's Indian "**pioneer**" (since 1986) "**still pleases**", thanks to actress/

chef Madhur Jaffrey's "**high-caliber**" cooking, "**graciously served**" in a "**quiet**", "**contemporary**" room that's "**conducive to conversation**"; it may look a little "tired", but fans say the tabs are "**worth the extra cost.**"

DB BISTRO MODERNE | French   4.4   4.1   4.3 $$$
West 40s | City Club Hotel | 55 W. 44th St. (6th Ave.)
212-391-2400 | www.dbbistro.com

"**Still a favorite**" in the Theater District, Daniel Boulud's "**energetic bistro**" delivers a "**top-drawer**" French menu led by that "**irresistible**" foie gras–stuffed burger in a "**sleek**" setting; "**assured service**" that's "**mindful**" of curtain time further helps justify the "**hefty**" price tag.

DBGB | French   4.2   4.1   4.1 $$
East Village | 299 Bowery (bet. 1st & Houston Sts.)
212-933-5300 | www.dbgb.com

"**Astonishingly good**" housemade sausages, "**amped-up**" burgers and a "**massive**" craft beer selection define Daniel Boulud's Bowery French; "**more relaxed**" than its brethren, the "**casual**" space includes a somewhat "**spacious**" dining room and "**convivial**" front bar area, making it a solid "**anytime**" pick.

DEAD RABBIT | Pub Food   4.2   4.3   4.0 $$$
Financial District | 30 Water St. (bet. Pearl & Water Sts.)
646-422-7906 | www.deadrabbitnyc.com

While this Irish-inspired FiDi duplex has a "**well-deserved**" rep as a "**cocktail mecca**" with a "**Bible**" of "**enviable**" craft drinks, its "**well-prepared**" pub fare is "**not just an afterthought**"; manned by an "**excellent**" staff, the saloonish digs "**get busy quickly**" and "**just need more elbow room**" when it hops

DEAR IRVING | Eclectic   ▽ 3.8   4.7   4.4 $$$
Gramercy Park | 55 Irving Pl. (bet. 17th & 18th Sts.)
no phone | www.dearirving.com

"**Elegant**" and "**beautiful**", this Gramercy Park speakeasy from the Raines Law Room team features an "**extensive**" list of specialty cocktails poured by "**sage bartenders**" alongside creative small bites; the "**uniquely decorated**" rooms reflect different time periods with tabletop bells to summon staffers.

DECOY | Chinese   4.7   3.7   4.1 $$$
West Village | 529½ Hudson St., downstairs (bet. Charles & W. 10th Sts.)
212-691-9700 | www.decoynyc.com

The Peking duck "**soars**" at this underground West Village Chinese beneath RedFarm, where the "**succulent**" specialty is the star of "**awe-inspiring**" prix fixes enhanced by "**craveable**" sides and "**crafty cocktails**"; the "**cramped space**" has just a single "**long**" communal table, but there's also a bar for à la carte eating.

DEE'S | Pizza   4.3   3.9   4.1 $$
Forest Hills | 107-23 Metropolitan Ave. (74th Ave.) | Queens
718-793-7553 | www.deesnyc.com

Dee-votees depend on this "**homey**" Forest Hills outlet for "**especially good**" brick-oven pizzas, Mediterranean "**comfort**" classics and other grill items; "**fair prices**", a "**huge**" space and "**ample seating**" bolster the "**amicable**", "**family-friendly**" mood.

DEFONTE'S | Sandwiches   4.5   2.9   3.8 $
Red Hook | 379 Columbia St. (Luquer St.) | Brooklyn | 718-625-8052

continued

Stapleton | 95 Water St. (bet. Beach & Canal Sts.) | Staten Island | 718-285-4310
www.defontesofbrooklyn.com

"**Don't eat for a week**" before attacking the "**two-handed**" "**Dagwood**" sandwiches at these "**lip-smacking**" Italian sub shops; the '20s-era Red Hook original "**used to feed the longshoremen**" and still exudes a whiff of "**old-fashioned Brooklyn**", while its Staten Island outpost continues the tradition.

DEGREZIA | Italian   4.4   4.2   4.4 $$$

East 50s | 231 E. 50th St. (bet. 2nd & 3rd Aves.)
212-750-5353 | www.degreziaristorante.com

A "**hidden jewel**" below street level, this East Midtowner is a model of "**old-world elegance**", offering "**first-rate**" Italian food, "**experienced**" service and a "**civilized**" milieu where "**one can actually talk**"; though a "**bit costly**", it's "**worth it for special occasions**" and "**business lunches.**"

DEGUSTATION | American   4.6   3.9   4.4 $$$$

East Village | 239 E. Fifth St. (bet. 2nd & 3rd Aves.)
212-979-1012 | www.degustation-nyc.com

Grace and Jack Lamb's East Village tasting bar is still "**firing on all cylinders**" with its "**exquisite**", Franco-Spanish–accented New American small plates served in bite-sized quarters; for most, the "**cramped**" counter seating and "**pricey**" tabs are offset by the "**fun**" of "**watching the chefs**" work their magic.

DELAWARE & HUDSON | American   4.5   3.9   4.4 $$$

Williamsburg | 135 N. Fifth St. (Bedford Ave.) | Brooklyn
718-218-8191 | www.delawareandhudson.com

A "**constantly changing**" prix fixe menu "**honors the seasons**" at this Williamsburg American where "**elevated**" takes on Mid-Atlantic comfort food are "**delicious**" and "**well presented**" by an "**accommodating**" crew; the "**warm, cozy**" surrounds fill up fast, but an attached tavern offering à la carte bites adds more room.

DEL FRISCO'S | Steak   4.5   4.2   4.2 $$$

West 40s | 1221 Sixth Ave. (bet. 48th & 49th Sts.) | 212-575-5129 |
www.delfriscos.com

DEL FRISCO'S GRILLE | Steak

West 50s | Rockefeller Ctr. | 50 Rockefeller Plaza (51st St.) | 212-767-0371 |
www.delfriscosgrille.com

"**A hit all around**", these "**energetic**" Midtown steakhouses hum like "**a well-oiled machine**" as an "**engaged**" staff sets down "**premium**" beef in "**sprawling**" surrounds with "**urbane**" vibes and a "**power bar scene**"; they're perpetually "**packed**" with "**suits**" wielding the "**corporate Amex**" to cover the "**splurge**"; P.S. "**definitely try the lemon cake.**"

DELICATESSEN | American   4.1   3.9   4.0 $$

NoLita | 54 Prince St. (Lafayette St.)
212-226-0211 | www.delicatessennyc.com

NoLita is home to this "**cool**" spot slinging "**solid**" American comfort food with an "**upscale twist**" (including "**really good**" mac 'n' cheese); the "**relaxed**" digs are outfitted with retractable walls for "**great people-watching on a nice day**", and the "**good-looking**" staff is "**friendly**" enough.

	FOOD	DECOR	SERVICE	COST

DELL'ANIMA | Italian — 4.5 3.9 4.2 $$$

West Village | 38 Eighth Ave. (Jane St.)
212-366-6633 | www.dellanima.com

"Exceptional pastas" come out of the "tiniest of open kitchens" at this "energetic" West Village Italian, where a "fun" chef's counter gives "lucky" diners a glimpse of the "show"; "small" dimensions result in waits, but you can always pass the time in its adjacent wine bar, Anfora.

DELMONICO'S | Steak — 4.4 4.3 4.3 $$$

Financial District | 56 Beaver St. (William St.) | 212-509-1144 | www.delmoniconsy.com

DELMONICO'S KITCHEN | Steak

West 30s | 207 W. 36th St. (bet. 7th & 8th Aves.) | 212-695-5220 | www.delmonicosrestaurantgroup.com

You can "turn back time" at this "iconic" FiDi steakhouse that preserves "the glories of old NY" with "top-of-the-line" meat and more (it's the birthplace of baked Alaska and lobster Newburg) delivered in "robber baron" surrounds; at the offshoot near Penn Station, the cuts are "just as good" and just as "pricey."

DEL POSTO | Italian — 4.7 4.7 4.7 $$$$

Chelsea | 85 10th Ave. (bet. 15th & 16th Sts.)
212-497-8090 | www.delposto.com

"Hard to top", this "magnifico" Chelsea Italian showcases the Batali-Bastianich "magic" with "inspired" cuisine and an "extraordinary" wine list in a "glamour palace" setting where "gracious" servers leave you "feeling totally pampered"; just expect to "spend a whopping amount", or try the lunch prix fixe for "a true bargain."

DELUXE GREEN BO RESTAURANT | Chinese — 4.2 2.7 3.5 $$

Chinatown | 66 Bayard St. (bet. Elizabeth & Mott Sts.)
212-625-2359 | www.deluxegreenbo.com

"Hungry hordes" hit this Chinatown "hole-in-the-wall" to nosh on "some of NY's best soup dumplings" and other "classic", "bargain-priced" Shanghai specialties; too bad "dumpy" digs and "grumpy" staffers are part of the experience.

DENINO'S PIZZERIA | Pizza — 4.5 3.2 3.8 $$

NEW **Greenwich Village** | 93 MacDougal St. (Bleecker St.)
646-838-6987 | www.deninosgreenwichvillage.com
Elm Park | 524 Port Richmond Ave. (bet. Hooker Pl. & Walker St.) | Staten Island
718-442-9401 | www.deninos.com

"Always a contender for Staten Island's best", this circa-1937 Elm Park pizzeria (with a Greenwich Village offshoot) turns out "phenomenal" pies with "the most remarkable" crispy crusts (not to mention "out-of-this-world" fried calamari); it's cash only and the space is "no-frills" to put it mildly, but "bargain" tabs help keep it perennially packed.

DESNUDA | South American — ▽ 4.4 4.1 4.1 $$$

East Village | 122 E. Seventh St. (Ave. A) | 212-254-3515 | www.desnudany.com
Williamsburg | 221 S. First St. (Roebling St.) | Brooklyn | 718-387-0563 | www.desnudawbk.com

These snug South American wine bars specialize in Latin vinos and "delicious" "variations" on ceviche bolstered by oysters from a "great raw bar"; for most they're an "adventure" with a "fun vibe", though the "bill can rack up."

	FOOD	DECOR	SERVICE	COST

DEUX AMIS | French 4.1 3.8 4.2 $$$
East 50s | 356 E. 51st St. (1st Ave.)
212-230-1117 | www.deuxamisnyc.com

The "**warm**" owner and "**agreeable staff**" lend a "**feel-at-home**" air to this East
Midtown bistro, an approximation of "**side-street-Paris**" dining featuring
"**solid**" French country cuisine; the interior's "*plaisant*" if "**a bit close**", so some
find it's "**best sitting outside.**"

DHABA | Indian 4.3 3.3 3.6 $$
Murray Hill | 108 Lexington Ave. (bet. 27th & 28th Sts.)
212-679-1284 | www.dhabanyc.com

"**Delicious and different**", this "**simple**" Curry Hill Indian turns out
"**impressive**", "**pungently spiced**" specialties – even "**'regular' is hot, hot, hot**"
– at "**terrific-value**" tabs; there's "**always a line**" at the "**sliver**" of a space for
the "**bargain**" lunch buffet.

DI FARA | Pizza 4.6 2.5 3.0 $$
Midwood | 1424 Ave. J (15th St.) | Brooklyn
718-258-1367 | www.difara.com

Pizzaiolo "**legend**" Dom DeMarco is "**a master plying his art**" at this 1965
Midwood "**institution**", where his "**lovingly handmade**" pies are "**a must for
the pizza addicted**"; despite "**unappealing**" digs, "**interminable waits**" and
service with "**zero sense of urgency**", it's "**thronged**" with those who urge
"**patience – it's worth it.**"

DIMES | Californian 4.3 3.7 3.7 $
Lower East Side | 49 Canal St. (Orchard St.)
212-240-9410 | www.dimesnyc.com

"**Almost like being in California**", this LES "**hipster hangout**" specializes in
"**healthy-ish**", "**simple**" fare like "**delicious**" grain bowls, toasts and big salads;
it's especially known for its popular brunch ("**expect waits**") when an "**under
30 crowd**" packs into the basic but cheerful space.

DIM SUM GO GO | Chinese 4.1 3.1 3.4 $$
Chinatown | 5 E. Broadway (bet. Catherine St. & Chatham Sq.)
212-732-0797 | www.dimsumgogo.com

"**Cheap**", "**tasty**" dim sum ordered off a menu rather than snagged from a
trolley makes this "**utilitarian**" Chinese "**less chaotic**" than the typical C-town
outfits; however, traditionalists "**miss the ladies schlepping the carts**" and
report "**perfunctory service**" and "**run-of-the-mill**" decor.

DINER | American 4.5 3.9 4.3 $$
Williamsburg | 85 Broadway (Berry St.) | Brooklyn
718-486-3077 | www.dinernyc.com

"**Handwritten menus**" announce the daily roster of "**consistently excellent**"
New American bites (including a "**phenomenal**" burger) at this "**funky**" local
fixture in Williamsburg; set in a 1920s dining car and overseen by a
"**knowledgeable**" crew, it has a "**quintessential hipster**" vibe that carries over
to the outside seating area.

NEW **DINNERTABLE** | American/Italian — — — $$$
East Village | The Garret East | 206 Ave. A (13th St.)
no phone | www.dinnertable.nyc

Hidden inside The Garret East bar behind a doorbell entrance, this East

Village supper spot offers an Italian-American menu by alums of Quality Italian. The tiny space has a communal table adorned with cloth placemats, votive candles and other quaint trappings.

DINOSAUR BAR-B-QUE | BBQ — **4.2 3.6 3.8 $$**

Morningside Heights | 700 W. 125th St (12th Ave.) | 212-694-1777
Gowanus | 604 Union St. (4th Ave.) | Brooklyn | 347-429-7030
www.dinosaurbarbque.com

"**Funky**" is the word on these "**high-volume**" smoke joints where the BBQ is "**tender**" and "**juicy**", and the settings "**loud, crowded**" and "**great for groups**"; they're "**welcoming to both bikers and families**" alike, but be prepared for "**hectic**" atmospheres and "**long lines.**"

DIRT CANDY | Vegetarian — **4.3 4.0 4.4 $$$**

Lower East Side | 86 Allen St. (Broome St.)
212-228-7732 | www.dirtcandynyc.com

Chef-owner Amanda Cohen shows "**serious skills**" at this "**vegetarian mecca**" on the LES where "**exciting, innovative**" dishes are "**beautifully presented**" by a "**knowledgeable**" crew; the airy space has a "**buzzy**" vibe, and tabs include an administrative fee (no tipping).

DIRTY FRENCH | French — **4.1 4.2 4.0 $$$**

Lower East Side | Ludlow Hotel | 180 Ludlow St. (bet. Houston & Stanton Sts.)
212-254-3000 | www.dirtyfrench.com

This "**funky**" LES "**hot spot**" from the Carbone team delivers "**fun**" French fare "**reimagined**" with Moroccan, Cajun and Southeast Asian influences in a "**sexy**" brasserie setup with "**pink neon accents**"; it's a "**tough**" reservation and you're "**definitely going to pay for what you get,**" but the "**buzzy**" (read: "**loud**") crowd doesn't mind.

NEW **DIZENGOFF** | Israeli — — — **$**

Chelsea | Chelsea Mkt. | 75 Ninth Ave. (bet. 15th & 16th Sts.)
646-833-7097 | www.cooknsolo.com

A sequel to the popular Philly spot, this Chelsea Market counter emphasizes the house's famed hummus – served with freshly baked pita and chef-driven toppings – plus shakshuka and changing selections for dinner. There's counter seating along with Israeli wines by the glass.

DOCKS OYSTER BAR | Seafood — **4.0 3.8 3.9 $$$**

East 40s | 633 Third Ave. (40th St.)
212-986-8080 | www.docksoysterbar.com

A "**safe bet**" for seafood, this "**cavernous**" Midtown fish house offers "**simple, straightforward**" fare to a "**business crowd**" that goes for "**power lunches**" and a "**bustling**" happy hour; live jazz on Sundays also makes it "**feel special**" for brunch.

D.O.C. WINE BAR | Italian ∇ **4.4 4.2 4.3 $$**

Williamsburg | 83 N. Seventh St. (Wythe Ave.) | Brooklyn
718-963-1925 | www.docwinebar.com

"**Delicious**" Sardinian plates are "**the perfect accompaniment**" to the all-Italian vino selection at this "**cozy**" Williamsburg enoteca, known to admirers as a "**secret gem**"; the "**welcoming**" vibes, rustic decor and "**decent prices**" provide extra incentive to "**go back again.**"

	FOOD	DECOR	SERVICE	COST

DO HWA | Korean 4.2 4.0 4.1 $$
West Village | 55 Carmine St. (bet. Bedford St. & 7th Ave.)
212-414-1224 | www.dohwanyc.com

"**Authentic**" eats packing "**lots of spice**" chased with "**creative**" cocktails fuel the "**cool vibe**" at this "**hip**" West Village Korean, a slightly "**upscale**" take on the "**traditional**" with grill-equipped tables on hand for hands-on types; sure, it may cost "**a little more than K-town**", but it's a much "**sexier**" experience.

DOMINICK'S | Italian 4.4 3.0 3.9 $$
Arthur Avenue/Belmont | 2335 Arthur Ave. (bet. 184th & 187th Sts.) | Bronx
718-733-2807

Patrons have been filling the communal tables of this "**iconic**" Arthur Avenue Italian since 1962, despite no decor, "**no menus**" ("**you eat what they're cooking**"), "**no checks**" ("**trust the waiter**") and no reservations or credit cards; "**off-the-charts**" food and "**cost performance**" make the "**daunting waits**" bearable, but to save time, go early.

DOMINIQUE ANSEL BAKERY | Bakery/French 4.5 3.6 3.6 $
SoHo | 189 Spring St. (bet. Sullivan & Thompson Sts.)
212-219-2773 | www.dominiqueansel.com

Pastry chef "**extraordinaire**" Dominique Ansel and his "**cult-status**" Cronuts draw "**crazy morning lines**" to this SoHo "**fantasy land of desserts**" where you'll also find other "**transcendent innovations**" plus "**exceptional**" French classics too; the counter crew can be "**slow**" and the "**small**" space gets "**super-packed**", but if you head to the back garden, "**it's like leaving the city.**"

DOMINIQUE ANSEL KITCHEN | Bakery/French 4.4 3.7 4.0 $
West Village | 137 Seventh Ave. S. (bet. Charles & 10th Sts.)
212-242-5111 | www.dominiqueanselkitchen.com

Pastry star Dominique Ansel "**goes beyond the Cronut**" at this "**small but mighty**" West Village bakery, which "**delivers a big payoff**" with "**exceptional**" French pastries and savory noshes made to order "**with Instagram in mind**"; there's also a walk-up window for ice cream and a second floor space called U.P. for themed dessert tasting menus.

DON ANTONIO | Pizza 4.5 3.6 4.0 $$
West 50s | 309 W. 50th St. (bet. 8th & 9th Aves.)
646-719-1043 | www.donantoniopizza.com

Fans ascend to "**pie heaven**" via the dozens of varieties built on "**light, flaky**" crusts (its flash-fried rendition is especially "**scrumptious**") at this "**excellent**" Midtown Neapolitan; the setting can be "**cramped**" and "**hectic**", yet in the end those "**tasty**" wood-fired pizzas "**overcome all.**"

DONOVAN'S | American 4.1 3.8 4.0 $$
Bayside | 214-16 41st Ave. (Bell Blvd.) | Queens | 718-423-5353 |
www.donovansofbayside.com
Woodside | 57-24 Roosevelt Ave. (58th St.) | Queens | 718-429-9339 |
www.donovansny.com

"**Something-for-everyone**" menus draw the "**family**" trade to these separately owned Queens Americans lauded for "**perfect**" hamburgers along with "**solid**", "**Irish-tinged**" pub grub; "**bargain**" tabs and "**pleasant**" service come with the territory.

	FOOD	DECOR	SERVICE	COST

DON PEPPE | Italian   4.7   3.2   3.9 $$

South Ozone Park | 135-58 Lefferts Blvd. (149th Ave.) | Queens
718-845-7587

"**Bring a crowd**" to this circa-1968 South Ozone Park Italian that's "**still cranking out**" the "**fantastic**" old-world comfort classics ("**clams! clams! clams!**") in portions to "**feed an army**", washed down with "**lotsa house wine**"; it's cash only, the interior's "**tired**" and service can be "**snippy**", but fans shrug "**so what?**"

DON'S BOGAM BBQ & WINE BAR | Korean   4.4   3.9   3.8 $$

Murray Hill | 17 E. 32nd St. (bet. 5th & Madison Aves.)
212-683-2200 | www.donsbogam.com

"**Excellent Korean BBQ**" that you cook yourself ("**make sure you get a grill table**") is the main event at this "**trendy**" spot off the Koreatown strip that also offers staples like bibimbop, noodles and more; a stylish bar adds to the "**cool**" experience.

THE DONUT PUB | Donuts   4.2   3.1   3.8 $

Chelsea | 203 W. 14th St. (7th Ave.)
212-929-0126 | www.donutpub.com

"**Sit at the counter and watch the world go by**" at this "**old-time throwback**" in Chelsea, doling out "**shiny glazed donuts**", black-and-white cookies and other "**guilty pleasures**" 24/7; "**cramped quarters add to the charm**" – as do "**old-fashioned**" prices.

DOS CAMINOS | Mexican   3.9   3.8   3.8 $$$

East 50s | 825 Third Ave. (bet. 50th & 51st Sts.) | 212-336-5400
Meatpacking District | 675 Hudson St. (bet. 13th & 14th Sts.) | 212-699-2400
Murray Hill | 373 Park Ave. S. (bet. 26th & 27th Sts.) | 212-294-1000
SoHo | 475 W. Broadway (bet. Houston & Prince Sts.) | 212-277-4300
West 40s | 1567 Broadway (47th St.) | 212-918-1330
www.doscaminos.com

The "**tasty if simple**" lineup kicks off with "**flavorful**" tableside guac and "**killer margaritas**" at these "**exuberant**" Mexican "**favorites**"; maybe the "**typical**" cantina style holds "**no surprises**", but they're "**always busy and it's easy to see why.**"

NEW **OO & CO** | Pizza/Vegan   4.1   4.0   4.0 $$

East Village | 65 Second Ave. (4th St.)
212-777-1608 | www.matthewkenneycuisine.com

"**Innovative**" vegan pizzas are what it's about at Matthew Kenney's East Village hang where "**flavorful**" wood-fired pies are made with superfine flour (for which it's named) and nut-based cheeses (the "**greatest surprise**"); communal table seating can feel "**super-tight**", but it's still a "**cool**" spot overall.

DOUGH | Donuts   4.4   3.3   3.7 $

NEW **East 40s** | Urbanspace Vanderbilt | 230 Park Ave. (45th St.)
646-747-0806
Flatiron | 14 W. 19th St. (5th Ave.) | 212-243-6844
West 40s | City Kitchen | 700 Eighth Ave. (bet. 44th & 45th Sts.) |
917-338-1420

continued

Bedford-Stuyvesant | 448 Lafayette Ave. (Franklin Ave.) | Brooklyn |
347-533-7544
www.doughdoughnuts.com

Taking donuts to "**a whole other level**", these bakeshops turn out their
"**extra-large**" yeast version with a "**ridiculously good**" variety of "**fancy**"
glazes and fillings ("**hibiscus, anyone?**"); the modest cafes are joined by
"**strategically located**" stalls in City Kitchen and Urbanspace Vanderbilt.

DOUGHNUT PLANT | Donuts   4.3   3.4   3.7 $
Chelsea | 220 W. 23rd St. (7th Ave.) | 212-505-3700
Lower East Side | 379 Grand St. (Norfolk St.) | 212-505-3700
Prospect Heights | 245 Flatbush Ave. (bet. Bergen St. & 6th Ave.) | Brooklyn |
212-505-3700
Sunnyside | Falchi Bldg. | 31-00 47th Ave. (bet. 31st Pl. & 31st St.) | Queens |
212-505-3700
www.doughnutplant.com

The "**designer donuts**" are "**dangerously delicious**" at this LES-based bakery
chain, where the "**intriguing flavors**" include the "**life-changing**" likes of tres
leches and crème brûlée ("'**nuff said**"); the goods run "**expensive**" and you
may end up "**waiting in line**", but "**you'll regret not stopping in.**"

DOVER | American   4.5   3.9   4.2 $$$
Carroll Gardens | 412 Court St. (bet. 1st & 2nd Pls.) | Brooklyn
347-987-3545 | www.doverbrooklyn.com

"**Wow**" is the word on this Carroll Gardens American where the "**innovative**",
ambitious American fare is "**remarkably good**" (ditto the "**first-rate**" cocktails)
and service is "**super-attentive**"; its "**simple**" (some say "**stark**") surrounds
may be an "**odd match**" for the "**fine-dining**" fare, but the "**pricey**" tabs are
right in line.

DOVETAIL | American   4.6   4.4   4.6 $$$$
West 70s | 103 W. 77th St. (Columbus Ave.)
212-362-3800 | www.dovetailnyc.com

Something of a "**surprise gem**" on the UWS, John Fraser's "**sophisticated**"
New American delivers "**terrific**" tasting menu–only cuisine in "**chic, modern**"
and "**serene**" environs via an "**intelligent, caring**" crew; "**wonderful for special
occasions**", it's unsurprisingly "**expensive**" – though the 'Sunday Suppa' and
"**veggie-focused Monday**" are relative "**bargains.**"

DUCKS EATERY | Eclectic   4.3   3.6   3.9 $$
East Village | 351 E. 12th St. (1st Ave.)
212-432-3825 | www.duckseatery.com

This "**cool**" East Villager "**wows**" with "**exotic**" dishes like "**succulent**" smoked
meats (chicken wings, duck, goat neck) with "**huge**" Asian, Creole and
Southern flavors; "**interesting**" drinks are another reason the small,
"**hipster**"-friendly space is "**crowded at peak hours.**"

DUDLEY'S | American/Australian   ∇ 4.2   3.8   4.1 $$
Lower East Side | 85 Orchard St. (Broome St.)
212-925-7355 | www.dudleysnyc.com

Local ingredients drive a menu of Australian-inspired American eats at this
"**cozy**" LES all-day cafe and bar serving everything from pancakes to steaks,
plus custom cocktails and regional brews; "**cool without being pretentious**",
the "**tiny**" corner spot has a marble bar and sidewalk tables.

	FOOD	DECOR	SERVICE	COST
DUE	Italian	4.1	3.7	4.1	$$$

East 70s | 1396 Third Ave. (bet. 79th & 80th Sts.)
212-772-3331 | www.duenyc.com

Locals tout the "**simple**", "**satisfying**" Northern Italian cooking and "**feel-at-home**" atmosphere at this longtime "**low-profile**" Upper Eastsider; "**rustic**" looks and "**warm**" service enhance its "**unpretentious**" air, and fair prices seal the deal.

DUMONT BURGER	Burgers	▽ 4.3	3.4	3.7	$$

Williamsburg | 314 Bedford Ave. (bet. 1st & 2nd Sts.) | Brooklyn
718-384-6127 | www.dumontnyc.com

Williamsburg's burger fans insist the "**prime**" patties at this "**hip**" hideaway are "**definitely high up there**", especially matched with "**amazing**" boozy shakes; the "**very small**" space has limited seating, but sidewalk tables double its size in summer.

DUMPLING GALAXY	Chinese	4.1	3.7	3.7	$

Flushing | 42-35 Main St. (Franklin Ave.) | Queens
718-461-0808 | www.dumplinggalaxy.com

The "**rich and juicy**" dumplings attract daytrippers to this mall-based Flushing Chinese whose "**mind-boggling**" selection includes plenty of "**unusual options**"; it's a "**no-frills venue**", but given "**speedy service**" and "**great prices**", "**it makes kitschy work.**"

DUMPLING MAN	Chinese	4.2	3.0	3.8	$

East Village | 100 St. Marks Pl. (bet. Ave. A & 1st Ave.)
212-505-2121 | www.dumplingman.com

Steamed or seared, the "**delicious**" dumplings at this East Village Chinese make for a "**super-cheap**", cash-only snack that's handmade "**right in front of you**" (a "**show in itself**"); many prefer to "**stuff themselves**" on the run since the premises "**aren't much to look at.**"

DUN-WELL DOUGHNUTS	Donuts/Vegan	▽ 4.3	4.0	4.4	$

East Village | 102 St. Marks Pl. (1st Ave.)
no phone
Williamsburg | 222 Montrose Ave. (Bushwick Ave.) | Brooklyn
347-294-0871
www.dunwelldoughnuts.com

Artisanal donuts get the vegan treatment at these shops that offer a "**delicious**" rotating selection of classic and "**quirky**" flavors; dairy-free soft-serve ice cream is also on tap in the "**hip**" digs, with "**excellent**" coffee drinks too.

THE DUTCH	American	4.2	4.1	4.1	$$$

SoHo | 131 Sullivan St. (Prince St.)
212-677-6200 | www.thedutchnyc.com

"**Just what one hopes for in SoHo**", this "**happening**" American presents chef Andrew Carmellini's "**innovative takes on classic dishes**" in an "**attractive**" "**retro setting**" where "**Downtown**" types can "**see and be seen**"; skeptics say it's "**noisy**" and "**expensive for what it is**", but expect "**bustling**" business "**at all times.**"

	FOOD	DECOR	SERVICE	COST

E&E GRILL HOUSE | Steak   4.3   3.9   4.2 $$$

West 40s | 233 W. 49th St. (bet. B'way & 8th Ave.)
212-505-9909 | www.eegrillhouse.com

"**Darn-good steaks**" and seafood are the headliners at this "**heart-of–Times Square**" chophouse where a minimalist, "**modern**" setting and "**eager-to-please**" staffers set a "**delightful**" mood; throw in tabs that "**won't break the bank**", and showgoers say this baby's got star "**potential.**"

EARL'S BEER & CHEESE | American   4.3   3.4   4.0 $$

East 90s | 1259 Park Ave. (bet. 97th & 98th Sts.)
212-289-1581 | www.earlsny.com

"**The name says it all**" at this "**warm little hole-in-the-wall**" on the UES serving a "**small**" but "**quality**" menu of "**well-chosen**" craft beer and "**delicious**" cheese-based eats; the "**laid-back**" space has an "**easy vibe**", so it's an all-around "**great local spot.**"

THE EAST POLE | American/British   4.1   4.0   3.9 $$$

East 60s | 133 E. 65th St. (bet. Lexington & Park Aves.)
212-249-2222 | www.theeastpolenyc.com

"**Downtown moves Uptown**" via this Fat Radish offshoot that's "**enchanting**" Upper Eastsiders with its "**farm-to-table-done-right**", British-accented New American fare and "**original**" cocktails served in airy, "**hip**" quarters; despite "**pricey**" tabs, it's generally "**crowded**" – especially at the "**fantastic brunch.**"

E.A.T. | American   4.0   3.1   3.6 $$

East 80s | 1064 Madison Ave. (bet. 80th & 81st Sts.)
212-772-0022 | www.elizabar.com

Before "**Madison Avenue shopping**" or hitting the Museum Mile, "**East Side ladies**" and others drop by Eli Zabar's "**high-style**" American cafe for "**tastefully prepared**" sandwiches and salads; despite "**money-is-no-object**" tabs, "**rushed**" service and "**glamorized deli**" digs, it's "**always busy.**"

EATALY | Food Hall/Italian   4.3   3.8   3.7 $$

NEW **Financial District** | 101-125 Liberty St. (Greenwich St.)
212-897-2895
Flatiron | 200 Fifth Ave. (bet. 23rd & 24th Sts.)
212-229-2560
www.eataly.com

A "**high temple of *la dolce vita***", these marketplace and dining "**wonderlands**" from the Batali-Bastianich team trade in "**Italian bliss**" via an "**overwhelming**" variety of gourmet food stalls, take-out counters and "**innovative**" sit-down restaurants, including a "**delightful**" rooftop beer garden at the Flatiron locale; those who can stomach the "**crowds**", "**chaos**" and "**tourist prices**" consider it foodie "**paradiso.**"

ECCO | Italian   4.1   3.9   4.2 $$$

TriBeCa | 124 Chambers St. (bet. B'way & Church St.)
212-227-7074 | www.eccorestaurantny.com

"**Still going strong**", this "**old-school**" TriBeCan turns out "**true-to-its-roots**" Italian fare in mahogany-paneled "**publike**" surrounds with a "**bustling bar**"; "**friendly**" staffers add to the "**classic**" neighborhood vibe, making "**Uptown prices**" the only kink.

	FOOD	DECOR	SERVICE	COST

EDDIE'S SWEET SHOP | Ice Cream   4.5   4.0   4.0 $

Forest Hills | 105-29 Metropolitan Ave. (72nd Rd.) | Queens
718-520-8514

The "**good 'ol days are alive and well**" at this Forest Hills soda shop that has been making its own "**first-rate**" ice cream and toppings ("**real whipped cream**", "**don't-miss**" hot fudge) for over 100 years; the space "**could use some sprucing up**", but there's no denying it's "**high on charm.**"

THE EDDY | American   4.5   4.2   4.4 $$

East Village | 342 E. Sixth St. (bet. 1st & 2nd Aves.)
646-895-9884 | www.theeddynyc.com

This "**charming**" East Village New American "**nails it**" with "**exciting**" plates "**executed with perfect flavors**" plus some of the "**most creative**" cocktails around; despite "**expensive**" tabs and an "**itty-bitty**" space that can feel a "**bit tight**", most still "**can't say enough great things.**"

EDI & THE WOLF | Austrian   4.2   4.2   4.1 $$$

East Village | 102 Ave. C (bet. 6th & 7th Sts.)
212-598-1040 | www.ediandthewolf.com

"**Unique**" is the word on this "**funky**" East Village Austrian offering "**rich**", "**authentic**" fare paired with super suds and wines; the hipster "**cozy-cottage**" design seems straight out of a fractured fairy tale, while the "**cute**" garden is a quiet alternative to the "**loud**" goings-on inside.

ED'S CHOWDER HOUSE | Seafood   4.0   4.0   4.0 $$$

West 60s | Empire Hotel | 44 W. 63rd St. (bet. B'way & Columbus Ave.)
212-956-1288 | www.edschowderhouse.nyc

For "**civilized dining by Lincoln Center**", this "**reliable**" seafood spot in the Empire Hotel fits the ("**pricey**") bill with "**skillfully prepared**" catch and a "**courteous**" staff; "**nicely spaced**" tables make for a "**comfortable**" meal, and there's also an "**inviting**" bar area too.

ED'S LOBSTER BAR | Seafood   4.3   3.6   4.1 $$

SoHo | 222 Lafayette St. (bet. Broome & Spring Sts.)
212-343-3236 | www.lobsterbarnyc.com

A "**seafood bonanza**" awaits at this "**tiny**" SoHo fish house, where "**consistently fresh**" fare includes a "**loaded**" lobster roll that "**tops the charts**"; space is "**tight**" in the "**beachy**" room, but the front bar can be quite "**pleasant.**"

EGG | Southern   4.3   3.7   3.8 $$

Williamsburg | 109 N. Third St. (bet. Berry St. & Wythe Ave.) | Brooklyn
718-302-5151 | www.eggrestaurant.com

Known for "**one of the best brunches in town**", this Williamsburg daytimer packs 'em in for "**very good**", "**simple**" Southern dishes made with ingredients from its own upstate farm; there are "**lengthy**" waits on weekends, but given the "**hip**"crowd, at least there's good "**people-watching.**"

EGG SHOP | American   4.1   3.6   3.9 $

NoLita | 151 Elizabeth St. (Kenmare St.)
646-666-0810 | www.eggshopnyc.com

"**Creative**" egg dishes are "**on point**" at this all-day NoLita American supplying "**Instagram-friendly**" sandwiches and bowls alongside "**very good**" cocktails; seating's limited in the "**sunny-side-up**" space, so weekend wait times are an "**investment**", but the "**good price point**" helps.

83.5 | Italian　　　　　　　　　4.2　3.8　4.1　$$

East 80s | 345 E. 83rd St. (1st Ave.)
212-737-8312 | www.eighty-threeandahalf.com

This "**charming**" UES "**hideaway**" puts a "**creative**" modern spin on classic Italian fare with its "**flavorful**" dishes (including "**to-die-for**" Brussels sprouts) and "**enticing**" specials; "**gracious**" staffers preside over the "**intimate**" space, where an open kitchen allows a glimpse of "**the chefs at work.**"

EISENBERG'S SANDWICH SHOP | Sandwiches　4.0　3.1　3.6　$

Flatiron | 174 Fifth Ave. (22nd St.)
212-675-5096 | www.eisenbergsnyc.com

A "**bygone**" ode to the "**greasy spoon**", this circa-1929 Flatiron luncheonette is known for "**basics**" like tuna sandwiches and "**old-style**" egg creams; some may moan about "**shabby**" decor and "**rickety**" service, but for many, this remains a "**sentimental**" favorite.

NEW EL ATORADERO | Mexican　　　▽　4.3　3.6　3.9　$$
BROOKLYN

Prospect Heights | 708 Washington Ave. (Prospect Pl.) | Brooklyn
718-399-8226 | www.elatoraderobrooklyn.com

This Bronx-born destination for "**authentic**" Mexican home cooking resurfaces in Prospect Heights with "**delicious**" familiar favorites and unexpected offerings that are "**not for the meek palate**", plus a full bar; the "**small**" space "**can get crowded super-fast**" and doesn't take reservations.

EL CENTRO | Mexican　　　　　　4.0　3.7　3.9　$$

West 50s | 824 Ninth Ave. (54th St.)
646-763-6585 | www.elcentro-nyc.com

This "**upbeat**" Midtown Mexican throws a "**hip**", "**loud**" fiesta ramped up by "**awesome**" margaritas and, oh yeah, "**satisfying**" south-of-the-border fare that's "**decently priced**"; the "**kitschy**" setting is "**always packed**", though regulars wish the "**music could be lowered a few decibels.**"

ELEVEN MADISON PARK | American　4.7　4.8　4.8　$$$$

Flatiron | 11 Madison Ave. (24th St.)
212-889-0905 | www.elevenmadisonpark.com

"**Brilliant as ever**", Daniel Humm's New American "**knockout**" on Madison Square Park is "**a total indulgence**" where a "**spectacular**" tasting menu with pairings from a "**massive**" wine list provides a "**culinary adventure**" that's "**expertly**" served in a "**magnificent**" art deco space; the "**jumbo bill**" is a given, but "**throw the budget out the window**" – "**you can't afford to miss this place.**"

ELIÁ | Greek　　　　　　　　　4.5　4.0　4.3　$$

Bay Ridge | 8611 Third Ave. (bet. 86th & 87th Sts.) | Brooklyn
718-748-9891 | www.eliarestaurant.com

Bringing Bay Ridge an "**exceptional**" "**taste of the Mediterranean**", this Greek neighborhood fixture produces "**perfectly cooked**" whole fish and other "**innovative**" specials; sure, it's a "**splurge**", but the staff is "**hospitable**" and there are bonus "**outdoor seats**" on the garden deck.

ELIAS CORNER | Greek/Seafood　　4.5　3.1　3.7　$$

Astoria | 24-02 31st St. (24th Ave.) | Queens
718-932-1510 | www.eliascorner.com

Grilled fish so fresh it tastes like it was "**caught an hour ago**" is the specialty of this "**no-frills**" Astoria Greek with not much decor and "**no menus**" (just check out the **"cold case"** and point); though it only accepts cash and service is **"so-so"**, the tabs are sure **"hard to beat."**

ELIO'S | Italian   4.5   3.9   4.1 $$$

East 80s | 1621 Second Ave. (bet. 84th & 85th Sts.)
212-772-2242

A magnet for **"media"** moguls, **"Page Six regulars"** and **"monied"** UES types, this **"old-school"** Italian dispenses food **"delectable"** enough to justify the **"through-the-nose"** tabs; expect the **"cold shoulder"** if you're not a **"member of the club"**, but at least the **"cheek-to-jowl"** seating bolsters the chance of rubbing elbows with **"Matt Lauer."**

ELI'S ESSENTIALS | Eclectic   3.8   3.2   3.4 $$

East 70s | 922 Madison Ave. (73rd St.) | 646-790-2333
East 70s | 939 Madison Ave. (74th St.) | 212-988-4506
East 80s | 1291 Lexington Ave. (87th St.) | 212-348-4940

ELI'S ESSENTIALS WINE BAR | Eclectic

East 90s | Eli's Essentials | 1270 Madison Ave. (91st St.) | 646-755-3999
www.elizabar.com

"Good for a quick grab", these UES market/cafes from Eli Zabar are **"convenient"** stops to pick up soup, salad or a sandwich along with **"fresh"** breads and baked goods; they're **"audaciously"** priced, but for the **"upscale"** locals **"easy"** is the watchword here; P.S. the East 90s locale turns into a wine bar at night.

ELI'S TABLE | American   4.3   3.8   4.0 $$$

East 80s | 1413 Third Ave. (80th St.)
212-717-9798 | www.elistablenyc.com

"There's a lot to like" at this modern UES American from Eli Zabar, whose **"fine-tuned"** sourcing from the neighboring gourmet shop informs a **"market-driven"** menu (brunch included) matched with **"very good wines"**; even with **"high prices"**, fans say it's an **"underrated" "gem."**

EL LUCHADOR | Mexican   ▽ 4.3   4.2   4.0 $

Financial District | 87 South St. (John St.) | 646-398-7499
NEW **Lower East Side** | 132 Ludlow St. (Rivington St.) | 646-398-7499
www.elluchador.nyc

"Bravo"-worthy tacos, burritos and quesadillas are **"worth toughing out the line"** for at these Mexican counter serves with a lucha libre wrestling motif; summer brings a few outdoor seats to the otherwise takeout-oriented surrounds.

EL PARADOR CAFE | Mexican   4.2   3.8   4.1 $$$

Murray Hill | 325 E. 34th St. (bet. 1st & 2nd Aves.)
212-679-6812 | www.elparadorcafe.com

A **"locals' hideout"** since 1959, this **"warm"** Murray Hill **"standard"** keeps regulars **"coming back"** with **"true Mexican food"** that's consistently **"solid"**; the **"retro"** setting has **"a certain charm"**, and the staff is as **"friendly"** as the drinks are **"potent."**

EL PASO | Mexican   4.2   3.5   3.9 $$

East 90s | 64 E. 97th St. (bet. Madison & Park Aves.) | 212-996-1739
East Harlem | 1643 Lexington Ave. (104th St.) | 212-831-9831
www.elpasony.com

Eastsiders count on these **"solid"**, unpretentious Uptown Mexicans for "**terrific**" tacos and other standards ("**try the aguas frescas**") made "**fresh**" with "**quality ingredients**"; "**tight quarters**" and "**so-so**" service are offset by "**unbelievable-value**" prices.

EL PORRÓN | Spanish   4.2   3.7   4.0 $$$

East 60s | 1123 First Ave. (bet. 61st & 62nd Sts.)
212-207-8349 | www.elporronnyc.com

Tapas "**like you'd find in Barcelona**" make for "**real-thing**" dining at this UES Spaniard sporting a "**something-for-everyone**" menu; "**winning wine**" arrives in the namesake pitcher, and the crowd's a mix of "**lively**" types who "**come hungry, thirsty and often.**"

EL POTE | Spanish   4.2   3.4   4.1 $$

Murray Hill | 718 Second Ave. (bet. 38th & 39th Sts.)
212-889-6680 | www.elpote.com

"**Home away from home**" for Murray Hill amigos since '77, this Spanish stalwart keeps business brisk with "**fantastic paella**" and other "**fine**" Iberian standards; maybe it's looking a bit "**shabby**", but locals count themselves "**lucky**" to have it.

EL QUIJOTE | Spanish   4.1   3.6   4.0 $$

Chelsea | 226 W. 23rd St. (bet. 7th & 8th Aves.)
212-929-1855 | www.elquijoterestaurant.com

"**Old school to the hilt**", this "**colorful**" Hotel Chelsea octogenarian may be "**faded**" but is still "**memorable**" for Spanish food plated in "**gut-buster portions**"; the decor lies somewhere between "**tacky**" and "**kitschy**", but the prices are "**decent**" and that "**lobster deal can't be beat.**"

EL QUINTO PINO | Spanish   4.5   3.8   4.2 $$

Chelsea | 401 W. 24th St. (bet. 9th & 10th Aves.)
212-206-6900 | www.elquintopinonyc.com

Alex Raij's Spanish small plates "**pack an incredible flavor punch**" (especially the much "**raved-about**" uni panini) at this compact Chelsea tapas bar also known for its "**delicious**" wines; the "**laid-back**" space might not be fancy, but it's just right for "**cozy conversation**" or a "**casual**" date.

EL REY COFFEE BAR & | American   ∇ 4.4   3.8   3.8 $
LUNCHEONETTE

Lower East Side | 100 Stanton St. (Ludlow St.)
212-260-3950 | www.elreynyc.com

"**Cute and cozy**" during the day for "**healthy and delicious**" bites, this "**trendy**" vegetarian-friendly Lower Eastsider is also "**killing it**" at night with ambitious New American small plates; the "**tiny, tiny**" space can be a "**zoo during brunch**", but there's always draft beer and "**interesting**" wines to help distract.

EL TORO BLANCO | Mexican   4.2   4.0   4.0 $$

West Village | 257 Sixth Ave. (bet. Bedford & Downing Sts.)
212-645-0193 | www.eltoroblanconyc.com

A "**great place to hang**", this "**chill**" West Villager from Josh Capon (Burger & Barrel, Lure) offers "**delicious**" Mexican fare like "**creative**" tacos and "**fresh**" guac alongside "**fabulous**" margaritas; it might be a bit "**pricey**" for the genre, but the outdoor seating is a "**real boon.**"

EL VEZ | Mexican   3.8   4.0   3.9 $$
Battery Park City | 259 Vesey St. (bet. North End Ave. & West St.)
212-233-2500 | www.elveznyc.com

The Battery Park City outpost of a Philly original, this "**spacious**" Mexican provides "**big flavors**" via a classic menu with "**modern**" twists served amid "**quirky**" cantina decor; given a "**busy bar**" pouring "**well-mixed**" drinks with a "**preponderance of mezcal**", "**expect suits after work**" – and during the day at the burrito bar.

EMILIA'S | Italian   4.2   3.8   4.2 $$
Arthur Avenue/Belmont | 2331 Arthur Ave. (Crescent Ave.) | Bronx
718-367-5915 | www.emiliasrestaurant.com

"**In the heart of**" Arthur Avenue's "**food mecca**", this longtime Italian "**mainstay**" delivers "**delicious**" "**red-sauce standards**" in "**generous portions**", including "**wonderful daily specials**"; happily there's "**minimal frenzy**" within its "**cozy**", nothing-fancy digs, which are presided over by a "**friendly**" staff.

EMILIO'S BALLATO | Italian   4.6   3.9   4.2 $$$
NoLita | 55 E Houston St. (Mott St.)
212-274-8881

The "**food sings**" at this "**back-in-the-day**" NoLita "**red-sauce**" joint that "**looks like an Italian farmhouse hallway**" and is "**one of the last of a breed**" (it's been around since 1956); owner Emilio is "**always there**", and his presence "**makes the evening complete.**"

EMILY | Pizza   4.7   3.7   4.2 $$
Clinton Hill | 919 Fulton St. (bet. Clinton & Waverly Aves.) | Brooklyn
347-844-9588 | www.pizzalovesemily.com

A "**smash hit**" for Clinton Hill, this "**vibrant**" pizzeria built its name on "**out-of-this-world**" Neapolitan pies with "**perfectly charred**" crusts and "**inventive**" toppings – though some swear the "**killer**" (but limited-supply) burger is the real "**showstopper**"; "**tight**" quarters spell "**absurdly long**" waits, but fans say "**it's all worth it.**"

🆕 **EMMY SQUARED** | Pizza   —   —   — $$
Williamsburg | 364 Grand St. (Marcy Ave.) | Brooklyn
718-360-4535 | www.pizzalovesemily.com

An offshoot of Clinton Hill's Emily, this modern Williamsburg pizza place specializes in Detroit-style square pies plus Italian sandwiches and one notable burger. The spacious interior with white-washed brick walls has high-top and standard tables as well as a downstairs burger bar.

EMPANADA MAMA | Colombian   4.4   3.3   3.8 $
Lower East Side | 95 Allen St. (bet. Broome & Delancey Sts.)
212-673-0300 | www.empmamanyc.com

Worth "**driving across town for**", the "**impressive**" array of "**delicious**" empanadas features a "**perfect filling-to-dough ratio**" at this "**busy**" LES joint; there's plenty of other "**hearty**" Colombian food on the menu, and while the space is "**sparse**", "**super**" sangria helps distract.

EMPELLÓN AL PASTOR | Mexican   3.9   3.4   3.5 $
East Village | 132 St. Marks Pl. (Ave. A)
646-833-7039 | www.empellon.com

"**Fun for a pit stop**" when you're in the East Village, this "**lively**" counter-service Mexican specializes in tacos al pastor featuring spit-roasted pork shoulder and housemade tortillas; there are other "**creative**" options and "**seriously good**" drinks too, plus graffiti art lends a "**trendy**" feel to the "**no-nonsense**" digs.

EMPELLÓN COCINA	Mexican	4.5	4.0	4.0	$$$

East Village | 105 First Ave. (bet. 6th & 7th Sts.)
212-780-0999 | www.empellon.com

The "**high-end**" takes on Mexican cooking are both "**inventive**" and "**excellent**" at this "**vibrant**" East Villager, where a chef's table is also an option for "**incredible**" tasting menus; "**delicious**" drinks are another reason it's a "**sure**" bet – and can be a bit "**noisy**."

EMPELLÓN TAQUERIA	Mexican	4.2	3.8	3.9	$$$

West Village | 230 W. Fourth St. (W. 10th St.)
212-367-0999 | www.empellon.com

"**First-rate**" ingredients in "**imaginative**" combinations make for some seriously "**haute**" tacos at this "**trendy**" West Village Mexican where the "**strong**" margaritas are just as "**creative**"; "**slightly upscale**" pricing doesn't deter those who keep its "**barlike**" space "**crowded and noisy**."

EMPIRE STEAKHOUSE	Steak	4.3	3.9	4.3	$$$$

NEW **East 50s** | 151 E. 50th St. (3rd Ave.) | 212-586-9700
West 50s | 237 W. 54th St. (bet. B'way & 8th Ave.) | 212-586-9700
www.empiresteakhousenyc.com

Though they're "**under the radar**", these "**conveniently located**" steakhouses provide "**ample**" portions of "**prime**" beef via "**professional**" staffers who'll make you "**feel like a regular in no time**"; "**unobtrusive**" surroundings keep the focus on the "**pricey**" plates.

EN JAPANESE BRASSERIE	Japanese	4.4	4.6	4.3	$$$

West Village | 435 Hudson St. (Leroy St.)
212-647-9196 | www.enjb.com

"**Sexy**", "**serene**" surroundings provide the backdrop for "**innovative**" Japanese fare at this "**consistently excellent**" West Village "**date spot**", where highlights include "**killer**" housemade tofu and "**work-of-art**" kaiseki meals; a "**superb**" sake list and "**gracious**" service are more reasons it's "**worth what it costs**."

ENOTECA MARIA	Italian	4.4	3.8	4.1	$$$

St. George | 27 Hyatt St. (Central Ave.) | Staten Island
718-447-2777 | www.enotecamaria.com

A cast of "**rotating nonnas**" in the kitchen "**lovingly**" prepare "**fabulous**" regional Italian specialties at this "**convivial**", cash-only Staten Island enoteca where a "**strong selection**" of affordable wines and "**blasting rock 'n' roll**" contribute to the "**warm, appealing**" atmosphere; though "**seating is tight**", supporters swear the food is "**worth any discomfort**."

ENZO'S	Italian	4.4	3.8	4.2	$$

Morris Park | 1998 Williamsbridge Rd. (Neill Ave.) | Bronx | 718-409-3828 | www.enzosbronxrestaurant.com

ENZO'S OF ARTHUR AVENUE | Italian

Arthur Avenue/Belmont | 2339 Arthur Ave. (bet. 184th & 187th Sts.) | Bronx | 718-733-4455

These separately owned "**blue-ribbon**" "**red-sauce palaces**" in the Bronx dish out **"down-home"** Italian standards in mammoth portions and toss in some **"old-school charm"** on the side; the **"unpretentious"** staff **"treats you like family"**, so embrace the **"time warp"** – and **"don't fill up on the bread."**

ÉPICERIE BOULUD | French
4.2   3.4   3.7 $$

West 50s | Plaza Food Hall | 1 W. 59th St. (Grand Army Plaza) | 212-794-2825
West 60s | 1900 Broadway (bet. 63rd & 64th Sts.) | 212-595-9606
www.epicerieboulud.com

"Grab-and-go was never so delicious" say fans of Daniel Boulud's **"high-class"** counter-serve stops for **"incredible"** French pastries, **"inventive"** sandwiches and other **"light meals"**; the Lincoln Center flagship includes a raw bar, and **"prices are a bit steep"** all around.

ERAWAN | Thai
4.3   3.8   4.1 $$

Bayside | 42-31 Bell Blvd. (bet. 42nd & 43rd Aves.) | Queens
718-428-2112 | www.erawanthaibayside.com

Bayside locals tout this **"go-to Thai"** for its **"aromatic"** offerings with **"interesting modern twists"**, abetted by **"gentle"** service and a **"Manhattan atmosphere"**; though prices lie on the **"premium"** side for the genre, it's ever **"crowded"** at prime times.

ERMINIA | Italian
4.4   4.3   4.4 $$$

East 80s | 250 E. 83rd St. (bet. 2nd & 3rd Aves.)
212-879-4284 | www.erminiaristorante.com

If you're looking for **"romance"**, try this **"transporting"** UES Roman **"hideaway"** where a **"cavelike"**, candlelit setting sets the mood for **"knockout"** Italian cooking, while **"attentive"** service and a **"leisurely"** pace do the rest; sure, it's **"expensive"**, but there are **"only a few tables"**, lending exclusivity to this **"special experience."**

ESCA | Italian/Seafood
4.4   4.0   4.2 $$$

West 40s | 402 W. 43rd St. (bet. 9th & 10th Aves.)
212-564-7272 | www.esca-nyc.com

"Heaven for fish lovers", this **"classy"** Hell's Kitchen Italian from the Batali-Bastianich-Pasternack team crafts **"thoughtfully prepared"** seafood and **"irresistible"** pastas in **"relaxed"** surrounds; **"accommodating"** service, **"excellent"** wines and a relatively **"convenient"** pre-theater location further justify the **"high tab."**

ESME | American
▽ 4.4   3.8   3.9 $$

Greenpoint | 999 Manhattan Ave. (Huron St.) | Brooklyn
718-383-0999 | www.esmebk.com

Updated American classics deliver **"big taste"** at this relaxed Greenpoint bistro, whose understated style features reclaimed church pews and subdued hues; craft (and draft) cocktails are mixed at a wooden-ceilinged bar under exposed-filament bulbs that create a soft, **"romantic"** glow.

ESS-A-BAGEL | Bagels
4.4   2.9   3.5 $

East 50s | 831 Third Ave. (51st St.) | 212-980-1010
NEW **Gramercy Park** | 324 First Ave. (20th St.) | 212-260-2252
www.ess-a-bagel.com

The **"giant"** bagels are so **"fresh, chewy and flavorful"** they **"don't even need a schmear"**, though you'll still find **"interesting"** spreads and **"tons"** of deli fixin's at these at these daytime **"madhouses"**; lines can be **"ridiculous"** and the ambiance is **"minimal"**, but after one **"delicious"** bite **"nothing else matters."**

	FOOD	DECOR	SERVICE	COST

ESTELA | American/Mediterranean   **4.6**   **3.8**   **4.2**   **$$$**
NoLita | 47 E. Houston St. (bet. Mott & Mulberry Sts.)
212-219-7693 | www.estelanyc.com

You "**can't go wrong**" at this NoLita "**hot spot**" from Ignacio Mattos, where the "**beautifully executed**" American menu includes "**highly original**" Med-influenced share plates; the "**small**", "**loud**" space is "**less than thrilling**" and bills do "**run up**", but scoring reservations is still a "**challenge.**"

ETCETERA ETCETERA | Italian   **4.2**   **3.8**   **4.2**   **$$**
West 40s | 352 W. 44th St. (bet. 8th & 9th Aves.)
212-399-4141 | www.etcetcnyc.com

"**Casual**" but "**lively**", this Midtown Italian features a "**modern**" menu that's a match for its "**contemporary**" looks; "**splendid**", "**get-you-to-the-theater-on-time**" service makes up for "**noisy**" acoustics, though regulars say it's "**quieter upstairs.**"

ETHOS | Greek/Seafood   **4.2**   **3.8**   **3.9**   **$$$**
East 50s | 905 First Ave. (51st St.) | 212-888-4060
Murray Hill | 495 Third Ave. (bet. 33rd & 34th Sts.) | 212-252-1972
www.ethosrestaurants.com

"**Count on**" Greek seafood "**done right**" at these "**deservedly popular**" joints, where the "**fulfilling**" meals come at "**fair prices**"; the Murray Hill locale is "**relaxed**" if "**a little tight**" while the separately owned Midtown outpost's roomier, "**whitewashed**" digs draw a "**hopping**" crowd that "**gets very loud.**"

EXCELLENT DUMPLING HOUSE | Chinese   **4.0**   **2.5**   **3.2**   **$$**
Chinatown | 111 Lafayette St. (bet. Canal & Walker Sts.)
212-219-0212 | www.excellentdumplinghouse.com

There's "**no false advertising**" at this Chinatowner where the "**name-says-it-all**" dumplings are served with equally "**worthwhile**" Shanghainese plates; true, there's "**no atmosphere**" and service is of the "**rush-you-out**" variety, but "**at these prices, who cares?**"

EXTRA FANCY | Seafood   ▽ **4.2**   **4.1**   **4.2**   **$$**
Williamsburg | 302 Metropolitan Ave. (Roebling St.) | Brooklyn
347-422-0939 | www.extrafancybklyn.com

Williamsburg "**meets New England**" at this "**swinging**" seafood joint whose clam shack–inspired menu features "**fine oysters**" and "**fun comfort food**" backed by "**expertly made**" cocktails; the "**lovely**" garden makes it a "**perfect day-drinking**" destination, but it's also "**great for late-night nosh.**"

EXTRA VIRGIN | Mediterranean   **4.2**   **3.8**   **3.8**   **$$**
West Village | 259 W. Fourth St. (Perry St.)
212-691-9359 | www.extravirginrestaurant.com

The "**young**" and "**glamorous**" hobnob at this "**fashionable**" West Villager over "**dependable**" Med fare that "**won't break the bank**"; although the place is usually "**crowded**" and the no-rez policy (for fewer than six) leads to "**waits**", amusing "**people-watching**" helps pass the time.

F & J PINE RESTAURANT | Italian   **4.3**   **3.8**   **4.0**   **$$**
Van Nest | 1913 Bronxdale Ave. (bet. Matthews & Muliner Aves.) | Bronx
718-792-5956 | www.fjpine.com

"**Gigantic portions**" are the name of the game at this "**doggy bag**"–

guaranteed Van Nest Italian ladling out **"loads of red sauce"** for fans of **"old-time"** carbo-loading, **"checkered"** tablecloths, **"old Yankee"** memorabilia and Bronx Bomber sightings are all part of the **"colorful"** package here.

FARM ON ADDERLEY | American   4.2   3.9   4.1 $$

Ditmas Park | 1108 Cortelyou Rd (bet. Stratford & Westminster Rds.) | Brooklyn
718-287-3101 | www.thefarmonadderley.com

With its **"inventive"** New American fare showcasing **"farm-fresh"** ingredients, this **"quaint"** Ditmas Park **"favorite"** is something of an **"oasis"** in the **"wilds of Brooklyn"**; it **"gets super-crowded"** ("and with reason") during weekend brunch, but summer brings access to a **"gorgeous"** backyard.

FARO | Italian   ▽ 4.4   4.0   4.1 $$$

Bushwick | 436 Jefferson St. (bet. St. Nicholas & Wyckoff Aves.) | Brooklyn
718-381-8201

"Hyper-local ingredients" are the basis for the **"beautiful"** Italian offerings – **"excellent"** pastas, **"fabulous wood-fired"** dishes – at this **"cool"** Bushwick eatery with an **"innovative"** tasting menu and **"good wine program"**; **"warm"** service and a **"hip but homey"** space are other pluses.

THE FAT RADISH | American   4.1   3.9   4.0 $$

Lower East Side | 17 Orchard St. (bet. Canal & Hester Sts.)
212-300-4053 | www.thefatradishnyc.com

"Veggie fanatics" get the royal treatment at this **"funky"** Lower Eastsider that **"oozes cool"** with its **"creative"**, locavore-oriented New American cooking and **"hiptastic"** **"art-crowd"** following; sure, it's a **"tad pricey"** and can feel **"cramped"**, but thanks to **"friendly"** servers and **"interesting cocktails"**, it **"doesn't matter."**

FATTY FISH | Asian   4.0   3.5   3.9 $$

East 60s | 406 E. 64th St. (bet. 1st & York Aves.)
212-813-9338 | www.fattyfishnyc.com

Upper Eastsiders are hooked on this Asian-fusion practitioner boasting **"surprisingly creative"** cooking (and sushi) served by **"solicitous"** staffers who just **"keep smiling"**; a **"Zen-like"** mood and **"beautiful"** enclosed garden distract from the **"small"** dimensions.

NEW FAUN | American/Italian   —   —   — $$$

Prospect Heights | 606 Vanderbilt Ave. (bet. Prospect Pl. & St Marks Ave.) | Brooklyn
718-576-6120 | www.faun.nyc

A veteran of Vinegar Hill House helms the kitchen at this Prospect Heights locale with an Italian-American menu emphasizing locally sourced ingredients. Whitewashed brick walls and a wood bar lend a comfortable feel, and service is included in the bill.

FEAST | American   ▽ 4.2   4.1   4.3 $$$

Greenwich Village | 102 Third Ave. (13th St.)
212-529-8880 | www.eatfeastnyc.com

"Fabulous" servers **"make you feel like longtime friends"** at this **"charmingly rustic"** Village American that showcases its **"delicious"** seasonal dishes with a **"tasting menu concept"** (à la carte is also an option); it's **"not cheap"**, but given the **"cool but not hipster-y vibe"**, most **"look forward to future feasts"** nonetheless.

FEDORA | American   4.3   3.9   4.2 $$$

West Village | 239 W. Fourth St., downstairs (bet. Charles & W. 10th Sts.)
646-449-9336 | www.fedoranyc.com

Gabe Stulman's "**low-key chic**" West Village basement earns a tip of the cap for its "**delicious**" upscale American fare, "**tasty cocktails**" and "**beautiful neon sign**"; blending a "**speakeasy vibe**" with some "**Wisconsin hospitality**", it's "**an all-around win**", except perhaps for the cost.

FELICE | Italian   4.2   4.0   4.1 $$$

East 60s | 1166 First Ave. (64th St.) | 212-593-2223 | www.felice64.com
East 80s | 1593 First Ave. (83rd St.) | 212-249-4080 | www.felice83.com
Financial District | 15 Gold St. (Platt St.) | 212-785-5950 |
www.felice15goldstreet.com

These "**moderately hip**" wine bars spice up "**date nights**" with "**affordable**", "**well-chosen**" vinos paired with "**tasty**" Italian plates; the "**gracious**" service and "**sexy**" ambiance "**appeal to multiple generations**", though they mainly draw "**younger**" folks.

FELIDIA | Italian   4.6   4.2   4.4 $$$$

East 50s | 243 E. 58th St. (bet. 2nd & 3rd Aves.)
212-758-1479 | www.felidia-nyc.com

Lidia Bastianich "**does it right**" at this "**grown-up**" Midtowner providing "**exquisite**" Italian cuisine, including "**delicate**" pastas, via a "**gracious**" staff in "**elegant**" townhouse surrounds; it's "**nothing but a delight**", at least until the check comes – though you really "**can't lose**" with the "**bargain**" lunch prix fixe.

FERRARA | Bakery   4.3   3.6   3.7 $$

Little Italy | 195 Grand St. (bet. Mott & Mulberry Sts.)
212-226-6150 | www.ferraracafe.com

Open 120-plus years "**and counting**", this Little Italy bakery is a "**legend**" famed for its "**heaven-on-a-plate**" cannoli and "**pick-me-up**" espresso; "**crowds of tourists**" and "**expensive**"-for-what-it-is tabs draw some complaints, yet most agree this NYC relic "**still has charm.**"

FETTE SAU | BBQ   4.5   3.5   3.6 $$

Williamsburg | 354 Metropolitan Ave. (bet. Havemeyer & Roebling Sts.) | Brooklyn
718-963-3404 | www.fettesaubbq.com

It's the "**quintessential Williamsburg experience**" to "**join the hipsters**" at this "**serious foodie**" "**heaven**" for "**awesome**" dry-rub, by-the-pound BBQ paired with "**artisanal**" beers and bourbons; no rezzies means "**crazy lines**" for "**cafeteria-style**" service in a "**former garage**" outfitted with "**communal picnic tables**" – but to most it's so "**worth it.**"

15 EAST | Japanese   4.6   4.2   4.4 $$$

Union Square | 15 E. 15th St. (5th Ave.)
212-647-0015 | www.15eastrestaurant.com

"**Inventive**" preparations and "**top-quality**" fish result in "**sublime**" sushi at this "**classy**" Union Square Japanese also known for its wide sake selection; "**personable**" service and a "**serene**", "**minimalist**" setting up its appeal for "**adult dinners**", though the tabs have some saving it for "**big occasions.**"

FIG & OLIVE | Mediterranean   4.2   4.0   4.0 $$$

East 50s | 10 E. 52nd St. (bet. 5th & Madison Aves.) | 212-319-2002
East 60s | 808 Lexington Ave. (bet. 62nd & 63rd Sts.) | 212-207-4555

continued

Meatpacking District | 420 W. 13th St. (bet. 9th Ave. & Washington St.) | 212-924-1200
www.figandolive.com

"**Accessible**" meals built around "**well-crafted**" small plates and "**eye-opening**" olive oil tastings ensure a "**constant hum**" at these "**easy-on-the-eyes**" Mediterraneans; the Eastsiders are "**handy**" for a "**biz lunch**" or a "**respite from shopping**" while the "**airy**" Meatpacking outpost creates a "**happening**" "**scene**" near the Whitney.

THE FINCH | American   ∇   4.6   4.4   4.5 $$$

Clinton Hill | 212 Greene Ave. (bet. Cambridge Pl. & Grand Ave.) | Brooklyn
718-218-4444 | www.thefinchnyc.com

A Gramercy Tavern alum "**flies high**" with "**sophisticated, creative and delicious**" seasonal American dishes at this Clinton Hill brownstoner, overseen by a "**friendly**" team; though "**small**"-ish portions come at "**Manhattan**" prices, the "**minimalist**" space with a marble bar exudes "**neighborhood charm.**"

FIRENZE | Italian   4.1   4.0   4.3 $$$

East 80s | 1594 Second Ave. (bet. 82nd & 83rd Sts.)
212-861-9368 | www.firenzeny.com

Candlelight and exposed-brick walls set a "**romantic**" mood at this longtime UES Italian that evokes Florence with "**solid**" Tuscan cooking delivered by a "**couldn't-be-nicer**" crew; the "**small**" confines can feel "**cramped**" or "**cozy**" depending on who you ask, but everyone agrees it's a neighborhood "**favorite.**"

FISH | Seafood   4.2   3.5   3.8 $$

West Village | 280 Bleecker St. (Jones St.)
212-727-2879 | www.fishrestaurantnyc.com

Like the simple implies, there's "**nothing fancy**" going on at this West Village seafood shack, just "**truly good**" catch delivered with great shuck for your buck; trade-offs include "**rough-around-the-edges**" looks and "**tight-squeeze**" seating.

FISHTAG | Mediterranean   4.2   3.8   4.1 $$$

West 70s | 222 W. 79th St. (bet. Amsterdam Ave. & B'way)
212-362-7470 | www.michaelpsilakis.com

This "**worthy**" Upper Westsider from Michael Psilakis is "**not your usual fishbar**" thanks to "**creative, tasty**" seafood prepared with Mediterranean "**flair**" along with a "**diverse wine list**"; a "**welcoming bar**" and "**friendly**" servers also help make the "**intimate**" space a "**neighborhood go-to.**"

FIVE LEAVES | American   4.3   3.9   3.6 $$

Greenpoint | 18 Bedford Ave. (Lorimer St.) | Brooklyn
718-383-5345 | www.fiveleavesny.com

This all-day Greenpoint "**staple**" "**remains a favorite**" in "**hipsterville**" for "**out-of-this-world**" burgers, "**incredible pancakes**" and other "**reliable**" New American eats; despite often-"**crowded**" digs and occasional "**attitude**", it's pretty "**perfect for brunch**" – with the "**long lines**" to prove it.

5 NAPKIN BURGER | Burgers   4.0   3.5   3.7 $$

East 60s | 1325 Second Ave. (70th St.) | 212-249-0777
Greenwich Village | 150 E. 14th St. (3rd Ave.) | 212-228-5500
West 40s | 630 Ninth Ave. (45th St.) | 212-757-2277
West 80s | 2315 Broadway (84th St.) | 212-333-4488
www.5napkinburger.com

You "**definitely need five napkins**" to tackle the "**massive**", "**juicy**" burgers at this "**dependable**" chain where the "**diverse menu**" includes sushi at some locations; the "**comfortable**", chophouse-inspired digs can get "**jammed**", but the "**energy**" (and "**decibel level**") boosts the "**kid-friendly**" factor.

FLATBUSH FARM | American   ▽ 4.0   3.8   3.7 $$

Park Slope | 76 St. Marks Ave. (Flatbush Ave.) | Brooklyn
718-622-3276 | www.flatbushfarm.com

"**Farm-to-table**" bounties are the draw at this affordable Park Slope American where the "**solid**" menu is assembled from "**wholesome**" local ingredients; the less-enthused cite "**uneven**" service, but it wins kudos for a "**super-brunch**" and a "**little-piece-of-heaven**" garden.

FLETCHER'S BROOKLYN BARBECUE | BBQ   4.1   3.4   3.9 $

Gowanus | 433 Third Ave. (bet. 7th & 8th Sts.) | Brooklyn
347-763-2680 | www.fletchersbklyn.com

There's "**real BBQ**" in store at this locavore-friendly Gowanus joint smoking the classics (St. Louis ribs, brisket) as well as more "**unique items**"; the "**super-casual**" setup features "**friendly**" counter service, by-the-pound pricing and communal seating.

FLEX MUSSELS | Seafood   4.4   3.7   4.0 $$

East 80s | 174 E. 82nd St. (bet. Lexington & 3rd Aves.) | 212-717-7772
West Village | 154 W. 13th St. (bet. 6th & 7th Aves.) | 212-229-0222
www.flexmussels.com

"**Steamy pots of mussels**" are served with "**exotic sauces**" and "**crusty bread**" at these "**fast-moving**" seafood specialists also touted for their "**standout**" donuts and "**won't-break-the-bank**" tabs; not much decor and "**noisy**", "**highly social**" scenes come with the territory.

FLINDERS LANE | Australian   ▽ 4.3   4.0   4.3 $$

East Village | 162 Ave. A (bet. 10th & 11th Sts.)
212-228-6900 | www.flinderslane-nyc.com

A "**rare find**" in the East Village outback, this "**approachable**" Australian produces "**well-prepared**" dishes with a "**burst of Asian flair**"; "**sweet**" service lends a "**welcoming**" vibe to "**intimate**" digs that get bigger when floor-to-ceiling windows open and it feels like "**you're dining outdoors.**"

FLOR DE MAYO | Chinese/Peruvian   4.1   3.1   3.8 $$

West 100s | 2651 Broadway (bet. 100th & 101st Sts.)
212-663-5520 | www.flordemayo.com

"**Divine**" rotisserie chicken draws "**believers**" to this "**consistent**" Upper Westsider where "**homestyle**" Peruvian-Chinese fare comes at "**value**" prices; the "**nothing-fancy**" surrounds are "**not for date night**", but the "**mixed crowd**" digs the "**true New York**" experience.

FLORIAN | Italian   4.1   4.1   4.2 $$$

Gramercy Park | 225 Park Ave. S. (18th St.)
212-869-8800 | www.floriannyc.com

Owner Shelly Fireman (Trattoria Dell'Arte, Brooklyn Diner) brings a little flash down to Gramercy with this upscale Italian where menu highlights include "**crisp**" thin-crust pizza and "**simple**" pastas "**done well**"; the "**cavernous**" space is either "**beautiful**" or "**over the top**" depending on who you ask, but most agree it's a "**welcome addition.**"

	FOOD	DECOR	SERVICE	COST

FOGO DE CHÃO | Brazilian   4.2   4.2   4.2 $$$
West 50s | 40 W. 53rd St. (bet. 5th & 6th Aves.)
212-969-9980 | www.fogo.com

An all-you-can-eat "**meat extravaganza**" awaits at this big Brazilian churrascaria near Rock Center offering "**delicious**" skewers (along with a "**vast**" salad bar) in a "**beautiful**" triplex setting; true, the tabs are "**not inexpensive**", but it's "**paradise**" for those bent on "**protein overload.**"

FONDA | Mexican   4.3   3.8   3.9 $$
Chelsea | 189 Ninth Ave. (bet. 21st & 22nd Sts.) | 917-525-5252
East Village | 40 Ave. B (3rd St.) | 212-677-4096
Park Slope | 434 Seventh Ave. (bet. 14th & 15th Sts.) | Brooklyn | 718-369-3144
www.fondarestaurant.com

These "**humming**" Mexican "**charmers**" put a "**modern**" spin on things using "**unexpected**" ingredients in the "**consistently**" "**delicioso**" dishes; thanks to "**excellent margaritas**" and "**great happy-hour options**" things can get "**loud**", but in Park Slope the patio provides a respite.

FORAGERS CITY TABLE | American   4.1   3.7   3.7 $$$
Chelsea | 300 W. 22nd St. (8th Ave.)
212-243-8888 | www.foragersmarket.com

"**You can really taste the difference**" in "**creative**" farm-to-table fare that "**bursts with freshness**" at this Chelsea New American, an "**informal**" eatery and locally sourced grocer spun off from a Dumbo market; it's an "**easy**" dinner option and "**good for brunch**", though some find it "**a little pricey for what you get.**"

FORNINO | Pizza   4.4   3.9   4.1 $
Brooklyn Heights | Brooklyn Bridge Park Pier 6 (Joralemon St.) | Brooklyn | 718-422-1107
Greenpoint | 849 Manhattan Ave. (bet. Milton & Noble Sts.) | Brooklyn | 718-389-5300
Williamsburg | 187 Bedford Ave. (7th St.) | Brooklyn | 718-384-6004
www.forninopizza.com

In the eternal "**NY pizza wars**", these Brooklyn "**favorites**" are "**strong players**" thanks to "**decadent**" toppings and "**perfectly done**" wood-fired crusts; "**price-is-right**" tabs enhance their "**can't-go-wrong**" reputations.

FORT DEFIANCE | American   ∇ 4.2   3.7   4.2 $$
Red Hook | 365 Van Brunt St. (bet. Coffey & Dikeman Sts.) | Brooklyn
347-453-6672 | www.fortdefiancebrooklyn.com

Named for a Revolutionary War fort that once stood nearby, this "**funky**" Red Hook haunt dishes up "**solid**" American food, including a "**great**" brunch, washed down with "**terrific**" classic cocktails; the menu is "**small**", but "**excellent-value**" pricing makes it a "**home base**" for locals.

FORTUNATO BROTHERS | Bakery/Italian   4.3   3.7   3.9 $$
Williamsburg | 289 Manhattan Ave. (bet. 110th & 111th Sts.) | Brooklyn
718-387-2281 | www.fortunatobrothers.com

"**When it comes to Italian pastries**", fans in Williamsburg say "**there's nothing better**" than this "**old-school**" bakery where the cannoli and other "**fantastic**" sweets transport you "**back to Italy**"; the "**casual**" cafe setup has an "**authentic accent**", meaning you can "**linger over your latte.**"

44 & X | American | 4.2 | 4.0 | 4.1 | $$$

West 40s | 622 10th Ave. (bet. 44th & 45th Sts.) | 212-977-1170 | www.44andx.com

44½ | American

West 40s | 626 10th Ave. (bet. 44th & 45th Sts.) | 212-399-4450 | www.44andahalf.com

"**Gaiety abounds**" at these Hell's Kitchen "**go-to**" spots where "**well-toned**" waiters in "**tight, witty**" T-shirts serve "**consistently delicious**" American fare; "**inviting**" havens in an area with "**limited**" options, they host a "**popular**" brunch and "**fit the bill**" before or after a play at the nearby Signature Theatre complex.

FOUR & TWENTY BLACKBIRDS | Bakery | 4.5 | 3.4 | 3.8 | $

Gowanus | 439 Third Ave. (8th St.) | Brooklyn | 718-499-2917
Prospect Heights | Brooklyn Public Library | 10 Grand Army Plaza (Plaza St.) | Brooklyn | 718-230-2100
www.birdsblack.com

"**If you're a pie lover**", you "**won't regret**" seeking out the "**sublime**" renditions – think decadent fillings and a "**divine**" crust – offered by the slice at this Brooklyn bakery; the Gowanus flagship has cafe tables "**if you can snag a seat**", and there's a basic "**snack**" counter at the Brooklyn Public Library.

456 SHANGHAI CUISINE | Chinese | 4.1 | 3.2 | 3.7 | $$

Chinatown | 69 Mott St. (bet. Bayard & Canal Sts.) | 212-964-0003

"**Wonderful**" soup dumplings are the draw at this busy Chinatown "**find**" that's also a "**reliable**" source for "**ample portions**" of "**authentic Shanghainese**" chow; the "**tight quarters**" sport "**minimal**" decor, but prices are so "**reasonable**" that no one minds.

THE FOUR HORSEMEN | American | ∇ 4.5 | 4.2 | 4.3 | $$$

Williamsburg | 295 Grand St. (Eldridge St.) | Brooklyn | 718-599-4900 | www.fourhorsemenbk.com

A "**killer wine list**" filled with "**quirky**" finds is the headliner at this Williamsburg nook from musician James Murphy (LCD Soundsystem), but the seasonal American fare is "**spot-on**" too; "**sleek**" and "**perfectly dimmed**" with a front bar, it draws "**hip, but mature**" types who keep the mood "**convivial.**"

FRAGOLE | Italian | 4.4 | 3.7 | 4.2 | $$

Carroll Gardens | 394 Court St. (bet. Carroll St. & 1st Pl.) | Brooklyn | 718-522-7133 | www.fragoleny.com

This veteran Carroll Gardens Italian remains a "**neighborhood favorite**" for its "**solid**" cooking "**with an eye toward authenticity**", "**quality wine list**" and overall "**charm**"; "**affordable**" tabs keep it filled with "**happy**" customers – but as it's "**small**", be "**prepared to wait**" for a table at prime times.

FRANCHIA | Korean | 4.4 | 4.2 | 4.2 | $$

Murray Hill | 12 Park Ave. (bet. 34th & 35th Sts.) | 212-213-1001 | www.franchia.com

"**Innovative**" vegan cuisine is the hallmark of this Midtown Korean "**favorite**" where the "**wonderful, filling**" offerings ("**I didn't miss meat at all**") are complemented by "**friendly**" service and a "**Zen-like ambiance**" that suffuses the "**jewel-box**" teahouse setting; thanks to "**value**" pricing, it's an "**affordable oasis.**"

	FOOD	DECOR	SERVICE	COST

FRANCISCO'S CENTRO | Seafood/Spanish   4.4   3.3   3.9 $$
VASCO
Chelsea | 159 W. 23rd St. (bet. 6th & 7th Aves.)
212-645-6224 | www.franciscoscentrovasco.com

"Monster-size" lobsters at "fair prices" are the highlight of this longtime
Chelsea Spaniard that also offers "wonderful paella" and "potent sangria";
"dumpy" digs and "noisy, crowded" conditions don't deter fans who feel it's
"cheaper to come here than to cook your own."

FRANÇOIS PAYARD BAKERY | Dessert/French   4.3   3.4   3.7 $
Battery Park City | 210 Murray St. (End Way) | 212-566-8300
Greenwich Village | 116 W. Houston St. (bet. Sullivan & Thompson Sts.) |
212-995-0888
West 50s | 1775 Broadway (bet. 57th & 58th Sts.) | 212-995-0888
www.fpbnyc.com

Pastry master François Payard still "has the touch" at these "petite
patisseries", where the "light-as-air macarons", croissants, cakes and other
"delectable" treats "will remind you of being in France"; it's not cheap, but
"your sweet tooth will say merci."

FRANK | Italian   4.4   3.4   3.8 $$
East Village | 88 Second Ave. (bet. 5th & 6th Sts.)
212-420-0202 | www.frankrestaurant.com

This cash-only East Villager is a longtime standby for "da best" Italian
"home cooking" at "solid-value" prices; it's a "jam-packed", no-frills joint
that sometimes has a wait at prime times, but you can always pass the time
at its next door Vera Bar.

NEW **FRANKEL'S DELICATESSEN** | Deli/Jewish   —   —   — $
Greenpoint | 631 Manhattan Ave. (bet. Bedford & Nassau Aves.) | Brooklyn
718-389-2302 | www.frankelsdelicatessen.com

Two brothers are behind this modern Greenpoint deli devoted to top-tier
bagels with smoked salmon and egg-and-cheese combos. The counter also
dishes up hot brisket and pastrami on rye, among other Jewish specialties, in
a polished space with white subway tiles and colorfully stocked shelves.

FRANKIE & JOHNNIE'S | Steak   4.2   3.7   4.1 $$$
West 30s | 32 W. 37th St. (bet. 5th & 6th Aves.) | 212-947-8940
West 40s | 269 W. 45th St., 2nd fl. (8th Ave.) | 212-997-9494
www.frankieandjohnnies.com

To experience "days long past", fans dig these long-running "throwbacks"
(the 37th Street outpost is set in John Barrymore's former townhouse) known
for "delectable" steaks, "career" waiters and "rough-around-the-edges"
decor; just note the prices are decidedly up to date.

FRANKIES SPUNTINO | Italian   4.4   3.8   4.0 $$
West Village | 570 Hudson St. (11th St.) | 212-924-0818
Carroll Gardens | 457 Court St. (bet. 4th Pl. & Luquer St.) | Brooklyn |
718-403-0033
www.frankiesspuntino.com

"Special local places", these "homey" Italians serve "delicate" dishes with a
"modern spin", including "main-attraction" meatballs, at prices that won't
"break the bank"; although they trend "noisy", Carroll Gardens' "enchanting"
patio is a summer "plus."

FRANNY'S | Italian/Pizza   4.3   3.7   3.9 $$
Park Slope | 348 Flatbush Ave. (bet. 8th Ave. & Sterling Pl.) | Brooklyn
718-230-0221 | www.frannysbrooklyn.com

"**Out-of-this-world**" wood-fired pizzas, pastas and other Italian dishes built around "**wonderful local ingredients**" mean you "**can't lose**" at this Park Slope "**go-to**"; "**fantastic**" wines and cocktails are another plus, but just note the "**hip**", "**rustic**" space gets "**noisy**" (especially at "**kid-friendly**" brunch).

FRAUNCES TAVERN | Pub Food   3.9   4.3   4.0 $$
Financial District | 54 Pearl St. (Broad St.)
212-968-1776 | www.frauncestavern.com

Have a side of "**history**" with dinner at this FiDi "**landmark**" where George Washington bid farewell to his troops in 1783; today, it's a "**refurbished**" tavern serving "**decent**" pub grub and "**diverse**" beers in a "**faux-Revolutionary**" setting.

FRED'S AT BARNEYS NY | American/Italian   4.2   4.0   4.0 $$$
`NEW` **Chelsea** | Barneys Chelsea | 101 Seventh Ave. (16th St.)
646-264-6402
East 60s | Barneys NY | 660 Madison Ave., 9th fl. (61st St.)
212-833-2200
www.barneys.com

"**Shopping is hard work**" and "**sustenance is necessary**", so "**well-Botoxed**" types unwind and "**pick at a salad**" at these "**chichi**" department-store canteens in Barneys; the "**consistently good**" Italian-American fare may be "**pricey for what it is**", but no one cares – it's "**fun to be chic**" here.

`NEW` **FREEK'S MILL** | American   —   —   — $$$
Gowanus | 285 Nevins St. (Sackett St.) | Brooklyn
718-852-3000 | www.freeksmill.com

Named for an 18th-century mill on nearly the same site, this Gowanus American draws on local farms and producers for a menu that spans veggie-based plates, seafood and meat, including some wood-roasted options. Rough brick walls lend a semi-industrial look to the simple space, which also has a bar dispensing wine and seasonal cocktails.

FREEMANS | American   4.1   4.2   3.9 $$$
Lower East Side | Freeman Alley (off Rivington St., bet. Bowery & Christie St.)
212-420-0012 | www.freemansrestaurant.com

"**Hidden**" down a Lower East Side alley, this "**homey**" American feels like a "**hunting-lodge wonderland**" with its "**curiosity-cabinet**" decor ("**embrace the taxidermy**"); "**hearty**" cooking, "**killer**" cocktails and an "**especially great**" brunch are all popular with the "**cool kids**" who keep it "**totally fun**" (and "**crowded**").

FRENCH LOUIE | American/French   4.4   4.1   4.3 $$
Boerum Hill | 320 Atlantic Ave. (bet. Hoyt & Smith Sts.) | Brooklyn
718-935-1200 | www.frenchlouienyc.com

Particularly "**popular for brunch**", this "**busy**" Boerum Hill bistro offers "**seasonally changing**" French-American dishes that are "**imaginative**" and "**elegant**" but "**without pretension**"; the "**attractive**" space, boasting a "**lovely**" backyard and "**small but fun**" front bar is overseen by an "**enthusiastic**" staff.

FRESCO BY SCOTTO | Italian   4.3   4.0   4.2 $$$
East 50s | 34 E. 52nd St. (bet. Madison & Park Aves.)
212-935-3434 | www.frescobyscotto.com

Thanks to "**beautifully prepared**" Tuscan dishes and "**hands-on attention**"

from the "**welcoming**" Scotto family, this "**old standby**" in Midtown "**doesn't lose its appeal**" for "**corporate**" types and "local celebs"; "**expense-account**" pricing is no deterrent to "**crazy**" lunch crowds who say it's "**worth every penny.**"

NEW **FREUD** | Austrian   4.3   4.1   4.1 $$$
Greenwich Village | 506 LaGuardia Pl. (bet. Bleecker & Houston Sts.)
212-777-0327 | www.freudnyc.com

"**After deep analysis**", fans find the "**modern**" Austrian cuisine "**insanely delicious**" at this "**more grown-up**" Village cousin to Edi & the Wolf; the "**comfortable**" farmhouse-chic space "**gets busy**" (plus "**noisy**"), but overall it's considered a "**great addition to the neighborhood.**"

FRIEDMAN'S | American   4.2   3.7   4.0 $$
Chelsea | Chelsea Mkt. | 75 Ninth Ave. (bet. 15th & 16th Sts.) | 212-929-7100
Morningside Heights | 1187 Amsterdam Ave. (118th St.) | 212-932-0600
West 30s | 132 W. 31st St. (bet. 6th & 7th Aves.) | 212-971-9400
West 30s | 450 10th Ave. (35th St.) | 212-268-1100
www.friedmansrestaurant.com

"**Inventive**" touches and seasonal ingredients make for "**higher-end**" takes on "**consistently good**" comfort food at these "**reasonably priced**" Americans also known for "**excellent**" gluten-free options; the simple digs can get "**pretty packed**", especially during the "**madhouse**" lunches, but "**accommodating**" servers are another reason many "**dig**" 'em.

FRIEND OF A FARMER | American   4.0   3.8   3.8 $$
Gramercy Park | 77 Irving Pl. (bet. 18th & 19th Sts.) | 212-477-2188
NEW **Brooklyn Heights** | 76 Montague St. (Hicks St.) | Brooklyn |
718-643-6600
www.friendofafarmer.com

With their "**Vermont**" feel, these "**quaint**" American "**country kitchens**" have fans crowing about their "**farm-fresh**" fare and "**hippie**" air; citified pricing, "**slow service**" and a "**jammed**" weekend brunch come with the territory.

FUKU | Chicken/Sandwiches   4.2   3.4   3.6 $
East Village | 163 First Ave. (10th St.) | no phone
NEW **Willets Point** | Citi Field | 123-01 Roosevelt Ave. (126th St.) | Queens |
no phone

NEW **FUKU+** | Chicken/Sandwiches
West 50s | 15 W. 56th St. (5th Ave.) | 212-757-5878
www.momofuku.com

Momofuku mastermind David Chang's "**brilliant**" "**riff**" on the fried chicken sandwich showcases "**succulent**" dark meat and a "**spicy kick**" at these "**busy**" quick-serve spots; the "**simple**" menu also includes chicken fingers, sides and bar drinks, and the "**sparse**" setups are "**mostly standing room.**"

FUNG TU | American/Chinese   4.3   3.7   4.1 $$
Lower East Side | 22 Orchard St. (bet. Canal & Hester Sts.)
212-219-8785 | www.fungtu.com

"**Adventurous**" eaters say it's "**not your mama's egg roll**" at this "**artful**" LES Chinese-American where "**tasty**", "**completely original**" dishes are matched with "**well-chosen**" wines and "**delicious**" cocktails; "**nicely timed**" service and "**understated-chic**" decor complete the "**upscale**" picture.

FUSHIMI | Japanese   4.2   4.2   3.9 $$
Bay Ridge | 9316 Fourth Ave. (bet. 93rd & 94th Sts.) | Brooklyn | 718-833-7788

continued

Williamsburg | 475 Driggs Ave. (bet. 10th & 11th Sts.) | Brooklyn |
718-963-2555

Grant City | 2110 Richmond Rd. (bet. Colfax & Lincoln Aves.) | Staten Island |
718-980-5300

www.fushimigroup.com

These "**sexy**" Japanese standouts are "**an experience**" complete with "**sleek**"
settings, "**fun atmospheres**", "**city-quality**" sushi and "**inventive**" cocktails";
maybe tabs are "**not the cheapest**", but then again these are "**not your
regular around-the-corner sushi**" joints.

| **GABRIEL KREUTHER** | French | 4.8 | 4.7 | 4.7 | $$$ |

West 40s | 41 W. 42nd St. (bet. 5th & 6th Aves.)
212-257-5826 | www.gknyc.com

Prepare to be "**wowed by**" this French "**standout**" opposite Bryant Park,
where chef Gabriel Kreuther produces "**inspired**" tasting menus with his
signature "**Alsatian twists**", served by a "**seamless staff**" in an "**impressive**"
setting with "**snazzy**" "**rustic**" accents; though it's "**costly**", there's also an à la
carte bar menu if you're "**mindful of your pocketbook.**"

| **GABRIEL'S** | Italian | 4.3 | 3.9 | 4.3 | $$$ |

West 60s | 11 W. 60th St. (bet. B'way & Columbus Ave.)
212-956-4600 | www.gabrielsbarandrest.com

"**Caring**" service overseen by "**natural host**" Gabriel Aiello sets the "**classy**" tone
at this "**even-keeled**" Columbus Circle Italian known for "**delicious**" cooking, a
"**comfortable**" setting and proximity to Lincoln Center; given the rather "**hefty**"
tabs, "**media**" types from nearby CBS and CNN prefer it for lunch.

| **GALLAGHERS** | Steak | 4.4 | 4.0 | 4.2 | $$$ |

West 50s | 228 W. 52nd St. (bet. B'way & 8th Ave.)
212-586-5000 | www.gallaghersnysteakhouse.com

A "**true New York steakhouse**" with "**history**", this circa-1927 Theater District
"**institution**" delivers "**melt-in-your-mouth**" meat and "**first-rate**" wine in
"**clubby**" surrounds watched over by a "**polished**" crew; the "**old-school**"
package is "**everything you'd expect**" – right down to the "**pricey**" bill.

| **THE GANDER** | American | 4.1 | 4.1 | 4.2 | $$ |

Flatiron | 15 W. 18th St. (bet. 5th & 6th Aves.)
212-229-9500 | www.thegandernyc.com

An upscale but "**relaxed**" offering from Jesse Schenker (ex Recette), this Flatiron
New American delivers "**well-prepared**" dishes "**without much pretension**" in
"**comfortable**" confines; prices skew "**pretty expensive**" in the "**fine-dining**" main
room, but the "**lively**" bar's gastropub menu is easier on the wallet.

| **GANSO** | Japanese/Noodle Shop | 4.4 | 3.7 | 4.0 | $$ |

Downtown Brooklyn | 25 Bond St. (Livingston St.) | Brooklyn
718-403-0900 | www.gansonyc.com

"**Truly addictive**" noodles are what it's about at this Downtown Brooklyn
Japanese, which slings "**well-made**" ramen and other quick bites ("**you can't
go wrong with the wings**"); a streamlined setup with a "**friendly**" "**hipster
staff**", it's "**much needed in the neighborhood.**"

| **GANSO YAKI** | Japanese | 4.3 | 3.9 | 4.0 | $$ |

Downtown Brooklyn | 515 Atlantic Ave. (3rd Ave.) | Brooklyn
646-927-0303 | www.gansonyc.com

The "**Mouthwatering Japanese street food**" at this "**hip**" Downtown Brooklyn izakaya ranges from **"artfully prepared"** grill dishes to what may be **"the city's best okonomiyaki"**, plus there's sushi from next-door sib Ganso Sushi; **"impressive"** sakes and craft beers, killer **"happy hour deals"** and an all-around **"friendly atmosphere"** seal the deal.

GAONNURI | Korean   4.1   4.5   4.2 $$$

West 30s | 1250 Broadway (32nd St.)
212-971-9045 | www.gaonnurinyc.com

Its **"biggest appeal"** is the **"stellar"** panoramic Midtown vistas from its **"chic"**, 39th-floor space, but this **"upmarket"** player on the K-town scene also **"holds its own"** with **"stylishly prepared"** Korean fare, including **"traditional"** tabletop BBQ; service is variable and you **"pay for the view"**, but that **"sunset over the Hudson"** is more than **"worth it."**

GARGIULO'S | Italian   4.2   4.0   4.2 $$

Coney Island | 2911 W. 15th St. (bet. Mermaid & Surf Aves.) | Brooklyn
718-266-4891 | www.gargiulos.com

After a **"swim at the beach"**, have a **"swim in red sauce"** at this circa-1907 Coney Island **"time warp"**, a **"catering hall"**–sized arena for **"consistently good"** **"old-fashioned"** Neapolitan cooking ferried by **"tuxedo-clad"** waiters; the **"colorful"** crowd feels its **"reputation is deserved"**, while a nightly raffle means **"you could eat for free."**

GATO | Mediterranean   4.5   4.2   4.3 $$$

NoHo | 324 Lafayette St. (bet. Bleecker & Houston Sts.)
212-334-6400 | www.gatonyc.com

Bobby Flay **"hits the nail on the head"** at this **"happening"** NoHo Med where his **"wonderfully creative"** dishes **"burst"** with **"bold flavors"**; a **"Downtown sceney"** crowd keeps the **"Industrial"** digs feeling **"cool"**, and a large front bar area offers a **"fun vibe"** along with the full menu.

GAZALA'S | Mideastern   4.1   2.9   3.6 $$

West 40s | 709 Ninth Ave. (bet. 48th & 49th Sts.)
212-245-0709 | www.gazalaplace.com

"Dependably good" Druze fare at **"value"** prices makes this **"tiny"** Hell's Kitchen BYO a **"reliable"** standby; the **"humble"** digs **"lack atmosphere"** and seating is **"tight"** ("prepare to get cozy with your neighbor"), but the grub **"more than makes up"** for all that.

GEMMA | Italian   4.3   4.3   4.0 $$

East Village | Bowery Hotel | 335 Bowery (bet. 2nd & 3rd Sts.)
212-505-7300 | www.theboweryhotel.com

Primo **"people-watching"** abounds at this **"fun"**, all-day Bowery Hotel Italian that lures **"scenesters"** with a **"romantic"**, **"country-chic"** setting festooned with **"hundreds of candles"**, plus a sidewalk patio; **"tasty"** fare, **"attentive service"** and **"fair prices"** make the **"no-rez"** policy (except for hotel guests) less of a drag.

GENNARO | Italian   4.5   3.6   4.1 $$

West 90s | 665 Amsterdam Ave. (bet. 92nd & 93rd Sts.)
212-665-5348 | www.gennaronyc.com

The **"early bird gets the table"** at this **"homey"** UWS **"star"** that's **"busy, like the trattorias in Italy"** thanks to its **"fresh"** classics, **"wonderful"** pasta and daily specials **"that'll make your head spin"**; it takes no reservations and no credit cards but is still **"worth it."**

	FOOD	DECOR	SERVICE	COST

GENUINE SUPERETTE | Californian/Diner ▽ 4.6 4.4 4.3 $

Little Italy | 191 Grand St. (Mulberry St.)
646-726-4633 | www.eatgenuine.com

A "**super-fun**" faux "**throwback**" inspired by California's classic roadside diners, this all-day Little Italy counter-serve joint offers "**terrific**" "**casual eats**" (burgers, fish tacos, salads) plus "**interesting**" juices and cocktails; it's "**perfect for a quick bite**", while "**sneaky surprise bar**" Genuine Liquorette below is more of a "**scene**."

GG'S | American/Pizza ▽ 4.3 3.7 4.2 $$

East Village | 511 E. Fifth St. (bet. Aves. A & B)
212-687-3641 | www.ggsnyc.com

"**Delicious**", "**innovation**"-prone pizzas (the square grandma pie is a "**revelation**") lead a roster running from pastas to burgers at this East Village American; a "**neighborhood joint**" with a marble bar furnishing "**awesome drinks**", it's a "**go-to**" for a "**quality**" meal that's "**not super-expensive**."

GIGINO AT WAGNER PARK | Italian 4.1 4.0 3.9 $$$

Battery Park City | 20 Battery Pl. (Little West St.)
212-528-2228 | www.gigino-wagnerpark.com

GIGINO TRATTORIA | Italian

TriBeCa | 323 Greenwich St. (Duane St.)
212-431-1112 | www.gigino-trattoria.com

An "**unpretentious**" taste of Tuscany, these "**affordable**" standbys deliver "**above-average**" food from a "**friendly**" staff; the TriBeCa original has a "**farmhouselike**" feel while its "**off-the-beaten-path**" Battery Park sibling offers outdoor dining with "**outstanding views**" of the harbor and Statue of Liberty.

GINO'S | Italian 4.4 3.8 4.2 $$

Bay Ridge | 7414 Fifth Ave. (bet. Bay Ridge Pkwy. & 74th St.) | Brooklyn
718-748-1698 | www.ginosbayridge.com

A neighborhood "**staple**" since 1964, this ever-"**crowded**" Bay Ridge Italian serves up "**generous portions**" of "**terrific**" classics "**just like mom makes**", in "**casual**" environs; "**get ready to wait in line**" at prime times, but the all-around "**enjoyable**" experience and "**reasonable**" tab ensure it's "**well worth it**."

GIORGIO'S OF GRAMERCY | American/Italian 4.3 3.8 4.2 $$

Flatiron | 27 E. 21st St. (bet. B'way & Park Ave. S.)
212-477-0007 | www.giorgiosofgramercy.com

The epitome of a "**true sleeper**", this longtime Flatiron "**hideaway**" features "**consistently good**" New American cooking that suggests "**unsung talent in the kitchen**"; "**gracious**" service and "**cozy**" surrounds that are "**never overcrowded**" are other incentives.

GIOVANNI RANA | Italian 4.3 3.9 4.0 $$$
PASTIFICIO & CUCINA

Chelsea | 75 Ninth Ave. (16th St.)
212-370-0975 | www.rananyc.com

The "**fresh-cut**" pastas "**justify the carb hit**" at this Chelsea Market eatery from an Italy-based pasta maker, offering "**darn tasty**" Italiana for on-site dining alongside a carry-away market; a "**rustic**", roomy space with "**hanging pots and pans**" complements the "**real homemade**" style.

	FOOD	DECOR	SERVICE	COST

GIOVANNI VENTICINQUE | Italian   4.3   3.9   4.2 $$$

East 80s | 25 E. 83rd St. (bet. 5th & Madison Aves.)
212-988-7300 | www.giovanniventicinque.com

"**Well-prepared**" Tuscan fare and a "**gracious**" staff keep this UES Italian popular with a "**neighborhood**" crowd; "**intimate**" and "**hushed**" enough for "**real conversation**", it boasts "**proximity to the Met**" and an "**unbeatable**" lunch prix fixe that offsets otherwise "**pricey**" tabs.

GLADY'S | Caribbean   ▽ 4.3   4.0   4.1 $

Crown Heights | 788 Franklin Ave. (Lincoln Pl.) | Brooklyn
718-622-0249 | www.gladysnyc.com

"**Like going back to your roots**" say fans of the "**delicious**" "**homestyle**" fare off a well-edited menu at this "**affordable**" Crown Heights Caribbean; tropical drinks, rum flights and a turquoise palette add to the "**cool**" island feel.

GLASSERIE | Mediterranean   ▽ 4.6   4.4   3.9 $$

Greenpoint | 95 Commercial St. (bet. Box St. & Manhattan Ave.) | Brooklyn
718-389-0640 | www.glasserienyc.com

"**Imaginative**" and "**delicious**" sum up the fare at this "**hip**" Greenpoint Mediterranean where a "**small but complete**" seasonal menu gets an assist from "**well-balanced**" cocktails; the "**comfortable**", vintage-industrial space jibes with its glass-factory past, and the neighborhood's skyline views are another reason it's "**worth the trek.**"

GLASS HOUSE TAVERN | American   3.9   3.7   4.0 $$$

West 40s | 252 W. 47th St. (bet. B'way & 8th Ave.)
212-730-4800 | www.glasshousetavern.com

Something "**calming**" in the "**hectic**" Theater District, this "**solid performer**" provides New Americana that tastes even better when Broadway "**stars**" are seated alongside you; "**cordial**" service also draws applause, though conversationalists advise "**eat upstairs.**"

GNOCCO | Italian   ▽ 4.3   3.9   4.2 $$

East Village | 337 E. 10th St. (bet. Aves. A & B)
212-677-1913 | www.gnocco.com

"**Authentic Emilian fare**" is the focus of this East Village Italian praised for its "**tasty pizza**", "**lengthy wine list**" and "**excellent**" namesake dish; the "**most prized tables**" are in its "**lovely**", all-seasons garden, though "**modest**" pricing and "**helpful**" service are available throughout.

GOLDEN SHOPPING | Chinese/Food Hall   ▽ 4.4   2.4   3.1 $
MALL

Flushing | 41-36 Main St. (41st Rd.) | Queens
no phone

An "**adventure**" for the "**intrepid**", this bi-level Flushing food court offers a "**variety**" of "**tasty**" Chinese "**delights**" from vendors like "**terrific**" dumpling shops and the original Xi'an Famous Foods; it's "**crazy**" "**crowded**" with "**no ambiance**", but never mind – the eats are "**really cheap.**"

GOLDEN UNICORN | Chinese   4.1   3.3   3.4 $$

Chinatown | 18 E. Broadway (Catherine St.)
212-941-0911 | www.goldenunicornrestaurant.com

"**Mobbed and noisy**" is a given at this "**huge**" C-town Cantonese featuring "**endless carts**" stocked with "**heavenly**" dim sum; "**hurried**" service and "basic Chinatown wedding party decor" are forgiven since it's a lot "cheaper than flying to Hong Kong."

GOOD | American	4.1	3.7	4.1	$$

West Village | 89 Greenwich Ave. (bet. Bank & W. 12th Sts.)
212-691-8080 | www.goodrestaurantnyc.com

"Should be named 'great'" say fans of this West Village American "respite" that's still something of a "hidden gem" despite "simple", "hearty" cooking and "kind service"; some may find the decor "boring", but there's always a "weekend line" for its "amazing brunch."

GOOD ENOUGH TO EAT | American	3.9	3.5	3.7	$$

West 80s | 520 Columbus Ave. (85th St.)
212-496-0163 | www.goodenoughtoeat.com

This "great-value" UWS "favorite" offers all-day dining à la "Vermont" via a "simple" American comfort-food menu; the "no-frills" setting sports "cute farm decor" and also offers outdoor seating, although "painful waits" are the norm at weekend brunch.

GOOD FORK | American	4.4	3.8	4.2	$$

Red Hook | 391 Van Brunt St. (bet. Coffey & Van Dyke Sts.) | Brooklyn
718-643-6636 | www.goodfork.com

"Hidden away" in Red Hook, this "funky" New American maintains a "loyal following" for its "excellent", Korean-influenced cooking dispensed in "cozy" digs with an "amazing" back garden; "warm" service and a "small but fine" drinks list are other reasons reservations are a "must."

GOTHAM BAR & GRILL | American	4.8	4.7	4.7	$$$$

Greenwich Village | 12 E. 12th St. (bet. 5th Ave. & University Pl.)
212-620-4020 | www.gothambarandgrill.com

"Longevity tells it all" at this circa-1984 Village "treasure" where Alfred Portale's "picture-perfect" New American plates plus "savvy service" and a "gothamy" setting add up to "superior dining with no corners cut"; longtime fans are "glad to pay the tariff" for an experience that "refuses to disappoint", and the $38 greenmarket lunch "truly is a steal."

GOTHAM WEST MARKET | Food Hall	4.1	3.6	3.6	$$

West 40s | 600 11th Ave. (bet. 44th & 45th Sts.)
212-582-7940 | www.gothamwestmarket.com

Some of the city's best-regarded chefs – including Seamus Mullen and Ivan Orkin – whip up "everything from burgers to tapas to noodles" at this "industrial-chic" Hell's Kitchen food hall offering both counter and communal table seating; it's perfect for "grazing" and definitely "worth the trip to 11th Avenue."

GRADISCA | Italian	4.4	3.9	4.2	$$$

West Village | 126 W. 13th St. (bet. 6th & 7th Aves.)
212-691-4886 | www.gradiscanyc.com

"Superb" hand-rolled pastas (sometimes made by the owner's mama) are the "main attraction" at this "low-key" West Village Italian, but other "savory" dishes shine as well; a "strong wine list", a "casual ambiance" and "friendly" service further secure its standing as an area "favorite."

GRAFFITI | Indian	4.6	3.7	4.4	$$$

East Village | 224 E. 10th St. (bet. 1st & 2nd Aves.)
212-464-7743 | www.graffitinyc.com

Chef Jehangir Mehta "really puts his heart" into the "fantastic" Indian-inspired share plates at this "**tiny**" East Village joint where "**vibrant, global flavors**" make for seriously "**innovative**" dishes; the "**hole-in-the-wall**" space is "**cramped**", but given the "**reasonable**" prices (especially the wines), the "**squeeze**" is more than "**justified.**"

NEW GRAFFITI EARTH | Indian/Persian   —   —   — $$$

TriBeCa | Duane Street Hotel | 190 Church St. (Duane St.)
212-542-9440 | www.graffitiearthnyc.com

This TriBeCa sib to chef Jehangir Mehta's Graffiti in the Duane Street Hotel serves a vegetable-centric Indian- and Persian-inspired menu that brings sustainability to the fore, with a similarly simple pricing structure as the original. Designed with woods and soft gray tones, the 20-seater has communal and two-top tables, along with a small private dining room.

GRAMERCY TAVERN | American   4.8   4.6   4.7 $$$$

Flatiron | 42 E. 20th St. (bet. B'way & Park Ave. S.)
212-477-0777 | www.gramercytavern.com

You can rely on "**top-class**" dining with "**no gimmicks**" at Danny Meyer's enduring Flatiron New American, where chef Michael Anthony's "**outstanding**" set menus are presented by "**eminently suave**" staffers in an "**upscale-country**" dining room arrayed with "**gorgeous**" flower displays; it's "**not cheap by any means**", though the front tavern offers a "**reasonable**" à la carte menu in a "**colorful**" walk-in setting.

GRAND ARMY | Seafood   ∇ 3.9   4.3   4.1 $$

Downtown Brooklyn | 338 State St. (Hoyt St.) | Brooklyn
718-422-7867 | www.grandarmybar.com

This "**lively**" Downtown Brooklyn hangout from Noah Bernamoff (Mile End) and crew pairs an "**imaginative**" seafood-centric menu with "**cocktail wizardry**" and a "**killer**" wine list; "**snagging a table**" in the "**cozy**" space can be difficult but seats at the vintage bar provide another option.

GRAND CENTRAL OYSTER BAR | Seafood   4.2   3.8   3.7 $$$

East 40s | Grand Central | 89 E. 42nd St., Lower Level (Park Ave.)
212-490-6650 | www.oysterbarny.com

"**Justly beloved**", this "**boisterous**" seafood "**legend**" in Grand Central stays "**faithful to its 1913 origins**" with "**terrific**" oysters and pan roasts that provide a taste of "**true NY**"; a "**venerable**" sublevel sprawl with a "**dramatically**" vaulted ceiling, "**classic**" dining counters and a "**throwback**" saloon, it's "**not to be missed**" even if it "**costs a pretty penny.**"

GRAND SICHUAN | Chinese   4.0   3.0   3.6 $$

Chelsea | 229 Ninth Ave. (24th St.) | 212-620-5200 | www.grandsichuan.com
Chelsea | 172 Eighth Ave. (bet. 18th & 19th Sts.) | 212-243-1688 |
www.grandsichuaneasternnyc.com
East 50s | 1049 Second Ave. (bet. 55th & 56th Sts.) | 212-355-5855 |
www.grandsichuaneasternnyc.com
East Village | 19-23 St. Marks Pl. (bet. 2nd & 3rd Aves.) | 212-529-4800 |
www.ordergrandsichuan.com
West 70s | 307 Amsterdam Ave. (bet. 74th & 75th Sts.) | 212-580-0277 |
www.grandsichuan74.com
West Village | 15 Seventh Ave. S. (bet. Carmine & Leroy Sts.) | 212-645-0222 |
www.grandsichuannyc.com
Forest Hills | 98-108 Queens Blvd. (bet. 66th & 67th Aves.) | Queens |
718-268-8833

"**Hot stuff**" seekers tout the "**mouth-numbing**" Sichuan fare served at this all-over-town mini-chain where the "**huge**" plates are on par with the "**extensive**" menu; service is "**perfunctory**" and there's "**no ambiance**", but otherwise it's "**fast**", "**reliable**" and "**doesn't hurt the wallet.**"

| **GRAND TIER** | American | 4.1 | 4.7 | 4.4 | $$$$ |

West 60s | Metropolitan Opera House | 30 Lincoln Center Plaza (65th St.)
212-799-3400 | www.patinagroup.com

Those long performance nights have a "**delightful**" prelude at this Lincoln Center New American (open during opera season only to all ticket-holders), where the "**tasty**" if "**limited**" menu is served in a "**dramatic**", chandeliered setting overlooking the Met foyer; tabs are "**expensive**", but payoffs include "**efficiency**" and "**dessert at intermission.**"

| **GRAN ELECTRICA** | Mexican | 4.3 | 4.2 | 4.3 | $$ |

Dumbo | 5 Front St. (Old Fulton St.) | Brooklyn
718-852-2700 | www.granelectrica.com

"**Simple but super-delicious**", the Mexican eats at this "**pleasant**" Dumbo denizen under the Brooklyn Bridge pair well with its extensive list of mezcals, tequilas and "**killer**" margaritas; Day of the Dead–inspired wallpaper adds to the "**festive**" vibrations, while the "**fun patio**" provides a "**civilized respite from the noisy interior.**"

| **GRAY'S PAPAYA** | Hot Dogs | 4.0 | 2.5 | 3.4 | $ |

West 70s | 2090 Broadway (72nd St.)
212-799-0243 | www.grayspapayanyc.com

This 24/7 UWS hot dog stand vends "**surprisingly good**" wieners washed down with "**frothy**" papaya drinks; "**quick**" turnaround and "**chump-change**" tabs offset the "**gruff**" service, "**what-a-dump**" decor and lack of seats at this "**quintessential**" NY "**institution.**"

| **GRAZIE** | Italian | 4.0 | 3.7 | 4.1 | $$$ |

East 80s | 26 E. 84th St. (Madison Ave.)
212-717-4407 | www.grazienyc.com

With its "**cozy**" townhouse setting and "**quite creditable**" Italian cooking, this veteran UES duplex off Museum Mile is a "**relaxing**" respite "**before, after or instead of the Met**"; maybe it's "**a bit pricey**", but the set-price bento box lunch is a "**bargain considering the neighborhood.**"

| **NEW** **GREAT NORTHERN** | Food Hall | — | — | — | $ |
| **FOOD HALL** | | | | | |

East 40s | Grand Central | 89 E. 42nd St. (Park Ave.)
646-568-4020 | www.greatnorthernfood.com

This casual extension of Agern by Claus Meyer (Copenhagen's Noma) in Grand Central Terminal features five vendors selling Scandinavian fare that's largely based on local produce. Crisp tilework sets off the space in Vanderbilt Hall, which offers Danish open-faced sandwiches, hot dogs, salads and pastries, along with house-roasted coffee and after-work beer and cocktails.

| **GREAT NY NOODLE TOWN** | Noodle Shop | 4.3 | 2.5 | 3.2 | $$ |

Chinatown | 28 Bowery (Bayard St.)
212-349-0923 | www.greatnynoodletown.com

"**Surrender to the crowd experience**" and "**sit with strangers**" at this "**chaotic**" C-town noodle shop known for "**dirt-cheap**" Cantonese eats (and "**delicious**" salt-baked seafood) served into the wee hours; not so great is "**zero decor**", no credit cards and "**difficult**" service.

	FOOD	DECOR	SERVICE	COST

GREEK KITCHEN | Greek 3.9 3.4 4.0 $$

West 50s | 889 10th Ave. (58th St.)
212-581-4300 | www.greekkitchennyc.com

"Trustworthy", "economical" eats in "generous" portions make this "real Greek" a "staple" on the edge of Hell's Kitchen, a location "convenient to Lincoln Center"; the nautical space is "pleasant" enough, and a "glassed-in" patio offers sidewalk views.

GREENPOINT FISH & | Seafood 4.4 3.6 3.9 $$
LOBSTER CO.

Greenpoint | 114 Nassau Ave. (Eckford St.) | Brooklyn
718-349-0400 | www.greenpointfish.com

The seafood is "fresh, fresh, fresh" at this "combo" fishmonger/dinette in Greenpoint where the "interesting" menu features "terrific" raw-bar eats, "delicious" fish tacos and one "fantastic" lobster roll; despite "tiny" digs with "not much" atmosphere, it's still "packed" at prime times.

GREY DOG | American 4.0 3.6 3.7 $

Chelsea | 242 W. 16th St. (8th Ave.) | 212-229-2345
Greenwich Village | 90 University Pl. (E. 12th St.) | 212-414-4739
NoLita | 244 Mulberry St. (bet. Prince & Spring Sts.) | 212-966-1060
West Village | 49 Carmine St. (Bedford St.) | 212-462-0041
www.thegreydog.com

Folks find a "sweet throwback" to what neighborhood coffee stops "used to be" in these "comfortable" hangouts for "relaxing" and "people-watching" over "inexpensive", "reliably good" American comfort food and java; yes, "brunch lines" can be "over the top", but staffers "know how to work the crowd."

GRIFONE | Italian 4.4 3.8 4.4 $$$

East 40s | 244 E. 46th St. (2nd Ave.)
212-490-7275

A "tried-and-true" East Side "sleeper", this "old-line" Northern Italian near the U.N. fields an "extensive" menu of "outstanding" dishes in "intimate" if somewhat "dated" surrounds; "captains-of-industry" price tags detract, but fans dig the "discreet" service and "calm, quiet" vibe.

GRIMALDI'S | Pizza 4.1 3.3 3.6 $$

Coney Island | 1215 Surf Ave. (bet. Stillwell Ave. & 12th St.) | Brooklyn |
718-676-2630
Dumbo | 1 Front St. (bet. Dock & Old Fulton Sts.) | Brooklyn | 718-858-4300
Douglaston | 242-02 61st Ave. (Douglaston Pkwy.) | Queens | 718-819-2133
www.grimaldis-pizza.com

Brace yourself for "endless crowds" at this Dumbo pizzeria–cum–"tourist" magnet where the payoff is "delicious" "thin-crust", coal-fired pies; the other branches can usually be accessed "without the wait", but they share the mother ship's no-plastic, no-reservations, no-slices rules.

GROM | Ice Cream 4.5 3.2 3.6 $

West 50s | 1796 Broadway (58th St.) | 212-974-3444
West Village | 233 Bleecker St. (Carmine St.) | 212-206-1738
www.grom.it

"Some of the best gelato around" (plus "outrageously rich" hot chocolate too) is found at these artisanal gelaterias whose "heavenly" product incorporates ingredients imported from Italy, including the water for its sorbets; despite *molto* grumbling about "**long lines**" and "**exorbitant prices**", most agree it's "**worth the extra bucks.**"

NEW GRÜNAUER BISTRO | Austrian   ▽ 3.9   4.1   4.1 $$$

East 80s | 1578 First Ave. (82nd St.)
212-988-1077 | www.grunauernyc.com

"**You can almost hear the sounds of a Strauss waltz**" at this UES Austrian bistro where a "**caring team**" serves "**traditional**" Viennese fare like spaetzle, Wiener schnitzel and sauerbraten complemented by hard-to-find Alsatian wines; the "**old-world**" "**wood-paneled interior**" is as "**authentic**" as the cooking.

NEW GÜNTER SEEGER NY | European   —   —   — $$$$

Meatpacking District | 641 Hudson St. (bet. Gansevoort & Horatio Sts.)
646-657-0045 | www.gunterseegerny.com

High-profile German chef Günter Seeger, whose onetime Atlanta restaurant influenced the regional food scene, leads this prix fixe-only Meatpacking European emphasizing changing menus based around the day's produce. Done in white brick, the interior holds nicely spaced round tables, as well as a long table at the open kitchen and a bar cart by the entrance for drinks.

GYU-KAKU | Japanese   3.9   3.6   3.8 $$$

East 40s | 805 Third Ave., 2nd fl. (bet. 49th & 50th Sts.) | 212-702-8816
Greenwich Village | 34 Cooper Sq. (bet. Astor Pl. & 4th St.) | 212-475-2989
West 40s | 321 W. 44th St. (bet. 8th & 9th Aves.) | 646-692-6297
www.gyu-kaku.com

"**Novelty**"-seekers hype this "**delicious, do-it-yourself**" Japanese yakiniku franchise where you cook your own BBQ on tabletop charcoal braziers; since the "**small portions**" can add up to "**pricey**" tabs, bargain-hunters show up for the happy-hour specials.

NEW HAIL MARY | Diner   —   —   — $$

Greenpoint | 68 Greenpoint Ave. (bet. Franklin & West Sts.) | Brooklyn
347-422-0645 | www.hailmarybk.com

Reinterpreting the American diner, this Greenpoint eatery by a married team offers an upscale take on sandwiches, comforting plates and small bites. There are also fountain drinks and housemade candy bars served in a kitschy yet chic setting, with wine, beer and cocktails too.

HAKATA TONTON | Japanese   ▽ 4.5   3.6   4.2 $$

West Village | 61 Grove St. (7th Ave. S.)
212-242-3699

You'll feel "**instantly transported**" at this West Village Japanese where the "**refreshing**" menu of "**obscure**" and "**imaginative**" small plates "**pays homage**" to pork via "**fantastic**" dishes including "**must-have**" pig's feet; a "**warm**" staff "**eager to educate**" first-timers elevates the "**casual**" space.

HAKKASAN | Chinese   4.4   4.6   4.3 $$$$

West 40s | 311 W. 43rd St. (bet. 8th & 9th Aves.)
212-776-1818 | www.hakkasan.com

"**Spectacular**" Shanghai-chic surrounds "**transport you**" away from the Theater District at this "**massive**" branch of the London-born chain, where the "**modern**" Cantonese-inspired fare and "**epic**" dim sum also "**impress**"; "**fabulously expensive**" prices are part of the "**high-end**" package, but after a few "**fancy**" cocktails you might "**not mind.**"

THE HALAL GUYS | Mideastern   3.9   2.8   3.6 $

Gramercy Park | 307 E. 14th St. (2nd Ave.) | 347-527-1505

continued

West 90s | 722 Amsterdam Ave. (95th St.) | no phone
www.thehalalguysny.com

For a "**fast**" Middle Eastern "**fix**", these food-cart offshoots dispense "**satisfying**" gyros, falafel and chicken rice platters with their "**famous**" white sauce; the "**small storefronts**" are decidedly "**nothing fancy**", but portions are "**plentiful**" and "**your wallet won't even feel it.**"

HAMPTON CHUTNEY CO.	Indian	4.1	3.1	3.6	$

SoHo | 143 Grand St. (bet. Crosby & Lafayette Sts.) | 212-226-9996
West 80s | 464 Amsterdam Ave. (bet. 82nd & 83rd Sts.) | 212-362-5050
www.hamptonchutney.com

"**Crispy and light**", the "**super**" dosas with "**nonconventional**" fillings offer an "**affordable**" taste of "**something different**" at these "**casual**" Indian standbys; it's a "**cool concept**", but the "**basic**" counter-service setups have many turning to them for takeout.

HANCO'S	Vietnamese	4.0	2.9	3.4	$

Brooklyn Heights | 147 Montague St. (bet. Clinton & Henry Sts.) | Brooklyn | 347-529-5054
Cobble Hill | 134 Smith St. (bet. Bergen & Dean Sts.) | Brooklyn | 718-858-6818
Park Slope | 350 Seventh Ave. (10th St.) | Brooklyn | 718-499-8081

"**Addictive**" banh mi sandwiches washed down with "**excellent**" bubble teas (plus pho in Park Slope and Brooklyn Heights) ensure these Vietnamese storefronts are "**always busy**"; "**no-frills**" sums up both the decor and service, but few mind given the price.

HAN DYNASTY	Chinese	4.2	3.4	3.7	$$

Greenwich Village | 90 Third Ave. (bet. 12th & 13th Sts.) | 212-390-8685
West 80s | 215 W. 85th St. (B'way) | 212-858-9060
www.handynasty.net

"**Hot in just the right way**" these "**awesome Philly transplants**" offer "**unapologetically spicy**" Sichuan dishes including "**knockout**" dan dan noodles; the Villager is "**always crowded**" while the UWS offshoot is much more "**spacious**", and though both are "**no-frills**", they're priced for "**value.**"

HANGAWI	Korean/Vegetarian	4.5	4.4	4.4	$$$

Murray Hill | 12 E. 32nd St. (bet. 5th & Madison Aves.)
212-213-0077 | www.hangawirestaurant.com

A "**wonderful respite**" in "**honky-tonk**" K-town, this "**transporting**" Korean provides "**exquisite**" vegan fare that tastes even better in its "**Zen-like atmosphere**"; "**knowledgeable**" service is also part of the "**relaxing**" package, but "**be willing to take your shoes off**" – it's a "**requirement**" here.

HANJAN	Korean	4.4	3.9	4.1	$$$

Flatiron | 36 W. 26th St. (bet. B'way & 6th Ave.)
212-206-7226 | www.hanjan26.com

"**Modern twists**" elevate the Korean small plates to "**really delicious**" levels at this "**casual**" Flatiron gastropub; "**interesting**" cocktails and "**not-to-be-missed**" rice beer add to the "**fun atmosphere**" – and keep things "**lively.**"

NEW **HAO NOODLE & TEA BY**	Chinese	—	—	—	$$
MADAM ZHU'S KITCHEN					

West Village | 401 Sixth Ave. (bet. Greenwich Ave. & Waverly Pl.)
212-633-8900

A Sichuanese impresario behind restaurant chains in China touches down in the West Village with this eatery serving dishes drawing from different Chinese regions, a number of which incorporate housemade noodles and seasonal ingredients. The warm, brick-walled space has both communal and two-top tables.

HARLEM SHAKE | Burgers   3.9   3.9   3.7 $$

NEW   **East Harlem** | 2162 Second Ave. (111th St.) | 212-222-8311
Harlem | 100 W. 124th St. (Lenox Ave.) | 212-222-8300
www.harlemshakenyc.com

"**Solid**" griddled burgers are the signature of these "**fun**" all-day Harlem joints with "**malt-shop-meets-*Jet***-magazine" decor and a neighborhood-centric "**wall of fame**"; "**out-of-this-world**" shakes and "**affordable**" tabs add to their popularity.

HARRY & IDA'S MEAT & SUPPLY CO. | Deli   4.4   3.6   4.0 $

East Village | 189 Ave. A (12th St.)
646-864-0967 | www.meatandsupplyco.com

The "**pastrami is for real**" at this "**hip**" East Village deli from the Ducks Eatery team, where the "**outstanding**" signature sandwich is offered alongside other "**thrilling**" options (e.g. smoked eel); the vintage-inspired space also has "**interesting**" smoked and pickled goods to take out.

HARRY CIPRIANI | Italian   4.3   4.2   4.2 $$$$

East 50s | Sherry-Netherland Hotel | 781 Fifth Ave. (bet. 59th & 60th Sts.)
212-753-5566 | www.cipriani.com

"**Vanderbilts**" and other "**VIPs**" feel "**right at home**" at this "**classy**" Sherry-Netherland "**landmark**" modeled after the Venice original; the Italian fare is "**on-point**" and the Bellinis are "**excellent**" but some feel you're paying the "**stratospheric**" tabs to see "**who might walk in.**"

HARRY'S CAFE & STEAK | Steak   4.3   4.1   4.2 $$$

Financial District | 1 Hanover Sq. (bet. Pearl & Stone Sts.)
212-785-9200 | www.harrysnyc.com

Long "**Wall Street's go-to eatery**", this FiDi "**throwback**" beneath the historic India House attracts "**captains of industry**" with "**mouthwatering**" steaks and more backed by one of the best wine cellars in the city; it's "**busy**" for lunch, quieter at dinner and "**expense account**"–worthy all the time.

HARRY'S ITALIAN | Italian   4.1   3.7   3.9 $$

Battery Park City | 225 Murray St. (West St.) | 212-608-1007
Financial District | 2 Gold St. (Platt St.) | 212-747-0797
West 50s | 30 Rockefeller Plaza, Concourse Level (bet. 49th & 50th Sts.) |
212-218-1450
www.harrysitalian.com

"**Sterling**" pizzas figure among the "**Italian favorites**" at these "**welcoming**" fallbacks from the Harry's Cafe folks; "**ample portions**" and "**reasonable pricing**" cement their "**go-to**" status for "**less-than-formal lunches**" at the Downtown locations or eats on the move from the "**busy**", takeout-only Rock Center outlet.

HARU | Japanese   4.0   3.6   3.8 $$

NEW   **Chelsea** | 176 Eighth Ave. (19th St.) | 212-739-9740
East 70s | 1329 Third Ave. (76th St.) | 212-452-2230
Financial District | 1 Wall Street Ct. (Pearl St.) | 212-785-6850
Union Square | 220 Park Ave. S. (18th St.) | 646-428-0989
West 40s | 229 W. 43rd St. (bet. 7th & 8th Aves.) | 212-398-9810

continued

West 80s | 433 Amsterdam Ave. (bet. 80th & 81st Sts.) | 212-579-5655
www.harusushi.com

This "**bustling**" Japanese mini-chain is an "**easy**" option thanks to its
"**comprehensive**" menu, "**inventive**" sushi rolls and "**nothing fancy**" settings;
OK, so it's "**not extraordinary**" and service can turn "**harried**" at prime times,
but the "**happening**" happy hour is always a total "**steal.**"

HATSUHANA | Japanese   4.5   3.7   4.2 $$$

East 40s | 17 E. 48th St. (bet. 5th & Madison Aves.)
212-355-3345 | www.hatsuhana.com

The "**real deal**" for "**traditional**" sushi, this "**been-there-forever**" Midtown
Japanese "**still holds its own**" with "**top-quality**" fish "**served without
flourish**" by a "**first-rate**" staff; the "**simple**" digs may seem "**sparse**", but it
remains a "**favorite**", especially for the "**business crowd.**"

HAVANA CENTRAL | Cuban   4.0   4.0   3.9 $$

West 40s | 151 W. 46th St. (bet. 6th & 7th Aves.)
212-398-7440 | www.havanacentral.com

A "**festive**" pick for "**entertaining friends**", this Midtown Cuban "**escape**"
offers "**well-prepared**" food and "**delicious**" drinks in a "**tropical**" setting
where "**Desi Arnaz**" would feel at home; too bad the "**party atmosphere**" and
"**spirited**" live music can make for "**jet-airplane**" noise levels.

HAVELI | Indian   ▽ 4.3   3.6   4.1 $$

East Village | 100 Second Ave. (bet. 5th & 6th Sts.)
212-477-5956 | www.haveliny.com

East Village kitchens Banjara and Haveli have "**joined forces**" at this bi-level
Indian offering "**cut-above**" cooking from a "**goes-on-forever**" menu in the
former Haveli space; the ambiance is "**not the best**" but "**attentive**" service
and "**reasonable**" bills help make the merger a "**success.**"

HEARTH | American/Italian   4.4   4.0   4.3 $$$

East Village | 403 E. 12th St. (1st Ave.)
646-602-1300 | www.restauranthearth.com

"**Given new life**" after an update to its menu and space, Marco Canora's
upscale East Villager still "**delivers**" via "**gutsy**", "**market-driven**" Tuscan-
American plates with a "**more healthful**" bent; the "**subtly redone**" room has
the same "**lively**" vibe, complete with a "**caring staff.**"

HECHO EN DUMBO | Mexican   4.1   3.4   3.6 $$

NoHo | 354 Bowery (bet. 4th & Great Jones Sts.)
212-937-4245 | www.hechoendumbo.com

A generally "**innovative**" take on Mexican cooking can be found at this NoHo
hang where "**elevated**" small plates are paired with "**amazing**" margaritas;
maybe it's no longer the neighborhood "**star**" it once was, but it's still "**good
for groups.**"

HEIDELBERG | German   4.2   3.7   4.0 $$

East 80s | 1648 Second Ave. (bet. 85th & 86th Sts.)
212-628-2332 | www.heidelbergrestaurant.com

When it comes to "**delicious**", "**stick-to-your-ribs**" German classics, this
vintage-1936 Yorkville "**time capsule**" fields a "**heavy**", "**no-apologies**" menu
washed down with "**boots of beer**"; "**costumed**" staffers and a "**kitschy**",
"*oompah-pah*" setting are part of the "**fun**" package.

	FOOD	DECOR	SERVICE	COST

HELL'S KITCHEN | Mexican — 4.0 3.6 3.9 $$
West 50s | 754 Ninth Ave. (51st St.)
212-977-1588 | www.hellskitchen-nyc.com

"Satisfying", "updated Mexican" food draws a "lively crowd" to this "high-concept" Hell's Kitchen cantina where the "margaritas keep flowing" as the "noise" levels rise; the "pre-theater crush" can be "overwhelming", but "friendly" service helps keep fans "happy."

HENRY PUBLIC | Pub Food — 4.0 4.1 3.9 $$
Cobble Hill | 329 Henry St. (Pacific St.) | Brooklyn
718-852-8630 | www.henrypublic.com

"Trendy in a late-1800s sort of way", this "olde-timey" Cobble Hill pub serves a "small" menu anchored by an "off-the-charts" turkey-leg sandwich; "suspendered" bartenders shake "sophisticated" cocktails, leaving a limited reservations policy and sometimes "crowded" conditions as the only downsides.

HENRY'S END | American — 4.5 3.6 4.3 $$$
Brooklyn Heights | 44 Henry St. (bet. Cranberry & Middagh Sts.) | Brooklyn
718-834-1776 | www.henrysend.com

A "neighborhood fixture" since 1973, this "cozy" Brooklyn Heights American mixes "delicious" "old-school" favorites (including "superb wild game" in season) with more "inventive" options; if the "closet-size" space seemingly "hasn't changed since the Nixon administration", most don't mind, especially given the "friendly" service and relatively "reasonable prices."

NEW **HER NAME IS HAN** | Korean — ▽ 4.5 4.3 4.1 $$
Murray Hill | 17 E. 31st St. (bet. 5th & Madison Aves.)
212-779-9990 | www.hernameishan.com

A "refreshing addition" to Murray Hill, this "fantastic" Korean kitchen delivers "excellent", "homestyle" cooking with "modern" touches in a warm setting overseen by the "nicest" staff; economical lunch specials and "on-point" house-infused soju add to the draw.

HIBINO | Japanese — 4.6 3.6 4.1 $$
Cobble Hill | 333 Henry St. (Pacific St.) | Brooklyn | 718-260-8052 |
www.hibino-brooklyn.com
Long Island City | 10-70 Jackson Ave. (bet. 49th & 50th Aves.) | Queens |
718-392-5190 | www.hibino-lic.com

"Fresh-as-one-can-get" sushi vies for the spotlight with the "daily changing" obanzai (small plates) and "compelling" housemade tofu at these "unusual", Kyoto-style Japanese eateries; "budget-friendly" tabs and "unobtrusive" service embellish the "subdued" mood.

HIDE-CHAN | Japanese/Noodle Shop — 4.4 3.5 3.9 $$
East 50s | 248 E. 52nd St., 2nd fl. (bet. 2nd & 3rd Aves.)
212-813-1800 | www.hidechanramen.com

The sound of diners "noisily slurping" "cooked-to-perfection" noodles swimming in "flavorful" broth provides the background music at this "authentic" East Midtown Japanese ramen joint; alright, the service can be "a bit rushed" and the setting "cramped", but "low costs" keep the trade brisk.

	FOOD	DECOR	SERVICE	COST

**NEW HIGH STREET | American/Bakery   4.5   4.1   4.1 $$
ON HUDSON**

Meatpacking District | 637 Hudson St. (Horatio St.)
917-388-3944 | www.highstreetonhudson.com

"**They do everything right**" at this Meatpacking District cafe (sequel to a Philly original), where the "**stellar**" lineup spans especially "**heavenly**" homemade breads and pastries, "**great sandwiches**" for a "**casual lunch**" and more "**adventuresome**" Americana for dinner; "**cheerful**" staffers heighten the "**lively**" neighborhood feel.

HILL COUNTRY | BBQ   4.2   3.6   3.6 $$

Flatiron | 30 W. 26th St. (bet. B'way & 6th Ave.) | 212-255-4544 | www.hillcountry.com

Downtown Brooklyn | 345 Adams St. (bet. Fulton & Johnson Sts.) | Brooklyn | 718-885-4608 | www.hillcountrybk.com

"**Hip BBQ**" is yours at these "**cafeteria-style**" joints where patrons order the "**messy**", "**smoky**" 'cue from a counter, then find a communal table and dig in; "**toe-tapping**" live music, a "**good bourbon selection**" and "**friendly**" vibrations make it the "**next best thing to being in Austin.**"

HILL COUNTRY CHICKEN | Chicken/Southern   4.1   3.4   3.6 $$

Flatiron | 30 W. 26th St. (bet. B'way & 6th Ave.) | 212-255-4544 | www.hillcountryny.com

Downtown Brooklyn | 345 Adams St. (bet. Fulton & Johnson Sts.) | Brooklyn | 718-885-4609 | www.hillcountrychicken.com

"**Crispy-crunchy**" fried chicken (including a "**fabulous**" skinless version) and "**decent sides**" make it hard to "**save room for pie**" at these low-budget Southerners; regulars ignore the "**service hiccups**" and "**groan-inducing**", "**rec-room**" decor, since those desserts "**are worth the trip alone.**"

HILLSTONE | American   4.2   4.0   4.1 $$$

East 50s | 153 E. 53rd St. (enter on 3rd Ave. & 54th St.) | 212-888-3828

NoMad | 378 Park Ave. S. (27th St.) | 212-689-1090
www.hillstone.com

"**Corporate crowds**" head to these "**busy**" Americans for "**well-executed**" food (including a "**must-have**" spinach-artichoke dip) served in "**dark**", "**modern**" digs suitable for everything from "**business lunches**" to "**date nights**"; just be ready for "**noisy**" bar scenes, particularly "**after work.**"

HOMETOWN BAR-B-QUE | BBQ   4.6   3.7   3.8 $$

Red Hook | 454 Van Brunt St. (Reed St.) | Brooklyn
347-294-4644 | www.hometownbarbque.com

A "**destination-worthy**" home to "**honest**" BBQ, this Red Hook "**champ**" supplies "**terrific**" Texas-style meats (think "**melt-in-your-mouth**" brisket and "**caveman-sized**" ribs) in a "**converted garage**" with a "**roadhouse party vibe**"; "**energetic**" crowds line up for the counter service, but the "**smoky**" "**excellence**" "**rewards the wait.**"

HOMETOWN HOTPOT & BBQ | Chinese   ∇ 4.2   4.0   3.9 $$

Little Italy | 194 Grand St. (Mott St.)
212-219-8833 | www.hometownhotpot.com

True to its name, this bi-level Little Italy Chinese offers "**cook-your-own**" hot pots with an "**amazing**" choice of broths and a separate BBQ menu for tabletop grilling; given the roomy digs, "**reasonable**" pricing and servers who "**don't rush you**", it's "**fantastic for groups.**"

HOP KEE | Chinese   4.1   2.7   3.5 $$
Chinatown | 21 Mott St., downstairs (bet. Chatham Sq. & Mosco St.)
212-964-8365 | www.hopkeenyc.com

This "**old-guard**", cash-only Chinatown cellar has been slinging "**traditional**"
Cantonese food – "**and plenty of it**" – since 1968; the "**dank**" decor and often
"**crowded**" conditions are offset by "**late**"-night hours, "**rock-bottom**" tabs and
an "**Anthony Bourdain**" endorsement.

HOUDINI KITCHEN LABORATORY | Pizza   ▽ 4.5   3.8   4.0 $$
Ridgewood | 1563 Decatur St. (Wyckoff Ave.) | Queens
718-456-3770 | www.houdinikitchenlaboratoryridgewood.com

"**Far off any tourist map**", this "**cool**", cash-only Ridgewood pizzeria turns out
a "**fantastic**" array of "**fancy**" wood-fired pies alongside Italian-leaning apps;
set in a former brewery, the "**funky**" space maintains an "**industrial**" feel and
there's also a "**pleasant**" back patio.

THE HOUSE | American   4.0   4.4   4.0 $$$
Gramercy Park | 121 E. 17th St. (bet. Irving Pl. & Park Ave. S.)
212-353-2121 | www.thehousenyc.com

This tri-level Gramercy standout delivers "**solid**" New American cooking
but "**even better ambiance**" given its "**romantic**", "**candlelit**" setting in a
"**gorgeous**" 1854 carriage house; factor in "**attentive**" service, and you've
got a "**perfect**" date place – though you'll pay to "**impress**" here.

HOUSEMAN | American   4.2   3.8   4.1 $$$
Hudson Square | 508 Greenwich St. (Spring St.)
212-641-0654 | www.housemanrestaurant.com

A "**true neighborhood**" place, this Hudson Square American from a Prune
veteran offers a "**short, quirky**" daily menu of "**satisfying**" fare headlined by
"**succulent**" roast chicken; a "**relaxed**" crew steers the "**calm**", white-brick
space, which works as well for weekday lunch as "**date**" night.

HUDSON CLEARWATER | American   4.1   3.9   4.0 $$
West Village | 447 Hudson St. (Morton St.)
212-989-3255 | www.hudsonclearwater.com

Set in a "**quasi-hidden**" West Village space, this "**buzzy**" New American "**date
spot**" delivers "**inventive**" plates to a "**trendy**" clientele; a "**lovely**" back patio
comes in handy when the "**cozy**" confines get "**a little cramped**" – and is
another reason it's a real "**find.**"

HUDSON EATS | Food Hall   4.1   4.0   3.7 $$
Battery Park City | Brookfield Pl. | 230 Vesey St. (West St.)
www.brookfieldplaceny.com

There's "**something for everyone**" at this "**fancy food court**" in Battery Park
City's Brookfield Place, where the "**substantial**" variety includes local vendors
like Mighty Quinn's BBQ, Blue Ribbon Sushi and Num Pang; though it's
"**packed at lunch**", "**fantastic**" harbor views and "**tons of seating**" are assets.

HUDSON GARDEN GRILL | American   ▽ 4.2   4.2   4.2 $$
Bronx Park | 2900 Southern Blvd. (Bronx Park Rd.) | Bronx
646-627-7711 | www.nybg.org

Arched windows looking out to the arboretum help define the "**lovely**" setting
at this New American by Stephen Starr, a full-service first for the New York
Botanical Garden; offering "**high-quality**", locally sourced lunch and light bites,
it's open to both garden visitors and the general public.

	FOOD	DECOR	SERVICE	COST

HUERTAS | Spanish   4.5   4.1   4.4 $$$

East Village | 107 First Ave. (bet. 6th & 7th Sts.)
212-228-4490 | www.huertasnyc.com

"**Impressive**" Basque fare (including "**inventive**" tapas) and "**creative**" drinks make for an "**exciting**" meal at this "**cool**" East Village joint; the "**helpful**" staff "**makes navigating the menu easy**", and while it "**can get pricey**" (gratuity is included), it's a solid pick "**with friends or a date.**"

HUGO & SONS | Italian   3.8   3.8   3.6 $$

Park Slope | 367 Seventh Ave. (11th St.) | Brooklyn
718-499-0020

Though its "**airy**" dining room is done up like a retro "**French bistro**", the "**varied**" menu skews Italian at this "**upbeat**" "**neighborhood joint**" on Park Slope's Seventh Avenue strip; there's also a "**neat**" little side pizzeria turning out "**savory, thin-crust**" pies from a wood-burning oven.

HU KITCHEN | Health Food   4.1   3.5   3.7 $

East 80s | 1536 Third Ave. (bet. 86th & 87th Sts.) | 212-335-2105
Greenwich Village | 78 Fifth Ave. (bet. 13th & 14th Sts.) | 212-510-8919
www.hukitchen.com

It's "**paleo paradise**" as these organic-leaning joints deliver "**solid**" gluten-free grub all day, including "**interesting**" veggie-based dishes, prepackaged snacks and smoothies; the "**cafeteria-style**" setups suit "**health-conscious**" types "**on-the-go**", though there's also seating with a "**casual, coffee-shop vibe.**"

HUMMUS PLACE | Israeli/Kosher/Vegetarian   4.2   3.0   3.7 $$

West 70s | 305 Amsterdam Ave. (bet. 74th & 75th Sts.) | 212-799-3335
West Village | 71 Seventh Ave. S. (bet. Barrow & Bleecker Sts.) | 212-924-2022
www.hummusplace.com

Those who like their hummus "**silky**" and their pita bread "**fresh**" and "**warm**" kvell over the vegetarian offerings at these "**popular**" Israelis (the Upper Westsider is kosher to boot); decor is nearly "**nonexistent**", but the grub's "**filling**" and tabs are "**terrific.**"

HUNDRED ACRES | American   4.2   4.0   4.1 $$

SoHo | 38 MacDougal St. (Prince St.)
212-475-7500 | www.hundredacresnyc.com

"**Farm-fresh**" New American "**home cooking**" arrives in an appropriately "**country-road**" setting at this SoHo charmer that's kin to Cookshop; its "**cult following**" commends its "**delicious brunch**" and "**awesome**" garden room, only wishing there were "**more menu options.**"

HUNT & FISH CLUB | Steak   4.2   4.4   4.3 $$$

West 40s | 125 W. 44th St. (bet. 6th & 7th Aves.)
212-575-4949 | www.hfcnyc.com

"**Sleek and sexy**", this marbled, mirrored Times Square chophouse offers "**solid**" steaks, seafood and game to a crowd of "**heavy hitters**" – and "**wannabes**" – who don't mind the "**big price tags**"; the "**glamour**" gets a boost from "**impressive**" scenery at the bar.

ICE & VICE | Ice Cream   ▽ 4.5   3.4   4.2 $

Lower East Side | 221 E. Broadway (Clinton St.)
646-678-3687 | www.iceandvice.com

A staple at outdoor markets goes brick-and-mortar at this LES ice cream shop, handcrafting small-batch scoops in a "**rotating**" lineup of "**knockout flavors**" featuring "**fabulously inventive**" combos (like crème fraîche and rose petal jam); "**very cool**" staffers help sweeten a "**pricey**" treat.

IL BAMBINO | Italian   4.5   3.8   4.1 $$

NEW **Greenwich Village** | 48 W. 8th St. (bet. MacDougal St. & 6th Ave.) | 212-228-2466

Astoria | 34-08 31st Ave. (bet. 34th & 35th Sts.) | Queens | 718-626-0087
www.ilbambinonyc.com

Panini fans and "**pork lovers**" dig these "**homey**" Italian "**nooks**" serving "**imaginative**" pressed sandwiches (many that are pig-centric) on "**crunchy**" bread, plus small plates, wines and "**fantastic**" brunch; backyards and "**cheap**" tabs are more reasons "**locals flock there.**"

IL BUCO | Italian/Mediterranean   4.5   4.3   4.3 $$$

NoHo | 47 Bond St. (bet. Bowery & Lafayette St.)
212-533-1932 | www.ilbuco.com

"**Marvelous**" "*cucina rustica*" pairs with a "**well-crafted**" wine list in "**intimate farmhouse-inspired**" surrounds that'll "**transport**" you to a "**Tuscan home**" at this NoHo Med-Italian; if it gets "**loud**", the downstairs wine cellar is a "**beautiful**" alternative, though it's "**not cheap**" no matter where you sit.

IL BUCO ALIMENTARI | Italian/Mediterranean   4.5   4.1   4.1 $$$$
E VINERIA

NoHo | 53 Great Jones St. (bet. Bowery & Lafayette St.)
212-837-2622 | www.ilbucovineria.com

"**Unpretentious**" but with a "**pure NY vibe**", this Il Buco spin-off is a "**go-to**" for "**simple yet refined**" Italian-Med fare – "**especially the pastas**" and "**ridiculously good**" short ribs – in a "**homey**" NoHo setup with a front market area/coffee bar; communal seats and somewhat "**pricey**" tabs aside, it's "**comfortable**" for just about "**every occasion.**"

IL CANTINORI | Italian   4.4   4.3   4.3 $$$

Greenwich Village | 32 E. 10th St. (bet. B'way & University Pl.)
212-673-6044 | www.ilcantinori.com

"**Top-of-the-line**" Tuscan cooking is the draw at this "**classy**" Village "**favorite**", "**still going strong**" after more than three decades; it's known as a "**celebrity hangout**" with a concordant "**price factor**", but "**genuine**" hospitality and "**gorgeous flowers**" make it a "**special-occasion**" destination for all.

IL CORTILE | Italian   4.3   4.0   4.1 $$$

Little Italy | 125 Mulberry St. (bet. Canal & Hester Sts.)
212-226-6060 | www.ilcortile.com

"*Buongusto* is an understatement" at this "**memory-lane**" Italian, a "**good bet on Mulberry**" since 1975 thanks to "**hearty**" food served by waiters who've "**been there forever**"; though it's "**a bit pricey**" for the area, regulars report a seat in the "**delightful**" garden atrium is "**worth the trip**" alone.

IL FALCO | Italian   4.4   4.0   4.5 $$$

Long Island City | 21-50 44th Dr. (23rd St.) | Queens
718-707-0009 | www.ilfalcolic.com

"**First-rate**" service boosts the "**classy**" feel of this "**real find**" in Long Island City, where the "**delicious**" Italian dishes come courtesy of two Il Mulino alums; tucked into "**cozy**" white-tablecloth surrounds, it's "**a winner**" all around.

	FOOD	DECOR	SERVICE	COST

IL GATTOPARDO | Italian $\qquad$ 4.4 $\quad$ 4.2 $\quad$ 4.3 $\quad$ $$$
West 50s | 13-15 W. 54th St. (bet. 5th & 6th Aves.)
212-246-0412 | www.ilgattopardonyc.com

"**Formal dining in the European manner**" comes via a "**terrific**" Southern Italian menu, "**smooth**" service and an "**elegant**" townhouse setting at this Midtown "**gem**"; its atrium is especially "**lovely**" for a "**unique**" brunch or lunch, but be prepared for "**hold-on-to-your-wallet**" tabs.

ILILI | Lebanese $\qquad$ 4.5 $\quad$ 4.2 $\quad$ 4.2 $\quad$ $$$
NoMad | 236 Fifth Ave. (bet. 27th & 28th Sts.)
212-683-2929 | www.ililinyc.com

"**Modern takes**" on "**traditional**" Lebanese cooking come with "**creative enhancements**" at this NoMad "**scene**", where the cocktails are equally "**inventive**"; the "**cathedral-sized**", wood-lined space is made for "**big groups**", but its "**nightclub vibe**" has "**noise**" to match (hint: upstairs nooks are "**more sedate**").

IL LABORATORIO DEL GELATO | Ice Cream $\quad$ 4.6 $\quad$ 3.4 $\quad$ 3.8 $\quad$ $
Lower East Side | 188 Ludlow St. (Houston St.)
212-343-9922 | www.laboratoriodelgelato.com

Whether you go "**adventurous**" or "**classic**", the artisan gelati and sorbetti is "**consistently excellent**" at this LES gelateria where you'll find "**flavors you never dreamed of before**" ("**but will dream of after**"); just note the "**sleek industrial**" space is designed for grabbing and going.

IL MULINO | Italian $\qquad$ 4.6 $\quad$ 4.0 $\quad$ 4.3 $\quad$ $$$$
Greenwich Village | 86 W. Third St. (bet. Sullivan & Thompson Sts.) | 212-673-3783 | www.ilmulino.com

IL MULINO UPTOWN | Italian
East 60s | 37 E. 60th St. (bet. Madison & Park Aves.) | 212-750-3270 | www.ilmulino.com

"**As good as ever**", these "**old-school**" Italians "**don't miss**", offering "**overabundant portions**", "**loads of freebies**" and all-around "**luscious**" fare; servers must "**perform a ballet**" to get around the "**cramped**" Village "**landmark**" (UES is roomier), and though it's "**memorable**" for sure, your wallet may "**hurt afterwards.**"

IL MULINO PRIME | Italian/Steak $\quad$ 4.3 $\quad$ 4.0 $\quad$ 4.1 $\quad$ $$$
SoHo | 331 W. Broadway (Grand St.)
212-226-0020 | www.ilmulino.com

"**Delicious**" prime beef is offered alongside "**wonderful**" Italian classics at this SoHo steakhouse; the white-on-white space has an "**appealing**" vibe, though a few say it's "**not on the same level**" as the original (except for price).

IL POSTINO | Italian $\qquad$ 4.5 $\quad$ 4.1 $\quad$ 4.4 $\quad$ $$$
East 40s | 337 E. 49th St. (bet. 1st & 2nd Aves.)
212-688-0033 | www.ilpostinony.com

Waiters inhale, then recite a "**huge list of daily specials**" at this "**old-world**" U.N.-area Italian that'll also "**cook anything you want**"; an "**intimate**", "**opera**"-enhanced space boosts the "**charming**" vibe, though "**reliably expensive**" tabs have some opting for the lunchtime prix fixe.

IL RICCIO | Italian   4.2   3.7   4.1 $$$

East 70s | 152 E. 79th St. (Lexington Ave.)
212-639-9111 | www.eatilriccionyc.com

Upper Eastsiders "**of a certain age**" patronize this "**clubby**" Italian for "**above-average**" Amalfi Coast food served by a "**cheerful**" staff; if the compact main room gets "**tight**", there's also an enclosed garden in back.

IL TINELLO | Italian   4.4   4.1   4.5 $$$

West 50s | 16 W. 56th St. (bet. 5th & 6th Aves.)
212-245-4388 | www.iltinellony.com

"**Serenity**" reigns at this Midtown "**grande dame**" exuding "**senior appeal**" and patrolled by "**conscientious**" waiters in "**black tie**"; everyone agrees that the Northern Italian cooking is "**superb**", but given the "**corporate-checkbook**" tabs, many save it for "**special occasions.**"

IL VALENTINO OSTERIA | Italian   4.4   4.4   4.6 $$

East 50s | 1078 First Ave. (59th St.)
212-784-0800 | www.ilvalentinonyc.com

"**Warm and welcoming**", this East Midtown Italian draws locals with its "**fantastic**" brick-oven pizzas, "**delicious**" pastas (including half portions) and "**elegant**" wine selection; the "**casual**" Tuscan-like feel further explains its appeal as the "**perfect neighborhood spot**" for the "**whole family.**"

IMPERO CAFFÈ | Italian   ∇ 4.2   3.9   4.2 $$$

Chelsea | INNSIDE New York | 132 W. 27th St. (bet. 6th & 7th Aves.)
917-409-5171 | www.imperorestaurants.com

Chef Scott Conant's all-day Italian at Chelsea's Innside New York hotel provides an upmarket menu starring "**heavenly**" housemade pastas and his "**signature**" ragu; accessed via a glass staircase leading below street level, the "**airy**" "**modern**" space works for anything from "**a business meal to a romantic dinner.**"

INAKAYA | Japanese   4.0   3.8   4.0 $$$

West 40s | NY Times Bldg. | 231 W. 40th St. (bet. 7th & 8th Aves.)
212-354-2195 | www.inakayany.com

It's always "**showtime**" at this "**high-drama**" Japanese robatayaki specialist in the NY Times building, where staffers dish out "**grilled delights**" (plus "**swanky sushi**") while engaging in ritualized "**yelling and screaming**"; however, all the "**fun**" – which is most intense at the robata counter – can add up to "**big bucks.**"

INDAY | Indian   ∇ 4.3   3.9   4.0 $

Flatiron | 1133 Broadway (26th St.)
917-521-5012 | www.indaynyc.com

This counter-serve Flatiron Indian offers build-your-own rice, grain and veggie bowls for a "**relatively healthy**" fix; a sleek setup with both communal and two-top seating means it's not just for takeout.

NEW **INDIAN ACCENT** | Indian   4.7   4.5   4.7 $$$$

West 50s | Le Parker Meridien | 123 W. 56th St. (6th Ave.)
212-842-8070 | www.indianaccent.com

You'll "**completely change**" the way you look at Indian dining at this contemporary Parker Meridien offshoot of a New Delhi original, which "**kicks it up several notches**" with "**exceptionally creative**" prix fixe menus; it's undeniably "**expensive, but totally worth it**" for an "**elegant**" culinary "**adventure.**"

INDOCHINE | French/Vietnamese   4.3   4.2   4.0 $$$
Greenwich Village | 430 Lafayette St. (bet. Astor Pl. & 4th St.)
212-505-5111 | www.indochinenyc.com

Ever "**sexy**" – even "**timeless**" – this "**'80s hot spot**" opposite the Public Theater still lures "**attractive thin**" folk with "**on-target**" French-Vietnamese fare served in "**exotic**" digs à la 1930s Saigon; perhaps its "**elegance is slightly worn**", but the "**people-watching**" is as stellar as ever.

NEW INSA KOREAN BBQ | Korean   ▽ 4.3   4.3   4.0 $$
Gowanus | 328 Douglass St. (4th Ave.) | Brooklyn
718-855-2620 | www.insabrooklyn.com

"**Particularly great for groups**", this Gowanus Korean BBQ spot is furnished with communal tables for "**awesome**" grill-your-own spreads washed down with "**outstanding cocktails**" and "**handcrafted soju**"; the mood is "**low-key hip**", and post-meal the private karaoke rooms are "**a hoot.**"

IPPUDO | Japanese/Noodle Shop   4.5   3.9   3.9 $$
Greenwich Village | 65 Fourth Ave. (bet. 9th & 10th Sts.) | 212-388-0088
West 50s | 321 W. 51st St. (bet. 8th & 9th Aves.) | 212-974-2500
www.ippudony.com

"**Rich**", "**category-defining**" ramen and "**incredible**" pork buns make for "**insanely packed**" conditions (and "**ridiculously long waits**") at these Japanese joints; digs are "**more spacious**" in Midtown, while the Village original is "**darker**" with "**interesting**" Asian-inspired decor, but expect a "**warm**", "**shouted**" greeting at both.

ISABELLA'S | American/Mediterranean   4.0   3.9   3.9 $$
West 70s | 359 Columbus Ave. (77th St.)
212-724-2100 | www.isabellas.com

"**Convenient**" for a "**post Museum of Natural History**" meal, this "**UWS staple**" delivers "**dependable**" American-Mediterranean fare for "**reasonable**" sums; "**go early**" if you want a seat on the "**large**" sidewalk patio, because the "**light, airy**" interior can feel a bit "**frantic**", especially during brunch.

ISLE OF CAPRI | Italian   4.1   3.7   4.1 $$$
East 60s | 1028 Third Ave. (61st St.)
212-223-9430 | www.isleofcapriny.com

A "**little slice of Italy**" near Bloomingdale's, this "**throwback**" Italian has been serving "**classic**" red-sauce fare via "**old-world**" staffers since 1955; OK, so it's "**nothing exciting**", but the "**rustic**" trattorialike setting is "**cozy**", and it's "**been around forever**" – with a "**loyal following**" – for "**good reason.**"

I SODI | Italian   4.6   3.8   4.2 $$$
West Village | 105 Christopher St. (bet. Bleecker & Hudson Sts.)
212-414-5774 | www.isodinyc.com

"**Incredible pastas**" and other "**truly authentic**" Tuscan dishes are "**made with love**" at this "**quaint**" West Villager, where the "**well-put-together wine list**" and "**superb**" Negronis boost the "**neighborly**" vibes; since it's "**always busy**", the "**only drawback**" is a "**squished**" space where it's "**tough to get a table.**"

ITHAKA | Greek/Seafood   4.2   3.7   4.1 $$

East 80s | 308 E. 86th St. (bet. 1st & 2nd Aves.)
212-628-9100 | www.ithakarestaurant.com

"**Neighborhood tavernas**" don't get much more "**relaxed**" than this "**quiet**" Yorkville Greek where the "**honest**" food and "**wonderful grilled fish**" channel Santorini – or at least "**Astoria**"; maybe the whitewashed setting could be "**spiffed up**", but thankfully the tables are "**far enough apart**" and service is "**attentive.**"

I TRULLI | Italian   4.3   4.0   4.2 $$$

Murray Hill | 122 E. 27th St. (bet. Lexington & Park Ave. S.)
212-481-7372 | www.itrulli.com

"**An old standby**", this Murray Hill Southern Italian purveys a trulli "**special**" Puglian menu in "**rustic**" quarters with a "**crackling**" fireplace and an "**expansive**" garden; "**smooth**" service and "**costly**" tabs complete the picture; P.S. it's now adjoined by Nic & Dora's, a quick-serve sub shop.

IVAN RAMEN | Japanese/Noodle Shop   4.1   3.4   3.7 $$

Lower East Side | 25 Clinton St. (bet. Houston & Stanton Sts.) |
646-678-3859

IVAN RAMEN SLURP SHOP | Japanese/Noodle Shop

West 40s | Gotham West Mkt. | 600 11th Ave. (bet. 44th & 45th Sts.) |
212-582-7942
www.ivanramen.com

"**Master**" chef Ivan Orkin "**brings Tokyo to NYC**" with his namesakes where "**interesting**" takes on traditional ramen yield "**soul-satisfying**" bowls; the LES flagship is "**small but comfortable**" with "**funky**" Japanese pop decor and a back patio, while the Hell's Kitchen counter has communal tables – but both get "**very busy.**"

NEW **IZI** | Japanese   —   —   — $$$$

West 40s | W Times Square | 1567 Broadway (47th St.)
212-918-1405 | www.izinewyork.com

Tucked into Blue Fin inside the W Times Square, this upscale Japanese izakaya complements sushi with group-friendly selections (mini lobster rolls, shellfish towers). The polished wooden space is equally focused on drinks, including hard-to-find Japanese and American whiskeys and sakes.

JACKSON DINER | Indian   3.9   3.1   3.5 $$

Bellerose | 256-01 Hillside Ave. (256th St.) | Queens | 718-343-7400
Jackson Heights | 37-47 74th St. (bet. 37th Ave. & 37th Rd.) | Queens |
718-672-1232
www.jacksondiner.com

"**Cheap and tasty**" eats earn these "**spartan**" Indians "**a loyal following**" among fans of "**well-seasoned**" "**comfort**" cooking; the decades-old Jackson Heights original is the "**favorite**", but both host lunch buffets that are "**especially noteworthy**" for "**value.**"

JACK'S STIR BREW COFFEE | Coffee   ▽ 4.2   3.6   4.0 $

South Street Seaport | 222 Front St. (bet. Beekman St. & Peck Slip) |
212-227-7631
NEW **TriBeCa** | 2 Sixth Ave. (bet. Walker & White Sts.) | 212-519-6600
West Village | 138 W. 10th St. (bet. Greenwich Ave. & Waverly Pl.) |
212-929-0821

continued

West Village | 10 Downing St. (6th Ave.) | 212-929-6011
www.jacksstirbrew.com

The pioneering stir-brew technique and signature Fair Trade roast yield a "**rich and smooth**" "**cup o' joe**" at these "**cozy**" cafes; "**fresh-baked**" vegan treats add incentive to stay and "**chill**" if you can "**snag a seat.**"

JACK'S WIFE FREDA | American   4.2   3.7   3.9 $$

SoHo | 224 Lafayette St. (Spring St.) | 212-510-8550
West Village | 50 Carmine St. (Bedford St.) | 646-669-9888
www.jackswifefreda.com

"**Simple but delicious**" American fare gets a "**modern**" and often "**Mediterranean spin**" at these "**well-priced**" bistros, making them a "**pretty-people**" favorite; they're especially "**sceney**" at brunch ("**if you can get in, you've made it in life**") when the "**cozy**" digs fill up fast.

JACK THE HORSE TAVERN | American   4.2   3.9   4.0 $$

Brooklyn Heights | 66 Hicks St. (Cranberry St.) | Brooklyn
718-852-5084 | www.jackthehorse.com

A "**cozy, taverny**" vibe, "**terrific cocktails**" and "**upscale**" American comfort fare delivered by a "**cheerful**" crew make a "**neighborhood go-to**" of this Brooklyn Heights "**hideaway**"; some find the menu "**limited**" and "**slightly pricey**", but all welcome the next-door Oyster Room dispensing bivalves and small plates.

JACOB'S PICKLES | Southern   4.2   3.8   3.9 $$

West 80s | 509 Amsterdam Ave. (bet. 84th & 85th Sts.)
212-470-5566 | www.jacobspickles.com

"**Gigantic portions**" of "**serious comfort food**" like "**life-changing**" fried chicken, biscuits and pickles have fans saying "**calories be damned**" at this "**upbeat**" UWS Southern; "**darn good cocktails**" are another reason the "**young crowd**" keeps the place "**packed**" (especially during the "**unbelievable**" brunch).

JACQUES | French   3.9   3.6   3.9 $$$

East 80s | 206 E. 85th St. (bet. 2nd & 3rd Aves.) | 212-327-2272 |
www.jacquesbrasserie.com
NoLita | 20 Prince St. (bet. Elizabeth & Mott Sts.) | 212-966-8886 |
www.jacques1534.com

"**Don't-miss**" mussels stand out on the "**simple menu**" at these "**traditional**" French brasseries; though a few find the settings "**old-fashioned**" and "**noisy**", the "**reasonable**" pricing is fine as is; P.S. the NoLita branch has a downstairs cocktail bar called Shorty.

JACQUES TORRES CHOCOLATE | Dessert   4.6   3.8   4.0 $

East 50s | 110 E. 57th St. (bet. Lexington & Park Aves.) | 646-852-6624
East 60s | 1186 Third Ave. (69th St.) | 212-204-7040
Hudson Square | 350 Hudson St. (bet. Charlton & King Sts.) | 212-414-2462
NoHo | 327 Lafayette St. (bet. Bleecker & Houston Sts.) | 646-370-4719
West 50s | Rockefeller Ctr. | 30 Rockefeller Plaza (bet. 49th & 50th Sts.) |
212-664-1804
West 70s | 285 Amsterdam Ave. (bet. 73rd & 74th Sts.) | 212-787-3256
Dumbo | 62 Water St. (Front St.) | Brooklyn | 718-875-1269

"**Chocolate lovers**" reach "**nirvana**" at Jacques Torres' shops where the "**rich, silky**" hot chocolate (the Wicked is "**to die for**"), "**killer**" cookies and "**artfully decorated**" truffles "**redefine the description of decadent**"; seats are "**limited**" and prices "**high**", but it's the "**ultimate guilty pleasure**" so "**just savor it.**"

	FOOD	DECOR	SERVICE	COST

JAIYA | Thai — 4.2 — 3.9 — 3.8 — $$

East 80s | 1553 Second Ave. (bet. 80th & 81st Sts.) | 212-717-8877
Murray Hill | 396 Third Ave. (28th St.) | 212-889-1330
www.jaiya.com

Whether you prefer "**spicy**" or "**incendiary**", these East Side Thais offer "**authentic**" Siamese food running the gamut from standards to "**challenging, take-no-hostages**" dishes; "**decent**" price points trump the "**noisy**" settings and less-than-stellar service.

JAKE'S STEAKHOUSE | Steak — 4.3 — 3.9 — 4.1 — $$$

Fieldston | 6031 Broadway (242nd St.) | Bronx
718-581-0182 | www.jakessteakhouse.com

"**Scenic views**" of Van Cortlandt Park make the "**Manhattan-quality**" steaks taste even juicier at this Fieldston chophouse where the service is "**professional**" and the beer selection "**vast**"; although "**expensive**", it's "**cheaper than the city**", and there's evening "**valet parking**" to boot.

JAMES | American — 4.4 — 4.0 — 4.1 — $$

Prospect Heights | 605 Carlton Ave. (St Marks Ave.) | Brooklyn
718-942-4255 | www.jamesrestaurantny.com

"**Creative**" American fare with a "**local**" focus matches with an "**awesome**" drink list at this "**charming**" Prospect Heights haunt also known for its "**top-notch**" burgers; quartered in "**welcoming**" whitewashed-brick digs, it's "**convenient to BAM**" and the Barclays Center, but also a local brunch magnet.

JAMS | Californian — 3.8 — 3.8 — 3.8 — $$$

West 50s | 1 Hotel Central Park | 1414 Sixth Ave. (58th St.)
212-703-2007 | www.jamsrestaurant.nyc

Jonathan Waxman's revival of his '80s-era Californian gets mixed reviews ("**delish**" vs. "**meh**"), though most agree the "**famous**" roast chicken is "**as good as you've heard**"; a "**lovely**" airy space in Midtown's 1 Hotel Central Park and "**fun bar area**", are reasons to hope he works out the "**kinks.**"

JANE | American — 4.2 — 3.7 — 4.0 — $$

Greenwich Village | 100 W. Houston St. (bet. LaGuardia Pl. & Thompson St.)
212-254-7000 | www.janerestaurant.com

The "**girl-next-door**" of Village restaurants, this "**reliable**" American turns out "**solid**" cooking in "**warm**" surrounds watched over by a "**low-key**" staff; its "**unassuming**" vibe during the week changes completely during the "**always packed**" brunch – a "**noisy**" but "**not-to-be-missed**" affair.

JAPONICA | Japanese — 4.4 — 3.7 — 4.2 — $$$

Greenwich Village | 90 University Pl. (12th St.)
212-243-7752 | www.japonicanyc.com

A Village "**fave**" for decades, this circa-1978 Japanese is ever-"**dependable**" for "**generous**" cuts of "**quality**" sushi ("**fresh is the magic word**") served by "**accommodating**" staffers; it's "**not ridiculously expensive**" ("**though it could be**"), so the "**tight**" quarters are typically "**busy.**"

JEAN-GEORGES | French — 4.8 — 4.7 — 4.8 — $$$$

West 60s | Trump Int'l Hotel | 1 Central Park W. (61st St.)
212-299-3900 | www.jean-georgesrestaurant.com

"**Time after time**", Jean-Georges Vongerichten's CPW flagship "**lives up to its billing**" with "**exquisite**" New French cuisine that "**dazzles your palate**" served "**with balletlike precision**" in "**a serene, luxurious**" setting that requires a jacket; it'll cost a "**king's ransom**" to settle the tab, but those "**willing to splurge**" can count on an "**unforgettable**" meal.

JEAN-GEORGES' NOUGATINE | French   4.7   4.4   4.6 $$$

West 60s | Trump Int'l Hotel | 1 Central Park W. (61st St.)
212-299-3900 | www.jean-georgesrestaurant.com

"**Jean-Georges style**" extends to its "**less formal**" but "**still stellar**" front dining area, known for "**superlative**" New French fare and "**on-point**" service in a "**smart**" setting with a "**lovely**" terrace; "**substantial savings**" over the main room include a prix fixe lunch that's "**an outstanding deal.**"

JEEPNEY | Filipino   ▽ 3.9   3.6   3.7 $$$

East Village | 201 First Ave. (bet. 12th & 13th Sts.)
212-533-4121 | www.jeepneynyc.com

You can "**be as adventurous (or as cautious) as you want**" at this "**dope**" East Village gastropub offering "**equal parts daring and gourmet**" takes on traditional Filipino comfort food; a "**knowledgeable**" crew can help guide "**neophytes**" through the menu, and the colorful decor (e.g. pin-up photos) keeps the space "**interesting.**"

THE JEFFREY CRAFT BEER | Pub Food   ▽ 4.2   3.7   4.0 $$
& BITES

East 60s | 311 E. 60th St. (bet. 1st & 2nd Aves.)
212-355-2337 | www.thejeffreynyc.com

A "**carefully curated**" lineup of craft brews lures "**beer lovers**" to this "**hip**" UES pub beside the Queensboro Bridge, which also offers "**surprisingly great**" bar food (burgers to oysters); the "**cool vibe**" in its tumbledown-chic space extends to the back garden filled with picnic tables.

JEFFREY'S GROCERY | American   4.4   4.1   4.1 $$$

West Village | 172 Waverly Pl. (Christopher St.)
646-398-7630 | www.jeffreysgrocery.com

"**Totally casual**" and "**charming**", Gabe Stulman's West Village American offers a "**tight menu**" in close quarters, with a "**focus on fresh fish done well**" and "**tasty oysters**"; "**one heck of a brunch**" seals the deal, making this local spot a "**great find.**"

JEWEL BAKO | Japanese   4.4   4.2   4.2 $$$

East Village | 239 E. Fifth St. (bet. 2nd & 3rd Aves.)
212-979-1012 | www.jewelbakosushi.com

"**Casually elegant**" and "**expensively**" priced, this bamboo-lined East Village Japanese slices a "**flawless symphony**" of "**incredibly fresh fish**"; for best results, insiders "**sit at the sushi bar**" and go the omakase route, though no matter where you land, owners Jack and Grace Lamb "**really take care of you.**"

J.G. MELON | Pub Food   4.1   3.4   3.7 $$

East 70s | 1291 Third Ave. (74th St.) | 212-744-0585
Greenwich Village | 89 MacDougal St. (Bleecker St.) | 212-460-0900

"**Now and forever**", this circa-1972 UES "**preppy haven**" is a "**fixture**" where the "**classic burgers**", "**addictive cottage fries**" and "**mob scene**" are as much a "**tradition**" as the cash-only policy"; the separately owned Village outpost "**authentically replicates**" the menu, and "**you can usually get a table without waiting.**"

JING FONG | Chinese   4.1   3.2   3.3 $$

Chinatown | 20 Elizabeth St. (bet. Bayard & Canal Sts.)
212-964-5256 | www.jingfongny.com

Set in a "**football field–sized**" hall, this "**bustling**" Chinatown Cantonese rolls
out "**delectable**" dim sum "**à la Hong Kong**" on "**quickly moving carts**"
propelled by "**brusque**" staffers; it's "**crowded at peak hours**", a "**hectic
madhouse**" on weekends and "**affordable**" all the time.

JIN RAMEN | Japanese/Noodle Shop   4.3   3.6   3.8 $

Morningside Heights | 3183 Broadway (bet. 125th St. & Tiemann Pl.) |
646-559-2862
West 80s | 462 Amsterdam Ave. (82nd St.) | 646-657-0755
www.jinramen.com

"**Slurp-alicious**" bowls of hand-pulled noodles will "**warm you up**" at these
"**inexpensive**" ramen shops where the "**limited**" menu is dispatched in
"**timely**" fashion; the wood-lined spaces are "**small and cramped**", so prepare
for a "**wait at peak times.**"

JOE | Coffee   4.1   3.3   3.9 $

Chelsea | 405 W. 23rd St. (9th Ave.) | 212-206-0669
Chelsea | 131 W. 21st St. (bet. 6th & 7th Aves.) | 212-924-7400
East 40s | 44 Grand Central Terminal (Lexington Ave.) | 212-661-8580
East 70s | 1045 Lexington Ave. (75th St.) | 212-988-2500
Greenwich Village | 9 E. 13th St. (bet. 5th Ave. & University Pl.) |
212-924-3300
Greenwich Village | 37 E. Eighth St. (University Pl.) | 212-466-2800
Morningside Heights | 550 W. 120th St. (B'way) | 212-924-7400
West 60s | 187 Columbus Ave. (68th St.) | 212-877-0244
West 80s | 514 Columbus Ave. (85th St.) | 212-875-0100
West Village | 141 Waverly Pl. (Gay St.) | 212-924-6750
www.joetheartofcoffee.com

"**Cheerful**" baristas whip up "**high-quality**" coffee drinks at this
"**unpretentious**" mini-chain that also serves a "**small selection of nice
pastries**"; the settings are "**unassuming**", though Flatiron's Pro Shop offers
classes and the chance to sample "**beans from guest roasters.**"

JOE ALLEN | American   3.9   3.8   4.0 $$$

West 40s | 326 W. 46th St. (bet. 8th & 9th Aves.)
212-581-6464 | www.joeallenrestaurant.com

The "**ultimate**" Theater District haunt, this "**clubby**" American has been
turning out "**consistently tasty**" pub grub ("**terrific burgers**") since "**forever**";
posters of "**famous Broadway failures**" line the space and a long bar offers
"**serious**" cocktails and "**great people-watching**" ("**look, there's Liza**").

JOE & PAT'S | Italian/Pizza   4.4   3.2   3.7 $$

Castleton Corners | 1758 Victory Blvd. (bet. Manor Rd. & Winthrop Pl.) |
Staten Island | 718-981-0887

It's all about the "**deliciously thin, crispy**" pizzas at this Castleton Corners
"**staple**" that's been dishing up "**delicious**" Italian family meals for "**generations**"
of Staten Island folks; there's "**not much atmosphere**" to speak of, but "**fast**"
service and modest tabs go a long way.

JOE'S GINGER | Chinese   4.1   2.9   3.5 $$

Chinatown | 25 Pell St. (Mott St.)
212-285-0999 | www.joeginger.com

"**Slightly slicker**" and "**less crazy**" than its nearby sibling, Joe's Shanghai, this

C-town contender features the "**same great soup dumplings**", "**rushed service**" and lack of decor; "**individual tables**" and "**less waiting in line**" are additional benefits.

JOE'S PIZZA | Pizza   4.5   2.8   3.6 $

Greenwich Village | 150 E. 14th St. (bet. Irving Pl. & 3rd Ave.) | 212-388-9474
West Village | 7 Carmine St. (bet. Bleecker St. & 6th Ave.) | 212-366-1182
Williamsburg | 216 Bedford Ave. (5th St.) | Brooklyn | 718-388-2216
www.joespizzanyc.com

"**Iconic for a reason**", this local chain delivers "**reliably excellent**" "**old-school**" slices "**straight from the oven**"; "**divey**" surroundings and "**stand-up**" tables mean many take it "**on the go**", but when you want "**classic NY pizza**", it's "**still one of the best.**"

JOE'S SHANGHAI | Chinese   4.2   3.0   3.5 $$

Chinatown | 9 Pell St. (bet. Bowery & Doyers St.) | 212-233-8888
West 50s | 24 W. 56th St. (bet. 5th & 6th Aves.) | 212-333-3868
Flushing | 136-21 37th Ave. (bet. Main & Union Sts.) | Queens | 718-539-3838
www.joeshanghairestaurants.com

"**Delicate, savory and fun to eat**", the "**signature**" soup dumplings at these Chinese "**staples**" are "**justly famous**"; trade-offs include "**long lines**", "**perfunctory service**" and "**no atmosphere**", yet they're "**always packed for a reason.**"

JOHN BROWN SMOKEHOUSE | BBQ   4.3   3.1   3.5 $$

Long Island City | 10-43 44th Dr. (bet. 10th & 11th Sts.) | Queens
347-617-1120 | www.johnbrownseriousbbq.com

"**No-nonsense**" BBQ (including "**awesome burnt ends**") is the specialty of this Kansas City–style joint in Long Island City that also provides "**plentiful sides**" and a "**great craft beer selection**"; it's a "**simple setup**", i.e. you "**order at the counter and pick up your tray when it's ready.**"

JOHN DORY OYSTER BAR | Seafood   4.2   3.9   3.8 $$$

NoMad | Ace Hotel | 1196 Broadway (29th St.)
212-792-9000 | www.thejohndory.com

"**A must for oyster lovers**", this "**boisterous**" seafood spot from April Bloomfield and Ken Friedman (The Spotted Pig) rolls out "**fabulous**" bivalves and "**tasty**" small plates in a bright, "**hip**" space in the NoMad's happening Ace Hotel; yes, it can be a "**splurge**", but fans affirm it's always a "**treat.**"

JOHN'S OF 12TH STREET | Italian   4.1   3.5   4.0 $$

East Village | 302 E. 12th St. (2nd Ave.)
212-475-9531 | www.johnsof12thstreet.com

"**Upholding the art of Italian cooking**" since 1908, this East Village "**institution**" endures thanks to "**no-nonsense**" red-sauce meals (plus some vegan selections), all at "**fair prices**"; no credit cards and "**nothing-fancy**" decor – think Chianti bottles and "**melted candle wax**" – add to the "**time-warp**" vibe.

JOHN'S PIZZERIA | Pizza   4.3   3.5   3.7 $$

West 40s | 260 W. 44th St. (bet. 7th & 8th Aves.) | 212-391-7560 |
www.johnspizzerianyc.com
West Village | 278 Bleecker St. (Jones St.) | 212-243-1680 |
www.johnsbrickovenpizza.com

"**True**" NY-style pizza emerges from the coal-fired brick ovens of these separately owned "**bang-for-the-buck**" pie joints; the West Village "institution" is "worth the wait in line" ("forget the decor"), while the "huge" Theater District outlet is set in an old church with "beautiful" stained-glass windows.

JOJO | French   4.4   4.1   4.3 $$$

East 60s | 160 E. 64th St. (bet. Lexington & 3rd Aves.)
212-223-5656 | www.jojorestaurantnyc.com

The French fare is "still heavenly" at this UES "jewel" in the Jean-Georges Vongerichten "crown", backed up by an "excellent" wine list and a "lovely townhouse setting"; the "intimate" rooms prompt "romance aplenty", helping to "makes the prices easier to swallow."

JONES WOOD FOUNDRY | British   4.1   3.9   4.0 $$

East 70s | 401 E. 76th St. (bet. 1st & York Aves.)
212-249-2700 | www.joneswoodfoundry.com

An "inviting" "neighborhood 'haunt'", this Yorkville pub supplies "solid" British staples (think "fish 'n' chips as it should be") chased with a "big selection of craft brews"; the "spot-on" staff and "unhurried" style suit the regulars found in the "lively bar" and garden out back.

JORDANS LOBSTER DOCK | Seafood   4.2   2.8   3.5 $$

Sheepshead Bay | 3165 Harkness Ave. (Plumb 2nd St.) | Brooklyn
718-934-6300 | www.jordanslobster.com

Locals "pretend they're in Maine" at this longtime Sheepshead Bay seafood spot where live lobsters in "big tanks" make for ultra-"fresh" eating; sure, the "decor's as minimal as the service", but tabs aren't high and an on-site retail market means you can "eat your goodies at home."

JOSEPH LEONARD | American   4.3   4.2   4.2 $$$

West Village | 170 Waverly Pl. (Grove St.)
646-429-8383 | www.josephleonard.com

"Original", "deeply satisfying" takes on New American standards draw "super-cool" folks to Gabe Stulman's West Village "neighborhood joint" that ups the ante with open-all-day hours; the "hiply rustic", "lumberjacky" setting is so "tiny" that "crowded" conditions and long "waits" are a given.

JOYA | Thai   4.2   3.7   3.9 $$

Cobble Hill | 215 Court St. (bet. Warren & Wyckoff Sts.) | Brooklyn
718-222-3484

Always "lively", this Cobble Hill Thai attracts "young" throngs with a mix of "solid" food, "cheap" tabs and "sleek" design; "dance-club" acoustics send regulars to the "more peaceful" back garden, but there's no sidestepping the cash-only rule.

JUBILEE | French   4.1   3.8   4.0 $$$

East 50s | 948 First Ave. (bet. 52nd & 53rd Sts.)
212-888-3569 | www.jubileeny.net

A "clientele of a certain age" touts this "longtime" Sutton Place–area bistro as a haven of "relaxed sophistication" that's like a "quick trip to Paris"; it's "not noisy" and the seafood-oriented French fare (including "claim-to-fame" moules) is "tasty", so reservations are recommended.

NEW JUE LAN CLUB | Chinese   ∇ 4.1   4.4   4.2 $$$

Flatiron | 49 W. 20th St. (6th Ave.)
646-524-7409 | www.juelanclub.com

In the old Limelight space, this "elegant" Flatiron Chinese offers "high-end" cooking with modern touches plus a raw bar that "**shouldn't be missed**", sake and a lengthy cocktail list; the "**cool**" bi-level setting is "**on point**" with plush booths, elaborate lighting, and multiple rooms and bars.

JULIANA'S | Pizza   4.7   3.9   4.2 $$

Dumbo | 19 Old Fulton St. (bet. Front & Water Sts.) | Brooklyn
718-596-6700 | www.julianaspizza.com

From "**pizza legend**" Patsy Grimaldi, this "**old-school**" joint turns out "**premium**" pies via a coal oven ("**it's the char!**") in "**casual**" digs beneath the Brooklyn Bridge; since it "**looks like everyone knows**", don't be surprised to see lines "**down the block.**"

JUNGSIK | Korean   4.7   4.5   4.6 $$$$

TriBeCa | 2 Harrison St. (Hudson St.)
212-219-0900 | www.jungsik.kr

"**Each dish is a piece of art**" at this "**high-end**" TriBeCa Korean whose "**meticulously prepared**" fusion bites take "**many twists and turns**" and can be sampled in "**sublime**" yet "**accessible**" tasting menus presented by an "**attentive**" staff; the subtle, "**elegant**" space suits the "**special experience**", though "**you'll pay for it**" when the bill arrives.

JUNIOR'S | Dessert/Diner   3.8   3.4   3.7 $$

West 40s | 1515 Broadway (45th St.) | 212-302-2000
Downtown Brooklyn | 386 Flatbush Ave. Extension (Dekalb Ave.) | Brooklyn | 718-852-5257
www.juniorscheesecake.com

"**World famous**" for its "**stupendous**" cheesecakes, this Brooklyn "**icon**" and its Midtown offshoot also sling a "**huge menu**" of "**decent**" American diner fare, served in "**gigantic portions**" by "**swift**" staffers; sure, the atmosphere's "**frenetic**" and the decor "**bland**", but the "**fair prices**" alone make it "**worth a visit.**"

JUN-MEN | Noodle Shop   ▽   4.4   3.8   4.0 $$

Chelsea | 249 Ninth Ave. (bet. 25th & 26th Sts.)
646-852-6787 | www.junmenramen.com

"**Tasty**", "**flavorful**" ramen is the thing at this "**super-tiny**" Chelsea noodle shop, a "**neighborhood asset**" putting forth traditional (pork or spicy miso) and a couple of thoughtful creations (uni mushroom is a "**treat**"); the "**elegantly spare**" space has an open kitchen dispensing steamed buns and other appetizers that "**excel.**"

JUNOON | Indian   4.3   4.4   4.2 $$$

Flatiron | 27 W. 24th St. (bet. 5th & 6th Aves.)
212-490-2100 | www.junoonnyc.com

You can "**dine like a prince**" at this "**upmarket**" Flatiron "**oasis**" offering "**innovative**" Indian food with "**rich, complex flavors**" in a "**gorgeous**" front lounge and main dining room; tabs are "**higher than average**", but "**precise**" service and a sommelier who "**knows his stuff**" up the appeal.

KAFANA | E European   ▽   4.4   3.7   3.7 $$

East Village | 116 Ave. C (bet. 7th & 8th Sts.)
212-353-8000 | www.kafananyc.com

"**As authentic as it comes**", this East Village Serbian kitchen turns out "**perfectly prepared**" renditions of "**hearty**" meat-centric fare that'll take you right "**back to Belgrade**"; though still a "**best-kept secret**", it's a true "**find**", especially given the "**reasonably priced**" tabs.

KAJITSU | Japanese/Vegetarian   ▽ 4.6   4.2   4.6 $$$$
Murray Hill | 125 E. 39th St. (bet. Lexington & Park Aves.)
212-228-4873 | www.kajitsunyc.com

This wood-lined, "**Zen**"-like Japanese vegetarian in Murray Hill is a "**hushed**" oasis for "**excellent**" ancient Buddhist shojin cuisine, served kaiseki-style at dinner by an "**impeccable**" staff (and priced "**as if it were Harry Winston jewels**"); the more casual first-floor adjunct goes by the name Kokage, and offers non-vegetarian, à la carte dishes for lunch and dinner.

KANG HO DONG BAEKJEONG | Korean   4.4   3.4   4.0 $$$
Murray Hill | 1 E. 32nd St. (5th Ave.)
212-966-9839

You can "**taste the difference**" in the "**top-notch**" meats at this K-town "**winner**" from a South Korea-based chain, where the "**elevated**" BBQ is grilled tableside by "**efficient**" servers; since it's "**so crazy popular**", be ready for "**crowded**" conditions and a "**wait time.**"

KANG SUH | Korean   3.9   3.0   3.3 $$
West 30s | 1250 Broadway (bet. 31st & 32nd Sts.)
212-564-6845 | www.kangsuhnyc.com

"**After-hours**" types tout this 30-plus-year-old Garment Center Korean for its "**authentic**" BBQ, low tabs and "**24/7**" open-door policy; since it's "**not much to look at**" and "**you'll smell like it when you leave**", maybe it's good that the staff "**rushes you through your meal.**"

KANOYAMA | Japanese   4.6   3.8   4.1 $$
East Village | 175 Second Ave. (bet. 11th & 12th Sts.)
212-777-5266 | www.kanoyama.com

The sushi is "**always fresh**" and "**wonderful**" at this no-frills East Village Japanese, where "**unusual**" specials and "**excellent oysters**" are other reasons to go; though not cheap, it's considered a "**pretty good value**" given the "**quality**" – no wonder it's "**frequently full.**"

KAO SOY | Thai   ▽ 4.2   2.6   3.5 $$
Red Hook | 283 Van Brunt St. (Pioneer St.) | Brooklyn
718-875-1155

The namesake noodle dish is a "**must**" at this simple Red Hook stop specializing in "**spicy**" Northern Thai fare highlighted by "**bold**" flavors; "**small**" digs mean there may be a wait during peak hours, but at least prices are "**reasonable.**"

KAPPO MASA | Japanese   ▽ 4.3   4.2   4.2 $$$$
East 70s | 976 Madison Ave. (76th St.)
212-906-7141 | www.kappomasanyc.com

You're "**in the hands of a master**" at chef Masa Takayama's "**serene**" UES Japanese below Gagosian Gallery, where "**delicate**" sushi made from the "**freshest-quality**" fish is offered alongside a diverse array of cooked dishes; "**painfully expensive**" tabs are no surprise given the "**elegant**" surrounds and ritzy zip code.

NEW **KARASU** | Japanese   —   —   — $$$
Fort Greene | Walter's | 166 Dekalb Ave. (Cumberland St.) | Brooklyn
347-223-4811 | www.karasubk.com

Hidden behind a door at Walter's in Fort Greene, this elegant Japanese izakaya serves eclectic contemporary bites to go with sake, whiskey and beautifully presented cocktails. The setting is dark and softly lit, with vinyl records adding to the speakeasy mood.

KASHKAVAL GARDEN | Mediterranean   4.3   3.6   4.1 $$
West 50s | 852 Ninth Ave. (bet. 55th & 56th Sts.)
212-245-1758 | www.kashkavalgarden.com

A "**good first-date place**", this "**casual**" Midtown Med offers a "**wide selection**" of "**terrific**" tapas (plus some "**quality**" fondues), all for "**reasonable**" dough; an "**inviting**" interior and a small, "**under-the-radar**" back garden are other reasons it's a "**local favorite.**"

KAT & THEO | American/Mediterranean   4.1   4.3   4.2 $$$
Flatiron | 5 W. 21st St. (5th Ave.)
212-380-1950 | www.katandtheo.com

"**Cool**" industrial-modern decor "**works well**" with the "**distinctive**", Med inspired plates from an ex elBulli chef at this Flatiron American; the "**informed staff**" oversees the fireplace-equipped space, where the "**vibrant bar scene**" is fueled by "**great craft cocktails.**"

KATI ROLL COMPANY | Indian   4.2   2.9   3.4 $
East 50s | 229 E. 53rd St. (bet. 2nd & 3rd Aves.) | 212-888-1700
Greenwich Village | 99 MacDougal St. (Bleecker St.) | 212-420-6517
West 30s | 49 W. 39th St. (bet. 5th & 6th Aves.) | 212-730-4280
www.thekatirollcompany.com

"**Grab-and-go**" Indian street food is the concept at these counter-service joints specializing in "**tasty**", "**flavorful**" kati wraps stuffed with "**fragrant ingredients**"; "**exceptional value**" keeps them as "**busy as Bombay**" at lunchtime, "**no-decor**" settings notwithstanding.

KATSU-HAMA | Japanese   4.0   3.3   3.6 $$
East 40s | 11 E. 47th St. (bet. 5th & Madison Aves.) | 212-758-5909
West 50s | 43-45 W. 55th St. (bet. 5th & 6th Aves.) | 212-541-7145
www.katsuhama.com

"**Deep-fried comfort food**" in pork-cutlet form is the specialty of these Midtown Japanese tonkatsu parlors where the goods are "**tender and juicy**" and the accompanying sauce, "**addictive**"; "**easy-on-the-pocketbook**" tabs trump "**not much decor**" and "**indifferent**" service.

KATZ'S DELICATESSEN | Deli   4.5   3.1   3.5 $$
Lower East Side | 205 E. Houston St. (Ludlow St.)
212-254-2246 | www.katzsdelicatessen.com

A "**legendary**" LES landmark since 1888, this cash-only "**bucket lister**" remains the "**gold standard**" for "**sky-high**" pastrami sandwiches and other "**real-deal**" Jewish deli eats; resembling a "**high school cafeteria**", the "**crowded, hectic**" space is "**nothing to talk about**", but for a "**classic NYC**" experience it still has many joining *When Harry Met Sally* fans in shouting "**yes, yes, yes!**"

KEENS STEAKHOUSE | Steak   4.5   4.4   4.4 $$$
West 30s | 72 W. 36th St. (bet. 5th & 6th Aves.)
212-947-3636 | www.keens.com

The "**granddaddy of all NYC steakhouses**", this circa-1885 Midtown "**temple to meat**" remains "**rock solid**", with "**sinful**" "*Flintstones*-size" mutton chops and other "**succulent**" slabs of beef in "**masculine**" "**museum**"-like surrounds with "**lines upon lines**" of antique pipes on the ceiling; it's "**not for the weak of wallet", but "**welcoming**" service and an "**endless**" scotch selection are other reasons you "**won't regret splurging.**"

KEFI | Greek   4.1   3.5   3.7 $$
West 80s | 505 Columbus Ave. (bet. 84th & 85th Sts.)
212-873-0200 | www.michaelpsilakis.com

For "**generous**" portions of "**well-prepared**" Greek comfort food at "**über-reasonable prices**", locals head to this "**relaxed**" UWS "**staple**"; while service can seem "**bewildered**" and the "**too-close-for-comfort**" main room can get "**noisy**" (downstairs is "**quieter**"), most still think it's "**very good indeed.**"

KELLARI TAVERNA | Greek/Seafood   4.2   4.1   4.1 $$$
West 40s | 19 W. 44th St. (bet. 5th & 6th Aves.)
212-221-0144 | www.kellariny.com

"**Mouthwatering**" displays of "**fresh fish on ice**" beckon at this "**sophisticated**" Midtown Greek seafood spot offering "**next-flight-to-Athens**"-quality cooking; though some menu items are "**pricey**", the pre-theater prix fixe is a "**steal**" – and "**efficient**" staffers "**make sure you make your curtain.**"

KESTE PIZZA E VINO | Pizza   4.4   3.3   3.7 $$
West Village | 271 Bleecker St. (Morton St.)
212-243-1500 | www.kestepizzeria.com

"**Blow-you-away**" Neapolitan pizzas ("**oh, that crust!**") with "**fresh, flavorful toppings**" are the draw at this "**popular**", "**no-frills**" West Village pizzeria; but while the goods may be "**hard to beat**", trade-offs include "**so-so service**", no reservations and "**super-cramped**" digs.

KHE-YO | Laotian   4.3   4.0   4.1 $$
TriBeCa | 157 Duane St. (bet. Hudson St. & W. B'way)
212-587-1089 | www.kheyo.com

The "**underexposed, underappreciated**" cuisine of Laos gets its due at this Marc Forgione–backed TriBeCan where the "**helpful**" staff guides diners through the "**bold**", "**adventurous**" menu; the "**down-to-earth**" space has a "**hip**" feel, and there's a daytime cafe, Khe-Yosk, that serves banh mi sandwiches.

KIKI'S | Greek   ▽ 4.5   3.7   4.1 $$
Lower East Side | 130 Division St. (Orchard St.)
646-882-7052

Behind the Chinese-characters signage, this LES hang is an "**amazing Greek find**" where "**truly excellent**" taverna staples ("**plan to share**") arrive "**at a decent price**" in an "**authentic rustic**" setting; since reservations aren't taken and "**it fills up fast**", waits can be "**significant.**"

NEW **KING** | Mediterranean   —   —   — $$
Hudson Square | 18 King St. (6th Ave.)
917-825-1618 | www.kingrestaurantnyc.com

Run by expats from London, this Hudson Square Mediterranean presents a concise daily menu of seasonal plates that take a rustic slant. The light-filled corner digs sport whitewashed brick walls, a hardwood floor and a front bar mixing house cocktails with names like Marquis de Sade.

KINGS' CARRIAGE HOUSE | American   4.3   4.6   4.4 $$$
East 80s | 251 E. 82nd St. (bet. 2nd & 3rd Aves.)
212-734-5490 | www.kingscarriagehouse.com

Best known for its "**charming**" setting, this Upper East Side "**hideaway**" is nestled in a "**romantic**" townhouse "**lovingly furnished**" like an "**English country manor**"; the prix fixe–only New American menu is also "**excellent**", with "**gracious**" service, "**quiet**" decibels and "**dainty**" afternoon tea as bonuses.

KINGS COUNTY IMPERIAL | Chinese ▽ 4.4 4.1 4.2 $$

Williamsburg | 20 Skillman Ave. (Meeker Ave.) | Brooklyn
718-610-2000 | www.kingscoimperial.com

Local ingredients go into the "**delicious**", "**eclectic**" Chinese fare at this "**lively**" Williamsburg hangout, where a "**warm**" crew serves family-style plates and tiki-inspired cocktails; decked in mahogany, the "**cool**" digs feature red booths, a curved bar and laser-cut light boxes with vintage Chinese landscapes.

NEW KINGSLEY | American/French 4.8 4.8 4.8 $$$

East Village | 190 Ave. B (12th St.)
212-674-4500 | www.kingsleynyc.com

Fit "**for foodies or fun times**", this "**sleek**" East Villager "**distinguishes itself**" as "**passionate**" staffers deliver "**masterful**" French-American cuisine that takes market ingredients "**to another level**"; add "**fancy infused cocktails**" from the "**spectacular**" bar, and those who "**can't get enough**" confide it's a "**best-kept secret – but not for long.**"

KI SUSHI | Japanese 4.5 4.0 4.3 $$

Cobble Hill | 122 Smith St. (bet. Dean & Pacific Sts.) | Brooklyn
718-935-0575

This "**intimate**" Cobble Hill Japanese serves "**exceptional**" sushi including "**memorable signature rolls**" made with "**high-quality fish**" in a "**modern**", "**cheerful**" setting; "**extremely hospitable**" service adds to the reasons it's a "**consistent pleaser.**"

KITCHENETTE | Southern 4.0 3.7 4.0 $$

Morningside Heights | 1272 Amsterdam Ave. (bet. 122nd & 123rd Sts.)
212-531-7600 | www.kitchenetterestaurant.com

Southern "**comfort**" cooking is the specialty of this "**kitschy**" "**country farmhouse**"–inspired standby in Morningside Heights where both the menu and the portions are "**big**"; the "**cutesy**", "**tiny**" digs can feel "**cramped**", but "**friendly**" service and "**fair prices**" help compensate.

KNICKERBOCKER BAR & GRILL | American 4.1 3.9 4.2 $$$

Greenwich Village | 33 University Pl. (9th St.)
212-228-8490 | www.knickerbockerbarandgrill.com

"**Time warps**" don't get more "**lovable**" than this 1977-vintage Villager, an "**old-school**" source of "**solid**", "**no-surprises**" American fare highlighted by "**gargantuan**" steaks; though the "**clubby**" digs are a tad "**tattered**", "**warm**" service and "**surprisingly good**" weekend jazz make it a "**neighborhood favorite.**"

KOA | Asian ▽ 4.2 4.4 4.2 $$

Flatiron | 12 W. 21st St. (5th Ave.)
212-388-5736 | www.koanyc.com

Yuji Wakiya (aka "**Iron Chef Chinese**") crafts "**delicious**", "**Nouvelle**" Asian cuisine at this "**sophisticated and sexy**" Flatiron kitchen dispensing Japanese-inspired noodle dishes, small plates and sushi; a "**beautifully designed**" space and "**knowledgeable**" service are other reasons it's "**recommended.**"

	FOOD	DECOR	SERVICE	COST

KOI | Japanese ⎯ 4.4 4.2 4.0 $$$
Hudson Square | Trump Soho Hotel | 246 Spring St. (bet. 6th Ave. &
Varick St.) | 212-842-4550
West 40s | Bryant Park Hotel | 40 W. 40th St. (bet. 5th & 6th Aves.) |
212-921-3330
www.koirestaurant.com

"**Pretty people**" and other "**trendy**" types nibble "**Japanese delicacies**"
(including "**beautiful**" sushi and "**otherworldly crispy rice**") at these "**glitzy**"
hotel "**scenes**"; while the "**buzzing**" vibe can feel "**far too loud**" to some,
and you don't want to get "**stuck with the bill**", most say it's "**still hitting
all the right notes.**"

NEW KOSAKA | Japanese ∇ 4.6 4.6 4.6 $$$$
West Village | 220 W. 13th St. (bet. Greenwich & 7th Aves.)
212-727-1709 | www.kosakanyc.com

From a former chef of Jewel Bako, this West Village Japanese offers
"**exceptional**" multicourse dining options including omakase featuring
"**top-quality**" sushi only or an "**impressive**" chef's tasting menu adding
cooked dishes; the "**simple, comfortable**" surrounds are elevated by an
"**excellent**" staff, making it a "**perfect escape.**"

NEW KOSSAR'S BAGELS & BIALYS | Bagels 4.3 3.2 3.7 $
Lower East Side | 367 Grand St. (bet. Essex & Norfolk Sts.)
212-473-4810 | www.kossars.com

Back after a renovation, this circa-1936 LES "**classic**" is a "**carb-fueled
heaven**" thanks to "**old-world good**" bialys and bagels offered alongside
housemade cream cheese and smoked fish for a "**taste of real NYC**"; the
"**bright**" space has a window with views of the baking action.

KO SUSHI | Japanese 4.1 3.4 4.1 $$
East 70s | 1329 Second Ave. (70th St.) | 212-439-1678
East 80s | 1619 York Ave. (85th St.) | 212-772-8838
www.newkosushi.com

These "**no-frills**", separately owned Japanese Upper Eastsiders furnish a
"**neighborhood**" following with "**tasty**" raw fish that's "**priced right**"; "**quick**"
service makes the "**cafeteria**"-like settings more palatable, though aesthetes
recommend the "**reliable delivery.**"

KOUZAN | Japanese 4.1 3.7 4.1 $$
West 90s | 685 Amsterdam Ave. (93rd St.)
212-280-8099 | www.kouzanjapanese.com

"**Well-prepared**", "**traditional**" sushi and more "**inventive rolls**" distinguish
this "**reliable**" Upper West Side Japanese where the "**pleasant**" staff instills
a "**warm atmosphere**"; throw in tabs geared to the "**99%**" and no wonder it's
such a "**neighborhood asset.**"

K RICO SOUTH | S American ∇ 4.4 4.0 4.3 $$$
AMERICAN STEAKHOUSE
West 50s | 772 Ninth Ave. (bet. 51st & 52nd Sts.)
212-757-9393 | www.kriconyc.com

"**Very good**" plancha-grilled steaks, including the tomahawk (a "**major
winner**") headline the menu at this Hell's Kitchen South American chophouse;
the sleek, pampas-inspired ambiance, complete with deer skulls, a courtyard
and sidewalk seating, make it a "**great find**" for a pre-theater dinner.

	FOOD	DECOR	SERVICE	COST

KRISTALBELLI | Korean — 4.3 | 4.1 | 4.4 | $$$

West 30s | 8 W. 36th St. (bet. 5th & 6th Aves.)
212-290-2211 | www.kristalbelli.com

An "**elegant**" yet "**modern**" vibe matches the "**high-end**" Korean cuisine offered at this "**classy**" K-town restaurant/lounge where the "**refined**" dishes include meats that diners barbecue on "**cool**", smoke-free crystal grills; "**attentive**" staffers help distract from the "**pricey**" tabs.

KRUPA GROCERY | American — ▽ 4.2 | 3.8 | 3.9 | $$

Windsor Terrace | 231 Prospect Park W. (Windsor Pl.) | Brooklyn
718-709-7098 | www.krupagrocery.com

This "**neighborhood find**" in Windsor Terrace supplies "**tasty**" American fare breakfast through dinner (plus a "**creative brunch**") in an "**unassuming**" space with a back patio; with the "**upbeat**" staff also dispensing "**tasty**" cocktails, it's a "**local secret**" where those in the know "**keep coming back.**"

KUMA INN | Filipino/Thai — ▽ 4.3 | 3.3 | 3.9 | $$

Lower East Side | 113 Ludlow St., 2nd fl. (bet. Delancey & Rivington Sts.)
212-353-8866 | www.kumainn.com

One of NYC's "**best hidden gems**", this "**unusual**" Filipino-Thai accessed up a flight of LES stairs puts out an "**avant-garde**" small-plates menu "**exploding with flavor**"; the "**hole-in-the-wall**" setup is "**tight**" and cash only, but the "**price is right**" and "**BYO makes it even better.**"

KUM GANG SAN | Korean — 4.2 | 3.7 | 3.9 | $$

Flushing | 138-28 Northern Blvd. (bet. Bowne & Union Sts.) | Queens
718-461-0909 | www.kumgangsan.net

This 24/7 "**kitsch**" palace in Flushing slings "**solid**", "**traditional**" Korean BBQ in a "**cavernous**" setting equipped with a waterfall and piano; the decor is a tad "**age-worn**", but "**helpful**" service makes it "**fun**", especially "**for first-timers**" and "**out-of-towners.**"

KUNG FU LITTLE STEAMED BUNS RAMEN | Noodle Shop — 4.4 | 2.6 | 3.5 | $

West 40s | 811 Eighth Ave. (49th St.)
917-388-2555 | www.kungfulittlesteamedbunsramen.com

It's "**kind of a dump**", but this West Midtowner is "**always packed**" thanks to its "**excellent**" roster of hand-cut noodles, "**hearty**" soups and "**super**" dumplings; you'll have "**barely enough table space for the plate**", but the "**bargain prices**" are "**worth the squeeze.**"

KUNJIP | Korean — 4.2 | 3.2 | 3.3 | $$

West 30s | 32 W. 32nd St. (5th Ave.)
212-564-8238 | www.thekunjip.com

Always open and "**always crowded**", this "**popular**" 24/7 K-town venue plies an "**extensive menu**" of "**traditional**" Korean cooking in a "**no-frills**" atmosphere; while seating's "**cramped**" and servers "**rush you out the door**", the "**solid**" chow largely redeems all.

KURUMAZUSHI | Japanese — ▽ 4.6 | 3.3 | 4.1 | $$$$

East 40s | 7 E. 47th St., 2nd fl. (bet. 5th & Madison Aves.)
212-317-2802 | www.kurumazushi.com

The "**ethereal, next-level**" sushi "**couldn't be fresher or more delicious**" at chef Toshihiro Uezu's pioneering Midtown eatery, perched in a "**simple**", second-floor space; tabs may be "**extravagant**", but the prices are "**warranted**" for a "**traditional experience**" on par with "**high-end places in Japan.**"

KYOCHON CHICKEN | Chicken — 4.0 3.4 3.5 $$

Murray Hill | 319 Fifth Ave. (bet. 32nd & 33rd Sts.) | 212-725-9292
Flushing | 156-50 Northern Blvd. (bet. 156th & 157th Sts.) | Queens
718-939-9292 | www.kyochonus.com

Fried chicken gets an "**oh-so-spicy**" Korean spin – and some "**soy-garlic**" inflections – at these "**addictive**" satellites of the global poultry chain; "**modern**" food-court design distracts from the "**small portions**" and tabs that are "**a bit pricey for wings.**"

KYO YA | Japanese — 4.7 4.4 4.6 $$$$

East Village | 94 E. Seventh St., downstairs (1st Ave.)
212-982-4140

At this East Village Japanese in a below-ground space, the Kyoto-style seasonal specialties are "**as good as the finest in Tokyo**" and the reservations-only kaiseki dinners are a "**meal to remember**"; "**wonderful**" servers and calm surroundings are more reasons its admirers spend big and "**leave satisfied.**"

LA BARAKA | French — 4.3 3.9 4.5 $$

Douglaston | 255-09 Northern Blvd. (2 blocks east of Little Neck Pkwy.) | Queens
718-428-1461 | www.labarakarest.com

Renowned for the "**hospitality**" of "**lovely hostess**" Lucette, this Douglaston "**old-timer**" follows through with "**terrific**" Tunisian-accented French fare; though the decor "**needs an update**", tabs are "**reasonable**" and the overall mood definitely "**enjoyable.**"

LA BERGAMOTE | Bakery/French — 4.3 3.7 3.8 $$

Chelsea | 177 Ninth Ave. (20th St.) | 212-627-9010
West 50s | 515 W. 52nd St. (bet. 10th & 11th Aves.) | 212-586-2429
www.labergamotenyc.com

These "**buttery**" patisserie/cafes supply "**dynamite**" French pastries that are "**gorgeous to look at and just as delicious to taste**", along with other savory "**light meals**"; "**neighborhoody**" vibes and "**easy-on-the-wallet**" pricing make up for the "**spare seating.**"

LA BOÎTE EN BOIS | French — 4.1 3.7 4.0 $$$

West 60s | 75 W. 68th St. (bet. Columbus Ave. & CPW)
212-874-2705 | www.laboitenyc.com

A longtime "**pre-theater favorite**" near Lincoln Center, this "**tiny**" French boîte turns out "**classic**" bistro dishes in a "**congenial**" setting overseen by "**fast-moving**" staffers; "**sardine**"-can dimensions, "**old-fashioned**" decor and kinda "**pricey**" tabs come with the territory.

LA BONNE SOUPE | French — 3.9 3.4 3.8 $$

West 50s | 48 W. 55th St. (bet. 5th & 6th Aves.)
212-586-7650 | www.labonnesoupe.com

"**Serviceable**" enough for a "**quick bite**", this longtime Midtown "**pinch hitter**" is best known for its "**divine onion soup**", though the rest of its French bistro menu is certainly "**reliable**"; "**brusque**" service, "**crowded**" conditions and "**no-frills**" looks are blunted by good "**value**" (and a seat on the tiny balcony is a "**treat**").

	FOOD	DECOR	SERVICE	COST

LA CHINE | Chinese 4.4 4.4 4.2 $$$
East 40s | Waldorf Astoria Hotel | 540 Lexington Ave. (bet. 49th & 50th Sts.)
212-872-4913 | www.lachinenyc.com

A "**stunner**", this "**high-style**" Chinese in Midtown's Waldorf Astoria produces a "**wow**"-worthy multiregional menu with "**imaginative**" French accents in an "**elegant**", chandeliered setting; "**solicitous**" service rounds out the "**rewarding**" experience, but be ready for "**a splurge.**"

LA COLOMBE COFFEE ROASTERS | Coffee 4.4 3.8 4.0 $
Chelsea | 601 W. 27th St. (11th Ave.) | 646-885-0677
Financial District | 67 Wall St. (Pearl St.) | 212-220-0415
Greenwich Village | 400 Lafayette St. (4th St.) | 212-677-5834
Hudson Square | 75 Vandam St. (Hudson St.) | 212-929-9699
SoHo | 154 Prince St. (W. B'way) | 646-690-7340
SoHo | 270 Lafayette St. (Prince St.) | 212-625-1717
TriBeCa | 319 Church St. (Lispenard St.) | 212-343-1515
www.lacolombe.com

"**Meccas**" for the "**coffee connoisseur**", these "**friendly**" outposts of the Philly-based artisanal roaster dispense "**strong, smooth**" java and pastries to go; they're seemingly "**always busy**", but the "**lines move pretty quickly**" thanks to the "**efficient**" staff.

LA CONTENTA | Mexican ▽ 4.4 4.2 4.3 $$
Lower East Side | 102 Norfolk St. (bet. Delancey & Rivington Sts.)
212-432-4180 | www.lacontentanyc.com

An "**unexpected**" LES find, this "**intimate**" Mexican shines with "**foodie-worthy**" nachos and other "**delicious**", "**constantly changing**" plates; the "**micro-small**" space has a handful of tables and a small bar mixing "**excellent**" agave-based cocktails and micheladas.

LADURÉE | Bakery/French 4.3 4.3 3.9 $$
East 70s | 864 Madison Ave. (bet. 70th & 71st Sts.) | 646-558-3157
SoHo | 398 W. Broadway (bet. Broome & Spring Sts.) | 646-392-7868
www.laduree.com

"**If you can't get to Paris**", these patisseries from the "**froufrou**" French bakery are sites to "**indulge**" in "**gold-standard**" macarons and other "**first-rate**" sweets, provided you can "**pay up**"; the SoHo branch also serves "**OK**" Gallic staples in an "**elegant**" dining room and "**beautiful**" outdoor courtyard.

NEW **LADYBIRD** | Vegetarian — — — $$$
Greenwich Village | 127 MacDougal St. (3rd St.)
212-475-2246 | www.ladybirdny.com

This modern Village tapas spot embraces vegetarian eating with creative, globally accented fare, plus cocktails in a similarly creative vein. Marble surfaces, plush emerald-green barstools and gilded mirrors are some of the decorous touches.

LADY M CAKE BOUTIQUE | Dessert/Japanese 4.6 3.7 3.8 $
East 70s | 41 E. 78th St. (Madison Ave.) | 212-452-2222
West 40s | 36 W. 40th St. (bet. 5th & 6th Aves.) | 212-452-2222
West 50s | Plaza Food Hall | 1 W. 58th St. (Grand Army Plaza) | 212-452-2222
www.ladym.com

The "**sublime**" mille crêpes gateau (try the "**totally addictive**" green tea version) seems to be made from "**thousands**" of "**delicate**" layers at these "**civilized**" Japanese-influenced cake shops; prices match the "**genteel environment**", and the "**tiny**" UES flagship is also "**lovely for a quick lunch.**"

LADY MENDL'S | Teahouse   4.0   4.4   4.1 $$$

Gramercy Park | Inn at Irving Pl. | 56 Irving Pl. (bet. 17th & 18th Sts.)
212-533-4600 | www.ladymendls.com

Ladies live it up à la "*Downton Abbey*" at this "**mahvelous**" Gramercy tearoom in the Inn at Irving Place where "**excellent**" servers present "**tasty**" sandwiches and sweets along with "**wonderful**" brews in an "**elegant**" Victorian setting; it's "**pricey**", but a "**pampered afternoon**" is the reward.

LA ESQUINA | Mexican   4.3   4.1   3.9 $$$

SoHo | 114 Kenmare St. (bet. Cleveland Pl. & Lafayette St.) | 646-613-7100 | www.esquinanyc.com

CAFE DE LA ESQUINA | Mexican

Williamsburg | 225 Wythe Ave. (3rd St.) | Brooklyn | 718-393-5500 | www.esquinabk.com

"**Straight-up *delicioso***" describes both the food and the scene at this ever-"**trendy**" SoHo Mexican comprising a "**dive**"-like taqueria, casual indoor/outdoor cafe and "**ultracool**", hard-to-access underground grotto; the Williamsburg spin-off set in a "**futuristic retro diner**" comes equipped with a moody back room and "**huge outdoor patio.**"

LAFAYETTE | French   4.3   4.4   4.1 $$$

NoHo | 380 Lafayette St. (Great Jones St.)
212-533-3000 | www.lafayetteny.com

A "**gorgeous**", "**expansive**" space with "**plenty of room to breathe**" lures "**beautiful people**" to this "**bustling**" all-day NoHo cafe that's a showcase for Andrew Carmellini's "**hearty**" French cooking; insiders say it "**shines best at breakfast**", though the front bakery is a "**great pit stop**" for "**delicious bread**" and "**delectable**" pastries any time.

LA FONDA DEL SOL | Spanish   4.1   4.0   4.0 $$$

East 40s | 200 Park Ave. (enter on 44th St. & Vanderbilt Ave.)
212-867-6767 | www.patinagroup.com

Conveniently sited above Grand Central, this reincarnation of a "**classic**" '60s Spaniard offers both a "**lively after-work bar**" serving "**upscale tapas**" and a "**soothing**", more "**sophisticated**" back room; it's "**a bit high-priced**", but at least the service is "**professional.**"

LA GAMELLE | French   4.2   4.0   4.2 $$

Lower East Side | 241 Bowery (Stanton St.)
212-388-0052 | www.lagamellenyc.com

Like "**a touch of Paris**", this LES spot offers "**classic**" French fare and charcuterie matched by a "**charming**" bistro setting (zinc bar, tiled floors, globe lights); the staffers are "**welcoming as can be**" to those in on the "**find.**"

LA GRENOUILLE | French   4.7   4.8   4.7 $$$$

East 50s | 3 E. 52nd St. (bet. 5th & Madison Aves.)
212-752-1495 | www.la-grenouille.com

Ever "**intoxicating**", this Midtown "**bastion**" of "**fine-dining nonpareil**" remains a "**top-tier**" source of "**fantastique**" French classics and "**exemplary service**" in a "**dressy**", jackets-required setting heightened by "**stunning floral displays"; the **"steep tabs"** are **"not for the timid"**, but the consistent **"level of taste"** makes you **"feel special."**

LA LANTERNA DI VITTORIO | Italian ▽ 3.9 4.3 4.1 $$

Greenwich Village | 129 MacDougal St. (bet. 3rd & 4th Sts.)
212-529-5945 | www.lalanternacaffe.com

It's all about the **"romantic feel"** at this Village Italian **"slice of heaven"** purveying **"enjoyable"**, **"affordable"** light bites and standout desserts in **"quaint"** quarters lit by a fireplace and **"lantern-filled"** garden; **"live jazz"** in the adjoining bar adds further **"first-date"** appeal.

L' ALBERO DEI GELATI | Ice Cream ▽ 4.4 3.8 4.1 $$

Park Slope | 341 Fifth Ave. (bet. 33rd & 34th Sts.) | Brooklyn
718-788-2288 | www.alberodeigelati.com

A walk-up window for **"delectable"** gelato in flavors both **"classic"** and **"unique"** (**"saffron, blue cheese"**) lures 'em to this Park Slope offshoot of a Lombardy, Italy, favorite; inside, it's a **"delightful"** coffee/wine bar with a **"sustainable/slow cooking"** ethos serving **"serious"** panini and more – and the **"magic"** back garden seals the deal.

LA MANGEOIRE | French 4.3 4.0 4.3 $$$

East 50s | 1008 Second Ave. (bet. 53rd & 54th Sts.)
212-759-7086 | www.lamangeoire.com

If you **"can't get to Provence"**, check out this next-best-thing East Midtowner offering **"imaginative takes on traditional country French dishes"**; its longevity (since 1975) may be due to the **"warm"** service and **"transporting"** South-of-France decor.

LA MASSERIA | Italian 4.4 4.0 4.3 $$$

West 40s | 235 W. 48th St. (bet. B'way & 8th Ave.) | 212-582-2111 | www.lamasserianyc.com

MASSERIA DEI VINI | Italian

West 50s | 887 Ninth Ave. (bet. 57 & 58th Sts.) | 212-315-2888 | www.masseriadeivini.com

"Like a visit to Puglia", these **"elevated"** Italians offer **"consistently very good"** cuisine via a staff that's **"on top of things"**; the **"rustic"** Theater District **"favorite"** is **"lively"** and **"speedy"** before a show, while the Hell's Kitchen follow-up matches more contemporary vibes with a **"strong wine list."**

LAMAZOU | Sandwiches ▽ 4.5 3.4 4.2 $$

Murray Hill | 370 Third Ave. (27th St.)
212-532-2009 | www.lamazoucheese.com

The **"terrific"** sandwiches come close to **"perfection"** at this **"little"** European cheese and prepared-foods shop in Murray Hill, also a **"gem"** for **"excellent"** soups and imported goods; lunchtime lines can go **"out the door"**, but locals still find a lot to **"love"** here.

LAMBS CLUB | American 4.3 4.4 4.2 $$$

West 40s | Chatwal Hotel | 132 W. 44th St. (bet. 6th & 7th Aves.)
212-997-5262 | www.thelambsclub.com

A **"clubby sanctuary"**, Geoffrey Zakarian's art deco New American **"stands out"** in the Theater District with **"swanky-in-red"** decor and a **"fabulous fireplace"** setting the stage for **"equally impressive"** fare and **"polished"** service; it **"nails"** the **"elegant throwback"** feel, **"but it's not cheap."**

	FOOD	DECOR	SERVICE	COST

LA MELA | Italian   3.8   3.2   3.8 $$

Little Italy | 167 Mulberry St. (bet. Broome & Grand Sts.)
212-431-9493 | www.lamelarestaurant.com

"**Belly-busting**", multicourse meals are the backbone of this "**old-school Little Italy**" vet where the "**solid**" Southern Italian cooking can be ordered either à la carte or in family-style prix fixes; maybe the decor "**leaves much to be desired**" (though it still "**hooks the tourists**"), but service is "**prompt**" and pricing "**fair.**"

L'AMICO | American/Italian   4.4   4.1   3.9 $$

Chelsea | Eventi Hotel | 849 Sixth Ave. (bet. 29th & 30th Sts.)
212-201-4065 | www.lamico.nyc

The pastas and wood-oven pizzas are "**off-the-charts**" at this "**buzzy**" eatery in Chelsea's Eventi Hotel where chef Laurent Tourondel offers a "**solid**" Italian-influenced American menu; since the "**rustic**" space is often "**packed**", be prepared for "**loud**" acoustics and a "**slow**" pace.

LAM ZHOU HANDMADE | Chinese   ▽ 4.3   2.3   3.2 $
NOODLE & DUMPLING

Lower East Side | 144 E. Broadway (bet. Essex & Pike Sts.)
212-566-6933

"**Delightful**" noodles and "**some of the best dumplings**" in town draw fans to this no-frills LES Chinese where a "**skilled**" chef hand-pulls dough on the spot; "**dirt-cheap**" prices help compensate for the seriously "**hole-in-the-wall**" digs.

L&B SPUMONI GARDENS | Ice Cream/Pizza   4.4   3.2   3.7 $$

Gravesend | 2725 86th St. (bet. W. 10th & 11th Sts.) | Brooklyn
718-449-1230 | www.spumonigardens.com

This circa-1939 Gravesend "**icon**" is beloved for its "**twin legends**" – Sicilian square pizza that "**rules**" and "**creamy, refreshing**" spumoni in portions big enough to feed "**all the families in your building**"; there's a "**dated**" dining room, but in summer most opt to order at the window and "**eat outside**" with the "**neighborhood characters.**"

LANDMARC | French   3.9   3.8   3.9 $$$

TriBeCa | 179 W. Broadway (bet. Leonard & Worth Sts.) | 212-343-3883
West 50s | Time Warner Ctr. | 10 Columbus Circle, 3rd fl. (60th St. at B'way) |
212-823-6123
www.landmarc-restaurant.com

An "**extensive**" menu, "**reliable**" French-leaning fare and "**big tables**" make Marc Murphy's "**upbeat**" bistros "**good for large groups**"; you'll find "**gorgeous views**" and an after-work bar scene at TWC, while TriBeCa is a "**neighborhood standby**" – but brunch at both is a "**stroller-fest.**"

LANDMARK TAVERN | Pub Food   3.9   4.0   4.0 $$

West 40s | 626 11th Ave. (46th St.)
212-247-2562 | www.thelandmarktavern.org

Around since 1868, this "**off-the-beaten-path**" Hell's Kitchen tavern is deemed "**worth the detour**" for its "**cozy olde NY**" atmosphere alone; grab a pint and some "**standard**" pub grub delivered by a "**caring**" crew – "**they don't make 'em like this anymore.**"

LAND THAI KITCHEN | Thai   4.2   3.3   3.8 $$

West 80s | 450 Amsterdam Ave. (bet. 81st & 82nd Sts.)
212-501-8121 | www.landthaikitchen.com

"**Big on flavor**" but not in decor or size, this UWS neighborhood Thai offers "**delicious**" standards "**quick**" at "**wallet-friendly**" rates; since "**waits**" are the norm at peak times, many elect for takeout/delivery.

LA PALAPA	Mexican	4.3	4.0	4.1	$$

East Village | 77 St. Marks Pl. (bet. 1st & 2nd Aves.)
212-777-2537 | www.lapalapa.com

The "**authenticity shows**" at this East Village cocina, where a chef-owner who "**knows her stuff**" prepares Mexican fare that's "**a cut above the usual**"; between the "**accommodating**" staff and "**fabulous**" margaritas, expect a "**festive**" scene.

LA PECORA BIANCA	Italian	4.4	4.4	4.2	$$$

Flatiron | 1133 Broadway (26th St.)
212-498-9696 | www.lapecorabianca.com

"**Exciting**" locavore spins "**hit the target**" at this all-day Flatiron Italian, where the "**delicious**" pastas and other "**elevated**" dishes arrive in an "**airy**" "**country kitchen**" setting; "**innovative**" cocktails boost the "**lively**" buzz, and the brunch is "**not to be missed.**"

L'APICIO	Italian	4.4	4.2	4.3	$$$

East Village | 13 E. First St. (bet. Bowery & 2nd Ave.)
212-533-7400 | www.lapicio.com

"**Marvelous pastas**" are "**the strong suit**" at this East Villager from the folks behind dell'anima and L'Artusi, which produces a "**very good**" Italian lineup in "**chic**", "**spacious**" surroundings; the "**cool vibe**" extends to the sizable bar area.

LA PIZZA FRESCA	Italian/Pizza	4.4	4.1	4.2	$$

Flatiron | 31 E. 20th St. (bet. B'way & Park Ave. S.)
212-598-0141 | www.lapizzafresca.com

It was a "**granddaddy of the artisanal pizza trend**", and this "**cozy**" Flatiron "**favorite**" continues to turn out "**superior**" Neapolitan pies along with "**terrific pasta**"; "**attentive**" staffers with "**smiles on all faces**" help maintain the "**relaxed**" mood.

LARB UBOL	Thai	∇ 4.4	3.0	3.8	$

West 30s | 480 Ninth Ave. (37th St.)
212-564-1822 | www.larbubol.com

It's the "**real deal**" say supporters of this "**tasty**" Hell's Kitchen Thai supplying Isan specialties from the country's northeast region that pack an "**incendiary punch**"; the bare-bones space jibes with the wallet-friendly tabs, while "**friendly**" servers add to the overall "**pleasant**" vibe.

L'ARTUSI	Italian	4.7	4.3	4.4	$$$

West Village | 228 W. 10th St. (bet. Bleecker & Hudson Sts.)
212-255-5757 | www.lartusi.com

"**Incredible**" pastas and other "**creative**" Italian dishes are "**done with great care**" at this "**happening**" West Village "**standout**" where the "**polished**" staffers also curate an "**impeccable wine list**"; the "**intimate**" bi-level digs "**bustle**" with a "**youngish crowd**", so "**bring ear plugs**" – and good luck getting a reservation.

NEW **LA SIRENA**	Italian	4.2	4.4	4.1	$$$

Chelsea | Maritime Hotel | 88 Ninth Ave. (bet. 16th & 17th Sts.)
212-977-6096 | www.lasirena-nyc.com

The "**latest hit**" from the Batali-Bastianich team, this "**high-end**" hot spot in Chelsea's Maritime Hotel delivers a "**refined Italian**" menu led by "**first-rate**" pastas; the "**gorgeous**" layout includes a sprawling patio and "**huge, airy bar**" that mixes "**ambitious**" cocktails and hosts a "**happening**" scene.

LA SIRÈNE | French   4.4   3.7   4.2 $$$

Hudson Square | 558½ Broome St. (Varick St.)
212-925-3061 | www.lasirenenyc.com

"**Decadent**" preparations of "**traditional**" French cuisine shuttled by "**charming**" staffers are the lures at this "**small**" Hudson Square bistro; though seating is "**tight**", fans call it "**cozy**" and all agree on the "**exceptional**" service; P.S. BYO Sunday through Thursday only.

L'ASSO | Pizza   ▽ 4.4   3.8   4.2 $$

NoLita | 192 Mott St. (Kenmare St.)
212-219-2353 | www.lassopizza.com

"**State of the art**" wood-fired pizza ("**that cheese! that crust!**") is a hit at this "**buzzing**" NoLita stop where the pastas and salads are also "**worth trying**"; graffiti-like murals on the exterior belie the "**cozy**" brick-walled digs within.

LATTANZI | Italian   4.3   4.0   4.2 $$$

West 40s | 361 W. 46th St. (bet. 8th & 9th Aves.)
212-315-0980 | www.lattanzinyc.com

Something "**special**" on Restaurant Row, this "**better-than-average**" Italian separates itself from the pack with an unusual post-theater menu of Roman-Jewish specialties; otherwise, it's a strictly "**old-guard**" experience with "**gracious**" service and a "**charming**" setting featuring lots of "**dining nooks and crannies.**"

LAUT | Malaysian/Thai   4.2   3.3   3.7 $$

Union Square | 15 E. 17th St. (bet. B'way & 5th Ave.)
212-206-8989 | www.lautnyc.com

"**Legit**" Southeast Asian fare comes with "**no frills**" at this Union Square stop, home to a "**diverse**" lineup of "**kickass**" Malaysian, Singaporean and Thai bites; since it's "**easy on the wallet**", fans put up with "**cramped quarters**" and a laut of "**noise.**"

LAVAGNA | Italian   4.4   3.7   4.2 $$

East Village | 545 E. Fifth St. (bet. Aves. A & B)
212-979-1005 | www.lavagnanyc.com

This "**intimate**" Alphabet City "**fave**" delivers "**value for the quality**" with "**delicious**", trattoria-style Tuscan fare set down by a "**warm**" staff; as it's "**consistently packed**" ("**for good reason**"), followers only wish for "**a tad more elbow room.**"

LA VARA | Spanish   4.7   3.9   4.4 $$$

Cobble Hill | 268 Clinton St. (bet. Verandah Pl. & Warren St.) | Brooklyn
718-422-0065 | www.lavarany.com

"**Quality and originality**" merge at this Cobble Hill Spanish "**delight**", which "**hits new heights**" with "**exceptional**" tapas that highlight Moorish and Jewish influences; the "**passionate staff**" maintains a "**warm, casual vibe**", so it's "**no wonder**" the "**tight quarters**" are typically "**packed.**"

LA VIGNA | Italian   4.4   3.8   4.3 $$

Forest Hills | 100-11 Metropolitan Ave. (70th Ave.) | Queens
718-268-4264 | www.lavignany.com

Forest Hills locals "**can't say enough about**" this Italian charmer that enjoys a "**well-earned reputation**" for "**authentic**", "**premium-quality**" cooking;

the "**cozy**", brick-walled quarters and "**thoughtful**" service add to its "**dependable**" reputation.

| **LA VILLA PIZZERIA** | Pizza | 4.1 | 3.6 | 4.0 | $$ |

Mill Basin | 6610 Ave. U (66th St.) | Brooklyn | 718-251-8030
Park Slope | 261 Fifth Ave. (bet. 1st St. & Garfield Pl.) | Brooklyn |
718-499-9888
Howard Beach | 8207 153rd Ave. (82nd St.) | Queens | 718-641-8259
www.lavillaparkslope.com

These "**basic neighborhood red-sauce**" joints dish out "**first-rate**" pizzas along with a "**lengthy**" roster of "**comfort**" Italian items; nondescript settings and "**loud**" acoustics are offset by "**modest**" tabs.

| **LAVO** | Italian | 3.9 | 4.0 | 3.8 | $$$ |

East 50s | 39 E. 58th St. (bet. Madison & Park Aves.)
212-750-5588 | www.lavony.com

It's one "**crazy**" scene at this "**pricey**" Midtown Italian that rivals nearby sibling Tao as a "**meet-and-mingle**" hub for the "**Botox-and-high-heels**" set and the "**expense-account suits**" who love them; just bring "**earplugs**" and an appetite – the "**garlicky**" fare is "**surprisingly good**" – and then "**go party**" in the "**thumping**" downstairs club.

| **LE BARRICOU** | French | ▽ 4.4 | 4.2 | 4.0 | $$ |

Williamsburg | 533 Grand St. (bet. Lorimer St. & Union Ave.) | Brooklyn
718-782-7372 | www.lebarricouny.com

"**A local favorite**" known for its "**great brunch experience**", this "**old-school**" East Williamsburg bistro offers "**more-than-solid**" French staples at "**cost-effective**" rates; just "**expect to wait**" when weekends roll around ("**it's totally worth it**").

| **LE BERNARDIN** | French/Seafood | 4.9 | 4.8 | 4.9 | $$$$ |

West 50s | 155 W. 51st St. (bet. 6th & 7th Aves.)
212-554-1515 | www.le-bernardin.com

Prepare to dine on "**a higher plane**" at this "**dazzling**" Midtown "**star**" where Eric Ripert's "**world-class**" tasting menus highlight "**transcendent**" French seafood, earning it No. 1 Food honors in NYC for the eighth year in a row; a "**deep**" wine list, "**exemplary**" staff and "**soigné**" surrounds further justify the "**sky-high**" tabs, so for a "**dream-come-true**" meal, this is "**as good as it gets.**"

| **LE BILBOQUET** | French | 4.1 | 4.0 | 3.9 | $$$ |

East 60s | 20 E. 60th St. (bet. Madison & Park Aves.)
212-751-3036

"**One does not go for the meal alone**" to this "**see-and-be-seen**" UES French bistro that functions as a clubhouse for "**power**" types, "**Euro locals**" and "**Park Avenue dowagers**"; the food's "**consistently good**" and the service "**rude**" if you're not a regular, but the "**outrageous**" pricing extends to all.

| **LE CIRQUE** | French | 4.4 | 4.5 | 4.4 | $$$$ |

East 50s | 151 E. 58th St. (bet. Lexington & 3rd Aves.)
212-644-0202 | www.lecirque.com

"**Impressive**" is the word for this "**iconic**" destination in the Bloomberg Tower, where Sirio Maccioni and his "**gracious**" staff deliver "**outstandingly prepared**" French fare with a side of "**VIP treatment**"; the "**astronomical**" prices befit Adam Tihany's "**spectacular**", circus-themed main dining room, where "**well-dressed**" "**millionaires**" and "**oligarchs**" feel right at home.

	FOOD	DECOR	SERVICE	COST

LE COLONIAL | French/Vietnamese   4.2   4.4   4.1 $$$
East 50s | 149 E. 57th St. (bet. Lexington & 3rd Aves.)
212-752-0808 | www.lecolonialnyc.com

At this "**gorgeous**" East Midtowner, you'll be "**transported to an exotic place**" where the spirit of 1920s "**colonial Indochine**" is in the air and on the plate in the form of "**terrific**" French-Vietnamese fare; the "**old Saigon**" sensibility extends to a "**comfortable upstairs lounge**", though prices are strictly modern day.

NEW   **LE COQ RICO** | French   4.4   4.2   4.4 $$$
Flatiron | 30 E. 20th St. (bet. B'way & Park Ave. S.)
212-267-7426 | www.lecoqriconyc.com

It's "**whole chicken heaven**" at acclaimed chef Antoine Westermann's Flatiron offshoot of a Paris standout where "**French country–style**" dishes featuring responsibly farmed birds (including hens, duck and squab) are "**seriously delicious**" (as are the egg starters); tabs run "**pricey**", but "**lovely**" service is another reason this newcomer is "**taking off.**"

NEW   **LE COUCOU** | French   —   —   — $$$$
SoHo | 11 Howard Hotel | 138 Lafayette St. (Howard St.)
212-271-4252 | www.lecoucou.com

Stephen Starr and star-chef Daniel Rose of the Paris hits Spring and La Bourse et La Vie have created this high-end SoHo French in the 11 Howard hotel offering contemporary takes on classic dishes. Designed with softly toned wood and brick with white tablecloths and specially designed chandeliers, it also offers a pared-down selection of cocktails and a well thought-out wine list.

LE DISTRICT | Food Hall/French   4.1   4.1   3.8 $$
Battery Park City | Brookfield Pl. | 230 Vesey St. (West St.)
212-981-8588 | www.ledistrict.com

The "**French answer to Eataly**", this "**lively**" food hall in Battery Park City's Brookfield Place lets you "**stroll, shop and eat**" amid an "**amazing**" variety of "**quality**" venues, from take-out vendors to cafes to the sit-down brasserie Beaubourg; some find it "**overly pricey**", but le "**fun factor is high.**"

LEFT BANK | American   4.3   4.2   4.4 $$$
West Village | 117 Perry St. (Greenwich St.)
212-727-1170 | www.leftbanknewyork.com

"**Imaginatively prepared**" New American fare with European influences is paired with a "**terrific wine selection**" at this "**relaxed**" West Village "**home away from home**"; "**outstanding**" service and a "**quiet, cozy**" ambiance further burnish this "**neighborhood gem.**"

LE GIGOT | French   4.5   3.8   4.4 $$
West Village | 18 Cornelia St. (bet. Bleecker & 4th Sts.)
212-627-3737 | www.legigotrestaurant.com

A little piece of the "**Left Bank**" in the West Village, this "**lovely**" French bistro offers "**beautifully cooked**" Provençal dishes, a "**superb**" wine list and "**warm**" service; the "**petite**" space can feel "**tight**", but "**flattering lighting**" adds to the "**romantic**" appeal.

LE MARAIS | French/Kosher/Steak   4.2   3.6   3.7 $$$
West 40s | 150 W. 46th St. (bet. 6th & 7th Aves.)
212-869-0900 | www.lemarais.net

"**If you're a kosher carnivore**", this Theater District French "**staple**" comes across with "**excellent steaks**" that pass muster with the highest authority; maybe the service "**doesn't match**" the food quality and the surrounds are "**forgettable**", but it's generally "**packed**" all the same.

LEMON ICE KING OF CORONA | Ice Cream	4.6	2.6	3.6	$

Corona | 52-02 108th St. (52nd Ave.) | Queens
718-699-5133 | www.thelemoniceckingofcorona.com

A "**delicious**" way to "**cool off**" since the 1940s, this Corona "**landmark**" draws "**long lines**" with its "**vast assortment**" of "**real-deal**" Italian ices that fans dub the "**city's best**"; there's no seating, so regulars head for nearby Flushing Meadows Park.

LEOPARD AT DES ARTISTES | Italian	4.3	4.6	4.3	$$$

West 60s | 1 W. 67th St. (bet. Columbus Ave. & CPW)
212-787-8767 | www.theleopardnyc.com

Hailed as a "**worthy heir to Café des Artistes**", this Lincoln Center–area Italian occupies a "**spiffed-up**" space where Howard Chandler Christy's "**gorgeous**" murals make it "**hard to keep your eyes**" on the "**lovingly prepared**" plates; it'll "**stretch your budget**", but the "**Hermès**"-clad crowd hardly blinks.

LEO'S BAGELS | Bagels	4.3	2.8	3.6	$

Financial District | 3 Hanover Sq. (William St.)
212-785-4700 | www.leosbagels.com

"**Awesome**" "**freshly baked bagels**", an "**interesting variety of spreads**" and "**generously sized**" sandwiches are a welcome "**surprise**" at this FiDi breakfast-and-lunch stop; more predictably, service is "**a little rough**" and things get "**chaotic during the morning rush.**"

LEO'S LATTICINI | Italian/Sandwiches	4.6	3.2	4.0	$

Corona | 46-02 104th St. (46th Ave.) | Queens | 718-898-6069

MAMA'S OF CORONA | Italian/Sandwiches

Willets Point | Citi Field | 12301 Roosevelt Ave. (behind the scoreboard) | Queens | no phone

"**Nobody makes a sandwich**" like this Corona "**old-school Italian deli**", where the subs are "**fit for royalty**" and the mozzarella is among the "**best in the boroughs**"; its Citi Field stand services Mets fans on game days, but, unfortunately, without those "**adorable ladies**" behind the counter.

LE PARISIEN | French	4.2	3.5	4.0	$$

Murray Hill | 163 E. 33rd St. (bet. Lexington & 3rd Aves.)
212-889-5489 | www.leparisiennyc.com

"**Teleport**" to the "**banks of the Seine**" via this "**cozy**" Murray Hill French bistro offering "**excellent**", "**well-priced**" renditions of "**all the classics**"; "**charming**" staffers compensate for "**tiny**" dimensions and help seal its standing as a local "**winner.**"

LE PERIGORD | French	4.5	4.2	4.5	$$$$

East 50s | 405 E. 52nd St. (bet. FDR Dr. & 1st Ave.)
212-755-6244 | www.leperigord.com

"**White glove**" all the way, this Sutton Place "**bastion of civility**" has been a "**treat for adults**" since 1964 thanks to a menu of "**exquisite**" French classics and an "**impeccable**" wine list, "**served with grace**" by an "**old-school**" staff; *bien sûr*, it's a "**splurge**", but still less costly than a "**trip to Paris.**"

LE RELAIS DE VENISE | French/Steak   4.1   3.7   4.0 $$
L'ENTRECÔTE

East 50s | 590 Lexington Ave. (52nd St.)
212-758-3989 | www.relaisdevenise.com

It's all about "**value**" at this "**unique**" East Midtown French brasserie where the "**one-trick-pony**" menu consists only of steak frites and salad for a $30 fixed price; there's a no-reservations rule, but fans generally find it "**quick and easy.**"

LE RIVAGE | French   4.1   3.7   4.2 $$$

West 40s | 340 W. 46th St. (bet. 8th & 9th Aves.)
212-765-7374 | www.lerivagenyc.com

"**Old-school**" French dining is alive and well at this circa-1958 Restaurant Row survivor where the "**middle-of-the-road**" Gallic offerings are "**consistent**" and the staff "**understands curtain time**"; the digs may be "**dated**", but the post-theater $29 prix fixe is quite the "**deal.**"

LES HALLES | French/Steak   4.0   3.7   3.8 $$$

Financial District | 15 John St. (bet. B'way & Nassau St.)
212-285-8585 | www.leshalles.net

"**Even without Anthony Bourdain**", this "**solid**" FiDi French brasserie stays "**busy**" thanks to "**reliably good**" steak frites and other "**simple**" but "**well-prepared**" traditional dishes served in "**dark-wood**" quarters with a "**classic feel**"; "**loud**" acoustics are part of the "**convivial**" package.

NEW LE TURTLE | French   ▽ 4.1   4.1   4.0 $$$

Lower East Side | 177 Chrystie St. (Rivington St.)
646-918-7189 | www.leturtle.fr

"**One cool place**", this joint effort from the owners of Freemans and The Smile offers a "**fascinating**" menu of modern French fare in a LES space both "**funky and sleek**" that's staffed by "**jumpsuit**"-clad waiters; though some say it's "**trying too hard**" with "**trendy ingredients**" and mixed results, at least it ensures a "**memorable**" meal.

LEVAIN BAKERY | Bakery   4.7   2.8   3.9 $

Harlem | 2167 Frederick Douglass Blvd. (bet. 116th & 117th Sts.) |
646-455-0952
West 70s | 167 W. 74th St. (Amsterdam Ave.) | 212-874-6080
www.levainbakery.com

"**All hail**" the "**just-out-of-the-oven**" chocolate chip cookies at these simple bakeries where the "**hockey puck–sized**" treats are "**dense, gooey and decadent**"; "**exceptional**" breads, pastries and sandwiches are other reasons to go, just be ready for "**impressively long lines**" at the "**tiny**" Upper West Side flagship.

LE VEAU D'OR | French   3.8   3.5   3.9 $$$

East 60s | 129 E. 60th St. (bet. Lexington & Park Aves.)
212-838-8133

"**Forgotten**" French bistro classics work their "**throwback**" magic on loyal patrons of this circa-1937 Eastsider; though it's "**had a full life**" – and it shows – here's hoping it'll "**continue forever.**"

L'EXPRESS | French   3.9   3.7   3.9 $$

Gramercy Park | 249 Park Ave. S. (20th St.)
212-254-5858 | www.lexpressnyc.com

One of the "**classiest 24-hour operations**" around, this Gramercy Park "**go-to** for brunch and late nights" has "**that real Paris bistro feel**", from the "**bustling**" atmosphere to "**satisfying**" French classics; the noise may "**coddle your brain**", but for most, it's part of the "**happy**" vibe.

	FOOD	DECOR	SERVICE	COST

LE ZIE | Italian | | 4.1 | 3.7 | 4.0 | $$

Chelsea | 172 Seventh Ave. (bet. 20th & 21st Sts.)
212-206-8686 | www.lezie.com

"**High-end in quality but not in price**" sums up the Venetian cuisine at this "**lively**" Chelsea Italian; regulars suggest the "**back room**" if quiet dining is preferred, and say "**beware**" the "**daily specials**" that sell for "**much more**" than the regular fare.

THE LIBRARY AT THE PUBLIC | American | 3.8 | 4.1 | 4.0 | $$

Greenwich Village | 425 Lafayette St. (bet. Astor Pl. & 4th St.)
212-539-8777 | www.thelibraryatthepublic.com

"**Hidden away**" upstairs at the Public Theater is this "**gem**" providing "**pricey**" American fare from chef Andrew Carmellini in "**dark**", "**clubby**" quarters with a "**vibrant**" bar scene; opinions are mixed on the food ("**terrific**" vs. "**nothing special**"), but all agree it "**couldn't be easier before the show.**"

LIC MARKET | American | 4.3 | 3.7 | 3.8 | $$

Long Island City | 21-52 44th Dr. (23rd St.) | Queens
718-361-0013 | www.licmarket.com

LIC denizens feel "**lucky to have**" this rustic American "**gem**" providing "**lick-your-plate**" good farm-to-table fare and "**personable service**" at a "**reasonable**" price point; since it's both "**small**" and "**popular**", seating can be "**scarce**" – particularly for the "**delicious**" brunch.

LIDO | Italian | 4.1 | 3.8 | 4.0 | $$

Harlem | 2168 Frederick Douglass Blvd. (117th St.)
646-490-8575 | www.lidoharlem.com

"**Skillfully prepared**" Italian dishes draw Harlemites to this "**solid**" player on the neighborhood's "**Restaurant Row**"; the "**relaxed**" environs are peopled by "**friendly**" staffers, with no letup in "**quality**" during the popular "**bottomless-mimosa**" brunch.

LIEBMAN'S DELICATESSEN | Deli/Kosher | 4.3 | 3.1 | 3.9 | $

Riverdale | 552 W. 235th St. (Johnson Ave.) | Bronx
347-227-0776 | www.liebmansdeli.com

If "**you're nostalgic**", this Riverdale kosher deli is a circa-1953 destination for "**the gamut of Jewish comfort food**" – notably "**excellent**" overstuffed sandwiches – dispensed by an equally "**old-fashioned**" staff; even though the decor's "**completely lacking**", it's "**a real treasure**" in the nabe.

LIL' FRANKIE'S PIZZA | Italian/Pizza | 4.3 | 3.6 | 3.9 | $$

East Village | 19 First Ave. (bet. 1st & 2nd Sts.)
212-420-4900 | www.lilfrankies.com

Really "**solid**" Italian fare "**without frills**" at an "**affordable price**" is the signature of this "**casual**", cash-only East Villager, a sibling of Frank, Sauce and Supper; it offers "**standout**" Neapolitan pizzas, late hours and a "**garden room**", so it's no wonder it gets way- "**crowded**" at peak times.

NEW **LILIA** | Italian | 4.6 | 4.4 | 4.4 | $$$

Williamsburg | 567 Union Ave. (Frost St.) | Brooklyn
718-576-3095 | www.lilianewyork.com

Missy Robbins' "**mind-blowing**" housemade pastas and wood-fired entrees are declared **"exactly what Italian food should be"** at this **"outstanding"** arrival to the Williamsburg dining scene; the **"spare-but-warm"** space – complete with **"lovely open kitchen"**, **"sweeping bar"** and plenty of **"buzz"** – is overseen by an **"excellent"** staff, so the only real problem is **"getting a reservation."**

LIMANI | Mediterranean

	4.4	4.5	4.3	$$$

West 50s | 45 Rockefeller Plaza (5th Ave.)
212-858-9200 | www.limani.com

A **"surprise"** in Rock Center, this **"swanky"** offshoot of a Long Island original offers a Mediterranean menu highlighting **"superb"** seafood that measures up to a **"dramatic all-white room"** with an infinity pool in the middle; though tabs can be **"extremely pricey"**, the **"bargain"** prix fixes help make it **"a repeater."**

LINCOLN | Italian

	4.5	4.6	4.5	$$$$

West 60s | Lincoln Ctr. | 142 W. 65th St. (bet. Amsterdam Ave. & B'way)
212-359-6500 | www.lincolnristorante.com

A **"calm oasis"** on the Lincoln Center campus, Jonathan Benno's Italian **"showstopper"** rolls out a **"marvelous"** menu in a **"sleek"**, glass-walled space built around a **"gleaming"** open kitchen; **"polished"** service and ultra-**"proximity"** to the various concert halls are part of the **"superb"** package, but be prepared to spend **"many Lincolns"** for the privilege.

LINCOLN SQUARE STEAK | Steak

	4.3	4.2	4.3	$$$

West 70s | 208 W. 70th St. (Amsterdam Ave.)
212-875-8600 | www.lincolnsquaresteak.com

A **"high-end steakhouse"** comes to the Upper West Side via this **"welcoming"** venue where **"charming"** servers set down **"delicious"** prime cuts in a **"well-spaced"** room with a **"colorful"** mural, barside pianist and **"bordellolike"** crimson walls; sure, the tabs skew **"pricey"**, but it gives rivals **"a run for their money."**

THE LITTLE BEET | American

	4.0	3.3	3.7	$

`NEW` **NoMad** | 1140 Broadway (bet. 26th & 27th Sts.) | 212-367-8015
West 50s | 135 W. 50th St. (7th Ave.) | 212-459-2338
www.thelittlebeet.com

"Healthy foodies" hit up these **"boffo"** Americans, which supply **"extremely fresh"**, gluten-free, veggie-friendly fare in a **"quick-service cafeteria format"**; granted, **"the line can be hellish at lunch"**, but **"your cells will thank you."**

LITTLE BEET TABLE | American

	4.0	3.3	3.7	$

Murray Hill | 333 Park Ave. S. (bet. 24th & 25th Sts.)
212-466-3330 | www.thelittlebeettable.com

It's **"hard to believe it's so healthy"** say diners **"pleasantly surprised"** by the **"tasty, original"** gluten-free menu at this Murray Hill American, where the seasonal roster highlights **"creative"** uses of veggies; the **"cute little"** space has a communal feel with a small front bar.

LITTLENECK | Seafood

	4.1	3.7	4.0	$$

Gowanus | 288 Third Ave. (bet. Carroll & President Sts.) | Brooklyn |
718-522-1921

LITTLENECK OUTPOST | Seafood

Greenpoint | 128 Franklin St. (Milton St.) | Brooklyn | 718-363-3080
www.littleneckbrooklyn.com

New England–style seafood washes up at these **"friendly"** clam shacks where the "**well-priced**" roster ranges from "**always fresh**" raw-bar items to steamers and "**delicious**" rolls; a "**mean brunch**", "**great-deal**" happy-hour oysters and "**cozy**", marine-themed digs keep its "**hipster**" crowd content.

LITTLE OWL	American/Mediterranean	4.5	3.9	4.4	$$$

West Village | 90 Bedford St. (Grove St.)
212-741-4695 | www.thelittleowlnyc.com

A definite "**bucket-list**" candidate, this "**tiny**" but "**stellar**" West Villager offers chef Joey Campanaro's "**elevated**" Med–New American cuisine served by an "**expert**" team in "**extremely tight quarters**"; reservations remain "**ever-elusive**" even a month in advance, but wised-up admirers just "**keep trying.**"

LITTLE PARK	American	4.4	4.2	4.2	$$$

TriBeCa | Smyth Hotel | 85 W. Broadway (Chambers St.)
212-220-4110 | www.littlepark.com

"**Another hit**" from chef Andrew Carmellini (Locanda Verde, The Dutch), this all-day TriBeCa American delivers a "**beautifully conceived**" seasonal menu with "**veg-centric**" twists in "**classy**" contemporary digs; it'll "**cost you a pretty penny**", but the "**Condé Nast chic**" clientele confirms "**there's a good reason.**"

LITTLE POLAND	Diner/Polish	4.1	2.9	3.8	$$

East Village | 200 Second Ave. (bet. 12th & 13th Sts.)
212-777-9728

"**Heaping portions**" of "**filling**" Polish "**diner food**" comes "**cheap as can be**" at this "**old-time**" East Village "**greasy spoon**"; "**drab**" the interior may be, but wait till you taste those "**perfect pierogi**" – you couldn't do better in Gdansk.

NEW **LLAMA INN**	Peruvian	4.5	4.2	4.1	$$

Williamsburg | 50 Withers St. (Meeker Ave.) | Brooklyn
718-387-3434 | www.llamainnnyc.com

"**Big, bold**" flavors come across in the "**devilishly creative**" Peruvian dishes at this Williamsburg hot spot where the mix of "**inventive**" pisco cocktails and an "**in-the-know**" crowd makes for a "**great bar scene**"; the "**cool**" airy space has lots of counter seating (plus some tables), and there's also a rooftop for drinks and snacks.

LOBSTER JOINT	New England/Seafood	4.4	3.8	4.1	$$

Greenpoint | 1073 Manhattan Ave. (bet. Dupont & Eagle Sts.) | Brooklyn
718-389-8990 | www.lobsterjoint.com

Bringing some "**Bar Harbor**" to the boroughs, this "**laid-back**" Greenpoint seafood shack offers "**delicious**" lobster rolls and other "**quality**" New England–style fare, plus "**no-nonsense**" cocktails, "**without cleaning out your wallet**"; come summer, a "**picnic-table backyard**" expands the "**simple**" setup.

THE LOBSTER PLACE	Seafood	4.5	3.2	3.6	$$

Chelsea | Chelsea Mkt. | 75 Ninth Ave. (bet. 15th & 16th Sts.)
212-255-5672 | www.lobsterplace.com

Part fish market, part raw bar, this Chelsea Market destination is "**unbeatable**" for its "**fresh-out-of-the-ocean**" seafood, including "**top-grade**" steamed lobsters, sushi and "**freshly shucked**" oysters; few seats at the marble bar mean many take it to go – or end up "**sitting on the hallway floor**" outside.

LOCANDA VERDE	Italian	4.5	4.3	4.2	$$$

TriBeCa | Greenwich Hotel | 377 Greenwich St. (N. Moore St.)
212-925-3797 | www.locandaverdenyc.com

"**Energetic**" is the word on chef Andrew Carmellini's "**grand-slam**" TriBeCa

Italian offering a "**delectable**", all-day menu to a "**swinging**" clientele basking in its "**trendiness factor**"; despite an "**overcrowded**", somewhat "**frantic**" scene at prime times, reservations can still be "**hard to get.**"

LOCANDA VINI & OLII | Italian   4.4   4.3   4.2 $$$

Clinton Hill | 129 Gates Ave. (bet. Cambridge Pl. & Grand Ave.) | Brooklyn
718-622-9202 | www.locandaviniieolii.com

The "**former pharmacy**" setting lends "**old-fashioned but stylish appeal**" to this "**refreshingly distinctive**" Clinton Hill Northern Italian, home to "**expertly prepared**" pastas and other "**authentic**" fare delivered by a "**hands-on**" staff; it's a bona fide "**hidden gem**" where regulars "**leave full and happy.**"

LOI ESTIATORIO | Greek   4.4   3.7   4.2 $$$

West 50s | 132 W. 58th St. (6th Ave.)
212-713-0015 | www.loiestiatorio.com

"**High-end Greek**" cuisine is chef Maria Loi's signature at her Midtown namesake, where the "**out-of-this-world**" menu centers on seafood "**done to perfection**" set down by staffers who "**want you to be happy**"; while it "**can get expensive**", loyal fans liken it to "**a tiny vacation.**"

LOLO'S SEAFOOD | Caribbean/Seafood   ▽ 4.3   3.6   3.9 $
SHACK

Harlem | 303 W. 116th St. (Frederick Douglass Blvd.)
646-649-3356 | www.lolosseafoodshack.com

This "**tiny**" Harlem seafood specialist rolls out "**delectable**" takes on Caribbean street eats, offering "**sloppy-casual**" dishes like conch fritters and steampots with an array of sauces; while the counter-order space is "**rough**", it suits the eats, and there's patio seating out back.

LOMBARDI'S | Pizza   4.5   3.5   3.8 $$

NoLita | 32 Spring St. (bet. Mott & Mulberry Sts.)
212-941-7994 | www.firstpizza.com

This 1905-vintage NoLita pizza "**shrine**", which claims to be America's first pizzeria, still draws throngs with its "**real-deal**" coal-fired pies; it doesn't take plastic or reservations, and you may have to "**tussle with the tourists to get a table**", but it's a true "**slice of NY**" – even though it "**doesn't do slices.**"

LONDON LENNIE'S | Seafood   4.3   3.8   4.1 $$$

Middle Village | 63-88 Woodhaven Blvd. (bet. Fleet Ct. & Penelope Ave.) |
Queens
718-894-8084 | www.londonlennies.com

It's been in operation since 1959, and this Middle Village seafood joint "**hasn't lost its touch**", putting forth a "**wide selection**" of "**fresh**", "**unfussy**" shore fare in "**big**", "**down-to-earth**" digs; "**fast**" service and "**fair prices**" are two more reasons it's "**always crowded.**"

LORENZO'S | Italian   4.1   4.5   4.3 $$$

Bloomfield | 1100 South Ave. (Lois Ln.) | Staten Island
718-477-2400 | www.lorenzosdining.com

"**Food and entertainment**" go hand in hand at this Staten Island Italian in Bloomfield, where the "**weekend cabarets**" and "**jazz brunch**" are big hits with "**locals**" looking for a "**classy**" outing "**without city hassles**"; service also rates high, but grumbles about "**uneven**" cuisine persist.

	FOOD	DECOR	SERVICE	COST

LOS TACOS | Mexican   4.7   3.1   3.8 $

Chelsea | Chelsea Mkt. | 75 Ninth Ave. (bet. 15th & 16th Sts.)
212-256-0343 | www.lostacos1.com

"**Outrageously good**" tacos made with "**super-fresh**" fillings headline the short, "**top-notch**" Mexican menu at this Chelsea Market stall ("**just look for the long line**"); there's "**zero seating**", but eats this bueno and "**cheap**" are "**worth standing for.**"

LOUKOUMI TAVERNA | Greek   4.5   4.0   4.4 $$

Astoria | 45-07 Ditmars Blvd. (bet. 45th & 46th Sts.) | Queens
718-626-3200 | www.toloukoumi.com

"**Excellent**", "**authentic**" taverna fare leads the charge at this "**warm, inviting**" Astoria Greek; it's located "**a bit away**" from the main neighborhood action, but "**affordable**" tabs and a back garden clinch the "**good-on-all-counts**" endorsement.

LUCALI | Pizza   4.7   3.9   4.1 $$

Carroll Gardens | 575 Henry St. (bet. Carroll St. & 1st Pl.) | Brooklyn
718-858-4086 | www.lucali.com

It's "**hard to beat**" the "**ethereal**" pizzas and "**league-of-their-own**" calzones that emerge from the brick oven at this cash-only Carroll Gardens joint; the BYO policy "**makes it a great value**", but the trade-off is notoriously "**insane waits.**"

LUCIEN | French   4.3   3.8   4.1 $$$

East Village | 14 First Ave. (1st St.)
212-260-6481 | www.luciennyc.com

"**A neighborhood taste of Paris**", Lucien Bahaj's East Village bistro is an "**old standby**" for "**traditional**" French fare "**done right**" in a "**congenial**" setting; while the "**narrow room**" is "**a tight fit**", it only "**adds to the experience**" for its "**devoted following.**"

NEW **THE LUCKY BEE** | SE Asian   —   —   — $$

Lower East Side | 252 Broome St. (bet. Ludlow & Orchard Sts.)
844-364-4286 | www.luckybeenyc.com

Seasonal Thai curries and spicy Southeast Asian street snacks are prepared with local ingredients at this upbeat Lower Eastsider from a pair of Aussie owners (including a former Fat Radish chef). The vibrantly colored space boasts a black-and-white bar pouring attractively garnished cocktails.

LUCKY STRIKE | French   3.8   3.5   3.7 $$

SoHo | 59 Grand St. (bet. W. B'way & Wooster St.)
212-941-0772 | www.luckystrikeny.com

Part of the McNally empire, this circa-1989 mainstay "**off the beaten SoHo path**" caters to a "**casual, young**" crowd in the mood for "**standard**" French bistro fare and late-night burgers at "**fair**" prices; a few find it "**nothing special**", and the "**shabby-chic**" interior can feel "**cramped**", but it's still a "**magnet**" for fans who come back "**time and again.**"

LUIGI'S | Italian   4.3   3.7   4.1 $$

Glen Oaks | 265-21 Union Tpke. (266th St.) | Queens
718-347-7136 | www.luigisnewhydepark.com

The "**diverse**" menu of "**delicious**" dishes draws a "**well-deserved supper crowd**" to this Glen Oaks Italian where fans tout homemade pastas "**to die** for"; the "**small**" space has a "**cozy**" vibe, and affordable tabs add to its "**consistent**" appeal.

	FOOD	DECOR	SERVICE	COST

LUKE'S LOBSTER | Seafood   4.3   3.1   3.7 $$

East 40s | 685 Third Ave. (bet. 43rd & 44th Sts.) | 646-657-0066
East 80s | 242 E. 81st St. (bet. 2nd & 3rd Aves.) | 212-249-4241
East Village | 93 E. Seventh St. (bet. Ave. A & 1st Ave.) | 212-387-8487
Financial District | 26 S. William St. (bet. Beaver & Broad Sts.) | 212-747-1700
West 40s | City Kitchen | 700 Eighth Ave. (bet. 44th & 45th Sts.) | 917-338-0928
West 50s | Plaza Food Hall | 1 W. 59th St. (5th Ave.) | 646-755-3227
West 80s | 426 Amsterdam Ave. (bet. 80th & 81st Sts.) | 212-877-8800
Dumbo | 11 Water St. (bet. New Dock & Old Fulton Sts.) | Brooklyn | 917-882-7516
Park Slope | 237 Fifth Ave. (Carroll St.) | Brooklyn | 347-457-6855
www.lukeslobster.com

When "**you can't make it to Maine**", this "**standout**" seafood chain's "**real-deal**" lobster rolls – "**chock-full**" of "**succulent**" meat with "**no filler**" – are just about the "**closest you'll get**" (and "**priced accordingly**"); the "**utilitarian**", counter-serve setups suggest "**takeout**", though wine and beer poured at some branches encourages lingering.

LUKSUS | American   ▽ 4.5   4.2   4.4 $$$$

Greenpoint | 615 Manhattan Ave. (bet. Driggs & Nassau Aves.) | Brooklyn 718-389-6034 | www.luksusnyc.com

They "**keep your palate entertained**" at this Greenpoint New American (set in the "**intimate back room**" at Tørst), where the "**incredible**", Scandinavian-inspired creations out of an open kitchen are offered in tasting menu format only ($125); the "**original**" beer pairing option and "**amazing show put on by the chefs**" make it a natural for a foodie "**special occasion.**"

LUPA | Italian   4.6   3.9   4.2 $$$

Greenwich Village | 170 Thompson St. (bet. Bleecker & Houston Sts.) 212-982-5089 | www.luparestaurant.com

"**They're still doing it right**" at Mario Batali's "**unpretentious**" Village trattoria, an "**all-time favorite**" for "**superior**" Roman dishes, "**terrific**" Italian vinos and service that "**never slacks**" – "**at fairly reasonable prices**" to boot; but even those who "**love the warmth**" warn it's a "**squeeze**" with molto "**bustle and noise.**"

LUPULO | Portuguese   4.3   4.1   4.0 $$$

Chelsea | 835 Sixth Ave. (29th St.) 212-290-7600 | www.lupulonyc.com

Chef George Mendes' "**utterly delicious**" Portuguese fare and a suds selection "**for beer nerds**" make for an "**exciting**" meal at this Aldea sibling in Chelsea; it's a "**crowded**", "**noisy scene**" built around a dining-friendly bar, but you'll still "**wanna hang here**"; P.S. a take-out window called Bica offers coffee and snacks.

LURE FISHBAR | Seafood   4.4   4.2   4.1 $$$

SoHo | 142 Mercer St. (Prince St.) 212-431-7676 | www.lurefishbar.com

Still "**trendy**" and filled with "**beautiful people**", this SoHo staple wins 'em over with "**fresh seafood par excellence**" and a "**swank**", "**yachtlike**" setting tucked below street level; tabs "**on the pricier side**" don't seem to dampen the "**active bar scene**" or "**challenging**" decibels.

LUSARDI'S | Italian · · · 4.4 · 3.9 · 4.3 · $$$
East 70s | 1494 Second Ave. (bet. 77th & 78th Sts.)
212-249-2020 | www.lusardis.com

"**Friendly**" owners oversee the "**vintage poster**"–lined room at this longtime UES "**institution**" where the Tuscan food is as "**terrific**" as the "**gracious**" service and "**old-fashioned style**"; its "**adult**", "**well-heeled crowd**" doesn't mind the "**expensive**" checks, given that it has "**maintained its quality over the years.**"

LUZZO'S | Pizza · · · 4.5 · 3.5 · 3.9 · $$
East Village | 211-13 First Ave. (bet. 12th & 13th Sts.) | 212-473-7447 | www.luzzospizza.com
Brooklyn Heights | 145 Atlantic Ave. (bet. Clinton & Henry Sts.) | Brooklyn | 718-855-6400 | www.luzzosbk.com

Fans "**thank the pizza gods**" for these separately owned joints, where "**superior**" Neapolitan-style pies emerge from coal-fired ovens with enough "**authenticity**" to "**make an Italian grandma proud**"; they're "**no-frills**" and often "**jammed**", but the Brooklyn Heights locale has a back patio.

LYCHEE HOUSE | Chinese · · · 4.0 · 3.4 · 3.9 · $$
East 50s | 141 E. 55th St. (bet. Lexington & 3rd Aves.)
212-753-3900 | www.lycheehouse.com

Ranking a "**notch above most**", this East Midtown Chinese offers a "**wide variety**" of "**well-prepared**" dishes, plus "**inventive dim sum**", backed by cocktails from a full bar; although it's "**tiny in size**", fans feel it's "**big in heart.**"

MACAO TRADING CO. | Chinese/Portuguese · · · 4.0 · 4.3 · 3.8 · $$$
TriBeCa | 311 Church St. (bet. Lispenard & Walker Sts.)
212-431-8750 | www.macaonyc.com

Channeling a 1940s "**Macao gambling parlor**", this "**dazzling**", bi-level TriBeCan offers plentiful "**eye candy**" to go with its Chinese-Portuguese chow; late-night, it turns "**club**"-like – "**loud and crowded**" with uneven service – but most are having too much "**fun**" to care.

MACHIAVELLI | Italian · · · 4.3 · 4.4 · 4.2 · $$$
West 80s | 519 Columbus Ave. (85th St.)
212-724-2658 | www.machiavellinyc.com

"**Dine like a prince**" at this "**elegant**", all-day UWS Italian, where candelabras, plush upholstered chairs and "**gorgeous**" "**Renaissance**"-inspired murals – not to mention live music most nights – set a "**romantic**" tone; the "**pricey**", "**carefully prepared**" Northern Italian food is somewhat more down to earth (think pastas, pizzas).

MADIBA | S African · · · 4.2 · 3.9 · 4.0 · $$
Fort Greene | 195 Dekalb Ave. (bet. Adelphi St. & Carlton Ave.) | Brooklyn
718-855-9190 | www.madibarestaurant.com

The "**down-home**" South African dishes are "**strangely addicting**" at this pioneering Fort Greene "**original**", where "**friendly**" folks bring on the "**hearty**" traditional meals; "**fun**" digs with plenty of "**relaxed**" personality help keep "**everyone very happy.**"

MADISON BISTRO | French · · · 4.1 · 3.5 · 4.1 · $$$
Murray Hill | 238 Madison Ave. (bet. 37th & 38th Sts.)
212-447-1919 | www.madisonbistro.com

"**Every neighborhood should have a local bistro**" like this Murray Hill "**sleeper**" that's appreciated for its "**quality**" French cooking and prix fixe deals; "**well-behaved**" locals are drawn to its "**friendly**" vibe and "**relaxing**" (if "**generic**") dining room that's "**conducive to conversation.**"

MADONIA BROTHERS BAKERY | Bakery   4.5   3.3   4.0 $

Arthur Avenue/Belmont | 2348 Arthur Ave. (186th St.) | Bronx
718-295-5573

Get ready to "**splurge**" at this "**old-school**" Arthur Avenue bakery known for "**real-deal**" breads (olive, prosciutto, fennel raisin) so "**tremendous**" you'll "**eat half the loaf on the way home**"; with "**excellent**" freshly filled cannoli, biscotti and pastries too, it's no wonder it's been drawing "**hordes**" since 1918.

MAHARLIKA | Filipino   ▽ 4.3   3.8   4.1 $$

East Village | 111 First Ave. (bet. 6th & 7th Sts.)
646-392-7880 | www.maharlikanyc.com

Filipino food gets "**redefined**" at this "**hip**" East Village Jeepney sibling that jump-starts the "**not-mainstream**" cuisine with some modern "**twists**" (Spam fries, anyone?); its "**enthusiastic audience**" happily overlooks the kinda "**tight**" conditions given the overall "**cozy**" mood, "**warm**" service and bargain tabs.

MAIALINO | Italian   4.6   4.4   4.4 $$$

Gramercy Park | Gramercy Park Hotel | 2 Lexington Ave. (21st St.)
212-777-2410 | www.maialinonyc.com

"**Danny Meyer does things right, as usual**" at this "**love song to Rome**" overlooking Gramercy Park, where "**sublime**" farm-to-table Italian fare and "**stellar wines**" come in "**delightful**", "**buzzing**" digs via a "**welcoming**" pro staff; scoring a reservation can be "**challenging**" (though the "**bustling**" front bar welcomes "**drop-ins**"), and while prices run "**high**", at least "**the tip is included.**"

MAIELLA | Italian   4.5   4.5   4.5 $$

Long Island City | 4610 Center Blvd. (46th Ave.) | Queens
718-606-1770 | www.maiellalic.com

With "**first-rate**" fare from Rocco Sacramone (Trattoria L'incontro) and "**stunning**" skyline views, this Italian "**sleeper**" on the LIC waterfront delivers an "**exceptional**" Queens experience; "**attentive**" service, an "**inviting**" rustic-chic space and a patio are other reasons many swear it's "**worth the drive from the city.**"

MAISON HARLEM | French   ▽ 4.0   3.7   3.9 $$

Manhattanville | 341 St. Nicholas Ave. (127th St.)
212-222-9224 | www.maisonharlem.com

Like a little "**chunk of Paris**" transported to NYC, this all-day bistro on the Harlem/Manhattanville border supplies "**solid**" French classics in "**super-cozy**" quarters with a "**vintage**" vibe; it's a "**bustling scene**" that expands out onto the sidewalk in warmer months.

MAISON HUGO | French   4.0   3.8   4.0 $$$

East 60s | 132 E. 61st St. (Lexington Ave.)
212-832-0500 | www.maisonhugo.com

A "**discovery**" on the UES, this "**smart**" brasserie gives chef Florian Hugo a chance to "**shine**" with "**refreshing updates**" to "**traditional**" French fare served in a "**modern setting**"; the bill can run "**a little pricey**" – but that comes with the real estate.

	FOOD	DECOR	SERVICE	COST

MAISON KAYSER | Bakery/French   4.2   3.7   3.7 $$
East 80s | 1535 Third Ave. (74th St.) | 212-348-8400
Flatiron | 921 Broadway (21st St.) | 212-979-1600
TriBeCa | 355 Greenwich St. (Harrison St.) | no phone
West 40s | 8 W. 40th St. (bet. 5th & 6th Aves.) | 212-354-2300
West 50s | 1800 Broadway (bet. CPS & 58th St.) | 212-245-4100
West 70s | 2161 Broadway (76th St.) | 212-873-5900
West Village | 326 Bleecker St. (Christopher St.) | 212-645-7900
www.maison-kayser-usa.com

You'll "**feel transported to the Left Bank**" at these Paris-based cafes where the "**just-right**" baguettes, "**flaky**" croissants and "**high-end**" pastries are a "**highlight**", though the French "**bistro-style**" fare is "**tasty**" too; "**uneven**" service and "**deafening**" noise levels are reasons to go at off-hours.

MAISON PREMIERE | Seafood   4.5   4.6   4.3 $$
Williamsburg | 298 Bedford Ave. (1st St.) | Brooklyn
347-335-0446 | www.maisonpremiere.com

It "**really feels like the Big Easy**" at this "**gorgeous**" Williamsburg hang offering "**beautiful, plump**" oysters and "**serious**" cocktails (including "**creative**" absinthe options) alongside other "**delicious**" seafood-focused dishes in "**old New Orleans**" digs; snagging a seat is "**tough**", but a seasonal garden helps.

MALAPARTE | Italian   4.3   3.7   3.9 $$
West Village | 753 Washington St. (Bethune St.)
212-255-2122 | www.malapartenyc.com

"**High quality**" and "**low frills**" mark this West Village sibling to Malatesta, where the "**delizioso**" Italian "**country cuisine**" (read pizza and pasta) draws a "**hopping**" crowd into ultra-"**cozy**" digs; if the cash-only rule is a "**drawback**", at least "**the prices are right.**"

MALATESTA TRATTORIA | Italian   4.3   3.6   3.8 $$
West Village | 649 Washington St. (Christopher St.)
212-741-1207 | www.malatestatrattoria.com

"**Wonderful**" trattoria staples at "**reasonable**", cash-only rates make this "**friendly**", "**popular**" way West Village Northern Italian well "**worth**" the "**waits**" at prime times; the "**simple**" interior gets "**crowded and noisy**", but in the summertime, "**sidewalk dining**" offers a bit more elbow room.

MALECON | Dominican   4.2   3.2   3.7 $$
Washington Heights | 4141 Broadway (175th St.) | 212-927-3812
West 90s | 764 Amsterdam Ave. (bet. 97th & 98th Sts.) | 212-864-5648
Kingsbridge | 5592 Broadway (231st St.) | Bronx | 718-432-5155
www.maleconrestaurants.com

When "**you're looking for a fix**" of "**super-good**" "**traditional**" Dominican fare, it's "**hard to beat**" these "**favorites**" known especially for their "**mmm**" rotisserie chicken slathered in "**garlicky goodness**"; "**huge portions**" at "**bargain**" prices mean most don't mind if the settings are on the "**tacky**" side.

MALONEY & PORCELLI | Steak   4.5   4.2   4.4 $$$
East 50s | 37 E. 50th St. (bet. Madison & Park Aves.)
212-750-2233 | www.maloneyandporcelli.com

"**High quality all around**" marks Alan Stillman's Midtown "**classic**", a *Mad Men*-ish" cow palace where "**marvelous**" "**old-school**" servers ferry "**extraordinary steaks**", "**superb**" crackling pork shank and "**killer martinis**";

the "**mighty expensive**" tabs are somewhat eased by the nightly $85 wine dinner.

MAMAN | American/French   ∇   3.9   4.0   3.7 $

Little Italy | 239 Centre St. (bet. Broome & Grand Sts.) | 212-226-0770
NEW **NoLita** | 250 Bowery (bet. Houston & Prince Sts.) | no phone
TriBeCa | 211 W. Broadway (Franklin St.) | 646-882-8682
NEW **Greenpoint** | 80 Kent St. (Franklin St.) | Brooklyn | 347-689-9195
www.mamannyc.com

With a "**you're-in-Paris**" feel, these "**cozy**" bakery/cafes offer "**tasty**" French and American bites for breakfast and lunch, plus sweet stuff à la its "**famous chocolate chunk cookie**"; the "**cute**", shabby-chic spaces have rustic wood tables, and there's a to-go version in the International Center of Photography Museum.

MAMO | Italian   ∇   4.3   4.4   4.3 $$$

SoHo | 323 W. Broadway (bet. Canal & Grand Sts.)
646-964-4641 | www.mamonyc.com

Spun off from the celeb favorite in Antibes – a longtime staple for Cannes Film Festival attendees – this chic SoHo duplex offers pricey, "**well-executed**" Italian standards, including dishes from "**truffle heaven**"; with whitewashed walls and vintage movie posters, the "**beautiful**" space brings a "**bit of the South of France.**"

MAMOUN'S | Mideastern   4.4   2.8   3.8 $

East Village | 30 St. Marks Pl. (bet. 2nd & 3rd Aves.) | 212-387-7747
Greenwich Village | 119 MacDougal St. (bet. Minetta Ln. & W. 3rd St.) | 212-674-8685
www.mamouns.com

"**Tasty and hasty**" sums up these cross-Village Middle Eastern "**favorites**", whose "**awesome**" falafel and shawarma "**can't be beat**" for "**cheap, filling eats**" served into the "**wee hours**"; "**bare-bones**" digs with a serious "**space crunch**" don't keep them from "**bustling.**"

MANDUCATIS | Italian   4.3   3.7   4.1 $$

Long Island City | 13-27 Jackson Ave. (47th Ave.) | Queens | 718-729-4602 | www.manducatis.com

MANDUCATIS RUSTICA | Ice Cream/Pizza

Long Island City | 46-33 Vernon Blvd. (bet. 46th & 47th Sts.) | Queens | 718-937-1312 | www.manducatisrustica.com

"**You expect Tony Bennett to arrive**" any minute at this "**warm**", "**family-run**" LIC Italian supplying "**wonderful**" "**homestyle**" fare and wines from a "**deep**" list (plus there's the "**scaled-down**" Rustica offshoot focusing on pizza and gelato); yes, the look may be "**dated**", but fans say that only "**adds to the charm.**"

MANETTA'S | Italian   4.4   3.8   4.1 $$

Long Island City | 10-76 Jackson Ave. (11th St.) | Queens
718-786-6171 | www.manettaslic.com

"**Go with family**" to this LIC "**favorite**", a "**friendly**" "**neighborhood staple**" offering "**excellent**" wood-fired brick-oven pizza and "**everyday Italian**" eats likened to "**mom's cooking**"; while rather "**dated**" in the decor department, it's "**affordable**" and has a fireplace that's perfect on a "**cold winter's night.**"

	FOOD	DECOR	SERVICE	COST

MANHATTAN VALLEY | Indian   4.3   3.6   3.9 $$
West 90s | 2636 Broadway (100th St.)
212-222-9222 | www.manhattanvalleynyc.com

A **"neighborhood standby"**, this UWS Indian **"does the trick"** thanks to **"tasty"** standards and a **"plentiful"** weekend lunch buffet; a full bar, **"reasonable"** prices and **"friendly service"** further qualify it as a **"go-to."**

MANOUSHEH | Lebanese   ▽ 4.4   3.4   3.9 $
Greenwich Village | 193 Bleecker St. (MacDougal St.)
347-971-5778 | www.manousheh.com

"The freshest" housemade flatbreads are the trademark of this Greenwich Village Lebanese, which turns out **"excellent"** sandwiches and **"hand food"** via an **"engaged"** counter crew; rates are **"inexpensive"**, though the compact space makes a case for takeout.

MANZO | Italian/Steak   4.5   3.6   3.9 $$$
Flatiron | Eataly | 200 Fifth Ave. (bet. 23rd & 24th Sts.)
212-229-2180 | www.eataly.com

A **"walled-off oasis"** amid the **"flurry of Eataly"**, this full-service Italian steakhouse within the Batali-Bastianich food hall shows a **"nice range"** with **"terrific"** chops bolstered by **"excellent"** pastas and an **"extensive wine list"**; the venue's upmarket pricing carries over, but most report being **"well fed"** for the money.

MÁ PÊCHE | American   4.3   3.7   4.0 $$$
West 50s | Chambers Hotel | 15 W. 56th St. (bet. 5th & 6th Aves.)
212 757 5878 | www.momofuku.com

It's **"all about sharing"** at David Chang's **"innovative"** New American in Midtown's Chambers Hotel, where **"flavor-packed"** plates for the table join **"clever" "twists on dim sum"** (just **"flag down a trolley"**); **"blah"** decor may detract, but **"the food more than makes up for it."**

MAPO KOREAN B.B.Q. | Korean   ▽ 4.5   3.0   4.0 $$
Flushing | 149-24 41st Ave (149th Pl.) | Queens
718-886-8292

It's all about the tabletop barbecue at this **"tasty"** Flushing Korean, where the **"meats are everything"** and grilled over lump charcoal (insiders **"go for the fabulous marinated kalbi"**); maybe it **"needs improvement"** in the decor department, but at least the staff is **"patient"** and the pricing modest.

MARC FORGIONE | American   4.6   4.4   4.4 $$$
TriBeCa | 134 Reade St. (bet. Greenwich & Hudson Sts.)
212-941-9401 | www.marcforgione.com

This TriBeCa **"charmer"** from **"talented"** Iron Chef Marc Forgione **"excels in every way"** with **"superlative"** New American cooking and **"warm"**, **"knowledgeable"** service in a **"rustic"** space with **"romantic"** vibes; it's usually **"mobbed"** despite **"platinum-card"** pricing, so reservations are a foregone conclusion.

MARCONY | Italian   4.5   4.3   4.5 $$$
Murray Hill | 184 Lexington Ave. (bet. 31st & 32nd Sts.)
646-837-6020 | www.marconyusa.com

When an **"Italian vacation"** isn't in the cards, there's always this Murray Hill **"standout"** whose **"fantastic"** classic dishes with **"service to match"** arrive in

"**Capri-comes-to-NY**" digs (including "**sidewalk seating**"); given the "**all-around wonderful**" experience, fans don't blink at the "**pricey**" tab.

MARCO POLO | Italian   4.2   4.0   4.3 $$
Carroll Gardens | 345 Court St. (Union St.) | Brooklyn
718-852-5015 | www.marcopoloristorante.com

"**Old-school Italian in every respect**", this Carroll Gardens vet presents "**upscale red-sauce**" fare in a "**warm**" space complete with fireplace and murals; "**treat-you-like-family**" service and an "**amazing happy hour**" are two more reasons locals keep coming.

MAREA | Italian/Seafood   4.7   4.6   4.6 $$$$
West 50s | 240 Central Park S. (bet. B'way & 7th Ave.)
212-582-5100 | www.marea-nyc.com

"**Excellence abounds**" at Michael White's Italian "**star**" on Central Park South, where the "**adventurous**" seafood and "**heavenly**" housemade pastas "**never fail to wow**"; the "**impeccable**" service matches the "**sleek**", "**convivial**" setting – as well as the "**power broker**" prices (lunchtime set menus are a comparative "**steal**").

MARGAUX | French/Mediterranean   ▽ 4.1   3.9   4.0 $$
Greenwich Village | Marlton Hotel | 5 W. Eighth St. (bet. 5th & 6th Aves.)
212-321-0111 | www.marltonhotel.com

Breakfast through dinner, this Village cafe in the "**charming**" Marlton Hotel fields an "**original**" roster of seasonal French-Med fare served "**with no drama**" in "**comfortable**", faux-Parisian surrounds; there's a skylit "**garden room**", and the "**lively**" bar is apt to be "**jammed with hip sippers.**"

MARIA PIA | Italian   4.0   3.7   4.1 $$
West 50s | 319 W. 51st St. (8th Ave.)
212-765-6463 | www.mariapianyc.com

"**Geared to the pre-theater crowd**", this "**reliable**" Hell's Kitchen "**red-sauce**" Italian keeps 'em coming back with "**quick**" service, a "**charming garden**" and "**reasonable**" rates (especially the $27 dinner prix fixe); non-showgoers hit it "**off-hours**" to avoid the "**noisy**" crush.

MARIETTA | Southern   ▽ 4.3   3.9   4.2 $$$
Clinton Hill | 285 Grand Ave. (Clifton Pl.) | Brooklyn
718-638-9500 | www.bcrestaurantgroup.com

The "**fried chicken is a must**" at this Clinton Hill "**hit**", a Peaches sibling whose "**creative**", carefully sourced takes on Southern classics are "**super-satisfying**" and "**won't hurt your pocket**"; the "**comfortable**" space done up in Americana gets particularly packed during weekend brunch.

MARIO'S | Italian   4.1   3.7   4.1 $$
Arthur Avenue/Belmont | 2342 Arthur Ave. (bet. Crescent Ave. & 184th St.) | Bronx
718-584-1188 | www.mariosrestarthurave.com

A Neapolitan "**home away from home**" on the Arthur Avenue "**tourist strip**", this "**iconic red-sauce**" joint is nearly a century old and still "**never steers you wrong**"; "**friendly**" waiters working the "**bustling**", "**no-pretense**" digs ensure regulars remain in their "**comfort zone.**"

	FOOD	DECOR	SERVICE	COST

MARI VANNA | Russian   4.2   4.3   4.2 $$$
Flatiron | 41 E. 20th St. (bet. B'way & Park Ave. S.)
212-777-1955 | www.marivanna.ru

Like "**stepping into your grandmother's house in Moscow**" – but with
a "**party**" vibe fueled by "**flowing vodka**" – this "**fabulous**" Flatiron magnet
for "**expats**" and "**beautiful young things**" serves up "**hearty**" Russian
staples; "**attentive**" service and a "**unique-in-NY**" experience help justify
the "**pricey**" tab.

THE MARK | American   4.3   4.5   4.2 $$
East 70s | Mark Hotel | 25 E. 77th St. (bet. 5th & Madison Aves.)
212-744-4300 | www.themarkrestaurantnyc.com

Jean-Georges Vongerichten "**hits a high mark**" at this "**chic**" Upper Eastsider,
where "**well-heeled**" types "**expect nothing less**" than "**deft**" New American
cuisine at prices that "**push the envelope**", "**civility reigns**" in the "**fancy**"
dining room, but "**check out the action**" in the "**hopping bar.**"

MARKET TABLE | American   4.4   4.1   4.3 $$$
West Village | 54 Carmine St. (Bedford St.)
212-255-2100 | www.markettablenyc.com

A "**solid farm-to-table**" approach makes for "**engaging dishes**" at this West
Village New American, a corner outfit with "**big picture windows**", "**warm**"
service and an "**unpretentious**" vibe; it "**continues to amaze**" a wide following,
meaning it's on the "**crowded**" side at prime times.

MARKJOSEPH STEAKHOUSE | Steak   4.3   3.8   4.2 $$$
South Street Seaport | 261 Water St. (bet. Dover St. & Peck Slip)
212-277-0020 | www.markjosephsteakhouse.com

Pack a "**huge appetite**" and a "**corporate card**" to best enjoy this chop shop
"**on the fringe of the Financial District**", where "**lunch is a better value**";
"**no-frills**", "**standard steakhouse**" digs put the focus on the "**outstanding**"
beef (and "**even better**" bacon appetizer) delivered by "**friendly pro**" staffers.

MARLOW & SONS | American   ▽ 4.4   4.1   4.2 $$
Williamsburg | 81 Broadway (Berry St.) | Brooklyn
718-384-1441 | www.marlowandsons.com

An "**upscale**" Williamsburg "**hipster**" joint from way back, this "**market-to-table**"
pioneer puts forth a daily changing menu of "**delicious-in-every-detail**" New
American fare, matched with an "**excellent**" drinks list; factor in the "**appropriately
Brooklyn**" staff and vibe, and no wonder it's "**always a good time.**"

MARSEILLE | French/Mediterranean   4.0   3.9   3.9 $$$
West 40s | 630 Ninth Ave. (44th St.)
212-333-2323 | www.marseillenyc.com

"**Like being in Paris – but with better service**" – this Theater District French-
Med brasserie serves a "**well-priced**", "**quality**" menu in a rather "**hectic**" room
that suggests "*Casablanca*"; its trump card is "**convenience**" to Broadway
shows, and they know how to "**get you out in time for your curtain.**"

THE MARSHAL | American   4.3   3.3   4.0 $$$
West 40s | 628 10th Ave. (bet. 44th & 45th Sts.)
212-582-6300 | www.the-marshal.com

A "**serious farm-to-table experience**", this Hell's Kitchen "**find**" reliably "**packs
a wallop**" with its "**well-crafted**", sustainably sourced New American dishes

and "**NY-purveyed**" wines; yes, the "**teeny**", brick-lined storefront space is a "**tight fit**", but to most it's "**worth the squeeze.**"

MARTA | Italian/Pizza   4.4   4.1   4.2 $$
NoMad | The Redbury New York | 29 E. 29th St. (bet. Madison & Park Aves.)
212-651-3800 | www.martamanhattan.com

Another "**stunner**" from Danny Meyer, this "**happening**" Italian in NoMad's Redbury Hotel is known for its "**perfectly crisp**" Roman pizzas adorned with "**first-rate**" toppings, but the wood-fired entrees are considered "**just as good**"; the "**high-ceiling, high-energy**" space and "**hip crowd**" add up to a "**noisy**", "**fun**" time.

MARUZZELLA | Italian   4.2   3.6   4.2 $$$
East 70s | 1483 First Ave. (bet. 77th & 78th Sts.)
212-988-8877 | www.maruzzellanyc.com

There's "**nothing fancy**" about this UES "**quintessential neighborhood Italian**", just "**surprisingly good**" cooking brought to the table by "**old-school**" servers; "**friendly owners**" on the scene and "**reasonable**"-for-the-zip-code rates make the "**modest**" decor easy to overlook.

MARY'S FISH CAMP | Seafood   4.4   3.5   4.0 $$
West Village | 64 Charles St. (4th St.)
646-486-2185 | www.marysfishcamp.com

With its "**fresh-off-the-boat**" seafood, "**killer**" lobster roll and "**laid-back**" vibe, it's like being at a "**New England fish house**" at this "**dependable**" West Village joint; "**tiny**" digs, "**elbow-to-elbow**" seating and "**tough**" waits (no reservations) are a "**small price to pay**" given the "**wonderful**" grub.

MASA | Japanese   4.5   4.5   4.4 $$$$
West 50s | Time Warner Ctr. | 10 Columbus Circle (bet. 58th & 59th Sts.)
212-823-9800 | www.masanyc.com

"**If you don't mind spending**", chef Masayoshi Takayama's omakase meals are mighty "**delectable**" at this "**Zen-like**" Japanese in the Time Warner Center that fans dub a "**once-in-a-lifetime**" experience; the $450-and-up set price strikes most as "**prohibitive**", though à la carte tabs are somewhat more "**tolerable**" in the "**less formal**" bar.

MAS (FARMHOUSE) | American   4.7   4.5   4.7 $$$$
West Village | 39 Downing St. (Bedford St.)
212-255-1790 | www.masfarmhouse.com

Chef Galen Zamarra brings a "**magic touch**" to "**farm-to-table**" American cuisine at this "**splurge-worthy**" West Villager, which exudes "**understated rustic elegance**" from the "**quietish**", "**romantic**" setting to the "**relaxed-but-stellar**" service; pro tip: tasting menus are where the kitchen's "**talents really shine;**" P.S. closed at press time due to a fire.

MASTRO'S STEAKHOUSE | Steak   4.4   4.2   4.3 $$$
West 50s | 1285 Sixth Ave. (52nd St.)
212-459-1222 | www.mastrosrestaurants.com

The mood's "**upbeat**" at this Midtown outlet of the national chophouse chain, where "**perfectly cooked**" steaks and "**plentiful**" sides are delivered by "**attentive**" servers in "**noisy**" digs complete with live music upstairs ("**downstairs is quieter**"); the tabs are "**not for the faint of heart**", but most maintain you "**get your money's worth.**"

	FOOD	DECOR	SERVICE	COST

MAYA | Mexican   4.1   3.9   3.9 $$$
East 60s | 1191 First Ave. (bet. 64th & 65th Sts.)
212-585-1818 | www.richardsandoval.com

"Not your usual Mexican" cucina, this "elevated" Upper Eastsider supplies "exciting" cooking with "full flavor in every bite" via a "solicitous" staff; the "smart setting" (with a "vibrant" tequileria attached) "tends to get loud" and it runs "a little pricey", "but hey, you get what you pay for."

MAYFIELD | American   ▽ 4.2   4.0   4.1 $$
Crown Heights | 688 Franklin Ave. (Prospect Pl.) | Brooklyn
347-318-3643 | www.mayfieldbk.com

"A real find" in Crown Heights, this "comfortable" New American offers a "creative" lineup of "Southern-influenced" plates in charmingly "rough-and-tumble" digs; staffers who "know what they're doing" suit the happening neighborhood, but the "price point is vintage Brooklyn."

MAYSVILLE | American   4.2   4.0   4.2 $$$
NoMad | 17 W. 26th St. (bet. B'way & 6th Ave.)
646-490-8240 | www.maysvillenyc.com

An "awe-inspiring" bourbon and whiskey selection, "great cocktails" and "inventive" Southern-accented dishes draw a "younger crowd" to this NoMad New American; the "chill but grown-up" space includes a lively front bar area, and brunch is popular as well.

MAZ MEZCAL | Mexican   4.1   3.8   4.1 $$
East 80s | 316 E. 86th St. (bet. 1st & 2nd Aves.)
212-472-1599 | www.mazmezcal.com

"Hits all the right spots" say Yorkville locals of this "family-owned" Mexican "standby" where a "lively neighborhood crowd" assembles for "tasty" classics; "reasonable prices" and "friendly" service are further reasons why it's "still packed after all these years."

MEADOWSWEET | American   4.7   4.5   4.6 $$$
Williamsburg | 149 Broadway (bet. Bedford & Driggs Aves.) | Brooklyn
718-384-0673 | www.meadowsweetnyc.com

The flavors are "on point" at this Williamsburg "standout" from former Dressler chef Polo Dobkin whose "ever-changing" New American menu highlights his "ingenuity"; the "bright, airy" space has a "hip", "laid-back" vibe, and the "attentive" staff is another big plus.

MEATBALL SHOP | Sandwiches   3.9   3.4   3.7 $$
Chelsea | 200 Ninth Ave. (bet. 22nd & 23rd Sts.) | 212-257-4363
East 70s | 1462 Second Ave. (bet. 76th & 77th Sts.) | 212-257-6121
Lower East Side | 84 Stanton St. (bet. Allen & Orchard Sts.) | 212-982-8895
West 80s | 447 Amsterdam Ave. (81st St.) | 212-422-1752
West Village | 64 Greenwich Ave. (11th St.) | 212-982-7815
Williamsburg | 170 Bedford Ave. (bet. N. 7th & 8th Sts.) | Brooklyn | 718-551-0520
www.themeatballshop.com

"Meatballs rule" at these sandwich shops slinging "reliable" "mix-and-match" balls (meat, chicken, veggie) paired with "lots" of sauces, plus "snappy cocktails", "nice beers on tap" and "sinful" ice cream sandwiches; "millennials" and the stroller set keep things "boisterous", but at least tabs are "gentle."

	FOOD	DECOR	SERVICE	COST

MEIJIN RAMEN | Japanese/Noodle Shop   4.2   3.9   4.1 $
East 80s | 1574 Second Ave. (82nd St.)
212-327-2800

Upper Eastsiders craving "**noodle slurping goodness**" hail this Japanese joint's "**flavorful**" ramen and izakaya-style small plates (a next-door annex offers desserts and cocktails); the seating's mostly "**communal**", but no one cares given the "**reasonable**" tabs and "**hits-the-spot**" cooking.

MELBA'S | American/Southern   4.3   4.0   4.1 $$
Harlem | 300 W. 114th St. (8th Ave.)
212-864-7777 | www.melbasrestaurant.com

"**Down-home**" Southern dishes including a "**fan-favorite**" chicken 'n' waffles ensure this "**comforting**" Harlem American remains "**loved by all**"; indeed, the "**friendly**" atmosphere trumps the "**cramped**" setting and "**long waits**" for its "**to-die-for**" brunch.

MÉMÉ | Mediterranean/Moroccan   4.4   3.8   4.3 $$
NEW **West 40s** | 607 10th Ave. (44th St.) | 917-262-0827
West Village | 581 Hudson St. (Bank St.) |646-692-8450
www.mememediterranean.com

It's "**great to go with folks and share**" to these "**affordable**" "**neighborhood**" Mediterraneans dispensing "**wonderful**" small plates and entrees with "**Moroccan flair**"; "**friendly**" service and an appealing "**bohemian**" vibe will "**keep you returning**", unless the "**tight-packed tables**" make you feel like you're "**flying coach.**"

MERCATO | Italian   4.3   3.7   4.0 $$
West 30s | 352 W. 39th St. (bet. 8th & 9th Aves.)
212-643-2000 | www.mercatonyc.com

A "**pleasant surprise**" in a restaurant-"**barren**" zone a few blocks from the Port Authority, this "**well-kept secret**" slings "**genuine homestyle**" Italian food in a "**cozy**", "**rustic**" setting; factor in "**reasonable**" rates and to most it's "**worth seeking out**" when in the area.

MERCER KITCHEN | American/French   4.2   4.1   3.8 $$$
SoHo | Mercer Hotel | 99 Prince St. (Mercer St.)
212-966-5454 | www.themercerkitchen.com

Ever "**chic**", Jean-Georges Vongerichten's "**still buzzy**" SoHo vet in the Mercer Hotel is touted for "**enjoyable**" Franco-American cooking offered in "**dimly lit**" subterranean digs; despite some "**snobbish**" 'tudes and "**pricey**" tabs, the "**great location**" and "**models-'r'-us**" vibe keep it ever "**bustling.**"

MERMAID INN | Seafood   4.2   3.9   4.1 $$$
East Village | 96 Second Ave. (bet. 5th & 6th Sts.) | 212-674-5870
West 80s | 570 Amsterdam Ave. (bet. 87th & 88th Sts.) | 212-799-7400

MERMAID OYSTER BAR | Seafood
Greenwich Village | 79 MacDougal St. (bet. Bleecker & Houston Sts.) |
212-260-0100
www.themermaidnyc.com

Like dining "**at the shore**", these New England–inspired "**standbys**" supply "**spot-on**" seafood highlighted by a most "**worthy lobster roll**"; trade-offs include "**high decibels**" and "**tight quarters**" (although the expanded UWS outpost is "**more comfortable**"), especially when the "**unbeatable happy hour**" rolls around with its "**swell**" oyster deals.

MESA COYOACAN | Mexican   4.4   4.2   4.2 $$

Williamsburg | 372 Graham Ave. (bet. Conselyea St. & Skillman Ave.) | Brooklyn

718-782-8171 | www.mesacoyoacan.com

There's **"always something to discover"** at this **"upbeat"** Williamsburg Mexican, a dispenser of **"sensational"** Mexico City–style cuisine and **"absolutely killer margaritas"** at an **"affordable"** cost; a **"very cool"** staff and **"creative"** decor help keep the mood **"warm"** and **"inviting."**

NEW **METROGRAPH** | American   —   —   — $$$
COMMISSARY

Lower East Side | The Metrograph | 7 Ludlow St. (bet. Canal & Hester Sts.)

212-660-0312 | www.metrograph.com

Inside the Lower East Side cinema, this American eatery with two bars (one in the lobby) is designed to evoke Hollywood's old-time studio hangouts, with elegant couches and potted palms setting the mood. The menu offers straightforward entrees and classic salads, plus a few modern touches.

NEW **METROPOLIS** | Seafood   —   —   — $$

Union Square | 31 Union Sq. W., downstairs (16th St.)

212-533-2500 | www.metropolisnewyork.com

Nestled beneath Blue Water Grill, this swank spot offers oysters and share-worthy seafood alongside an impressive cocktail program (think martinis for two mixed tableside). Jazz combos perform in a low-lit room done up with gray hues, hand-painted murals and velvet drapes.

MEXICO LINDO | Mexican   3.9   3.7   4.3 $$

Murray Hill | 459 Second Ave. (26th St.)

212-679-3665 | www.mexicolindonyc.com

A Murray Hill **"fixture"** since 1972, this neighborhood **"hidden gem"** is touted for its **"down-to-earth"** Mexican cooking, **"friendly"** service and **"best-buy"** prices; maybe it **"needs a makeover"**, but no one cares **"after a margarita or two."**

NEW **MEYERS BAGERI** | Bakery   —   —   — $

Williamsburg | 667 Driggs Ave. (Fillmore Pl.) | Brooklyn

no phone

Spun off from the Denmark original, this petite Williamsburg bakery by Claus Meyer (Agern, Copenhagen's Noma) sells hearty Nordic breads and a few sandwiches as well as serious cinnamon swirls, tarts and, yes, Danishes. There's a window onto the work area behind the counter, and just a few wooden tables with seating on white benches.

MEZZALUNA | Italian   4.2   3.6   3.9 $$

East 70s | 1295 Third Ave. (74th St.)

212-535-9600 | www.mezzalunanyc.com

Despite the **"tiniest"** of dimensions, this 1984-vintage UES Italian boasts a **"strong"** track record, **"swiftly"** sending out wood-oven pizzas (**"the highlight"**) and other **"soulful"** standards; regulars who keep it **"crowded"** confirm it's **"what a neighborhood place should be."**

MICHAEL JORDAN'S | Steak   3.9   3.9   3.9 $$$
THE STEAK HOUSE NYC

East 40s | Grand Central | 23 Vanderbilt Ave. (42nd St.)

212-655-2300 | www.michaeljordansnyc.com

It's the **"unusual location"** – a balcony overlooking the **"scurrying"** masses in Grand Central's Main Concourse – that's the hook at this **"reliable"** chophouse, where the beef is **"aged"** and the prices **"high"**; critics find **"nothing original"** here, but to fans the **"cool setting"** alone is a **"slam dunk."**

MICHAEL'S | Californian 4.3 4.1 4.2 $$$

West 50s | 24 W. 55th St. (bet. 5th & 6th Aves.)
212-767-0555 | www.michaelsnewyork.com

"Media titans" and other **"heavy hitters"** collect at this **"classy"** Midtowner that's known more for its breakfast and lunch **"power"** scenes than its **"fresh"**, **"premium-priced"** Californian fare and **"pro"** service; **"relaxed"** dinners come **"without the hot crowd"**, but there's always the **"lovely"** room's **"fresh flowers and art"** to look at.

MIGHTY QUINN'S BARBECUE | BBQ 4.3 3.3 3.6 $

Battery Park City | Hudson Eats | 230 Vesey St. (West St.) | 646-649-2777
NEW **East 70s** | 1492 Second Ave. (78th St.) | 646-484-5691
East Village | 103 Second Ave. (6th St.) | 212-677-3733
West Village | 75 Greenwich Ave. (bet. Bank & 11th Sts.) | 646-524-7889
Crown Heights | Berg'n | 899 Bergen St. (bet. Classon & Franklin Aves.) |
Brooklyn | 718-857-2337
www.mightyquinnsbbq.com

Those who **"hail the meat god"** rely on this **"no-fuss"** counter-serve chain for **"delicious"** BBQ **"fixes"** (including **"perfectly toothsome brisket"**) offered **"cafeteria-style"**; **"barebones"** setups and **"insane"** lines are part of the package, but so are **"reasonable"** prices.

MIKE'S BISTRO | American/Kosher ∇ 4.5 4.1 4.2 $$$$

East 50s | 127 E. 54th St. (bet. Lexington & Park Aves.)
212-799-3911 | www.mikesbistro.com

An **"upscale"** endeavor from a namesake chef-owner **"who cares"**, this East Midtowner offers **"creative"** New American fare prepared with such **"elegance"** that you'd **"never know it was kosher"**; overseen by a **"helpful"** staff, it's typically **"busy"** despite the **"high prices."**

MILE END | Deli 4.2 3.3 3.8 $$

Boerum Hill | 97 Hoyt St. (bet. Atlantic Ave. & Pacific St.) | Brooklyn |
718-852-7510

MILE END SANDWICH SHOP | Sandwiches

NoHo | 53 Bond St. (bet. Bowery & Lafayette St.) | 212-529-2990
www.mileenddeli.com

Prepare for a **"different kind"** of fress at these **"hip, low-key"** spots where the Montreal-style Jewish deli menu is highlighted by **"killer"** house-smoked meats; sure, the **"bare-bones"** settings can get a bit **"cramped"**, but even purists admit they give the old guard **"a run for their money."**

MILK BAR | Dessert 4.1 3.3 3.7 $

NEW **Chelsea** | 220 Eighth Ave. (21st St.) | 347-577-9504
East Village | 251 E. 13th St. (2nd Ave.) | 347-577-9504
West 50s | 15 W. 56th St. (5th Ave.) | 347-577-9504
West 80s | 561 Columbus Ave. (87th St.) | 347-577-9504
Carroll Gardens | 360 Smith St. (bet. 1st & 2nd Pl.) | Brooklyn | 347-577-9504
Williamsburg | 382 Metropolitan Ave. (bet. Havenmeyer St. & Marcy Ave.) |
Brooklyn | 347-577-9504
www.milkbarstore.com

"Get your sugar fix" on at these **"destinations"** for pastry chef Christina Tosi's "**weirdly delicious concoctions**" like compost cookies, cereal milk ice cream and appropriately "**addictive**" crack pie; the setups are simple, and while "**too sweet**" for a few, most embrace the "**sinfulness.**"

MILKFLOWER | Pizza   ▽ 4.5   3.8   4.0 $$

Astoria | 34-12 31st Ave. (bet. 34th & 35th Sts.) | Queens
718-204-1300 | www.milkflowernyc.com

"**Artisanal**" Neapolitan pies with "**crispy**", wood-oven crusts and locavore toppings have pizza fans "**on a cloud**" over this "**hipster-chic**" Astoria storefront, also home to pastas and small plates that "**pair nicely**" with craft beer and wine; the narrow, brick-lined space with a "**relaxed**" feel is adjoined by a back garden.

MILL BASIN DELI | Deli/Kosher   4.3   3.5   4.0 $$

Flatlands | 5823 Ave. T (bet. 58th & 59th Sts.) | Brooklyn
718-241-4910 | www.millbasindeli.com

"**Old-style deliciousness**" lives on at this '70s-era deli on the Flatlands–Mill Basin border, home to Jewish "**standard-bearers**" like "**overstuffed sandwiches**" piled high with pastrami; a wall of paintings for sale lends "**arty**" appeal, and though costs skew "**high**", the "**hearty**" fare leaves most "**satisfied.**"

MILLING ROOM | American   4.3   4.3   4.1 $$

West 80s | 446 Columbus Ave. (bet. 81st & 82nd Sts.)
212-595-0380 | www.themillingroom.com

A "well-curated" New American menu with "flair" is matched by a "gorgeous" dining room at this "sprawling" Upper Westsider; the "**welcoming**" vibe spills over to the "**big**" bar where "**delicious cocktails**" help keep things "**lively.**"

MILOS | Greek/Seafood   4.7   4.4   4.3 $$$$

West 50s | 125 W. 55th St. (bet. 6th & 7th Aves.)
212-245-7400 | www.milos.ca

A "**class act**", this "**glorious**" Midtown Greek specializes in "**fresh-as-it-gets**" seafood served up in a "**cavernous**" white-on-white space that gets especially "**energetic**" at lunch; "**by-the-ounce**" pricing can add up ("**buying your own boat may be less expensive**"), but the prix fixe options are a relative "**bargain.**"

NEW **MIMI** | French   —   —   — $$$

Greenwich Village | 185 Sullivan St. (bet. Bleecker & Houston Sts.)
212-418-1260 | www.miminyc.com

A young team takes on traditional Gallic fare at this tiny Greenwich Village French delivering modern interpretations of high-end classics. There's both bar and banquette seating, with mod pendant lights and marble surfaces accenting the charming space.

MIMI CHENG'S DUMPLINGS | Taiwanese   4.3   3.4   3.8 $

East Village | 179 Second Ave. (12th St.)
no phone | www.mimichengs.com

"**Simply delicious**" dumplings made with local, "**healthy ingredients**" keep this "**super-friendly**" East Villager's "**minimalist**" counter-serve digs "**busy**"; "**inspired combos**" and "**fun**" seasonal specials are two more reasons fans say it's "**worth**" the somewhat "**high**" prices for the genre.

	FOOD	DECOR	SERVICE	COST

MIMI'S HUMMUS | Mideastern   4.3   3.4   4.0 $
Gramercy Park | 245 E. 14th St. (2nd Ave.) | 212-951-1105
Ditmas Park | 1209 Cortelyou Rd. (bet. Argyle & Westminster Rds.) |
Brooklyn | 718-284-4444
www.mimishummus.com

"**Who knew hummus could be so extravagant?**" say fans who "**dream**"
of the namesake dish at these "**cozy**" nooks that "**keep it simple**" with
Middle Eastern small plates, bowls and sweets, plus beer and wine;
"**reasonable**" prices are the icing on the cake, though "**tiny**" digs mean
many opt for "**takeout.**"

MINCA | Japanese/Noodle Shop   ∇ 4.3   3.1   3.5 $$
East Village | 536 E. Fifth St. (bet. Aves. A & B)
212-505-8001 | www.newyorkramen.com

There are "**no pretenses**" at this "**traditional**" Japanese noodle shop in the
East Village, just the "**charming simplicity**" of "**delicious**" ramen featuring
"**rich**", "**slurp-worthy**" broth, plus gyoza "**just like in Tokyo**"; its "**tiny**", "**basic**"
space is "**perpetually packed**", but "**fast**" servers keep things on track.

MINETTA TAVERN | French   4.4   4.1   4.1 $$$
Greenwich Village | 113 MacDougal St. (Minetta Ln.)
212-475-3850 | www.minettatavernny.com

"**Nostalgia trip**" meets "**trendiness**" at Keith McNally's "**energetic**" Village
"**standout**" that revives a circa-1937 tavern with "**vintage**" knickknacks,
"**snappy**" service and "**excellent**" French fare including a "**mind-blowing**"
Black Label burger ("**holy cow!**"); the prospect of "**famous**" faces in the back
room keeps it a "**tough table**", despite digs "**more crowded than the subway.**"

MIRIAM | Israeli/Mediterranean   4.1   3.7   3.8 $$
Park Slope | 79 Fifth Ave. (Prospect Pl.) | Brooklyn
718-622-2250 | www.miriamrestaurant.com

"**Dinner is a pleasure**" but Park Slopers flock to this "**affordable**" Israeli-
Mediterranean mainly for its daily brunch; since it's usually a "**mob scene**"
on weekends, insiders "**go at off times**" for a calmer taste of the "**tasty**" fare.

MISSION CANTINA | Chinese/Mexican   3.7   3.3   3.6 $$
Lower East Side | 172 Orchard St. (Stanton St.)
212-254-2233 | www.missioncantinany.com

"**Untraditional**" spins on Mexican classics plus a few Chinese dishes fill the
ever-changing menu at Danny Bowien's "**funky**" LES follow-up to Mission
Chinese; though "**memorably hip**" to many, a few who find it "**overhyped**"
say it "**doesn't work as well**" as its sibling.

MISSION CHINESE FOOD | Chinese   4.3   3.9   3.9 $$
Lower East Side | 171 E. Broadway (bet. Jefferson & Rutgers Sts.)
no phone | www.missionchinesefood.com

"**Exciting takes**" on Chinese cooking can be found at Danny Bowien's "**hip**"
LES hang that offers "**crazy delicious**" Californian Sichuan fare known for
its "**mouth-tingling**" spice; a "**cool crowd**" fills the "**boisterous**" digs, where
"**powerful**" cocktails come in handy during the "**long waits.**"

MISS KOREA BBQ | Korean   4.0   3.5   3.6 $$
West 30s | 10 W. 32nd St. (bet. B'way & 5th Ave.)
212-594-4963 | www.on3rd.misskoreabbq.com

This second-floor Korean BBQ specialist is a "**K-town favorite**" for "**authentic**" classics in a "**spacious**", Zen-like setting; it feels "**a cut above**" others "**without being more expensive**" – no wonder it's "**always packed.**"

MISS LILY'S | Jamaican   4.1   3.9   3.9 $$
Greenwich Village | 132 W. Houston St. (Sullivan St.) | 646-588-5375

MISS LILY'S 7A CAFE | Jamaican
East Village | 109 Ave. A (7th St.) | 212-812-1482
www.misslilys.com

Serge Becker's "**sexy**" Jamaican joints are set in "**fun**" rooms pulsing with "**hip**" island tunes and overseen by "**beautiful**" staffers; the well-priced Caribbean eats are "**tasty**", while "**fresh**", green juices from Melvin's Juice Box ice the cake.

MISS MAMIE'S | Soul Food   4.3   3.3   3.8 $$
SPOONBREAD TOO
West 100s | 366 W. 110th St. (Columbus Ave.)
212-865-6744 | www.spoonbreadinc.com

"**Real Southern comfort food**" in "**tremendous portions**" keeps fans of "**homestyle cooking**" loyal to this UWS soul fooder; OK, the decor's "**kind of plain**" and the "**friendly**" servers "**can be slow**", but no one minds given the "**fair prices.**"

THE MODERN | American/French   4.6   4.6   4.6 $$$$
West 50s | Museum of Modern Art | 9 W. 53rd St. (bet. 5th & 6th Aves.)
212-333-1220 | www.themodernnyc.com

"**Reliably superb**" French–New American cuisine "**as modern as the art**" is the deal at Danny Meyer's "**effortlessly chic**" eatery inside MoMA, where the "**tranquil**" dining room boasts "**lovely**" sculpture garden views and service is "**impeccable**" ("**refreshing**" no-tipping policy notwithstanding); such "**high-end sophistication**" is unsurprisingly "**pricey**", but the "**more casual**" front bar area is "**easier on the wallet.**"

MOLLY'S | Pub Food   4.3   3.9   4.3 $$
Gramercy Park | 287 Third Ave. (22nd St.)
212-889-3361 | www.mollysshebeen.com

A burger that "**could vie for best in town**" served by "**lovely Colleens**" make this "**step-back-in-time**" Irish pub a Gramercy "**favorite**"; with a "**like-in-Dublin**" feel that includes a "**sawdust-covered floor**" and "**wood-burning fireplace**", it's the "**real deal.**"

MOLYVOS | Greek   4.3   4.0   4.1 $$$
West 50s | Wellington Hotel | 871 Seventh Ave. (bet. 55th & 56th Sts.)
212-582-7500 | www.molyvos.com

An "**oh-so-convenient location**" to Carnegie Hall and City Center is one of the draws at this "**perennial favorite**" that follows through with "**top-notch**" Greek grub and "**amiable**" service; "**bearable**" acoustics and a "**spacious-by-Manhattan-standards**" setting complete the "**solid**" picture.

MOMOFUKU KO | American   4.7   4.3   4.6 $$$$
East Village | 8 Extra Pl. (1st. St.)
212-203-8095 | www.momofuku.com

A "**phenomenal experience**" for an "**open-minded foodie**", David Chang's East Village "**event**" provides a "**fascinating tour**" of Asian-inspired American cuisine via "**extraordinary**" tasting menus crafted at a sleekly "**comfortable**" chef's counter; the "**steep**" price tag is considered "**well worth**" it, so reservations are still as "**tough**" as "**getting past heaven's gates.**"

NEW **MOMOFUKU NISHI** | Asian/Italian   4.3   3.7   3.9 $$

Chelsea | 232 Eighth Ave. (22nd St.)
646-518-1919 | www.nishi.momofuku.com

An "**adventurous**" blend of Italian and Asian influences make for "**mostly delish**" dishes, including an "**epic**" riff on cacio e pepe, at this "**hype**"-generating David Chang joint; the "**minimalist**" Chelsea digs and "**tight**" communal tables aren't for everyone (especially given "**expensive**" pricing), but most agree it's "**something to try**" – at least once.

MOMOFUKU NOODLE BAR | American   4.5   3.6   3.9 $$

East Village | 171 First Ave. (bet. 10th & 11th Sts.)
212-777-7773 | www.momofuku.com

"**Noodle bliss**" awaits at this "**lively**" East Village American where "**master**" chef David Chang offers specialties like his "**hallmark pork buns**" and "**complex**" ramen bowls; "**crammed**" quarters and "**long waits**" detract, but the payoff is "**awesome**" eating "**without breaking the bank.**"

MOMOFUKU SSÄM BAR | Asian   4.5   3.6   4.0 $$

East Village | 207 Second Ave. (13th St.)
212-254-3500 | www.momofuku.com

The "**bold**" dishes are always "**a wow**" at David Chang's East Village Asian, which remains "**as good as advertised**", especially if you get the "**addictive**" pork buns or "**grab a few friends**" for the large-format pork shoulder spread; predictably, the "**bare-bones**" setup is typically "**mobbed**" with groupies who "**can't get enough**"; P.S. a renovation is in the works.

NEW **MOMOSAN RAMEN** | Noodle Shop   ∇ 4.6   4.3   4.3 $$
& SAKE

Murray Hill | 342 Lexington Ave. (bet. 39th & 40th Sts.)
646-201-5529 | www.momosanramen.com

An "**authentic ramen**" joint by Iron Chef Masaharu Morimoto, this Murray Hill spot focuses on four types of "**phenomenal**" bowls – including Tokyo-style chicken and pork with spicy coconut curry – plus "**top-notch**" appetizers; communal seating creates a "**nice buzz**", and set lunches and happy-hour specials bolster the "**reasonable**" cost.

MOMO SUSHI SHACK | Japanese   ∇ 4.6   4.4   4.4 $$

Bushwick | 43 Bogart St. (Moore St.) | Brooklyn
718-418-6666 | www.momosushishack.com

Understated but "**definitely not a shack**", this Bushwick Japanese "**go-to**" serves "**interesting, delicious**" small plates and "**unconventional**" sushi (including lots of veggie options); its wooden communal tables "**fill up fast**" at prime times, so regulars "**get there early.**"

MOMOYA | Japanese   4.4   3.8   4.0 $$

Chelsea | 185 Seventh Ave. (21st St.) | 212-989-4466
West 80s | 427 Amsterdam Ave. (bet. 80th & 81st Sts.) | 212-580-0007
www.momoyanyc.com

"**Sublimely fresh**" sushi and "**inventive**" cooked dishes keep these "**sophisticated**" Japanese eateries "**packed**" with "**neighborhood**" types; "**prompt, friendly**" servers man the "**modern**" surrounds, further justifying prices deemed slightly "**more expensive**" than some competitors.

MONKEY BAR | American   4.0   4.3   4.0 $$$

East 50s | Elysée Hotel | 60 E. 54th St. (bet. Madison & Park Aves.)
212-288-1010 | www.monkeybarnewyork.com

The "**jazz-age ambiance**" endures at Graydon Carter's "**old-school**" Midtown canteen lined with Ed Sorel's "**wonderful**" murals of 1920s-era celebs; its American grub is "**better than it needs to be**" and accompanied by "**expertly crafted**" cocktails, so even though the "**see-and-be-seen**" scene has cooled, it still works for a "**special night out.**"

MON PETIT CAFE | French   4.0   3.6   4.0 $$

East 60s | 801 Lexington Ave. (62nd St.)
212-355-2233 | www.monpetitcafe.com

A "**bit of Paris in the shadow of Bloomingdale's**", this "**tiny**" fixture offers "**homey French**" staples that especially hit the spot during an "**intense shopping day**"; its tearoom-style space "**may not meet the standards of the Designers Guild**", but to fans it has a certain "**charm.**"

MONTANA'S TRAIL HOUSE | Southern   ▽ 4.5   4.3   4.3 $$

Bushwick | 445 Troutman St. (Scott Ave.) | Brooklyn
917-966-1666 | www.montanastrailhouse.com

"**Elevated**" takes on Southern faves like fried chicken go down well with "**creative**" cocktails ("**try the switchel**") at this "**Appalachian-chic**" Bushwick spot that stays open late; the digs are done in "**rustic**" style, but the bookcase that spins open to the outdoors steals the show.

MONTEBELLO | Italian   4.3   4.0   4.4 $$$

East 50s | 120 E. 56th St. (bet. Lexington & Park Aves.)
212-753-1447 | www.montebellonyc.com

One of the "**best-kept secrets in Midtown**" is this "**oasis of peace and quiet**" where "**personalized**" service and "**fantastic**" Northern Italian fare keep a "**dedicated clientele**" returning; it's "**a bit on the expensive side**", but hey, at least "**you can linger.**"

MONTE CARLO | French   4.0   3.8   4.0 $$$

East 70s | 181 E. 78th St. (3rd Ave.)
646-863-3465 | www.monte-carlo.nyc

"**Classic**" French dishes are rendered "**extremely well**" at this "**neighborly**" Upper Eastsider with a simple, traditional style; while "**not overly ambitious**", it's a "**comfortable**" spot that's "**quiet enough to hear your companions.**"

MONUMENT LANE | American   4.2   4.0   4.0 $$$

West Village | 103 Greenwich Ave. (W. 12th St.)
212-255-0155 | www.monumentlane.com

The "**care is clear**" at this West Village tavern where a "**rough-hewn**" "**Old NY atmosphere**" sets the scene for "**accomplished**" New American cooking that's "**often sourced locally**" and prepared "**with little fuss**"; a "**nice staff**" adds appeal to this "**not-so-well-kept secret.**"

MORANDI | Italian   4.2   4.0   4.0 $$$

West Village | 211 Waverly Pl. (bet. Charles St. & 7th Ave. S.)
212-627-7575 | www.morandiny.com

"**Tasty, satisfying**" Italian fare and a "**totally Village vibe**" still bring the "**beautiful people**" to this "**cozy**" all-day hangout from Keith McNally; it's "**a bit pricey**" and you may need "**earplugs**" to cope with the "**buzz**", but the "**lovely outdoor seating**" and "**fabulous people-watching**" overcome all.

	FOOD	DECOR	SERVICE	COST

MORGAN DINING ROOM | American — 3.9 4.3 4.1 $$

Murray Hill | 225 Madison Ave. (bet. 36th & 37th Sts.)
212-683-2130 | www.themorgan.org

For a "**civilized**" repast while taking in the "**wonders of the Morgan Library**", this lunch-only Murray Hill museum option offers "**limited**" but "**satisfatory**" American bites served in the "**light-filled**" atrium or J. Pierpont's "**elegant**" former dining room; it's all very "**genteel**" – with "**prices to match.**"

MORGANS BBQ | BBQ — 4.1 3.5 3.7 $

Prospect Heights | 267 Flatbush Ave. (St. Marks Ave.) | Brooklyn
718-622-2224 | www.morgansbrooklynbarbecue.com

"**Legit Texas BBQ**" distinguishes this Prospect Heights smokehouse, where the "**satisfying**" choices include brisket and pulled pork, plus sides like Frito pie; the no-frills interior is joined by a sidewalk seating area in summer, and the adjacent Elbow Room stall supplies "**inventive**" mac 'n' cheese.

MORGENSTERN'S FINEST | Ice Cream — 4.4 3.9 3.9 $
ICE CREAM

Lower East Side | 2 Rivington St. (bet. Bowery & Chrystie St.)
212-209-7684 | www.morgensternsnyc.com

A "**wild and wonderful mix of flavors**" ("**four different types of vanilla!**") awaits at Nick Morgenstern's cash-only LES storefront, where "**real-deal**" ice cream and sorbet is "**meticulously**" scooped into cones and sundaes; despite an "**old-time**" vibe, prices are up-to-date.

MORIMOTO | Japanese — 4.6 4.5 4.4 $$$$

Chelsea | 88 10th Ave. (bet. 15th & 16th Sts.)
212-989-8883 | www.morimotonyc.com

"**Sushi master**" Masaharu Morimoto's "*Iron Chef*-quality" omakase and other "**unbelievably good**" Japanese dishes are served in a "**striking**", ultramodern setting at this West Chelsea destination; it's true, you'll "**pay handsomely**", but when you need "**to impress**", this is "**as good as it gets.**"

MORSO | Italian — 4.4 4.1 4.2 $$$

East 50s | 420 E. 59th St. (bet. 1st Ave. & Sutton Pl.)
212-759-2706 | www.morso-nyc.com

Pino Luongo "**knows what he's doing**" at this "**classy**" East Midtown "**oasis**", a "**dependable**" source of "**marvelous**" Italian cuisine served by staffers who "**genuinely care**"; the "**contemporary**" room features Pop Art on the walls and a "**dramatic**" view of the Queensboro Bridge from the outdoor terrace.

MORTON'S THE STEAKHOUSE | Steak — 4.4 4.1 4.3 $$$$

East 40s | 233 Park Ave. S. (19th St.) | 212-220-9200
Financial District | 136 Washington St. (Albany St.) | 212-608-0171
www.mortons.com

"**Go hungry**" to these "**corporate**" chophouses where "**huge**" steaks with "**just the right char**" arrive with bountiful sides; it's predictably "**expensive**", but "**classy**" service and "**upmarket**" confines keep its "**expense-account**" crowd content.

MOTI MAHAL DELUX | Indian — 4.3 3.6 3.7 $$

East 60s | 1149 First Ave. (63rd St.)
212-371-3535 | www.motimahaldelux.us

"**Innovative**" tandoor cooking – including a "**to-die-for**" signature butter chicken – is the specialty of this UES Indian; although it's part of an international chain, its "**simple**" setting has a "**friendly neighborhood vibe.**"

MOTORINO | Pizza   4.3   3.4   3.8 $$

East Village | 349 E. 12th St. (bet. 1st & 2nd Aves.) | 212-777-2644
NEW **West 80s** | 510 Columbus Ave. (85th St.) | 917-675-7581
Williamsburg | 139 Broadway (bet. Bedford & Driggs Aves.) | Brooklyn | 718-599-8899
www.motorinopizza.com

These "**effortlessly cool**" parlors turn out "**dynamite**" Neapolitan-style pies that wed a "**perfectly charred**", "**wood smoke-kissed**" crust to "**top-of-the-line ingredients**" (e.g. the "**awesome**" Brussels sprouts-pancetta version); "**squeezed**" seating and "**minimal**" service are the trade-offs.

MOUNTAIN BIRD | French   ∇ 4.5   4.0   4.4 $$

East Harlem | 251 E. 110th St. (2nd Ave.)
212-744-4422 | www.tastingsnyc.com

"**A true standout**", this Harlem bistro presents rich head-to-foot cooking on an "**excellent**" French menu that highlights "**creative**" preparations of poultry (primarily chicken); "**expertly overseen**" by a chef-owner couple and an "**attentive**" team, the space is "**cute**" but "**small**" – so "**don't tell anyone.**"

MOUSTACHE | Mideastern   4.2   3.4   4.0 $$

East Harlem | 1621 Lexington Ave. (102nd St.) | 212-828-0030
East Village | 265 E. 10th St. (bet. Ave. A & 1st Ave.) | 212-228-2022
West Village | 90 Bedford St. (bet. Barrow & Grove Sts.) | 212-229-2220
www.moustachepitza.com

"**Straightforward**", "**delicious**" Middle Eastern staples come at a "**low price**" at these "**popular**" places; service is "**nonchalant**" and the "**no-decor**" setups tilt "**tiny and cramped**", but the minute that "**just-baked pita**" arrives, "**all is forgiven.**"

MP TAVERNA | Greek   4.3   4.0   4.1 $$

Williamsburg | 470 Driggs Ave. (10th St.) | Brooklyn | 929-250-2312
Astoria | 31-29 Ditmars Blvd. (33rd St.) | Queens | 718-777-2187
www.michaelpsilakis.com

A "**modern**" approach to Greek cooking yields "**memorable**" results at Michael Psilakis's "**consistent**" tavernas, where the "**knowledgeable**" staff can guide you through the "**creative**" options; there's a "**festive**" vibe within the "**sleek**" spaces, and relatively "**affordable**" prices only add to the good mood.

MR. CHOW | Chinese   4.3   4.2   4.1 $$$

East 50s | 324 E. 57th St. (bet. 1st & 2nd Aves.) | 212-751-9030

MR. CHOW TRIBECA | Chinese

TriBeCa | 121 Hudson St. (Moore St.) | 212-965-9500
www.mrchow.com

"**Upper-crust dining**" endures at these swanky Chinese dining rooms offering a "**delicious**", "**classic**" menu; voters split on its buzz factor – "**still glamorous**" vs. "**lost its luster**" – but there's agreement on the "**elegant**" settings and "**high**" price tags.

NEW **MR. DONAHUE'S** | American   —   —   — $$

NoLita | 203 Mott St. (Spring St.)
646-850-9480 | www.mrdonahues.com

The chef-owners of Uncle Boons tap into Americana at this NoLita nook focused on diner-style plates that highlight meats with a choice of two sides. With just a handful of seats in the vintage-style space, it's geared toward both eat-in and takeout; P.S. cash is not accepted.

MULBERRY & VINE | American ▽ 4.0   3.5   3.5 $

NEW NoMad | 55 W. 27th St. (bet. B'way & 6th Ave.) | 212-791-6300
TriBeCa | 73 Warren St. (W. B'way) | 212-791-6300
www.mulberryandvine.com

These sunny, fashionable cafes offer largely organic, quick-serve American meals made up of three plates (your choice of three veggie sides, or two veggie and one meat) that get some zing from global spices. Flavored lemonades, juice blends and iced teas, plus gluten-free sweets, are also sold.

MULINO A VINO | Italian ▽ 4.1   3.9   4.2 $$$

Chelsea | 337 W. 14th St. (bet. 8th & 9th Aves.)
855-343-4513 | www.mulinoavino.com

A sibling to Italy's Combal.Zero restaurant, this Chelsea Italian has a "**fun**" wine-centric twist – customers order from the "**extensive**" vino list first, then "**helpful**" staffers suggest pairings from traditional pastas to more adventurous combos; the below-ground space is "**cool**" and makes for a "**relaxing time.**"

MU RAMEN | Japanese/Noodle Shop 4.5   4.2   4.2 $$

Long Island City | 12-09 Jackson Ave. (bet. 47th Rd. & 48th Ave.) | Queens
917-868-8903 | www.muramennyc.com

"**Transcendent slurping**" lures noodle enthusiasts to this LIC cash-only ramen shop serving "**amazing**" bowls and "**innovative**" Japanese apps; unsurprisingly, the "**tight**" quarters are "**often jam-packed**", while the no-rezzie rule causes "**daunting**" waits.

MURRAY'S BAGELS | Bagels 4.3   3.0   3.5 $

Chelsea | 242 Eighth Ave. (bet. 22nd & 23rd Sts.) | 646-638-1335 |
www.murraysbagelschelsea.com
Greenwich Village | 500 Sixth Ave. (13th St.) | 212-462-2830 |
www.murraysbagels.com

The "**seriously fresh bagels**" are "**huge, crusty**" and so "**gratifying**" they "**don't need to be toasted**" at these "**no-nonsense**" shops, which "**deliver the goods**" accompanied by "**lip-smacking**" smoked fish and schmears "**galore**"; the counter folks are "**efficient**", but expect "**killer lines on weekends.**"

MURRAY'S CHEESE BAR | American 4.4   3.7   4.0 $$

West Village | 264 Bleecker St. (bet. Leroy & Morton Sts.)
646-476-8882 | www.murrayscheesebar.com

This West Village American from the famous nearby shop showcases "**serious**" fromages ("**creamy, stinky, crumbly**") with faves like "**outstanding fondue**", "**the best grilled cheese ever**" and wine-paired flights; the "**bright**" space can be "**cramped and noisy**", but for "**cheese lovers**" "**it doesn't get any better than this.**"

MUSKET ROOM | New Zealand 4.5   4.2   4.4 $$

NoLita | 265 Elizabeth St. (bet. Houston & Prince Sts.)
212-219-0764 | www.musketroom.com

A "**wonderful**" Down Under "**experience**", this NoLita "**find**" rates "**excellent on all fronts**" with "**serious**" New Zealand cuisine matched with a "**Kiwi-focused wine list**", dispatched by a "**top-notch**" team; fans of its "**sophisticated**" yet "**comfy**" style are "**hooked**" despite the "**high prices.**"

	FOOD	DECOR	SERVICE	COST

M. WELLS DINETTE | Québécois   4.1   3.5   3.9 $

Long Island City | MoMA PS1 | 22-25 Jackson Ave. (46th Ave.) | Queens
718-786-1800 | www.magasinwells.com

French-Canadian chef Hugue Dufour and wife Sarah Obraitis deliver
a "**charming**" experience at this cafeteria inside LIC's MoMA PS1
(museum admission is not required for entry); the "**rich, delicious**" Québécois
fusion fare arrives in a "**funky**" former classroom complete with chalkboard
menus and cubbyhole desks; in summer, there's a rooftop annex for
drinks and snacks.

M. WELLS STEAKHOUSE | Steak   4.3   4.1   4.2 $$$

Long Island City | 43-15 Crescent St. (bet. 43rd Ave. & 44th Rd.) | Queens
718-786-9060 | www.magasinwells.com

Located in an LIC "**converted auto-body shop**", this Québécois-accented
take on the classic steakhouse from Hugue Dufour and Sarah Obraitis
presents "**terrific**" chops from a "**wood-burning grill**" in the open kitchen
(where there's also a live trout tank); a patio with its own bar and a pétanque
court only adds to the "**unique**" – and "**pricey**" – experience; P.S. it's only open
Thursday–Saturday.

NEW **NAKAMURA** | Noodle Shop   ∇ 4.3   3.7   4.1 $

Lower East Side | 172 Delancey St. (bet. Attorney & Clinton Sts.)
212-614-1810 | www.nakamuranyc.com

Vanguard Japanese ramen specialist Shigetoshi Nakamura leads this "**classic**"
Lower East Side noodle shop, offering a "**limited**" menu of "**meticulously
prepared**" bowls (including chicken-based torigara and yuzu dashi) plus
"**don't-skip**" pork gyoza; the narrow, brick-walled interior is "**small**", but fans
still "**drink the broth until the very end.**"

NAKED DOG | Italian   ∇ 4.5   4.4   4.4 $$$

Greenpoint | 47 Java St. (West St.) | Brooklyn
929-337-8096 | www.nakeddogbrooklyn.com

From "**wonderful**" housemade pastas to brick-pressed pork belly, this
Greenpoint Italian provides "**delicious**" hearty Pugliese cooking with seasonal
touches; a "**friendly**" team inhabits the "**cozy**" rustic-chic space, which
includes a small bar hung with many Edison bulbs.

NARCISSA | American   4.5   4.2   4.2 $$$

East Village | The Standard East Village Hotel | 25 Cooper Sq. (bet. 5th & 6th
Sts.)
212-228-3344 | www.narcissarestaurant.com

"**Talented**" chef John Fraser puts forth "**inspired**", "**veggie-forward**" New
American cuisine at this "**upscale**" destination in the Standard East Village
Hotel with serious "**farm-to-table**" cred (some produce is "**grown Upstate**" at
the co-owner's farm); its "**lovely**", "**sunny**" interior and garden have a "**relaxed**"
vibe, and the "**fun crowd**" adds "**energy.**"

THE NATIONAL | American   3.8   3.8   3.7 $$

East 50s | Benjamin Hotel | 557 Lexington Ave. (50th St.)
212-715-2400 | www.thenationalnyc.com

A "**business lunch**" standby, Geoffrey Zakarian's "**cozy**" American bistro in
East Midtown's Benjamin Hotel serves "**straightforward**" American fare that
ranges from "**solid**" to "**meh**"; "**scattered**" service and "**noisy**" decibels don't
deter the weekday "**crowds**" (brunch is more "**pleasant**").

NATSUMI | Japanese · · · · · · · · · · · · · · · · 4.1 · 3.8 · 4.0 · $$$

West 50s | Amsterdam Court Hotel | 226 W. 50th St. (bet. B'way & 8th Ave.)
212-258-2988 | www.natsuminyc.com

Amid the Theater District "**madness**" lies this Japanese "**sleeper**" that "**exceeds expectations**" with its "**wonderful**" selction of sushi, "**helpful**" service and "**reasonable**" rates; other endearments include a "**sleek**" room "**not filled to the brim with tourists**" and a "**tolerable noise level.**"

NAYA | Lebanese · · · · · · · · · · · · · · · · · 4.2 · 3.5 · 3.8 · · $$

East 50s | 1057 Second Ave. (bet. 55th & 56th Sts.) | 212-319-7777 |
www.nayarestaurants.com

NAYA EXPRESS | Lebanese

East 40s | 688 Third Ave. (43rd St.) | 212-557-0007
NEW **Financial District** | One NY Plaza | 1 FDR Dr. (bet. Broad &
Whitehall Sts.) | 212-760-8888
West 50s | 54 W. 56th St. (bet. 5th & 6th Aves.) | 212-944-7777
www.nayaexpress.com

"**Appealing**" meze leads the "**winning**" lineup at these "**popular**" Lebanese stops, also favored for its "**amiable**" service and "**reasonable prices**"; the East Side flagship sports a "**clever**", white-toned space while the quick-serve Express stops draw "**epic**" lunch lines.

NEARY'S | Pub Food · · · · · · · · · · · · · · · 3.9 · 3.6 · 4.3 · $$$

East 50s | 358 E. 57th St. (1st Ave.)
212-751-1434

"**Consummate host**" Jimmy Neary and his "**welcoming**" "**old-school staff**" keep loyal "**seniors**" coming back to this "**frozen-in-time**" Midtown watering hole; it's a "**cozy place**" to relax and have a drink, with "**dependable**" Irish bar food playing a supporting role.

NEGRIL | Caribbean/Jamaican · · · · · · ▽ 4.3 · 3.7 · 3.8 · · $$

Greenwich Village | 70 W. Third St. (bet. La Guardia Pl. & Thompson St.)
212-477-2804 | www.negrilvillage.com

"**Hot food, hot crowd**" sums up this "**modern**" Village Caribbean-Jamaican where the "**lively**" scene is fueled by "**phenomenal**" cocktails and "**flavorful**", "**dressed-up**" fare; sure, other competitors are "**less expensive**", but you're paying for the "**upscale**" setting here.

NELLO | Italian · · · · · · · · · · · · · · · · · 3.7 · 3.8 · 3.6 · $$$$

East 60s | 696 Madison Ave. (bet. 62nd & 63rd Sts.)
212-980-9099 | www.nello-hub.com

Money is no object at this one-of-a-kind UES Italian, famed for serving "**nothing-out-of-this-world**" food for "**mortgage-the-house**" sums; fans jockey for the "**sidewalk seats**" on Madison Avenue ("*the place to be seen*"), where a "**too-tan**" crowd is tolerated by staffers who "**think they're celebs.**"

NERAI | Greek · · · · · · · · · · · · · · · · · · 4.4 · 4.3 · 4.4 · $$$

East 50s | 55 E. 54th St. (bet. Madison & Park Aves.)
212-759-5554 | www.nerainyc.com

"**Elegant and quiet**", this "**upscale**" Midtown Greek caters to "**business**" types with "**thoughtfully prepared**", seafood-focused fare delivered by an "**accommodating**" crew in "**sleek**", breezy digs; though it's not cheap, there's a prix fixe lunch to "**provide value.**"

	FOOD	DECOR	SERVICE	COST

NETA | Japanese — 4.5 — 4.0 — 4.4 — $$

Greenwich Village | 61 W. Eighth St. (6th Ave.)
212-505-2610 | www.netanyc.com

"**Exceptional**" sushi and "**innovative**" small plates figure at this "**intimate**" Village Japanese standout, known for its "**exquisite**" omakase; the "**minimalist**" surrounds keep the focus on the "**magic**" at the sushi bar, and "**solicitous**" service enhances the "**rewarding experience**" – for which unsurprisingly you'll spend "**a lot.**"

NEW WONJO | Korean — 4.3 — 3.3 — 3.7 — $$

West 30s | 23 W. 32nd St. (bet. B'way & 5th Ave.)
212-695-5815 | www.newwonjo.com

"**Korean awesomeness**" 24/7 is the deal at this Koreatown vet whose "**crave**"-worthy specialties include tableside BBQ; you "**gotta love**" the charcoal grills (vs. more typical gas ones) – but "**no atmosphere**" and "**long lines**" at peak hours are also part of the package.

NEW WORLD MALL | Asian/Food Hall — 4.1 — 2.8 — 3.0 — $

Flushing | 136-20 Roosvelt Ave. (Main St.) | Queens
718-353-0551 | www.newworldmallny.com

For the "**curious and adventuresome**", this basement Flushing food hall is "**like a mini-trip to Asia**" with vendors turning out handmade dumplings, noodles, hot pots and other "**amazing**" "**cheap bites**"; sure, there's "**no service**" and it can be "**intimidating if you don't speak the language**", but regulars know to just "**point and enjoy the ride.**"

NEW YORK SUSHI KO | Japanese — — — — — — $$$$

Lower East Side | 91 Clinton St. (Rivington St.)
917-734-5857 | www.newyorksushiko.com

You may "**never see sushi in the same way**" after visiting this "**tiny**" LES Japanese for a "**delicious**", omakase-only spread via a "**personable**" chef who "**knows what he's doing**"; the $165-and-up set price is steep, but the "**overall flow**" at the 11-seat counter is "**absolutely perfect.**"

NGAM | Thai — 4.3 — 3.5 — 3.7 — $$

East Village | 99 Third Ave. (bet. 12th & 13th Sts.)
212-777-8424 | www.ngamnyc.com

Chef Hong Thaimee is "**usually on-site sharing the love**" at this "**small**" East Villager known for its "**imaginative**" twists on Thai comfort classics; "**interesting**" cocktails and a "**hip**", "**casual**" vibe are additional reasons why it's an all-around "**favorite.**"

NHA TRANG | Vietnamese — 4.2 — 2.8 — 3.5 — $$

Chinatown | 148 Centre St. (bet. Walker & White Sts.) | 212-941-9292
Chinatown | 87 Baxter St. (bet. Bayard & Canal Sts.) | 212-233-5948
www.nhatrangnyc.com

"**Fantastic**" pho and other "**authentic**" Vietnamese eats trump "**institutional decor**" and the "**rushed service you'd expect**" at these "**hole-in-the-wall**" Chinatown joints; the "**incredibly reasonable**" prices alone make them "**worth a stop**" even if you're not on jury duty.

NICE MATIN | French/Mediterranean — 3.9 — 3.8 — 3.9 — $$$

West 70s | 201 W. 79th St. (Amsterdam Ave.)
212-873-6423 | www.nicematinnyc.com

"**Always running full throttle**", this all-day UWS "**hive**" doles out "**reliable**"

French-Med eats in a "**casual**" space channeling the "**South of France**", complete with "**sidewalk seating**" to "**watch the passing scene**"; however, given the prime-time "**noise**" and "**crush**", regulars say it's "**best off-peak.**"

NICK & STEF'S STEAKHOUSE | Steak   4.2   3.7   4.1 $$$
West 30s | 9 Penn Plaza (bet. 7th & 8th Aves.)
212-563-4444 | www.patinagroup.com

"**Incredibly convenient to MSG**" – diners can even use a private arena entrance – this "**comfortable**" Penn Plaza steakhouse boasts "**tasty**" chops served by a "**fast**" team; even if the decor seems "**sort of a decade ago**", it's ultimately a "**bright spot**" in a dining-challenged nabe.

NICK & TONI'S CAFE | Italian/Mediterranean   4.0   3.6   3.9 $$
West 60s | 100 W. 67th St. (bet. B'way & Columbus Ave.)
212-496-4000 | www.nickandtoniscafe.com

Just a "**short walk**" from Lincoln Center, this "**low-key**" offshoot of the "**popular**" East Hampton standby offers "**delicious pizzas**" and other "**straightforward**" Italian-Med fare; it's a good bet "**pre-movie or -show**", with the bonus of possibly spotting "**journalists from nearby ABC.**"

NICK'S | Pizza   4.5   3.5   4.0 $$
East 90s | 1814 Second Ave. (94th St.) | 212-987-5700 | www.nicksnyc.com
Murray Hill | 365 Third Ave. (bet. 26th & 27th Sts.) | 646-918-6553 |
www.nickspizzabar.com
Forest Hills | 108-26 Ascan Ave. (bet. Austin & Burns Sts.) | Queens |
718-263-1126

A "**step above your everyday pizza place**", these "**neighborhood joints**" specialize in "**charred**", thin-crust pies with "**perfect sauce**" and some "**gourmet flair**"; true, the decor and service are strictly "**no-frills**", but they fill the bill for "**family**"-friendly dining.

NICOLA'S | Italian   4.3   3.7   4.2 $$$
East 80s | 146 E. 84th St. (Lexington Ave.)
212-249-9850 | www.nicolasnyc.com

"**Yes, it's like a private club**" and that's fine with the "**well-heeled**" regulars who seek out this "**unhurried**" Upper Eastsider for "**delicious**", "**old-time**" Italian cooking and "**warm welcomes**"; it's "**expensive**" and "**a wee bit dated**", but at least you can "**develop membership status**" with return visits.

NICOLETTA | Italian/Pizza   ∇ 3.9   3.7   3.9 $$
East Village | 160 Second Ave. (10th St.)
212-432-1600 | www.nicolettapizza.com

Chef Michael White is behind this East Village pizzeria, a "**no-frills**" joint ("**so different from Marea**") for "**tasty**" thick-crust pies topped with intriguingly "**different combinations**", along with "**standout**" meatballs and wings; while some call it a "**ripoff**", others can't wait to "**go back.**"

99 FAVOR TASTE | Chinese/Korean   4.1   3.7   4.0 $$
Lower East Side | 285 Grand St. (Eldridge St.) | 646-682-9122
Sunset Park | 732 61st St. (FDR Dr.) | Brooklyn | 718-439-0658
www.favortaste.com

"**Unlimited food = unlimited fun**" at these "**all-you-can-eat**" Chinese-Koreans supplying "**heaps of fresh vegetables, meats and seafood**" you cook yourself at tabletop hot pots or BBQ grills; they're "**open late**" and especially "**good for groups**", with "**vast**", "**Chinatown-standard**" interiors and "**unbeatable**" prices, but reserve ahead or endure "**a long wait.**"

	FOOD	DECOR	SERVICE	COST

NINO'S | Italian   4.0 3.9 4.2 $$$

East 70s | 1354 First Ave. (bet. 72nd & 73rd Sts.) | 212-988-0002 |
www.ninosnyc.com

NINO'S TUSCANY STEAK HOUSE | Italian/Steak

West 50s | 117 W. 58th St. (bet. 6th & 7th Aves.) | 212-757-8630 |
www.ninostuscany.com

"**More than typical neighborhood Italians**", these "**civilized**" standbys exude
"**old-world charm**" from the "**comfortable**" settings to the "**reliably good**",
"**traditional**" cooking, maybe they're "**a little pricey**", but "**smiling**" servers
always "**enhance the experience.**"

NINTH STREET ESPRESSO | Coffee   4.3 3.4 3.8 $

Chelsea | 75 Ninth Ave. (bet. 15th & 16th Sts.) | 212-228-2930
East 50s | 109 E. 56th St. (bet. Lexington & Park Aves.) | 646-559-4793
East Village | 700 E. 9th St. (Ave. C) | 212-358-9225
East Village | 341 E. 10th St. (Ave. B) | 212-777-3508
Gowanus | 333 Douglass St. (4th Ave.) | Brooklyn | 212-358-9225
www.ninthstreetespresso.com

This pioneering "**coffee-lover's coffeehouse**" mini-chain is a "**go to**" for
"**meticulously prepared**", "**damn good**" java – notably "**espresso that packs
some punch**"; its spaces featuring a "**simple aesthetic**" are staffed by
"**serious**" yet "**mellow**" baristas; P.S. they're cash only.

NIPPON | Japanese   4.4 3.7 4.1 $$$

East 50s | 155 E. 52nd St. (bet. Lexington & 3rd Aves.)
212-688-5941

"**One of NYC's oldest**" Japanese restaurants, this circa-1963 Midtown
"**favorite**" still turns out "**excellent**", "**traditional**" fare – including sushi – with
"**no glitz, no glam**", just "**gracious**" attention; maybe the decor's a bit "**tired**",
but nearly everyone likes its "**quiet, pleasant**" feel.

NISHIDA SHOTEN | Noodle Shop   ∇ 4.2 3.3 4.1 $

East 40s | 302 E. 49th St. (2nd Ave.)
212-308-0791 | www.nishidasho-ten.com

A "**strong ramen contender**", this Midtown "**hole-in-the-wall**" offers
"**delicious**" noodle soups plus Japanese small bites and sake in a setting fit
for "**a Tokyo side street**"; if the compact space could be "**more comfortable**",
fans would rather focus on the "**good value.**"

🆕 **NIX** | Vegetarian   ∇ 4.5 4.2 4.2 $$$

Greenwich Village | 72 University Pl. (bet. 10th & 11th Sts.)
212-498-9393 | www.nixny.com

Chef John Fraser (Dovetail, Narcissa) uses a "**global palate of flavors
and techniques**" to craft "**delicious, interesting**" vegetarian cuisine at
this "**grown-up**" Greenwich Villager; a "**fresh**" modern space and
"**conscientious**" team boost the "**class**" factor – "**too bad it's already an
impossible reservation.**"

NIZZA | Italian   4.0 3.5 3.9 $$

West 40s | 630 Ninth Ave. (bet. 44th & 45th Sts.)
212-956-1800 | www.nizzanyc.com

"**Won't-break-the-bank**" prices for "**solid**" classics from the Italian Riviera
(including "**impressive**" gluten-free options) ensure this "**casual**" Theater
District spot is plenty "**popular**" pre- or post-curtain; the noise level can be
"**a bit much**", but in warm weather there's always the sidewalk seating.

NOBU | Japanese   4.7   4.4   4.3 $$$$
TriBeCa | 105 Hudson St. (Franklin St.) | 212-219-0500

NOBU 57 | Japanese
West 50s | 40 W. 57th St. (bet. 5th & 6th Aves.) | 212-757-3000

NOBU NEXT DOOR | Japanese
TriBeCa | 105 Hudson St. (Franklin St.) | 212-334-4445
www.noburestaurants.com

"**One-of-a-kind terrific**", Nobu Matsuhisa's "**iconic**" TriBeCa namesake
continues to "**tantalize your palate**" with "**distinctive**" Japanese-Peruvian
plates "**sleekly delivered**" to a "**sceney**" crowd in a "**beautiful space**" via
David Rockwell; the "**cool little**" next-door annex and "**over-the-top**" Midtown
outpost are equally "alluring", "**especially if someone else is paying.**"

NOCELLO | Italian   4.1   3.8   4.2 $$$
West 50s | 257 W. 55th St. (bet. B'way & 8th Ave.)
212-713-0224 | www.nocello.net

"**Enduring and endearing**" – not to mention "**convenient**" if you're bound
for Carnegie Hall or City Center – this "**cozy**" Tuscan turns out "**plentiful**"
helpings of "**fine**" "**traditional**" fare; "**charming owners**" add "**warmth**" to
the "**unassuming**" setting.

NOHO STAR | American/Asian   3.9   3.6   3.9 $$
NoHo | 330 Lafayette St. (Bleecker St.)
212-925-0070 | www.nohostar.com

The "**offbeat**" menu "**should just say 'everything, plus Chinese'**" at this
"**long-standing**" NoHo "**favorite**" that "**cheerfully**" offers Asian specialties
side by side with "**kicked-up**" American eats; tabs "**priced right**" and a
"**comfy**" setting are other reasons this "**star keeps shining.**"

THE NOMAD | American/European   4.6   4.5   4.4 $$$$
NoMad | NoMad Hotel | 1170 Broadway (28th St.)
347-472-5660 | www.thenomadhotel.com

This "**stylish**" "**trendsetter**" in the NoMad Hotel draws a "**chic crowd**" that's
"**blown away**" by Daniel Humm's "**superb**" American-European menu (the
roast chicken is "**one for the books**"); "**spot-on service**" and a "**beautifully
designed**" space spread out over several cozy rooms help distract from
the "**heavy**" tabs.

THE NOMAD BAR | American   4.4   4.5   4.3 $$
NoMad | NoMad Hotel | 10 W. 28th St. (B'way)
347-472-5660 | www.thenomadhotel.com

"**More relaxed**" than The NoMad but still "**chic**", this "**dark**" "**retreat**" in the
namesake hotel dispenses "**top-notch**" craft cocktails alongside a "**limited**"
lineup of "**upgraded**" bar bites, including a "**sublime**" burger; the "**beautiful**"
bi-level space is ever "**buzzing**" (verging on "**madhouse**" at prime times) –
"**glitterati**" watchers say it's "**quite the scene.**"

NOM WAH TEA PARLOR | Chinese   4.1   3.2   3.5 $$
Chinatown | 13 Doyers St. (bet. Chatham Sq. & Pell St.)
212-962-6047 | www.nomwah.com

You may "**need Google Maps**" to find it, but it's worth seeking out this
"**time-warp**" Chinatown vet (around since 1920) for "**surprisingly good**",
"**real-deal**" dim sum at "**bargain**" rates; despite a "**nondescript ambiance**"

and "**no-frills**" service, it's still a "**favorite**" – "**go early or really late**" to avoid a wait.

NOODLE PUDDING | Italian   4.4   3.8   4.3 $$
Brooklyn Heights | 38 Henry St. (bet. Cranberry & Middagh Sts.) | Brooklyn
718-625-3737

An "**enduring favorite**" that "**never gets old**", this cash-only Brooklyn Heights "**winner**" is a hit with locals thanks to its "**sublime**" traditional Italian cooking and "**wonderful energy**"; the "**crowds never cease**" and regulars "**wish they took reservations**", but "**moderate**" tabs are the payoff.

NOREETUH | Hawaiian   4.2   3.6   4.1 $$
East Village | 128 First Ave. (bet. 7th St. & St. Marks Pl.)
646-892-3050 | www.noreetuh.com

"**Elevated**" Hawaiian fare is the "**unexpected**" specialty of this East Village "**up-and-comer**", where the "**refreshing**" Asian-inspired plates are backed by a "**stellar wine list**"; amiable servers add "**warmth**" to the somewhat "**sterile**" digs, so despite "**high**" noise levels, fans "**put on that flower-print shirt**" and say "**aloha!**"

NORMA'S | American   4.4   3.9   4.0 $$$
West 50s | Le Parker Meridien | 119 W. 56th St. (bet. 6th & 7th Aves.)
212-708-7460 | www.normasnyc.com

"**Lavish**" breakfasts and brunches are the specialty of this Midtown American in the Parker Meridien, where the "**memorable**" morning fare arrives in "**large, easily shareable**" portions; no kidding, the tabs are "**out of this world**" (e.g. that $1,000 frittata) and it's a "**bit of a tourist factory**", but it's still a "**highly recommended**" experience.

NEW **THE NORM AT** | Eclectic   —   —   — $$$
BROOKLYN MUSEUM
Prospect Heights | Brooklyn Museum | 200 Eastern Pkwy. (Washington Ave.) | Brooklyn
718-230-0897 | www.thenormbkm.com

Chef Saul Bolton remains at the helm of this Eclectic eatery replacing Saul at the Brooklyn Museum, preparing dishes that draw on the borough's global roots. The interior is designed to resemble a museum storage area (complete with jumbled paintings and stamped crates) and opens up to a terrace overlooking the sculpture garden.

NORTH END GRILL | American/Seafood   4.5   4.4   4.5 $$$
Battery Park City | 104 North End Ave. (bet. Murray & Vesey Sts.)
646-747-1600 | www.northendgrillnyc.com

Battery Park City is home to this "**smart, upscale**" American via Danny Meyer, where the "**outstanding**" seafood-focused menu arrives via an "**on-point**" staff that's "**really on its game**"; the "**civilized**", "**modern**" space features a "**lively**" bar popular with "**suits**", and a no-tipping policy.

NORTH SQUARE | American   4.3   4.0   4.3 $$$
Greenwich Village | Washington Sq. Hotel | 103 Waverly Pl. (MacDougal St.)
212-254-1200 | www.northsquareny.com

Although a "**favorite**" of "**NYU profs**" and other "**Washington Square regulars**", this "**swell little neighborhood place**" mostly flies under the radar; "**superior**" New American cuisine, "**civilized**" service and a "**grown-up**", "**comfy**" setting where you "**can talk without going hoarse**" keep it a "**neighborhood standby.**"

NO. 7 | American   4.1   3.5   3.8 $$

Fort Greene | 7 Greene Ave. (bet. Cumberland & Fulton Sts.) | Brooklyn |
718-522-6370 | www.no7restaurant.com

NO. 7 SUB | Sandwiches

Dumbo | 11 Water St. (bet. New Dock & Old Fulton Sts.) | Brooklyn |
917-618-4399

NoMad | 1188 Broadway (29th St.) | 212-532-1680

West 50s | Plaza Food Hall | 1 W. 59th St., lower level (5th Ave.) |
646-755-3228

www.no7sub.com

This "**cool**", BAM-handy Fort Greene number is a "**local favorite**" for
"**intriguing**" New American innovations ("**two words: broccoli tacos!**");
its counter-serve outlets follow up with "**can't-be-beat**" sub sandwiches
whose "**quality ingredients**" and "**wacky combos**" likewise venture "**beyond
the common herd.**"

NOVITÁ | Italian   4.5   3.8   4.2 $$$

Gramercy Park | 102 E. 22nd St. (bet. Lexington Ave. & Park Ave. S.)
212-677-2222 | www.novitanyc.com

A true neighborhood "**standby**", this longtime Gramercy Northern Italian
offers a "**top-notch**" menu dispatched by an "**attentive**" staff; despite "**small**"
dimensions and "**shoehorned**" seating, the "**crowds still come**", drawn by
the "**pleasant**" atmosphere.

NUCCI'S | Italian   4.1   3.6   4.1 $$

Tottenville | 4842 Arthur Kill Rd. (S. Bridge St.) | Staten Island | 718-967-3600

West Brighton | 616 Forest Ave. (Oakland Ave.) | Staten Island | 718-815-4882
www.nuccis.net

"**Delicious pizza**" and other Italian basics have locals "**dining regularly**" at
these "**reliable**" Staten Islanders; "**fair prices**" and "**make-you-feel-like-
family**" service trump "**mediocre**" atmospherics, so most consider them
decent enough "**neighborhood**" fallbacks.

NUMERO 28 | Pizza   4.3   3.3   3.8 $$

East 70s | 1431 First Ave. (bet. 74th & 75th Sts.) | 212-772-8200

East Village | 176 Second Ave. (bet. 11th & 12th Sts.) | 212-777-1555

West 90s | 660 Amsterdam Ave. (92nd St.) | 212-706-7282

West Village | 28 Carmine St. (bet. Bedford & Bleecker Sts.) | 212-463-9653

Park Slope | 137 Seventh Ave. (bet. Carroll St. & Garfield Pl.) | Brooklyn |
718-398-9198

Cobble Hill | 68 Bergen St. (Smith St.) | Brooklyn | 347-987-4819
www.numero28.com

"**In a sea of neighborhood pizza joints**", these "**homey**" outlets produce
"**crispy**", real-deal Neapolitan pies fired up in "**blazing**", wood-fired brick
ovens; the "**unpretentious**" style is more reason to be "**pleasantly surprised
by the quality.**"

NUM PANG | Cambodian/Sandwiches   4.2   2.9   3.5 $

Battery Park City | Hudson Eats | 230 Vesey St. (West St.) | 212-227-1957

Chelsea | Chelsea Mkt. | 75 Ninth Ave. (bet. 15th & 16th Sts.) | 212-390-8851

East 40s | 140 E. 41st St. (bet. Lexington & 3rd Aves.) | 212-867-8889

Financial District | 75 Broad St. (bet. Beaver & William Sts.) | 646-964-4150

NEW **Financial District** | 200 Pearl St. (bet. Fulton & John Sts.) | 917-475-1854

Flatiron | 1129 Broadway (bet. 25th & 26th Sts.) | 212-647-8889

continued

Greenwich Village | 21 E. 12th St. (bet. 5th Ave. & University Pl.) | 212-255-3271
West 40s | 148 W. 48th St. (bet. 6th & 7th Aves.) | 212-421-0743
www.numpangnyc.com

"**Cambodia's answer**" to the banh mi craze, this local chain dispenses "**damn good**" sandwiches "**worth standing in line**" for, with "**more-than-fair**" prices and "**speedy service**" to sweeten the deal; though the setups are "**fast food**"–style, most feel "**you can't go wrong**" here.

NURNBERGER BIERHAUS | German   4.2   3.8   4.0 $$
Randall Manor | 817 Castleton Ave. (Regan Ave.) | Staten Island
718-816-7461

Staten Islanders in the mood for Wiener schnitzel and beer turn up at this "**festive**" Randall Manor take on Bavaria, where the German grub is matched with "**wonderful**" brews on tap; it's "**authentic**" right down to the "**hokey decor**", dirndl-clad staff and back biergarten.

NYONYA | Malaysian   4.3   3.3   3.5 $$
Little Italy | 199 Grand St. (bet. Mott & Mulberry Sts.) | 212-334-3669
Bath Beach | 2322 86th St. (Bay 34th St.) | Brooklyn | 718-265-0888
Sunset Park | 5323 Eighth Ave. (54th St.) | Brooklyn | 718-633-0808
www.ilovenyonya.com

When you crave "**exotic flavors**", these "**favorite**" Malaysians fill the bill with "**generous**" servings of "**delicious**" standards at "**ridiculously good**" rates (just "**bring cash**"), "**assembly-line**" service and "**packed**", "**no-frills**" quarters are part of the experience.

NYY STEAK | Steak   4.3   4.2   4.1 $$$
West 50s | 7 W. 51st St. (bet. 5th & 6th Aves.) | 646-307-7910
Concourse/Downtown | Yankee Stadium | 1 E. 161st St., Gate 6 (River Ave.) |
Bronx | 646-977-8325
www.nyysteak.com

There's "**no other place like**" this ticket holders–only chophouse within Yankee Stadium, where "**solid**" steaks served in a room "**adorned with memorabilia**" are a "**grand slam**" for pinstripe patrons who can swing the "**high prices**"; there's also a sprawling, all-seasons offshoot that pinch-hits in Rock Center.

OBAO | Asian   4.1   3.6   3.7 $$
East 50s | 222 E. 53rd St. (bet. 2nd & 3rd Aves.) | 212-308-5588
Financial District | 38 Water St. (Broad St.) | 212-361-6313
West 40s | 647 Ninth Ave. (45th St.) | 212-245-8880
www.obaony.com

"**Elevated**" Southeast Asian street food is the specialty at these "**local go-to**" joints that supply an "**array**" of "**tasty**" plates at "**affordable prices**"; the setups are informal, though the Hell's Kitchen locale "**stands out**" with its "**cool**", nightclubbish decor.

OBICÀ MOZZARELLA BAR | Italian   4.1   3.8   3.8 $$
East 50s | 590 Madison Ave. (56th St.) | 212-355-2217
Flatiron | 928 Broadway (bet. 21st & 22nd Sts.) | 212-777-2754
www.obica.com

A "**delicious sampling**" of diverse mozzarellas "**freshly flown in**" from Italy is the draw at these links of an international chain; the IBM atrium counter offers Midtowners artfully prepared "**quick bites**", while the full-service Flatiron branch adds "**awesome pizza**" to the mix in an "**industrial-sleek**" space.

OCEANA | American/Seafood 4.5 4.3 4.4 $$$
West 40s | 120 W. 49th St. (bet. 6th & 7th Aves.)
212-759-5941 | www.oceanarestaurant.com

"**First-class**" fish is the hook at this "**fancy**" Rock Center seafood spot, whose "**huge**", "**civilized**" space includes a "**lively**" bar and a "**pleasant**" patio, all overseen by an "**aim-to-please**" crew; "**expense-account**"–ready prices have many reserving it for "**entertaining clients**", though the pre-theater prix fixes are a comparative "**bargain.**"

OCEAN PRIME | Seafood/Steak 4.4 4.3 4.3 $$$$
West 50s | 123 W. 52nd St. (bet. 6th & 7th Aves.)
212-956-1404 | www.ocean-prime.com

"**Delectable seafood**" and "**fabulous steaks**" share the "**broad menu**" at this "**modern**" Midtown link of an upscale surf 'n' turf chain; an "**excellent**" staff helps make the "**chic**", "**sprawling**" space feel "**inviting**", further ensuring it's "**worth the pricey tab.**"

ODA HOUSE | Georgian ∇ 4.3 3.4 3.9 $$
East Village | 76 Ave. B (5th St.)
212-353-3838 | www.odahouse.com

"**For something a little different**", there's this East Village nook specializing in "**delicious**" Georgian classics – "**think Tbilisi, not Atlanta**" – including "**divine**" khachapuri cheese bread; the space is basic and often "**busy**", but given the modest prices, most don't seem to mind.

ODDFELLOWS ICE CREAM CO. | Ice Cream 4.4 3.7 3.9 $
East Village | 75 E. 4th St. (bet. Bowery & 2nd Ave.) | 917-475-1812
Williamsburg | 175 Kent Ave. (3rd St.) | Brooklyn | 347-599-0556
www.oddfellowsnyc.com

You'll find "**adventurous**" ice cream flavors that are "**insanely delish**" at these "**wonderful**" artisan scoop shops; the "**bigger**" Williamsburg flagship has a "**quaint**" soda-fountain feel, while its East Village sequel focuses on ice cream sandwiches.

THE ODEON | American/French 4.0 3.9 4.0 $$
TriBeCa | 145 W. Broadway (bet. Duane & Thomas Sts.)
212-233-0507 | www.theodeonrestaurant.com

"**Historical hipness**" clings to this "**sexy-smart**" TriBeCa bistro that's enjoying something of a rebirth with the renaissance of the Financial District; "**solid**" Franco-American fare, a "**vibrant**" mood and the addition of breakfast service are reasons why it "**seems fresher**" than ever to its perpetually "**cool crowd.**"

OFRENDA | Mexican 4.1 3.5 3.8 $$
West Village | 113 Seventh Ave. S. (bet. 4th & 10th Sts.)
212-924-2305 | www.ofrendanyc.com

"**Creative**" Mexican fare – and "**even better margaritas**" – delivered by a friendly" staff keeps this "**bar-esque**" West Villager "**bustling**"; the "**tiny**" space can be "**deafeningly loud**", but "**fun**" outdoor seating provides summertime relief, and the "**amazing**" happy hour is among the "**best deals in town.**"

OIJI | Korean 4.5 3.9 4.1 $$$
East Village | 119 First Ave. (7th St.)
646-767-9050 | www.oijinyc.com

Specializing in "**out-of-the-box**" Korean fare, this East Villager matches "**excellent renditions**" of "**modern**" dishes (the "**honey butter chips are a must**") with "**high-quality sojus**"; the "**pint-sized**" space is "**tight**", but once you "**cram yourself in**" the food "**speaks for itself.**"

OKONOMI/YUJI RAMEN | Japanese ▽ 4.4 3.9 4.0 $

Williamsburg | 150 Ainslie St. (bet. Leonard & Lorimer Sts.) | Brooklyn
no phone | www.okonomibk.com

"**Talk about originality**", this "**tiny**" Williamsburg Japanese from chef Yuji Haraguchi provides "**traditional**" ichiju-sansai set meals for breakfast and lunch, then segues into Yuji Ramen at night, offering "**cutting-edge**" noodle soups; seats can be scarce in the "**minimal**" space, which doesn't take reservations.

OLD HOMESTEAD | Steak   4.5 4.0 4.2 $$$$

Chelsea | 56 Ninth Ave. (bet. 14th & 15th Sts.)
212-242-9040 | www.theoldhomesteadsteakhouse.com

Still serving a "**hell of a steak**", this "**legendary**" Chelsea chophouse has been drawing "**big spenders**" in "**big suspenders**" since 1868, and its "**clubby**" (soon to be expanded) quarters "**capture a bygone era**"; "**robber baron**" prices are part of the package, but given the "**William Howard Taft**"–worthy portions, some call it a "**comparative value.**"

OLD TBILISI GARDEN | Georgian ▽ 4.2 3.6 3.7 $$

Greenwich Village | 174 Bleecker St. (Sullivan St.)
212-470-6064

Fans of Georgian food – "**the country, not the state**" – seek out this "**different**" Villager, where the "**tasty**" khachapuri and other "**hearty**" dishes are served with "**old-world charm**"; if the "**decor's nothing much**", tabs are "**reasonable**" and there's a garden with a "**funky**" waterfall.

OLEA | Mediterranean   4.5 4.1 4.3 $$

Fort Greene | 171 Lafayette Ave. (Adelphi St.) | Brooklyn
718-643-7003 | www.oleabrooklyn.com

"**On the keeper list**" in Fort Greene, this BAM-area "**favorite**" features "**delightful**" Med plates (including notably "**wonderful tapas**") set down in "**cozy**", "**colorful**" digs by an "**accommodating**" crew; since "**everyone in the neighborhood**" knows about it, be ready for "**bustling**" crowds and "**long waits**", especially for brunch.

OLEANDERS | American   — — — $$

Williamsburg | McCarren Hotel | 160 N. 12th St. (Berry St.) | Brooklyn
718-218-7500 | www.oleandersnyc.com

This casual New American in Williamsburg's McCarren Hotel offers modern twists on classic dishes and house-concocted cocktails (riffs on gimlets and Negronis). The breezy interior is lined with plants galore, including a wall of namesake shrubs, and faux Tiffany light fixtures.

NEW OLMSTED | American   — — — $$$

Prospect Heights | 659 Vanderbilt Ave. (bet. Park & Prospect Pls.) | Brooklyn
718-552-2610 | www.olmstednyc.com

A chef with an all-star history (Per Se, Blue Hill at Stone Barns, Chicago's Alinea) has teamed up with a farmer to open this Prospect Heights American drawing from super-local sources, including its own backyard garden. The woodsy interior brings nature inside with the beginnings of a live green wall, and has a chef's counter for watching the action.

OMAI | Vietnamese   4.2   3.4   3.9 $$
Chelsea | 158 Ninth Ave. (bet. 19th & 20th Sts.)
212-633-0550 | www.omainyc.com

A longtime "**solid**" neighborhood "**go-to**", this "**pleasant**", "**low-key**" Chelsea Vietnamese serves up "**delicious**", "**delicate**" standards; "**reasonable prices**" and a location "**close to the Joyce Theater**" are pluses, though the "**little**" space is on the "**tight**" side.

ONE IF BY LAND, TWO IF BY SEA | American   4.4   4.7   4.4 $$$$
West Village | 17 Barrow St. (bet. 7th Ave. S. & W. 4th St.)
212-255-8649 | www.oneifbyland.com

"**Steeped in history**" and "**romance**", this "**historic**" Village "**rendezvous**" set in Aaron Burr's former carriage house offers "**excellent**" American cuisine delivered by staffers who "**take their job seriously**"; "**mood-setting**" touches – "**candlelit rooms**", four fireplaces, a piano bar – distract from the "**special occasion**"–level tabs.

1 OR 8 | Japanese   4.5   4.2   4.3 $$$
Williamsburg | 66 S. Second St. (Wythe Ave.) | Brooklyn
718-384-2152 | www.oneoreightbk.com

Representing the "**new cool**" in Williamsburg, this Japanese "**find**" turns out "**exceptional sushi**" and other "**original**" "**culinary creations**" in an "**inviting space**" with all-white, "**modern**" decor; also touted for "**telepathic service**" and an "**under-the-radar omakase**" deal, it's "**a real treat**" for those in the know.

OOTOYA | Japanese/Noodle Shop   4.3   4.0   4.1 $$
Flatiron | 8 W. 18th St. (bet. 5th & 6th Aves.) | 212-255-0018
Greenwich Village | 41 E. 11th St. (University Pl.) | 212-473-4300
West 40s | 141 W. 41st St. (bet. B'way & 6th Ave.) | 212-704-0833
www.ootoya.us

Turning out "**Japanese comfort food**" that's "**consistently delicious**", these "**nothing-fancy**" branches of a Tokyo-based izakaya chain provide "**down-to-earth**" favorites like yakitori, soba and soup bowls; given the "**reasonable**" pricing (and no-tipping policy), the only hitch is the occasional "**wait.**"

ORIENTAL GARDEN | Chinese/Seafood   4.3   3.3   3.7 $$
Chinatown | 14 Elizabeth St. (bet. Bayard & Canal Sts.)
212-619-0085 | www.orientalgardenny.com

"**Don't let the drab decor fool you**" at this C-town Cantonese vet, because its "**wonderful**" dim sum and seafood fresh "**from the tanks**" just might "**knock your socks off**"; the mood gets "**manic**" at prime times, but at least the "**banquet**" comes "**without an insane price.**"

THE ORIGINAL CHINATOWN | Ice Cream   4.4   2.8   3.7 $
ICE CREAM FACTORY
Chinatown | 65 Bayard St. (bet. Elizabeth & Mott Sts.)
212-608-4170 | www.chinatownicecreamfactory.com

This Chinatown "**institution**" dishes out "**yummy**" ice cream in Asian-accented flavors like green tea, taro and red bean, along with more standard ones (chocolate, strawberry); "**tiny but big on flavor**", it's takeout-only with "**lines out the door**" on warm days – thankfully they "**usually move fast.**"

ORIGINAL CRAB SHANTY | Italian/Seafood   4.2   3.5   4.0 $$
City Island | 361 City Island Ave. (Tier St.) | Bronx
718-885-1810 | www.originalcrabshanty.com

They "**pile it on**" at this "**informal**" City Island vet where the "**king-sized**"

Italian seafood servings are both "**tasty**" and "**affordable**"; the catch is certainly "**fresh**", but the nautical decor may have been out of the water too long.

ORSAY | French   3.9   4.1   3.9 $$$

East 70s | 1057 Lexington Ave. (75th St.)
212-517-6400 | www.orsayrestaurant.com

An UES facsimile of "**bygone France**", this French brasserie offers the "**expected**" dishes (at "**unexpectedly high prices**") to a "**boisterous**", "**multigenerational**" crowd; a "**lovely**" art nouveau setting cements the "**classique**" feel.

ORSO | Italian   4.3   3.9   4.2 $$$

West 40s | 322 W. 46th St. (bet. 8th & 9th Aves.)
212-489-7212 | www.orsorestaurant.com

A "**Theater District standard**" for decades, this "**crowded-but-convivial**" Restaurant Row Italian still supplies "**reliably delicious**", "**upscale**" fare via a "**quick**" staff of "**would-be actors**"; it's on the "**plain**" side and "**reserving way ahead is a must**", but to fans it's "**worth it**" for the "**Broadway star**"–gazing alone.

ORWASHER'S BAKERY | Bakery/Kosher   4.5   3.3   4.1 $

East 70s | 308 E. 78th St. (2nd Ave.)
212-288-6569
NEW **West 80s** | 440 Amsterdam Ave. (81st St.) | 646-461-7929
www.orwashers.com

A "**traditional**" kosher bakery "**the way it should be**", this circa-1916 UES vet and its UWS spin-off offer "**outstanding**" Jewish-style loaves ("**best raisin-pumpernickel ever**", "**off-the-charts challah**") and sweet "**treats galore**", including custom-filled jelly donuts that some could "**kill for**"; while the original has an **old-time**" feel, the newer locale is more modern with seats and expanded offerings (sandwiches, salads).

OSTERIA AL DOGE | Italian   4.1   3.8   4.0 $$$

West 40s | 142 W. 44th St. (bet. B'way & 6th Ave.)
212-944-3643 | www.osteria-doge.com

Exuding "**old-world charm**", this Times Square duplex rolls out "**tasty**" Venetian standards at a "**reasonable-for-Midtown**" price; the space is "**cozy**" (even if some say it "**could use a face-lift**"), while the "**speedy**" staff "**gets you to the theater on time.**"

NEW **OSTERIA DELLA PACE** | Italian   —   —   — $$$

Financial District | Eataly | 4 World Trade Ctr., 3rd fl. (Fulton St.)
646-677-8580 | www.eataly.com

A chef hailing from Italy's Veneto region leads the kitchen at this upscale Southern Italian inside the FiDi branch of Eataly, preparing housemade pastas, meats and large plates for the table to share, complemented by a brief but lively selection of wines and cocktails. The space is stylish with leather banquettes, marble tables and tile floors, as well as decorative ceramic plates.

OSTERIA LAGUNA | Italian   4.1   3.9   4.0 $$

East 40s | 209 E. 42nd St. (bet. 2nd & 3rd Aves.)
212-557-0001 | www.osteria-laguna.com

Offering a "**welcome**" "**neighborhood feel in a non-neighborhood area**", this "**busy**" Italian parked between Grand Central and the U.N. serves "**straight-ahead**" Venetian eats at relatively "**reasonable**" rates; it's a "**perfect lunch** spot for on-the-go execs", with a "**people-watching**" bonus when the French doors are open.

OSTERIA MORINI | Italian   4.5   3.9   4.2 $$$

SoHo | 218 Lafayette St. (bet. Broome & Spring Sts.)
212-965-8777 | www.osteriamorini.com

The "**fabulous pasta**" is a "**real draw**" at Michael White's "**low-key**" SoHo Italian where the rest of the Emilia-Romagna menu is "**spot-on**" too; "**space is tight**" in the "**rustic**" room, but "**consistency**" from the kitchen means it's still a "**winner.**"

OTTO | Italian/Pizza   4.3   3.8   3.9 $$

Greenwich Village | 1 Fifth Ave. (8th St.)
212-995-9559 | www.ottopizzeria.com

"**Another winner**" from the Batali-Bastianich team, this "**reasonable**", "**kid-friendly**" Village enoteca/pizzeria delivers "**excellent**" pizzas and pastas matched with an "**incredible**" wine list; meanwhile, the "**cavernous**" space includes an "**amazing**" front bar, whose "**vibrant scene**" kicks up "**lots of noise.**"

OTTO'S TACOS | Mexican   3.9   3.2   3.6 $

East Village | 141 Second Ave. (9th St.) | 646-678-4018
West 40s | 705 Ninth Ave. (bet. 48th & 49th Sts.) | 646-918-7681
West Village | 131 Seventh Ave. S. (10th St.) | 646-657-0646
www.ottostacos.com

"**Tasty**" LA-inspired tacos made with housemade tortillas ("**the key**") are "**on target**" at these "**popular**" Mexican joints, offering "**solid**", "**nicely seasoned**" eats on the "**cheap**"; the settings are "**no-frills**", but they're "**reliable**" for a "**quick bite**" on the go.

OVELIA | Greek   4.2   3.8   3.8 $$

Astoria | 34-01 30th Ave. (34th St.) | Queens
718-721-7217 | www.ovelia-ny.com

A "**go-to**" for Astorians seeking "**Greek chic**", this bar/eatery offers "**fresh**" Hellenic specialties with a "**modern twist**"; "**hospitable**" owners, modest tabs and a "**casual**", "**pleasant**" setting with outdoor seating help keep it "**popular.**"

OVEST PIZZOTECA | Pizza   ▽ 4.4   4.1   4.1 $$

Chelsea | 513 W. 27th St. (bet. 10th & 11th Aves.)
212-967-4392 | www.ovestnyc.com

"**Fantastic**" wood-oven pizza that tastes "**like Naples**" is the specialty of this West Chelsea pie parlor, a cousin of Luzzo's that also offers pastas and panini; "**appropriate**" tabs and a "**relaxed**" vibe tempt regulars to "**hang out**" well into the night.

O YA | Japanese   4.6   4.1   4.5 $$$$

Murray Hill | Park South Hotel | 120 E. 28th St. (Lexington Ave.)
212-204-0200 | www.o-ya.restaurant

"**Flavors like you'd never believe**" are found in the "**beautifully presented**" omakase meals at this modern Japanese in Murray Hill's Park South Hotel; the "**highly original**" fare is available à la carte too, but either way expect a "**huge price tag.**"

	FOOD	DECOR	SERVICE	COST

PACHANGA PATTERSON | Mexican ▽ 4.0 4.0 4.2 $$
Astoria | 33-17 31st Ave. (bet. 33rd & 34th Sts.) | Queens
718-554-0525 | www.pachangapatterson.com

This "**hip**" Astoria Mexican from the Vesta folks puts a "**cool spin**" on tacos
and other classics – but some say the sophisticated cocktails are its real
"**strong suit**"; "**multicolored string lights and candles**" enliven its "**low-key**"
interior, while the "**sunny**" backyard is a warm-weather "**find.**"

PACIFICANA | Chinese 4.5 3.7 3.9 $$
Sunset Park | 813 55th St. (8th Ave.) | Brooklyn
718-871-2880 | www.sunset-park.com

"**Authentic and delicious**" dim sum draws "**throngs**" to this huge, "**you're-in–
Hong Kong**" Sunset Park banquet hall, where a well-priced Cantonese menu
backs up what's on the "**rolling carts**"; on weekends it's a "**madhouse**" packed
with "**big, multigenerational parties**", but "**be patient**" – it's "**worth the wait.**"

THE PALM | Steak 4.4 3.9 4.2 $$$
TriBeCa | 206 West St. (bet. Chambers & Warren Sts.) | 646-395-6393
West 50s | 250 W. 50th St. (bet. B'way & 8th Ave.) | 212-333-7256

PALM TOO | Steak
East 40s | 840 Second Ave. (bet. 44th & 45th Sts.) | 212-697-5198
www.thepalm.com

"**Continuing the tradition**" of the now closed 1926 original, these "**top-end**"
links of the national steakhouse chain deliver "**superior**" beef and "**giant**"
lobsters in "**clubby**" quarters "**full of characters and caricatures**"; "**huge
prices**" come with the territory, but "**old-school service**" is another reason
it's a "**memorable experience.**"

PALMA | Italian 4.5 4.4 4.3 $$$
West Village | 28 Cornelia St. (bet. Bleecker & 4th Sts.)
212-691-2223 | www.palmanyc.com

Italian food made with "**loving care**" tastes like "**nonna's**" at this "**charming**"
West Villager with a "**like-you're-in-Italy**" vibe; its "**lovely garden**" is a
"**summer favorite**", the private party–only carriage house is "**perfect for a
special occasion**" and there's also a next-door wine bar, Aperitivo di Palma.

PALM COURT | American 4.2 4.6 4.3 $$$$
West 50s | Plaza Hotel | 768 Fifth Ave. (59th St.)
212-546-5300 | www.theplazany.com

A "**step into Old New York**", this "**sumptuous**", palm-filled atrium in The Plaza
serves breakfast, cocktails and evening American snacks, plus famed
afternoon tea that's "**a Belle Époque dream**" (including a menu for "**little
Eloises**"); for a trip to the "**glorious past**", fans gladly pony up for the
"**gazillion-dollar**" tab.

PAMPANO | Mexican/Seafood 4.4 4.1 4.1 $$$
East 40s | 209 E. 49th St., 2nd fl. (bet. 2nd & 3rd Aves.)
212-751-4545 | www.richardsandoval.com

"**Refined**" Mexican dishes highlighting "**excellent**" seafood are the stars at this
"**classy**" East Midtowner from Richard Sandoval and tenor Plácido Domingo,
it's "**not cheap**", but the "**beachy**", "**whitewashed**" decor and "**creative**" drinks
help make it "**feel like a vacation**", especially out on the "**beautiful terrace.**"

	FOOD	DECOR	SERVICE	COST

PAM REAL THAI FOOD | Thai — 4.1 2.9 3.7 $$
West 40s | 404 W. 49th St. (bet. 9th & 10th Aves.)
212-333-7500 | www.pamrealthaifood.com

"**Reliable**" Thai food, "**spiced to your taste**", comes via a "**speedy**" staff at this cash-only Hell's Kitchen "**favorite**" that makes an "**excellent pre-theater**" choice; the interior is "**kinda dumpy**", but to most that's "**worth tolerating**" given pricing that's among the area's "**best values.**"

PANEANTICO | Bakery/Italian — 4.5 3.6 3.7 $
Bay Ridge | 9124 Third Ave. (92nd St.) | Brooklyn
718-680-2347 | www.paneantico.com

It's "**more than great bread**" that draws Bay Ridgers to this "**marvelous**" Italian bakery/cafe – the panini, salads and pastries are all rated "**delish**" as well; its "**small**", blue-tiled space, with tables indoors and out, is "**always jammed**" on weekends – clearly "**they're doing something right.**"

PAOLA'S | Italian — 4.3 3.9 4.2 $$$
East 90s | Wales Hotel | 1295 Madison Ave. (92nd St.)
212-794-1890 | www.paolasrestaurant.com

As a "**sophisticated**" haunt for "**ritzy**" Upper Eastsiders, this "**attractive**" Carnegie Hill Italian wins favor with "*delizioso*" cuisine and "**hospitality**" via the "**gracious**" eponymous owner and her "**tip-top**" staff; some dub it "**Payola's**" – but it's "**thriving**" (and "**loud**") for a reason.

NEW **PAOWALLA** | Indian — — — $$$
SoHo | 195 Spring St. (Sullivan St.)
212-235-1098 | www.paowalla.com

Celebrated chef Floyd Cardoz has opened this Soho Indian devoted to dishes with Goan roots, as well as a variety of breads from the wood-burning oven. The space is largely unadorned, with neutral tones and whitewashed brick walls setting the stage for vibrant presentations.

PAPAYA KING | Hot Dogs — 4.1 2.7 3.4 $
East 80s | 179 E. 86th St. (3rd Ave.) | 212-369-0648
East Village | 3 St. Marks Pl. (bet. 2nd & 3rd Aves.) | 646-692-8482
www.papayaking.com

"**Easier than a trip to Coney Island**", these wiener wonderlands supply "**happiness in a tube**" via "**damn fine**" hot dogs and papaya drinks on the "**cheap**" (even for "**fast food**"); OK, you're "**not going for the ambiance**", but as an "**only-in-NYC-baby**" experience, "**nothing beats**" 'em.

PAPPARDELLA | Italian — 4.1 3.7 4.0 $$
West 70s | 316 Columbus Ave. (75th St.)
212-595-7996 | www.pappardella.com

This "**inviting**" UWS "**neighborhood joint**" is "**long established**" as a "**not-too-expensive**" fallback for "**tasty pastas**" and other "**solid**" Italian standards; whether you "**relax**" indoors or sit outside and take in the Columbus Avenue scene, count on "**no pressure.**"

PARDON MY FRENCH | French ∇ 4.3 4.0 4.2 $$$
East Village | 103 Ave. B (7th St.)
212-358-9683 | www.pmf.nyc

A remake of Casimir by the same owners, this New Wave French bistro offers "**delicious**" small plates and upscale entrees until the wee hours, as well as a bottomless weekend brunch; the "**inviting**", softly lit setting "**oozes charm**" and includes a tiled communal table and spiffy cocktail bar.

THE PARK | Mediterranean · · · · · · · · 3.7 · 4.4 · 3.7 · · $$
Chelsea | 118 10th Ave. (bet. 17th & 18th Sts.)
212-352-3313 | www.theparknyc.com

A "**beautiful**" multitiered setting is the draw at this Chelsea vet that's a "**relaxing**" stop "**before or after the High Line**" thanks to its "**fantastic**" year-round garden "**dressed up like Central Park**"; the Med fare is just "**OK**", but it's a relative "**bargain**" compared to "**higher-priced neighbors.**"

PARK AVENUE SPRING/ | American · · · · 4.4 · 4.5 · 4.3 · · $$$
SUMMER/AUTUMN/WINTER
Flatiron | 360 Park Ave. S. (26th St.)
212-951-7111 | www.parkavenyc.com

Set in an "**airy**" Flatiron space, this "**smooth**" New American "**keeps things fresh**" with an "**inspiring menu**" and "**transporting**", AvroKO-conceived decor that both change quarterly to reflect the four seasons; it's "**not cheap**", but compensations include a "**first-rate**" staff and a "**thoughtful wine list.**"

PARKER & QUINN | American · · · · · · · 4.0 · 3.9 · 3.9 · · $$
West 30s | Refinery Hotel | 64 W. 39th St. (6th Ave.)
212-729-0277 | www.ingoodcompanyhg.com

"**Much needed**" in the dining-deprived Garment District, the Refinery Hotel's spacious bar/eatery supplies "**surprisingly good**" American fare that's "**satisfying**" if "**not necessarily inventive**"; a "**nicely decorated**", vintage-style space with "**vantage points**" from raised booths makes for a "**fun**" vibe

PARK SIDE | Italian · · · · · · · · · · · 4.5 · 3.9 · 4.2 · · $$$
Corona | 107-01 Corona Ave. (bet. 51st Ave. & 108th St.) | Queens
718-271-9321 | www.parksiderestaurantny.com

"**Local color**" abounds at this "**Corona landmark**" beloved for its "**old-school**" Italian cooking and "**energetic**" following, from "**politicians**" to "**goodfellas**"; with "**valet parking**", "**plentiful**" portions and "**classy**" "**waiters in tuxes**", it "**rivals Arthur Avenue**" – down to the "**bocce games in the park across the street.**"

PARLOR STEAKHOUSE | Steak · · · · · · 4.1 · 3.9 · 4.0 · · $$$
East 80s | 1600 Third Ave. (90th St.)
212-423-5888 | www.parlorsteakhouse.com

"**One of the few decent options above 86th Street**", this "**much-needed**" Carnegie Hill steakhouse serves "**quality**" surf 'n' turf in a "**lovely**" modern setting; a "**hopping bar scene**" and convenience to the 92nd Street Y compensate for the "**pricey**" tabs.

PARM | Italian/Sandwiches · · · · · · · · 3.8 · 3.4 · 3.6 · · $$
Battery Park City | 250 Vesey St. (North End Ave.) | 212-776-4927
NoLita | 248 Mulberry St. (bet. Prince & Spring Sts.) | 212-993-7189
West 70s | 235 Columbus Ave. (71st St.) | 212-776-4921
NEW **Williamsburg** | 162 N. Fourth St. (Bedford Ave.) | Brooklyn |
718-408-7240
www.parmnyc.com

That "**can't-miss**" namesake sandwich stars on the "**limited menu**" of "**Carbone-on-the-cheap**" Italian-American classics at this "**relaxed**" mini-chain from the Torrisi crew, some unimpressed with the "**dinerlike**" setups and "**spotty**" service call it "**overhyped**", but the fact that it's "**always crowded**" speaks for itself.

PARMA | Italian	4.1	3.4	4.2	$$$

East 70s \| 1404 Third Ave. (80th St.)
212-535-3520 \| www.parmanyc.com

This longtime UES Italian is a bastion of "**hearty**" cooking delivered by a seasoned staff that's clearly "**there to please**"; maybe it's "**pricey**" and "**not much to look at**", but it just "**feels right**" to loyal patrons.

PASCALOU \| French 4.2 3.5 4.1 $$

East 90s \| 1308 Madison Ave. (bet. 92nd & 93rd Sts.)
212-534-7522 \| www.pascalou.info

So long as you don't mind sitting "**elbow-to-elbow**", this UES vet is "**dependable**" for "**authentic**" French fare served in the "**tiniest**" space; a "**welcoming**" vibe and "**cost-conscious**" tabs – "**especially the early-bird**" – are additional bonuses.

PASHA \| Turkish 4.0 3.8 4.1 $$

West 70s \| 70 W. 71st St. (bet. Columbus Ave. & CPW)
212-579-8751 \| www.pashanewyork.com

It's a bit like being "**magically transported**" to the "**Bosphorus**" at this "**sedate**" UWS retreat where "**solid**" Turkish staples are enhanced by "**attentive**" service; set in "**civilized**" surroundings, it's a "**fairly priced**" fallback near Lincoln Center.

NEW **PASQUALE JONES** \| Italian ▽ 4.5 4.4 4.4 $$$

NoLita \| 187 Mulberry St. (Kenmare St.)
no phone \| www.pasqualejones.com

"**Another winner**" from the Charlie Bird team, this "**hot**" NoLita Italian "**lives up to the fanfare**" with "**exceptional**" pizzas and other "**inventive**" dishes from a wood-burning oven; there's a "**nice buzz**" in the "**relaxed**" space courtesy of a hip-hop soundtrack and a staff that's like a "**well-oiled machine**" – but "**good luck getting a table.**"

PASQUALE RIGOLETTO \| Italian 4.0 3.6 4.0 $$$

Arthur Avenue/Belmont \| 2311 Arthur Ave. (184th St.) \| Bronx
718-365-6644 \| www.pasqualesrigoletto.com

For an "**authentic Bronx experience**", this Arthur Avenue "**landmark**" offers "**generous**" helpings of "**real Italian**" classics seasoned with "**a lot of local color**"; it's a post–Yankee game "**favorite**", though it might be time for a decor "**makeover.**"

PASTRAMI QUEEN \| Deli/Kosher 4.2 2.7 3.5 $$

East 70s \| 1125 Lexington Ave. (78th St.)
212-734-1500 \| www.pastramiqueen.com

"**Outstanding pastrami**" is the claim to fame at this "**reliable**" UES deli that's the "**real thing**" for "**overstuffed sandwiches**" and other kosher "**basics done right**"; seating is "**almost an afterthought**" in its "**cramped, dingy**" space, so regulars say "**takeout is best.**"

PATRICIA'S \| Italian 4.3 3.9 4.1 $$

Morris Park \| 1082 Morris Park Ave. (bet. Haight & Lurting Aves.) \| Bronx
718-409-9069

Bronx-based fans of this Morris Park Italian say it "**satisfies**" any hankering for "**solid**" "**homestyle cooking**" and "**excellent**" wood-fired pizzas; "**comfortable,** "relatively quiet" environs, "friendly" service and good "bang for the buck" round out the "dependable" picture.

PATSY'S | Italian   4.2   3.7   4.2 $$$

West 50s | 236 W. 56th St. (bet. B'way & 8th Ave.)
212-247-3491 | www.patsys.com

It "doesn't get more old-school" than this 1944-vintage Midtown "throwback", a "favorite of Sinatra's" that still offers "delicious" Neapolitan cooking and "quality service"; maybe it could stand a "refresh", but the "heaping" portions and Theater District proximity are fine as is.

PATSY'S PIZZERIA | Pizza   4.1   3.2   3.7 $$

East 40s | 801 Second Ave. (43rd St.) | 212-878-9600 | www.patsyspizzeria.us
East 60s | 206 E. 60th St. (bet. 2nd & 3rd Aves.) | 212-688-9707 |
www.patsyspizzerianewyork.com
East 60s | 1279 First Ave. (69th St.) | 212-639-1000 |
www.patsyspizzerianewyork.com
East Harlem | 2287 First Ave. (bet. 117th & 118th Sts.) | 212-534-9783 |
www.thepatsyspizza.com
Greenwich Village | 67 University Pl. (bet. 10th & 11th Sts.) | 212-533-3500 |
www.patsyspizzeria.us
West 70s | 61 W. 74th St. (bet. Columbus Ave. & CPW) | 212-579-3000 |
www.patsyspizzeria.us
Park Slope | 450 Dean St. (Flatbush Ave.) | Brooklyn | 718-622-2268 |
www.patsyspizza.nyc

Turning out "Naples-good" thin-crust pizza since 1933, this East Harlem "treasure" and its separately owned offshoots offer "generous portions" of "hit-the-spot" Italian-American fare as well as an "excellent variety of salads"; while "nothing compares" to the original, all the "dependable" locales are "magnets" for families.

PAUL & JIMMY'S | Italian   4.1   3.8   4.1 $$$

Gramercy Park | 123 E. 18th St. (Irving Pl.)
212-475-9540 | www.paulandjimmys.com

"They know what they're doing" at this "been-there-for-ages" Gramercy Italian where a "welcoming" crew delivers "solid", "old-school" staples; it's particularly "appreciated" by locals since the lunch and dinner prix fixes are quite the "deal."

PAULIE GEE'S | Pizza   4.6   3.9   4.1 $$

Greenpoint | 60 Greenpoint Ave. (bet. Franklin & West Sts.) | Brooklyn
347-987-3747 | www.pauliegee.com

The "crowds" prove the "hype" at this Greenpoint pizzeria where "seriously good" pies (especially the "addictive" Hellboy) are offered with "original" toppings varied enough "to please anyone"; the "dimly lit" digs feel especially "inviting" when Paulie "drops by to say hello."

PEACEFOOD CAFÉ | Kosher/Vegan/Vegetarian   4.0   3.5   3.7 $$

Greenwich Village | 41 E. 11th St. (bet. B'way & University Pl.) | 212-979-2288
West 80s | 460 Amsterdam Ave. (82nd St.) | 212-362-2266
www.peacefoodcafe.com

"Fresh, creative" (and kosher) vegan fare – including "terrific baked goods" – keeps "health-conscious" types returning to these "relaxed" neighborhood joints, though service may be "spacey", the "affordable" tabs and "guilt-free" feeling are fine as is.

	FOOD	DECOR	SERVICE	COST

PEACHES | Southern   4.3   3.7   4.0 $$
Bedford-Stuyvesant | 393 Lewis Ave. (MacDonough St.) | Brooklyn |
718-942-4162

PEACHES HOTHOUSE | Southern
Bedford-Stuyvesant | 415 Tompkins Ave. (Hancock St.) | Brooklyn |
718-483-9111
www.bcrestaurantgroup.com

Easier than keeping "**granny in the kitchen all day**", these Bed-Stuy "**local
beacons**" win "**three thumbs up**" for their "**delicious**" Southern staples;
whether for "**delightful**" platters at Peaches or "**spicy**" fried chicken at The
HotHouse, they're "**well worth**" the frequent wait.

PEARL & ASH | American   4.3   3.8   4.1 $$$
NoLita | 220 Bowery (bet. Prince & Spring Sts.)
212-837-2370 | www.pearlandash.com

While the "**original**" New American small plates are "**exciting**" at this Bowery
hideaway, the "**true find**" is its "**jumbo**" wine list with countless "**back
vintages**" decanted by "**personable**" staffers; a "**cool clientele**" keeps the
slender room "**buzzy**", so expect "**moderate noise.**"

PEARL OYSTER BAR | New England/Seafood   4.6   3.5   4.1 $$$
West Village | 18 Cornelia St. (bet. Bleecker & W. 4th Sts.)
212-691-8211 | www.pearloysterbar.com

"**Just get the lobster roll**" say fans of this "**nothing-fancy**" West Village
"**landmark**" and its "**luscious**" signature sandwich – though pretty much
"**everything's delicious**" on the classic New England seafood menu here; it
doesn't take rezzies, and the "**cute**" space can get "**cramped**", so just "**go
early or expect to wait.**"

PEARL ROOM | Seafood   4.1   3.9   4.0 $$$
Bay Ridge | 8201 Third Ave. (82nd St.) | Brooklyn
718-833-6666 | www.thepearlroom.com

"**As fancy as it gets in Bay Ridge**", this seafaring "**surprise**" provides
"**consistently good**" preparations of "**fresh**" marine cuisine served by an
"**attentive**" crew; factor in a white-tablecloth setting suitable for "**romantic**"
encounters and "**celebrations**", and it's no surprise the tab can skew "**pricey.**"

PEASANT | Italian   4.5   4.3   4.1 $$$
NoLita | 194 Elizabeth St. (bet. Prince & Spring Sts.)
212-965-9511 | www.peasantnyc.com

From the "**warm**", rustic setting to the "**fabulous**", wood-fired cuisine, this
"**unforgettable**" Italian "**outshines**" many of its NoLita neighbors; "**romantic**"
types on a "**dinner date**" finish up the meal in the "**civilized**" cellar wine bar
for after-dinner drinks.

PEKING DUCK HOUSE | Chinese   4.3   3.4   3.7 $$
Chinatown | 28 Mott St. (bet. Chatham Sq. & Pell St.) | 212-227-1810
East 50s | 236 E. 53rd St. (bet. 2nd & 3rd Aves.) | 212-759-8260
www.pekingduckhousenyc.com

With its "**juicy**" meat and "**savory, crispy skin**", the signature Peking duck
carved tableside is a "**real treat**" at these "**old-fashioned**" Chinese spots;
decor and service may be somewhat "**lacking**", but "**wine lovers**" applaud the
BYO policy at the Chinatown location, which also received a facelift.

	FOOD	DECOR	SERVICE	COST

PELLEGRINO'S | Italian — 4.4 3.8 4.2 $$

Little Italy | 138 Mulberry St. (bet. Grand & Hester Sts.)
212-226-3177 | www.pellegrinosristorante.com

"High-quality" "red-sauce" cooking and "personal service" foster the "happy ambiance" at this Little Italy "winner"; regulars prefer sitting outside and taking in the only-in-NY Mulberry Street "scene."

PENELOPE | American — 4.0 3.6 3.7 $$

Murray Hill | 159 Lexington Ave. (30th St.)
212-481-3800 | www.penelopenyc.com

Murray Hill locals tout this "adorable" neighborhood "favorite" for "tasty", "comfort"-oriented New American at a "reasonable cost" served in a "country-cafe" setting; there's "high demand" for the "amazing brunch", so bring "patience" to deal with the inevitable "waits."

NEW THE PENNSY | Food Hall — 3.9 3.4 3.6 $

West 30s | 2 Pennsylvania Plaza (31st St.)
917-475-1830 | www.thepennsy.nyc

To the "historically abysmal" dining zone around Penn Station comes this "upscale food hall" offering "something for everyone", from "vegan to carnivore" (vendors include Mario Batali, Pat LaFrieda, Marc Forgione, Little Beet and Cinnamon Snail); there's "plenty of space to sit and linger", indoors and out, plus a bar for pre-train or post-MSG drinks.

THE PENROSE | American — 4.1 3.9 3.7 $

East 80s | 1590 Second Ave. (bet. 82nd & 83rd Sts.)
212-203-2751 | www.penrosebar.com

A "hip spot" in the "otherwise unhip Upper East Side", this "lively" gastropub lures "younger" types with a "trendy" scene fueled by "delicious burgers" and other "enjoyable" American bar bites; a "Brooklyn vibe" and "rustic" looks make it a "welcome alternative" in the neighborhood.

PEPOLINO | Italian — 4.5 3.7 4.3 $$$

TriBeCa | 281 W. Broadway (bet. Canal & Lispenard Sts.)
212-966-9983 | www.pepolino.com

"Hiding in plain sight" on the fringes of TriBeCa, this "charming" trattoria delivers a "magic combination" of "savory" Tuscan farm cuisine and "attentive" service amid "rustic" surrounds; the experience is "not cheap", but given the "high quality", insiders still consider it a "deal."

PERA | Mediterranean — 4.0 3.9 3.8 $$$

East 40s | 303 Madison Ave. (bet. 41st & 42nd Sts.) | 212-878-6301 |
www.peranyc.com

SoHo | 54 Thompson St. (bet. Broome & Spring Sts.) | 212-878-6305 |
www.soho.peranyc.com

These "attractive" eateries make "civilized" choices for Turkish-accented Mediterranean fare – including a "lovely range" of meze – served in "modern" surrounds; the Midtown original is a "no-brainer for business", while the stylin' SoHo spin-off sports a "stunning outdoor deck."

PERIYALI | Greek — 4.4 4.1 4.4 $$$

Flatiron | 35 W. 20th St. (bet. 5th & 6th Aves.)
212-463-7890 | www.periyali.com

"Dependably rewarding" since 1987, this Flatiron "Greek classic" remains a "refined" refuge for "superb fresh fish" and "gracious service" in "soothing", "not-too-loud" surrounds; fans say the "like-you're-in-Greece" experience is "worth the high price."

PERLA CAFE | Italian   4.3   4.0   4.2 $$$

West Village | 24 Minetta Ln. (bet. MacDougal St. & 6th Ave.)
212-933-1824 | www.perlanyc.com

Settled into new digs on a "**trendy**" West Village corner, Gabe Stulman's Italian "**gem**" delivers the same trademark "**excellent pastas**" and other "**delicious**" fare (including lighter options) in "**artsy**" surrounds with "**more of a cafe**" feel; the "**wait**" for a table remains, but "**sitting at the bar**" is a "**fun**" option.

PERRY ST. | American   4.6   4.5   4.5 $$$

West Village | 176 Perry St. (West St.)
212-352-1900 | www.perrystrestaurant.com

It's "**serenity defined**" at this Jean-Georges Vongerichten "**retreat**" in the far West Village, where "**superb**" New American cooking from chef (and chip off the old block) Cedric Vongerichten comes in "**sleek**" Richard Meier–designed quarters "**overlooking the Hudson**"; "**caring**", pro service completes the "**refined**" picture – and helps justify the "**not cheap**" tab.

PER SE | American/French   4.6   4.7   4.7 $$$$

West 50s | Time Warner Ctr. | 10 Columbus Circle (bet. 58th & 60th Sts.)
212-823-9335 | www.perseny.com

Thomas Keller's Time Warner Center "**high temple**" of French–New American cuisine is "**truly an event**" given the "**fabulous**" tasting menu, "**unimpeachable**" service and "**posh**", jackets-required surrounds overlooking Central Park; while the "**through-the-roof**" set price may limit visits to "**once in a blue moon**", those of more limited means "**love the à la carte option**" in the lounge.

PERSEPOLIS | Persian   4.1   3.7   4.0 $$

East 70s | 1407 Second Ave. (bet. 73rd & 74th Sts.)
212-535-1100 | www.persepolisnewyork.com

A "**standout**" among the "**few Persians**" in town, this Upper Eastsider offers "**interesting**", "**well-spiced**" Iranian dishes (the signature "**sour-cherry rice is a treat**") in an "**understated**" setting; given the "**personal service**" and overall "**value**", it's "**easy to relax and enjoy**" here.

PETER LUGER STEAK HOUSE | Steak   4.8   3.7   4.2 $$$$

Williamsburg | 178 Broadway (Driggs Ave.) | Brooklyn
718-387-7400 | www.peterluger.com

"**Still the one and only**", this circa-1887 Williamsburg "**monument to meat**" sets the bar with its "**buttery**" house-aged beef ("**they define porterhouse**") served by "**cantankerous**" career waiters in a "**busy**" "**old-time**" German beer hall setting; the "**rough-and-tumble**" style "**only adds to the charm**", but prices are "**stiff**" and they don't take plastic, so come with "**a lot of cash.**"

PETER PAN DONUT   4.5   3.7   4.1 $
& PASTRY SHOP | Donuts

Greenpoint | 727 Manhattan Ave. (bet. Meserole & Norman Aves.) | Brooklyn
718-389-3676 | www.peterpandonuts.com

"**Policemen, elder locals, foodies and hipsters**" come together at this Greenpoint "**legend**", a "**bustling**" "**throwback**" for "**traditional**" donuts in more than 20 "**fabulous**" flavors; "**old-school**" prices match the "**old-fashioned**" space where you can also snag a counter seat and get "**one of the best egg creams**" around.

	FOOD	DECOR	SERVICE	COST

PETE'S TAVERN | American/Italian — 3.6 | 3.8 | 3.8 | $$$

Gramercy Park | 129 E. 18th St. (Irving Pl.)
212-473-7676 | www.petestavern.com

A "**Gramercy Park tradition**", this circa-1864 "**landmark**" turns out "**gently priced**" Italian-American pub grub in an "**old-time**" space where former regular O. Henry "**would still be comfortable**"; though the food's "**passable**", it's the "**history, charm**" and "**lively**" front bar that "**brings you back.**"

PETROSSIAN BOUTIQUE | Continental/French — 4.4 | 4.3 | 4.3 | $$$$

West 50s | 911 Seventh Ave. (58th St.) | 212-245-2217
West 50s | 182 W. 58th St. (7th Ave.) | 212-245-2214
www.petrossian.com

When you're "**craving a caviar fix**", this Carnegie Hall–area "**grand dame**" is a "**sublime**" (albeit "**frightfully expensive**") pick, also offering "**high-quality**" French-Continental cuisine in a "**lovely**" space with "**art deco styling**"; meanwhile the adjacent cafe is a "**quiet enclave**" favored for "**light fare.**"

PHILIPPE | Chinese — 4.3 | 3.9 | 4.1 | $$$

East 60s | 33 E. 60th St. (bet. Madison & Park Aves.)
212-644-8885 | www.philippechow.com

"**Low-lit and high-class**", this East Side Chinese channels "**Mr. Chow**" with "**well-crafted**" cuisine served to a "**glamorous**" crowd in digs that turn "**cacophonous**" when going full tilt (the back room's more "**chill**"); expect a "**showy**" scene, and note that the $24 prix fixe lunch is one way around the "**sky-high**" tabs.

PHO BANG | Noodle Shop/Vietnamese — 4.1 | 2.7 | 3.3 | $

Little Italy | 157 Mott St. (bet. Broome & Grand Sts.) | 212-966-3797
Elmhurst | 82-90 Broadway (bet. 45th & Whitney Aves.) | Queens |
718-205-1500
Flushing | 41-07 Kissena Blvd. (bet. Barclay & 41st Aves.) | Queens |
718-939-5520

"**Just as the name says**", these "**no-nonsense**" Vietnamese joints cater to "**pho phans**" with "**delicious**" soup bowls and a "**big bang for the buck**"; otherwise they're "**dingy**" setups where the staffers "**could be a little more courteous.**"

PHOENIX GARDEN | Chinese — 4.2 | 2.8 | 3.4 | $$

East 40s | 242 E. 40th St. (bet. 2nd & 3rd Aves.)
212-983-6666 | www.phoenixgardennyc.com

"**Solid**" Cantonese cooking and the "**added benefit**" of a BYO policy make this "**unassuming**" Midtown vet a "**real find**" ("**save yourself a trip to Chinatown**"); fans overlook the "**attitude**", "**dreary decor**" and cash-only policy because you can't beat the "**value.**"

PICCOLA VENEZIA | Italian — 4.6 | 3.8 | 4.4 | $$$

Astoria | 42-01 28th Ave. (42nd St.) | Queens
718-721-8470 | www.piccola-venezia.com

The "**classic**" Northern Italian cooking is "**superb**" and "**they'll make whatever you want**" at this Astoria "**oldie but goodie**" that's kept "**regulars returning**" "**for generations**"; if "**the decor needs a redo**", that's "**easy to overlook**" given "**fabulous**" service from a staff out of "**central casting.**"

PICCOLO ANGOLO | Italian   4.4   3.3   4.1 $$$

West Village | 621 Hudson St. (Jane St.)
212-229-9177 | www.piccoloangolo.com

A longtime West Village "**family operation**" that still "**holds its own**", this "**old-school**" Northern Italian consistently "**wows**" with its "**excellent homestyle**" cooking and "**mama-loves-you**" service; the "**close**", "**no-frills**" quarters are "**always crowded**", so "**definitely have a reservation.**"

PICCOLO CAFE | Coffee/Italian   4.2   3.5   3.9 $$

Gramercy Park | 157 Third Ave. (bet. 15th & 16th Sts.) | 212-260-1175
Murray Hill | 238 Madison Ave. (37th St.) | 212-447-4399
West 40s | 274 W. 40th St. (8th Ave.) | 212-302-0143
West 70s | 313 Amsterdam Ave. (bet. 74th & 75th Sts.) | 212-873-0962
www.piccolocafe.us

These "**cheerful**" cafes are linked to an Italy-based coffee roaster, so count on espresso from imported beans and "**real Italian**" bites including "**delicious**" pastas and panini; just don't expect much seating because, as the name implies, they're "**teensy-weensy.**"

PIER A HARBOR HOUSE | American   3.8   4.3   3.7 $$

Battery Park City | 22 Battery Pl. (Little West St.)
212-785-0153 | www.piera.com

A circa-1886 pier is home to this "**big, beautiful**" Battery Park City hangout with a "**publike**" area for "**drinking and snacks**" at street level, plus a balcony bar and private rooms above; maybe the seafood-centric American fare "**could be better**", but the "**astonishing**" harbor views and sprawling outdoor space need no improvement.

PIES-N-THIGHS | Southern   4.3   3.3   3.7 $$

Williamsburg | 166 S. Fourth St. (Driggs Ave.) | Brooklyn
347-529-6090 | www.piesnthighs.com

"**Naps are required**" after visiting this "**popular**" Williamsburg storefront for "**perfectly fried**" chicken, "**fantastic**" homemade pies and other Southern "**comfort food**"; the "**down-and-dirty**" digs are "**a tight squeeze**" and "**service can lag**", so be ready for a "**long wait on weekends.**"

PIETRO'S | Italian/Steak   4.5   3.4   4.4 $$$

East 40s | 232 E. 43rd St. (bet. 2nd & 3rd Aves.)
212-682-9760 | www.pietrosnyc.com

In the Grand Central area since 1932, this "**old-school**" holdout rests its rep on "**excellent steaks**" and "**superior**" Italian basics served in "**copious amounts**" by a "**gracious**", "**been-there-for-years**" staff; the room's "**not glamorous**", but "**loyal**" regulars appreciate the "**quiet**" vibe – or more "**lively**" times at its "**great bar.**"

PIG AND KHAO | SE Asian   4.3   3.3   3.8 $$$

Lower East Side | 68 Clinton St. (bet. Rivington & Stanton Sts.)
212-920-4485 | www.pigandkhao.com

The "**adventurous will be rewarded**" at chef Leah Cohen's "**offbeat**" LES Southeast Asian where "**tongue-tingling**" Thai and Filipino flavors inspire an "**innovative array**" of pork-centric dishes (e.g. "**mouthwatering sisig**") that make for "**happy sharing**"; "**good-deal**" pricing helps keep the patio-equipped space "**bustling.**"

PIG HEAVEN | Chinese   4.1   3.6   4.0 $$

East 80s | 1420 Third Ave. (bet. 80th & 81 Sts.)
212-744-4333 | www.pigheavennyc.com

"If pig is what you want", this UES Chinese "favorite" run by "gracious" Nancy Lee is "heaven indeed" for "anything pork-related", with a lineup showcasing its "signature spareribs"; the word is definitely out, so expect "lots of company at the trough."

THE PINES | American   ▽ 4.4   4.0   4.0 $$

Gowanus | 284 Third Ave. (bet. Carroll & President Sts.) | Brooklyn
718-596-6560 | www.thepinesbrooklyn.com

"Ambitious", somewhat "edgy" New American cuisine and creative cocktails draw a "hipster" crowd to this Gowanus nook that also offers a "brilliant" all-natural wine list; despite "a lot of hype", it exudes a "down-to-earth" vibe, starting with its reclaimed church pew seating.

PING'S SEAFOOD | Chinese/Seafood   4.0   3.1   3.4 $$

Chinatown | 22 Mott St. (bet. Chatham Sq. & Mosco St.) | 212-602-9988
Elmhurst | 8302 Queens Blvd. (Goldsmith St.) | Queens | 718-396-1238

With "first-rate" seafood backed by "varied", "flavorful" dim sum, these Cantonese contenders stay "ping on target"; despite "simple" settings and "not-that-welcoming" service, they "pack 'em in", especially for that "madhouse" Sunday brunch.

PIO PIO | Chicken/Peruvian   4.3   3.3   3.7 $$

East 90s | 1746 First Ave. (bet. 90th & 91st Sts.) | 212-426-5800
Murray Hill | 210 E. 34th St. (bet. 2nd & 3rd Aves.) | 212-481-0034
West 40s | 604 10th Ave. (bet. 43rd & 44th Sts.) | 212-459-2929
West 90s | 702 Amsterdam Ave. (94th St.) | 212-665-3000
Mott Haven | 264 Cypress Ave. (bet. 138th & 139th Sts.) | Bronx | 718-401-3300
Gravesend | 282 Kings Hwy. (7th St.) | Brooklyn | 718-627-3744
Jackson Heights | 84-02 Northern Blvd. (bet. 84th & 85th Sts.) | Queens | 718-426-4900
Jackson Heights | 84-21 Northern Blvd. (85th St.) | Queens | 718-426-1010
Middle Village | 62-30 Woodhaven Blvd. (bet. Dry Harbor Rd. & 62nd Dr.) | Queens | 718-458-0606
www.piopio.com

"Succulent" rotisserie chicken slathered with an "excellent" green sauce makes these "quick-and-easy" Peruvians "popular" "go-tos", particularly given the "modest price"; the "bustling" setups are "not terribly comfy" and the acoustics "abysmal", but hey, "you won't leave hungry."

PIORA | American   4.6   4.5   4.5 $$$

West Village | 430 Hudson St. (bet. Morton St. & St. Lukes Pl.)
212-960-3801 | www.pioranyc.com

A "lovely" "find" that "buzzes with good energy", this "inventive" New American "sleeper" in the West Village showcases Korean and Italian influences in its "perfection-on-a-plate" menu; "attentive " service and a "romantic" setting help distract from the "expensive" prices.

PIPPALI | Indian   ▽ 4.4   3.6   4.1 $$

Murray Hill | 129 E. 27th St. (Lexington Ave.)
212-689-1999 | www.pippalinyc.com

Thanks to chef Peter Beck (ex Tamarind), this Curry Hill Indian rises "a cut

above" its rivals with a "**terrific**", "**nonstandard menu**" of "**regional specialties**" spanning the subcontinent (and it will "**adjust the heat for the timid**"); "**helpful**" service distracts from decor that's the "**usual**" for the genre.

PISTICCI | Italian	4.4	3.9	4.0	$$

Morningside Heights | 125 La Salle St. (B'way)
212-932-3500 | www.pisticcinyc.com

It "**doesn't get much better for local Italian**" than this "**warm, homey**" Columbia-area "**favorite**" for "**delicious**" food at "**reasonable prices**" (and free "**jazz on Sundays**"); the "**no-reservations**" rule can be "**a drag**", yet the "**long lines**" deter few.

PIZZA MOTO | Pizza	▽ 4.6	4.0	4.2	$$

Red Hook | 338 Hamilton Ave. (bet. Centre & Mill Sts.) | Brooklyn
718-834-6686 | www.pizzamoto.com

A mobile outfit plants brick-and-mortar roots at this Red Hook pizzeria near the BQE, a former bakery where "**delicious**" wood-fired pies in "**original versions**" emerge from a restored 19th-century oven; rustic accents and "**earnest**" service warm the space, as do custom cocktails from the bar.

PIZZARTE | Pizza	4.2	3.8	4.1	$$

West 50s | 69 W. 55th St. (bet. 5th & 6th Aves.)
212-247-3936 | www.pizzarteny.com

"**True**" Neapolitan pizzas and "**well-curated**" artwork, all for sale, make an "**intriguing**" combo at this Midtown Italian, also vending pastas and more; its "**modern**", "**bowling-lane-thin**" duplex digs can feel "**cramped**", but the location's hard to beat "**before Carnegie Hall**" or City Center.

NEW **PIZZERIA SIRENETTA** | Pizza	4.3	3.9	4.2	$$

West 80s | 568 Amsterdam Ave. (bet. 87th & 88th Sts.)
212-799-7401 | www.pizzeriasirenetta.com

An instant UWS "**staple**", this Mermaid Inn sibling fires up "**killer**" Neapolitan pizzas alongside "**creative**" pastas and "**simple yet delicious**" small plates; though it "**can be noisy**", the "**crisp**" white-brick space is sufficiently "**charming**" for a "**casual**" meal.

PIZZETTERIA BRUNETTI | Pizza	4.4	3.7	4.1	$

West Village | 626 Hudson St. (bet. Horatio & Jane Sts.)
212-255-5699 | www.pizzetteriabrunetti.com

The brick-oven pizzas "**rock**" at this West Village import from Westhampton Beach, where the "**distinctive**" Neapolitan pies include a signature clam version; "**warm, witty**" staffers keep the mood at the "**casual**", patio-equipped setting "**totally relaxed.**"

P.J. CLARKE'S | Pub Food	3.8	3.6	3.8	$$$

East 50s | 915 Third Ave. (55th St.) | 212-317-1616

P.J. CLARKE'S AT LINCOLN SQUARE | Pub Food
West 60s | 44 W. 63rd St. (Columbus Ave.) | 212-957-9700

P.J. CLARKE'S ON THE HUDSON | Pub Food
Battery Park City | 4 World Financial Ctr. (Vesey St.) | 212-285-1500

SIDECAR AT P.J. CLARKE'S | Pub Food
East 50s | 915 Third Ave. (55th St.) | 212-317-2044
www.pjclarkes.com

An "**NY institution**", these "**bustling**" taverns "**continue to satisfy**" with their "**juicy**" burgers, "**jovial**" atmosphere and "**big bar scenes**"; "**you can feel the history**" at the circa-1884 East Midtown original, while Lincoln Center is a "**staple**" for showgoers and Battery Park City offers "**outdoor seating by the Hudson.**"

NEW **PLANT LOVE HOUSE** | Thai — — — $$

Prospect Heights | 622 Washington Ave. (bet. Dean & Pacific Sts.) | Brooklyn
718-622-0026

Spun off from an Elmhurst sensation, this family-run Prospect Heights Thai offers noodles, soups and other spicy favorites, while taking more of a home-cooking approach to the menu. The petite space doubles in size on warm days when the patio opens up.

PLAZA FOOD HALL | Food Hall 4.1 3.8 3.7 $$$

West 50s | Plaza Hotel | 1 W. 59th St., lower level (5th Ave.)
212-986-9260 | www.theplazany.com

"**Tour the world in one meal**" at this "**gourmet**" food hall below The Plaza Hotel, offering a "**dizzying**" array of "**fancy foods**" from Todd English and vendors like Luke's Lobster and Épicerie Boulud; when "**madness**" prevails, or bar seating seems "**uncomfortable**", there's always the "**takeout**" route.

PÓ | Italian 4.5 3.7 4.2 $$$

West Village | 31 Cornelia St. (bet. Bleecker & W. 4th Sts.)
212-645-2189 | www.porestaurant.com

"**Delicious**", "**well-priced**" Italian classics delivered by "**personable**" staffers in "**teeny-tiny**" digs is the deal at this "**longtime**" West Village "**gem**"; fans declare it's well "**worth the lack of elbow room**" for such a "**lovely meal**" – especially if you "**go early**" or for lunch, when it's "**quieter.**"

POKE | Japanese 4.5 3.7 4.1 $$

East 80s | 343 E. 85th St. (bet. 1st & 2nd Aves.)
212-249-0569 | www.pokesushinyc.com

"**Tucked away**" on a UES side street, this cash-only Japanese BYO has earned a following for its "**high-quality**" sushi offered in "**conventional and innovative**" preparations; no reservations mean "**long waits**" and the setting is "**basic**", but still the "**positives far outweigh the negatives.**"

POK POK NY | Thai 4.4 3.6 3.8 $$

Columbia Street Waterfront District | 117 Columbia St. (Kane St.) | Brooklyn
718-923-9322 | www.pokpokny.com

"**Every bite is a revelation**" at Andy Ricker's Thai "**tour de force**" on the Columbia Street Waterfront, where the "**delectable**" regional dishes are "**different from the ordinary**" and "**totally reasonable**" costwise; since it's both "**tiny**" and very "**popular**", it still can be "**difficult to get in.**"

POK POK PHAT THAI | Thai 4.3 3.5 3.8 $

Columbia Street Waterfront District | 127 Columbia St. (bet. Degraw & Kane Sts.) | Brooklyn
718-923-9322 | www.pokpokny.com

A "**truer**"-than-usual "**rendition of pad Thai**" is the highlight of Andy Ricker's Columbia Street Waterfront offshoot of Pok Pok NY, which fields a "**small but mighty**" menu of "**vibrant**", noodle-centric dishes; a simple setup with garden seating, it's "**more laid-back**" and "**less crowded**" than the down-the-block sib.

POLO BAR | American

East 50s | 1 E. 55th St. (5th Ave.)
212-207-8562 | www.ralphlauren.com

FOOD	DECOR	SERVICE	COST
4.1	4.6	4.3	$$$

"**Ralph Lauren–ness**" runs high at the designer's subterranean Midtown lair, where a "**well-groomed**" crowd "**relishes**" the "**posh hunting lodge**" decor and "**dazzling people-watching**", not to mention "**solid**" American "**country-club**" fare ferried by "**Polo model**" staffers; reservations are an "**ordeal**" and tabs "**mortgage payment**"–size, but "**yes, darling**", it's "**worth it.**"

POMODORO ROSSO | Italian

West 70s | 229 Columbus Ave. (bet. 70th & 71st Sts.)
212-721-3009 | www.pomodororossonyc.com

4.2   3.6   4.2 $$

It's like "**mama's in the kitchen**" cooking up "**hearty**" Italian classics at this "**quaint**" UWS vet near Lincoln Center, a "**quintessential neighborhood gem**" run with "**loving care**"; since it's "**always busy**", insiders make reservations to dodge the "**wait for a table.**"

NEW PONDICHERI | Indian

NoMad | 15 W. 27th St. (5th Ave.)
646-878-4375 | www.pondichericafe.com

—   —   — $$

A Houston import, this NoMad Indian draws from different regions of the subcontinent for its order-at-the-counter breakfasts and lunches and table-service dinners with wine. Soft lighting, tile floors and a marble bar give it an elegant air.

PONTY BISTRO | African/French

Gramercy Park | 218 Third Ave. (bet. 18th & 19th Sts.) | 212-777-1616
Harlem | 144 W. 139th St. (Adam Clayton Powell Junior Blvd.) | 212-234-6474
www.pontybistro.com

4.2   3.5   4.1 $$$

When you want "**something different**", these "**lovely neighborhood bistros**" deliver, sending out "**deliciously prepared**" French-Senegalese dishes featuring an "**interesting combination of flavors**"; the "**casual**" digs are "**nothing special**", but they're "**comfortable**" enough and service is "**friendly.**"

PORCHETTA | Italian/Sandwiches

East Village | 110 E. Seventh St. (bet. Ave. A & 1st Ave.)
212-777-2151 | www.porchettanyc.com

4.4   2.8   3.6 $$

Famed for its "**crave-worthy**" namesake – "**divine**" Italian-style roast pork sandwiches and platters – Sara Jenkins' "**tiny**" East Villager offers a few other options, including soup, beans and greens; the setup is "**counter service with a few stools**", so most do "**takeout.**"

PORSENA | Italian

East Village | 21 E. Seventh St. (bet. 2nd & 3rd Aves.)
212-228-4923 | www.porsena.com

4.4   3.6   4.2 $$

The "**knowing hand**" of chef-owner Sara Jenkins elevates the "**heavenly pastas**" and other "**delicious, straightforward**" Italian staples at this "**friendly**" East Villager; it works as a "**down-to-earth**" "**date spot**", albeit a "**busy**" one.

PORTER HOUSE NEW YORK | Steak

West 50s | Time Warner Ctr. | 10 Columbus Circle (bet. 58th & 60th Sts.)
212-823-9500 | www.porterhousenewyork.com

4.6   4.5   4.5 $$$

They "**know how to cook a steak**" at Michael Lomonaco's "**chic**" Time Warner Center chophouse, where the beef is "**juicy and fork-tender**" and the "**modern**" surroundings get a boost from "**spectacular**" Central Park views; "**caring**" servers take the edge off the predictably "**big checks.**"

| **POSTO** | Pizza | 4.5 | 3.5 | 4.0 | $$ |

Gramercy Park | 310 Second Ave. (18th St.)
212-716-1200 | www.postothincrust.com

The "**thinnest**", "**winningest**" crust is the hallmark of this Gramercy pizzeria, a "**local hot spot**" cranking out "**splendid**" pies at "**accessible prices**"; its "**small**", "**publike**" digs are usually "**packed and noisy**", so the to-go trade stays brisk.

| **PRESS 195** | Sandwiches | 4.3 | 3.3 | 3.7 | $$ |

Bayside | 4011 Bell Blvd. (bet. 40th & 41st Aves.) | Queens
718-281-1950 | www.press195.com

The "**hardest part is choosing**" from the "**extensive list**" of "**amazing panini**" at this "**casual**" Bayside "**favorite**", where the "**terrific**" Belgian fries are a no-brainer; with a full bar, "**fun patio**" and some of the "**best craft beers**" around, it's no wonder locals "**love this place.**"

| **PRIME GRILL** | Kosher/Steak | 4.1 | 4.0 | 3.9 | $$$$ |

East 50s | 550 Madison Ave. (bet. 55th & 56th Sts.)
212-692-9292 | www.theprimegrill.primehospitalityny.com

Still a Midtown "**place to be seen**" following its move to the Sony Building, this "**high-end**" kosher steakhouse serves up "**respectable**" fare highlighted by "**flavorfully charred**" beef and "**top-notch**" sushi; spacious, "**private club**" surrounds help justify the "**OMG**" price tag.

| **PRIME MEATS** | American/Steak | 4.3 | 4.1 | 4.0 | $$ |

Carroll Gardens | 465 Court St. (Luquer St.) | Brooklyn
718-254-0327 | www.frankspm.com

A "**meat mecca**", this Carroll Gardens "**favorite**" is a "**solid performer**" for German-accented American fare ("**slammin'**" steaks, "**don't-skip**" spaetzle, an especially "**solid**" burger) and "**thoughtfully mixed**" cocktails; since the "**traditional Brooklyn**" setting is typically "**jammed**", you'll need a reservation.

| **PRIMOLA** | Italian | 4.4 | 3.8 | 4.2 | $$$ |

East 60s | 1226 Second Ave. (bet. 64th & 65th Sts.)
212-758-1775

No stranger to "**Page Six**" mentions, this "**clubby**" Italian satisfies its "**moneyed UES**" clientele with "**dependable**" pastas at "**steep prices**"; count on service "**with a smile**" if you're a regular, a "**celebrity**" or "**wearing dark glasses**", though first-timers may find the "**attitude**" "**intimidating.**"

| **PRINT** | American | 4.5 | 4.4 | 4.4 | $$$ |

West 40s | Ink48 Hotel | 653 11th Ave. (bet. 47th & 48th Sts.)
212-757-2224 | www.printrestaurant.com

Way "**out of the way**" in West Hell's Kitchen, this "**memorable**" New American is a "**first-rate**" option for "**locavoracious**" fare and "**smart**" service in "**stylish**" environs; insiders have cocktails after dinner at the "**rooftop lounge**" with its drop-dead, 360-degree "**skyline view.**"

| **PRUNE** | American | 4.6 | 3.6 | 4.3 | $$$ |

East Village | 54 E. First St. (bet. 1st & 2nd Aves.)
212-677-6221 | www.prunerestaurant.com

An "**innovator that's stood the test of time**", chef Gabrielle Hamilton's East Village "**standout**" serves a "**perfectly curated**" menu of "**exceptional**" New

American dishes in "**unfailingly professional**" style; the only drawbacks are a "**toooo small**" room with seating "**on top of your neighbors**" and long lines for the "**fabulous brunch.**"

PUBLIC | Eclectic   4.3   4.4   4.2 $$$$

NoLita | 210 Elizabeth St. (bet. Prince & Spring Sts.)
212-343-7011 | www.public-nyc.com

A "**beautiful crowd**" still frequents this "**impressive**" AvroKO-designed NoLita "**staple**" with an "**innovative**", Australian-accented approach, delivering "**well-executed**" Eclectic fare and "**outstanding wines**" via an "**attentive**" team; given the "**good-time**" vibe, it fits the bill for "**a date or a festive group.**"

PURE THAI COOKHOUSE | Thai   4.5   3.2   3.8 $$

West 50s | 766 Ninth Ave. (bet. 51st & 52nd Sts.)
212-581-0999 | www.purethaishophouse.com

"**Taste the essence of Thailand**" at this "**hole-in-the-wall**" Hell's Kitchen Thai that "**stands out**" thanks to the "**bold flavors**" of its "**excellent noodle dishes**" and other "**cheap**" eats; the only downside is a "**shoebox**" space with "**backless stools**" that's "**always packed.**"

PURPLE YAM | Asian   4.3   3.9   4.1 $$

Ditmas Park | 1314 Cortelyou Rd. (bet. Argyle & Rugby Rds.) | Brooklyn
718-940-8188 | www.purpleyamnyc.com

"**Sophisticated**" Pan-Asian fare with an emphasis on Filipino flavors – as in the "**superb**" chicken adobo – is the "**unusual**", "**totally approachable**" specialty of this "**cozy**" Ditmas Park "**gem**"; "**inexpensive**" tabs are another reason why it's generally "**packed.**"

PYLOS | Greek   4.5   4.4   4.2 $$$

East Village | 128 E. Seventh St. (bet. Ave. A & 1st Ave.)
212-473-0220 | www.pylosrestaurant.com

"**Not your run-of-the-mill Greek**", this "**more upscale**" East Villager offers "**unbeatable**" cuisine that's "**lovingly prepared**" and "**well priced**" for the quality; with a "**wonderful**" team overseeing a "**memorable**" space boasting a ceiling lined with terra cotta pots, it's a "**real find.**"

QI | Asian/Thai   4.1   4.2   3.8 $$

West 40s | 675 Eighth Ave. (43rd St.) | 212-247-8992

QI THAI GRILL | Asian/Thai

Williamsburg | 176 N. Ninth St. (bet. Bedford & Driggs Aves.) | Brooklyn |
718-302-1499
www.qirestaurant.com

Chef Pichet Ong delivers "**well-prepared**", "**beautifully presented**" Asian-Thai dishes at these "**trendy**" contenders; "**reasonable prices**" belie their "**glittery**", "**Buddhist temple**"–meets-"**nightclub**" decor, especially at the "**over-the-top**" Theater District outlet done up in "**chandeliers and holograms.**"

NEW QUALITY EATS | Steak   4.5   4.4   4.4 $$$

West Village | 19 Greenwich Ave. (10th St.)
212-337-9988 | www.qualityeats.com

"**Definitely not your father's steakhouse**", this more "**accessible**" Quality Meats spin-off in the West Village courts a "**young crowd**" with "**lesser-known**" but "**still delicious**" cuts of meat, plus "**inventive**" starters and sides; a "**chill**" vibe and an "**amazing bar**" further the "**great buzz.**"

	FOOD	DECOR	SERVICE	COST

QUALITY ITALIAN | Italian/Steak 4.4 4.2 4.3 $$$
West 50s | 57 W. 57th St. (6th Ave.)
212-390-1111 | www.qualityitalian.com

A "**home run**" from the folks at Quality Meats, this Midtown double-decker caters to the "**expense-account**" crowd with "**memorable**" steaks and Italian fare (notably the "**epic**" chicken parm pizza) served by an "**accommodating**" team; though the decibels in the "**lofty**" space are "**not for an intimate meal**", all that "**high energy**" suggests they're "**doing something right**" here.

QUALITY MEATS | American/Steak 4.5 4.3 4.3 $$$
West 50s | 57 W. 58th St. (bet. 5th & 6th Aves.)
212-371-7777 | www.qualitymeatsnyc.com

A "**steakhouse for the modern era**", this "**energetic**" Midtowner "**proves itself**" with "**really solid**" beef plus more "**offbeat**" sides and apps served in "**hipper than average**" surroundings ("**no mahogany here**"); "**high**" prices are a given, but you do "**pay for quality.**"

QUATORZE BIS | French 4.2 3.9 4.0 $$$
East 70s | 323 E. 79th St. (bet. 1st & 2nd Aves.)
212-535-1414

"**Steady**" and "**essential**", this "**longtime**" UES French bistro remains a local "**favorite**" for its "**delicious**" "**Left Bank menu**" and "**welcoming**" atmosphere; it's "**not cheap**" and could "**use a face-lift**", but its "**prosperous clientele**" deems it a "**pleasant experience**" all the same.

QUEEN | Italian 4.3 3.6 4.3 $$$
Brooklyn Heights | 84 Court St. (bet. Livingston & Schermerhorn Sts.) | Brooklyn
718-596-5955 | www.queenrestaurant.com

A circa-1958 "**Brooklyn Heights institution**" near the courthouses, this "**old-line**" Italian continues its reign as an area "**favorite**" for "**true red sauce**" fare minus culinary gimmicks; given the "**gracious service**" and "**reasonable**" tabs, most pardon the "**dated**" decor.

QUEEN OF SHEBA | Ethiopian 4.3 3.5 3.8 $$
West 40s | 650 10th Ave. (bet. 45th & 46th Sts.)
212-397-0610 | www.shebanyc.com

"**Hidden**" in Hell's Kitchen, this "**real-thing**" Ethiopian offers "**flavorful**" fare – "**numerous**" veggie dishes included – that's eaten with your hands and "**delicious injera**" bread; factor in "**affordable**" tabs and it's easy to overlook the "**small**" quarters and "**slow**" pacing.

QUEENS COMFORT | Southern 4.2 3.7 3.9 $$
Astoria | 40-09 30th Ave. (bet. Steinway & 41st Sts.) | Queens
718-728-2350 | www.queenscomfort.com

"**Get your comfort on**" at this Astoria joint dishing up Southern "**pig-out**" fare in "**simple**" digs with a "**wacky**", "**chill**" vibe; it's "**cash only but cheap and BYO**" – no wonder there are "**lines on weekends**", especially for the "**fun**" brunch with a live DJ.

QUEENS KICKSHAW | Coffee/Sandwiches 4.0 3.7 3.8 $$
Astoria | 40-17 Broadway (bet. 41st & Steinway Sts.) | Queens
718-777-0913 | www.thequeenskickshaw.com

"**Divine grilled cheese**" taken "**to the next level**" and other "**creative**", fromage-focused eats are the specialty of this all-day, "**all-vegetarian**" Astoria "**gem**"; its "**serious**" coffee drinks and craft beers are a "**huge plus**", as are the "**reasonable prices**", late-night hours and "**hip**", "**touch-of-Brooklyn**" vibe.

RACINES | French   4.3   3.8   4.2 $$

TriBeCa | 94 Chambers St. (bet. B'way & Church St.)
646-644-6255 | www.racinesny.com

Linked to a Parisian wine-bar outfit, this "**fine and funky**" TriBeCan offers a "**limited**" but "**well-executed**" lineup of French market fare accompanied by a "**wine geek**"–worthy vino list, featuring many "**obscure**" and biodynamic bottles; "**down-to-earth**" service and a "**mellow**" ambiance are other pluses.

RADIANCE TEA HOUSE | Teahouse   4.1   4.1   3.9 $$

East 40s | 208 E. 50th St. (3rd Ave.) | 212-888-8060
West 50s | 158 W. 55th St. (bet. 6th & 7th Aves.) | 212-217-0442
www.radiancetea.com

Radiating "**calm**" amid the "**Midtown madness**", these "**delightful**" teahouses match a "**huge**" selection of "**exotic**" brews with an affordable menu of "**light**", Chinese-accented bites; the "**very Zen**" surroundings lend "**spiritual quietude.**"

RAFELE | Italian   4.5   4.1   4.3 $$

West Village | 29 Seventh Ave. S. (Bedford St.)
212-242-1999 | www.rafele.com

"**Walk through the door and you're in Rome**" agree fans of this "**rustic**" Italian West Villager serving "*molte bene*" pastas and wood-oven pizzas made with "**super-fresh**" ingredients; sidewalk seating and service that remains solid even when it's "**crazy busy**" cement its status as a neighborhood "**gem.**"

RAINBOW ROOM | American   4.3   4.7   4.4 $$$$

West 40s | Rockefeller Ctr. | 30 Rockefeller Plaza, 65th fl. (bet. 5th & 6th Aves.)
212-632-5000 | www.rainbowroom.com

"**The glamour of yesteryear**" lives on at this "**iconic**" Rock Center supper club famed for its "**incredible art deco room**" and "**stunning**" 65th-floor views; now mostly hosting private events, it opens to the public for "**opulent**" Sunday brunch and dinner on select evenings ("**rob a bank**" first) – or you can take in the "**astonishing**" vista from the weeknights-only bar, SixtyFive.

RALPH'S FAMOUS ITALIAN ICES | Ice Cream   4.4   2.9   3.8 $

Bayside | 214-13 41st Ave. (Bell Blvd.) | Queens | 718-428-4578
Glen Oaks | 264-21 Union Tpke. (265th St.) | Queens | 718-343-8724
Middle Village | 73-01 Metropolitan Ave. (73rd Pl.) | Queens | no phone
Whitestone | 12-48 Clintonville St. (12th Rd.) | Queens | 718-746-1456
Arden Heights | 3285 Richmond Ave. (Gurley Ave.) | Staten Island |
718-967-1212
Elm Park | 501 Port Richmond Ave. (Catherine St.) | Staten Island |
718-273-3675
New Dorp | 2361 Hylan Blvd. (Otis Ave.) | Staten Island | 718-351-8133
Prince's Bay | 6272 Amboy Rd. (Bloomingdale Rd.) | Staten Island |
718-605-8133
Prince's Bay | 890 Huguenot Ave. (bet. Amboy & Drumgoole Rds.) |
Staten Island | 718-356-8133
www.ralphsices.com

There's "**nothing better on a hot summer day**" than the "**ah-mazing**" Italian ices in a "**dizzying**" array of flavors served at this "**beloved**" SI-based chain; you've gotta "**stand in line**" at the circa-1949 Elm Park original, but it "**goes quickly**" – fans only wish this "**NY highlight**" were "**open all year.**"

		FOOD	DECOR	SERVICE	COST

RAMEN LAB | Japanese/Noodle Shop ▽ 4.3 3.5 4.2 $$

NoLita | 70 Kenmare St. (Mulberry St.)
646-613-7522 | www.ramen-lab.com

Backed by artisan noodle maker Sun Noodle, this "**tiny**", "**Tokyo-style**"
NoLita nook features a 10-seat counter where visiting "**ramen artists**"
dispense a "**limited**" but "**super-authentic**" choice of "**robust**", "**affordable**"
bowls; the pop-up format makes each trip "**a different experience**", but fans
"**love the concept.**"

RANDAZZO'S | Seafood 4.2 3.1 3.7 $$

Sheepshead Bay | 2017 Emmons Ave. (21st St.) | Brooklyn
718-615-0010 | www.randazzosclambar.com

A "**real Brooklyn joint**" – "**packed**" and "**boisterous**" with lotsa "**local color**" –
this "**iconic**" Sheepshead Bay clam bar is beloved for its "**simple**", "**fresh**"
seafood plus "**red-sauce**" classics in "**ginormous portions**"; the "**dinerlike**"
interior is strictly "**no-frills**", but "**sitting outside as the boats come in**" is
hard to beat.

RAO'S | Italian 4.3 3.7 4.2 $$$$

East Harlem | 455 E. 114th St. (Pleasant Ave.)
212-722-6709 | www.raos.com

It practically "**takes an act of Congress**" to score a "**coveted table**", but if
you "**get lucky**", Frank Pellegrino's East Harlem Italian lives up to the
"**mystique**" with its "**terrific**" cooking and "**central-casting**" crowd; ordinary
folks who don't "**know someone**" can try the "**one in Las Vegas**" or just "**buy
the sauce in jars.**"

RAOUL'S | French 4.5 4.0 4.2 $$$

SoHo | 180 Prince St. (bet. Sullivan & Thompson Sts.)
212-966-3518 | www.raouls.com

"**One of the last outposts of bohemian SoHo**", this circa-1975 bistro remains
"**jam-packed**" with "**seen-it-all**" locals and other lovers of "**just perfect**"
"**old-style French**" fare served by "**pros**" in "**cozy, dim**" digs; yes, it's "**cramped**"
and "**not quiet**", but that's all part of the "**charm**" – it's a NY "**institution**" that
"**should be landmarked.**"

RARE BAR & GRILL | Burgers 4.1 3.7 3.8 $$

Chelsea | Fashion 26 Hotel | 152 W. 26th St. (bet. 6th & 7th Aves.) |
212-807-7273
Murray Hill | Affinia Shelburne Hotel | 303 Lexington Ave. (37th St.) |
212-481-1999
www.rarebarandgrill.com

A "**great variety of burgers**" and "**addicting**" fries make these "**relaxed**" hotel
eateries "**standbys**" for a casual meal; they can get "**noisy**" at prime times, but
the rooftop bars are "**excellent.**"

RAVAGH | Persian 4.3 3.4 3.9 $$

East 60s | 1237 First Ave. (bet. 66th & 67th Sts.) | 212-861-7900
East Village | 125 First Ave. (St. Marks Pl.) | 212-335-0207
www.ravaghpersiangrill.com

Among "**NYC's few**" options for classic Persian cooking, these Eastsiders dish
up "**flavorful**", "**stick-to-your-ribs**" fare including "**succulent kebabs**" and
"**delicious**" rice dishes; "**generous**" portions and "**value**" prices offset the
"**lacking decor.**"

	FOOD	DECOR	SERVICE	COST

RAYMI | Peruvian   4.3   4.1   4.1 $$$

Flatiron | 43 W. 24th St. (bet. 5th & 6th Aves.)
212-929-1200 | www.rayminyc.com

This Flatiron Peruvian "**gem**" features "**tasty, innovative**" dishes including "**outstanding**" ceviche, best accompanied by the bar's "**fantastic pisco cocktails**"; a "**big, buzzy, beautiful**" space and "**warm service**" help justify the "**pricey**" tabs; P.S. at lunch, the front area morphs into fast-casual joint Latin Beet Kitchen.

REAL MADRID | Spanish   4.2   3.6   4.2 $$

Mariners Harbor | 2703 Forest Ave. (Union Ave.) | Staten Island
718-447-7885

"**Always reliable**", this "**friendly**" longtimer in Staten Island's Mariners Harbor offers an "**extensive**" menu of "**real-thing**" Spanish standards served in "**very generous**" portions; it's easy to overlook "**dated**" decor since you get "**so much for your money.**"

REBELLE | French   4.3   3.9   4.2 $$$

NoLita | 218 Bowery (Rivington St.)
917-639-3880 | www.rebellenyc.com

An "**industry-leading**" wine list is a big draw at this "**cool**" Bowery follow-up to Pearl & Ash, though its "**inventive**" and "**refined**" French cooking also makes it a "**multiple-repeat candidate**"; the "**sleek**" space has an "**unpretentious vibe**", though the tabs trend "**expensive.**"

RED CAT | American/Mediterranean   4.3   3.9   4.2 $$$

Chelsea | 227 10th Ave. (bet. 23rd & 24th Sts.)
212-242-1122 | www.theredcat.com

"**Art gallery types**" and "**locals**" remain "**devoted**" to this Chelsea "**classic**" that's "**ideally located**" near the High Line and a "**go-to**" for "**consistently creative**" (if "**pricey**") Med-American fare and "**thoughtful**" service; a few say the "**cozy**" space has "**lost some of its sparkle**", but the atmosphere remains "**vibrant**" all the same.

NEW **RED COMPASS** | Georgian   ▽ 4.4   4.1   3.9 $$

Lower East Side | 154 Orchard St. (bet. Rivington & Stanton Sts.)
212-473-9100

A "**delicious**" introduction to "**traditional Georgian cuisine**" awaits at this LES hangout where the specialties like "**unique**" cheese bread are meant for sharing "**with friends**"; "**leisurely**" service and frequent live music encourages lingering in the "**warm, inviting**" digs.

REDEYE GRILL | American/Seafood   4.0   4.0   4.0 $$$

West 50s | 890 Seventh Ave. (56th St.)
212-541-9000 | www.redeyegrill.com

In a "**handy**" locale opposite Carnegie Hall, Shelly Fireman's "**upscale**" Midtown "**staple**" puts forth a "**dependable**" American menu featuring "**tons of seafood**", plus sushi and other "**Japanese-inspired**" dishes; "**prompt**" service and a "**dramatic**" setting with live music keep it "**bustling.**"

REDFARM | Chinese   4.4   3.7   4.0 $$$

West 70s | 2170 Broadway (bet. 76th & 77th Sts.) | 212-724-9700
West Village | 529 Hudson St. (bet. Charles & W. 10th Sts.) | 212-792-9700
www.redfarmnyc.com

"**Intense**" flavors and "**innovative**" preparations make for "**unbelievably good**"

Chinese plates and "**contemporary**" dim sum (a "**strong suit**") at these "**lively**" hangs from Ed Schoenfeld and Joe Ng; "**long waits**" (no reservations) and "**elbow-to-elbow**" seating are the downsides, but "**incredible**" cocktails help ensure "**everyone leaves happy.**"

| **THE REDHEAD** | Southern | 4.1 | 3.5 | 4.0 | $$ |

East Village | 349 E. 13th St. (bet. 1st & 2nd Aves.)
212-533-6212 | www.theredheadnyc.com

The mood is "**chill**" at this East Village bar/eatery slinging Southern-leaning comfort faves like "**killer fried chicken**" and "**fun drinks**" at "**relatively inexpensive**" rates; sure, it's a "**cramped**" "**hole-in-the-wall**", but "**courteous**" service is another reason it's "**worth the wait.**"

| **RED HOOK LOBSTER POUND** | Seafood | 4.3 | 3.3 | 3.8 | $$ |

East Village | 16 Extra Pl. (off 1st St., bet. Bowery & 2nd Ave.) | 212-777-7225
Red Hook | 284 Van Brunt St. (bet. Pioneer & Verona Sts.) | Brooklyn |
718-858-7650
www.redhooklobster.com

"**If you're jonesing for a lobster roll**", these "**cool**" seafood shacks fit the bill with "**really tasty**" varieties, including a warm and "**buttery**" Connecticut-style; the digs are simple, but the Red Hook original adds table service and "**delicious**" whole lobster dinners to the mix.

| **RED ROOSTER** | American | 4.2 | 4.1 | 4.1 | $$$ |

Harlem | 310 Lenox Ave. (bet. 125th & 126th Sts.)
212-792-9001 | www.redroosterharlem.com

"**A scene to say the least**", Marcus Samuelsson's "**electric**" Harlem joint provides "**delicious**" Southern-accented American fare and "**wow**" cocktails with a side of "**superb**" people-watching; maybe it's "**expensive for the neighborhood**", but nonetheless it's typically "**packed**"; P.S. there's often live music downstairs at Ginny's Supper Club.

| **REGENCY BAR & GRILL** | American | 4.0 | 4.2 | 4.2 | $$$ |

East 60s | Regency Hotel | 540 Park Ave. (61st St.)
212-339-4050 | www.regencybarandgrill.com

"**The power breakfast is no longer the only thing to write home about**" at this UES bastion in the Loews Regency Hotel, which also has a "**chic**", "**lively**" bar scene; "**fairly basic**" New American fare comes at "**first-rate**" prices, but it's still an "**elegant**" refuge for those seeking either "**to be seen or to hide.**"

| **REMI** | Italian | 4.2 | 4.2 | 4.1 | $$$ |

West 50s | 145 W. 53rd St. (bet. 6th & 7th Aves.)
212-581-4242 | www.remi-nyc.com

"**Reliable**" "**all-around quality**" marks this "**upscale**" Midtown Italian "**standby**", where "**delicious**" Venetian specialties are "**served with panache**" to "**pre-theater**" and "**business**" types; the "**serene**" space with its "**impressive**" Grand Canal mural is "**pretty**" enough to help you forget the "**expense account**"–ready prices.

| **REPUBLIC** | Asian | 3.8 | 3.4 | 3.6 | $$ |

Union Square | 37 Union Sq. W. (bet. 16th & 17th Sts.)
212-627-7172 | www.republicrestaurantnyc.com

Long a "**Union Square standby**", this Asian "**mess hall**" still "**does the trick**" with "**filling**" bowls of noodles and more at "**bargain-basement prices**"; the "**communal-style**" setup is "**awkward**" and "**noisy as all get-out**", but its "**young**" followers eat and exit "**in a flash.**"

		FOOD	DECOR	SERVICE	COST

RESERVE CUT | Kosher/Steak   4.3   4.5   4.1 $$$$

Financial District | The Setai Club & Spa Wall St. | 40 Broad St. (Exchange Pl.)
212-747-0300 | www.reservecut.com

"Who knew that kosher could taste, look and feel glamorous?" marvel fans of this "beautiful" Financial District steakhouse's "excellent" beef, sushi and French-influenced dishes; prices may induce "sticker shock", but the "knowledgeable" staff makes sure you're "happy."

REYNARD | American   ∇ 4.4   4.4   4.2 $$$

Williamsburg | Wythe Hotel | 80 Wythe Ave. (11th St.) | Brooklyn
718-460-8004 | www.reynardsnyc.com

This "vibrant" Williamsburg New American from Andrew Tarlow (Diner, Marlow & Sons) is a "hip" scene that's also "deeply serious" about its "creative" seasonal food and drink; factor in a "fabulous" setting in the converted-1901-factory Wythe Hotel, and it's an all-around "wow."

RIBALTA | Italian   4.5   3.8   4.1 $$

Greenwich Village | 48 E. 12th St. (B'way)
212-777-7781 | www.ribaltapizzarestaurant.com

A "true Italian experience", this "under-the-radar" Villager is "totally committed" to producing "authentic Neapolitan" pizza and other "high-quality" specialties from the Napoli region; run by a "helpful" crew, the "modern", high-ceilinged space is at its most "vibrant" during "giant-screen soccer-watching."

THE RIBBON | American   4.0   3.8   3.8 $$$

West 70s | 20 W. 72nd St. (bet. Columbus Ave. & CPW)
646-416-9080 | www.theribbonnyc.com

"Locals, Central Park visitors and yuppie-hip well-to-dos" mix at this UWS New American from the Blue Ribbon team where "on-point fried chicken", prime rib and other comfort fare is offered alongside "knock-out" cocktails; an "energetic bar scene" means it gets "loud", but at least it "saves a trip Downtown."

RICARDO STEAK HOUSE | Steak   ∇ 4.4   3.8   3.9 $$

East Harlem | 2145 Second Ave. (bet. 110th & 111th Sts.)
212-289-5895 | www.ricardosteakhouse.com

East Harlem has a "real gem" in this "well-done" steakhouse where "simply delicious" chops are served with "flair" to a crowd with "energy" to spare; the art-lined space includes a patio and "value" pricing boosts its appeal.

RICE TO RICHES | Dessert   4.4   3.8   3.8 $

NoLita | 37 Spring St. (bet. Mott & Mulberry Sts.)
212-274-0008 | www.ricetoriches.com

Get ready to enjoy the "riches of rice pudding" at this NoLita dessert shop that puts a "great twist on a throwback", offering "every kind" of "decadent" flavor combination imaginable ("and then some"); the "original" digs have a space-agey feel, which adds to the "fun."

RIDER | American   —   —   — $$$

Williamsburg | 80 N. 6th St. (Wythe Ave.) | Brooklyn
718-210-3152 | www.riderbklyn.com

At Williamsburg's National Sawdust music venue, this American bistro is big on boldly flavored eclectic small plates well matched with specialty cocktails.

The first floor has a light look with whitewashed brick and a bar, while upstairs is more dramatic with a tall banquette wrapping around the room.

RISOTTERIA MELOTTI | Italian   ▽ 4.4   3.6   4.0 $$

East Village | 309 E. Fifth St. (bet. 1st & 2nd Aves.)
646-755-8939 | www.risotteriamelottinyc.com

"**Heavenly risotto**" via the owner's Verona rice fields is served in an "**impressive**" variety at this East Village Italian, a "**find**" for gluten-free diners; "**well-taken-care-of**" regulars agree that the "**authentic**" cooking at a "**good price**" compensates for the "**tight quarters.**"

RISTORANTE MORINI | Italian   4.4   4.3   4.3 $$$$

East 80s | 1167 Madison Ave. (bet. 85th & 86th Sts.)
212-249-0444 | www.ristorantemorini.com

An "**oasis on Madison Avenue**", this "**civilized**" UES duplex from chef Michael White delivers "**beautifully prepared**" seasonal Italian fare headlined by "**superb**" handmade pastas; service is appropriately "**white-glove**", while happy hour at the downstairs bar offers an alternative to the otherwise "**special-occasion**" prices.

RIVER CAFÉ | American   4.6   4.8   4.6 $$$$

Dumbo | 1 Water St. (bet. Furman & Old Fulton Sts.) | Brooklyn
718-522-5200 | www.rivercafe.com

"**Is there a more beautiful setting in NYC?**" swoon fans of this Dumbo waterfront "**classic**" whose "**romantic**" dining room offers "**unbeatable**" views of Manhattan, as well as a fairy-lit "**Garden of Eden**" just outside; "**elegant**" prix fixe–only American cuisine and "**exceptional**" service complete the "**high-end**" experience – for which an "**expensive**" price tag is "**to be expected.**"

RIVERPARK | American   4.5   4.7   4.5 $$$

Murray Hill | 450 E. 29th St. (1st Ave.)
212-729-9790 | www.riverparknyc.com

"**Out of the way and hard to find**", this "**serene**" hideaway in a Murray Hill office park offers Tom Colicchio's "**sophisticated**" New American food showcasing "**divine**" seasonal dishes sourced from its own herb garden; the "**special-occasion**" pricing is offset by "**inexpensive parking**" and a "**spectacular**" East River view.

ROBERT | American   4.1   4.6   4.2 $$$

West 50s | Museum of Art & Design | 2 Columbus Circle (bet. B'way & 8th Ave.)
212-299-7730 | www.robertnyc.com

It's all about the "**wondrous**" Central Park views at this museum "**aerie**" high above Columbus Circle, though its "**pricey**" American fare is "**fine**" too – and frequent live jazz further boosts the "**special**" mood; fans say the experience is just as "**striking**" over cocktails in the lounge, but either way, a window table is "**key.**"

ROBERTA'S | Italian/Pizza   4.6   3.8   3.9 $$

Bushwick | 261 Moore St. (Bogart St.) | Brooklyn
718-417-1118 | www.robertaspizza.com

"**Legendary**" by now, this this "**hipster-chic**" Bushwick destination is a "**real standout**" thanks to "**expertly crafted**" pizzas (try the "**out-of-this-world**" bee sting) and "**equally amazing**" Italian dishes, enhanced by homegrown produce; perpetual "**crowds**" make for "**massive**" waits, but once you're in it's "**loads of fun.**"

	FOOD	DECOR	SERVICE	COST

ROBERTO'S | Italian 4.5 3.9 4.2 $$$
Arthur Avenue/Belmont | 603 Crescent Ave. (Hughes Ave.) | Bronx
718-733-9503 | www.robertos.roberto089.com

Fans "**love**" this "**real-deal**" Bronx Italian where Roberto Paciullo turns out "**superb**" housemade pastas and other "**expertly prepared**" dishes in "**quaint**", "**convivial**" surrounds; "**pricey**" tabs detract, but factor in "**charming service**" and most agree it's "**worth the splurge.**"

ROC | Italian 4.1 3.7 4.0 $$$
TriBeCa | 190 Duane St. (Greenwich St.)
212-625-3333 | www.rocrestaurant.com

"**Year after year**", this "**warm**" TriBeCa "**standby**" remains roc-"**solid**" for "**fancy**" Italian classics courtesy of "**delightful owners**" who "**make you feel at home**"; a "**comfortable**" atmosphere with "**fantastic**" outdoor seating distracts from prices that slant "**expensive.**"

ROCCO STEAKHOUSE | Steak ∇ 4.3 4.1 4.5 $$$
NoMad | 72 Madison Ave. (bet. 27th & 28th Sts.)
212-696-9660 | www.roccosteakhouse.com

The "**experienced**" staff treats you "**like family**" at this NoMad chophouse serving "**high-quality**" beef from a "**traditional**" menu that fits the "**beautiful**", mahogany setting; "**expensive**" tabs are a given, but it's still a "**nice addition**" to the neighborhood.

ROCKING HORSE CAFE | Mexican 4.2 3.6 3.9 $$
Chelsea | 182 Eighth Ave. (bet. 19th & 20th Sts.)
212-463-9511 | www.rockinghorsecafe.com

"**Handy**" in the neighborhood, this "**buoyant**" Chelsea veteran "**rocks on**" with "**creative**" Mexican eats and "**fab**" margaritas at "**value**" rates (especially the "**best-kept-secret**" $18 brunch); the "**lively scene**" can get "**noisy**", but in summer there's "**terrific**" sidewalk seating.

ROLF'S | German 3.5 4.3 3.6 $$$
Gramercy Park | 281 Third Ave. (22nd St.)
212-473-8718 | www.rolfsnyc.com

Best experienced "**around the holidays**", this circa-1968 Gramercy German "**time warp**" is a "**sight to see**" when the "**lavish**" Christmas decorations go up ("**bring your sunglasses**"); too bad the "**run-of-the-mill**" food makes a case for just a "**drink at the bar.**"

ROLL-N-ROASTER | Sandwiches 4.0 3.1 3.4 $
Sheepshead Bay | 2901 Emmons Ave. (bet. Nostrand Ave. & 29th St.) | Brooklyn
718-769-6000 | www.rollnroaster.com

"**Retro fast-food**" fans roll into this "**busy**" Sheepshead Bay "**institution**" to chow down on "**bangin'**" roast beef sandwiches and "**must-have**" cheese fries served into the wee hours; the aging digs are pretty "**beat up**", but "**there's a reason why they've been in business**" since 1970.

ROMAN'S | Italian ∇ 4.4 3.9 4.1 $$
Fort Greene | 243 Dekalb Ave. (bet. Clermont & Vanderbilt Aves.) | Brooklyn
718-622-5300 | www.romansnyc.com

Its seasonally attuned Italian menu "**changes every day, but the quality doesn't**" at this "**hip**", snug (and now tip-free) Fort Greene sibling of Marlow &

Sons that's a "**memorable**" blend of culinary "**passion**" and "**neighborhoody**" vibes; no reservations means waits are "**standard**", providing time to size up the bar's "**talented mixologists.**"

ROOM SERVICE | Thai   4.3   4.3   4.0 $$

West 40s | 690 Ninth Ave. (bet. 47th & 48th Sts.)
212-582-0999 | www.roomservicerestaurant.com

Decked out with mirrors and chandeliers, this "**eye-popping**" Theater District Thai is a "**cool**" destination for "**spot-on**" cooking at a "**fair price**"; an "**upbeat**" vibe and "**fun-loving**" crowd is all part of the "**like-a-nightclub**" atmosphere.

ROOT & BONE | Southern   4.4   3.9   4.1 $$

East Village | 200 E. Third St. (bet. Aves. A & B)
646-682-7076 | www.rootnbone.com

Fans "**can't get enough**" of this "**cute**" East Villager's "**incredible fried chicken**" and other "**OMG**"-"**delicious**" Southern comfort classics; "**excellent**" cocktails help fuel the "**fun**", "**cool**" scene, though the "**tiny**", "**tight**" space fills up fast, especially at brunch ("**a must**").

ROSA MEXICANO | Mexican   4.1   4.0   4.0 $$$

East 50s | 1063 First Ave. (58th St.) | 212-753-7407
Flatiron | 9 E. 18th St. (bet. B'way & 5th Ave.) | 212-533-3350
TriBeCa | 41 Murray St. (Church St.) | 212-849-2885
West 60s | 61 Columbus Ave. (62nd St.) | 212-977-7700
www.rosamexicano.com

You "**can't beat**" the "**famous tableside guacamole**" and "**potent**" pomegranate margaritas at this "**upbeat**" chain, a "**tried-and-true**" source for "**sophisticated**" Mexican cuisine; tabs run a "**bit high**", but the "**festive**" atmosphere makes for a "**fun scene**" that's "**especially good**" for groups.

ROSEMARY'S | Italian   4.3   4.2   4.1 $$

West Village | 18 Greenwich Ave. (10th St.)
212-647-1818 | www.rosemarysnyc.com

"**Delicious yet light**" Italian dishes are sourced "**straight from the rooftop garden**" at this "**energetic**", all-day West Village trattoria with a "**sunny**", "**rustic**" dining room; a no-reservations policy (for fewer than eight) makes it "**difficult to get a table**" and the big "**bar scene**" pumps out "**loud**" decibels, so insiders say it's best "**mid-afternoon.**"

ROSE'S | American   ▽   4.2   3.4   3.9 $$

Prospect Heights | 295 Flatbush Ave. (Prospect Pl.) | Brooklyn
718-230-0427 | www.rosesbklyn.com

"**Just what you want**" in a local hang, this Prospect Heights bar from the Franny's team offers a crowd-pleasing American menu including one "**excellent**" burger plus creative cocktails. The sports TV–equipped interior features repurposed high-school auditorium seats and a back garden.

ROSE WATER | American   4.6   4.0   4.4 $$$

Park Slope | 787 Union St. (bet. 5th & 6th Aves.) | Brooklyn
718-783-3800 | www.rosewaterrestaurant.com

An enduring Park Slope "**favorite**", this "**charming**" New American offers a "**beautiful representation of the seasons**" via "**excellent**" locavore fare, including a "**delicious**" brunch; the "**tight**" environs are "**worth squeezing into**", and there's a "**gorgeous**" patio in the summertime.

ROSIE'S | Mexican · · · · · · · · · · · · · · · · 4.0 · 4.0 · 3.9 · $$
East Village | 29 E. Second St. (2nd Ave.)
212-335-0114

"**Soulful**" Mexican eats and "**delicious**" margaritas lure a "**good-looking crowd**" to this "**boisterous**" East Village cantina, where both the "**creative**" menu and the "**open**" digs are built around a central comal grill; "**fair**" prices are one more thing keeping 'em coming "**back for more.**"

ROSSINI'S | Italian · · · · · · · · · · · · · · · · 4.4 · 4.1 · 4.5 · $$$
Murray Hill | 108 E. 38th St. (bet. Lexington & Park Aves.)
212-683-0135 | www.rossinisrestaurant.com

The "**good old days**" endure at this 1978-vintage Murray Hill Italian touted for its "**excellent**" Tuscan fare and "**seamless**" service from "**tuxedo**"-attired staffers; the nightly piano player and live "**opera music**" on Saturdays help soothe any "**sticker shock.**"

ROTISSERIE GEORGETTE | French · · · · · 4.1 · 4.1 · 4.2 · $$$
East 60s | 14 E. 60th St. (bet. 5th & Madison Aves.)
212-390-8060 | www.rotisserieg.com

"**Gracious**" owner Georgette Farkas is a "**charmer**" at her UES namesake, known for "**impressive**" rotisserie chicken and other "**home-inspired**" French cooking from an "**attentive**" staff; the "**comfortable**" atmosphere is "**always a pleasure**", "**but you do pay for it.**"

RUBIROSA | Italian/Pizza · · · · · · · · · · · · 4.5 · 3.8 · 4.1 · $$
NoLita | 235 Mulberry St. (bet. Prince & Spring Sts.)
212-965-0500 | www.rubirosanyc.com

"**Amazing**" thin-crust pizzas and "**to-die-for**" meatballs are the fortes of this "**charming**" NoLita Italian done up in "**rustic-chic**" style; "**cozy**" turns "**tight**" during prime times, and it can be "**hard to get a table**", but "**cool**" vibes and "**reasonable**" tabs compensate.

RUBY'S CAFE | Australian · · · · · · · ∇ · 4.4 · 4.0 · 4.1 · $$
NoLita | 219 Mulberry St. (Spring St.) | 212-925-5755
NEW **Murray Hill** | 442 Third Ave. (bet. 30th & 31st Sts.) | 212-300-4245
www.rubyscafe.com

"**Amazing**" burgers and "**delicious**" Aussie-inspired dishes top the blackboard menu at these "**trendy**" yet "**unpretentious**" "**hot spots**"; "**tiny**" digs mean you may have to cozy up to your mates at shared tables but never mind, most just "**love the vibe.**"

RUCOLA | Italian · · · · · · · · · · · · · · · · · 4.4 · 4.0 · 4.0 · $$
Boerum Hill | 190 Dean St. (Bond St.) | Brooklyn
718-576-3209 | www.rucolabrooklyn.com

There's "**Brooklyn**" in the air at this all-day Italian on a "**quiet leafy street**" in Boerum Hill offering "**knockout**" rustic fare served by a "**good-natured**" team; since it's "**crazy popular**" and takes no reservations (for fewer than five), expect to "**rub elbows**" in the "**intimate**" brick-and-plank space.

RUE 57 | French · · · · · · · · · · · · · · · · · 3.9 · 3.9 · 3.9 · $$
West 50s | 60 W. 57th St. (6th Ave.)
212-307-5656 | www.rue57.com

"**Convenience is key**" at this veteran brasserie that's "**well located**" on Billionaire's Row, turning out "**reliable**" if "**not outstanding**" French eats plus sushi; despite "**uneven**" service, "**noisy**" decibels and a "**tourist**"-centric crowd, it's usually "**bustling**" – verging on "**hectic.**"

	FOOD	DECOR	SERVICE	COST

RUNNER & STONE | American/Bakery   4.4   4.2   4.2 $$
Gowanus | 285 Third Ave. (bet. Carroll & President Sts.) | Brooklyn
718-576-3360 | www.runnerandstone.com

"**Artisanal in all respects**", this "**charming**" Gowanus bakery/bistro is best
known for its "**heavenly**" breads and "**sublime**" croissants, though it also offers
"**delicious**" New American fare and cocktails; the "**relaxed**" space and
"**mindful**" staff are other reasons to "**just go.**"

RUSS & DAUGHTERS | Deli/Jewish   4.7   3.5   4.0 $$
Lower East Side | 179 E. Houston St. (bet. Allen & Orchard Sts.)
212-475-4880 | www.russanddaughters.com

A "**New York classic**" dating to 1914, this "**incomparable**" LES "**temple of
noshes**" is a "**smoked fish heaven**" known for "**sublime salmon**" and a "**zillion
varieties of herring**", plus "**proper bagels**", sandwiches and sweets, all
courtesy of a "**knowledgeable**" counter crew; "**oy vey**" is it "**small**", "**crowded**"
and "**pricey**", but for "**old-world Jewish**" fare, there's "**no comparison.**"

RUSS & DAUGHTERS CAFE | Jewish   4.5   3.8   4.1 $$
Lower East Side | 127 Orchard St. (bet. Delancey & Rivington Sts.) |
212-475-4880 | www.russanddaughterscafe.com

NEW **RUSS & DAUGHTERS AT THE JEWISH MUSEUM** | Jewish
East 90s | 1109 Fifth Ave. (92nd St.) | 212-475-4880 |
www.russanddaughters.com

Sit-down spin-offs of the LES appetizing store, these "**modern**" riffs on a
"**classic Jewish deli**" serve "**top-shelf**" smoked fish and other "**real-deal**"
"**old-world**" eats; the "**spiffy**" digs are often "**busy**" (expect waits, especially at
brunch), and the certified kosher location at the Jewish Museum adds a
take-out counter.

RUSSIAN TEA ROOM | Continental/Russian   3.8   4.4   4.0 $$$
West 50s | 150 W. 57th St. (bet. 6th & 7th Aves.)
212-581-7100 | www.russiantearoomnyc.com

Its "**glamorously ostentatious**" decor intact, this "**legendary**" Russo-
Continental stunner by Carnegie Hall still provides a "**glitzy**" czarist backdrop
for "**posh**" noshing built around caviar and blini; "**outrageous**" prices for
"**so-so**" food have fans lamenting its "**former glory**", but it's hard to top as a
"**theatrical experience**" for "**out-of-towners.**"

RUTH'S CHRIS STEAK HOUSE | Steak   4.4   4.1   4.3 $$$
West 50s | 148 W. 51st St. (bet. 6th & 7th Aves.)
212-245-9600 | www.ruthschris.com

"**Melt-in-your-mouth**" chops arrive with a butter-induced "**sizzle**" at this
"**high-end**" Theater District steakhouse that's part of the New Orleans–born
chain; fans like the "**men's-club**" decor and "**eager-to-please**" servers, adding
that the food tastes even better when "**you're not the one paying.**"

RYE | American   4.4   4.1   4.1 $$
Williamsburg | 247 S. First St. (bet. Havemeyer & Roebling Sts.) | Brooklyn
718-218-8047 | www.ryerestaurant.com

This "**seemingly traditional**" Williamsburg American offers up "**quiet
luxury**" via "**reliably delicious**" cooking washed down with "**spectacular
cocktails**" mixed at a vintage bar; augmenting the "**comfy, romantic**"
vibe is an oak-paneled cellar (Bar Below Rye) and one of the "**best happy
hours**" around.

SABLE'S SMOKED FISH | Deli/Jewish   4.5   2.7   3.8 $$

East 70s | 1489 Second Ave. (bet. 77th & 78th Sts.)
212-249-6177 | www.sablesnyc.com

At this UES appetizing "**institution**" you'll find "**unbelievable**" smoked fish,
"**mile high**" pastrami sandwiches and "**unmatched**" lobster and whitefish
salads, plus a "**helpful**" staff known for "**giving out little noshes**"; despite
pricing that may require "**missing this month's rent**", the space is "**no-frills**",
so plan to "**grab and run.**"

SACRED CHOW | Kosher/Vegan/Vegetarian ▽ 4.3   3.5   4.1 $$

Greenwich Village | 227 Sullivan St (bet. Bleecker & 3rd Sts.)
212-337-0863 | www.sacredchow.com

The "**delicious**" organic, kosher and vegan offerings (think "**exceptional
fake meatballs**") at this "**quirky**" Villager may just make carnivores
"**believe**"; it's small in size and "**popular**" with the health-minded, so
"**definitely make a reservation.**"

SADELLE'S | European/Jewish   4.3   4.3   3.9 $$

SoHo | 463 W. Broadway (bet. Houston & Prince Sts.)
212-776-4926 | www.sadelles.com

The Torrisi crew has "**rocked the brunch world**" with this SoHo "**scene**",
an "**ode**" to "**classic**" Jewish appetizing appreciated for its "**lux**" towers of
house-cured smoked fish, "**fresh-from-the-oven**" bagels, "**to-die-for**" sticky
buns and more; the "**airy space**" becomes candlelit and "**less crowded**" at
dinner, when the menu switches to seafood and European specialties.

SAHARA | Turkish   4.0   3.5   3.7 $$

Sheepshead Bay | 2337 Coney Island Ave. (bet. Aves. T & U) | Brooklyn
718-376-8594 | www.saharanewyork.com

It's "**old school at this point**", but this durable Sheepshead Bay Turk is "**hard
to beat**" for "**seriously good**" grilled fare ("**kebab is king**") at the right price;
the "**huge**" space may be "**short on ambiance**", but that doesn't hurt its
"**popularity**" with "**groups and families**", and "**the garden is an oasis.**"

SAJU BISTRO | French   4.1   3.9   4.1 $$$

West 40s | Mela Hotel | 120 W. 44th St. (6th Ave.)
212-997-7258 | www.sajubistro.com

A "**slice of Paree**" in Times Square, this "**very French**" bistro is "**spot-on**"
for "**traditional Provençal dishes**" offered at "**fair**" prices; it's especially
"**convenient**" pre-theater with an "**engaging**" staff to get you in and out.

SAKAGURA | Japanese   4.5   4.2   4.1 $$

East 40s | 211 E. 43rd St. (bet. 2nd & 3rd Aves.)
212-953-7253 | www.sakagura.com

A "**portal to Tokyo**" "**hidden away**" beneath an "**anonymous**" office building
near Grand Central, this Japanese izakaya couples "**sophisticated**" small
plates with an "**amazing array**" of "**superb**" sakes in a "**calm**", bamboo-rich
setting; given "**dainty**"-by-design portions, be prepared to "**spend more
than you expect.**"

SAKE BAR HAGI | Japanese   4.1   3.0   3.3 $$

West 40s | 152 W. 49th St. (7th Ave.) | 212-764-8549 | www.sakebarhagi.com

SAKE BAR HAGI 46 | Japanese

West 40s | 358 W. 46th St. (9th Ave.) | 212-956-2429 | www.hagi46.com

Just off Times Square, these "**hole-in-the-wall**" izakayas "**fill up fast**" with

---

folks unwinding over "**down-home**" Japanese bar food and "**plenty of booze on the cheap**" – so get there soon after work or prepare to wait; there's "**no decor**" to speak of, but the crowd "**lends atmosphere.**"

SALA ONE NINE | Spanish   4.2   3.8   3.8 $$$
Flatiron | 35 W. 19th St. (bet. 5th & 6th Aves.)
212-229-2300 | www.salaonenine.com

"**Dependable**" tapas and sangria fuel the "**energetic**" scene at this "**inviting**", "**no-attitude**" Flatiron Spaniard that works for "**hanging out with friends**" or going on a "**fun date**"; just be aware the "**fantastic happy-hour**" deals make for "**crowded**" conditions in the after-work hours.

SALINAS | Spanish   4.5   4.6   4.3 $$$
Chelsea | 136 Ninth Ave. (bet. 18th & 19th Sts.)
212-776-1990 | www.salinasnyc.com

"**Who'd believe you were in NYC**" at this "**stunning**" Chelsea retreat where "**lush**" digs with "**gorgeous flowers**" and a retractable roof set the scene for "**inventive**" tapas that'll "**transport you to Spain**"; "**expensive**" tabs are forgiven considering the "**amazing ambiance.**"

SALT & FAT | American/Asian   4.3   3.5   4.0 $$
Sunnyside | 41-16 Queens Blvd. (bet. 41st & 42nd Sts.) | Queens
718-433-3702 | www.saltandfatny.com

The name shows a "**sense of humor**", but they "**take the food seriously**" at this Sunnyside "**rising star**" where "**inventive**" small plates showcase a "**delectable**" blend of New American and Asian flavors, offered at "**Queens prices**"; "**no reservations**" and "**tiny**" dimensions mean "**waits**" at prime times.

SALUMERIA ROSI PARMACOTTO | Italian   4.4   3.7   4.0 $
West 70s | 283 Amsterdam Ave. (73rd St.)
212-877-4800 | www.salumeriarosi.com

A taste of "**Italy on the UWS**", this "**authentic little gem**" is known for its "**vast**" charcuterie selection and "**high-end**" cheeses plus "**inventive**" Italian tapas too; the space is "**cramped**" but nevermind – "**score a table outside**" and "**watch the neighborhood go by.**"

SALVATION BURGER | Burgers   4.1   3.8   3.7 $$
East 50s | Pod 51 Hotel | 230 E. 51st St. (bet. 2nd & 3rd Aves.)
646-277-2900 | www.salvationburger.com

April Bloomfield and Ken Friedman's "**refreshing burger experience**" in Midtown's Pod 51 Hotel wood-grills "**juicy**" locavore patties with "**spot-on**" homemade toppings to pair with "**cool**" boozy shakes; though the prices are "**a big ask**" for a "**quite casual**" setup, it's typically "**super busy**"; P.S. closed at press time due to a fire.

SALVATION TACO | Mexican   3.8   3.9   3.4 $$
Murray Hill | Pod 39 Hotel | 145 E. 39th St. (bet. Lexington & 3rd Aves.)
212-865-5800 | www.salvationtaco.com

This "**totally fun**" Murray Hill Mexican from April Bloomfield and Ken Friedman offers "**different from the norm**" tacos and other "**interesting**" bites in a colorful space; OK, it's "**noisy**" and "**service could be better**", but the rooftop bar is "**terrific**" for "**boozy bonding.**"

SAMMY'S FISH BOX | Seafood   4.2   3.7   4.0 $$$

City Island | 41 City Island Ave. (Rochelle St.) | Bronx
718-885-0920 | www.sammysfishbox.com

"**You will not leave hungry**" could be the motto of this "**huge**" City Island vet, which has been churning out "**generous**" servings of seafood since 1966; though not cheap, it's something of a "**tourist**" magnet, so count on it being "**crowded in summer months.**"

NEW   **SAMMY'S HOUSE OF BBQ** | Barbecue   —   —   — $$

West 40s | 258 W. 44th St. (8th Ave.)
212-944-6900 | www.sammyshouseofbbq.com

Pitmaster Big Lou Elrose (ex Hill Country, Wildwood BBQ) delivers brisket, ribs and sides with different regional BBQ sauces at this three-story smoke joint with tacos on the menu too. Designed with tiled floors, reclaimed wood and burlap banquettes, it's a sprawling locale for a casual Times Square bite.

SAMMY'S ROUMANIAN | Jewish   4.0   3.2   3.7 $$$

Lower East Side | 157 Chrystie St. (Delancey St.)
212-673-0330 | www.sammysromanian.com

This LES "**heartburn city**" rolls out "**old-fashioned**" Jewish staples "**covered in schmaltz**" (and vodka in ice blocks) in a "**grungy basement**" setting where a keyboardist spouts "**nonstop shtick**"; like being in a "**perpetual bar mitzvah**", the clamorous "**cavorting**" could cause "**cardiac arrest**" – but it's a "**great way to go.**"

SAMMY'S SHRIMP BOX | Seafood   4.2   3.8   3.9 $$

City Island | 64 City Island Ave. (Horton St.) | Bronx
718-885-3200 | www.shrimpboxrestaurant.com

Docked "**at the end of the strip**" near its Fish Box forerunner, this "**casual**" City Islander dispenses "**down-to-earth**" fried seafood and "**lots of it**" at a "**nice price**"; it's a standard "**hang in the summer**", when you should expect "**very crowded**" conditions.

SANDRO'S | Italian   4.3   3.6   4.1 $$$

East 80s | 306 E. 81st St. (bet. 1st & 2nd Aves.)
212-288-7374 | www.sandrosnyc.com

"**If you want real Italian**", this Upper Eastsider provides "**really good**" Roman-style cooking courtesy of "**colorful**" chef-owner Sandro Fioriti, whose appearances "**add flair**" to the "**clubby**" scene; it may seem "**expensive**" given the "**dated interior**", but the regulars are "**always happy.**"

SANFORD'S | Diner   4.1   3.9   3.9 $$

Astoria | 30-13 Broadway (bet. 30th & 31st Sts.) | Queens
718-932-9569 | www.sanfordsnyc.com

In business since 1922, this revamped Astoria "**super-diner**" serves "**reliable**" American comfort food at "**reasonable**" rates; the formula is "**deservedly popular**", especially at the "**famous**" brunch when the "**only drawback is the wait.**"

SAN MATTEO | Italian/Pizza   4.6   3.4   4.1 $$

East 80s | 1559 Second Ave. (81st St.) | 212-861-2434
East 90s | 1739 Second Ave. (90th St.) | 212-426-6943
www.sanmatteopanuozzo.com

Bite into the "**first-rate**", "**real-deal**" Neapolitan pies or "**unusual**" panuozzi (sandwiches) at these "**popular**" Upper Eastsiders, and "**you're in Italy**"; tables are **"few"** in the **"tiny"**, **"basic"** flagship, but the **"expanded"** East 80s outpost boasts a **"lovely upstairs"** space with a **"fun vibe."**

SAN PIETRO | Italian
| | 4.5 | 4.2 | 4.5 | $$$$ |

East 50s | 18 E. 54th St. (bet. 5th & Madison Aves.)
212-753-9015 | www.sanpietroristorantenyc.com

"Filled with CEOs" and **"older sophisticates"** at lunch, this **"top-notch"** Southern Italian is a Midtown **"respite"** offering **"sumptuous"** cuisine and **"treat-you-like-royalty"** service; since its **"money-is-no-object"** tabs are **"wildly costly"**, some reserve it for **"special occasions."**

SANT AMBROEUS | Italian
| | 4.4 | 4.1 | 4.1 | $$$ |

East 70s | 1000 Madison Ave. (bet. 77th & 78th Sts.) | 212-570-2211
NoLita | 265 Lafayette St. (bet. Prince & Spring Sts.) | 212-966-2770
West Village | 259 W. Fourth St. (Perry St.) | 212-604-9254
www.santambroeus.com

"Sophisticated" sorts are drawn to these **"Milano-in-NY"** cafes where **"chichi"** Italian nibbles are served in a **"civilized"** atmosphere; the **"bustling"** digs draw a **"stylish"** crowd that doesn't mind paying **"sky-high prices"** to **"see and be seen."**

SANTINA | Italian
| | 4.2 | 4.3 | 4.0 | $$$ |

Meatpacking District | 820 Washington St. (Gansevoort St.)
212-254-3000 | www.santinanyc.com

Like **"summer on Capri"**, this **"hot hot hot"** Meatpacking Italian from the Torrisi team **"evokes an island off Italy"** with its **"breezy atmosphere"**, **"flavorful"** seafood-focused menu and **"sexy drinks"**; **"enchanting"** Murano chandeliers decorate the glass-walled setting, where **"tight"** seating and **"loud"** conditions carry over to the popular brunch.

SAPPHIRE INDIAN CUISINE | Indian
| | 4.1 | 3.8 | 3.8 | $$ |

West 60s | 1845 Broadway (bet. 60th & 61st Sts.)
212-245-4444 | www.sapphireny.com

This **"quiet"** Indian **"retreat"** off Columbus Circle is touted for its **"reliable"** kitchen, **"courteous"** service, **"comfortable"** quarters and convenience to Lincoln Center; though it's a tad **"more expensive"** than some, the $17 buffet lunch is a **"bargain."**

SARABETH'S | American
| | 4.0 | 3.8 | 3.8 | $$ |

Chelsea | Chelsea Mkt. | 75 Ninth Ave. (bet. 15th & 16th Sts.) | 212-989-2424 | www.sarabeth.com
East 90s | 1295 Madison Ave. (92nd St.) | 212-410-7335 | www.sarabeth.com
Murray Hill | 381 Park Ave. S. (27th St.) | 212-335-0093 | www.sarabeth.com
TriBeCa | 339 Greenwich St. (bet. Harrison & Jay Sts.) | 212-966-0421 | www.sarabeth.com
West 30s | Lord & Taylor | 424 Fifth Ave., 5th fl. (bet. 38th & 39th Sts.) | 212-827-5068 | www.sarabeth.com
West 50s | 40 Central Park S. (6th Ave.) | 212-826-5959 | www.sarabethscps.com
West 80s | 423 Amsterdam Ave. (bet. 80th & 81st Sts.) | 212-496-6280 | www.sarabethswest.com

Breakfast and brunch **"reign"** at these **"hugely popular"** American spots, **"a staple forever"** for **"wholesome"** comfort food and baked goods served in **"cheery"** surrounds; they can be **"fast-paced"** **"madhouses"** by day, though dinner is **"more civilized."**

		FOOD	DECOR	SERVICE	COST

SARAGHINA | Pizza ▽ 4.4 4.2 4.0 $$
Bedford-Stuyvesant | 435 Halsey St. (Lewis Ave.) | Brooklyn
718-574-0010 | www.saraghinabrooklyn.com

A Bed-Stuy "**hidden treasure**", this "**rustic**" all-day "**favorite**" stands out with "**wonderful**" Neapolitan pizzas and other Italian dishes showcasing "**top-quality ingredients**"; a "**crowded**" interior on weekends is alleviated in summer by the "**cool backyard.**"

SARAVANAA BHAVAN | Indian/Vegetarian 4.4 3.2 3.5 $$
Murray Hill | 81 Lexington Ave. (26th St.) | 212-679-0204
West 70s | 413 Amsterdam Ave. (80th St.) | 212-721-7755
www.saravanabhavan.com

"**Interesting**" dosas are "**delicious**" standouts at these "**bustling**" branches of a global chain, where the rest of the South Indian veggie fare is "**terrific**" too; the settings are "**uninspiring**" and "**service could improve**", but you do get "**excellent quality**" grub at "**reasonable prices.**"

SARDI'S | Continental 3.7 4.2 4.1 $$$
West 40s | 234 W. 44th St. (bet. 7th & 8th Aves.)
212-221-8440 | www.sardis.com

Sure, it's mainly a "**tourist joint**", but this circa-1921 "**showbiz institution**" is touted as a Theater District "**must-experience**" thanks to its celeb caricatures on the walls and "**Broadway stargazing**" in the seats; if its Continental fare and career waiters seem "**passionately outdated**", fans insist that's part of the "**charm.**"

SARGE'S DELI | Deli/Sandwiches 4.1 3.1 3.7 $$
Murray Hill | 548 Third Ave. (bet. 36th & 37th Sts.)
212-679-0442 | www.sargesdeli.com

This 24/7 Murray Hill "**staple**" (since 1964) maintains its "**across-the-board quality**" with a "**massive**" roster of "**traditional Jewish deli**" favorites including corned beef and pastrami sandwiches "**as big as your face**"; its "**nontouristy**" following ignores the "**tacky**" diner decor and focuses on the "**reasonable**" price tags.

SASABUNE | Japanese 4.6 3.2 4.2 $$$$
East 70s | 401 E. 73rd St. (1st Ave.)
212-249-8583 | www.sasabunenyc.com

Sushi "**masters**" craft "**absurdly delicious**" "**works of art**" at this UES Japanese from Kenji Takahashi, a "**tiny**" hideaway known for both à la carte options and an "**incredible**" omakase experience; though the "**decor's very basic**", sampling the "**first-class fish**" requires "**really deep pockets.**"

SAUCE | Italian 4.0 3.4 3.8 $$
Lower East Side | 78 Rivington St. (Allen St.)
212-420-7700 | www.saucerestaurant.com

"**Comfortable and always crowded**", this "**booming**" LES sibling of Lil' Frankie's and Supper provides "**fresh, flavorful**" Southern Italian eats in a "**tight**", wallpapered space with a vintage feel; though it's "**rather loud**", "**reasonable**" prices keep its "**hipster**" clientele happy.

NEW **SAUVAGE** | American — — — $$$
Greenpoint | 905 Lorimer St. (Nassau Ave.) | Brooklyn
718-486-6816 | www.sauvageny.com

The Maison Premiere team is behind this Greenpoint American emphasizing seafood (including oysters, of course), seasonal vegetables and eclectic dishes with French accents, along with cocktails made with hand-chiseled ice. The space has a crisp look, with tiled floors, a swerving bar and banquettes.

SAXON & PAROLE | American   4.3   4.3   4.2 $$$
NoHo | 316 Bowery (Bleecker St.)
212-254-0350 | www.saxonandparole.com

"Hip" "sophistication" marks this higher-end NoHo American, where "**lush decor**" with equestrian motifs sets the backdrop for "**well-executed**" fare with "**interesting twists**"; it's also a "**destination**" for "**killer cocktails**" from a bar "**where the action is.**"

SAZON | Puerto Rican   ▽ 4.3   4.1   4.1 $$$
TriBeCa | 105 Reade St. (bet. B'way & Church St.)
212-406-1900 | www.sazonnyc.com

"High-class" Puerto Rican fare is the draw at this "**sexy**" bi-level TriBeCa spot, where the popular pernil is "**as good as your *abuela's***"; "**upbeat**" music and sangria with the "**right amount of flair**" ratchet up the "**fun**", "**noisy**" vibe.

SCALETTA | Italian   4.1   3.8   4.2 $$$
West 70s | 50 W. 77th St. (bet. Columbus Ave. & CPW)
212-769-9191

Inventive it's not, but this "**dependable**" UWS "**favorite**" has been serving "**solid**", "**old-style**" Northern Italiana with "**simple elegance**" for more than a quarter century; the "**spacious seating**" and "**blissful quiet**" make conversation here a "**pleasure**", and "**no one pushes you out the door.**"

SCALINATELLA | Italian   4.4   3.8   4.2 $$$$
East 60s | 201 E. 61st St., downstairs (3rd Ave.)
212-207-8280

"A real Italian grotto", this subterranean UES lair attracts well-heeled admirers who "**rub elbows**" over "**superb**" Capri-style cuisine served with a "**personalized**" touch; it's bound to be "**memorable**", but "**beware of the specials**" or they'll "**empty out your wallet.**"

SCALINI FEDELI | Italian   4.7   4.5   4.7 $$$$
TriBeCa | 165 Duane St. (bet. Hudson & Staple Sts.)
212-528-0400 | www.scalinifedeli.com

"Simply a world apart", Michael Cetrulo's "**high-level**" TriBeCa Italian stands out with "**divine**" tasting menus and "**impeccable**" service in a "**beautifully arched**" "**European-style dining room**"; granted, the fixed price is "**a bit expensive**", but it "**sets the stage for an ideal romantic dinner.**"

SCALINO | Italian   4.3   3.5   4.2 $$
Greenpoint | 659 Manhattan Ave. (bet. Nassau & Norman Aves.) | Brooklyn | 718-389-8600 | www.scalinogp.com
Park Slope | 347 Seventh Ave. (10th St.) | Brooklyn | 718-840-5738 | www.scalinobrooklyn.com

It's "**endearing**" to be "**treated like a regular**" at these "small" but "**proud**" Brooklyn Italians serving "**generous**" plates of "**delicious**", "**earthy**" pastas and other staples; "**comfortable**" and "**no-frills**", they deliver "**value**" – and naturally "**fill up fast.**"

	FOOD	DECOR	SERVICE	COST

SCARLATTO | Italian — 3.9 3.8 3.9 $$$
West 40s | 250 W. 47th St. (bet. B'way & 8th Ave.)
212-730-4535 | www.scarlattonyc.com

Expect "**no gimmicks**" at this "**convenient**" Italian standby in the middle of the Theater District, just "**tasty**" standards delivered by a "**prompt**" crew; "**reasonable**"-for-the-neighborhood prices get even more so if you order the "**bargain**" prix fixe.

SCARPETTA | Italian — 4.5 4.2 4.3 $$$
Chelsea | 355 W. 14th St. (bet. 8th & 9th Aves.)
212-691-0555 | www.scarpettanyc.com

"**Especially fine**" pastas including that "**simple but perfect**" signature spaghetti headline the "**impressive**" menu at this Chelsea Italian, where a "**well-trained**" team delivers the "**first-rate**" fare; "**energy**" runs "**high**" in the "**sleek, modern**" space, as do the "**special-occasion**" bills.

SCHILLER'S | American — 3.8 3.8 3.8 $$
Lower East Side | 131 Rivington St. (Norfolk St.)
212-260-4555 | www.schillersny.com

A "**great late-night**" place, this LES hang from Keith McNally still draws the "**cool crowd**" for "**top**" drinks and American bistro fare in "**lively**" subway-tiled digs; even if the food's "**nothing to write home about**" and the decibels run "**high**", it always delivers "**a lot of fun.**"

NEW **SCHILLING** | Austrian/Mediterranean — — — $$$
Financial District | 109 Washington St. (bet. Carlisle & Rector Sts.)
212-406-1200 | www.schillingnyc.com

From Eduard Frauneder (Edi & the Wolf, Freud NYC) comes this FiDi eatery offering dishes that bring together Austrian and Mediterranean flavors. Weathered brick, wood and industrial fixtures feature in the space where front garage doors open for breezy warm-weather dining.

SCOTTADITO OSTERIA TOSCANA | Italian — 4.1 3.8 4.1 $$
Park Slope | 788 Union St. (bet. 6th & 7th Aves.) | Brooklyn
718-636-4800 | www.scottadito.com

Whether for an "**intimate dinner**" or brunch, this Park Sloper "**steals hearts**" with its "**tasty**" Northern Italian fare and "**Tuscan farmhouse**" setting ("**sit by the fireplace**"); "**warm**" service and well-priced wines complete the picture.

SEA | Thai — ∇ 4.0 4.3 3.8 $$
Williamsburg | 114 N. Sixth St. (Berry St.) | Brooklyn
718-384-8850 | www.seathainyc.com

It's all about the "**awe-inspiring interior**" at this "**nightclub**"-like Williamsburg Thai resembling a "**dreamy temple**" complete with a "**huge Buddha**"; "**party**" people swaying to the "**techno**" soundtrack report that the chow is as "**decent**" as the prices.

SEA FIRE GRILL | Seafood — 4.6 4.4 4.5 $$$
East 40s | 158 E. 48th St. (bet. Lexington & 3rd Aves.)
212-935-3785 | www.theseafiregrill.com

This East Midtown seafood "**oasis**" provides "**exceptional**" catch and "**premium**" steaks ("**the best of both worlds**"), backed by a "**limitless**" wine list and served in "**sophisticated**" confines complete with fireplace and "**high-energy**" bar; factor in "**a big welcome**" from the "**stellar**" team, and the upmarket prices are "**worth every penny.**"

	FOOD	DECOR	SERVICE	COST

SEA GRILL | Seafood — 4.4   4.4   4.3 $$$

West 40s | Rockefeller Ctr. | 19 W. 49th St. (bet. 5th & 6th Aves.)
212-332-7610 | www.theseagrillnyc.com

With a "**prime setting**" overlooking the skating rink and holiday Christmas tree, this "**iconic**" Rock Center seafood specialist is a "**treat**" that's "**not just for tourists**"; sure, the pricing is "**special-occasion**" level, but the "**quality**" fare and "**exceptional**" service are "**worth the occasional splurge.**"

SEAMORE'S | Seafood — 4.1   4.1   3.9 $$

Little Italy | 390 Broome St. (Mulberry St.)
212-730-6005 | www.seamores.com

Bringing a bit of the "**Hamptons**" to Little Italy, this "**modern**" fish shack from Michael Chernow (The Meatball Shop) spotlights sustainable seafood served in "**awesome**" fish tacos and other "**tasty**" bites; the "**light, airy**" space has a "**beachy**" feel, but because it's "**super-trendy**" don't be surprised when it's "**noisy.**"

SEA SHORE | Seafood — 4.0   3.8   4.2 $$

City Island | 591 City Island Ave. (Cross St.) | Bronx
718-885-0300 | www.seashorerestaurant.com

A City Island "**place to be**" since 1923, this "**friendly**" seafood spot dishes up "**hearty portions**" of "**classic**" catch in an "**old-fashioned**", shore-side setting; the outdoor dining and marina views reel in "**families**" and "**weekend**" visitors, as do the "**not-over-the-top prices.**"

2ND AVE DELI | Deli/Kosher — 4.2   3.3   3.8 $$

East 70s | 1442 First Ave. (75th St.) | 212-737-1700
Murray Hill | 162 E 33rd St. (bet. Lexington & 3rd Aves.) | 212-689-9000
www.2ndavedeli.com

Comfort food "**like Bubby used to make**" – "**insanely good**" "**overstuffed**" sandwiches, "**healing**" matzo ball soup, "**unbelievable**" knishes – are the claim to fame of these traditional kosher "**nosheries**"; the setups are "**basic**", the service "**no-nonsense**" and the tabs "**not cheap**", but for a "**true Jewish deli experience**" they're real "**crowd-pleasers.**"

NEW 2ND CITY | Filipino — —   —   — $

West Village | 525 Hudson St. (bet. Charles & 10th Sts.)
917-639-3262 | www.2ndcityusa.com

A chef-owner who first made his chops at Jean-Georges and The French Laundry is behind this Filipino eatery in the West Village that offers a playful modern menu (burritos, sandwiches, buns). The small space also has a bar for beer, wine and punch.

SEMILLA | American — 4.6   4.2   4.6 $$$$

Williamsburg | 160 Havemeyer St. (2nd St.) | Brooklyn
718-782-3474 | www.semillabk.com

"**Highly seasonal, highly original**" defines the "**vegetable-forward**" tasting menu at this "**petite**" Williamsburg New American where the "**interesting**" dishes are "**above all, incredibly delicious**"; the 18-seat counter setup is "**spare**", but a "**top-notch**" staff boosts the "**wow**"-factor.

SERAFINA | Italian — 3.8   3.6   3.7 $$$

East 50s | 38 E. 58th St. (bet. Madison & Park Aves.) | 212-832-8888
East 60s | 33 E. 61st St. (bet. Madison & Park Aves.) | 212-702-9898
East 70s | 1022 Madison Ave., 2nd fl. (79th St.) | 212-734-2676
Meatpacking District | 7 Ninth Ave. (Little W. 12th St.) | 646-964-4494

continued

Morningside Heights | 1260 Amsterdam Ave. (122nd St.) | 212-658-0226
West 40s | Time Hotel | 224 W. 49th St. (bet. B'way & 8th Ave.) | 212-247-1000
West 50s | Dream Hotel | 210 W. 55th St. (bet. B'way & 7th Ave.) |
212-315-1700
West 70s | On the Ave Hotel | 2178 Broadway (77th St.) | 212-595-0092
www.serafinarestaurant.com

"**Consistent and satisfying**", these Italians provide a "**wide-ranging**" menu of "**crispy**" thin-crust pizzas and "**reliable**" if "**nothing special**" pastas and salads; the "**comfortable**" digs are "**kid-friendly**" and "**accommodating to groups**" – other reasons they're "**handy**" for an "**easy eat out.**"

SERENDIPITY 3 | American/Dessert   4.0   4.2   3.7 $$
East 60s | 225 E. 60th St. (bet. 2nd & 3rd Aves.)
212-838-3531 | www.serendipity3.com

"**Must-try**" frozen hot chocolate is the signature and the other American comfort offerings are mere "**prelude**" at this "**whimsical**", circa-1954 East Side sweets 'n' gifts "**institution**"; despite "**high prices**", "**sassy**" service and "**crazy crowds**", it's a magnet for "**tourists**" and "**grandchildren**" alike.

SESSANTA | Italian   4.2   4.2   4.2 $$$
SoHo | Sixty Hotel | 60 Thompson St. (Broome St.)
212-219-8119 | www.sessantanyc.com

This "**charming**" retreat in SoHo's Sixty Hotel from restaurateur John McDonald (Lure Fishbar) pairs "**creative**" Sicilian-inspired coastal fare with a sizable Italian wine list; the "**beautiful**" midcentury setting includes plush banquettes and a streetside patio.

SETTE MEZZO | Italian   4.4   3.7   4.2 $$$
East 70s | 969 Lexington Ave. (bet. 70th & 71st Sts.)
212-472-0400

"**It helps to be a regular**" at this "**clubby**" UES Italian, which caters to "**well-to-do neighborhood patrons**" with "**surprisingly wonderful**" fare, "**accommodating**" service and house accounts to settle the "**expensive**" tabs; outsiders find "**they tend to rush you**", but it's still a "**dependable**" pick overall.

SEVA INDIAN CUISINE | Indian   ▽ 4.4   3.4   4.1 $$
Astoria | 30-07 34th St. (30th Ave.) | Queens
718-626-4440 | www.sevaindianrestaurant.com

Not your average curry house, this "**simple**" Astoria joint spotlights "**amazing**" Northern Indian cuisine that can be made "**as spicy as you want**"; everyone leaves "**happily full**", and the prix fixes and all-you-can-eat weekend brunch supply notable "**bang for the buck.**"

SEVILLA | Spanish   4.4   3.6   4.1 $$
West Village | 62 Charles St. (W. 4th St.)
212-929-3189 | www.sevillarestaurantandbar.com

"**They know what they're doing**" at this 1941-vintage West Village "**garlic haven**" delivering "**fabulous paellas**" and other low-cost Spanish classics via "**efficient**" staffers; maybe the decor's getting "**worn**", but patrons downing "**out-of-this-world sangria**" are having too much "**fun**" to notice.

SFOGLIA | Italian   4.4   3.8   4.2 $$$
East 90s | 1402 Lexington Ave. (92nd St.)
212-831-1402 | www.sfogliarestaurant.com

An "**oasis of class**", this Carnegie Hill standby near the 92nd Street Y is widely praised for its "**authentic**" Italian cooking, "**knowledgeable**" servers and "**romantic**" faux farmhouse digs; though "**pricey**", it's "**worth the money**" – "**getting a table**" is the real problem.

SHAKE SHACK | Burgers　　　　4.0　3.2　3.4　　$
Battery Park City | 215 Murray St. (bet. North End Ave. & West St.) | 646-545-4600
East 40s | Grand Central | 87 E. 42nd St. (bet. Lexington & Vanderbilt Aves.) | 646-517-5805
East 80s | 154 E. 86th St. (bet. Lexington & 3rd Aves.) | 646-237-5035
NEW **Financial District** | Fulton Ctr. | 200 Broadway, 2nd level (bet. Fulton & John Sts.) | 646-230-0320
Flatiron | Madison Square Park | 23rd St. (bet. B'way & Madison Ave.) | 212-889-6600
Murray Hill | 600 Third Ave. (40th St.) | 646-668-4880
NEW **West 30s** | 1333 Broadway (bet. 35th & 36th Sts.) | 646-230-0696
West 40s | 691 Eighth Ave. (bet. 43rd & 44th Sts.) | 646-435-0135
West 70s | 366 Columbus Ave. (77th St.) | 646-747-8770
Downtown Brooklyn | Fulton Street Mall | 409 Fulton St. (Adams St.) | Brooklyn | 718-307-7590
Dumbo | 1 Old Fulton St. (Water St.) | Brooklyn | 347-435-2676
Park Slope | 170 Flatbush Ave. (Pacific St.) | Brooklyn | 347-442-7721
www.shakeshack.com

"**Premium fast food**" is the draw at this "**widely syndicated**" Danny Meyer chain, offering "**mouthwatering**" burgers, "**rich shakes**" and other "**upgraded**" eats (plus beer and wine) at a "**manageable price**"; they're "a **magnet**" for "**legions of fans**" who can create "**hectic scenes**" and "**insane lines**", especially at the "**landmark**" Madison Square Park shack "**where it all started.**"

SHALOM JAPAN | Japanese/Jewish　　∇ 4.5　3.8　4.2　$$
Williamsburg | 310 S. Fourth St. (Rodney St.) | Brooklyn
718-388-4012 | www.shalomjapannyc.com

If you think Jewish-Japanese food is a "**strange concept**", the "**exciting**" "**marriage of cuisines**" at this cozy South Williamsburg standout may "**change your mind**"; converts advise: reserve ahead, check out the chalkboard menu and "**splurge**" a little.

SHANGHAI CAFE | Chinese　　　　4.3　2.9　3.3　$
Little Italy | 100 Mott St. (bet. Canal & Hester Sts.)
212-966-3988 | www.shanghaicafenyc.com

This "**tiny**" Little Italy Chinese churns out its signature "**succulent**" soup dumplings and other Shanghai treats "**fast**" and "**dirt-cheap**"; indeed, the "**flavorful**" eats distract from the "**barking**" service and inauspicious "**Formica-and-fluorescent-light**" decor.

SHELSKY'S OF BROOKLYN | Deli/Jewish　4.5　3.6　4.1　$$
Cobble Hill | 141 Court St. (bet. Atlantic Ave. & Pacific St.) | Brooklyn
718-855-8817 | www.shelskys.com

"**A real find**" for "**Manhattan-worthy**" noshes in Cobble Hill, this "**old-fashioned**" Jewish deli trades in "**a wide variety**" of "**first-rate**" staples, from "**tasty sandwiches**" to "**the smoked fish you know you want**"; a "**helpful staff**" dispenses "**the good stuff**", but "**be prepared to pay**" for it.

	FOOD	DECOR	SERVICE	COST

SHI | Asian   4.1   4.3   4.0 $$
Long Island City | 4720 Center Blvd. (Vernon Blvd.) | Queens
347-242-2450 | www.shilic.com

"Fantastic views of the NYC skyline" combine with "**tasteful**" Pan-Asian cuisine and "**amazing cocktails**" at this "**upscale**" LIC high-rise dweller; since it's "**stronger than most in the area**", insiders advise reserving in advance.

SHUKO | Japanese   4.6   4.4   4.4 $$$$
Greenwich Village | 47 E. 12th St. (B'way)
212-228-6088 | www.shukonyc.com

This "**tiny**", "**special-occasion**" Village Japanese limits itself to "**phenomenal omakase**", providing either "**top-tier**" sushi or traditional kaiseki spreads at a "**transporting**" bar that takes diners "**straight to Tokyo**"; options starting at $135 mean "**it ain't cheap**", but the payoff is a real "**wow experience.**"

SHUN LEE PALACE | Chinese   4.4   4.1   4.2 $$$
East 50s | 155 E. 55th St. (bet. Lexington & 3rd Aves.)
212-371-8844 | www.shunleepalace.net

The "**epitome**" of "**high-class Chinese**" dining, Michael Tong's circa-1971 East Midtowner delivers "**excellently prepared**", "**old-school**" fare in an "**elegant**" dining room; OK, so maybe it's a "**bit dated**", and prices are up there, but its "**charming**" vibe still works for a "**special**" night out.

SHUN LEE WEST | Chinese   4.1   4.0   4.0 $$$
West 60s | 43 W. 65th St. (bet. Columbus Ave. & CPW)
212-769-3888 | www.shunleewest.com

"Tried-and-true" for "**high-class**" Chinese dining, Michael Tong's UWS "**mainstay**" still "**runs like clockwork**" supplying "**elevated**" cuisine in a "**decorative setting**" adorned with golden dragons; though "**costly**" and "**sort of a throwback**", it claims "**many loyal customers – and it's easy to see why.**"

THE SIMONE | French   4.6   4.3   4.6 $$$
East 80s | 151 E. 82nd St. (bet. Lexington & 3rd Aves.)
212-772-8861 | www.thesimonerestaurant.com

A "**class act**", this "**tiny**" UES retreat pleases "**adults**" with "**exceptional**" French cooking and "**spot-on**" wine pairings in an "**elegant**" setting conducive to "**civilized conversation**"; though it's "**hard to get into**", "**flawless service**" is another reason it's "**worth the effort**" – and the "**splurge.**"

SINIGUAL | Mexican   4.0   3.9   3.8 $$
East 40s | 640 Third Ave. (41st St.)
212-286-0250 | www.sinigualrestaurants.com

Offering "**all the Mexican standards**" you'd expect ("**sizzling**" fajitas, "**tasty**" tableside guac), this "**jumping**" joint near Grand Central works for a "**fun business lunch**" or "**after-work**" margaritas; the "**large**", "**colorful**" space can get "**loud**", but moderate prices keep it group-friendly.

SIP SAK | Turkish   4.3   3.5   3.8 $$
East 40s | 928 Second Ave. (bet. 49th & 50th Sts.)
212-583-1900 | www.sip-sak.com

"Deliciously spiced" Turkish specialties come at "**fair**" rates at this U.N.-area "**standby**"; the "**Montparnasse-meets-the-Dardanelles**" decor is "**just OK**", but it's often "**busy**" with fans of the "**reliable**" performance.

	FOOD	DECOR	SERVICE	COST

SISTINA | Italian   4.4   3.7   4.2 $$$
East 80s | 24 E. 81st St. (Madison Ave.)
212-861-7660 | www.sistinany.com

Locals "**feel pampered**" at this recently relocated UES Italian, where "**excellent food**" pairs up with an "**extensive wine list**" and "**crisp**" service in a "**warm**" townhouse setting with a winter garden room; cash-conscious types favor it for "**special occasions**" given the "**expensive**" tabs.

THE SMILE | Mediterranean   4.3   4.0   4.0 $$
NoHo | 26 Bond St., downstairs (bet. Bowery & Lafayette St.)
646-329-5836 | www.thesmilenyc.com

"**Cozy and intimate**", this all-day NoHo cafe brings in a "**hip**" crowd for "**delicious**" Mediterranean-influenced fare at "**reasonable prices**"; "**warm lighting**" and "**charming decor**" make it equally "**comfortable**" for "**breakfast meetings**" or a "**date**", and brunch is "**fun**" too.

THE SMITH | American   3.9   3.6   3.7 $$
East 50s | 956 Second Ave. (bet. 50th & 51st Sts.) | 212-644-2700
East Village | 55 Third Ave. (bet. 10th & 11th Sts.) | 212-420-9800
NEW NoMad | 1150 Broadway (27th St.) | 212-685-4500
West 60s | 1900 Broadway (63rd St.) | 212-496-5700
www.thesmithnyc.com

"**Don't expect an intimate conversation**" at this "**million-decibel**" mini-chain that supplies "**basic**" but "**appealing**" American grub to "**under-35**" throngs out to "**eat and be merry**"; "**especially popular for brunch**", they're routinely "**bustling**" thanks to "**good value**" and "**upbeat**" vibes.

SMITH & WOLLENSKY | Steak   4.4   4.0   4.3 $$$
East 40s | 797 Third Ave. (49th St.)
212-753-1530 | www.smithandwollenskynyc.com

You can "**count on**" this "**time-honored**" East Midtown "**bastion of steak**" to deliver "**generous**" cuts of "**beef done right**" to a "**high-volume**" crowd of execs "**entertaining clients**" while downing "**manly**" cocktails; service with "**old-school**" flair seals the "**undeniable appeal**", especially "**if you can get someone else to pay.**"

SMOKE JOINT | BBQ   4.1   3.3   3.5 $$
Fort Greene | 87 S. Elliott Pl. (bet. Fulton St. & Lafayette Ave.) | Brooklyn
718-797-1011 | www.thesmokejoint.com

BBQ fixes are sated at this "**funky**" Fort Greene standby offering "**mouthwatering**", "**smoky**" pit meats washed down with "**top-shelf bourbons**"; maybe it's a bit "**rough around the edges**", but factor in "**budget**" prices and most will happily "**eat while standing**" – "**cuz it's so packed**" (especially "**pre-BAM and Barclays events**").

SMORGASBURG | Food Hall   4.3   3.5   3.5 $
South Street Seaport | 11 Fulton St. (Front St.) | no phone
Prospect Park | Breeze Hill | enter at Ocean Ave. & Lincoln Rd. | Brooklyn | no phone
Williamsburg | East River Waterfront (bet. 6th & 7th Sts.) | Brooklyn | no phone
www.smorgasburg.com

"**Eat yourself silly sampling everything**" at these seasonal open-air markets, where "**passionate vendors**" showcase "**innovative**", "**artisanal**" food "**from around the world"; "**insane crowds**" and "**long lines**" don't dampen the overall "**fun**" experience; P.S. check website for days and locations.

SMORGAS CHEF | Scandinavian   4.1   3.7   3.9 $$

Financial District | 53 Stone St. (William St.) | 212-422-3500
Murray Hill | Scandinavia House | 58 Park Ave. (bet. 37th & 38th Sts.) | 212-847-9745
www.smorgas.com

Fans would return "**just for the meatballs**", but these "**low-key**" Scandinavians also serve other "**tantalizing**" classics – many using ingredients from the owners' own upstate farm – at prices that offer "**value**"; the FiDi original is kinda "**spare**", but the Murray Hill spin-off within Scandinavia House is downright "**elegant.**"

SNACK EOS | Greek   4.3   3.6   4.1 $$

West 30s | 522 Ninth Ave. (39th St.) | 646-964-4964 | www.snackeos.com

SNACK TAVERNA | Greek

West Village | 63 Bedford St. (Morton St.) | 212-929-3499 | www.snacktaverna.com

They put "**interesting twists**" on Greek classics at these "**delightful**" tavernas where "**delicious**" mezes, salads and entrees pair with "**intriguing**" Hellenic wines; the West Village "**charmer**" is an "**intimate neighborhood spot**", while Hell's Kitchen has a prix fixe option that's "**compelling**" for theatergoers.

SOBA NIPPON | Japanese/Noodle Shop   4.3   3.5   4.1 $$

West 50s | 19 W. 52nd St. (bet. 5th & 6th Aves.)
212-489-2525 | www.sobanippon.com

They "**grow their own buckwheat**" to roll the "**authentic**" Japanese noodles at this Midtown soba standout, whose "**personal**" service and "**calm**" atmosphere make it "**perfect for stressed-out afternoons**"; if the decor looks a bit "**worn**", most focus on the "**properly done**" eats.

SOBA TOTTO | Japanese/Noodle Shop   4.5   3.9   4.2 $$$

East 40s | 211 E. 43rd St. (bet. 2nd & 3rd Aves.)
212-557-8200 | www.sobatotto.com

"**Stunning**" housemade soba and "**authentic**" yakitori (but no sushi) beckon Grand Central commuters to this "**dimly lit**" Midtown Japanese where it's a pleasure to "**sit at the bar and watch the charcoal pros work their magic**"; "**popular lunch specials**" seal the deal.

SOBA-YA | Japanese/Noodle Shop   4.3   3.9   4.1 $$

East Village | 229 E. Ninth St. (bet. 2nd & 3rd Aves.)
212-533-6966 | www.sobaya-nyc.com

At this "**low-key**" East Village Japanese, the "**perfectly made**" soba combines "**refreshing broths**" with "**delicious noodles**"; the no-reservations policy can cause "**weekend waits**", but "**affordable**" price tags more than compensate.

SOCARRAT PAELLA BAR | Spanish   4.2   3.7   3.8 $$$

Chelsea | 259 W. 19th St. (bet. 7th & 8th Aves.) | 212-462-1000
East 50s | 953 Second Ave. (bet. 50th & 51st Sts.) | 212-759-0101
NoLita | 284 Mulberry St. (bet. Houston & Prince Sts.) | 212-219-0101
www.socarratnyc.com

These "**low-key**" Spaniards dish up some of the best paella "**this side of Valencia**", along with "**hard-to-resist**" tapas and "**fantastic**" sangria choices;

the Chelsea original is on the "**cramped**" side, but there's more elbow room at the East Midtown and NoLita spin-offs.

SOJOURN | American | 4.1 | 3.8 | 3.9 | $$

East 70s | 244 E. 79th St. (bet. 2nd & 3rd Aves.)
212-537-7745 | www.sojournrestaurant.com

An "**attractive clientele**" frequents this UES American to sample "**creative**" small plates and varied vinos in "**dimly lit**" digs "**with a Downtown feel**"; just "**order carefully**" or the bill may be a "**shock.**"

NEW **SOLOMON & KUFF** | Caribbean | — | — | — | $$

Manhattanville | 2331 12th Ave. (133rd St.)
212-939-9443 | www.solomonandkuff.com

Caribbean food, drink and heritage are celebrated at this Manhattanville spot near the Hudson, where seafood favorites and other island dishes pair with a vast rum selection. The sizable space also hosts DJs who keep the party humming.

SOMTUM DER | Thai | 4.3 | 3.6 | 3.7 | $$

East Village | 85 Ave. A (bet. 4th & 6th Sts.)
212-260-8570 | www.somtumder.com

"**Nuanced**" Thai flavors – from "**subtle**" to "**bold**" to "**knock-your-socks-off spicy**" – mark this "**terrific**" East Village offshoot of a Bangkok eatery, specializing in "**authentic**" dishes from the Isan region; with "**reasonable**" prices and a "**lively**", "**modern**" interior, it's made for groups and "**sharing lots of plates.**"

SONG | Thai | 4.1 | 3.0 | 3.9 | $$

Park Slope | 295 Fifth Ave. (bet. 1st & 2nd Sts.) | Brooklyn
718-965-1108

Park Slopers sing the praises of this "**family-friendly**" Joya sibling, where the "**reliable**" Thai dishes are both "**inexpensive**" and "**generously portioned**"; if the high "**volume of music and chatter**" inside rankles, there's always the "**rear garden.**"

SONS OF ESSEX | American | 3.9 | 3.8 | 3.8 | $$$

Lower East Side | 133 Essex St. (Rivington St.)
212-674-7100 | www.sonsofessexnyc.com

Expect a "**vintage**" vibe – signaled by the "**cool**" delicatessen entrance – at this somewhat "**pricey**" Lower Eastsider; the "**happening bar scene**" threatens to overshadow New American fare that's "**nothing extraordinary**", but most are having too much "**fun**" to notice.

SONS OF THUNDER | Hawaiian/Seafood | ▽ 4.4 | 3.7 | 4.1 | $

Murray Hill | 204 E. 38th St. (bet. 3rd Ave. & Tunnel Exit St.)
646-863-2212 | www.sonsofthunder.com

"**Excellent poke**" hits Murray Hill via this "**fair-priced**" joint offering the Hawaiian specialty in customizable bowls built around salmon, tuna, octopus and tofu; the front counter-service space leads to "**simple seating**" in a "**skylit dining room.**"

SOTO | Japanese | 4.7 | 3.9 | 4.1 | $$$$

West Village | 357 Sixth Ave. (bet. 4th St. & Washington Pl.)
212-414-3088

An "**uni lovers' paradise**" given the many "**novel**" preparations, this tiny West Villager also offers "**sublime**" sushi and other Japanese bites courtesy of chef

Sotohiro Kosugi; the "**spare**" space has a "**serene**" vibe, which can come in handy when the bill arrives.

| **SOTTO 13** | Italian | 4.2 | 4.0 | 4.1 | $$ |

West Village | 140 W. 13th St. (bet. 6th & 7th Aves.)
212-647-1001 | www.sotto13.com

"**Solid in every aspect**", this "**hidden**" West Village Italian fields a small plate–centric menu stressing pasta and pizza; "**friendly**" service and a "**warm**" setting with a "**huge skylight**" burnish its "**cozy**" feel, while a "**sceney**" brunch seals the deal.

| **SPARKS STEAK HOUSE** | Steak | 4.5 | 4.1 | 4.4 | $$$$ |

East 40s | 210 E. 46th St. (bet. 2nd & 3rd Aves.)
212-687-4855 | www.sparkssteakhouse.com

A "**quintessential**" "**NY classic**", this 1966-vintage Midtown "**temple of beef**" "**still shines**" with "**huge**" cuts of "**mouthwatering**" meats and an "**exhaustive**" wine list administered by an "**experienced**" team; "**manly**" – bordering on "**stodgy**" – surrounds and "**power-lunch**" prices are all part of its "**old-world charm.**"

| **SPEEDY ROMEO** | Italian/Pizza | 4.5 | 4.1 | 4.0 | $$ |

NEW **Lower East Side** | 63 Clinton St. (bet. Rivington & Stanton Sts.) | 212-529-6300
Clinton Hill | 376 Classon Ave. (Greene Ave.) | Brooklyn | 718-230-0061
www.speedyromeo.com

Though it's "**tempting**" to stick to the "**amazing**" pizzas, regulars urge you to "**give some love**" to the other "**fantastic**" wood-grilled fare at these "**cool**" Italian kitchens; an "**unpretentious**" staff furthers the "**comfortable**" vibe, so the "**cozy**" setups suit "**kids**" and "**hipsters**" alike.

| **SPICY & TASTY** | Chinese | 4.4 | 3.1 | 3.5 | $$ |

Flushing | 39-07 Prince St. (Roosevelt Ave.) | Queens
718-359-1601 | www.spicyandtasty.com

The "**name says it all**" at this Flushing Chinese where the "**hot, hot, hot**" Sichuan cooking will "**open your sinuses**" but won't scorch your wallet; overlook the "**nonexistent**" decor, no-reservations rule and any "**communication problems**" with the staff – it's "**all about the food**" here.

| **SPIGA** | Italian | 4.2 | 3.6 | 4.1 | $$ |

West 80s | 200 W. 84th St. (bet. Amsterdam Ave. & B'way)
212-362-5506 | www.spiganyc.com

Among the "**best-kept secrets on the UWS**", this "**off-the-beaten-path**" trattoria is a "**tiny sanctuary**" of "**rich**", "**refined**" Italian cooking; OK, the seating's "**tight**" and tabs can run "**a little pricey**", but "**gracious**" service is an "**inviting**" plus.

| **SPOTTED PIG** | European | 4.4 | 3.9 | 3.9 | $$$ |

West Village | 314 W. 11th St. (Greenwich St.)
212-620-0393 | www.thespottedpig.com

A certified "**hot spot**", this West Village gastropub is a "**proven winner**" where nightly "**throngs**" convene for April Bloomfield's "**mouthwatering**" Modern European chow (including a "**killer**" burger) and sporadic "**celeb sightings**"; too bad the "**tight quarters**" are always "**jammed**" and the no-reservations policy makes for "**really long waits.**"

SPRING NATURAL KITCHEN | Health Food   4.1   3.7   3.9 $$
West 80s | 474 Columbus Ave (83rd St.) | 646-596-7434

SPRING NATURAL RESTAURANT | Health Food
NoLita | 98 Kenmare St. (Mulberry Pl.) | 212-966-0290
www.springnaturalkitchen.com

The "**interesting**" health-conscious menu "**covers all the bases**" with "**good, solid**" choices that'll work for "**omnivores, vegans and the gluten-free**"; "**decent**" prices and "**hospitable**" service are other payoffs, and the new NoLita location is especially "**attractive.**"

SPUNTO | Pizza   4.3   3.3   3.9 $$
West Village | 65 Carmine St. (7th Ave. S.)
212-242-1200 | www.spuntothincrust.com

"**Gorgeous thin-crust pizzas**" crowned with "**departure-from-the-usual**" toppings are the calling card of this West Village member of the Posto/Vezzo family; the "**relaxed**" digs are "**rather small**", so many try for the patio – or opt for "**speedy**" delivery.

SRIPRAPHAI | Thai   4.6   3.4   3.7 $$
Woodside | 64-13 39th Ave. (bet. 64th & 65th Sts.) | Queens
718-899-9599 | www.sripraphairestaurant.com

Worth the "**trek on the 7 train**", this Woodside "**holy grail of Thai food**" offers an "**enormous choice**" of "**memorable**" dishes at varied heat levels ("**make sure you really mean it if you ask for 'very spicy'**"); although cash only with "**perfunctory**" service and decor, it's affordable and "**out-of-this-world.**"

STAMATIS | Greek   4.2   3.3   3.8 $$
Astoria | 29-09 23rd Ave. (bet. 29th & 31st Sts.) | Queens
718-932-8596

"**If you can't get to Greece**", this "**well-established**", "**family-oriented**" Astoria taverna provides an "**authentic**" alternative with its "**reliable**" Hellenic cooking; maybe the "**stark**" decor is less transporting, but "**reasonable prices**" take the edge off.

THE STANDARD BIERGARTEN | German   3.7   3.9   3.7 $$
Meatpacking District | 848 Washington St. (bet. 12th & 13th Sts.)
212-645-4100 | www.standardhotels.com

When you want a "**cold beer in a hot spot**", this year-round beer garden under the High Line fills the bill with Bavarian brews, "**decent**" German snacks from Kurt Gutenbrunner (wursts, "**giant pretzels**") and even "**Ping-Pong**"; it's generally "**packed**" and "**noisy**", but fans say the summer scene is "**not to be missed.**"

STANDARD GRILL | American   4.1   4.1   3.9 $$$
Meatpacking District | The Standard Hotel | 848 Washington St. (bet. Little W. 12th & 13th Sts.)
212-645-4100 | www.thestandardgrill.com

A "**happening**" crowd collects at this "**festive**" scene in the Meatpacking's Standard Hotel, drawn by its "**reliably good**" American bites, "**fun people-watching**" and front cafe "**pickup scene**"; still, "**deafening**" decibels and "**shoulder-to-shoulder**" crowds lead some to dub it a "**place more to be seen than fed.**"

	FOOD	DECOR	SERVICE	COST

ST. ANSELM | American/Steak — 4.5   4.0   4.0 $$

Williamsburg | 355 Metropolitan Ave. (4th St.) | Brooklyn
718-384-5054

"Hipster" carnivores "leave smiling" from this "New Age" Williamsburg steakhouse supplying "mind-blowing" naturally raised beef and "excellent" sides in "rustic", brick-lined digs; "modest prices" make up for the "daunting" waits caused by the no-reservations policy, though regulars "kill time" at its neighboring "sister bar", Spuyten Duyvil.

STANTON SOCIAL | American — 4.5   4.2   4.0 $$$$

Lower East Side | 99 Stanton St. (Ludlow St.)
212-995-0099 | www.thestantonsocial.com

"Go with a group" and "order everything" say fans at this LES New American that puts a "creative spin on classic dishes" via "delicious" share plates; the sleek duplex space may "no longer be a place to be seen", but it remains "lively", with an "especially good brunch" and many who "still love the vibe."

STELLA 34 | Italian — 4.1   4.1   4.1 $$$

West 30s | Macy's | 151 W. 34th St. (bet. B'way & 7th Ave.)
212-967-9251 | www.stella34.com

"You forget you're in Macy's" while dining at this "stylish" Midtown "respite" from the Patina Group offering "tasty" pastas, pizzas and other Italian bites (including "don't-miss" gelati) in "airy", "modern" digs; "gorgeous" panoramic views of Herald Square "add to the charm."

STK | Steak — 4.2   4.3   4.0 $$$

Meatpacking District | 26 Little W. 12th St. (bet. 9th Ave. & Washington St.) |
646-624-2444
West 40s | 1114 Sixth Ave. (bet. 42nd & 43rd Sts.) | 646-624-2455
www.stkhouse.com

Rolling a steakhouse and a nightclub into one "slick" package, these "sexy" "scenes" dispense "surprisingly good" beef in "thumping", "lounge"-like settings full of "beautiful people"; pricing is "steep", so "bring the black card" and remember "you're paying for the vibe."

STONE PARK CAFÉ | American — 4.5   4.0   4.3 $$$

Park Slope | 324 Fifth Ave. (3rd St.) | Brooklyn
718-369-0082 | www.stoneparkcafe.com

Locally prized as a "culinary gem", this "charming" Park Slope New American owes its "popularity" to a "creatively prepared" menu "backed up by an informed staff"; the "casual but elevated" style extends to a "spectacular brunch" – "if you can get in."

STRAND SMOKEHOUSE | BBQ — 4.1   3.8   3.5 $

Astoria | 25-27 Broadway (bet. Crescent & 29th Sts.) | Queens
718-440-3231 | www.thestrandsmokehouse.com

"Solid" smokehouse eats are accompanied by craft suds at this "hip" Astoria BBQ where live bands on weekends provide a "raucous" soundtrack; the sprawling, counter-service setting lies somewhere between a "cafeteria" and a "glorified college beer hall."

STREETBIRD | Chicken — 3.8   4.1   3.8 $

Harlem | 2149 Frederick Douglass Blvd. (bet. 115th & 116th Sts.)
212-206-2557 | www.streetbirdnyc.com

"Delicious" rotisserie chicken is the "highlight" of Marcus Samuelsson's "**funky**" Harlem hangout, where "**solid**" soul-inspired fare comes in a space that will "**knock your hip-hop socks off**" thanks to boom boxes, graffiti and other "**nostalgia**" nods; if a few were "**expecting more**", the "**reasonable**" tabs get no complaints.

STRIP HOUSE | Steak   4.4   4.2   4.3 $$$$
Greenwich Village | 13 E. 12th St. (bet. 5th Ave. & University Pl.) | 212-328-0000
West 40s | 15 W. 44th St. (bet. 5th & 6th Aves.) | 212-336-5454
www.striphouse.com

STRIP HOUSE NEXT DOOR | Steak
Greenwich Village | 11 E. 12th St., downstairs (bet. 5th Ave. & University Pl.) | 212-838-9197 | www.striphousegrill.com

"**Sultry**", red-velvet decor provides the backdrop for "**off-the-charts delicious**" beef and "**amazing**" sides at these "**sexy**" steakhouses where "**expertly mixed**" cocktails help fuel an "**animated crowd**"; you'll need a "**fat wallet**", but service is "**attentive**", and it all makes for one "**darn good**" meal.

STUMPTOWN COFFEE ROASTERS | Coffee   4.0   3.6   3.8 $
Greenwich Village | 30 W. Eighth St. (MacDougal St.) | 855-711-3385
NoMad | Ace Hotel | 18 W. 29th St. (B'way) | 855-711-3385
www.stumptowncoffee.com

Experience a "**fine array**" of "**third-wave West Coast coffee**" at these Portland outposts brewing "**hipster**" java from "**meticulously selected**", "**freshly roasted**" beans; sure, "**endless crowds**" come with the territory, but the baristas keep the "**line moving fast.**"

SUGAR FREAK | Cajun/Creole   4.1   3.9   4.0 $$
Astoria | 36-18 30th Ave. (37th St.) | Queens
718-726-5850 | www.sugarfreak.com

A change of pace on the busy 30th Avenue strip, this "**bit of N'Awlins in Astoria**" traffics in "**real-deal**" Cajun-Creole favorites, "**kickass cocktails**" and "**desserts that'll make a sugar freak out of anyone**"; "**friendly service**" and "**kitschy-cute**" decor with a "**DIY feel**" seal the deal.

SULLIVAN STREET BAKERY | Bakery   4.5   3.4   3.9 $
Chelsea | 236 Ninth Ave. (bet. 24th & 25th Sts.) | 212-929-5900
West 40s | 533 W. 47th St. (bet. 10th & 11th Aves.) | 212-265-5580
www.sullivanstreetbakery.com

The "**outrageously good**" bread ("**crusty**" loaves, "**worth-a-detour**" olive rolls) tastes like it was "**baked by angels**" at Jim Lahey's bakeries, where "**top-notch**" offerings also include "**delicious**" thin-crust pizza and Italian pastries; though mostly for grab-and-go, the Chelsea locale has seating and an expanded menu of light bites.

SUNDAES & CONES | Ice Cream   ∇ 4.5   3.7   4.2 $
Greenwich Village | 95 E. 10th St. (3rd Ave.)
212-979-9398 | www.sundaescones.com

Some of "**the creamiest**" classic scoops can be found at this Greenwich Village parlor, but "**if you're feeling gutsy**", the more "**creative**" Asian-influenced flavors are "**delicious**" too; "**super-generous**" portions, along with "**friendly**" staffers (and prices) make the experience even sweeter.

	FOOD	DECOR	SERVICE	COST

NEW SUPERCROWN COFFEE | Coffee — — — $
ROASTERS

Bushwick | 8 Wilson Ave. (bet. Flushing Ave. & Noll St.) | Brooklyn
347-295-3161 | www.supercrown.coffee

From the founder of Gorilla Coffee, this Bushwick roaster and cafe offers espressos, pour-overs and other carefully brewed cups in a big, skylit space with roasting machinery on view. Collaborating with Roberta's, it serves a signature Magic Bialy plus pastries from local purveyors.

SUPERIORITY BURGER | Burgers/Vegetarian 4.4 3.1 3.9 $

East Village | 430 E. Ninth St. (Ave. A)
212-256-1192 | www.superiorityburger.com

"**Tiny place, huge taste**" sums up this East Village vegetarian where Brooks Headley has caused a craze – and "**long lines**" – with his "**famed**" veggie burgers; a handful of other items ("**interesting**" sides, "**special trip**" gelato) are available too, but since there are "**hardly any seats**" plan to take it to go.

SUPPER | Italian 4.3 3.6 3.8 $$$

East Village | 156 E. Second St. (bet. Aves. A & B)
212-477-7600 | www.supperrestaurant.com

This "**unpretentious**" East Villager from the Frank crew is a local "**favorite**" for "**homestyle**" Northern Italian fare; despite "**tight**" communal tables, "**long waits**" and a cash-only policy, the "**rustic**" digs are "**always bustling.**"

SUSHIDEN | Japanese 4.3 3.7 4.2 $$$

East 40s | 19 E. 49th St. (bet. 5th & Madison Aves.) | 212-758-2700
West 40s | 123 W. 49th St. (bet. 6th & 7th Aves.) | 212-398-2800
www.sushiden.com

Frequented by a Midtown "**business crowd**", these "**no-frills**" Japanese "**standbys**" provide "**traditional**" sushi and sashimi in "**serene**" settings; "**attentive**" service compensates for the "**wallet-capturing**" tabs, though they're decidedly cheaper than "**going to Tokyo.**"

SUSHI DOJO | Japanese 4.4 3.6 4.0 $$

East Village | 110 First Ave. (bet. 6th & 7th Sts.)
646-692-9398 | www.sushidojonyc.com

Though many "**miss**" founding chef David Bouhadana, this small East Village Japanese is still one of the "**best omakase values in NYC**", offering "**sublime**" sushi made with "**fresh**" fish at "**bang for the buck**" pricing; the only downside are "**underwhelming**" digs.

NEW SUSHI GANSO | Japanese — — — $$$

Downtown Brooklyn | 31 Third Ave. (bet. Atlantic Ave. & State St.) | Brooklyn
646-927-1776 | www.gansonyc.com

Next door to Ganso Yaki in Downtown Brooklyn, this sushi specialist offers Tokyo-style nigiri and sashimi (with housemade soy sauce), as well as Japanese small plates and salads. The space features thoughtfully designed woodwork and a striking mural of a sea bream by Momoyo Torimitsu.

NEW SUSHI GINZA ONODERA | Japanese — — — $$$$

East 40s | 461 Fifth Ave. (40th St.)
212-390-0925 | www.onodera-group.com

This extremely high-end Midtown branch of a Tokyo-based restaurant group serves an omakase-only sushi menu – with most of the fish flown in from

Tsukiji market – in a pared-down yet earthy setting with a wooden sushi counter and table seating.

SUSHI NAKAZAWA | Japanese   4.7   4.3   4.7 $$$$

West Village | 23 Commerce St. (bet. Bedford St. & 7th Ave. S.)
212-924-2212 | www.sushinakazawa.com

The "**ultimate showstopper**" from "**sushi master**" Daisuke Nakazawa, this "**extraordinary**" West Village Japanese specializes in "**breathtaking**" omakase meals served like "**a well-oiled machine**" at the bar and in a "**serene**" dining room; scoring reservations remains a "**difficult task**" and the cost is "**off the charts**", but an attached lounge should help on both fronts.

SUSHI OF GARI | Japanese   4.6   3.5   4.2 $$$$

East 70s | 402 E. 78th St. (bet. 1st & York Aves.) | 212-517-5340
TriBeCa | 130 W. Broadway (Duane St.) | 212-285-0130
West 40s | 347 W. 46th St. (bet. 8th & 9th Aves.) | 212-957-0046
West 70s | 370 Columbus Ave. (bet. 77th & 78th Sts.) | 212-362-4816
www.sushiofgari.com

The "**out-of-body**" omakase experience "**never fails to amaze**" at these Japanese "**standard-bearers**" from Gari Sugio, long known for their "**sublime bites**" of "**imaginative sushi**"; the "**cramped**" quarters and "**plain decor**" are less impressive, but regulars advise "**just open your wallet**" and "**eat at the bar.**"

SUSHISAMBA | Brazilian/Japanese   4.1   3.9   4.0 $$$

West Village | 87 Seventh Ave. S. (Barrow St.)
212-691-7885 | www.sushisamba.com

"**Youthful**" types favor this "**upbeat**" West Village standby for its "**Interesting**" Brazilian-Japanese fusion fare and "**wonderful**" cocktails (if not its "**premium prices**"); the "**bright and cheery**" interior is usually "**bustling**", and the rooftop is an extra "**treat.**"

SUSHI SEKI | Japanese   4.6   3.6   4.1 $$$$

Chelsea | 208 W. 23rd St. (bet. 7th & 8th Aves.) | 212-255-5988
East 60s | 1143 First Ave. (bet. 62nd & 63rd Sts.) | 212-371-0238
West 40s | 365 W. 46th St. (9th Ave.) | 212-262-8880
www.sushiseki.com

Renowned for its "**extraordinary**" omakase showcasing "**beyond-fresh**" fish, this "**spendy**" Japanese mini-chain slices "**spot-on**" sushi that's "**lovely to behold**"; though the settings can feel "**somewhat lacking in charm**", the bi-level Hell's Kitchen flagship has "**significantly better**" decor plus a "**fancy**" whiskey bar.

SUSHI SEN-NIN | Japanese   4.4   3.7   4.1 $$

Murray Hill | 30 E. 33rd St. (bet. Madison & Park Aves.)
212-889-2208 | www.sushisennin.com

Although a "**neighborhood favorite**", this Murray Hill Japanese remains an "**under-the-radar**" source of "**knee-knocking**" sushi at prices "**accessible**" enough for "**semi-regular**" dining; "**smiling**" service and recently spiffed-up digs add extra incentive.

SUSHI YASUDA | Japanese   4.8   4.2   4.4 $$$$

East 40s | 204 E. 43rd St. (bet. 2nd & 3rd Aves.)
212-972-1001 | www.sushiyasuda.com

"**Sushi of your dreams**" awaits at this "**hidden jewel**" near Grand Central, where disciples of the namesake master chef craft "**heavenly**" traditional cuts in a "**spare, Zen**" setting run by an "**efficiently courteous**" crew; "**the price matches the quality**", so "**be ready to spend a bundle**" – especially if you "**go for omakase**" at the bar.

NEW SUSHI ZO | Japanese   —   —   — $$$$

Greenwich Village | 88 W. Third St. (Sullivan St.)
646-405-4826 | www.sushizo.us

This LA import in the Village from top-tier sushi chef Keizo Seki showcases the day's catches with an omakase-only format in which trust is paramount (i.e. don't ask for soy sauce if it isn't presented). Behind the light-wood bar, an exposed-brick wall adorned with tree branches provides a simple, attractive backdrop to the high-end meal.

SWEET CHICK | Southern   4.3   3.7   4.0 $$

Lower East Side | 178 Ludlow St. (Houston St.) | 646-657-0233
Williamsburg | 164 Bedford Ave. (N. 8th St.) | Brooklyn | 347-725-4793
www.sweetchicknyc.com

"**Quirky**" takes on Southern staples – think "**creative chicken 'n' waffle combos**" – and "**seasonal**" cocktails make these "**droolworthy**" eateries "**excellent places to indulge**"; they get "**jam-packed**" at prime times, but "**friendly**" staffers help keep the feel "**fun.**"

SWEETGREEN | Health Food   4.4   3.5   3.8 $

Flatiron | 8 E. 18th St. (bet. B'way & 5th Ave.) | 646-692-3131
NEW Greenwich Village | 10 Astor Pl. (bet. B'way & Lafayette St.) | 646-692-3112
NEW Meatpacking District | 32 Gansevoort St. (Hudson St.) | 646-891-5100
NoLita | 100 Kenmare St. (Cleveland Pl.) | 646-964-5012
NoMad | 1164 Broadway (27th St.) | 646-449-8884
TriBeCa | 413 Greenwich St. (Hubert St.) | 646-922-8572
Williamsburg | 162 N. Fourth St. (bet. Bedford & Driggs Aves.) | Brooklyn | 347-987-3863
www.sweetgreen.com

A "**salad lover's delight**", this "**cheerful**" counter-serve chain tosses up "**super-delicious**" locally sourced ingredients in its "**crave**"-worthy greens; lines can be "**daunting**" and tabs "**expensive**", but true-blue fans agree it's "**worth all the hoopla.**"

SYLVIA'S | Soul Food/Southern   3.9   3.5   3.8 $$

Harlem | 328 Malcolm X Blvd. (bet. 126th & 127th Sts.)
212-996-0660 | www.sylviasrestaurant.com

A "**true icon of Harlem**", this circa-1962 soul food "**mainstay**" warms hearts with "**generous**" helpings of Southern classics and a "**rocking**" Sunday gospel brunch; old-timers say it's "**not what it used to be**" but allow it's still "**worth a visit**", as the "**tour buses out front**" suggest.

NEW SYNDICATED | American   —   —   — $$

Bushwick | 40 Bogart St. (Thames St.) | Brooklyn
718-386-3399 | www.syndicatedbk.com

This combination American restaurant, bar and movie theater in Bushwick serves burgers, sandwiches and crowd-pleasers like loaded tater tots, along with cocktails and seasonal beers. Separate from the dining area (but with its own menu), the 50-seat screening room shows a couple of films each night, often curated according to director or other themes.

	FOOD	DECOR	SERVICE	COST

SZECHUAN GOURMET | Chinese ⟶ 4.2   3.2   3.7 $$
East 70s | 1395 Second Ave. (bet. 72nd & 73rd Sts.) | 212-737-1838 |
www.szechuanchaletnyc.com
West 30s | 21 W. 39th St. (bet. 5th & 6th Aves.) | 212-921-0233 |
www.szechuan-gourmet.com
West 50s | 242 W. 56th St. (bet. B'way & 8th Ave.) | 212-265-2226 |
www.szechuangourmet56nyc.com
West 100s | 239 W. 105th St. (B'way) | 212-865-8808
Flushing | 135-15 37th Ave. (bet. Main & Prince Sts.) | Queens | 718-888-9388 |
www.szechuangourmetnyc.com

"**If you can take the heat**", head for these "**real Sichuans**" where the "**fiery**"
Chinese fare appeals to "**adventurous**" palates seeking "**unusual dishes**";
although the somewhat "**tired**" decor isn't nearly as sizzling, "**low prices**" and
"**fast**" takeout are pluses.

TABLE D'HÔTE | American/French ⟶ 4.4   3.7   4.2 $$$
East 90s | 44 E. 92nd St. (bet. Madison & Park Aves.)
212-348-8125 | www.tabledhote.info

Those "**unable to take that trip to Paris**" rely on this Carnegie Hill
"**tradition**" (since 1978) for an "**engaging**" French-American lineup served in
"**neighborly**" confines; given the très "**petite**" dimensions, however, consider
packing a "**shoehorn.**"

TABOON | Mediterranean/Mideastern ⟶ 4.5   3.9   4.2 $$$
West 50s | 773 10th Ave. (52nd St.)
212-713-0271 | www.taboononline.com

"**Consistently fantastic**", this "**popular**" Hell's Kitchen "**keeper**" provides
"**interesting**" Med–Middle Eastern cooking highlighted by "**extraordinary**"
bread "**fresh**" out of the namesake clay oven; if it's a "**bit pricey**", it's still
"**lovely for a pre-theater dinner.**"

TACI'S BEYTI | Turkish ⟶ 4.6   3.5   4.2 $$
Sheepshead Bay | 1955 Coney Island Ave (bet. Ave. P & Quentin Rd.) |
Brooklyn
718-627-5750 | www.tacisbeyti.com

In a refreshingly "**hipster-free corner of Brooklyn**", this long-standing Turk is
a Sheepshead Bay "**favorite**" for "**huge portions**" of "**delicious**" classics,
including "**juicy**" kebabs; the staff "**couldn't be nicer**", ditto the prices, so
never mind if the atmosphere is "**nothing special.**"

TACOMBI | Mexican ⟶ 4.1   4.0   3.8 $$
NoLita | 267 Elizabeth St. (bet. Houston & Prince Sts.) | 917-727-0179
West Village | 255 Bleecker St. (Cornelia St.) | 646-964-5984

TACOMBI CAFE EL PRESIDENTE | Mexican
Flatiron | Cafe El Presidente | 30 W. 24th St. (bet. 5th & 6th Aves.) |
212-242-3491
www.tacombi.com

These "**chill**" Mexican joints offer "**tasty**" tacos with "**big flavor**" in digs that
evoke a "**vacation in the Yucatán**"; the "**fun**" NoLita location stands out with
a "**cool, old VW van**" parked inside, but the others are just as "**lively**", and all
are "**reasonably priced.**"

	FOOD	DECOR	SERVICE	COST

TACUBA | Mexican   4.3 3.9 4.0 $$
West 50s | 802 Ninth Ave. (53rd St.) | 212-245-4500
Astoria | 35-01 36th St. (35th Ave.) | Queens | 718-786-2727
www.tacubanyc.com

Chef Julian Medina (Toloache, Yerba Buena) has some "**fun**" with these "**cool**"
Mexicans where highlights include "**excellent**" guac, "**interesting**" tacos and
"**killer**" margaritas; a "**festive**" crowd and "**spacious**" digs make them well
suited to "**group**" outings.

TAÏM | Israeli/Vegetarian   4.6 3.1 3.6 $
NoLita | 45 Spring St. (Mulberry St.) | 212-219-0600
West Village | 222 Waverly Pl. (bet. 11th & Perry Sts.) | 212-691-1287
www.taimfalafel.com

"**Fresh and fabulous**" falafel is "**the really real thing**" at chef Einat Admony's
hole-in-the-wall" Israeli joints, where "**glorious**" eats at "**gentle prices**"
are "**a vegetarian's dream come true**"; they're both "**fast**" and "**satisfying**", though
the West Village original's "**vest-pocket**" space means it's "**best to take away.**"

TAKAHACHI | Japanese   4.4 3.6 4.2 $$
East Village | 85 Ave. A (bet. 4th & 6th Sts.) | 212-505-6524
TriBeCa | 145 Duane St. (bet. B 'way & Church St.) | 212-571-1830
www.takahachi.net

"**Creative sushi**" and "**excellent**" Japanese home-cooking basics at a
favorable "**quality-to-price ratio**" earn these neighborhood spots "**favorite**"
status; a "**helpful**" staff adds warmth to the "**nothing-fancy**" setups, which
"**bustle**" at prime times.

TAKASHI | Japanese   4.6 3.8 4.1 $$$
West Village | 456 Hudson St. (bet. Barrow & Morton Sts.)
212-414-2929 | www.takashinyc.com

"**Adventurous**" eaters head to this West Village Japanese to grill "**insanely
good**" classic meats on tabletop BBQs, along with some "**crazy**" options
(intestines, calf's brains); on weekends, it adds "**out-of-this-world**" "**late-night
ramen**" to the mix.

TAKE ROOT | American   —   —   — $$$$
Carroll Gardens | 187 Sackett St. (bet. Henry & Hicks Sts.) | Brooklyn
347-227-7116 | www.take-root.com

Open Thursday–Saturday for one seating only, this "**tiny**" Carroll Gardens
American offers a "**seasonally changing**" tasting menu for a "**special-
occasion**" $125 set price; the simple, 12-seat space feels like an "**intimate**"
dinner party, albeit one that can be reserved 30 days in advance online.

TALDE | Asian   4.4 4.0 4.1 $$$
Park Slope | 369 Seventh Ave. (bet. 30th & 31st Sts.) | Brooklyn
347-916-0031 | www.taldebrooklyn.com

A "**seriously good**" Pan-Asian menu with a "**playful sensibility**" (e.g. the
"**fantastic**" pretzel pork dumplings) makes Dale Talde's Park Slope namesake
a "**hip**" neighborhood destination; reservations are now taken, but if there's a
wait, it's best spent sipping "**nifty**" cocktails from the bar.

TAMARIND | Indian   4.7 4.6 4.5 $$$
TriBeCa | 99 Hudson St. (bet. Franklin & Harrison Sts.)
212-775-9000 | www.tamarindrestaurantsnyc.com

The "**delight factor**" is high at this "**stylish**" TriBeCa stalwart whose

"**exquisite**" modern Indian cooking is served up in "**gorgeous**", bi-level digs where "**attentive waiters hover discreetly**"; yes, it's "**pricey**", but the "**plentiful**" prix fixe lunch is a "**bargain.**"

TANG PAVILION | Chinese   4.2   3.8   4.0 $$

West 50s | 65 W. 55th St. (bet. 5th & 6th Aves.)
212-956-6888 | www.tangpavilionnyc.com

"**Worthwhile**" traditional Shanghai cooking makes this "**sophisticated**" Midtown Chinese a "**top choice**" near City Center and Carnegie Hall; maybe its once-"**classy**" decor is "**getting a little frayed**", but the service remains "**polished**" and prices are as "**reasonable**" as ever.

TANOREEN | Mediterranean/Mideastern   4.7   4.1   4.4 $$

Bay Ridge | 7523 Third Ave. (76th St.) | Brooklyn
718-748-5600 | www.tanoreen.com

"**Complex flavors abound**" in the "**breathtaking**" Med–Middle Eastern dishes at this Bay Ridge "**local gem**", where chef Rawia Bishara's "**pride shows**" as she "**works the room**" alongside the "**skilled**" staff; the "**warm and hospitable**" room is typically "**packed – and that says it all.**"

TANOSHI SUSHI | Japanese   4.6   3.0   4.2 $$$

East 70s | 1372 York Ave. (bet. 73rd & 74th Sts.)
917-265-8254 | www.tanoshisushinyc.com

Known for "**fantastic**" omakase-only meals at "**bang-for-the-buck**" prices, this "**hole-in-the-wall**" Yorkville Japanese racks up the "**wows**" with an "**excellent assortment of fish and preparations**"; yes, the "**no-frills**" seating is "**tight**", but the BYO policy is a "**nice bonus.**"

TAO | Asian   4.3   4.6   4.1 $$$

East 50s | 42 E. 58th St. (bet. Madison & Park Aves.) | 212-888-2288 |
www.taorestaurant.com

TAO DOWNTOWN | Asian

Chelsea | Maritime Hotel | 92 Ninth Ave. (bet. 16th & 17th Sts.) |
212-888-2724 | www.taodowntown.com

Still "**delivering the wow factor**", these "**dramatic**" Pan-Asians feature "**mega-sized**" Buddhas anchoring "**impressive**", soaring spaces where attractions include "**imaginative**" food and cocktails and a chance "**to be seen**"; count on "**pulsing music**" and a "**vivacious**" "**scene**" that'll distract from the "**high-end**" tabs.

🆕 TAPESTRY | Indian   —   —   — $$$

West Village | 60 Greenwich Ave. (Perry St.)
212-373-8900 | www.tapestryrestaurant.com

Celebrated chef/co-owner Suvir Saran draws on his native Indian cuisine as well as global flavors at this modern West Village spot. Whitewashed brick walls and gridded woodwork provide a simple backdrop for the colorful, inventive plates, while a front bar adds to the nighttime energy.

TARTINE | French   4.2   3.4   3.7 $$

West Village | 253 W. 11th St. (4th St.)
212-229-2611 | www.tartinecafenyc.com

At this cash-only West Village bistro, "**delectable**" French basics and a "**could-be-in-Paris**" vibe come at an "**affordable**" price, helped along by the BYO policy; "**long waits**" are common, and since the "**teeny**" space can be "**tight**", regulars try for one of the sidewalk tables.

	FOOD	DECOR	SERVICE	COST

TASTY HAND-PULLED | Noodle Shop 4.3 2.4 3.2 $
NOODLES

Chinatown | 1 Doyers St. (Bowery)
212-791-1817 | www.tastyhandpullednoodlesnyc.com

Soups brimming with "**springy, chewy**" noodles and "**excellent**" dumplings are the stars at this Chinatown "**hole-in-the-wall**"; "**cheap**" tabs – plus a view of the chefs at work "**slamming and pulling**" dough – help distract from the seriously "**sketchy**" decor.

TAVERNA KYCLADES | Greek/Seafood 4.5 3.4 3.9 $$

East Village | 228 First Ave. (bet. 13th & 14th Sts.) | 212-432-0010
Astoria | 33-07 Ditmars Blvd. (33rd St.) | Queens | 718-545-8666
www.tavernakyclades.com

The "**excellently prepared**" fish and seafood ("**especially the octopus**") are "**the name of the game**" at these "**no-frills**" tavernas where "**traditional**" Greek specialties are "**delicious**" too; "**huge**" portions add "**value**", and while no reservations can make for "**painful**" waits, they're "**packed**" for a reason.

TAVERN ON THE GREEN | American 3.6 4.4 3.8 $$

Central Park | Central Park W. (bet. 66th & 67th Sts.)
212-877-8684 | www.tavernonthegreen.com

A Central Park "**landmark**", this "**storied**" American has a "**delightfully updated**" rustic interior and a "**splendid**" tree-lined courtyard; it may be a "**tourist**" magnet with "**serviceable**" food that "**doesn't soar as high as the prices**", but it's "**worth checking out**" for an experience that's "**so very NYC.**"

TAVOLA | Italian 4.3 3.9 4.1 $$$

West 30s | 488 Ninth Ave. (bet. 37th & 38th Sts.)
212-273-1181 | www.tavolahellskitchen.com

A "**great Hell's Kitchen find**", this "**casual**" Italian offers "**delicious**" Neapolitan pizzas, alongside "**well-prepared**" pastas and wood-fired specialties; yep, the "**small**" space can get "**loud**", but given the reasonable prices, there's "**no wonder it's always so busy.**"

T-BAR STEAK & LOUNGE | Steak 4.1 3.8 4.0 $$$

East 70s | 1278 Third Ave. (73rd St.)
212-772-0404 | www.tbarnyc.com

"**Lively**" and "**welcoming**", this "**rock-steady**" UES steakhouse via Tony Fortuna is "**where the locals go**" for "**well-prepared**" beef at "**serious but acceptable prices**"; just expect some "**noise**" and "**watch out for the cougars at the bar.**"

TEA & SYMPATHY | Teahouse 4.2 3.9 4.1 $$

West Village | 108 Greenwich Ave. (Jane St.)
212-989-9735 | www.teaandsympathynewyork.com

"**Get your Brit on**" at this "**tiny**" West Village teahouse where English "**comfort food**" arrives on "**charmingly varied china**"; "**helpful**"-but-"**cheeky**" service is a "**hallmark**", ditto the "**long wait**", but there's no doubt it's the "**perfect place for afternoon tea.**"

NEW **TEISUI** | Japanese — — — $$$$

NoMad | 246 Fifth Ave. (28th St.)
917-388-3596 | www.teisui.nyc

Sibling to a traditional inn (ryokan) in Japan, this NoMad Japanese serves a high-end yakitori tasting menu as well as a sushi course, with optional wine or sake pairings. Textured wood, brick and stone bring natural elements indoors, where the sleek bar wraps around the open kitchen and offers a less costly prix fixe option.

NEW TEKOÁ | Coffee   —   —   — $$

Cobble Hill | 264 Clinton St. (Verandah Pl.) | Brooklyn
347-987-3710 | www.tekoany.com

From the team behind near-neighbor La Vara (as well as Txikito and El Quinto Pino), this Cobble Hill coffee shop offers sandwiches, salads and breakfast bites with Mediterranean, Latin and Spanish accents in a space with a light palette and a smattering of indoor and outdoor tables.

TELLY'S TAVERNA | Greek/Seafood   4.4   3.8   4.1 $$

Astoria | 28-13 23rd Ave. (bet. 28th & 29th Sts.) | Queens
718-728-9056 | www.tellytaverna.com

"**Simple perfection**" via the "**freshest**" grilled fish is yours at this "**old-time**" Astoria Greek taverna, where the "**not-fancy**" setting is "**large**", "**relaxing**" and overseen by a "**friendly, never-rushed**" staff; factor in "**fair prices**", and no wonder it's a hands-down local "**favorite.**"

TEMPURA MATSUI | Japanese   4.6   4.5   4.6 $$$$

Murray Hill | 222 E. 39th St. (Tunnel Exit St.)
212-986-8885 | www.tempuramatsui.com

Tempura goes "**high-end**" at this Murray Hill Japanese presenting omakase menus starring "**deliciously delicate**" battered seafood and vegetables, along with small plates such as sashimi, presented in "**a lovely progression**" by "**gracious**" servers; "**expensive**" tabs match the "**elegant**" (albeit "**small**") space featuring a chef's counter and booths.

TENZAN | Japanese   4.1   3.4   3.8 $$

East 50s | 988 Second Ave. (bet. 52nd & 53rd Sts.) | 212-980-5900
East 80s | 1714 Second Ave. (89th St.) | 212-369-3600 |
www.tenzansushi89.com
West 70s | 285 Columbus Ave. (73rd St.) | 212-580-7300
Bensonhurst | 7117 18th Ave. (72nd St.) | Brooklyn | 718-621-3238

These "**neighborhood staples**" turn out "**solid sushi**" and other "**basic but tasty**" Japanese fare at a "**bang-for-your-buck**" price point; since the decor's "**nothing to write home about**", it's no surprise that they're "**go-to**" picks for delivery.

TERTULIA | Spanish   4.2   3.7   3.8 $$

West Village | 359 Sixth Ave. (Washington Pl.)
646-559-9909 | www.tertulianyc.com

Inspired by cider houses in Northern Spain, this West Villager from chef Seamus Mullen is a "**neighborhood standby**" for "**interesting**" tapas, "**delicious**" paella and cured meats; the "**cozy**", brick-walled space can host a "**happening**" scene, especially during its oyster happy hour.

TESSA | Mediterranean   4.3   4.1   4.2 $$

West 70s | 349 Amsterdam Ave. (bet. 76th & 77th Sts.)
212-390-1974 | www.tessanyc.com

A "**well-conceived**" menu of "**beautifully prepared**" grilled dishes and "**scrumptious pastas**" served by "**personable**" servers brings Upper Westsiders to this "**buzzy**" Mediterranean; though the "**dark**", industrial-chic dining room can be "**noisy**", locals dub it a "**keeper.**"

	FOOD	DECOR	SERVICE	COST

THAI MARKET | Thai — 4.3 3.7 3.8 $$

West 100s | 960 Amsterdam Ave. (bet. 107th & 108th Sts.)
212-280-4575 | www.thaimarketny.net

"**Authentic**" dishes that go way "**beyond pad Thai**" mean this "**no-frills**" UWS Thai "**fills up quick**" at prime times; the "**funky**" decor evokes "**street carts in Bangkok**", as do the "**reasonable**" prices – no surprise, it's a hit with the "**college crowd.**"

THALASSA | Greek/Seafood — 4.5 4.6 4.4 $$$

TriBeCa | 179 Franklin St. (bet. Greenwich & Hudson Sts.)
212-941-7661 | www.thalassanyc.com

"**Delicious upscale Greek dining**" with an emphasis on "**perfectly cooked**" seafood is offered in a "**gorgeous, expansive**" space with a "**floating on the Mediterranean**" feel at this TriBeCa standby; add in an "**incredible**" Hellenic wine list and "**even the gods of Mount Olympus would be pleased.**"

THALIA | American — 4.0 4.0 4.0 $$$

West 40s | 828 Eighth Ave. (50th St.)
212-399-4444 | www.restaurantthalia.com

A "**pre-show standby**", this "**reliable**" Theater District vet offers "**solid**", "**well-priced**" American fare delivered by "**pleasant**" staffers who ensure that you'll "**make your show**" on time; its "**lively crowd**" can kick up some "**noise**", but that comes with the "**friendly atmosphere.**"

THELEWALA | Indian — ∇ 4.4 3.1 3.6 $

Greenwich Village | 112 MacDougal St. (bet. Bleecker & 3rd Sts.)
212-614-9100 | www.thelewalany.com

Those seeking a "**cheap**", "**fresh**" bite make for this "**tiny**" Village "**nook**", where the "**beyond-delicious**" chaats, rolls and other Indian street faves are "**assertively spiced**" and offered into the wee hours; given its basic counter-serve setup with limited seating, many opt for takeout.

THIRD RAIL COFFEE | Coffee — ∇ 4.3 3.9 4.1 $

East Village | 159 Second Ave. (10th St.) | 646-580-1240
Greenwich Village | 240 Sullivan St. (3rd St.) | 646-580-1240
www.thirdrailcoffee.com

"**They take coffee seriously**" at these "**high-end**" cross-Village java shops that "**pack in the people**" with "**robust**" brews "**perfectly prepared**" by "**well-trained**" baristas who "**care deeply about your cup**" of joe; they're "**tight**" on space but still manage a "**relaxing, inviting**" vibe.

TÍA POL | Spanish — 4.4 3.4 4.0 $$$

Chelsea | 205 10th Ave. (bet. 22nd & 23rd Sts.)
212-675-8805 | www.tiapol.com

You "**could be in Barcelona**" at this "**tiny**" West Chelsea Spaniard, a neighborhood "**favorite**" for "**terrific**" tapas matched with a "**wonderful Spain-based wine list**"; it's a "**loud**", "**buzzing**" scene packed into "**very intimate digs**", but "**if you can squeeze in you won't be sorry.**"

TIELLA | Italian — 4.4 3.7 4.2 $$$

East 60s | 1109 First Ave. (bet. 60th & 61st Sts.)
212-588-0100 | www.tiellanyc.com

"**Tiny and special**", this "**hidden gem**" near the Queensboro Bridge fields "**superb**" takes on Neapolitan fare, notably its "**fabulous**" namesake mini-pizzas and "**homemade pastas**"; though the "**railway car–like**" setting can feel "**cramped**" at the dinner hour, insiders say it's "**more relaxed at lunch.**"

TILDA ALL DAY | Coffee ∇ 4.4 4.5 4.3 $

Clinton Hill | 930 Fulton St. (St. James Pl.) | Brooklyn
718-622-4300 | www.tildaallday.com

"**More than a coffee shop**", this "**bright**", "**airy**" Clinton Hill cafe offers a "**dreamy**" roster of "**delectable**" housemade pastries, sandwiches and other light bites for breakfast and lunch; java, craft beers and brunch-style cocktails boost the "**warm-hearted**" vibe.

TIMNA | Mediterranean ∇ 4.4 3.9 4.0 $$

East Village | 109 St. Marks Pl. (bet. Ave. A & 1st Ave.)
646-964-5181 | www.timna.nyc

Mediterranean fare gets a "**totally satisfying**" update with modern ingredients and "**inventive**", Middle East–inspired twists at this "**relaxed**" East Villager; the "**intimate setting**" and "**attentive service**" work equally well for "**a date night or a night out with friends.**"

TINY'S | American 4.1 4.0 3.8 $$

TriBeCa | 135 W. Broadway (bet. Duane & Thomas Sts.)
212-374-1135 | www.tinysnyc.com

This "**cool**" TriBeCan from nightlife czar Matt Abramcyk is indeed "**tiny**", but its "**rustic, bohemian**" interior tilts more "**cute**" than "**cramped**"; its equally compact American menu stars a "**to-die-for kale salad**", while upstairs the "**energetic, dark bar**" dispenses "**fun**" cocktails and nibbles.

TIPSY PARSON | Southern 3.9 3.8 3.8 $$

Chelsea | 156 Ninth Ave. (bet. 19th & 20th Sts.)
212-620-4545 | www.tipsyparson.com

You'll feel like you've "**traveled to the Old South**" at this "**laid-back**" Chelsea "**find**" near the High Line where the Southern grub is "**seriously decadent**"; "**delicious**" cocktails are another plus, so even if it's "**just OK**", it's still "**fun**" for happy hour.

TOBY'S ESTATE COFFEE | Coffee 4.1 3.9 3.7 $

Flatiron | 160 Fifth Ave. (bet. 20th & 21st Sts.) | 646-559-0161
West Village | 44 Charles St. (7th Ave.) | 646-590-1924
Williamsburg | 125 N. Sixth St. (bet. Bedford Ave. & Berry St.) | Brooklyn | 347-457-6160
www.tobysestate.com

When "**in need of a pick-me-up**", fans turn to these "**hipster**"-friendly cafes, links in an Australian chain providing "**smooth**" coffee made from single-origin, house-roasted beans plus light bites; they're "**zoos**" at prime hours, but the "**people-watching**" is solid.

TOCQUEVILLE | American/French 4.8 4.7 4.6 $$$$

Flatiron | 1 E. 15th St. (bet. 5th Ave. & Union Sq.)
212-647-1515 | www.tocquevillerestaurant.com

"**Sophisticated**" dining "**to be savored**" awaits at this "**top-of-the-line**" Flatiron "**oasis**", where chef Marco Moreira's "**knockout**" French–New American plates pair with a "**wine list that dazzles**" in a "**pristine**" "**adult**" setting; it runs "**expensive, of course**", but that makes a $29 prix fixe lunch even more of "**a steal.**"

	FOOD	DECOR	SERVICE	COST

TOLOACHE | Mexican — 4.4 | 3.8 | 4.0 | $$$

East 80s | 166 E. 82nd St. (bet. Lexington & 3rd Aves.) | 212-861-4505
Greenwich Village | 205 Thompson St. (bet. Bleecker & W. 3rd Sts.) |
212-420-0600
West 50s | 251 W. 50th St. (bet. B'way & 8th Ave.) | 212-581-1818
www.toloachenyc.com

"**Deservedly popular**", these "**haute cantinas**" offer "**thoughtful**" Mexican fare
that's a big "**step up from the ordinary**" served by an "**aim-to-please**" staff;
sure, the "**lively**" digs can be "**jammed and noisy**", but a "**dazzling array**" of
margaritas provides some distraction.

TOMMASO | Italian — 4.5 | 4.1 | 4.3 | $$$

Bath Beach | 1464 86th St. (bet. Bay 8th St. & 15th Ave.) | Brooklyn
718-236-9883 | www.tommasoinbrooklyn.com

Although touted for "**old-world**" red-sauce favorites the "**way you remember
them**", the real draw at this longtime Italian on the border of Bath Beach and
Dyker Heights is the "**opera floor show**" on certain nights; beyond the
"**festive**" vibe and "**friendly**" service, it also boasts an "**amazing**" wine cellar.

TOMOE SUSHI | Japanese — 4.5 | 2.9 | 3.7 | $$$

Greenwich Village | 172 Thompson St. (bet. Bleecker & Houston Sts.)
212-777-9346 | www.tomoesushi.com

There's "**often a line**" to get into this longtime Village Japanese touted for its
"**massive slabs**" of "**mouthwatering**" sushi; "**tiny**", "**nothing-fancy**" digs aside,
they "**do not skip on the quality.**"

TOMPKINS SQUARE BAGELS | Bagels — 4.4 | 3.3 | 3.8 | $

East Village | 165 Ave. A (bet. 10th & 11th Sts.)
646-351-6520 | www.tompkinssquarebagels.com

The "**options are endless**" at this East Village shop turning out "**fresh, fluffy**"
hand-rolled bagels and "**so many schmears**"; the weekend brings "**intimidating**"
lines, but at least the "**stacked**" sandwiches will "**fill you up for the whole day.**"

TONY'S DI NAPOLI | Italian — 4.0 | 3.7 | 4.0 | $$

East 60s | 1081 Third Ave. (bet. 63rd & 64th Sts.) | 212-888-6333
West 40s | Casablanca Hotel | 147 W. 43rd St. (bet. 6th & 7th Aves.) |
212-221-0100
www.tonysnyc.com

Made for "**large groups**", these "**welcoming**" Italians dish out
"**heaping**", "**family-style**" portions of "**reliable**" red-sauce standards at
"**affordable**" prices; "**tons of people**" turn up to kick up a "**din**" and leave
"**completely satiated.**"

TOPAZ | Thai — 4.2 | 3.2 | 3.7 | $$

West 50s | 127 W. 56th St. (bet. 6th & 7th Aves.)
212-957-8020 | www.newtopaznyc.com

Near Carnegie Hall and City Center, this "**simple**" Thai dishes out "**flavorful**"
classics priced way "**low**" for the zip code; "**drab**" digs with "**no elbow room**"
and variable service offset the "**bargain**" tabs, but still it's "**always packed.**"

TORISHIN | Japanese — 4.5 | 4.0 | 4.2 | $$$$

West 50s | 362 W. 53rd St. (9th Ave.)
212-757-0108 | www.torishinny.com

It's "**chicken heaven**" at this "**super-authentic**" Hell's Kitchen yakitori
specialist, whose "**exceptional**" skewers showcase poultry in its every

permutation; "**sit at the bar and watch the chefs**" for the full experience – it's "**expensive**", but cheaper than the "**plane ride**" to Tokyo.

TORO | Spanish   4.5   4.2   4.2 $$

Chelsea | 85 10th Ave. (bet. 15th & 16th Sts.)
212-691-2360 | www.toro-nyc.com

"**Crazy-creative**" small plates and other "**awesome**" Spanish dishes meet "**killer cocktails**" at this "**sceney**" Chelsea "**tapas heaven**" where "**well-informed**" staffers preside over a "**huge**", industrial-cool space; what's "**vibrant**" to some is "**deafening**" to others, but overall it's a pretty "**amazing experience.**"

TØRST | Danish   ∇ 4.5   4.3   4.4 $

Greenpoint | 615 Manhattan Ave. (Nassau Ave.) | Brooklyn
718-389-6034 | www.torstnyc.com

"**Daring to delicious**" describes the "**ever-changing**" beer lineup at this Greenpoint Danish hangout, whose "**minimal**" menu of Scandinavian small plates comes from its "**posh**" back-room sibling, Luksus; "**the best people**" work behind the marble bar, and the understated wood decor keeps all focus on the suds.

TORTILLERIA NIXTAMAL | Mexican   4.5   3.5   3.9 $

Corona | 104-05 47th Ave. (bet. 104th & 108th Sts.) | Queens
718-699-2434 | www.tortillerianixtamal.com

It's "**all about the masa**" ground in-house at this Corona Mexican renowned for the freshest tortillas "**this side of the Rio Grande**", as well as "**authentic**" tacos and "**melt-in-your-mouth**" tamales; sure, it's a "**hole-in-the-wall**", but compensations include "**friendly**" service and "**Queens prices.**"

TOTONNO'S PIZZERIA | Pizza   4.5   3.0   3.4 $$
NAPOLITANO

Coney Island | 1524 Neptune Ave. (bet. 15th & 16th Sts.) | Brooklyn
718-372-8606 | www.totonnosconeyisland.com

An "**old-fashioned place unchanged by time**", this 1924-vintage Coney Island pizzeria is renowned for "**terrific**" coal-oven pies "**lovingly made with the freshest ingredients**"; despite "**utilitarian**" service, "**not much atmosphere**" and a cash-only rule, fans insist it's a "**must-visit**" experience.

TOTTO RAMEN | Japanese/Noodle Shop   4.4   3.2   3.6 $

East 50s | 248 E. 52nd St. (2nd Ave.) | 212-421-0052
West 50s | 464 W. 51st St. (bet. 9th & 10th Aves.) | 646-596-9056
West 50s | 366 W. 52nd St. (bet. 8th & 9th Aves.) | 212-582-0052
www.tottoramen.com

"**Perfectly tender**" noodles in "**powerhouse**" broths draw fans to these "**fast-paced**", cash-only joints where you go for the "**soul-satisfying**" ramen, not the "**utilitarian**" digs; no reservations lead to "**crazy**" waits, but no one minds given the "**cheap**" tabs and "**real-deal**" grub.

TOURNESOL | French   4.3   3.6   4.1 $$

Long Island City | 50-12 Vernon Blvd. (bet. 50th & 51st Aves.) | Queens
718-472-4355 | www.tournesolnyc.com

For a taste of "**Paris in Queens**", check out this "**convivial**" LIC bistro offering "*magnifique*" French fare at "**easy-on-the-pocketbook**" rates; yes, the "**cramped space**" means "**you really have to like your neighbor**", but the "**warm welcome**" from a "**most pleasant**" staff compensates.

TRA DI NOI | Italian   4.3 3.4 4.0 $$
Arthur Avenue/Belmont | 622 E. 187th St. (bet. Belmont & Hughes Sts.) | Bronx
718-295-1784 | www.tradinoi.com

"Like a meal at grandma's house", this family-run "jewel" off Arthur Avenue might offer "not much decor" but is warmed by "welcoming" service; still, it's the "fresh", "cooked-just-right" Italian classics that make it "worth the trip."

TRAIF | Eclectic   4.6 3.8 4.1 $$$
Williamsburg | 229 S. Fourth St. (bet. Havemeyer & Roebling Sts.) | Brooklyn
347-844-9578 | www.traifny.com

Given its name (which roughly translates as 'non-kosher'), look for "lots of pork and shellfish" on the "innovative" Eclectic menu of this "intimate" Williamsburg "winner", featuring a small plates–centric format geared toward "sharing"; regulars say "splurging on the tasting menu" is the way to go.

TRATTORIA DELL'ARTE | Italian   4.3 4.1 4.2 $$$
West 50s | 900 Seventh Ave. (bet. 56th & 57th Sts.)
212-245-9800 | www.trattoriadellarte.com

A "perennial favorite" opposite Carnegie Hall, this "bustling" Tuscan is ever a "safe bet" with its "terrific" pizza, antipasti bar and "amusing" body-parts decor; it's "convenient" for a work lunch or "pre-theater", so "bring your appetite – and your credit card."

TRATTORIA IL MULINO | Italian   4.3 4.0 4.1 $$$
Flatiron | 36 E. 20th St. (bet. B'way & Park Ave. S.)
212-777-8448 | www.trattoriailmulino.com

A more "relaxed" version of the Village original, this "minimalist but chic" Flatiron trattoria is a "strong standby" for "quality" Italian cooking off a "something-for-everyone" menu; a huge bar adds to the "great vibe" and ups the group appeal.

TRATTORIA L'INCONTRO | Italian   4.7 4.0 4.6 $$$
Astoria | 21-76 31st St. (Ditmars Blvd.) | Queens
718-721-3532 | www.trattorialincontro.com

"Worth a trip to Astoria", this "special-occasion" Italian is a borough "institution" thanks to its "yuge" menu of "divine" "traditional" dishes, plus a specials list "longer than the Sunday *Times*" ("rattled off" by "patient" waiters); "multigenerational families" fill the "old-school" surrounds, where chef Rocco Sacramone can often be found "greeting each table."

TRATTORIA ROMANA | Italian   4.6 3.9 4.4 $$$
Dongan Hills | 1476 Hylan Blvd. (Benton Ave.) | Staten Island
718-980-3113 | www.trattoriaromanasi.com

A good "reason to visit Staten Island", this Dongan Hills Italian "favorite" offers "high-quality" cooking prepared by a chef who "makes you feel at home"; granted, it can be "noisy" and "congested" since it's "always filled with customers" who "only wish" it was "a bit larger."

TRATTORIA TRECOLORI | Italian   4.2 3.8 4.1 $$
West 40s | 254 W. 47th St. (B'way)
212-997-4540 | www.trattoriatrecolori.com

The staff "makes everyone feel at home" at this "inviting" Theater District Italian, a "red-sauce" mainstay that earns ovations for its "value" pricing and

| | FOOD | DECOR | SERVICE | COST |

"**lively**" atmosphere; it gets "**packed**" pre- and post-curtain, making reservations "**a must.**"

TRESTLE ON TENTH | American   4.0   3.8   4.0 $$$
Chelsea | 242 10th Ave. (24th St.)
212-645-5659 | www.trestleontenth.com

"**Rustic**" New American cuisine with Swiss inflections and an "**intelligent**" wine list appeal to gallery-goers and High Line strollers alike at this brick-lined Chelsea "**oasis**"; "**accommodating**" staffers and a "**pleasant little garden**" take the edge off of the slightly "**pricey**" tabs.

TRIBECA GRILL | American   4.3   4.2   4.3 $$$$
TriBeCa | 375 Greenwich St. (Franklin St.)
212-941-3900 | www.myriadrestaurantgroup.com

This "**steady**" TriBeCa "**mainstay**" from Drew Nieporent and Robert De Niro "**remains a favorite**" for "**dependably good**" (if "**pricey**") New American fare and a "**sick wine list**"; the "**warm**" surrounds ensure "**good people-watching**" and the "**attentive**" staff makes you "**feel at home.**"

TRIOMPHE | French   4.3   4.3   4.4 $$$
West 40s | Iroquois Hotel | 49 W. 44th St. (6th Ave.)
212-453-4233 | www.triomphe-newyork.com

A "**real find**" in the Theater District, this all-day French "**jewel box**" in the Iroquois Hotel turns out "**excellent**" cuisine in "**pleasing**" presentations; the "**superb service**" and "**civilized**" surrounds help take the sting out of "**expensive**" prices.

NEW   **TSURUTONTAN** | Japanese/Noodle Shop   —   — $$
Union Square | 21 E. 16th St. (bet. 5th Ave. & Union Sq. W.)
212-989-1000 | www.tsurutontan.com

Making a splashy entrance in Union Square Cafe's former digs, this first overseas outpost of a Japanese noodle chain serves variations on housemade udon plus sushi and tempura. The streamlined dining area has a communal feel and front bar.

TULSI | Indian   4.4   4.2   4.3 $$$
East 40s | 211 E. 46th St. (bet. 2nd & 3rd Aves.)
212-888-0820 | www.tulsinyc.com

"**Dazzling**" contemporary Indian cooking including some "**unusual**" specialties is yours at this "**classy**" standout near Grand Central; true, it's "**not cheap**", but compensations include a "**peaceful**" setting and "**service that makes you feel like a Raj.**"

TUOME | American   4.5   3.6   4.1 $$
East Village | 536 E. Fifth St. (Ave. B)
646-833-7811 | www.tuomenyc.com

"**Big**" flavors arrive in "**small**" digs at this "**inspired**" East Village New American fielding a "**progressive**", Asian-accented menu highlighted by its signature 'Pig Out', a "**killer**" pork belly dish for two; "**pleasant**" staffers and "**spare**" but "**cozy**" confines round out the "**happy surprise.**"

TURKISH KITCHEN | Turkish   4.3   3.9   4.0 $$
Murray Hill | 386 Third Ave. (bet. 27th & 28th Sts.)
212-679-6633 | www.turkishkitchen.com

"**As real as it gets**", this "**tried-and-true**" Murray Hill Turk earns "**undying** loyalty" with "**high-quality**" traditional eats at "**modest**" prices; "**courteous**" staffers oversee the "**comfortable**" setting, and the "**lavish**" Sunday brunch "**defeats all efforts at self-control.**"

| **TURKUAZ** | Turkish | 4.1 | 3.9 | 4.0 | $$ |

West 100s | 2637 Broadway (100th St.)
212-665-9541 | www.turkuazrestaurant.com

"**Tasty**", well-priced Turkish food presented by "**costumed**" servers in a room channeling a "**sultan's private tent**" draw "**armchair travelers**" and "**belly-dancing**" fans to this "**amenable**" Upper Westsider; the "**plentiful**" Sunday buffet is an additional lure.

| 🆕 **TURNSTYLE** | Food Hall | — | — | — | $ |

West 50s | 1000 Eighth Ave. (57th St.)
774-262-6095 | www.turn-style.com

Beneath Columbus Circle, this ambitious food hall and market in a modern, completely refurbished section of the subway station (with no fare required) features vendors providing everything from grilled-cheese sandwiches to savory salteña pastries plus a host of sweets.

| **TUSCANY GRILL** | Italian | 4.5 | 4.0 | 4.3 | $$ |

Bay Ridge | 8620 Third Ave. (bet. 86th & 87th Sts.) | Brooklyn
718-921-5633 | www.tuscanygrillbrooklyn.com

Beloved in Bay Ridge for its "**excellent**" contemporary Tuscan food at midrange prices, this "**quiet**", "**cozy little neighborhood**" Italian has a "**comfortable**" vibe perfect for "**dates**" and other "**happy occasions**"; valet parking and "**welcoming**" service are further reasons it's "**been around for years.**"

| **TUTTO IL GIORNO** | Italian | 4.3 | 4.5 | 4.1 | $$$ |

TriBeCa | 114 Franklin St. (bet. Church St. & W. B'way)
212-274-8100 | www.tuttoilgiorno.com

With its "**stunning**" sky-lit setting, this Hamptons transplant offers a semi-"**secret**" TriBeCa sanctum for a "**romantic date**" or a "**special occasion**"; the modern Italian fare is "**enjoyable**" enough, and "**expensive**" tabs are just a part of the "**stylish**" package.

| **12TH STREET BAR & GRILL** | American | 4.0 | 3.8 | 3.9 | $$ |

Park Slope | 1123 Eighth Ave. (12th St.) | Brooklyn
718-965-9526 | www.12thstreetbarandgrill.com

A locals' "**go-to**", this South Sloper is an "**old reliable**" for "**solid**", "**affordable**" American fare delivered by an "**accommodating**" crew; the "**pretty**" main dining room is fit for a casual "**date**", while the "**intimate**" round-the-corner pub offers the same menu with "**sports on the telly.**"

| **12 CHAIRS CAFE** | American/Mideastern | 4.3 | 3.8 | 4.1 | $$ |

SoHo | 56 MacDougal St. (bet. Houston & Prince Sts.)
212-254-8640 | www.12chairscafe.com

12 CHAIRS CAFE | American/Mideastern
Williamsburg | 342 Wythe Ave. (2nd St.) | Brooklyn
347-227-7077 | www.12chairscafe.com

"**Locals know**" about these "**comforting**" "**defaults**" for "**simple and delicious**" American-Middle Eastern eats at "**reasonable prices**"; while "**nothing fancy**", they're "**pretty enjoyable**", but "**definitely get busy.**"

	FOOD	DECOR	SERVICE	COST

21 CLUB | American   4.3   4.5   4.5 $$$$
West 50s | 21 W. 52nd St. (bet. 5th & 6th Aves.)
212-582-7200 | www.21club.com

A "**New York institution**" and "**class operation**", this circa-1929 former
speakeasy in Midtown turns out "**dependably good**" traditional American
dishes in an "**old-school**", "**dress-up**" setting (jackets required, no jeans) with
"**spectacular**" old toys hanging from the ceiling and "**serene**" private rooms
upstairs; an "**impeccable**" staff furthers the "**welcoming**" vibes, though you
may have to "**liquidate some stocks to cover the bill.**"

NEW TWIN SUNS | Deli   —   —   — $
Bushwick | 244 Himrod St. (Knickerbocker Ave.) | Brooklyn
718-484-9291 | www.twinsunsdeli.com

This Bushwick deli from the Montana's Trail House team provides amped-up
sandwiches filled with gourmet ingredients along with a few sides. The simple
space has wooden shelves stocked with retro groceries and candies for sale.

TWO HANDS | Australian   ∇ 4.3   4.1   3.9 $
Little Italy | 164 Mott St. (Broome St.) | no phone

TWO HANDS RESTAURANT & BAR | Australian
TriBeCa | 251 Church St. (bet. Franklin & Leonard Sts.) | no phone
www.twohandsnyc.com

Packed with "**super-chic**" diners, these "**always busy**" Aussie kitchens are
known for "**fresh but hearty**" fare including "**memorable**" breakfasts, standout
avocado toast and "**fantastic**" flat whites; the "**cute**" Little Italy original is
daytime-only while its sunny TriBeCa sequel adds dinner and a full bar.

TWO LITTLE RED HENS | Dessert   4.6   3.6   3.9 $$
East 80s | 1652 Second Ave. (86th St.)
212-452-0476 | www.twolittleredhens.com

A "**cut above**", this "**tiny**" UES dessert shop is "**the place to go**" for "**standout**"
cupcakes (and special-occasion cakes), "**tall, creamy**" cheesecakes and
"**incredible**" scones; it's also a "**popular**" stop for "**coffee and a biscuit**",
though there's "**not much seating**" and can have "**long lines**" on weekends.

212 STEAKHOUSE | Steak   4.2   3.9   4.1 $$$
East 50s | 316 E. 53rd St. (bet. 1st & 2nd Aves.)
212-858-0646 | www.212steakhouse.com

For "**true Kobe beef**", "**steak fans**" recommend this "**relaxed**" Midtown
chophouse also supplying "**great Wagyu**" and other "**well-cooked**" cuts in
"**cozy surroundings**"; if a few say it's "**not spectacular**", a "**casual
atmosphere**" and "**fair prices**" are still reasons to "**go back.**"

TXIKITO | Spanish   4.4   3.7   4.1 $$$
Chelsea | 240 Ninth Ave. (bet. 24th & 25th Sts.)
212-242-4730 | www.txikitonyc.com

Those "**dreaming of San Sebastián**" make for this "**lively**" Chelsea Spaniard
where "**smart**" staffers serve an "**absolutely delicious**", ever-evolving array of
"**real-deal**" Basque tapas; with "**so many wonderful choices**", the "**cute**",
plank-walled space "**can get expensive in a hurry**", but at least the "**terrific**"
wine selection is "**moderately priced.**"

NEW **TYGERSHARK** | Korean — — — $$

Prospect Heights | 581 Vanderbilt Ave. (Dean St.) | Brooklyn
718-576-6233 | www.tygershark.nyc

Korean-style seafood with colorful global touches stars on the dinner menu at this Prospect Heights hangout with both counter and table seating. By day it's a coffee and retail shop carrying surfboards and other indie gear, with brunch on the weekends.

NEW **ULIVO** | Italian — — — $$$

NoMad | 4 W. 28th St. (bet. B'way & 5th Ave.)
212-684-8000 | www.ulivonyc.com

This NoMad trattoria with a rustic bent specializes in housemade pastas, wood-fired dishes and aged cheeses and charcuterie. An array of Italian-accented cocktails, wines and after-dinner drinks is also on offer and the narrow space also includes a front bar and handful of sidewalk seats.

UMAMI BURGER | Burgers 4.0 3.3 3.6 $$

Battery Park City | Hudson Eats | 230 Vesey St. (West St.) | 917-728-4400
Greenwich Village | 432 Sixth Ave. (bet. 9th & 10th Sts.) | 212-677-8626
Williamsburg | 158 N. 4th St. (Bedford Ave.) | Brooklyn | 718-907-5680
www.umamiburger.com

Whether "**overhyped**" or "**living up to the hype**", this popular LA-based chain crafts "**unusual**", "**upscale**" burgers packing "**strong**", umami-rich flavors like Parmesan ("**dreamy**") and truffle ("**a must**"); the Village and Williamsburg outlets feature table service and a full bar, while the Hudson Eats counter offers beer.

UMBERTOS CLAM HOUSE | Italian 3.9 3.4 3.8 $$

Little Italy | 132 Mulberry St. (bet. Grand & Hester Sts.)
212-431-7545 | www.umbertosclamhouse.com

Fans "**dig the clams**" and pastas "**like mamma used to make**" at this "**casual**" Italian seafood spot on Mulberry Street; a few "**miss the original location**" and knock its "**tourist**" tendencies, but everyone appreciates prime "**people-watching**" from its seasonal sidewalk seating.

UNCLE BOONS | Thai 4.5 3.9 4.0 $$

NoLita | 7 Spring St. (bet. Bowery & Elizabeth St.)
646-370-6650 | www.uncleboons.com

Something "**different from the norm**", this "**cutting-edge**" NoLita hangout offers a "**new-school**" take on Thai cuisine via "**vibrant flavors**" and very "**serious spicing**"; an "**attentive**" team tends the "**knickknack**"-filled basement space, where "**must-try**" beer slushies can be ordered from the "**cozy**" bar.

UNCLE JACK'S STEAKHOUSE | Steak 4.3 4.0 4.2 $$$

West 30s | 440 Ninth Ave. (bet. 34th & 35th Sts.) | 212-244-0005
West 50s | 44 W. 56th St. (bet. 5th & 6th Aves.) | 212-245-1550
Bayside | 39-40 Bell Blvd. (40th Ave.) | Queens | 718-229-1100
www.unclejacks.com

"**Juicy**" beef plated in "**tremendous**" portions is the draw at these "**pleasing**" steakhouses with "**old-school**" looks and "**high**" but "**worth-every-penny**" tabs; bonus points go to an "**excellent**" staff that treats everyone like "**Uncle Jack's favorite niece or nephew.**"

	FOOD	DECOR	SERVICE	COST

UNCLE NICK'S | Greek — 4.0 3.2 3.8 $$

Chelsea | 382 Eighth Ave. (29th St.) | 212-609-0500
West 50s | 747 Ninth Ave. (bet. 50th & 51st Sts.) | 212-245-7992
www.unclenicksgreekrestaurant.com

Fans say there's "**no need to venture to Astoria**" given the "**tasty**", "**stick-to-your-ribs**" chow and "**affordable**" tabs at these "**casual**" Greek tavernas known for their "**wonderful flaming cheese**" dish; sure, the settings are on the "**shabby**" side, but they stay "**busy**" all the same.

NEW UNION FARE | American — — — $$$

Flatiron | 5 E. 17th St. (5th Ave.)
212-633-6003 | www.unionfare.com

Stretching out over a whole city block, this Union Square hang offers a wide-ranging American menu with group appeal. The dining and bar areas are abundant with pendant lights and exposed brick, and an adjoining food hall has a variety of stands for casual dining.

UNTAMED SANDWICHES | Sandwiches ▽ 4.6 3.8 4.3 $

West 30s | 43 W. 39th St. (bet. 5th & 6th Aves.)
646-669-9397 | www.untamedsandwiches.com

"**Bringing sandwiches to a new level**", this "**fun**" fast-casual spot near Bryant Park features "**creative combos**" of "**killer**" braised meats and veggies, plus beer and wine; "**friendly**" service and "**affordable**" tabs add to its "**understated**" appeal.

UNTITLED | American 4.4 4.1 4.2 $$$

Meatpacking District | Whitney Museum | 99 Gansevoort St. (bet. 10th Ave. & Washington St.) | 212-570-3670 | www.untitledatthewhitney.com

At Danny Meyer's "**sophisticated**" New American in the Whitney Museum, chef Michael Anthony offers an "**interesting**" menu of "**well-crafted**" "**farm-to-fork**" bites in "**arty**" presentations befitting the location; the "**airy**" windowed space has an "**unhurried**" atmosphere, while outdoor seats make you feel part of the Meatpacking "**scene.**"

UPHOLSTERY STORE | American 4.7 4.7 4.8 $$

West Village | 713 Washington St. (bet. 11th & Perry Sts.)
212-929-6384 | www.upholsterystore-ny.com

There's "**nothing stuffy about**" Kurt Gutenbrunner's "**wonderfully warm**" West Village wine bar, where the "**excellent**" American bites, "**stellar cocktails**" and "**well-chosen**" vinos are hailed as "**the perfect mix**"; a "**super**" staff and "**relaxed**" vibes round out "**a rare find.**"

UPLAND | Californian 4.4 4.4 4.3 $$

Murray Hill | 345 Park Ave. S. (26th St.)
212-686-1006 | www.uplandnyc.com

This "**upbeat**" Murray Hill Californian "**lives up to the hype**" with "**accessible**" but "**modern and creative**" Italian-inspired cooking; set in a "**beautiful, large room**" (try to "**score a booth**") with a "**busy**" front bar, it's an overall "**people-pleasing**" choice, which explains why it's "**tough to get in**" (the "**tantalizing**" brunch is easier).

UPSTATE | Seafood 4.5 3.8 4.2 $$

East Village | 95 First Ave. (bet. 5th & 6th Sts.)
917-408-3395 | www.upstatenyc.com

"**Oyster fans**" dig this "**lively**" East Village hangout for its "**first-rate**" seafood and "**revolving**" craft beer list; a no-rezzie rule and "**ridiculously small**" dimensions can make for "**long waits**," but payoffs include "**on-point**" service and "**fair prices.**"

	FOOD	DECOR	SERVICE	COST

URBANSPACE VANDERBILT | Food Hall   4.2   3.6   3.5 $$
East 40s | 230 Park Ave. (Vanderbilt Ave.)
646-747-0810 | www.urbanspacenyc.com

A Midtown "**revelation**", this "**upscale food court**" by Grand Central offers an "**awesome selection**" of basically "**whatever you crave**", with 20-plus vendors from Roberta's and Delaney Chicken to Dough; those looking to avoid the "**lunch crunch**" ("**lines**", "**tight seating**") go "**after work**" when it's "**more sane.**"

USHIWAKAMARU | Japanese   ▽ 4.5   3.9   4.2 $$$
Chelsea | 362 W. 23rd St. (9th Ave.)
917-639-3940 | www.ushiwakamarunewyork.com

Relocated from Greenwich Village to Chelsea, this "**simple**" Japanese by chef-owner Hideo Kuribara features the same "**melt-in-your-mouth**" sushi in larger digs anchored by a counter where you can "**enjoy the show**"; omakase dining is the main draw, and "**top prices**" come with the territory.

USKUDAR | Turkish   4.2   3.2   4.1 $$
East 70s | 1405 Second Ave. (bet. 73rd & 74th Sts.)
212-988-4046 | www.uskudarnyc.com

Although "**narrow**" with just a "**handful of tables**", this "**welcoming**" UES "**hole-in-the-wall**" does a brisk business thanks to its "**delicious**", "**straightforward**" Turkish cuisine and "**personal**" service; "**easy-on-the-wallet**" prices seal the deal.

UTSAV | Indian   4.0   3.8   3.9 $$
West 40s | 1185 Sixth Ave. (bet. 46th & 47th Sts.)
212-575-2525 | www.utsavny.com

Although somewhat "**difficult to find**", this Theater District Indian delivers "**satisfying**" classics in "**civilized**", "**modern**" digs tended by a "**gracious**" crew; if prices seem a "**little high**", the daily lunch buffet and $38 pre-theater prix fixe are a relative "**bargain.**"

UVA | Italian   4.2   3.8   4.0 $$
East 70s | 1486 Second Ave. (bet. 77th & 78th Sts.)
212-472-4552 | www.uvawinebar.com

"**Beautiful food**" and "**beautiful people**" collide at this "**bustling**", "**noisy**" UES "**date destination**" delivering "**delicious**" Italian dishes and "**wonderful wines**"; an "**enchanting**" back garden, "**decent**" prices and "**attentive**" service secure its standing as a "**neighborhood favorite.**"

VALBELLA | Italian   4.5   4.4   4.5 $$$$
East 50s | 11 E. 53rd St. (bet. 5th & Madison Aves.) | 212-888-8955 |
www.valbellamidtown.com
Meatpacking District | 421 W. 13th St. (bet. 9th Ave. & Washington St.) |
212-645-7777 | www.valbellarestaurants.com

Thanks to "**exceptional**" Italian cuisine, "**terrific**" wines, "**lavish**" settings and "**solicitous**" service, these "**classy**" destinations draw a "**mix of ages**" in the mood to "**celebrate**"; just "**bring an appetite**" and your "**expense account**" – and keep their "**unbelievable private rooms**" in mind for "**special occasions.**"

	FOOD	DECOR	SERVICE	COST

NEW VANDAL | Eclectic — 4.3 4.6 4.1 $$$

Lower East Side | 199 Bowery (Rivington St.)
212-400-0199 | www.vandalnewyork.com

Earning an "**A+ for creativity**", this "**so cool**" Lower Eastsider from the Tao Group and chef Chris Santos (Stanton Social) dispenses "**elevated**" global street fare offered tapas-style amid "**stunning**" murals (including one by Shepard Fairey); with a "**secret entrance**" and a downstairs DJ lounge, it's got "**hip**" types "**obsessed.**"

VANESSA'S DUMPLING HOUSE | Chinese — 4.0 2.6 3.2 $

East Village | 220 E. 14th St. (bet. 2nd & 3rd Aves.) | 212-529-1329
Lower East Side | 118 Eldridge St. (bet. Broome & Grand Sts.) | 212-625-8008
Williamsburg | 310 Bedford Ave. (bet. 1st & 2nd Sts.) | Brooklyn | 718-218-8809
www.vanessas.com

Just a few dollars fund a "**pig out**" at these "**always-busy**" dumpling joints whose "**amazing**" namesake specialty is fried or steamed "**while you wait**"; expect "**limited**" seating and "**minimal**" service in the "**utilitarian**" setups, but for a "**fast, filling**" nosh, you "**can't beat**" 'em.

VAN LEEUWEN ARTISAN ICE CREAM | Ice Cream — 4.4 3.7 4.0 $

East Village | 48 E. Seventh St. (2nd Ave.) | 718-701-1630
West Village | 152 W. 10th St. (Waverly Pl.) | 917-475-1448
Boerum Hill | 81 Bergen St. (Smith St.) | Brooklyn | 347-763-2979
Greenpoint | 620 Manhattan Ave. (123rd St.) | Brooklyn | 347-987-4774
Williamsburg | 204 Wythe Ave. (5th St.) | Brooklyn | 929-337-6907
www.vanleeuwenicecream.com

The "**premium**" ice cream earns "**wows**" at these parlors where "**creamy, rich**" scoops come in classic and more "**unusual**" flavors, including "**especially welcome**" vegan varieties; their small storefronts double as coffee bars, offering java from Toby's Estate as well as pastries.

VATAN | Indian/Vegetarian — 4.4 4.2 4.2 $$

Murray Hill | 409 Third Ave. (29th St.)
212-689-5666 | www.vatanny.com

An "**incredible variety of flavors**" from "**delicate**" to "**spicy**" emerges from the kitchen of this Murray Hill vegetarian Indian where the "**authentic Gujarati**" specialties come in an all-you-can-eat Thali format for $34; "**caring**" service and a transporting "**village**" setting complete the "**totally unique experience.**"

VAUCLUSE | French — 4.4 4.6 4.3 $$$

East 60s | 100 E. 63rd St. (Park Ave.)
646-869-2300 | www.vauclusenyc.com

A "**gorgeous**" backdrop sets the "**comfortably elegant**" tone at Michael White's "**true UES**" brasserie, where "**delectable**" French "**classics**" and the "**fabulous**" White Label Burger come via a "**caring**" staff; despite "**occasionally jaw-dropping**" tabs, the "**grown-up**" clientele declares it "**a winner.**"

VENIERO'S PASTRY | Dessert/Italian — 4.4 3.6 3.7 $$

East Village | 342 E. 11th St. (1st Ave.)
212-674-7070 | www.venierospastry.com

An "**Italian pastry institution**" since 1894, this East Village cafe is known for "**traditional**" desserts, like "**must-try**" cannoli, "**light, fluffy**" cheesecakes and a wide selection of cookies; "**atmosphere abounds**" in the "**old-world**" space where you can stay for a "**nice espresso**" when not too crowded.

	FOOD	DECOR	SERVICE	COST
VESELKA | Ukrainian	4.1	3.2	3.7	$$

East Village | 144 Second Ave. (9th St.)
212-228-9682 | www.veselka.com

The "**all-encompassing menu**" of "**hearty**", "**fair-priced**" Ukrainian staples (think "**handmade pierogi**", "**terrific borscht**") at this 24/7 East Village "**institution**" draws everyone from "**families**" to the "**post-party crowd**"; maybe there's "**no decor**" to speak of, but it's got "**old-time atmosphere**" to spare.

	FOOD	DECOR	SERVICE	COST
VESTA | Italian	4.4	3.7	4.1	$$

Astoria | 21-02 30th Ave. (21st St.) | Queens
718-545-5550 | www.vestavino.com

"**Neighborhood**" spots don't get much more "**cozy**" than this "**off-the-beaten-path**" Astoria Italian fielding "**spot-on**", "**farm-to-table**" fare dispatched by an "**attentive**" team; though the menu is rather "**limited**", it "**changes often**", while the "**welcoming**" vibe is a constant.

	FOOD	DECOR	SERVICE	COST
VESUVIO | Italian	4.2	3.6	4.1	$$

Bay Ridge | 7305 Third Ave. (bet. 73rd & 74th Sts.) | Brooklyn
718-745-0222 | www.vesuviobayridge.com

It may "**not have the name recognition**" of other Brooklyn pizza stalwarts, but this "**unpretentious**" neighborhood Italian in Bay Ridge has been slinging "**delicious**" pies since 1953, along with an "**abundance**" of pastas; "**friendly**" staffers, "**fair**" tabs and "**never a long wait**" keep regulars regular.

	FOOD	DECOR	SERVICE	COST
VEZZO | Pizza	4.4	3.5	3.9	$$

Murray Hill | 178 Lexington Ave. (31st St.)
212-839-8300 | www.vezzothincrust.com

"**Paper-thin**", "**crispy**"-crusted pies with "**toppings to suit any taste**" are the specialty of this "**friendly**", "**bargain-priced**" Murray Hill pizzeria; the digs are "**tight**" and often "**crowded**", but all's forgiven after a bite of that "**outstanding**" Shroomtown pie.

	FOOD	DECOR	SERVICE	COST
VIA CAROTA | Italian	4.6	4.2	4.3	$$

West Village | 51 Grove St. (bet. Bleecker St. & 7th Ave. S.)
no phone | www.viacarota.com

Jody Williams (Buvette) and Rita Sodi (I Sodi) put out "**distinctive**", "**dream**"-worthy dishes (including "**super-creative**" vegetables) at this West Village Italian, where the rustic setting will transport you "**miles from the city**"; "**excellent**" cocktails add to the "**magic**" – just "**go early**" as it's often "**packed**" and doesn't take reservations.

	FOOD	DECOR	SERVICE	COST
VIA EMILIA | Italian	4.2	3.5	4.0	$$

Flatiron | 47 E. 21st St. (bet. B'way & Park Ave. S.)
212-505-3072 | www.viaemilianyc.net

Known for its "**tasty**" Emilia-Romagnan food paired with "**excellent wines from the region**" (including "**the best Lambruscos**"), this "**friendly**" Flatiron Italian is also appreciated for its "**reasonable prices**"; the "**bright**" setting may be on the "**stark**" side, but a "**relaxing**" vibe prevails.

	FOOD	DECOR	SERVICE	COST
VIA QUADRONNO | Italian	4.1	3.5	3.8	$$$

East 70s | 25 E. 73rd St. (bet. 5th & Madison Aves.) | 212-650-9880

continued

East 80s | 1228 Madison Ave. (bet. 88th & 89th Sts.) | 212-369-9000
www.viaquadronno.com

Offering "**a little bit of Italy on the UES**" these "**fancy**" renditions of a Milanese bar draw "**swanky patrons**" for espresso, panini and Italian plates coupled with a "**European feel**"; tabs are "**pricey**" and the "**cozy**" digs can be "**tight**", but they're perfect "**before shopping or the museums.**"

VICEVERSA | Italian   4.3   4.2   4.4 $$$

West 50s | 325 W. 51st St. (bet. 8th & 9th Aves.)
212-399-9291 | www.viceversanyc.com

At this "**vibrant**" Theater District staple, the "**excellent**" Italian cooking garners as much praise as the "**attentive**" staffers who will "**get you out in time**" for your curtain; factor in a "**sleek**" interior augmented with a "**delightful**" back patio, and it's an all-around "**charmer.**"

VIC'S | Italian/Mediterranean   4.2   4.0   4.2 $$

NoHo | 31 Great Jones St. (bet. Bowery & Lafayette St.)
212-253-5700 | www.vicsnewyork.com

"**Special**" wood-fired pizzas and "**well-made pastas**" star on the menu of "**creatively imagined**" Italian-Med dishes at this "**buzzy**" NoHo bistro from the Cookshop team; relatively "**affordable**" given the "**hip neighborhood**", it draws an "**energetic**" crowd into its "**airy, light**" space with "**breezy outdoor seating.**"

VICTOR'S CAFE | Cuban   4.3   4.2   4.2 $$$

West 50s | 236 W. 52nd St. (bet. B'way & 8th Ave.)
212-586-7714 | www.victorscafe.com

In business since 1963, this Theater District Cuban "**doesn't rest on its laurels**", supplying "**terrific**" food and "**fantastic**" mojitos in "**energetic**" environs exuding classic "**Havana style**"; "**old-world**" service and live music boost the "**vacation**"-like vibe, but be prepared for "**noise**" and "**tourists.**"

VIETNAAM | Vietnamese   4.2   3.3   3.9 $$

East 80s | 1700 Second Ave. (88th St.)
212-722-0558 | www.vietnaam88.com

"**Well-prepared**" Vietnamese standards make this "**friendly**" Upper Eastsider a "**delightful**" find for classic satays and noodle dishes; it's "**not fancy**", but "**satisfying**" service and "**low prices**" further explain why locals are "**so glad to have it**" in the neighborhood.

THE VIEW | American   3.7   4.3   3.9 $$$$

West 40s | Marriott Marquis Hotel | 1535 Broadway (bet. 45th & 46th Sts.)
212-704-8900 | www.theviewny.com

"**As the name implies**", it's all about the "**second-to-none**" 360-degree views of Manhattan at this "**revolving**" Times Square hotel eatery; just "**be prepared to spend**" to dine on "**so-so**" prix fixe–only American fare with "**lots of tourists**", though even jaded natives admit it can be a "**fun experience.**"

VILLABATE ALBA | Dessert/Italian   ∇   4.7   4.2   4.2 $

Bensonhurst | 7001 18th Ave. (70th St.) | Brooklyn
718-331-8430 | www.villabate.com

The "**gorgeous**" cakes, pastries and cookies "**taste as good as they look**" at this family-run Italian pasticceria in Bensonhurst that "**does everything with love**"; marble counters and painted murals add to the "**traditional**" vibe, and while there's no seating, standing at the bar with a "**fabulous**" cup of espresso or housemade gelato can feel like being in Sicily.

VILLA BERULIA | Italian   4.4   4.0   4.5 $$$

Murray Hill | 107 E. 34th St. (bet. Lexington & Park Aves.)
212-689-1970 | www.villaberulia.com

"**Exceptional**" hospitality is the strong suit of this Murray Hill "**family affair**"
that follows through with "**excellent**" Italian cooking, "**exotic**" Croatian dishes
and "**even better specials**"; the "**throwback**" mood pleases its "**older crowd**",
and "**fair prices**" seal the deal.

VILLA MOSCONI | Italian   4.2   3.7   4.3 $$$

Greenwich Village | 69 MacDougal St. (bet. Bleecker & Houston Sts.)
212-674-0320 | www.villamosconi.com

"**Grandma would be proud**" of the "**real-deal**" Italian eats at this "**old-school**"
Villager, where a "**delightful**" staff has been slinging "**smack-your-lips-good**"
classics since 1976; maybe the "**old-world**" digs could "**use updating**", but
"**decent prices**" please its "**longtime**" regulars.

VINEGAR HILL HOUSE | American   4.4   3.8   4.0 $$$

Vinegar Hill | 72 Hudson Ave. (bet. Front & Water Sts.) | Brooklyn
718-522-1018 | www.vinegarhillhouse.com

On a "**charming cobblestone street**" in "**remote**" Vinegar Hill, this
"**comfortable**" hideaway stands out with "**inspired**" seasonal New American
fare and "**solid**" cocktails; the "**pleasant**", rustic digs with a "**fun garden**" work
equally well for date night or "**casual**" brunch, but reserve ahead or risk a wait.

VIRGIL'S REAL BARBECUE | BBQ   4.0   3.4   3.8 $$

West 40s | 152 W. 44th St. (bet. B'way & 6th Ave.)
212-921-9494 | www.virgilsbbq.com

"**Solid**" BBQ turns up in Times Square at this longtime "**crowd-pleaser**" that
rolls out "**huge portions**" of "**greasy**" grub in "**massive**" digs ideal "**for groups**";
OK, it's "**not Texas**" and the setup's "**nothing memorable**", but you'd never
know it from the hordes of "**tourists**" crowding in.

VIRGINIA'S | American   ∇ 4.4   4.0   4.0 $$$

East Village | 647 E. 11th St. (Ave. C)
212-658-0182 | www.virginiasnyc.com

"**Original**" and "**well crafted**" describes the fare at this "**cozy**" East Village ·
bistro where the somewhat "**limited**" New American menu changes frequently
for "**memorable**" results; the "**subdued**" space runs "**tight**", but "**great
camaraderie**" helps make it an overall "**winner.**"

VITAE | American   4.4   4.2   4.2 $$

East 40s | 4 E. 46th St. (bet. 5th & Madison Aves.)
212-682-3562 | www.vitaenyc.com

A "**beautiful**", "**modern**" bi-level space and "**even better**" seasonal American
cooking make this Midtown "**gem**" an ideal Grand Central–area "**business-
lunch**" spot; a roomy front bar offering lots of by-the-glass wines, a "**civilized**"
upstairs with a "**view of the scene below**" and "**personable**" service help
justify the "**expensive**" bill.

VIVOLO | Italian   4.0   3.8   4.1 $$

East 70s | 140 E. 74th St. (Lexington Ave.)
212-737-3533 | www.vivolo.vivolonyc.com

Though "**rather old-fashioned**", this circa-1977 UES Italian "**still holds up**" for
its longtime "**neighborhood clientele**" thanks to "**reliable**" dishes served
"**without the fanfare**" by a "**chummy**" staff; the wood-paneled townhouse digs
have an "**old-school**" feel and tabs are "**reasonable.**"

	FOOD	DECOR	SERVICE	COST

WA JEAL | Chinese   4.3   3.5   3.9 $$

East 80s | 1588 Second Ave. (bet. 82nd & 83rd Sts.)
212-396-3339 | www.wajeal.com

For a "**10-alarm fire**" of the taste buds, diners turn to this "**exotic**" UES Chinese offering "**incendiary**" but "**nuanced**" Sichuan cooking (there are also milder dishes for blander palates); factor in "**quick service**" and "**comfortable prices**", and the white-tablecloth space is a neighborhood "**go-to.**"

WALKER'S | Pub Food   3.9   3.5   4.0 $$

TriBeCa | 16 N. Moore St. (Varick St.)
212-941-0142 | www.walkersnyc.com

"**As local as it gets in TriBeCa**", this "**quintessential**" neighborhood pub is populated by everyone from area "**families**" to "**bankers**" who come for "**quality**" bar food at "**value**" rates; "**old NYC charm**" and "**engaging**" service boost the "**buoyant atmosphere.**"

WALLFLOWER | French   4.6   4.1   4.5 $$$

West Village | 235 W. 12th St. (Greenwich Ave.)
646-682-9842 | www.wallflowernyc.com

The menu may be "**small**", but "**the flavor isn't**" at this "**sweet**" West Village bistro where the French cuisine is "**inspired**" yet "**without pretension**", and the "**tiny**" space is "**well appointed**" and "**cozy**"; "**terrific**" cocktails and "**exceptional**" service further boost its "**date-night**" appeal, though it's also "**wonderful for brunch.**"

WALLSÉ | Austrian   4.6   4.4   4.5 $$$

West Village | 344 W. 11th St. (Washington St.)
212-352-2300 | www.kg-ny.com

An "**elegant**" "**taste of Vienna**", Kurt Gutenbrunner's West Village "**marvel**" crafts "**Nouvelle**" Austrian fare that's "**both hearty and delicate**", served by a "**talented**" team in a "**sophisticated**" space appointed with Julian Schnabel paintings; most agree the "**budget-busting**" bill is "**warranted**" for such a "**memorable**" meal.

WALTER FOODS | American   4.1   4.0   4.0 $$

Williamsburg | 253 Grand St. (Roebling St.) | Brooklyn | 718-387-8783

WALTER'S | American

Fort Greene | 166 Dekalb Ave. (Cumberland St.) | Brooklyn | 718-488-7800
www.walterfoods.com

Embodying Brooklyn's "**Socratic ideal of a neighborhood place**", these "**pub-ish**" spots supply "**solid**", spiffed-up American comfort fare and "**killer**" cocktails; "**reasonable**" prices and "**comfortable**" interiors seal the deal – they "**care about the details and it shows.**"

NEW **THE WARREN** | American   —   —   — $$$

West Village | 131 Christopher St. (bet. Greenwich & Hudson Sts.)
646-832-4956 | www.brunchrestaurantnewyork.com

With a nod to Admiral Sir Peter Warren (whose former estate is bordered by Christopher Street), this intimate West Village American beckons hearty eaters with a concise menu featuring chops, seafood and a namesake burger, as well as oysters and sharing plates. Model ships adorn a banquette-lined space with French doors that open in warm weather.

WASAN | Japanese   ▽ 4.3   3.7   4.3 $$$

East Village | 108 E. Fourth St. (bet. 1st & 2nd Aves.) | 212-777-1978

continued

Park Slope | 440 Bergen St. (5th Ave.) | Brooklyn | 347-725-3550
www.wasan-ny.com

These Japanese joints "**thoughtfully blend**" classic flavors with a "**modern approach**", using seasonal ingredients to prepare "**inventive, delicate**" small plates plus "**delicious**" sashimi; it's "**not cheap**", and the settings are simple, but the "**excellent**" sake program is another reason to go.

WASSAIL | American   4.2   3.7   4.0 $$
Lower East Side | 162 Orchard St. (Stanton St.)
646-918-6835 | www.wassailnyc.com

A "**fantastic choice of ciders**" complements the "**delightful**" New American fare at this "**warm, casual**" LES gastropub from the Queens Kickshaw team; factor in a "**passionate**" crew ready with cider "**tastes**" and suggestions and it "**fills a niche.**"

WATER CLUB | American   4.3   4.6   4.4 $$$
Murray Hill | East River & 30th St. (enter on 23rd St.)
212-683-3333 | www.thewaterclub.com

"**Inspiring water views**" from a barge docked on the East River off Murray Hill lend a "**romantic**" air to this "**charming**" destination, where a "**pro**" staff serves "**dependably good**" American fare (including a "**terrific**" Sunday brunch); sure, it's "**geared toward tourists**" and best enjoyed "**when your rich uncle is in town**", but it's hard to top for "**special-occasion**" dining.

WAVERLY INN | American   4.2   4.3   4.0 $$$
West Village | 16 Bank St. (Waverly Pl.)
917-828-1154 | www.waverlynyc.com

Maybe the "**celebrity buzz has slowed**", but Graydon Carter's "**clubby**" West Villager still offers "**high-end**" spins on American "**home cooking**" favorites in "**charming**" confines (adorned with droll Edward Sorel murals); in winter, regulars say a "**cozy booth by the fireplace**" is "**where it's at.**"

THE WEST 79TH STREET | American   3.4   4.1   3.5 $$
BOAT BASIN CAFÉ
West 70s | W. 79th St. (Riverside Dr.)
212-496-5542 | www.boatbasincafe.com

With its "**vacation-esque**" vibe and "**coveted view**" of the Hudson River, this "**unconventional**" alfresco venue on the UWS waterfront is favored for "**hanging**" during the warm seasons; the offerings are "**basic**" burgers, sandwiches and fries, but snag a "**prime riverside**" table, order a few "**adult beverages**" and "**you've got yourself a time.**"

WESTVILLE | American   4.1   3.3   3.8 $$
Chelsea | 246 W. 18th St. (8th Ave.) | 212-924-2223
East Village | 173 Ave. A (11th St.) | 212-677-2033
Hudson Square | 333 Hudson St. (bet. Charlton & Vandam Sts.) |
212-776-1404
West Village | 210 W. 10th St. (Bleecker St.) | 212-741-7971
www.westvillenyc.com

Popular with "**young 20s and 30s**", these "**local hangouts**" dish out "**New Wave**" American "**diner food**" with an emphasis on "**heavenly**" market-fresh veggies that make them a "**vegetarian's paradise**"; they're often "**crowded**" with "**elbow-to-elbow**" seating, but "**value**" prices keep the appeal high.

		FOOD	DECOR	SERVICE	COST

WHEATED | Pizza   ∇ 4.5   4.0   4.3 $

Ditmas Park | 905 Church Ave. (bet. Coney Island Ave. & 10th St.) | Brooklyn
347-240-2813 | www.wheatedbrooklyn.com

"Excellent", "artisanal" pizzas – built on "perfect" sourdough crusts and named for Brooklyn neighborhoods – are "what set apart" this "warm" Ditmas Park hangout; small and "pleasant" with an "energetic" bar dispensing "great whiskeys" and cocktails, it's a "nice option for the neighborhood."

WHITE BEAR | Chinese   ∇ 4.4   2.5   3.4 $$

Flushing | 135-02 Roosevelt Ave. (Prince St.) | Queens
718-961-2322

"Delish" and "addictive", the spicy chili oil wontons are the "signature dish" at this "must-stop" Flushing Chinese also known for its "awesome noodles" and "price-is-right" tabs; a "tiny", "hole-in-the-wall" setting make most "take it to go."

WHITE STREET | American   4.1   4.3   4.3 $$$

TriBeCa | 221 W. Broadway (bet. Franklin & White Sts.)
212-944-8378 | www.whitestreetnyc.com

An "opulent" setting for a "date" or "special occasion", this "posh" TriBeCan plates "tasty", "upscale" New American fare in "roomy", chandelier-rich environs overseen by a "pro" staff; given the "pricey" tab, some feel the food "underpunches", but to others it's just right for a "classy" evening.

WHITE TIGER | Korean   ∇ 4.1   3.6   3.9 $$

Prospect Heights | 601 Vanderbilt Ave. (Bergen St.) | Brooklyn
718-552-2272 | www.whitetiger.nyc

This "solid" Prospect Heights Korean uses largely organic produce and meats for its "modern" takes on classic snacks, and small and large plates; "unique and tasty" cocktails, along with Soju and sake complement the "lovely flavors" while colorful benches balance the room's woodsy tones.

WILDAIR | American   4.4   3.8   4.1 $$

Lower East Side | 142 Orchard St. (Rivington St.)
646-964-5624 | www.wildair.nyc

Little sister of the nearby Contra, this "hip" LES hang delivers a "carefully curated" American menu featuring "interesting" and "unexpected" dishes (including "amazing" housemade bread) plus natural wines; it's "small" and doesn't take reservations, so don't be surprised by "long" waits.

WILMA JEAN | Southern   ∇ 4.2   3.3   3.9 $$

Carroll Gardens | 345 Smith St. (Carroll St.) | Brooklyn
718-422-0444 | www.wilmajean345.com

"Greasy deliciousness" sums up the "perfectly edited menu" of "very tasty" fried chicken and "sides your mama wishes she could make" at this "casual" Carroll Gardens Southerner that's more than "worth the calories"; "excellent" beer and "good-value" tabs make this one a "neighborhood" keeper.

NEW WIN SON | American/Taiwanese   —   —   — $$

Williamsburg | 159 Graham Ave. (Montrose Ave.) | Brooklyn
347-457-6010 | www.winsonbrooklyn.com

This casual Williamsburg spot behind a bodega-style awning is devoted to Taiwanese American dishes like noodles and buns. There's a variety of vegetarian, vegan and gluten-free options, plus cocktails with sweet and savory touches.

NEW WISEFISH POKE | Hawaiian/Seafood   ▽ 4.1   3.5   3.7 $

Chelsea | 263 W. 19th St. (8th Ave.)
212-367-7653 | www.wisefishpoke.com

"**Fresh**" Hawaiian-style raw fish is celebrated at this Chelsea seafood spot offering buildable bowls of "**delicious**" poke; the "**small**" counter-serve space has a communal table, some window seats and a "**fun, laid-back surfer vibe.**"

WO HOP | Chinese   4.1   2.6   3.4 $$

Chinatown | 17 Mott St. (bet. Mosco & Worth Sts.)
212-962-8617 | www.wohopnyc.com

"**Old school**" is an understatement when it comes to this 1938-era Chinatown "**classic**" known for "**tried-and-true**" Cantonese cooking at "**rock-bottom**", cash-only rates; despite "**abrupt**" service and "**no-frills**" digs decorated with a "**zillion photos**", "**long lines**" are the norm – especially "**late-night.**"

WOLFGANG'S STEAKHOUSE | Steak   4.5   4.1   4.2 $$$$

East 40s | 16 E. 46th St. (bet. 5th & Madison Aves.) | 212-490-8300
East 50s | 200 E. 54th St. (3rd Ave.) | 212-588-9653
Murray Hill | 4 Park Ave. (33rd St.) | 212-889-3369
TriBeCa | 409 Greenwich St. (bet. Beach & Hubert Sts.) | 212-925-0350
West 40s | NY Times Bldg. | 250 W. 41st St. (bet. 7th & 8th Aves.) |
212-921-3720
www.wolfgangssteakhouse.net

"**Masterfully done**" steaks "**with all the trimmings**" lure "**business**" types and other "**enthusiastic carnivores**" to these "**high-energy**" chop shops also touted for their "**outstanding**" wine lists, "**old-school**" service and "**awesome ceilings**" in the Park Avenue outlet; "**holler**"-worthy noise and "**sticker-shock**" tabs notwithstanding, it's a "**top contender**" in its genre.

WOLLENSKY'S GRILL | Steak   4.4   3.9   4.2 $$$

East 40s | 201 E. 49th St. (3rd Ave.)
212-753-0444 | www.smithandwollenskynyc.com

"**Less highfalutin**" and somewhat "**cheaper**" than its next-door big brother, Smith & Wollensky, this "**casual**" East Midtowner serves "**dynamite**" steaks and burgers in "**high-energy**" environs; it's especially beloved for its "**late-dining**" hours – open nightly till 2 AM.

WONDEE SIAM | Thai   4.1   3.1   3.8 $$

West 50s | 792 Ninth Ave. (bet. 52nd & 53rd Sts.) | 212-459-9057
West 50s | 813 Ninth Ave. (bet. 53rd & 54th Sts.) | 917-286-1726
www.wondeesiam2.com

"**Consistently delicious**" Thai fare brings back "**memories of Bangkok**" at these "**hole-in-the-wall**" Westsiders; OK, they're "**not fancy**" and "**seating is limited**", but service is "**fast**" and regulars say the "**rock-bottom prices**" are the key to their enduring "**popularity.**"

WRITING ROOM | American   3.9   4.1   3.9 $$$

East 80s | 1703 Second Ave. (bet. 88th & 89th Sts.)
212-335-0075 | www.thewritingroomnyc.com

"**Paying homage to its predecessor, Elaine's**", this UES American is lined with photos of "**famous patrons**" from back in the day, while their literary works enjoy pride of place in the "**inviting**" rear study; expect "**solid**" food, "**friendly**" service and a bar "**packed**" with a "**fiftysomething crowd.**"

	FOOD	DECOR	SERVICE	COST

WU LIANG YE | Chinese   4.5   3.2   3.5 $$

West 40s | 36 W. 48th St. (bet. 5th & 6th Aves.)
212-398-2308 | www.wuliangyenyc.com

"One of the best Chinese restaurants north of C-town", this outfit just off Rock Center is known for "**lip-tingling**", "**real-deal**" Sichuan cooking ("**bring tissues to deal with your runny nose**"); "**bargain prices**" outweigh the "**glum**" decor and "**indifferent**" service.

XI'AN FAMOUS | Chinese/Noodle Shop   4.2   2.8   3.4 $
FOODS

Chinatown | 67 Bayard St. (bet. Bowery & Mott St.) | 718-885-7788
East 70s | 328 E. 78th St. (bet. 1st & 2nd Aves.) | 212-786-2068
East Village | 81 St. Marks Pl. (1st Ave.) | 212-786-2068
Murray Hill | 14 E. 34th St. (bet. 5th & Madison Aves.) | 212-786-2068
West 100s | 2675 Broadway (bet. 101st & 102nd Sts.) | 212-786-2068
West 40s | 24 W. 45th St. (bet. 5th & 6th Aves.) | 212-786-2068
Greenpoint | 648 Manhattan Ave. (bet. Nassau & Norman Aves.) | Brooklyn | 212-786-2068
Flushing | Golden Shopping Mall | 41-28 Main St. (41st Rd.) | Queens | 718-888-7713
www.xianfoods.com

Fans of "**banging**" hand-pulled noodles discover "**fiery**" "**nirvana**" at this "**burgeoning**" Western Chinese chain also famed for cumin-lamb burgers so "**insanely good**" that they have their own "**cult following**"; "**zero decor**" and "**cramped**" seating are offset by ultra-"**cheap**" tabs.

XIXA | Mexican   ∇ 4.6   3.8   4.2 $$

Williamsburg | 241 S. Fourth St. (Havemeyer St.) | Brooklyn
718-388-8860 | www.xixany.com

"**A Brooklyn foodie vibe**" marks this "**innovative**" Williamsburg Mexican from the Traif team, home to a "**unique**", small plates–centric menu paired with "**sinful**" cocktails; manned by a staff that's "**attentive without being annoying**", it's "**a bit pricey**" but "**worth it.**"

YAKITORI TOTTO | Japanese   4.4   3.5   3.8 $$

West 50s | 251 W. 55th St. (bet. B'way & 8th Ave.)
212-245-4555 | www.tottonyc.com

"**If it can be put on a skewer, they'll do it**" at this "**popular**" Midtown yakitori den where "**heavenly**" meats, veggies and "**chicken parts you never knew existed**" are grilled on sticks; it's a real "**excursion to Tokyo**" complete with "**cramped**", "**noisy**" digs, "**long waits**" and tabs that can "**add up quickly.**"

YAMA | Japanese   4.4   3.4   3.8 $$$

East 40s | 308 E. 49th St. (bet. 1st & 2nd Aves.) | 212-355-3370
Gramercy Park | 122 E. 17th St. (Irving Pl.) | 212-475-0969
www.yamasushinyc.com

"**Fresh and delicious**" sushi comes in "**giant-sized**" pieces at these East Side Japanese "**gems**"; "**cramped**", "**plain**" quarters are a "**downside**", but with the "**high-quality**" fare coming at a "**decent**" price, it's no surprise they're "**always jammed.**"

YEFSI ESTIATORIO | Greek   4.3   3.7   4.0 $$$

East 70s | 1481 York Ave. (bet. 78th & 79th Sts.)
212-535-0293 | www.yefsiestiatorio.com

Be "**transported to Greece**" at this "**real-deal**" Yorkville "**favorite**" where "**wonderful**" mezes are the focus and the service is "**warm and friendly**"; the "**rustic**", "**like-in-Athens**" setting can get "**noisy**", but in summer there's always the "**charming garden.**"

	FOOD	DECOR	SERVICE	COST

YERBA BUENA | Pan-Latin   4.3   3.8   4.0 $$

East Village | 23 Ave. A (bet. 1st & 2nd Sts.) | 212-529-2919
West Village | 1 Perry St. (Greenwich Ave.) | 212-620-0808
www.ybnyc.com

Chef Julian Medina delivers "**inventive**" Pan-Latin fare matched with "**creative drinks**" at these "**stylish**" crosstown siblings manned by a "**helpful**" crew; just be aware that the settings are "**tight**" and the "**noise level rises a few decibels**" as the night wears on.

YONAH SCHIMMEL KNISH BAKERY | Jewish   4.3   2.6   3.4 $

Lower East Side | 137 E. Houston St. (Forsyth St.)
212-477-2858 | www.knishery.com

Since 1910, this "**frozen-in-time**" LES "**relic**" has been offering "**can't-resist**" knishes so "**huge**" they'll "**hold you down in a hurricane**"; "**epic**" latkes, borscht and other Jewish classics are also available, and while the digs are "**outdated**", they'll take you on a "**real journey to the past.**"

YUCA BAR | Pan-Latin   4.1   3.5   3.5 $$

East Village | 111 Ave. A (7th St.)
212-982-9533 | www.yucabarnyc.com

"**Upbeat**" and "**crowded**" with "**good-looking**" types, this "**colorful**" East Villager mixes "**better-than-average**", well-priced Pan-Latin fare with "**killer**" drinks; it gets "**loud**" and service can lag, but for "**people-watching**" by the open doors and windows, it's hard to beat.

YUKA | Japanese   4.2   3.2   3.9 $$

East 80s | 1557 Second Ave. (81st St.)
212-772-9675 | www.yukasushi.com

"**Talk about a bargain**", this "**busy**" Yorkville Japanese vet offers "**super-fresh**", all-you-can-eat sushi for just $24 per person; the space and service are pretty basic, so most stay focused on the "**amazing deal.**"

YURA ON MADISON | Sandwiches   4.1   3.0   3.4 $$

East 90s | 1292 Madison Ave. (92nd St.)
212-860-1707 | www.yuraonmadison.com

A "**perfect pre-museum stop**", this "**upmarket**" Carnegie Hill cafe vending "**dependable**" sandwiches, salads and baked goods is also a "**hangout**" for local "**prep-school girls**" and their "**Madison Avenue moms**"; it "**needs more seating**", so many go the "**take-out**" route.

ZABB ELEE | Thai   4.1   3.0   3.5 $$

East Village | 75 Second Ave. (bet. 4th & 5th Sts.) | 212-505-9533
Elmhurst | 71-28 Roosevelt Ave. (72nd St.) | Queens | 718-426-7992
www.zabbelee.com

"**Complex flavors**" – some of them "**blistering hot**" – distinguish these "**affordable**" Thais that serve up "**tasty**" Northeastern Isan dishes; "**friendly**" staffers add warmth to the otherwise "**sterile**" environs.

NEW **ZADIE'S OYSTER ROOM** | Seafood   —   —   — $$$

East Village | 413 E. 12th St. (1st Ave.)
646-602-1300 | www.zadiesoysterroom.com

Honoring a forgotten tradition of old-time NYC watering holes, Marco Canora

(Hearth) devotes this East Villager to oysters prepared every which way (broiled, fried, pickled, poached). There's just a handful of other plates, plus a selection of ciders, beers and wines featuring a number of sparklers.

ZAITZEFF | Burgers

∇ 4.1 3.0 3.6 $

Financial District | 72 Nassau St. (John St.)
212-571-7272 | www.zaitzeffnyc.com

"**Tasty**" patties of all persuasions – Kobe beef, sirloin, turkey, vegetable – made with "**quality**" ingredients and served on "**terrific Portuguese rolls**" are the draw at this FiDi burger-and-beer purveyor; "**small**" dimensions make it more enjoyable either before or after the "**lunch crush.**"

ZAYTOONS | Mideastern

4.1 3.3 3.8 $$

Carroll Gardens | 283 Smith St. (Sackett St.) | Brooklyn | 718-875-1880
Clinton Hill | 472 Myrtle Ave. (bet. Hall St. & Washington Ave.) | Brooklyn | 718-623-5522
Prospect Heights | 594 Vanderbilt Ave. (St Marks Ave.) | Brooklyn | 718-230-3200
www.zaytoons.com

For "**tasty**", "**reliable**" Middle Eastern fare, stay tooned to these nothing-fancy Brooklyn standbys where "**tables are close**" but the prices are "**terrific**"; Carroll Gardens and Clinton Hill are BYOB (and the latter has a hookah bar), while Prospect Heights boasts a "**pleasant garden.**"

ZENGO | Pan-Latin

4.0 4.1 3.8 $$$

East 40s | 622 Third Ave. (40th St.)
212-808-8110 | www.richardsandoval.com

An "**upscale**" tri-level space designed by AvroKO sets the stage at this Grand Central–area Pan-Latin presenting Richard Sandoval's "**imaginative**" Asian-accented cuisine; "**pricey**" tabs and "**tiny portions**" can vex, but a "**cool**" downstairs tequila lounge tips the balance.

ZENKICHI | Japanese

4.6 4.5 4.4 $$$

Williamsburg | 77 N. Sixth St. (Wythe Ave.) | Brooklyn
718-388-8985 | www.zenkichi.com

"**Zen is the appropriate word**" for this "**special**" Williamsburg Japanese featuring "**peaceful**" private cubicles where "**mindful**" staffers can be summoned with the "**press of a button**"; adding to the "**romantic**" mood is an "**excellent**", izakaya-style small-plates menu paired with "**top-notch**" sakes.

ZERO OTTO NOVE | Italian/Pizza

4.3 4.1 4.2 $$

Flatiron | 15 W. 21st St. (bet. 5th & 6th Aves.) | 212-242-0899
Arthur Avenue/Belmont | 2357 Arthur Ave. (186th St.) | Bronx | 718-220-1027
www.roberto089.com

"**Fabulous pizzas and pastas**" top the list of "**hearty**" Southern Italian specialties offered at these "**reliable**" "**favorites**"; the Arthur Avenue original (done up like an "**old-fashioned**" courtyard) doesn't take reservations, so "**be prepared to wait**" – or check out the "**cavernous**" Flatiron offshoot.

ZIO | Italian

4.3 4.1 4.3 $$$

Flatiron | 17 W. 19th St. (5th Ave.)
212-352-1700 | www.zio-nyc.com

This "**welcoming**" Flatironer turns out "**classic**" Italian dishes "**with a little twist**", and its "**spacious**" modern setting includes a "**buzzing**" bar that's "**great for after work**"; factor in "**reasonable**" prices and "**friendly**" service, and no wonder it's considered a "**local gem.**"

ZONA ROSA | Mexican   ▽ 4.2   4.1   4.2 $$

Williamsburg | 571 Lorimer St. (Metropolitan Ave.) | Brooklyn
917-324-7423 | www.zonarosabrooklyn.com

"**Fabulous, quirky design**" – complete with a "**rooftop deck**" and kitchen
"**built inside an Airstream trailer**" – and a "**party**" vibe collide at this
Williamsburg taqueria; fueling the fiesta are "**delish**" Mexican staples and
"**incredible margaritas.**"

ZUCKER'S BAGELS & SMOKED FISH | Bagels   4.2   3.2   3.7 $

East 40s | 370 Lexington Ave. (41st St.) | 212-661-1080
TriBeCa | 146 Chambers St. (W. B'way) | 212-608-5844
www.zuckersbagels.com

These "**real-deal**" delis from the family behind Murray's Bagels supply
"**high-quality**" bagels with a "**nice, chewy texture**" alongside "**delicious
spreads**" including "**incredible**" smoked fish; service is "**no-nonsense**" and the
decor "**nonexistent**" but they're "**busy for a reason.**"

ZUMA | Japanese   4.3   4.6   4.0 $$$$

Murray Hill | 261 Madison Ave. (bet. 38th & 39th Sts.)
212-544-9862 | www.zumarestaurant.com

The first NYC outpost of the "**swank**" global chain, this "**high-energy**" Murray
Hill Japanese delivers "**inventive**" izakaya-style bites along with sushi and
robata-grilled dishes in a "**dramatic**" duplex space; "**sky-high**" tabs and
"**service kinks**" aren't keeping the "**good-looking**" crowd away from its
"**cool-as-can-be**" upstairs lounge.

ZUM SCHNEIDER | German   4.2   3.8   3.9 $$

East Village | 107 Ave. C (7th St.)
212-598-1098 | www.nyc.zumschneider.com

It's all about the "**humongous**" Bavarian steins of beer and German brats at
this affordable East Village "**slice of Munich**" that's a "**boisterous**" "**haus away
from home**" where "**every day's a party**"; hit the ATM first since it's "**cash
only**", and prepare to wait during Oktoberfest.

ZUM STAMMTISCH | German   4.5   3.9   4.2 $$

Glendale | 69-46 Myrtle Ave. (bet. 69th Pl. & 70th St.) | Queens
718-386-3014 | www.zumstammtisch.com

"**Go with an appetite**" to this 1972-vintage Glendale German, where the
"**hearty**" classics come in "**you-won't-leave-hungry**" portions for "**moderate**"
sums; "**pleasant frauleins in Alpine costume**" toting steins of "**frosty beer**"
bolster the kitschy "**hofbrauhaus-in-Bavaria**" vibe.

ZZ'S CLAM BAR | Seafood   ▽ 4.5   4.1   4.1 $$$

Greenwich Village | 169 Thompson St. (bet. Bleecker & Houston Sts.)
212-254-3000 | www.zzsclambar.com

You feel "**as if you're in a private club**" at this "**tiny**" Village hang from the
team behind Carbone and Parm, a "**stylish**" 12-seater where "**amazing**"
raw-bar offerings complement "**excellent**" craft cocktails; the "**roguish**"
staff "**makes you feel pampered**", but "**you'd better have a big wallet**"
and a reservation.

INDEXES

SPECIAL FEATURES

Listings cover the best in each category and include names, locations and Food ratings. Multi-location restaurants' features may vary by branch.

BAR/SINGLES SCENES

4.1 **ARLINGTON CLUB** | E 70s
4.3 **ATLANTIC GRILL** | E 70s
4.0 **BAGATELLE** | Meatpacking
4.2 **BEAUTY & ESSEX** | LES
3.9 **BERG'N** | Crown Hts
4.1 **BLACK BARN** | NoMad
4.4 **BLUE RIBBON** | Multi
4.3 **BLUE WATER** | Union Sq
4.1 **BODEGA NEGRA** | Chelsea
4.4 **BOWERY MEAT CO.** | E Vill
4.3 **BRESLIN** | NoMad
3.9 **BRYANT PK GRILL** | W 40s
4.4 **BUDDAKAN** | Chelsea
4.2 **CABANA** | Multi
4.3 **CATCH** | Meatpacking
4.4 **CECIL** | Harlem
4.3 **CLOCKTOWER** | Flatiron
4.3 **CRAVE FISHBAR** | UWS
4.2 **DBGB** | E Vill
4.5 **DEL FRISCO'S** | Multi
4.1 **DIRTY FRENCH** | LES
3.9 **DOS CAMINOS** | Multi
4.2 **DUTCH** | SoHo
4.1 **EAST POLE** | E 60s
4.2 **EL TORO BLANCO** | W Vill
4.1 **FREEMANS** | LES
4.3 **FREUD** | G Vill NEW
4.5 **GATO** | NoHo
4.2 **HILLSTONE** | Multi
4.1 **HUDSON CLEARWATER** | W Vill
4.2 **HUNT & FISH** | W 40s
4.2 **JOYA** | Cobble Hill
4.1 **JUE LAN CLUB** | Flatiron
4.3 **LA ESQUINA** | SoHo
4.3 **LAFAYETTE** | NoHo
4.4 **L'AMICO** | Chelsea
4.4 **LA PECORA BIANCA** | Flatiron
4.2 **LA SIRENA** | Chelsea NEW
3.9 **LAVO** | E 50s
4.5 **LLAMA INN** | W'burg NEW
4.4 **LURE FISHBAR** | SoHo
4.0 **MACAO TRADING** | TriBeCa

4.1 **MARGAUX** | G Vill
4.2 **MAYSVILLE** | NoMad
4.4 **MINETTA TAV.** | G Vill
4.1 **MISS LILY'S** | G Vill
4.6 **NOMAD** | NoMad
4.3 **OTTO** | G Vill
4.1 **PENROSE** | E 80s
4.3 **PERLA CAFE** | G Vill
3.6 **PETE'S TAV.** | Gramercy
3.8 **PIER A** | BPC
4.5 **QUALITY EATS** | W Vill NEW
4.2 **RED ROOSTER** | Harlem
4.4 **RIST. MORINI** | E 80s
4.3 **ROSEMARY'S** | W Vill
3.8 **SALVATION TACO** | Murray Hill
4.3 **SAXON & PAROLE** | NoHo
— **SAUVAGE** | Greenpt NEW
3.9 **SMITH** | Multi
4.3 **SPICE MKT.** | Meatpacking
3.7 **STANDARD BIERGARTEN** | Meatpacking
4.1 **STANDARD GRILL** | Meatpacking
4.5 **STANTON SOCIAL** | LES
4.2 **STK** | Meatpacking
4.3 **TAO** | Multi
4.5 **TORO** | Chelsea
4.4 **UPLAND** | Murray Hill
4.3 **VANDAL** | LES NEW
4.3 **ZUMA** | Murray Hill

BEER STANDOUTS

3.9 **BERG'N** | Crown Hts
4.2 **BIRRERIA** | Flatiron
4.1 **BLUE SMOKE** | Multi
4.3 **BRESLIN** | NoMad
4.1 **CAFÉ D'ALSACE** | E 80s
4.4 **CANNIBAL** | W 40s
4.5 **COLICCHIO/SONS** | Chelsea
4.2 **DBGB** | E Vill
4.2 **DINOSAUR BBQ** | Multi
4.7 **ELEVEN MADISON** | Flatiron
4.5 **FETTE SAU** | W'burg
4.6 **FINCH** | Clinton Hill

4.0 **5 NAPKIN BURGER** | Multi

4.4 **FLEX MUSSELS** | Multi

3.9 **FRAUNCES TAV.** | Financial

4.1 **GANDER** | Flatiron

4.8 **GRAMERCY TAV.** | Flatiron

4.2 **HEIDELBERG** | E 80s

4.2 **JACOB'S PICKLES** | W 80s

4.3 **JAKE'S STEAKHSE.** | Fieldston

4.2 **JEFFREY CRAFT BEER** | E 60s

4.3 **JOHN BROWN** | LIC

4.5 **LUKSUS** | Greenpt

4.3 **PRESS 195** | Bayside

4.0 **QUEENS KICKSHAW** | Astoria

4.4 **SPOTTED PIG** | W Vill

3.7 **STANDARD BIERGARTEN** | Meatpacking

4.5 **TØRST** | Greenpt

4.5 **UPSTATE** | E Vill

4.2 **WASSAIL** | LES

4.2 **ZUM SCHNEIDER** | E Vill

BREAKFAST

4.4 **BALTHAZAR** | SoHo

4.5 **BARNEY GREENGRASS** | W 80s

4.1 **BAZ BAGEL** | L Italy

4.3 **BRESLIN** | NoMad

4.0 **BUBBY'S** | Multi

4.1 **BUTTER** | W 40s

4.4 **BUVETTE** | W Vill

4.2 **CAFE LUXEMBOURG** | W 70s

4.0 **CAFE GITANE** | Multi

4.3 **CAFE MOGADOR** | E Vill

4.2 **CAFÉ SABARSKY/ FLEDERMAUS** | E 80s

4.3 **CARNEGIE DELI** | W 50s

4.4 **CASA LEVER** | E 50s

4.2 **CITY BAKERY** | Flatiron

4.5 **CLINTON ST. BAKING** | LES

— **COCO & CRU** | G Vill NEW

4.1 **COMMUNITY** | Morningside Hts

4.3 **COOKSHOP** | Chelsea

4.3 **COPPELIA** | Chelsea

4.2 **DUDLEY'S** | LES

4.0 **E.A.T.** | E 80s

4.3 **EGG** | W'burg

4.3 **FIVE LEAVES** | Greenpt

— **FRANKEL'S DELI** | Greenpt NEW

4.2 **FRIEDMAN'S** | Multi

4.5 **HIGH STREET/HUDSON** | Meatpacking NEW

4.1 **HUDSON CLEARWATER** | W Vill

4.1 **HUDSON EATS** | BPC

4.5 **IL BUCO ALIMENTARI** | NoHo

4.2 **IMPERO CAFFÈ** | Chelsea NEW

4.2 **JACK'S WIFE FREDA** | Multi

4.8 **JEAN-GEORGES** | W 60s

4.7 **JEAN-GEORGES' NOUG.** | W 60s

4.4 **JEFFREY'S GROCERY** | W Vill

4.3 **JOSEPH LEONARD** | W Vill

4.5 **KATZ'S DELI** | LES

4.0 **KITCHENETTE** | Morningside Hts

4.2 **KRUPA** | Windsor Terr.

4.3 **LADURÉE** | Multi

4.3 **LAFAYETTE** | NoHo

4.3 **LAMBS CLUB** | W 40s

3.9 **LANDMARC** | W 50s

4.4 **LA PECORA BIANCA** | Flatiron

4.2 **LA SIRENA** | Chelsea NEW

— **LE COUCOU** | SoHo NEW

4.4 **LITTLE PARK** | TriBeCa

4.5 **LOCANDA VERDE** | TriBeCa

4.3 **MACHIAVELLI** | W 80s

4.6 **MAIALINO** | Gramercy

4.2 **MAISON KAYSER** | Multi

4.1 **MARGAUX** | G Vill

4.4 **MARLOW/SONS** | W'burg

4.3 **MICHAEL'S** | W 50s

4.2 **MORANDI** | W Vill

3.9 **NICE MATIN** | W 70s

3.9 **NOHO STAR** | NoHo

4.6 **NOMAD** | NoMad

4.4 **NORMA'S** | W 50s

4.0 **ODEON** | TriBeCa

4.4 **OKONOMI** | W'burg

4.2 **PALM COURT** | W 50s

4.0 **PENELOPE** | Murray Hill

4.0 **REGENCY B&G** | E 60s

4.4 **REYNARD** | W'burg

4.3 **ROSEMARY'S** | W Vill

4.7 **RUSS & DAUGHTERS** | LES

4.3 **SADELLE'S** | SoHo

4.4 **SANT AMBROEUS** | Multi

4.0 **SARABETH'S** | Multi

4.1 **STANDARD GRILL** | Meatpacking

4.2 **TARTINE** | W Vill
— **TEKOÁ** | Cobble Hill `NEW`
4.4 **TILDA ALL DAY** | Clinton Hill
4.1 **VESELKA** | E Vill

BRUNCH

4.5 **ABC KITCHEN** | Flatiron
4.3 **AITA** | Multi
4.1 **ALLSWELL** | W'burg
3.9 **ALMOND** | Multi
4.4 **AMY RUTH'S** | Harlem
4.7 **AQUAGRILL** | SoHo
4.2 **ARTISANAL** | Murray Hill
4.3 **ATLANTIC GRILL** | E 70s
4.3 **A VOCE** | W 50s
4.0 **BAGATELLE** | Meatpacking
4.4 **BALABOOSTA** | NoLita
4.4 **BALTHAZAR** | SoHo
4.3 **BAR AMERICAIN** | W 50s
4.1 **BARBOUNIA** | Flatiron
4.5 **BARNEY GREENGRASS** | W 80s
4.1 **BAR TABAC** | Cobble Hill
4.1 **BAZ BAGEL** | L Italy
4.3 **BEEHIVE** | W'burg
4.0 **BLACK WHALE** | City Is
4.4 **BLUE RIBBON** | W Vill
4.3 **BLUE WATER** | Union Sq
4.2 **BRASSERIE 8½** | W 50s
4.0 **BUBBY'S** | Multi
4.6 **BUTTERMILK** | Carroll Gdns
4.2 **CAFE CLUNY** | W Vill
4.1 **CAFÉ D'ALSACE** | E 80s
3.9 **CAFE LOUP** | W Vill
4.2 **CAFE LULUC** | Cobble Hill
4.2 **CAFE LUXEMBOURG** | W 70s
4.3 **CAFE MOGADOR** | E Vill
4.2 **CARLYLE** | E 70s
4.2 **CEBU** | Bay Ridge
4.4 **CECIL** | Harlem
4.4 **CELESTE** | W 80s
4.2 **CHALK POINT** | SoHo
4.4 **CLAM** | W Vill
4.5 **CLINTON ST. BAKING** | LES
4.5 **COLICCHIO/SONS** | Chelsea
4.5 **COLONIE** | Bklyn Hts
4.1 **COMMUNITY** | Morningside Hts
4.3 **COOKSHOP** | Chelsea
3.8 **CORNELIA ST.** | W Vill
4.2 **CRAFTBAR** | Flatiron

4.4 **DB BISTRO MODERNE** | W 40s
4.2 **DBGB** | E Vill
4.5 **DELAWARE/HUDSON** | W'burg
4.5 **DELL'ANIMA** | W Vill
4.3 **DIMES** | LES
4.5 **DINER** | W'burg
4.2 **DUDLEY'S** | LES
4.2 **DUTCH** | SoHo
4.1 **EAST POLE** | E 60s
4.2 **EDI & THE WOLF** | E Vill
4.3 **EGG** | W'burg
4.5 **EL QUINTO PINO** | Chelsea
4.7 **EMILY** | Clinton Hill
4.2 **EMPELLÓN TAQ.** | W Vill
4.6 **ESTELA** | NoLita
4.2 **EXTRA VIRGIN** | W Vill
4.1 **FAT RADISH** | LES
4.3 **FIVE LEAVES** | Greenpt
4.0 **FLATBUSH FARM** | Park Slope
4.2 **44 & X/44½** | W 40s
— **FRANKEL'S DELI** | Greenpt `NEW`
— **FREEK'S MILL** | Gowanus `NEW`
4.1 **FREEMANS** | LES
4.4 **FRENCH LOUIE** | Boerum Hill
4.3 **FREUD** | G Vill `NEW`
4.0 **FRIEND/FARMER** | Multi
4.1 **GANDER** | Flatiron
4.1 **GOOD** | W Vill
4.4 **HEARTH** | E Vill
4.2 **HUNDRED ACRES** | SoHo
4.4 **IL GATTOPARDO** | W 50s
4.5 **ILILI** | NoMad
4.0 **ISABELLA'S** | W 70s
4.2 **JACK THE HORSE** | Bklyn Hts
4.2 **JACK'S WIFE FREDA** | Multi
4.2 **JACOB'S PICKLES** | W 80s
4.4 **JAMES** | Prospect Hts
4.2 **JANE** | G Vill
4.4 **JOJO** | E 60s
4.3 **JOSEPH LEONARD** | W Vill
4.0 **KITCHENETTE** | Morningside Hts
4.3 **LADURÉE** | Multi
4.3 **LAFAYETTE** | NoHo
4.3 **LAMBS CLUB** | W 40s
4.4 **LA PECORA BIANCA** | Flatiron
4.4 **L'APICIO** | E Vill
3.9 **LAVO** | E 50s
4.4 **LE COQ RICO** | Flatiron `NEW`

SPECIAL FEATURES

4.5 **LE GIGOT** | W Vill

4.3 **LEOPARD/DES ARTISTES** | W 60s

3.9 **L'EXPRESS** | Gramercy

4.3 **LIC MARKET** | LIC

4.1 **LIDO** | Harlem

4.5 **LOCANDA VERDE** | TriBeCa

4.6 **MAIALINO** | Gramercy

4.3 **MÁ PÊCHE** | W 50s

4.3 **MARK** | E 70s

4.3 **MARSHAL** | W 40s

4.7 **MEADOWSWEET** | W'burg

4.2 **MILE END** | Boerum Hill

4.4 **MINETTA TAV.** | G Vill

4.1 **MIRIAM** | Park Slope

4.1 **MISS LILY'S** | G Vill

4.0 **MON PETIT CAFE** | E 60s

4.4 **MURRAY'S CHEESE** | W Vill

4.5 **NARCISSA** | E Vill

3.9 **NICE MATIN** | W 70s

4.4 **NORMA'S** | W 50s

4.0 **ODEON** | TriBeCa

4.1 **OFRENDA** | W Vill

4.5 **OLEA** | Ft Greene

4.2 **PALM COURT** | W 50s

4.0 **PENELOPE** | Murray Hill

4.1 **PENROSE** | E 80s

4.3 **PERLA CAFE** | W Vill

4.4 **PETROSSIAN** | W 50s

4.6 **PRUNE** | E Vill

4.3 **PUBLIC** | NoLita

4.5 **QUALITY EATS** | W Vill NEW

4.2 **QUEENS COMFORT** | Astoria

4.3 **RAINBOW RM.** | W 50s

4.5 **RAOUL'S** | SoHo

4.2 **RED ROOSTER** | Harlem

— **RIDER** | W'burg NEW

4.4 **RIST. MORINI** | E 80s

4.6 **RIVER CAFÉ** | Dumbo

4.5 **RIVERPARK** | Murray Hill

4.6 **ROBERTA'S** | Bushwick

4.2 **ROCKING HORSE** | Chelsea

4.4 **ROOT & BONE** | E Vill

4.3 **ROSEMARY'S** | W Vill

4.6 **ROSE WATER** | Park Slope

4.4 **RUNNER & STONE** | Gowanus

4.5 **RUSS/DAUGHTERS CAFE** | LES

4.3 **SADELLE'S** | SoHo

3.8 **SALVATION TACO** | Murray Hill

4.1 **SANFORD'S** | Astoria

4.2 **SANTINA** | Meatpacking

4.0 **SARABETH'S** | Multi

4.3 **SAXON & PAROLE** | NoHo

4.1 **SCOTTADITO** | Park Slope

4.4 **SEVA INDIAN** | Astoria

4.5 **SHALOM JAPAN** | W'burg

4.3 **SMILE** | Multi

3.9 **SMITH** | Multi

4.4 **SPOTTED PIG** | W Vill

4.5 **STANTON SOCIAL** | LES

4.1 **STELLA 34** | W 30s

4.5 **STONE PARK** | Park Slope

3.9 **SYLVIA'S** | Harlem

4.2 **TARTINE** | W Vill

3.6 **TAVERN/GREEN** | Central Pk

4.2 **TERTULIA** | W Vill

4.4 **TIMNA** | E Vill

3.9 **TIPSY PARSON** | Chelsea

4.3 **TRIBECA GRILL** | TriBeCa

4.3 **TURKISH KIT.** | Murray Hill

4.3 **TWO HANDS** | Multi

4.4 **UPLAND** | Murray Hill

4.2 **VIC'S** | NoHo

4.3 **WATER CLUB** | Murray Hill

4.2 **WAVERLY INN** | W Vill

3.9 **WRITING ROOM** | E 80s

BYO

4.4 **AZURI CAFE** | W 50s

4.6 **DI FARA** | Midwood

4.1 **GAZALA'S** | W 40s

4.3 **KUMA INN** | LES

4.1 **LITTLE POLAND** | E Vill

4.7 **LUCALI** | Carroll Gdns

4.3 **PEKING DUCK** | Chinatown

4.2 **PHOENIX GDN.** | E 40s

4.5 **POKE** | E 80s

4.2 **QUEENS COMFORT** | Astoria

4.3 **RED HOOK LOBSTER** | Red Hook

4.0 **SAUCE** | LES

4.6 **TACI'S BEYTI** | Sheepshead

4.6 **TANOSHI** | E 70s

4.2 **TARTINE** | W Vill

4.1 **WONDEE SIAM** | W 50s

4.1 **ZAYTOONS** | Multi

CELEBRITY CHEFS

EINAT ADMONY
4.4 **BALABOOSTA** | NoLita
4.5 **BAR BOLONAT** | W Vill
4.6 **TAÏM** | Multi

MICHAEL ANTHONY
4.8 **GRAMERCY TAV.** | Flatiron
4.4 **UNTITLED** | Meatpacking

DAN BARBER
4.7 **BLUE HILL** | G Vill

LIDIA BASTIANICH
4.6 **FELIDIA** | E 50s

MARIO BATALI
4.6 **BABBO** | G Vill
4.6 **CASA MONO** | Gramercy
4.7 **DEL POSTO** | Chelsea
4.3 **EATALY** | Multi
4.4 **ESCA** | W 40s
4.2 **LA SIRENA** | Chelsea NEW
4.6 **LUPA** | G Vill
4.5 **MANZO** | Flatiron
4.3 **OTTO** | G Vill
3.9 **PENNSY** | W 30s NEW

JONATHAN BENNO
4.5 **LINCOLN** | W 00s

APRIL BLOOMFIELD
4.3 **BRESLIN** | NoMad
4.2 **JOHN DORY** | NoMad
3.8 **SALVATION TACO** | Murray Hill
4.4 **SPOTTED PIG** | W Vill

DAVID BOULEY
4.9 **BOULEY** | TriBeCa
4.6 **BRUSHSTROKE/ICHIMURA** | TriBeCa

DANIEL BOULUD
4.3 **BAR BOULUD** | W 60s
4.5 **BOULUD SUD** | W 60s
4.7 **CAFÉ BOULUD** | E 70s
4.8 **DANIEL** | E 60s
4.4 **DB BISTRO MODERNE** | W 40s
4.2 **DBGB** | E Vill

DANNY BOWIEN
3.7 **MISSION CANTINA** | LES
4.3 **MISSION CHINESE** | LES

DAVID BURKE
4.2 **DAVID BURKE FAB.** | W 30s
4.4 **DAVID BURKE KIT.** | SoHo

MARCO CANORA
4.4 **HEARTH** | E Vill
— **ZADIE'S OYSTER RM.** | E Vill NEW

MARIO CARBONE/RICH TORRISI
4.5 **CARBONE** | G Vill
4.1 **DIRTY FRENCH** | LES
3.8 **PARM** | Multi
4.3 **SADELLE'S** | SoHo
4.2 **SANTINA** | Meatpacking
4.5 **ZZ'S CLAM BAR** | G Vill

ANDREW CARMELLINI
4.4 **BAR PRIMI** | E Vill
4.2 **DUTCH** | SoHo
4.3 **LAFAYETTE** | NoHo
3.8 **LIBRARY/PUBLIC** | G Vill
4.4 **LITTLE PARK** | TriBeCa
4.5 **LOCANDA VERDE** | TriBeCa

DAVID CHANG
4.2 **FUKU** | Multi
4.3 **MÁ PÊCHE** | W 50s
4.7 **MOMOFUKU KO** | E Vill
4.3 **MOMOFUKU NISHI** | Chelsea NEW
4.5 **MOMOFUKU NOODLE** | E Vill
4.5 **MOMOFUKU SSÄM** | E Vill

REBECCA CHARLES
4.6 **PEARL OYSTER** | W Vill

AMANDA COHEN
4.3 **DIRT CANDY** | LES

TOM COLICCHIO
4.5 **COLICCHIO/SONS** | Chelsea
4.5 **CRAFT** | Flatiron
4.2 **CRAFTBAR** | Flatiron
4.5 **RIVERPARK** | Murray Hill

SCOTT CONANT
4.2 **IMPERO CAFFÈ** | Chelsea NEW

CHLOE COSCARELLI
4.3 **BY CHLOE** | Multi

ALAIN DUCASSE
4.2 **BENOIT** | W 50s

TODD ENGLISH
4.0 **ÇA VA** | W 40s
4.1 **PLAZA FOOD HALL** | W 50s

BOBBY FLAY
4.3 **BAR AMERICAIN** | W 50s
4.5 **GATO** | NoHo

MARC FORGIONE

4.4 **AMERICAN CUT** | Multi

4.3 **KHE-YO** | TriBeCa

4.6 **MARC FORGIONE** | TriBeCa

JOHN FRASER

4.6 **DOVETAIL** | W 70s

4.5 **NARCISSA** | E Vill

4.5 **NIX** | G Vill NEW

JOSE GARCES

— **AMADA** | BPC NEW

ALEX GUARNASCHELLI

4.1 **BUTTER** | W 40s

KURT GUTENBRUNNER

4.3 **BLAUE GANS** | TriBeCa

4.2 **CAFÉ SABARSKY/ FLEDERMAUS** | E 80s

4.7 **UPHOLSTERY STORE** | W Vill

4.6 **WALLSÉ** | W Vill

GABRIELLE HAMILTON

4.6 **PRUNE** | E Vill

DANIEL HUMM

4.7 **ELEVEN MADISON** | Flatiron

4.6 **NOMAD** | NoMad

4.4 **NOMAD BAR** | NoMad

EIJI ICHIMURA

4.6 **BRUSHSTROKE/ICHIMURA** | TriBeCa

SARA JENKINS

4.4 **PORCHETTA** | E Vill

4.4 **PORSENA** | E Vill

THOMAS KELLER

4.3 **BOUCHON BAKERY** | Multi

4.6 **PER SE** | W 50s

MARK LADNER

4.7 **DEL POSTO** | Chelsea

ANITA LO

4.7 **ANNISA** | W Vill

MICHAEL LOMONACO

4.6 **PORTER HOUSE** | W 50s

NOBU MATSUHISA

4.7 **NOBU** | Multi

JEHANGIR MEHTA

4.6 **GRAFFITI** | E Vill

CLAUS MEYER/GUNNAR GÍSLASON

— **AGERN** | E 40s NEW

— **GREAT NORTHERN FOOD HALL** | E 40s NEW

— **MEYERS BAGERI** | W'burg NEW

CARLO MIRARCHI

4.7 **BLANCA** | Bushwick

4.6 **ROBERTA'S** | Bushwick

MASAHARU MORIMOTO

4.6 **MOMOSAN** | Murray Hill NEW

4.6 **MORIMOTO** | Chelsea

SEAMUS MULLEN

4.2 **TERTULIA** | W Vill

MARC MURPHY

3.9 **LANDMARC** | Multi

DAISUKE NAKAZAWA

4.7 **SUSHI NAKAZAWA** | W Vill

ENRIQUE OLVERA

4.5 **COSME** | Flatiron

IVAN ORKIN

4.1 **IVAN RAMEN** | Multi

CHARLIE PALMER

4.6 **AUREOLE** | W 40s

4.4 **CHARLIE PALMER** | E 50s

4.2 **CHARLIE PALMER/KNICK** | W 40s

DAVID PASTERNACK

4.4 **ESCA** | W 40s

ALFRED PORTALE

4.8 **GOTHAM B&G** | G Vill

MICHAEL PSILAKIS

4.2 **FISHTAG** | W 70s

4.1 **KEFI** | W 80s

4.3 **MP TAVERNA** | Multi

CESAR RAMIREZ

4.8 **CHEF'S/BROOKLYN FARE** | Downtown Bklyn

MARY REDDING

4.4 **MARY'S FISH** | W Vill

ANDY RICKER

4.4 **POK POK NY** | Columbia St.

4.3 **POK POK PHAT** | Columbia St.

ERIC RIPERT

4.9 **LE BERNARDIN** | W 50s

MISSY ROBBINS

4.6 **LILIA** | W'burg NEW

MARCUS SAMUELSSON

4.2 **RED ROOSTER** | Harlem

3.8 **STREETBIRD** | Harlem

RICHARD SANDOVAL

4.1 **MAYA** | E 60s

4.4 **PAMPANO** | E 40s

4.0 **ZENGO** | E 40s

GUNTER SEEGER

— GUNTER SEEGER | Meatpacking NEW

ALEX STUPAK

3.9 EMPELLÓN/PASTOR | E Vill

4.5 EMPELLÓN COCINA | E Vill

4.2 EMPELLÓN TAQ. | W Vill

GARI SUGIO

4.6 GARI | Multi

MASAYOSHI TAKAYAMA

4.3 KAPPO MASA | E 70s

4.5 MASA | W 50s

DALE TALDE

4.4 TALDE | Park Slope

JEAN-GEORGES VONGERICHTEN

4.4 ABC COCINA | Flatiron

4.5 ABC KITCHEN | Flatiron

4.8 JEAN-GEORGES | W 60s

4.4 JOJO | E 60s

4.3 MARK | E 70s

4.2 MERCER KITCHEN | SoHo

4.6 PERRY ST. | W Vill

4.3 SPICE MKT. | Meatpacking

JONATHAN WAXMAN

4.6 BARBUTO | W Vill

3.8 JAMS | W 50s

ANTOINE WESTERMANN

4.4 LE COQ RICO | Flatiron NEW

MICHAEL WHITE

4.6 AI FIORI | W 30s

4.7 MAREA | W 50s

3.9 NICOLETTA | E Vill

4.5 OSTERIA MORINI | SoHo

4.4 RIST. MORINI | E 80s

4.4 VAUCLUSE | E 60s

JODY WILLIAMS

4.4 BUVETTE | W Vill

4.6 VIA CAROTA | W Vill

GEOFFREY ZAKARIAN

4.3 LAMBS CLUB | W 40s

3.8 NATIONAL | E 50s

4.2 PALM COURT | W 50s

GALEN ZAMARRA

4.7 MAS | W Vill

CELEBRITY SIGHTINGS

4.6 ANTICA PESA | W'burg

4.4 BALTHAZAR | SoHo

3.9 BAR CENTRALE | W 40s

4.4 BAR PITTI | G Vill

3.9 BEAUTIQUE | W 50s

4.5 BOND ST | NoHo

4.2 CAFE LUXEMBOURG | W 70s

4.5 CARBONE | G Vill

4.3 CATCH | Meatpacking

4.2 DA SILVANO | G Vill

4.5 ELIO'S | E 80s

4.2 HUNT & FISH | W 40s

3.9 JOE ALLEN | W 40s

4.2 LA SIRENA | Chelsea NEW

4.1 LE BILBOQUET | E 60s

4.3 LEOPARD/DES ARTISTES | W 60s

4.7 MAREA | W 50s

4.3 MICHAEL'S | W 50s

4.4 MINETTA TAV. | G Vill

4.6 NOMAD | NoMad

4.3 ORSO | W 40s

4.3 PHILIPPE | E 60s

4.1 POLO BAR | E 50s

4.4 PRIMOLA | E 60s

4.3 RAO'S | E Harlem

4.4 SPOTTED PIG | W Vill

4.2 WAVERLY INN | W Vill

CHILD-FRIENDLY

(* children's menu available)

3.9 ALICE'S TEA* | Multi

4.1 ALLSWELL | W'burg

4.3 AMORINA* | Prospect Hts

4.7 AMPLE HILLS | Multi

4.4 AMY RUTH'S | Harlem

4.4 ARTIE'S* | City Is

4.3 ATLANTIC GRILL* | Multi

4.3 BAMONTE'S | W'burg

3.9 BAREBURGER* | Multi

4.5 BARNEY GREENGRASS | W 80s

4.1 BAZ BAGEL | L Italy

4.1 BLUE RIBBON* | Multi

4.1 BLUE SMOKE* | Multi

4.3 BLUE WATER* | Union Sq

3.9 BOATHOUSE* | Central Pk

3.9 BRASSERIE COGNAC* | Multi

4.3 BRENNAN | Sheepshead

4.0 BROOKLYN CRAB | Red Hook

4.1 BROOKLYN FARMACY | Carroll Gdns

4.0 BUBBY'S* | Multi

4.6 **BUTTERMILK*** | Carroll Gdns

4.1 **CAFÉ HABANA** | Ft Greene

4.2 **CALEXICO** | Multi

4.1 **CARMINE'S*** | W 40s

4.0 **CHIPSHOP*** | Brooklyn Hts

4.2 **DBGB*** | E Vill

4.2 **DINOSAUR BBQ*** | Multi

4.5 **EDDIE'S SWEET SHOP** | Forest Hills

3.8 **EL VEZ** | Battery Pk

4.7 **EMILY** | Clinton Hill

4.2 **FARM/ADDERLEY*** | Ditmas Pk

4.0 **5 NAPKIN BURGER*** | Multi

4.0 **FLATBUSH FARM** | Park Slope

4.2 **FOGO DE CHÃO** | W 50s

4.3 **FRANNY'S** | Park Slope

4.0 **FRIEND/FARMER*** | Multi

4.4 **GANSO** | Downtown Bklyn

4.2 **GARGIULO'S** | Coney Is

4.1 **GIGINO*** | Multi

3.9 **GOOD ENOUGH*** | W 80s

4.0 **GREY DOG*** | Multi

4.2 **HAN DYNASTY*** | Multi

4.2 **HILL COUNTRY** | Multi

4.1 **HILL COUNTRY CHICKEN** | Multi

4.6 **HOMETOWN** | Red Hook

4.0 **ISABELLA'S*** | W 70s

4.2 **JACK THE HORSE** | Bklyn Hts

4.4 **JOE & PAT'S** | Castelton Cnrs

3.8 **JUNIOR'S*** | Multi

4.1 **KEFI** | W 80s

4.4 **L&B SPUMONI*** | Gravesend

3.9 **LANDMARC*** | W 50s

4.1 **LA VILLA PIZZERIA** | Multi

4.3 **LONDON LENNIE'S*** | Middle Vill

4.2 **MERMAID*** | Multi

4.5 **NICK'S** | Multi

4.4 **NOODLE PUDDING** | Bklyn Hts

4.3 **OTTO** | G Vill

4.5 **PALM** | W 50s

4.0 **PERA*** | E 40s

4.1 **ROSA MEXICANO*** | Multi

4.2 **SAMMY'S FISHBOX*** | City Is

4.2 **SAMMY'S SHRIMP*** | City Is

4.0 **SARABETH'S** | Multi

3.8 **SCHILLER'S*** | LES

4.4 **SEA GRILL*** | W 40s

4.2 **2ND AVE DELI** | Multi

4.0 **SERENDIPITY 3** | E 60s

4.0 **SHAKE SHACK** | Multi

4.1 **SMORGAS CHEF*** | Murray Hill

3.9 **SYLVIA'S*** | Harlem

4.0 **TONY'S DI NAPOLI** | W 40s

4.1 **VESELKA** | E Vill

3.7 **VIEW*** | W 40s

4.0 **VIRGIL'S*** | W 40s

4.3 **ZERO OTTO** | Arthur Ave./Belmont

4.5 **ZUM STAMMTISCH** | Glendale

COCKTAIL STARS

4.6 **ATERA** | TriBeCa

4.4 **BAR GOTO** | LES

4.4 **BAR PRIMI** | E Vill

4.1 **BEATRICE INN** | W Vill

3.9 **BEAUTIQUE** | W 50s

4.2 **BEAUTY & ESSEX** | LES

4.5 **BETONY** | W 50s

4.0 **BLACK ANT** | E Vill

— **BLACKTAIL** | BPC NEW

— **CAFÉ MEDI** | LES NEW

4.1 **CRIF DOGS** | E Vill

4.5 **DANTE** | G Vill

4.2 **DEAD RABBIT** | Financial

3.8 **DEAR IRVING** | Gramercy

4.7 **DECOY** | W Vill

4.2 **DUTCH** | SoHo

4.7 **ELEVEN MADISON** | Flatiron

4.2 **EMPELLÓN TAQ.** | W Vill

4.6 **ESTELA** | NoLita

4.2 **FORT DEFIANCE** | Red Hook

4.3 **FRANNY'S** | Park Slope

4.4 **FRENCH LOUIE** | Boerum Hill

4.3 **FUNG TU** | LES

4.6 **GENUINE SUPERETTE** | L Italy

3.9 **GRAND ARMY** | Downtown Bklyn

4.1 **HUDSON CLEARWATER** | W Vill

4.1 **KAT & THEO** | Flatiron

4.2 **LA SIRENA** | Chelsea NEW

4.5 **LLAMA INN** | W'burg NEW

4.0 **MACAO TRADING** | TriBeCa

4.2 **MAYSVILLE** | NoMad

— **METROPOLIS** | Union Sq NEW

4.4 **MINETTA TAV.** | G Vill

4.5 **MOMOFUKU SSÄM** | E Vill

4.0 **MONKEY BAR** | E 50s

4.3 **M. WELLS STEAKHSE.** | LIC

4.4 **NOMAD BAR** | NoMad

— **OLEANDERS** | W'burg

4.0 **PACHANGA PATTERSON**
Astoria

4.3 **PERLA CAFE** | G Vill

4.6 **PIORA** | W Vill

3.8 **P.J. CLARKE'S** | Multi

4.3 **PRIME MEATS** | Carroll Gdns

4.4 **REDFARM** | Multi

4.2 **RED ROOSTER** | Harlem

4.4 **ROOT & BONE** | E Vill

4.4 **RYE** | W'burg

3.8 **SALVATION TACO** | Murray Hill

4.2 **SANTINA** | Meatpacking

— **SAUVAGE** | Greenpt NEW

4.3 **SAXON & PAROLE** | NoHo

— **SYNDICATED** | Bushwick NEW

4.1 **TINY'S** | TriBeCa

4.5 **TORO** | Chelsea

4.3 **YERBA BUENA** | Multi

4.5 **ZZ'S CLAM BAR** | G Vill

COLLEGE-CENTRIC

COLUMBIA

4.0 **KITCHENETTE** |
Morningside Hts

4.4 **PISTICCI** | Morningside Hts

4.3 **THAI MARKET** | W 100s

NYU

4.1 **ARTICHOKE BASILLE** | Multi

4.1 **BAOHAUS** | E Vill

4.3 **BY CHLOE** | Multi

4.1 **CAFÉ HABANA** | NoLita

4.4 **CARACAS** | E Vill

4.1 **CRIF DOGS** | E Vill

3.9 **GYU-KAKU** | G Vill

4.5 **IPPUDO** | Multi

4.1 **JOHN'S/12TH ST.** | E Vill

4.3 **LA ESQUINA** | SoHo

4.4 **MAMOUN'S** | Multi

4.2 **NUM PANG** | G Vill

4.3 **OTTO** | G Vill

3.8 **REPUBLIC** | Union Sq

3.9 **SMITH** | Multi

4.0 **VANESSA'S DUMPLING** |
E Vill

4.1 **VESELKA** | E Vill

COMMUTER OASIS

GRAND CENTRAL

— **AGERN** | E 40s NEW

4.2 **AMMOS** | E 40s

4.3 **ARETSKY'S PATROON** |
E 40s

4.6 **BENJAMIN STEAK** | E 40s

4.2 **BOBBY VAN'S** | E 40s

4.1 **CAFE CENTRO** | E 40s

4.4 **CAPITAL GRILLE** | E 40s

4.3 **CIPRIANI** | E 40s

4.0 **DOCKS OYSTER** | E 40s

4.2 **GRAND CENTRAL OYSTER** |
E 40s

— **GREAT NORTHERN FOOD
HALL** | E 40s NEW

4.5 **HATSUHANA** | E 40s

3.8 **JUNIOR'S** | Multi

4.1 **LA FONDA/SOL** | E 40s

4.3 **LUKE'S LOBSTER** | E 40s

3.9 **MICHAEL JORDAN** | E 40s

4.4 **MORTON'S** | E 40s

4.2 **NAYA** | E 40s

4.2 **NUM PANG** | E 40s

4.1 **OSTERIA LAGUNA** | E 40s

4.4 **PALM** | E 40s

4.0 **PERA** | E 40s

4.5 **PIETRO'S** | E 40s

4.5 **SAKAGURA** | E 40s

4.0 **SHAKE SHACK** | E 40s

4.0 **SINIGUAL** | E 40s

4.5 **SOBA TOTTO** | E 40s

4.5 **SPARKS** | E 40s

4.8 **SUSHI YASUDA** | E 40s

4.4 **TULSI** | E 40s

4.2 **URBANSPACE VANDERBILT** |
E 40s

4.0 **ZENGO** | E 40s

PENN STATION

4.2 **ARNO** | W 30s

4.3 **CASA NONNA** | W 30s

4.2 **DAVID BURKE FAB.** | W 30s

4.4 **DELMONICO'S** | W 30s

4.2 **FRANKIE/JOHNNIE'S** | W 30s

4.1 **GAONNURI** | W 30s

4.5 **HER NAME IS HAN** |
Murray Hill NEW

SPECIAL FEATURES

4.5 **KEENS** | W 30s
4.4 **L'AMICO** | Chelsea
4.4 **LARB UBOL** | W 30s
4.2 **NICK & STEF'S** | W 30s
4.0 **PARKER & QUINN** | W 30s
3.9 **PENNSY** | W 30s NEW
4.3 **UNCLE JACK'S** | W 30s
4.0 **UNCLE NICK'S** | Chelsea

PORT AUTHORITY
4.0 **ÇA VA** | W 40s
4.1 **CHEZ JOSEPHINE** | W 40s
4.4 **CHIMICHURRI GRILL** | W 40s
4.0 **CITY KITCHEN** | W 40s
4.4 **ESCA** | W 40s
4.2 **ETC. ETC.** | W 40s
4.0 **5 NAPKIN BURGER** | W 40s
4.4 **HAKKASAN** | W 40s
4.0 **INAKAYA** | W 40s
4.3 **JOHN'S PIZZERIA** | W 40s
4.0 **MARSEILLE** | W 40s
4.3 **MERCATO** | W 30s
4.1 **QI** | W 40s
4.0 **SHAKE SHACK** | W 40s
4.5 **WOLFGANG'S** | W 40s

FIREPLACES
4.3 **ALBERTO** | Forest Hills
4.4 **ALTA** | G Vill
4.6 **ANTICA PESA** | W'burg
4.0 **BATTERY GDNS.** | Financial
4.1 **BEATRICE INN** | W Vill
4.6 **BENJAMIN STEAK** | E 40s
3.9 **BOATHOUSE** | Central Pk
4.9 **BOULEY** | TriBeCa
4.2 **BLOSSOM** | W Vill
4.0 **ÇA VA** | W 40s
4.2 **CEBU** | Bay Ridge
4.4 **CHRISTOS** | Astoria
4.5 **CLUB A STEAK** | E 50s
3.8 **CORNELIA ST.** | W Vill
4.1 **DONOVAN'S** | Bayside
4.2 **DUTCH** | SoHo
4.3 **F & J PINE** | Van Nest
4.0 **FRIEND/FARMER** | Multi
3.9 **GLASS HOUSE** | W 40s
4.0 **HOUSE** | Gramercy
4.3 **I TRULLI** | Murray Hill
4.4 **JOJO** | E 60s
4.5 **KEENS** | W 30s

4.0 **LADY MENDL'S** | Gramercy
3.9 **LA LANTERNA** | G Vill
4.3 **LAMBS CLUB** | W 40s
4.4 **MANETTA'S** | LIC
4.2 **MARCO POLO** | Carroll Gdns
4.6 **NOMAD** | NoMad
4.4 **NOMAD BAR** | NoMad
4.4 **ONE IF BY LAND** | W Vill
4.6 **PER SE** | W 50s
4.3 **PUBLIC** | NoLita
4.5 **QUALITY MEATS** | W 50s
4.5 **SALINAS** | Chelsea
4.1 **SCOTTADITO** | Park Slope
4.6 **SEA FIRE GRILL** | E 40s
4.4 **TELLY'S TAVERNA** | Astoria
4.1 **TINY'S** | TriBeCa
4.3 **TRIOMPHE** | W 40s
4.3 **21 CLUB** | W 50s
4.4 **VINEGAR HILL HSE.** | Vinegar Hill
4.3 **WATER CLUB** | Murray Hill
4.2 **WAVERLY INN** | W Vill
3.9 **WRITING ROOM** | E 80s

FOOD HALLS
3.9 **BERG'N** | Crown Hts
— **BOWERY MARKET** | NoHo NEW
4.0 **CITY KITCHEN** | W 40s
4.3 **EATALY** | Multi
4.4 **GOLDEN SHOPPING MALL** | Flushing
4.1 **GOTHAM WEST** | W 40s
— **GREAT NORTHERN FOOD HALL** | E 40s NEW
4.1 **HUDSON EATS** | BPC
4.1 **LE DISTRICT** | BPC
4.1 **NEW WORLD MALL** | Flushing
3.9 **PENNSY** | W 30s NEW
4.1 **PLAZA FOOD HALL** | W 50s
4.3 **SMORGASBURG** | Multi
— **TURNSTYLE** | W 50s NEW
4.2 **URBANSPACE VANDERBILT** | E 40s

GLUTEN-FREE OPTIONS
(Call to discuss specific needs)
4.4 **ALTA** | G Vill
4.3 **AMALI** | E 60s
4.2 **ANGELICA KIT.** | E Vill
4.4 **BALABOOSTA** | NoLita

3.9 **BAREBURGER** | Multi	— **AMADA** | BPC `NEW`
4.5 **BETONY** | W 50s	4.2 **ARTISANAL** | Murray Hill
4.0 **BISTANGO** | Multi	4.3 **ATLANTIC GRILL** | E 70s
4.1 **BLUE SMOKE** | Multi	4.5 **BABU JI** | E Vill
4.3 **BLUESTONE LANE** | Multi	4.4 **BALTHAZAR** | SoHo
4.3 **BY CHLOE** | Multi	4.3 **BAR AMERICAIN** | W 50s
— **CAFÉ MEDI** | LES `NEW`	4.2 **BEAUTY & ESSEX** | LES
4.4 **CANDLE 79** | E 70s	4.3 **BLAUE GANS** | TriBeCa
4.4 **CARACAS** | E Vill	4.5 **BLT PRIME** | Gramercy
4.6 **CHAIWALI** | Harlem	4.5 **BLT STEAK** | E 50s
4.2 **CHINA GRILL** | W 50s	4.2 **BLUE FIN** | W 40s
4.5 **COSME** | Flatiron	4.1 **BLUE SMOKE** | Multi
4.7 **DEL POSTO** | Chelsea	4.3 **BLUE WATER** | Union Sq
4.3 **DIRT CANDY** | LES	3.9 **BOATHOUSE** | Central Pk
4.5 **DON ANTONIO** | W 50s	4.4 **BUDDAKAN** | Chelsea
4.2 **ETC. ETC.** | W 40s	4.2 **CABANA** | Multi
4.0 **5 NAPKIN BURGER** | Multi	4.1 **CALLE OCHO** | W 80s
4.2 **FRIEDMAN'S** | Multi	4.1 **CARMINE'S** | Multi
4.4 **HEARTH** | E Vill	4.3 **CASA NONNA** | W 30s
4.2 **HILL COUNTRY** | Multi	4.4 **CECIL** | Harlem
4.1 **HU KITCHEN** | Multi	4.2 **CHINA GRILL** | W 50s
4.2 **HUMMUS PL.** | Multi	4.4 **CHURRASCARIA** | W 40s
4.4 **KESTE PIZZA** | W Vill	4.0 **CONGEE** | LES
4.4 **L'ASSO** | NoLita	4.3 **CRISPO** | W Vill
4.0 **LITTLE BEET TABLE** | Multi	4.2 **DBCD** | E Vill
4.7 **MAREA** | W 50s	4.7 **DECOY** | W Vill
4.0 **MULBERRY & VINE** | Multi	4.5 **DEL FRISCO'S** | Multi
3.9 **NICE MATIN** | W 70s	4.2 **DINOSAUR BBQ** | Multi
4.5 **NIX** | G Vill `NEW`	4.4 **DOMINICK'S** | Arthur Ave./Belmont
4.0 **NIZZA** | W 40s	4.7 **DON PEPPE** | S Ozone Pk
4.1 **NOM WAH** | Chinatown	3.9 **DOS CAMINOS** | Multi
4.2 **PALM COURT** | W 50s	3.8 **EL VEZ** | Battery Pk
4.1 **PAPPARDELLA** | W 70s	4.3 **F & J PINE** | Van Nest
4.0 **PEACEFOOD CAFÉ** | Multi	4.5 **FETTE SAU** | W'burg
3.9 **PENNSY** | W 30s `NEW`	4.2 **FIG & OLIVE** | Multi
4.4 **RISOTTERIA MELOTTI** | E Vill	4.2 **FOGO DE CHÃO** | W 50s
4.1 **ROSA MEXICANO** | Multi	4.1 **GOLDEN UNICORN** | Chinatown
4.5 **RUBIROSA** | NoLita	4.2 **GRAND CENTRAL OYSTER** | E 40s
3.9 **SMITH** | Multi	3.9 **GYU-KAKU** | G Vill
4.4 **SONS/THUNDER** | Murray Hill	4.0 **HAVANA CENTRAL** | W 40s
4.3 **TAO** | Multi	4.2 **HILL COUNTRY** | Multi
— **WIN SON** | W'burg `NEW`	4.5 **ILILI** | NoMad
4.1 **WISEFISH** | Chelsea `NEW`	4.3 **INSA** | Gowanus `NEW`
4.0 **ZENGO** | E 40s	4.1 **JING FONG** | Chinatown
	4.1 **JUE LAN CLUB** | Flatiron `NEW`
GROUP DINING	4.4 **KANG HO DONG** | Murray Hill
4.4 **ALMAYASS** | Flatiron	
3.9 **ALMOND** | Multi	
4.4 **ALTA** | G Vill	

4.3 **KUMA INN** | LES
4.2 **KUM GANG SAN** | Multi
3.9 **LANDMARC** | W 50s
4.3 **MÁ PÊCHE** | W 50s
4.3 **MISSION CHINESE** | LES
4.5 **MOMOFUKU SSÄM** | E Vill
4.6 **MORIMOTO** | Chelsea
4.4 **NOMAD BAR** | NoMad
4.3 **OTTO** | G Vill
4.5 **PACIFICANA** | Sunset Pk
4.4 **PARK AVENUE** | Flatiron
4.3 **PEKING DUCK** | Chinatown
4.8 **PETER LUGER** | W'burg
3.8 **PIER A** | BPC
4.3 **PUBLIC** | NoLita
4.5 **QUALITY MEATS** | W 50s
4.0 **REDEYE GRILL** | W 50s
4.2 **RED ROOSTER** | Harlem
4.1 **ROSA MEXICANO** | Multi
4.0 **ROSIE'S** | E Vill
4.0 **SAHARA** | Sheepshead
4.0 **SAMMY'S ROUMANIAN** | LES
4.1 **STANDARD GRILL** | Meatpacking
4.5 **STANTON SOCIAL** | LES
4.1 **STELLA 34** | W 30s
4.7 **TAMARIND** | TriBeCa
4.7 **TANOREEN** | Bay Ridge
4.3 **TAO** | Multi
3.6 **TAVERN/GREEN** | Central Pk
4.0 **TONY'S DI NAPOLI** | W 40s
4.5 **TORO** | Chelsea
4.3 **TRIBECA GRILL** | TriBeCa
— **UNION FARE** | Flatiron NEW
4.3 **VANDAL** | LES NEW
4.3 **VICTOR'S CAFE** | W 50s
4.3 **YERBA BUENA** | Multi
4.0 **ZENGO** | E 40s
4.3 **ZUMA** | Murray Hill

HAPPY HOURS

4.1 **ALLSWELL** | W'burg
4.0 **ATRIUM DUMBO** | Dumbo
— **BKW BY BROOKLYN WINERY** | Crown Hts NEW
4.4 **BROOKLYN STAR** | W'burg
4.1 **BURGER & LOBSTER** | Flatiron
4.4 **CLAM** | W Vill
4.3 **CRAVE FISHBAR** | E 50s

4.6 **CULL & PISTOL** | Chelsea
4.0 **DOCKS OYSTER** | E 40s
4.0 **ED'S CHOWDER** | W 60s
4.2 **FISHTAG** | W 70s
4.4 **FLEX MUSSELS** | Multi
4.3 **FONDA** | Multi
4.2 **GRAND CENTRAL OYSTER** | E 40s
3.9 **GYU-KAKU** | G Vill
4.0 **HARU** | Multi
3.9 **JACQUES** | Multi
4.2 **JOHN DORY** | NoMad
4.5 **KEENS** | W 30s
4.4 **L'ASSO** | NoLita
4.1 **LITTLENECK** | Gowanus
4.4 **LOBSTER JOINT** | Multi
4.6 **MAIALINO** | Gramercy
4.2 **MARCO POLO** | Carroll Gdns
4.2 **MERMAID** | Multi
4.3 **MOMOFUKU NISHI** | Chelsea NEW
4.3 **MP TAVERNA** | Multi
4.1 **OFRENDA** | W Vill
4.2 **RED ROOSTER** | Harlem
4.1 **ROSA MEXICANO** | Multi
4.4 **RYE** | W'burg
4.2 **SALA ONE NINE** | Flatiron
4.6 **SEA FIRE GRILL** | E 40s
4.0 **THALIA** | W 40s
4.1 **PENROSE** | E 80s
4.5 **UPSTATE** | E Vill

HISTORIC PLACES
(Year opened; * building)

3.9 1763 | **FRAUNCES TAV.*** | Financial
4.4 1787 | **ONE IF BY LAND*** | W Vill
3.6 1864 | **PETE'S TAV.** | Gramercy
3.9 1868 | **LANDMARK TAV.*** | W 40s
4.3 1870 | **KINGS' CARRIAGE*** | E 80s
3.8 1884 | **P.J. CLARKE'S** | Multi
4.5 1885 | **KEENS** | W 30s
3.8 1886 | **PIER A*** | BPC
4.8 1887 | **PETER LUGER** | W'burg
4.5 1888 | **KATZ'S DELI** | LES
4.3 1892 | **FERRARA** | L Italy
4.3 1896 | **RAO'S** | E Harlem

4.3 1900 | **BAMONTE'S** | W'burg

4.4 1902 | **ANGELO'S/MULBERRY** | L Italy

3.9 1905 | **MORGAN*** | Murray Hill

4.1 1906 | **BARBETTA** | W 40s

4.2 1907 | **GARGIULO'S** | Coney Is

4.5 1908 | **BARNEY GREENGRASS** | W 80s

4.1 1908 | **JOHN'S/12TH ST.** | E Vill

4.5 1910 | **WOLFGANG'S*** | Multi

4.2 1913 | **GRAND CENTRAL OYSTER** | E 40s

4.3 1917 | **LEOPARD/DES ARTISTES*** | W 60s

4.1 1919 | **MARIO'S** | Arthur Ave./Belmont

4.6 1920 | **LEO'S LATTICINI/ CORONA** | Corona

4.1 1920 | **NOM WAH** | Chinatown

4.2 1920 | **WAVERLY INN** | W Vill

3.7 1921 | **SARDI'S** | W 40s

4.1 1922 | **SANFORD'S** | Astoria

4.5 1924 | **TOTONNO'S** | Coney Is

4.2 1926 | **FRANKIE/JOHNNIE'S** | W 40s

4.4 1926 | **PALM** | E 40s

3.8 1927 | **ANN & TONY'S** | Arthur Ave./Belmont

3.8 1927 | **RUSSIAN TEA** | W 50s

4.0 1929 | **EISENBERG'S** | Flatiron

4.3 1929 | **JOHN'S PIZZERIA** | W 40s

4.3 1929 | **21 CLUB** | W 50s

4.2 1930 | **CARLYLE** | E 70s

4.1 1930 | **EL QUIJOTE** | Chelsea

4.1 1932 | **PAPAYA KING** | E 80s

4.5 1932 | **PIETRO'S** | E 40s

4.2 1933 | **PATSY'S** | W 50s

3.6 1934 | **TAVERN/GREEN** | Central Pk

4.2 1936 | **HEIDELBERG** | E 80s

4.0 1936 | **MONKEY BAR*** | E 50s

4.3 1937 | **CARNEGIE DELI** | W 50s

4.5 1937 | **DENINO'S** | Elm Pk

3.8 1937 | **LE VEAU D'OR** | E 60s

4.4 1937 | **MINETTA TAV.*** | G Vill

4.1 1938 | **WO HOP** | Chinatown

4.4 1941 | **SEVILLA** | W Vill

4.3 1942 | **B & H DAIRY** | E Vill

4.2 1944 | **PATSY'S** | W 50s

4.3 1945 | **BEN'S BEST** | Rego Pk

3.8 1950 | **JUNIOR'S** | W 40s

4.3 1953 | **LIEBMAN'S** | Riverdale

4.2 1953 | **VESUVIO** | Bay Ridge

4.0 1954 | **SERENDIPITY 3** | E 60s

4.1 1954 | **VESELKA** | E Vill

4.2 1957 | **ARTURO'S** | G Vill

4.3 1958 | **QUEEN** | Bklyn Hts

4.2 1959 | **EL PARADOR** | Murray Hill

4.3 1959 | **LONDON LENNIE'S** | Middle Vill

4.3 1960 | **BULL & BEAR** | E 40s

4.1 1960 | **CHEZ NAPOLÉON** | W 50s

4.4 1960 | **JOE & PAT'S** | Castelton Cnrs

4.2 1961 | **CORNER BISTRO** | W Vill

4.7 1962 | **LA GRENOUILLE** | E 50s

3.9 1962 | **SYLVIA'S** | Harlem

3.9 1963 | **JOE ALLEN** | W 40s

4.3 1963 | **VICTOR'S CAFE** | W 50s

4.6 1964 | **DI FARA** | Midwood

4.5 1964 | **LE PERIGORD** | E 50s

HOTEL DINING

ACE HOTEL

4.3 **BRESLIN** | NoMad

4.2 **JOHN DORY** | NoMad

4.1 **NO. 7 SUB** | NoMad

4.0 **STUMPTOWN** | NoMad

AFFINIA SHELBURNE HOTEL

4.1 **RARE B&G** | Murray Hill

AMSTERDAM COURT HOTEL

4.1 **NATSUMI** | W 50s

ARCHER HOTEL

4.2 **DAVID BURKE FAB.** | W 30s

BENJAMIN HOTEL

3.8 **NATIONAL** | E 50s

BOWERY HOTEL

4.3 **GEMMA** | E Vill

BRYANT PARK HOTEL

4.4 **KOI** | W 40s

CARLYLE HOTEL

4.2 **CARLYLE** | E 70s

CASABLANCA HOTEL

4.0 **TONY'S DI NAPOLI** | W 40s

CASSA HOTEL

4.1 **BUTTER** | W 40s

CHAMBERS HOTEL
4.3 MÁ PÊCHE | W 50s

CHATWAL HOTEL
4.3 LAMBS CLUB | W 40s

CITY CLUB HOTEL
4.4 DB BISTRO MODERNE | W 40s

DREAM DOWNTOWN HOTEL
4.1 BODEGA NEGRA | Chelsea

DREAM HOTEL
3.8 SERAFINA | W 50s

DUANE STREET HOTEL
— GRAFFITI EARTH | TriBeCa `NEW`

DYLAN HOTEL
4.6 BENJAMIN STEAK | E 40s

EDITION HOTEL
4.3 CLOCKTOWER | Flatiron

11 HOWARD HOTEL
— LE COUCOU | SoHo `NEW`

ELYSÉE HOTEL
4.0 MONKEY BAR | E 50s

EMPIRE HOTEL
4.0 ED'S CHOWDER | W 60s

EVENTI HOTEL
4.4 L'AMICO | Chelsea

EXCELSIOR HOTEL
4.1 CALLE OCHO | W 80s

GRAMERCY PARK HOTEL
4.6 MAIALINO | Gramercy

GREENWICH HOTEL
4.5 LOCANDA VERDE | TriBeCa

HILTON NY FASHION DISTRICT HOTEL
4.1 RARE B&G | Murray Hill

HOTEL INDIGO

HOTEL ON RIVINGTON
— CAFÉ MEDI | LES `NEW`

INK48 HOTEL
4.5 PRINT | W 40s

INN AT IRVING PL.
4.0 LADY MENDL'S | Gramercy

INNSIDE NEW YORK
4.2 IMPERO CAFFÈ | Chelsea `NEW`

INTERCONTINENTAL HOTEL TIMES SQ.
4.0 ÇA VA | W 40s

IROQUOIS HOTEL
4.3 TRIOMPHE | W 40s

JAMES HOTEL
4.4 DAVID BURKE KIT. | SoHo

JANE HOTEL
4.0 CAFE GITANE | W Vill

KNICKERBOCKER HOTEL
4.2 CHARLIE PALMER/KNICK | W 40s

LANGHAM PLACE FIFTH AVE. HOTEL
4.6 AI FIORI | W 30s

LE PARKER MERIDIEN
4.4 BURGER JOINT | W 50s
4.7 INDIAN ACCENT | W 50s `NEW`
4.4 NORMA'S | W 50s

LUDLOW HOTEL
4.1 DIRTY FRENCH | LES

MANDARIN ORIENTAL HOTEL
4.6 ASIATE | W 50s

MARITIME HOTEL
4.2 LA SIRENA | Chelsea `NEW`
4.3 TAO | Chelsea

MARK HOTEL
4.3 MARK | E 70s

MARLTON HOTEL
4.1 MARGAUX | G Vill

MARRIOTT MARQUIS HOTEL
3.7 VIEW | W 40s

MCCARREN HOTEL
— OLEANDERS | W'burg

MELA HOTEL
4.1 SAJU BISTRO | W 40s

MERCER HOTEL
4.2 MERCER KITCHEN | SoHo

NOMAD HOTEL
4.6 NOMAD | NoMad

NYLO HOTEL
3.8 SERAFINA | W 70s

1 HOTEL CENTRAL PARK
3.8 JAMS | W 50s

PARK HYATT HOTEL
4.3 BACK RM AT ONE57 | W 50s

PARK SOUTH HOTEL
4.4 COVINA | Murray Hill `NEW`
4.6 O YA | Murray Hill

PENINSULA HOTEL
4.6 CLEMENT REST. | W 50s

PLAZA HOTEL
4.2 PALM COURT | W 50s

HOT SPOTS

4.5 **PASQUALE JONES** | NoLita NEW

4.3 **PERLA CAFE** | G Vill

4.4 **POK POK NY** | Columbia St.

4.1 **POLO BAR** | E 50s

4.5 **QUALITY EATS** | W Vill NEW

4.2 **RED ROOSTER** | Harlem

4.4 **REYNARD** | W'burg

4.4 **RIST. MORINI** | E 80s

4.4 **ROOT & BONE** | E Vill

4.3 **ROSEMARY'S** | W Vill

4.3 **SADELLE'S** | SoHo

4.2 **SANTINA** | Meatpacking

4.7 **SUSHI NAKAZAWA** | W Vill

4.5 **TORO** | Chelsea

— **TSURUTONTAN** | Union Sq NEW

4.4 **UPLAND** | Murray Hill

4.3 **VANDAL** | LES NEW

JACKET REQUIRED

4.2 **CARLYLE** | E 70s

4.8 **DANIEL** | E 60s

4.8 **JEAN-GEORGES** | W 60s

4.7 **LA GRENOUILLE** | E 50s

4.9 **LE BERNARDIN** | W 50s

4.4 **LE CIRQUE** | E 50s

4.6 **PER SE** | W 50s

4.6 **RIVER CAFÉ** | Dumbo

4.3 **21 CLUB** | W 50s

MEET FOR A DRINK

4.4 **ABC COCINA** | Flatiron

4.2 **ACME** | NoHo

4.0 **ALDO SOHM** | W 50s

— **AMADA** | BPC NEW

4.4 **AMERICAN CUT** | Multi

4.3 **ARETSKY'S PATROON** | E 40s

4.2 **ARTISANAL** | Murray Hill

4.4 **ASIA DE CUBA** | G Vill

3.9 **ASTOR ROOM** | Astoria

4.3 **ATLANTIC GRILL** | E 70s

4.0 **ATRIUM DUMBO** | Dumbo

4.4 **AURORA** | Multi

4.3 **BAR BOULUD** | W 60s

4.1 **BARBOUNIA** | Flatiron

4.2 **BAR PLEIADES** | E 70s

4.3 **BAR SARDINE** | W Vill

4.5 **BETONY** | W 50s

— **BKW** | Crown Hts NEW

4.3 **BLUE WATER** | Union Sq

4.1 **BODEGA NEGRA** | Chelsea

4.5 **BOND ST** | NoHo

4.3 **BOQUERIA** | Multi

4.4 **BOWERY MEAT CO.** | E Vill

3.9 **BRYANT PK GRILL** | W 40s

4.4 **BUDDAKAN** | Chelsea

4.2 **CAFE LUXEMBOURG** | W 70s

4.4 **CASA LEVER** | E 50s

4.3 **CATCH** | Meatpacking

4.4 **CECIL** | Harlem

4.2 **CHALK POINT** | SoHo

— **CHERRY POINT** | Greenpt NEW

4.3 **CLOCKTOWER** | Flatiron

4.5 **COLICCHIO/SONS** | Chelsea

4.8 **DANIEL** | E 60s

4.2 **DBGB** | E Vill

4.2 **DEAD RABBIT** | Financial

3.8 **DEAR IRVING** | Gramercy

4.5 **DEL FRISCO'S** | Multi

3.9 **DOS CAMINOS** | Multi

4.2 **DUTCH** | SoHo

4.5 **EDDY** | E Vill

4.2 **EL TORO BLANCO** | W Vill

3.8 **EL VEZ** | Battery Pk

4.0 **FLATBUSH FARM** | Park Slope

4.1 **FREEMANS** | LES

4.4 **FRENCH LOUIE** | Boerum Hill

4.8 **GABRIEL KREUTHER** | W 40s

4.5 **GATO** | NoHo

3.9 **GLASS HOUSE** | W 40s

4.8 **GOTHAM B&G** | G Vill

4.8 **GRAMERCY TAV.** | Flatiron

3.9 **GRAND ARMY** | Downtown Bklyn

4.3 **GRAN ELECTRICA** | Dumbo

4.4 **HAKKASAN** | W 40s

4.3 **HARRY'S CAFE** | Financial

4.2 **HILLSTONE** | Multi

4.5 **HUERTAS** | E Vill

4.2 **JACK THE HORSE** | Bklyn Hts

4.8 **JEAN-GEORGES** | W 60s

4.1 **J.G. MELON** | Multi

4.5 **KEENS** | W 30s

4.2 **KELLARI TAVERNA** | W 40s

4.4 **KOI** | W 40s

4.3 **LAFAYETTE** | NoHo

4.1 **LA FONDA/SOL** | E 40s

4.3 **LAMBS CLUB** | W 40s
4.4 **L'AMICO** | Chelsea
3.9 **LANDMARC** | W 50s
4.4 **LA PECORA BIANCA** | Flatiron
4.2 **LA SIRENA** | Chelsea NEW
3.9 **LAVO** | E 50s
4.9 **LE BERNARDIN** | W 50s
4.4 **LE CIRQUE** | E 50s
4.2 **LE COLONIAL** | E 50s
4.4 **LE COQ RICO** | Flatiron NEW
3.8 **LIBRARY/PUBLIC** | G Vill
4.5 **LINCOLN** | W 60s
4.5 **LLAMA INN** | W'burg NEW
4.0 **MACAO TRADING** | TriBeCa
4.6 **MAIALINO** | Gramercy
4.2 **MARI VANNA** | Flatiron
4.3 **MARK** | E 70s
4.5 **MASA** | W 50s
4.2 **MAYSVILLE** | NoMad
3.9 **MICHAEL JORDAN** | E 40s
4.3 **MILLING RM.** | W 80s
4.4 **MINETTA TAV.** | G Vill
4.6 **MODERN** | W 50s
4.0 **MONKEY BAR** | E 50s
3.8 **NATIONAL** | E 50s
4.1 **NATSUMI** | W 50s
4.7 **NOBU** | Multi
4.6 **NOMAD** | NoMad
4.5 **NORTH END GRILL** | Battery Pk
4.0 **ODEON** | TriBeCa
— **OLEANDERS** | W'burg
3.9 **ORSAY** | E 70s
3.7 **PARK** | Chelsea
4.4 **PARK AVENUE** | Flatiron
4.1 **PENROSE** | E 80s
3.8 **PIER A** | BPC
4.3 **PIES-N-THIGHS** | W'burg
3.8 **P.J. CLARKE'S** | Multi
4.4 **QUALITY ITALIAN** | W 50s
4.5 **RAOUL'S** | SoHo
4.3 **REBELLE** | NoLita
4.2 **RED ROOSTER** | Harlem
4.4 **REYNARD** | W'burg
4.0 **RIBBON** | W 70s
— **RIDER** | W'burg NEW
4.6 **ROBERTA'S** | Bushwick
4.4 **ROMAN'S** | Ft Greene
3.8 **SALVATION TACO** | Murray Hill
— **SAUVAGE** | Greenpt NEW

4.3 **SAXON & PAROLE** | NoHo
4.1 **STANDARD GRILL** | Meatpacking
4.5 **STANTON SOCIAL** | LES
4.2 **STK** | Meatpacking
4.5 **STONE PARK** | Park Slope
4.4 **TALDE** | Park Slope
4.3 **TAO** | Multi
3.6 **TAVERN/GREEN** | Central Pk
4.3 **TESSA** | W 70s
4.5 **TORO** | Chelsea
4.3 **21 CLUB** | W 50s
4.4 **UNTITLED** | Meatpacking
— **UNION FARE** | Flatiron NEW
4.4 **UPLAND** | Murray Hill
4.2 **VIC'S** | NoHo
4.4 **WOLLENSKY'S** | E 40s
4.0 **ZENGO** | E 40s

MUSIC/LIVE ENTERTAINMENT

(Call for types and times of performances)

4.1 **BLUE SMOKE** | Murray Hill
4.1 **CHEZ JOSEPHINE** | W 40s
3.8 **CORNELIA ST.** | W Vill
4.1 **KNICKERBOCKER** | G Vill
3.9 **LA LANTERNA** | G Vill
— **METROPOLIS** | Union Sq NEW
4.6 **RIVER CAFÉ** | Dumbo
3.9 **SYLVIA'S** | Harlem

NEWCOMERS

— **AGERN** | E 40s
— **AMADA** | BPC
— **ASKA** | W'burg
— **ATOBOY** | NoMad
— **BARANO** | W'burg
— **BEASTS/BOTTLES** | Bklyn Hts
4.1 **BEDFORD & CO.** | E 40s
— **BKW** | Crown Hts
— **BLACKTAIL** | BPC
4.3 **BLU** | E 60s
4.3 **BOTTLE & BINE** | E 50s
— **BOWERY MARKET** | NoHo
4.4 **CAFÉ ALTRO** | Hudson Sq
— **CAFÉ MEDI** | LES
4.3 **CAPRI** | L Italy
— **CASA APICII** | G Vill
— **CARLA HALL'S** | Columbia St.

- **CHERRY POINT** | Greenpt
- **CHIKARASHI** | L Italy
- **COCO & CRU** | G Vill
- 4.1 **COPPER KETTLE** | E 70s
- 4.4 **COVINA** | Murray Hill
- **DINNERTABLE** | E Vill
- **DIZENGOFF** | Chelsea
- 4.1 **OO & CO** | E Vill
- 4.3 **EL ATORADERO** | Prospect Hts
- **EMMY SQUARED** | W'burg
- **FAUN** | Prospect Hts
- **FRANKEL'S DELI** | Greenpt
- **FREEK'S MILL** | Gowanus
- 4.3 **FREUD** | G Vill
- **GRAFFITI EARTH** | TriBeCa
- **GREAT NORTHERN FOOD HALL** | E 40s
- 3.9 **GRÜNAUER BISTRO** | E 80s
- **GUNTER SEEGER** | Meatpacking
- **HAIL MARY** | Greenpt
- 4.5 **HER NAME IS HAN** | Murray Hill
- **HAO NOODLE** | W Vill
- 4.5 **HIGH STREET/HUDSON** | Meatpacking
- 4.7 **INDIAN ACCENT** | W 50s
- 4.3 **INSA** | Gowanus
- **IZI** | W 40s
- 4.1 **JUE LAN CLUB** | Flatiron
- **KARASU** | Ft Greene
- **KING** | Hudson Sq
- 4.8 **KINGSLEY** | E Vill
- 4.6 **KOSAKA** | W Vill
- 4.3 **KOSSAR'S BAGELS** | LES
- **LADYBIRD** | G Vill
- 4.2 **LA SIRENA** | Chelsea
- 4.4 **LE COQ RICO** | Flatiron
- **LE COUCOU** | SoHo **NEW**
- 4.1 **LE TURTLE** | LES
- 4.6 **LILIA** | W'burg
- 4.5 **LLAMA INN** | W'burg
- **LUCKY BEE** | LES
- **METROGRAPH COMMISSARY** | LES
- **MEYERS BAGERI** | W'burg
- **MIMI** | G Vill
- 4.3 **MOMOFUKU NISHI** | Chelsea
- 4.6 **MOMOSAN** | Murray Hill
- **MR. DONAHUE'S** | NoLita

- 4.3 **NAKAMURA** | LES
- 4.5 **NIX** | G Vill
- **NORM** | Prospect Hts
- **OLMSTED** | Prospect Hts
- **OSTERIA DELLA PACE** | FiDi
- **PAOWALLA** | SoHo
- 4.5 **PASQUALE JONES** | NoLita
- 3.9 **PENNSY** | W 30s
- 4.3 **PIZZERIA SIRENETTA** | W 80s
- **PLANT LOVE** | Prospect Hts
- **PONDICHERI** | NoMad
- 4.5 **QUALITY EATS** | W Vill
- 4.4 **RED COMPASS** | LES
- **SAMMY'S HSE.** | W 40s
- **SAUVAGE** | Greenpt
- **SCHILLING** | Financial
- **2ND CITY** | W Vill
- **SOLOMON & KUFF** | Manhattanville
- **SUPERCROWN** | Bushwick
- **SUSHI GANSO** | Downtown Bklyn
- **SUSHI GINZA** | E 40s
- **SUSHI ZO** | G Vill
- **SYNDICATED** | Bushwick
- **TAPESTRY** | W Vill
- **TEISUI** | NoMad
- **TEKOÁ** | Cobble Hill
- **TSURUTONTAN** | Union Sq
- **TURNSTYLE** | W 50s
- **TWIN SUNS** | Bushwick
- **TYGERSHARK** | Prospect Hts
- **ULIVO** | NoMad
- **UNION FARE** | Flatiron
- 4.3 **VANDAL** | LES
- **WARREN** | W Vill
- **WIN SON** | W'burg
- 4.1 **WISEFISH** | Chelsea
- **ZADIE'S OYSTER RM.** | E Vill

NOTEWORTHY CLOSINGS

ABBOCCATO

ALMANAC

ÁPIZZ

A VOCE (W 50S)

BACK FORTY WEST

BAR CHUKO

BOURGEOIS PIG

BUTTERFLY
CAFE ASEAN
CHERRY
CHERRY IZAKAYA
CHEVALIER
CIBO
COLICCHIO & SONS
COSTATA
DANNY BROWN WINE BAR/KIT.
DAVID BURKE FISHTAIL
DO OR DINE
EATERY
ÉLAN
EMPIRE DINER
FATTY CRAB
FORCELLA
FOUR SEASONS
GRAND CENTRAL OYSTER (BKLYN)
HARLOW
IL VAGABONDO
KIN SHOP
LA LUNCHONETTE
LE PHILOSOPHE
LES HALLES (MURRAY HILL)
LION
MEAT HOOK SANDWICH SHOP
MEHTAPHOR
MONTMARTRE
MR. K'S
NORTHERN SPY FOOD CO.
OCEAN GRILL
PEACOCK
PERILLA
PICHOLINE
PROSPERITY DUMPLING
RECETTE
RESTO
RUBY FOO'S
SAUL
SIRIO
SPICE MARKET
SPIGOLO
SWIFTY'S
TELEPAN
TEODORA

OUTDOOR DINING

4.3 **AGNANTI** | Astoria
4.0 **ALMA** | Columbia St.

— **AMADA** | BPC **NEW**
4.1 **A.O.C.** | W Vill
4.7 **AQUAGRILL** | SoHo
4.4 **AURORA** | W'burg
4.6 **AVRA** | E 40s
4.1 **BACCHUS** | Downtown Bklyn
4.1 **BARBETTA** | W 40s
4.4 **BAR CORVO** | Prospect Hts
4.0 **BATTERY GDNS.** | Financial
3.9 **BEAUBOURG** | BPC
3.9 **BERG'N** | Crown Hts
4.3 **BLUE WATER** | Union Sq
3.9 **BOATHOUSE** | Central Pk
4.3 **BOBO** | W Vill
4.2 **BOGOTA** | Park Slope
4.0 **BOTTEGA** | E 70s
3.9 **BRASS. RUHLMANN** | W 50s
3.9 **BRYANT PK GRILL** | W 40s
4.2 **CACIO E PEPE** | E Vill
4.1 **CAFE CENTRO** | E 40s
4.3 **CAFE MOGADOR** | E Vill
4.3 **CATCH** | Meatpacking
4.6 **CONVIV. OSTERIA** | Park Slope
4.1 **DA NICO** | L Italy
4.2 **DINOSAUR BBQ** | Multi
4.5 **DOMINIQUE ANSEL BAKERY** | SoHo
4.4 **DOMINIQUE ANSEL KIT.** | W Vill
4.2 **EDI & THE WOLF** | E Vill
4.4 **ESCA** | W 40s
4.2 **FARM/ADDERLEY** | Ditmas Pk
— **FAUN** | Prospect Hts **NEW**
4.0 **FLATBUSH FARM** | Park Slope
4.2 **44 & X/44½** | W 40s
4.4 **FRANKIES** | Multi
4.4 **FRENCH LOUIE** | Boerum Hill
4.3 **FREUD** | G Vill **NEW**
4.1 **GIGINO** | BPC
4.3 **GNOCCO** | E Vill
4.4 **GOOD FORK** | Red Hook
4.3 **GRAN ELECTRICA** | Dumbo
4.1 **HUDSON EATS** | BPC
4.0 **ISABELLA'S** | W 70s
4.3 **I TRULLI** | Murray Hill
4.1 **IVAN RAMEN** | Multi
4.3 **LADURÉE** | Multi
4.3 **LA ESQUINA** | SoHo
3.9 **LA LANTERNA** | G Vill

4.3 **LA MANGEOIRE** | E 50s
4.4 **L&B SPUMONI** | Gravesend
4.2 **LA SIRENA** | Chelsea NEW
4.5 **LLAMA INN** | W'burg NEW
4.3 **M. WELLS STEAKHSE.** | LIC
4.0 **PACHANGA PATTERSON** | Astoria
4.5 **PALMA** | W Vill
4.0 **PERA** | SoHo
4.0 **PIER A HARBOR HSE.** | BPC
4.4 **PINES** | Gowanus
4.4 **PIZZETTERIA BRUNETTI** | W Vill
4.5 **RIVERPARK** | Murray Hill
4.6 **ROBERTA'S** | Bushwick
4.0 **ROSIE'S** | E Vill
4.5 **SALINAS** | Chelsea
4.5 **SAN PIETRO** | E 50s
4.2 **SANTINA** | Meatpacking
4.6 **SRIPRAPHAI** | Woodside
4.2 **TARTINE** | W Vill
3.6 **TAVERN/GREEN** | Central Pk
4.0 **TRESTLE ON 10TH** | Chelsea
4.3 **VICEVERSA** | W 50s
4.4 **VINEGAR HILL HSE.** | Vinegar Hill
4.3 **WATER CLUB** | Murray Hill
4.6 **TRAIF** | W'burg
4.4 **UNTITLED** | Meatpacking
4.2 **ZONA ROSA** | W'burg

PEOPLE-WATCHING

4.2 **AMARANTH** | E 60s
4.6 **ANTICA PESA** | W'burg
4.0 **BAGATELLE** | Meatpacking
4.4 **BALTHAZAR** | SoHo
3.9 **BEAUTIQUE** | W 50s
4.1 **BEATRICE INN** | W Vill
4.3 **BRESLIN** | NoMad
4.7 **CAFÉ BOULUD** | E 70s
4.0 **CAFE GITANE** | Multi
4.4 **CASA LEVER** | E 50s
4.3 **CATCH** | Meatpacking
4.2 **CHERCHE MIDI** | NoLita
4.3 **CIPRIANI** | SoHo
4.2 **DA SILVANO** | G Vill
4.5 **ELIO'S** | E 80s
4.2 **FRED'S AT BARNEYS** | Multi
4.3 **INDOCHINE** | G Vill

3.9 **JOE ALLEN** | W 40s
4.5 **KATZ'S DELI** | LES
4.2 **LA SIRENA** | Chelsea NEW
3.9 **LAVO** | E 50s
4.1 **LE BILBOQUET** | E 60s
4.4 **LE CIRQUE** | E 50s
4.3 **LEOPARD/DES ARTISTES** | W 60s
4.1 **LE TURTLE** | LES NEW
4.7 **MAREA** | W 50s
4.1 **MARGAUX** | G Vill
4.3 **MICHAEL'S** | W 50s
4.4 **MINETTA TAV.** | G Vill
3.7 **NELLO** | E 60s
4.3 **NICOLA'S** | E 80s
4.6 **NOMAD** | NoMad
4.3 **ORSO** | W 40s
— **PAOWALLA** | SoHo NEW
4.5 **PASQUALE JONES** | NoLita NEW
4.3 **PHILIPPE** | E 60s
4.1 **POLO BAR** | E 50s
4.3 **RAO'S** | E Harlem
4.2 **RED ROOSTER** | Harlem
4.4 **REYNARD** | W'burg
4.6 **ROBERTA'S** | Bushwick
4.3 **ROSEMARY'S** | W Vill
4.4 **SANT AMBROEUS** | Multi
4.2 **SANTINA** | Meatpacking
4.4 **SETTE MEZZO** | E 70s
4.5 **SPARKS** | E 40s
4.3 **SPICE MKT.** | Meatpacking
4.4 **SPOTTED PIG** | W Vill
4.1 **STANDARD GRILL** | Meatpacking
4.3 **21 CLUB** | W 50s
4.3 **VANDAL** | LES NEW
4.1 **VIA QUADRONNO** | E 70s

POWER SCENES

4.5 **ABC KITCHEN** | Flatiron
4.6 **AI FIORI** | W 30s
4.2 **AMARANTH** | E 60s
4.4 **BALTHAZAR** | SoHo
3.9 **BEAUTIQUE** | W 50s
4.5 **BETONY** | W 50s
4.1 **BLACK BARN** | NoMad
4.5 **BLT PRIME** | Gramercy
4.5 **BLT STEAK** | E 50s

4.2 **BOBBY VAN'S** | Multi
4.3 **BULL & BEAR** | E 40s
4.2 **CARLYLE** | E 70s
4.4 **CASA LEVER** | E 50s
4.2 **CHINA GRILL** | W 50s
4.3 **CIPRIANI** | Financial
4.8 **DANIEL** | E 60s
4.5 **DEL FRISCO'S** | Multi
4.7 **DEL POSTO** | Chelsea
4.5 **ELIO'S** | E 80s
4.3 **FRESCO** | E 50s
4.8 **GABRIEL KREUTHER** | W 40s
4.8 **GOTHAM B&G** | G Vill
4.3 **HARRY'S CAFE** | Financial
4.2 **HUNT & FISH** | W 40s
4.8 **JEAN-GEORGES** | W 60s
4.3 **KAPPO MASA** | E 70s
4.5 **KEENS** | W 30s
4.7 **LA GRENOUILLE** | E 50s
4.3 **LAMBS CLUB** | W 40s
4.2 **LA SIRENA** | Chelsea NEW
4.9 **LE BERNARDIN** | W 50s
4.1 **LE BILBOQUET** | E 60s
4.4 **LE CIRQUE** | E 50s
4.3 **LEOPARD/DES ARTISTES** | W 60s
4.7 **MAREA** | W 50s
4.3 **MICHAEL'S** | W 50s
4.6 **MODERN** | W 50s
4.4 **MORTON'S** | E 40s
4.7 **NOBU** | Multi
4.6 **NOMAD** | NoMad
4.4 **NORMA'S** | W 50s
4.5 **NORTH END GRILL** | Battery Pk
4.8 **PETER LUGER** | W'burg
4.3 **RAO'S** | E Harlem
4.0 **REGENCY B&G** | E 60s
4.4 **RIST. MORINI** | E 80s
3.8 **RUSSIAN TEA** | W 50s
4.5 **SAN PIETRO** | E 50s
4.4 **SANT AMBROEUS** | Multi
4.4 **SMITH/WOLLENSKY** | E 40s
4.5 **SPARKS** | E 40s
4.3 **21 CLUB** | W 50s

PRIVATE ROOMS/ PARTIES

4.2 **ACME** | NoHo
4.6 **AI FIORI** | W 30s

4.5 **ALDEA** | Flatiron
4.4 **ALTA** | G Vill
4.7 **AMPLE HILLS** | Multi
4.5 **AQUAVIT** | E 50s
4.3 **ARETSKY'S PATROON** | E 40s
3.9 **ASTOR ROOM** | Astoria
4.6 **AUREOLE** | W 40s
4.3 **A VOCE** | W 50s
4.2 **BACARO** | LES
4.3 **BAR AMERICAIN** | W 50s
4.1 **BARBETTA** | W 40s
4.3 **BAR BOULUD** | W 60s
4.0 **BATTERY GDNS.** | Financial
4.2 **BEAUTY & ESSEX** | LES
4.2 **BENOIT** | W 50s
4.5 **BETONY** | W 50s
4.5 **BLT PRIME** | Gramercy
4.5 **BLT STEAK** | E 50s
4.7 **BLUE HILL** | G Vill
4.1 **BLUE SMOKE** | Multi
4.3 **BLUE WATER** | Union Sq
4.1 **BODEGA NEGRA** | Chelsea
4.5 **BOND ST** | NoHo
4.9 **BOULEY** | TriBeCa
4.3 **BRESLIN** | NoMad
4.4 **BUDDAKAN** | Chelsea
4.7 **CAFÉ BOULUD** | E 70s
4.4 **CAPITAL GRILLE** | E 40s
4.4 **CASA LEVER** | E 50s
4.3 **CASA NONNA** | W 30s
4.3 **CATCH** | Meatpacking
4.0 **ÇA VA** | W 40s
4.2 **CELLINI** | E 50s
4.5 **COLICCHIO/SONS** | Chelsea
4.6 **CONVIV. OSTERIA** | Park Slope
4.5 **CRAFT** | Flatiron
4.8 **DANIEL** | E 60s
4.4 **DAVID BURKE KIT.** | SoHo
4.4 **DB BISTRO MODERNE** | W 40s
4.5 **DEL FRISCO'S** | Multi
4.4 **DELMONICO'S** | W 30s
4.7 **DEL POSTO** | Chelsea
4.2 **DINOSAUR BBQ** | Multi
4.0 **DOCKS OYSTER** | E 40s
4.7 **ELEVEN MADISON** | Flatiron
4.4 **EN JAPANESE** | W Vill
4.6 **FELIDIA** | E 50s
4.2 **FIG & OLIVE** | Multi

SPECIAL FEATURES

4.4 **FRANKIES** | Multi

3.9 **FRAUNCES TAV.** | Financial

4.1 **FREEMANS** | LES

4.3 **FRESCO** | E 50s

4.8 **GABRIEL KREUTHER** | W 40s

4.3 **GABRIEL'S** | W 60s

4.1 **GANDER** | Flatiron

4.8 **GRAMERCY TAV.** | Flatiron

4.4 **HAKKASAN** | W 40s

4.3 **HARRY'S CAFE** | Financial

4.1 **HECHO EN DUMBO** | NoHo

4.1 **HUDSON CLEARWATER** | W Vill

4.5 **IL BUCO** | NoHo

4.5 **IL BUCO ALIMENTARI** | NoHo

4.3 **IL CORTILE** | L Italy

4.5 **ILILI** | NoMad

4.3 **INSA** | Gowanus NEW

4.8 **JEAN-GEORGES** | W 60s

4.7 **JUNGSIK** | TriBeCa

4.5 **KEENS** | W 30s

4.3 **LAFAYETTE** | NoHo

4.7 **LA GRENOUILLE** | E 50s

4.9 **LE BERNARDIN** | W 50s

4.4 **LE CIRQUE** | E 50s

4.5 **LE PERIGORD** | E 50s

4.1 **LE ZIE** | Chelsea

4.5 **LINCOLN** | W 60s

4.5 **LOCANDA VERDE** | TriBeCa

4.6 **LUPA** | G Vill

4.4 **LURE FISHBAR** | SoHo

4.6 **MAIALINO** | Gramercy

4.5 **MALONEY & PORCELLI** | E 50s

4.5 **MARCONY** | Murray Hill

4.7 **MAREA** | W 50s

4.7 **MAS** | W Vill

4.3 **MICHAEL'S** | W 50s

4.7 **MILOS** | W 50s

4.6 **MODERN** | W 50s

4.3 **MR. CHOW** | F 50s

3.8 **NATIONAL** | E 50s

4.4 **NERAI** | E 50s

4.7 **NOBU** | Multi

4.6 **NOMAD** | NoMad

4.5 **OCEANA** | W 40s

4.5 **PALMA** | W Vill

3.7 **PARK** | Chelsea

4.1 **PARLOR STEAKHSE.** | E 80s

4.0 **PERA** | SoHo

4.4 **PERIYALI** | Flatiron

4.6 **PERRY ST.** | W Vill

4.6 **PER SE** | W 50s

4.5 **PRINT** | W 40s

4.3 **PUBLIC** | NoLita

4.5 **QUALITY MEATS** | W 50s

4.5 **RAOUL'S** | SoHo

4.0 **REDEYE GRILL** | W 50s

4.2 **REMI** | W 50s

4.6 **RIVER CAFÉ** | Dumbo

4.1 **ROTISSERIE GEORGETTE** | E 60s

3.8 **RUSSIAN TEA** | W 50s

4.5 **SALINAS** | Chelsea

4.3 **SAXON & PAROLE** | NoHo

4.5 **SCARPETTA** | Chelsea

4.1 **SCOTTADITO** | Park Slope

4.6 **SEA FIRE GRILL** | E 40s

4.4 **SEA GRILL** | W 40s

4.4 **SHUN LEE PALACE** | E 50s

4.4 **SISTINA** | E 80s

4.5 **SPARKS** | E 40s

4.3 **SPICE MKT.** | Meatpacking

4.5 **STANTON SOCIAL** | LES

4.5 **STONE PARK** | Park Slope

4.7 **TAMARIND** | TriBeCa

4.3 **TAO** | Multi

3.6 **TAVERN/GREEN** | Central Pk

— **TEISUI** | NoMad NEW

4.5 **THALASSA** | TriBeCa

4.5 **TORO** | Chelsea

4.7 **TRATT. L'INCONTRO** | Astoria

4.8 **TOCQUEVILLE** | Flatiron

4.3 **TRIBECA GRILL** | TriBeCa

4.3 **21 CLUB** | W 50s

4.3 **UNCLE JACK'S** | W 50s

4.2 **UVA** | E 70s

4.5 **VALBELLA** | Meatpacking

4.3 **VICTOR'S CAFE** | W 50s

4.4 **VITAE** | E 40s

4.3 **WATER CLUB** | Murray Hill

4.3 **YERBA BUENA** | Multi

4.0 **ZENGO** | E 40s

QUICK BITES

4.3 **AREPAS** | Astoria

4.2 **A SALT & BATTERY** | W Vill

4.4 **AZURI CAFE** | W 50s

4.1 **BAOHAUS** | E Vill
4.1 **BAZ BAGEL** | L Italy
4.3 **BOBWHITE** | Multi
4.3 **BOUCHON BAKERY** | Multi
4.6 **BREADS BAKERY** | Multi
4.3 **BY CHLOE** | Multi
4.2 **CALEXICO** | Multi
4.4 **CARACAS** | Multi
— **CARLA HALL'S** |
Columbia St. NEW
4.2 **CHOBANI** | SoHo
4.0 **CHOMP CHOMP** | W Vill
4.2 **CITY BAKERY** | Flatiron
4.1 **CRIF DOGS** | Multi
4.1 **DAISY MAY'S** | W 40s
— **FRANKEL'S DELI** | Greenpt NEW
4.2 **FUKU** | Multi
4.1 **GOTHAM WEST** | W 40s
4.0 **GRAY'S PAPAYA** | W 70s
3.9 **HALAL GUYS** | Multi
3.9 **HARLEM SHAKE** | Multi
4.1 **HUDSON EATS** | BPC
4.1 **HU KITCHEN** | Multi
4.2 **HUMMUS PL.** | Multi
4.5 **JOE'S PIZZA** | Multi
4.2 **KATI ROLL** | Multi
3.9 **LA BONNE SOUPE** | W 50s
4.3 **LA ESQUINA** | SoHo
4.1 **LE DISTRICT** | BPC
4.5 **LOBSTER PLACE** | Chelsea
4.7 **LOS TACOS** | Chelsea
4.3 **LUKE'S LOBSTER** | Multi
3.9 **MAMAN** | Multi
4.4 **MAMOUN'S** | Multi
3.9 **MEATBALL SHOP** | Multi
4.3 **MIMI CHENG'S** | E Vill
4.1 **MISS LILY'S** | Multi
4.0 **MULBERRY & VINE** | Multi
4.1 **PAPAYA KING** | Multi
4.1 **PLAZA FOOD HALL** | W 50s
4.4 **PORCHETTA** | E Vill
4.0 **SHAKE SHACK** | Multi
4.4 **SONS/THUNDER** | Murray Hill
4.4 **SUPERIORITY BURGER** | E Vill
4.4 **SWEETGREEN** | Multi
4.6 **TAÏM** | Multi
4.6 **UNTAMED SANDWICHES** |
W 30s
4.0 **VANESSA'S DUMPLING** | Multi

4.1 **VIA QUADRONNO** | Multi
4.1 **WISEFISH** | Chelsea NEW

QUIET CONVERSATION

4.2 **AMMOS** | E 40s
4.7 **ANNISA** | W Vill
4.6 **ASIATE** | W 50s
4.6 **AUREOLE** | W 40s
4.1 **BASSO56** | W 50s
4.7 **BLUE HILL** | G Vill
4.1 **BOSIE TEA PARLOR** | W Vill
4.2 **BRASSERIE 8½** | W 50s
4.2 **CELLINI** | E 50s
4.2 **CHARLIE PALMER/KNICK** |
W 40s
4.8 **CHEF'S/BROOKLYN FARE** |
Downtown Bklyn
4.6 **CLEMENT REST.** | W 50s
4.5 **DA UMBERTO** | Chelsea
4.4 **DAWAT** | E 50s
4.4 **EN JAPANESE** | W Vill
4.8 **GABRIEL KREUTHER** | W 40s
4.3 **GIOVANNI** | E 80s
3.9 **GRÜNAUER BISTRO** |
E 80s NEW
4.4 **IL TINELLO** | W 50s
4.8 **JEAN-GEORGES** | W 60s
4.7 **JUNGSIK** | TriBeCa
4.3 **KAPPO MASA** | E 70s
4.3 **KINGS' CARRIAGE** | E 80s
4.7 **LA GRENOUILLE** | E 50s
4.9 **LE BERNARDIN** | W 50s
4.3 **LEFT BANK** | W Vill
4.1 **MADISON BISTRO** | Murray Hill
4.7 **MAREA** | W 50s
4.7 **MAS** | W Vill
4.5 **MASA** | W 50s
— **MIMI** | G Vill NEW
4.3 **MONTEBELLO** | E 50s
4.5 **MOUNTAIN BIRD** | E Harlem
4.4 **NERAI** | E 50s
4.3 **NORTH SQ.** | G Vill
4.2 **PALM COURT** | W 50s
4.4 **PERIYALI** | Flatiron
4.6 **PERRY ST.** | W Vill
4.6 **PER SE** | W 50s
4.4 **PETROSSIAN** | W 50s
4.5 **PIETRO'S** | E 40s
4.1 **RADIANCE TEA** | Multi

4.2 **REMI** | W 50s
4.1 **SAPPHIRE INDIAN** | W 60s
4.1 **SCALETTA** | W 70s
4.4 **SFOGLIA** | E 90s
4.8 **TOCQUEVILLE** | Flatiron
4.3 **TRIOMPHE** | W 40s
4.4 **VILLA BERULIA** | Murray Hill
4.6 **ZENKICHI** | W'burg

RAW BARS

4.2 **AMMOS** | E 40s
4.1 **ANASSA TAVERNA** | E 60s
4.7 **AQUAGRILL** | SoHo
4.3 **ATLANTIC GRILL** | E 70s
4.4 **BALTHAZAR** | SoHo
4.3 **BAR AMERICAIN** | W 50s
3.9 **BEAUBOURG** | BPC
4.2 **BLUE FIN** | W 40s
4.4 **BLUE RIBBON** | Multi
4.3 **BLUE WATER** | Union Sq
4.1 **BLACK BARN** | NoMad NEW
4.0 **BROOKLYN CRAB** | Red Hook
4.3 **CATCH** | Meatpacking
3.9 **CITY LOBSTER/STEAK** | W 50s
4.4 **CLAM** | W Vill
4.3 **CRAVE FISHBAR** | Multi
4.6 **CULL & PISTOL** | Chelsea
4.0 **DOCKS OYSTER** | E 40s
4.2 **DUTCH** | SoHo
4.0 **ED'S CHOWDER** | W 60s
4.3 **ED'S LOBSTER BAR** | SoHo
4.4 **ESCA** | W 40s
4.2 **FISH** | W Vill
4.4 **FLEX MUSSELS** | Multi
4.2 **GRAND CENTRAL OYSTER** | E 40s
4.4 **GREENPOINT FISH** | Greenpt
4.2 **JACK THE HORSE** | Bklyn Hts
4.4 **JEFFREY'S GROCERY** | W Vill
4.2 **JOHN DORY** | NoMad
4.2 **JORDANS LOBSTER** | Sheepshead
4.6 **KANOYAMA** | E Vill
4.1 **LITTLENECK** | Multi
4.3 **LONDON LENNIE'S** | Middle Vill
4.4 **LURE FISHBAR** | SoHo
4.5 **MAISON PREMIERE** | W'burg
4.3 **MARK** | E 70s
4.4 **MARLOW/SONS** | W'burg

4.2 **MERCER KITCHEN** | SoHo
4.2 **MERMAID** | Multi
4.3 **M. WELLS STEAKHSE.** | LIC
4.5 **OCEANA** | W 40s
4.1 **PARLOR STEAKHSE.** | E 80s
4.6 **PEARL OYSTER** | W Vill
4.1 **PEARL ROOM** | Bay Ridge
3.8 **P.J. CLARKE'S** | Multi
4.1 **PLAZA FOOD HALL** | W 50s
4.2 **RANDAZZO'S** | Sheepshead
— **SAUVAGE** | Greenpt NEW
4.1 **STANDARD GRILL** | Meatpacking
4.0 **THALIA** | W 40s
4.3 **21 CLUB** | W 50s
4.3 **UNCLE JACK'S** | Multi
4.5 **UPSTATE** | E Vill
4.1 **WALTER** | Multi
4.5 **ZZ'S CLAM BAR** | G Vill

ROMANTIC PLACES

4.6 **AL DI LA** | Park Slope
4.4 **ALTA** | G Vill
4.7 **ANNISA** | W Vill
4.6 **ANTICA PESA** | W'burg
4.6 **ASIATE** | W 50s
4.4 **AURORA** | Multi
4.2 **BACARO** | LES
4.1 **BARBETTA** | W 40s
4.7 **BLUE HILL** | G Vill
3.9 **BOATHOUSE** | Central Pk
4.3 **BOBO** | W Vill
4.9 **BOULEY** | TriBeCa
4.5 **CAVIAR RUSSE** | E 50s
4.6 **CONVIV. OSTERIA** | Park Slope
4.8 **DANIEL** | E 60s
4.7 **DEL POSTO** | Chelsea
4.7 **ELEVEN MADISON** | Flatiron
4.5 **EL QUINTO PINO** | Chelsea
4.4 **ERMINIA** | E 80s
4.1 **FIRENZE** | E 80s
4.8 **GABRIEL KREUTHER** | W 40s
4.3 **GEMMA** | E Vill
4.4 **GOOD FORK** | Red Hook
4.8 **GRAMERCY TAV.** | Flatiron
4.0 **HOUSE** | Gramercy
4.5 **IL BUCO** | NoHo
4.6 **I SODI** | W Vill

4.3 **I TRULLI** | Murray Hill
4.4 **JOJO** | E 60s
4.3 **KINGS' CARRIAGE** | E 80s
4.7 **LA GRENOUILLE** | E 50s
3.9 **LA LANTERNA** | G Vill
4.3 **LA MANGEOIRE** | E 50s
4.3 **LAMBS CLUB** | W 40s
4.7 **L'ARTUSI** | W Vill
4.7 **LA VARA** | Cobble Hill
4.9 **LE BERNARDIN** | W 50s
— **LE COUCOU** | SoHo `NEW`
4.5 **LE GIGOT** | W Vill
4.5 **LITTLE OWL** | W Vill
4.7 **MAS** | W Vill
— **MIMI** | G Vill `NEW`
4.6 **MORIMOTO** | Chelsea
4.5 **MOUNTAIN BIRD** | E Harlem
4.6 **NOMAD** | NoMad
4.5 **OLEA** | Ft Greene
4.4 **ONE IF BY LAND** | W Vill
4.2 **OVELIA** | Astoria
4.5 **PALMA** | W Vill
4.3 **PAOLA'S** | E 90s
4.5 **PEASANT** | NoLita
4.3 **RAINBOW RM** | W 50s
4.5 **RAOUL'S** | SoHo
4.6 **RIVER CAFÉ** | Dumbo
4.4 **RYE** | W'burg
4.5 **SALINAS** | Chelsea
4.7 **SCALINI FEDELI** | TriBeCa
4.5 **SCARPETTA** | Chelsea
4.6 **SHUKO** | G Vill
4.4 **SISTINA** | E 80s
4.2 **SPIGA** | W 80s
4.8 **TOCQUEVILLE** | Flatiron
4.2 **UVA** | E 70s
3.7 **VIEW** | W 40s
4.4 **VINEGAR HILL HSE.** | Vinegar Hill
4.6 **WALLSÉ** | W Vill
4.3 **WATER CLUB** | Murray Hill
4.6 **ZENKICHI** | W'burg
4.5 **ZZ'S CLAM BAR** | G Vill

SENIOR APPEAL

4.4 **ARTIE'S** | City Is
4.6 **AUREOLE** | W 40s
4.3 **BAMONTE'S** | W'burg
4.1 **BARBETTA** | W 40s

4.5 **BARNEY GREENGRASS** | W 80s
4.2 **BENOIT** | W 50s
4.4 **CARAVAGGIO** | E 70s
4.1 **CHEZ NAPOLÉON** | W 50s
4.5 **CLUB A STEAK** | E 50s
4.4 **DAWAT** | E 50s
4.4 **DEGREZIA** | E 50s
4.4 **DELMONICO'S** | W 30s
4.7 **DEL POSTO** | Chelsea
4.1 **DUE** | E 70s
4.6 **FELIDIA** | E 50s
4.3 **GABRIEL'S** | W 60s
4.3 **GIOVANNI** | E 80s
4.4 **GRIFONE** | E 40s
3.9 **GRÜNAUER BISTRO** | E 80s `NEW`
4.4 **IL GATTOPARDO** | W 50s
4.4 **IL TINELLO** | W 50s
4.2 **ITHAKA** | E 80s
4.1 **JUBILEE** | E 50s
4.3 **KINGS' CARRIAGE** | E 80s
3.9 **LA BONNE SOUPE** | W 50s
4.7 **LA GRENOUILLE** | E 50s
4.3 **LA MANGEOIRE** | E 50s
4.3 **LATTANZI** | W 40s
4.4 **LE CIRQUE** | E 60s
4.3 **LEOPARD/DES ARTISTES** | W 60s
4.5 **LE PERIGORD** | E 50s
4.4 **LUSARDI'S** | E 70s
4.3 **MARK** | E 70s
4.4 **NERAI** | E 50s
4.3 **NICOLA'S** | E 80s
4.4 **NIPPON** | W 50s
4.4 **PICCOLO ANGOLO** | W Vill
4.5 **PIETRO'S** | E 40s
4.4 **PRIMOLA** | E 60s
4.2 **QUATORZE BIS** | E 70s
4.3 **RAINBOW RM.** | W 50s
4.2 **REMI** | W 50s
4.4 **RIST. MORINI** | E 80s
4.6 **RIVER CAFÉ** | Dumbo
4.4 **ROSSINI'S** | Murray Hill
4.1 **ROTISSERIE GEORGETTE** | E 60s
3.8 **RUSSIAN TEA** | W 50s
4.5 **SAN PIETRO** | E 50s
3.7 **SARDI'S** | W 40s
4.1 **SCALETTA** | W 70s

4.1 **SHUN LEE WEST** | W 60s
4.4 **SISTINA** | E 80s
4.3 **TRIOMPHE** | W 40s
4.5 **TUSCANY GRILL** | Bay Ridge
4.4 **VILLA BERULIA** | Murray Hill
4.0 **VIVOLO** | E 70s

TOUGH TICKETS

4.5 **ABC KITCHEN** | Flatiron
4.6 **BABBO** | G Vill
4.7 **BLANCA** | Bushwick
4.4 **CAFÉ ALTRO** | Hudson Sq **NEW**
4.5 **CARBONE** | G Vill
4.8 **CHEF'S/BROOKLYN FARE** | Downtown Bklyn
4.5 **COSME** | Flatiron
— **DINNERTABLE** | E Vill **NEW**
— **EMMY SQUARED** | W'burg **NEW**
4.5 **GATO** | NoHo
4.2 **LA SIRENA** | Chelsea **NEW**
— **LE COUCOU** | SoHo **NEW**
4.6 **LILIA** | W'burg **NEW**
4.5 **LUKSUS** | Greenpt
4.4 **MINETTA TAV.** | G Vill
4.7 **MOMOFUKU KO** | E Vill
4.3 **MOMOFUKU NISHI** | Chelsea **NEW**
4.6 **MOMOSAN** | Murray Hill **NEW**
4.5 **NIX** | G Vill **NEW**
— **OLMSTED** | Prospect Hts **NEW**
4.5 **PASQUALE JONES** | NoLita **NEW**
4.1 **POLO BAR** | E 50s
4.5 **QUALITY EATS** | W Vill **NEW**
4.3 **RAO'S** | E Harlem
4.3 **SADELLE'S** | SoHo
4.2 **SANTINA** | Meatpacking
4.6 **SHUKO** | G Vill
4.7 **SUSHI NAKAZAWA** | W Vill
— **TAKE ROOT** | Carroll Gdns
4.5 **ZZ'S CLAM BAR** | G Vill

TRANSPORTING EXPERIENCES

4.6 **ASIATE** | W 50s
4.4 **BALTHAZAR** | SoHo
4.2 **BEAUTY & ESSEX** | LES
3.9 **BOATHOUSE** | Central Pk
4.4 **BUDDAKAN** | Chelsea

4.4 **CAFE CHINA** | Murray Hill
4.5 **IL BUCO** | NoHo
4.5 **ILILI** | NoMad
4.5 **KEENS** | W 30s
4.7 **LA GRENOUILLE** | E 50s
4.3 **LAMBS CLUB** | W 40s
4.2 **LE COLONIAL** | E 50s
3.8 **LIBRARY/PUBLIC** | G Vill
4.4 **LIMANI** | W 50s
4.5 **MASA** | W 50s
4.0 **MONKEY BAR** | E 50s
4.6 **PER SE** | W 50s
4.1 **QI** | W'burg
4.3 **RAINBOW RM.** | W 50s
4.3 **RAO'S** | E Harlem
4.3 **SPICE MKT.** | Meatpacking
4.3 **TAO** | Multi
3.6 **TAVERN/GREEN** | Central Pk
4.2 **WAVERLY INN** | W Vill

24-HOUR DINING

4.2 **BCD TOFU** | W 30s
3.9 **CAFETERIA** | Chelsea
4.3 **COPPELIA** | Chelsea
4.0 **GRAY'S PAPAYA** | W 70s
4.2 **KUM GANG SAN** | Multi
4.2 **KUNJIP** | W 30s
3.9 **L'EXPRESS** | Gramercy
4.3 **NEW WONJO** | W 30s
4.1 **SANFORD'S** | Astoria
4.1 **SARGE'S DELI** | Murray Hill
4.1 **VESELKA** | E Vill

VIEWS

4.0 **ALMA** | Columbia St.
4.1 **ANGELINA'S** | Tottenville
4.6 **ASIATE** | W 50s
4.3 **A VOCE** | W 50s
4.0 **BATTERY GDNS.** | Financial
3.9 **BEAUBOURG** | BPC
4.2 **BIRRERIA** | Flatiron
3.9 **BOATHOUSE** | Central Pk
4.0 **BROOKLYN CRAB** | Red Hook
3.9 **BRYANT PK GRILL** | W 40s
4.1 **CITY IS. LOBSTER** | City Is
4.1 **GAONNURI** | W 30s
4.1 **GIGINO** | BPC
4.1 **HUDSON EATS** | BPC
4.3 **JAKE'S STEAKHSE.** | Fieldston

4.5 **LINCOLN** | W 60s

4.5 **MAIELLA** | LIC

3.9 **MICHAEL JORDAN** | E 40s

4.6 **MODERN** | W 50s

4.4 **MORSO** | E 50s

4.6 **PER SE** | W 50s

3.8 **PIER A** | BPC

3.8 **P.J. CLARKE'S** | Multi

4.6 **PORTER HOUSE** | W 50s

4.2 **RANDAZZO'S** | Sheepshead

4.1 **RARE B&G** | Murray Hill

4.6 **RIVER CAFÉ** | Dumbo

4.5 **RIVERPARK** | Murray Hill

4.1 **ROBERT** | W 50s

4.4 **SEA GRILL** | W 40s

4.1 **SHI** | LIC

4.1 **STELLA 34** | W 30s

3.7 **VIEW** | W 40s

4.3 **WATER CLUB** | Murray Hill

VISITORS ON EXPENSE ACCOUNT

— **AGERN** | E 40s NEW

4.6 **AI FIORI** | W 30s

4.4 **AMERICAN CUT** | Multi

4.6 **AUREOLE** | W 40s

4.6 **BABBO** | G Vill

4.5 **BÂTARD** | TriBeCa

4.9 **BOULEY** | TriBeCa

4.7 **CAFÉ BOULUD** | E 70s

4.5 **CARBONE** | G Vill

4.5 **CRAFT** | Flatiron

4.8 **DANIEL** | E 60s

4.5 **DEL FRISCO'S** | Multi

4.7 **DEL POSTO** | Chelsea

4.6 **DOVETAIL** | W 70s

4.7 **ELEVEN MADISON** | Flatiron

4.8 **GRAMERCY TAV.** | Flatiron

— **GUNTER SEEGER** | Meatpacking NEW

4.4 **HAKKASAN** | W 40s

4.6 **IL MULINO** | G Vill

4.7 **INDIAN ACCENT** | W 50s NEW

4.8 **JEAN-GEORGES** | W 60s

4.3 **KAPPO MASA** | E 70s

4.5 **KEENS** | W 30s

4.6 **KOSAKA** | W Vill NEW

4.6 **KURUMAZUSHI** | E 40s

4.4 **LA CHINE** | E 40s

4.7 **LA GRENOUILLE** | E 50s

4.2 **LA SIRENA** | Chelsea NEW

4.9 **LE BERNARDIN** | W 50s

4.4 **LE CIRQUE** | E 50s

4.4 **LE COQ RICO** | Flatiron NEW

— **LE COUCOU** | SoHo NEW

4.7 **MAREA** | W 50s

4.5 **MASA** | W 50s

4.7 **MILOS** | W 50s

4.6 **MODERN** | W 50s

4.7 **NOBU** | Multi

4.6 **O YA** | Murray Hill

4.4 **PALM** | E 40s

4.6 **PER SE** | W 50s

4.8 **PETER LUGER** | W'burg

4.4 **RIST. MORINI** | E 80s

4.6 **RIVER CAFÉ** | Dumbo

4.6 **SHUKO** | G Vill

— **SUSHI GINZA** | E 40s NEW

4.7 **SUSHI NAKAZAWA** | W Vill

4.8 **SUSHI YASUDA** | E 40s

— **SUSHI ZO** | G Vill NEW

— **TEISUI** | NoMad NEW

— **TEKOÁ** | Cobble Hill NEW

WINE BARS

3.9 **ABV** | E 90s

4.0 **ALDO SOHM** | W 50s

4.4 **ALTA** | G Vill

4.2 **BACARO** | LES

4.1 **BACCHUS** | Downtown Bklyn

4.3 **BAR BOULUD** | W 60s

4.5 **BAR JAMÔN** | Gramercy

— **BEASTS/BOTTLES** | Bklyn Hts NEW

4.4 **CASELLULA** | W 50s

4.0 **CORKBUZZ** | Multi

4.4 **DESNUDA** | Multi

4.4 **D.O.C. WINE BAR** | W'burg

3.8 **ELI'S ESSENTIALS** | E 90s

4.5 **EL QUINTO PINO** | Chelsea

4.2 **FELICE** | E 60s

4.5 **FOUR HORSEMEN** | W'burg

4.5 **IL BUCO ALIMENTARI** | NoHo

4.3 **I TRULLI** | Murray Hill

4.9 **LE BERNARDIN** | W 50s

4.4 **MURRAY'S CHEESE** | W Vill

4.3 **OTTO** | G Vill

4.5 **PALMA** | W Vill

4.5 **PEASANT** | NoLita

4.3 **RACINES** | TriBeCa

4.7 **UPHOLSTERY STORE** | W Vill

4.2 **UVA** | E 70s

4.4 **VESTA** | Astoria

WINNING WINE LISTS

4.4 **ABC COCINA** | Flatiron

4.5 **ABC KITCHEN** | Flatiron

4.5 **ALDEA** | Flatiron

4.4 **ALTA** | G Vill

4.3 **AMALI** | E 60s

4.7 **ANNISA** | W Vill

4.6 **ASIATE** | W 50s

4.6 **AUREOLE** | W 40s

4.3 **A VOCE** | W 50s

4.6 **BABBO** | G Vill

4.4 **BALTHAZAR** | SoHo

4.1 **BARBETTA** | W 40s

4.3 **BAR BOULUD** | W 60s

4.5 **BÂTARD** | TriBeCa

— **BEASTS/BOTTLES** | Bklyn Hts NEW

4.2 **BECCO** | W 40s

4.5 **BETONY** | W 50s

4.2 **BIRDS & BUBBLES** | LES

— **BKW** | Crown Hts NEW

4.5 **BLT PRIME** | Gramercy

4.5 **BLT STEAK** | E 50s

4.2 **BLUE FIN** | W 40s

4.7 **BLUE HILL** | G Vill

4.2 **BOBBY VAN'S** | Multi

4.9 **BOULEY** | TriBeCa

4.6 **BRUSHSTROKE/ICHIMURA** | TriBeCa

4.4 **CAFÉ ALTRO** | Hudson Sq NEW

4.7 **CAFÉ BOULUD** | E 70s

4.4 **CAFE KATJA** | LES

4.4 **CAPITAL GRILLE** | E 40s

4.5 **CARBONE** | G Vill

4.6 **CASA MONO** | Gramercy

4.2 **'CESCA** | W 70s

4.2 **CHARLIE BIRD** | SoHo

4.8 **CHEF'S/BROOKLYN FARE** | Downtown Bklyn

4.2 **CLAUDETTE** | G Vill

4.5 **CRAFT** | Flatiron

4.8 **DANIEL** | E 60s

4.4 **DB BISTRO MODERNE** | W 40s

4.5 **DEL FRISCO'S** | Multi

4.5 **DELL'ANIMA** | W Vill

4.7 **DEL POSTO** | Chelsea

4.7 **ELEVEN MADISON** | Flatiron

4.4 **ESCA** | W 40s

4.6 **ESTELA** | NoLita

4.6 **FELIDIA** | E 50s

4.5 **FOUR HORSEMEN** | W'burg

4.4 **FRANKIES** | Multi

4.3 **FRANNY'S** | Park Slope

4.8 **GABRIEL KREUTHER** | W 40s

4.1 **GANDER** | Flatiron

4.5 **GATO** | NoHo

4.8 **GOTHAM B&G** | G Vill

4.8 **GRAMERCY TAV.** | Flatiron

— **GUNTER SEEGER** | Meatpacking NEW

4.3 **HARRY'S CAFE** | Financial

4.4 **HEARTH** | E Vill

4.5 **IL BUCO** | NoHo

4.3 **I TRULLI** | Murray Hill

4.8 **JEAN-GEORGES** | W 60s

4.3 **JUNOON** | Flatiron

4.3 **LAFAYETTE** | NoHo

4.3 **LAMBS CLUB** | W 40s

3.9 **LANDMARC** | W 50s

4.4 **LA PIZZA FRESCA** | Flatiron

4.7 **LA VARA** | Cobble Hill

4.9 **LE BERNARDIN** | W 50s

4.4 **LE CIRQUE** | E 50s

4.6 **LUPA** | G Vill

4.6 **MAIALINO** | Gramercy

4.6 **MARC FORGIONE** | TriBeCa

4.7 **MAREA** | W 50s

4.4 **MARTA** | NoMad

4.7 **MAS** | W Vill

4.3 **MICHAEL'S** | W 50s

4.7 **MILOS** | W 50s

4.4 **MINETTA TAV.** | G Vill

4.6 **MODERN** | W 50s

4.3 **MOMOFUKU NISHI** | Chelsea NEW

4.1 **MULINO A VINO** | Chelsea

4.5 **MUSKET ROOM** | NoLita

4.3 **M. WELLS STEAKHSE.** | LIC

4.5 **NARCISSA** | E Vill

3.9 **NICE MATIN** | W 70s

4.6 **NOMAD** | NoMad

4.5 **OCEANA** | W 40s

4.5 **OSTERIA MORINI** | SoHo

4.3 **OTTO** | G Vill

4.6 **O YA** | Murray Hill

4.3 **PEARL & ASH** | NoLita

4.6 **PER SE** | W 50s

4.6 **PORTER HOUSE** | W 50s

4.3 **RACINES** | TriBeCa

4.5 **RAOUL'S** | SoHo

4.3 **REBELLE** | NoLita

4.4 **REYNARD** | W'burg

4.4 **RIST. MORINI** | E 80s

4.6 **RIVER CAFÉ** | Dumbo

4.1 **ROTISSERIE GEORGETTE** | E 60s

4.5 **SAN PIETRO** | E 50s

4.7 **SCALINI FEDELI** | TriBeCa

4.5 **SCARPETTA** | Chelsea

4.6 **SIMONE** | E 80s

4.4 **SISTINA** | E 80s

4.4 **SMITH/WOLLENSKY** | E 40s

4.5 **SPARKS** | E 40s

4.5 **THALASSA** | TriBeCa

4.4 **TÍA POL** | Chelsea

4.5 **TOMMASO** | Bath Bch

4.8 **TOCQUEVILLE** | Flatiron

4.0 **TRESTLE ON 10TH** | Chelsea

4.3 **TRIBECA GRILL** | TriBeCa

4.3 **21 CLUB** | W 50s

4.4 **TXIKITO** | Chelsea

4.5 **VALBELLA** | Meatpacking

4.2 **VIA EMILIA** | Flatiron

4.4 **VINEGAR HILL HSE** | Vinegar Hill

4.6 **WALLSÉ** | W Vill

4.4 **WILDAIR** | LES

CUISINES

Includes Food ratings, names and locations.

AFRICAN
4.4 **CECIL** | Harlem
4.2 **PONTY BISTRO** | Multi

AMERICAN
4.5 **ABC KITCHEN** | Flatiron
4.0 **ABIGAEL'S** | W 30s
3.9 **ABV** | E 90s
3.9 **ALICE'S TEA** | Multi
3.9 **ALOBAR** | LIC
4.7 **ANNISA** | W Vill
4.3 **ARETSKY'S PATROON** | E 40s
4.6 **ASIATE** | W 50s
3.9 **ASTOR ROOM** | Astoria
4.6 **ATERA** | TriBeCa
4.0 **ATRIUM DUMBO** | Dumbo
4.6 **AUREOLE** | W 40s
4.3 **BACK RM AT ONE57** | W 50s
4.3 **BAR AMERICAIN** | W 50s
3.9 **BAR CENTRALE** | W 40s
4.2 **BAR PLEIADES** | E 70s
4.3 **BAR SARDINE** | W Vill
4.5 **BÂTARD** | TriBeCa
4.6 **BATTERSBY** | Boerum Hill
4.0 **BATTERY GDNS.** | Financial
4.1 **BEATRICE INN** | W Vill
3.9 **BEAUTIQUE** | W 50s
4.2 **BEAUTY & ESSEX** | LES
4.1 **BEDFORD & CO.** | E 40s **NEW**
4.2 **BENCHMARK** | Park Slope
4.5 **BETONY** | W 50s
— **BKW** | Crown Hts **NEW**
4.1 **BLACK BARN** | NoMad
— **BLACKTAIL** | BPC **NEW**
4.3 **BLACK TREE** | Multi
4.0 **BLACK WHALE** | City Is
4.7 **BLANCA** | Bushwick
4.0 **BLENHEIM** | W Vill
4.7 **BLUE HILL** | G Vill
4.4 **BLUE RIBBON** | Multi
4.4 **BLUE RIBBON** | Multi
4.1 **BLUE RIBBON FRIED** | E Vill
4.1 **BLUJEEN** | Harlem
3.9 **BOATHOUSE** | Central Pk
4.3 **BOTTLE & BINE** | E 50s **NEW**

4.0 **BOULTON & WATT** | E Vill
4.2 **BRINDLE ROOM** | E Vill
3.9 **BRYANT PK GRILL** | W 40s
4.0 **BUBBY'S** | Multi
4.1 **BURGER & LOBSTER** | Flatiron
4.1 **BUTTER** | W 40s
4.6 **BUTTERMILK** | Carroll Gdns
4.1 **CAFE CLOVER** | W Vill
4.2 **CAFE CLUNY** | W Vill
4.2 **CAFE ORLIN** | E Vill
3.9 **CAFETERIA** | Chelsea
4.4 **CASELLULA** | W 50s
4.5 **CAVIAR RUSSE** | E 50s
4.4 **CECIL** | Harlem
4.4 **CHADWICK'S** | Bay Ridge
4.2 **CHALK POINT** | SoHo
4.2 **CHARLIE BIRD** | SoHo
4.2 **CHARLIE PALMER/KNICK** | W 40s
4.5 **CHEFS CLUB** | NoLita
— **CHERRY POINT** | Greenpt **NEW**
4.6 **CLEMENT REST.** | W 50s
4.5 **CLINTON ST. BAKING** | LES
4.3 **CLOCKTOWER** | Flatiron
3.6 **COFFEE SHOP** | Union Sq
4.5 **COLONIE** | Bklyn Hts
4.1 **COMMUNITY** | Morningside Hts
4.6 **CONTRA** | LES
4.3 **COOKSHOP** | Chelsea
4.1 **COPPER KETTLE** | E 70s **NEW**
3.8 **CORNELIA ST.** | W Vill
4.4 **COVINA** | Murray Hill **NEW**
4.5 **CRAFT** | Flatiron
4.2 **CRAFTBAR** | Flatiron
4.2 **DAVID BURKE FAB.** | W 30s
4.4 **DAVID BURKE KIT.** | SoHo
4.6 **DEGUSTATION** | E Vill
4.5 **DELAWARE/HUDSON** | W'burg
4.1 **DELICATESSEN** | NoLita
4.5 **DINER** | W'burg
— **DINNERTABLE** | E Vill **NEW**
4.1 **DONOVAN'S** | Multi
4.5 **DOVER** | Carroll Gdns
4.6 **DOVETAIL** | W 70s
4.2 **DUDLEY'S** | LES

4.2 **DUTCH** | SoHo

4.3 **EARL'S BEER/CHEESE** | E 90s

4.1 **EAST POLE** | E 60s

4.0 **E.A.T.** | E 80s

4.5 **EDDY** | E Vill

4.1 **EGG SHOP** | NoLita

4.7 **ELEVEN MADISON** | Flatiron

4.3 **ELI'S TABLE** | E 80s

4.4 **EL REY** | LES

4.4 **ESME** | Greenpt

4.6 **ESTELA** | NoLita

4.2 **FARM/ADDERLEY** | Ditmas Pk

4.1 **FAT RADISH** | LES

— **FAUN** | Prospect Hts NEW

4.2 **FEAST** | G Vill

4.3 **FEDORA** | W Vill

4.6 **FINCH** | Clinton Hill

4.3 **FIVE LEAVES** | Greenpt

4.0 **FLATBUSH FARM** | Park Slope

4.1 **FORAGERS CITY TABLE** | Chelsea

4.2 **FORT DEFIANCE** | Red Hook

4.2 **44 & X/44½** | W 40s

4.5 **FOUR HORSEMEN** | W'burg

4.2 **FRED'S AT BARNEYS** | Multi

— **FREEK'S MILL** | Gowanus NEW

4.1 **FREEMANS** | LES

4.4 **FRENCH LOUIE** | Boerum Hill

4.2 **FRIEDMAN'S** | Multi

4.0 **FRIEND/FARMER** | Multi

4.1 **GANDER** | Flatiron

4.3 **GIORGIO'S** | Flatiron

4.3 **GG'S** | E Vill

3.9 **GLASS HOUSE** | W 40s

4.1 **GOOD** | W Vill

3.9 **GOOD ENOUGH/EAT** | W 80s

4.8 **GOTHAM B&G** | G Vill

4.8 **GRAMERCY TAV.** | Flatiron

4.1 **GRAND TIER** | W 60s

4.0 **GREY DOG** | Multi

4.4 **HEARTH** | E Vill

4.5 **HENRY'S END** | Bklyn Hts

4.5 **HIGH STREET/HUDSON** | Meatpacking NEW

4.2 **HILLSTONE** | Multi

4.0 **HOUSE** | Gramercy

4.2 **HOUSEMAN** | Hudson Sq

4.1 **HUDSON CLEARWATER** | W Vill

4.2 **HUDSON GARDEN** | Bronx Park

4.2 **HUNDRED ACRES** | SoHo

4.0 **ISABELLA'S** | W 70s

4.2 **JACK'S WIFE FREDA** | Multi

4.2 **JACK THE HORSE** | Bklyn Hts

4.2 **JACOB'S PICKLES** | W 80s

4.4 **JAMES** | Prospect Hts

4.2 **JANE** | G Vill

4.4 **JEFFREY'S GROCERY** | W Vill

3.9 **JOE ALLEN** | W 40s

4.3 **JOSEPH LEONARD** | W Vill

4.1 **KAT & THEO** | Flatiron

4.3 **KINGS' CARRIAGE** | E 80s

4.8 **KINGSLEY** | E Vill NEW

4.1 **KNICKERBOCKER** | G Vill

4.2 **KRUPA** | Windsor Terr.

4.3 **LAMBS CLUB** | W 40s

4.4 **L'AMICO** | Chelsea

4.3 **LEFT BANK** | W Vill

3.8 **LIBRARY/PUBLIC** | G Vill

4.3 **LIC MARKET** | LIC

4.0 **LITTLE BEET** | Multi

4.5 **LITTLE OWL** | W Vill

4.4 **LITTLE PARK** | TriBeCa

4.5 **LUKSUS** | Greenpt

4.3 **MÁ PÊCHE** | W 50s

4.6 **MARC FORGIONE** | TriBeCa

4.3 **MARK** | E 70s

4.4 **MARKET TABLE** | W Vill

4.4 **MARLOW/SONS** | W'burg

4.3 **MARSHAL** | W 40s

4.7 **MAS** | W Vill

4.2 **MAYFIELD** | Crown Hts

4.2 **MAYSVILLE** | NoMad

4.7 **MEADOWSWEET** | W'burg

4.3 **MELBA'S** | Harlem

4.2 **MERCER KITCHEN** | SoHo

— **METROGRAPH COMMISSARY** | LES NEW

4.5 **MIKE'S BISTRO** | E 50s

4.3 **MILLING RM.** | W 80s

4.6 **MODERN** | W 50s

4.7 **MOMOFUKU KO** | E Vill

4.5 **MOMOFUKU NOODLE** | E Vill

4.5 **MOMOFUKU SSÄM** | E Vill

4.0 **MONKEY BAR** | E 50s

4.2 **MONUMENT LANE** | W Vill

3.9 **MORGAN DINING RM.** | Murray Hill

— **MR. DONAHUE'S** | NoLita `NEW`	4.3 **SALT & FAT** | Sunnyside
4.0 **MULBERRY & VINE** | Multi	4.1 **SANFORD'S** | Astoria
4.4 **MURRAY'S CHEESE** | W Vill	4.0 **SARABETH'S** | Multi
4.5 **NARCISSA** | E Vill	— **SAUVAGE** | Greenpt `NEW`
3.8 **NATIONAL** | E 50s	4.3 **SAXON & PAROLE** | NoHo
3.9 **NOHO STAR** | NoHo	3.8 **SCHILLER'S** | LES
4.6 **NOMAD** | NoMad	4.6 **SEMILLA** | W'burg
4.4 **NOMAD BAR** | NoMad	4.0 **SERENDIPITY 3** | E 60s
4.4 **NORMA'S** | W 50s	3.9 **SMITH** | Multi
4.5 **NORTH END GRILL** | Battery Pk	4.1 **SOJOURN** | E 70s
4.3 **NORTH SQ.** | G Vill	3.9 **SONS OF ESSEX** | LES
4.5 **OCEANA** | W 40s	4.1 **STANDARD GRILL** | Meatpacking
4.0 **ODEON** | TriBeCa	4.5 **ST. ANSELM** | W'burg
— **OLEANDERS** | W'burg	4.5 **STANTON SOCIAL** | LES
— **OLMSTED** | Prospect Hts `NEW`	4.5 **STONE PARK** | Park Slope
4.4 **ONE IF BY LAND** | W Vill	— **SYNDICATED** | Bushwick `NEW`
4.2 **PALM COURT** | W 50s	4.4 **TABLE D'HÔTE** | E 90s
4.4 **PARK AVENUE** | Flatiron	— **TAKE ROOT** | Carroll Gdns
4.0 **PARKER & QUINN** | W 30s	3.6 **TAVERN/GREEN** | Central Pk
4.3 **PEARL & ASH** | NoLita	4.0 **THALIA** | W 40s
4.0 **PENELOPE** | Murray Hill	4.1 **TINY'S** | TriBeCa
4.1 **PENROSE** | E 80s	4.8 **TOCQUEVILLE** | Flatiron
4.6 **PERRY ST.** | W Vill	4.0 **TRESTLE ON 10TH** | Chelsea
4.6 **PER SE** | W 50s	4.3 **TRIBECA GRILL** | TriBeCa
3.6 **PETE'S TAV.** | Gramercy	4.5 **TUOME** | E Vill
3.8 **PIER A** | BPC	4.0 **12TH ST. B&G** | Park Slope
4.4 **PINES** | Gowanus	4.3 **12 CHAIRS** | Multi
4.6 **PIORA** | W Vill	4.3 **21 CLUB** | W 50s
4.1 **POLO BAR** | E 50s	— **UNION FARE** | Flatiron `NEW`
4.3 **PRIME MEATS** | Carroll Gdns	4.4 **UNTITLED** | Meatpacking
4.5 **PRINT** | W 40s	4.7 **UPHOLSTERY STORE** | W Vill
4.6 **PRUNE** | E Vill	3.7 **VIEW** | W 40s
4.5 **QUALITY MEATS** | W 50s	4.4 **VINEGAR HILL HSE.** | Vinegar Hill
4.3 **RAINBOW RM.** | W 40s	4.4 **VIRGINIA'S** | E Vill
4.3 **RED CAT** | Chelsea	4.4 **VITAE** | E 40s
4.0 **REDEYE GRILL** | W 50s	4.1 **WALTER** | Multi
4.2 **RED ROOSTER** | Harlem	— **WARREN** | W Vill `NEW`
4.0 **REGENCY B&G** | E 60s	4.2 **WASSAIL** | LES
4.4 **REYNARD** | W'burg	4.3 **WATER CLUB** | Murray Hill
4.0 **RIBBON** | W 70s	4.2 **WAVERLY INN** | W Vill
— **RIDER** | W'burg `NEW`	3.4 **W. 79TH ST. BOAT BASIN** | W 70s
4.6 **RIVER CAFÉ** | Dumbo	4.1 **WESTVILLE** | Multi
4.5 **RIVERPARK** | Murray Hill	4.1 **WHITE STREET** | TriBeCa
4.1 **ROBERT** | W 50s	4.4 **WILDAIR** | LES
4.2 **ROSE'S** | Prospect Hts	— **WIN SON** | W'burg `NEW`
4.6 **ROSE WATER** | Park Slope	
4.4 **RUNNER & STONE** | Gowanus	
4.4 **RYE** | W'burg	

CUISINES

ARGENTINEAN
4.5 **BALVANERA** | LES
4.4 **BUENOS AIRES** | E Vill
4.4 **CHIMICHURRI GRILL** | W 40s

ARMENIAN
4.4 **ALMAYASS** | Flatiron

ASIAN
4.4 **ASIA DE CUBA** | G Vill
4.6 **ASIATE** | W 50s
4.4 **BUDDAKAN** | Chelsea
4.2 **CHINA GRILL** | W 50s
4.0 **FATTY FISH** | E 60s
4.2 **KOA** | Flatiron
— **LUCKY BEE** | LES NEW
4.3 **MOMOFUKU NISHI** |
Chelsea NEW
4.5 **MOMOFUKU SSÄM BAR** | E Vill
4.1 **NEW WORLD MALL** | Flushing
4.1 **OBAO** | Multi
4.3 **PIG AND KHAO** | LES
4.3 **PURPLE YAM** | Ditmas Pk
4.1 **QI** | Multi
4.3 **SALT & FAT** | Sunnyside
4.1 **SHI** | LIC
4.4 **TALDE** | Park Slope
4.3 **TAO** | Multi
4.0 **ZENGO** | E 40s

AUSTRALIAN
4.3 **BLUESTONE LANE** | Multi
4.3 **BURKE & WILLS** | W 70s
— **COCO & CRU** | G Vill NEW
4.2 **DUDLEY'S** | LES
4.3 **FLINDERS LANE** | E Vill
4.4 **RUBY'S CAFE** | Multi
4.3 **TWO HANDS** | Multi

AUSTRIAN
4.3 **BLAUE GANS** | TriBeCa
4.4 **CAFE KATJA** | LES
4.2 **CAFÉ SABARSKY/
FLEDERMAUS** | E 80s
4.2 **EDI & THE WOLF** | E Vill
4.3 **FREUD** | G Vill NEW
3.9 **GRÜNAUER BISTRO** |
E 80s NEW
— **SCHILLING** | Financial NEW
4.6 **WALLSÉ** | W Vill

BAGELS
4.6 **ABSOLUTE BAGELS** | W 100s
4.3 **BAGELWORKS** | E 60s
4.1 **BAZ BAGEL** | L Italy
4.1 **BLACK SEED** | Multi
4.4 **ESS-A-BAGEL** | Multi
4.3 **KOSSAR'S BAGELS** | LES NEW
4.3 **LEO'S BAGELS** | Financial
4.3 **MURRAY'S BAGELS** | Multi
4.7 **RUSS & DAUGHTERS** | LES
4.3 **SADELLE'S** | SoHo
4.4 **TOMPKINS SQUARE BAGELS** |
E Vill
4.2 **ZUCKER'S BAGELS** | Multi

BAKERIES
4.4 **AMY'S BREAD** | Multi
4.5 **ARCADE BAKERY** | TriBeCa
4.4 **BAKED** | Multi
4.3 **BAKERI** | Multi
4.4 **BALTHAZAR** | SoHo
4.1 **BAZ BAGEL** | L Italy
4.3 **BILLY'S BAKERY** | Multi
4.3 **BOUCHON BAKERY** | Multi
4.6 **BREADS BAKERY** | Multi
4.4 **CECI-CELA** | Multi
4.5 **CHIKALICIOUS** | Multi
4.2 **CITY BAKERY** | Flatiron
4.5 **CLINTON ST. BAKING** | LES
4.5 **DOMINIQUE ANSEL
BAKERY** | SoHo
4.4 **DOMINIQUE ANSEL KIT.** | W
Vill
4.3 **FERRARA** | L Italy
4.3 **FORTUNATO BROTHERS** |
W'burg
4.5 **FOUR & TWENTY** | Multi
4.5 **HIGH STREET/HUDSON** |
Meatpacking NEW
4.3 **LA BERGAMOTE** | Multi
4.3 **LADURÉE** | Multi
4.3 **LAFAYETTE** | NoHo
4.7 **LEVAIN BAKERY** | Multi
4.5 **MADONIA BROS. BAKERY** |
Arthur Ave./Belmont
4.2 **MAISON KAYSER** | Multi
— **MEYERS BAGERI** | W'burg NEW
4.5 **ORWASHER'S** | Multi
4.5 **PANEANTICO** | Bay Ridge

4.4 **RUNNER & STONE** | Gowanus
4.5 **SULLIVAN ST.** | Multi

BARBECUE

4.1 **BLUE SMOKE** | Multi
4.3 **BRISKETTOWN** | W'burg
4.3 **BUTCHER BAR** | Astoria
4.1 **DAISY MAY'S** | W 40s
4.2 **DINOSAUR BBQ** | Multi
4.5 **FETTE SAU** | W'burg
4.1 **FLETCHER'S** | Multi
4.2 **HILL COUNTRY** | Multi
4.6 **HOMETOWN** | Red Hook
4.3 **JOHN BROWN** | LIC
4.3 **MIGHTY QUINN'S** | Multi
4.1 **MORGANS BBQ** | Prospect Hts
— **SAMMY'S HSE.** | W 40s NEW
4.1 **SMOKE JOINT** | Ft Greene
4.1 **STRAND SMOKEHSE.** | Astoria
4.0 **VIRGIL'S** | W 40s

BELGIAN

— **BRASSERIE WITLOF** | W'burg
4.4 **CANNIBAL** | Multi

BRAZILIAN

4.4 **CHURRASCARIA** | W 40s
3.6 **COFFEE SHOP** | Union Sq
4.2 **FOGO DE CHÃO** | W 50s
4.1 **SUSHISAMBA** | W Vill

BRITISH

4.2 **A SALT & BATTERY** | W Vill
4.3 **BRESLIN** | NoMad
4.0 **CHIPSHOP** | Brooklyn Hts
4.1 **EAST POLE** | E 60s
4.1 **JONES WOOD** | E 70s
4.2 **TEA & SYMPATHY** | W Vill

BURGERS

4.3 **AMSTERDAM BURGER CO.** | W 90s
3.9 **BAREBURGER** | Multi
4.4 **BLACK IRON BURGER** | Multi
4.2 **BLACK TAP** | Multi
4.1 **BONNIE'S GRILL** | Park Slope
4.4 **BURGER JOINT** | Multi
4.1 **BURGER & LOBSTER** | Flatiron
4.2 **CORNER BISTRO** | Multi
4.4 **DB BISTRO MODERNE** | W 40s

4.1 **DONOVAN'S** | Multi
4.3 **DUMONT BURGER** | W'burg
4.7 **EMILY** | Clinton Hill
— **EMMY SQUARED** | W'burg NEW
4.0 **5 NAPKIN BURGER** | Multi
3.9 **HARLEM SHAKE** | Multi
4.1 **J.G. MELON** | Multi
4.5 **KEENS** | W 30s
4.4 **MINETTA TAV.** | G Vill
4.8 **PETER LUGER** | W'burg
3.8 **P.J. CLARKE'S** | Multi
4.1 **RARE B&G** | Multi
4.1 **SALVATION BURGER** | E 50s
4.0 **SHAKE SHACK** | Multi
4.4 **SPOTTED PIG** | W Vill
4.4 **SUPERIORITY BURGER** | E Vill
4.3 **21 CLUB** | W 50s
4.0 **UMAMI BURGER** | Multi

CAJUN/CREOLE

4.3 **BAYOU** | Rosebank
4.1 **SUGAR FREAK** | Astoria

CALIFORNIAN

4.3 **DIMES** | LES
4.6 **GENUINE SUPERETTE** | L Italy
4.3 **MICHAEL'S** | W 50s
4.4 **UPLAND** | Murray Hill

CAMBODIAN

4.2 **NUM PANG** | Multi

CARIBBEAN

4.4 **ALI'S ROTI** | Multi
4.3 **GLADY'S** | Crown Hts
4.3 **NEGRIL** | G Vill
— **SOLOMON & KUFF** | Manhattanville NEW

CAVIAR

4.5 **CAVIAR RUSSE** | E 50s
4.4 **PETROSSIAN** | W 50s
3.8 **RUSSIAN TEA** | W 50s
4.3 **SADELLE'S** | SoHo

CHEESE SPECIALISTS

4.2 **ARTISANAL** | Murray Hill
4.4 **CASELLULA** | W 50s
4.3 **EARL'S BEER/CHEESE** | E 90s
4.5 **LAMAZOU** | Murray Hill

CUISINES

4.4 **MURRAY'S CHEESE** | W Vill

4.4 **SALUMERIA ROSI PARMACOTTO** | W 70s

CHICKEN

— **BEASTS/BOTTLES** | Bklyn Hts NEW

4.2 **BIRDS & BUBBLES** | LES

4.1 **BLUE RIBBON FRIED** | E Vill

4.3 **BOBWHITE** | Multi

4.2 **BONCHON** | Multi

— **CARLA HALL'S** | Columbia St. NEW

4.0 **COCO ROCO** | Multi

4.2 **COMMODORE** | W'burg

4.1 **FLOR/MAYO** | Multi

4.2 **FUKU** | Multi

4.1 **HILL COUNTRY CHICKEN** | Multi

4.0 **KYOCHON** | Multi

4.2 **MALECON** | Multi

4.3 **PEACHES** | Bed-Stuy

4.3 **PIES-N-THIGHS** | W'burg

4.3 **PIO PIO** | Multi

3.8 **STREETBIRD** | Harlem

4.5 **TORISHIN** | W 50s

4.4 **YAKITORI TOTTO** | W 50s

CHINESE

(* dim sum specialist)

4.1 **AMAZING 66** | Chinatown

4.2 **BAO** | E Vill

4.1 **BAOHAUS** | E Vill

4.2 **BIG WONG** | Chinatown

4.4 **CAFE CHINA** | Murray Hill

4.0 **CAFE EVERGREEN*** | E 70s

4.3 **CHEF HO'S** | E 80s

4.1 **CHINA BLUE** | TriBeCa

4.0 **CONGEE** | LES

4.7 **DECOY** | W Vill

4.1 **DIM SUM GO GO*** | Chinatown

4.1 **DUMPLING GALAXY** | Flushing

4.2 **DUMPLING MAN** | E Vill

4.0 **EXCELLENT DUMPLING*** | Chinatown

4.1 **FLOR/MAYO** | Multi

4.1 **456 SHANGHAI** | Chinatown

4.3 **FUNG TU** | LES

4.4 **GOLDEN SHOPPING MALL** | Flushing

4.1 **GOLDEN UNICORN*** | Chinatown

4.0 **GRAND SICHUAN** | Multi

4.3 **GREAT NY NOODLE** | Chinatown

4.4 **HAKKASAN** | W 40s

4.2 **HAN DYNASTY** | Multi

— **HAO NOODLE** | W Vill NEW

4.2 **HOMETOWN HOTPOT & BBQ** | L Italy

4.1 **HOP KEE** | Chinatown

4.1 **JING FONG*** | Chinatown

4.1 **JOE'S GINGER** | Chinatown

4.2 **JOE'S SHANGHAI** | Multi

4.1 **JUE LAN CLUB** | Flatiron NEW

4.4 **LA CHINE** | E 40s

4.3 **LAM ZHOU** | LES

4.0 **LYCHEE HOUSE*** | E 50s

4.4 **KINGS COUNTY IMPERIAL** | W'burg

4.0 **MACAO TRADING** | TriBeCa

3.7 **MISSION CANTINA** | LES

4.3 **MISSION CHINESE** | LES

4.3 **MR. CHOW** | Multi

4.1 **99 FAVOR TASTE** | Multi

3.9 **NOHO STAR** | NoHo

4.1 **NOM WAH*** | Chinatown

4.3 **ORIENTAL GDN.*** | Chinatown

4.5 **PACIFICANA*** | Sunset Pk

4.3 **PEKING DUCK** | Multi

4.3 **PHILIPPE** | E 60s

4.2 **PHOENIX GDN.** | E 40s

4.1 **PIG HEAVEN** | E 80s

4.0 **PING'S SEAFOOD*** | Multi

4.4 **REDFARM*** | Multi

4.3 **SHANGHAI CAFE** | L Italy

4.4 **SHUN LEE PALACE** | E 50s

4.1 **SHUN LEE WEST** | W 60s

4.4 **SPICY & TASTY** | Flushing

4.2 **SZECHUAN GOURMET** | Multi

4.2 **TANG PAVILION** | W 50s

4.3 **TASTY HAND-PULLED** | Chinatown

4.0 **VANESSA'S DUMPLING** | Multi

4.3 **WA JEAL** | E 80s

4.4 **WHITE BEAR** | Flushing

4.1 **WO HOP** | Chinatown

4.5 **WU LIANG YE** | W 40s

4.2 **XI'AN** | Multi

COFFEE

4.6 **ABRAÇO ESPRESSO** | E Vill
4.3 **BAKERI** | Multi
4.2 **BLUE BOTTLE** | Multi
4.1 **BIRCH COFFEE** | Multi
4.3 **BLUESTONE LANE** | Multi
4.0 **CAFE LALO** | W 80s
4.2 **CAFÉ SABARSKY/ FLEDERMAUS** | E 80s
4.4 **CULTURE ESPRESSO** | W 30s
4.4 **EL REY** | LES
4.3 **FIVE LEAVES** | Greenpt
4.0 **GREY DOG** | Multi
4.2 **JACK'S STIR BREW** | Multi
4.4 **LA COLOMBE** | Multi
4.1 **MARGAUX** | G Vill
4.3 **NINTH ST ESPRESSO** | Multi
4.0 **QUEENS KICKSHAW** | Astoria
4.4 **RUCOLA** | Boerum Hill
4.6 **SAN MATTEO** | E 90s
4.4 **SANT AMBROEUS** | Multi
4.4 **SARAGHINA** | Bed-Stuy
4.3 **SMILE** | Multi
4.0 **STUMPTOWN** | Multi
— **SUPERCROWN** | Bushwick **NEW**
4.1 **TOBY'S ESTATE** | Multi
— **TEKOÁ** | Cobble Hill **NEW**
4.3 **THIRD RAIL COFFEE** | Multi
4.4 **TILDA ALL DAY** | Clinton Hill
4.1 **VIA QUADRONNO** | Multi

COLOMBIAN

4.4 **EMPANADA MAMA** | LES

CONTINENTAL

4.0 **BATTERY GDNS.** | Financial
4.2 **CEBU** | Bay Ridge
4.4 **PETROSSIAN** | W 50s
3.8 **RUSSIAN TEA** | W 50s
3.7 **SARDI'S** | W 40s

CUBAN

4.3 **AMOR CUBANO** | E Harlem
4.4 **ASIA DE CUBA** | G Vill
4.1 **CAFÉ HABANA** | Multi
4.3 **CUBA** | G Vill
4.0 **HAVANA CENTRAL** | W 40s
4.3 **VICTOR'S CAFE** | W 50s

DANISH

4.5 **TØRST** | Greenpt

DELIS

4.3 **B & H DAIRY** | E Vill
4.5 **BARNEY GREENGRASS** | W 80s
4.3 **BEN'S BEST** | Rego Pk
4.0 **BEN'S KOSHER** | Multi
4.3 **CARNEGIE DELI** | W 50s
4.3 **DAVID'S BRISKET** | Multi
— **FRANKEL'S DELI** | Greenpt **NEW**
4.4 **HARRY & IDA'S** | E Vill
4.5 **KATZ'S DELI** | LES
4.6 **LEO'S LATTICINI/CORONA** | Multi
4.3 **LIEBMAN'S** | Riverdale
4.2 **MILE END** | Multi
4.3 **MILL BASIN DELI** | Flatlands
4.2 **PASTRAMI QUEEN** | E 70s
4.7 **RUSS & DAUGHTERS** | LES
4.5 **SABLE'S SMOKED FISH** | E 70s
4.1 **SARGE'S DELI** | Murray Hill
4.2 **2ND AVE DELI** | Multi
4.5 **SHELSKY'S OF BROOKLYN** | Clinton Hill
— **TWIN SUNS** | Bushwick **NEW**

DESSERT

4.3 **BOUCHON BAKERY** | Multi
4.1 **BROOKLYN FARMACY** | Carroll Gdns
4.0 **CAFE LALO** | W 80s
4.2 **CAFÉ SABARSKY/ FLEDERMAUS** | E 80s
4.5 **CHIKALICIOUS** | Multi
4.4 **CHOCOLATE ROOM** | Multi
4.2 **CITY BAKERY** | Flatiron
4.5 **COURT PASTRY SHOP** | Clinton Hill
4.5 **DOMINIQUE ANSEL BAKERY** | SoHo
4.4 **DOMINIQUE ANSEL KIT.** | W Vill
4.2 **DONUT PUB** | Chelsea
4.4 **DOUGH** | Multi
4.3 **DOUGHNUT PLANT** | Multi
4.3 **DUN-WELL DOUGHNUTS** | Multi
4.3 **FERRARA** | L Italy
4.3 **FRANÇOIS PAYARD** | Multi

CUISINES

3.8 **JUNIOR'S** | Multi
4.6 **LADY M** | Multi
4.0 **LADY MENDL'S** | Gramercy
4.4 **L&B SPUMONI** | Gravesend
4.7 **LEVAIN BAKERY** | Multi
4.1 **MILK BAR** | Multi
4.5 **PETER PAN** | Greenpt
4.4 **RICE TO RICHES** | NoLita
4.4 **SANT AMBROEUS** | Multi
4.0 **SERENDIPITY 3** | E 60s
4.6 **TWO LITTLE RED** | E 80s
4.4 **VENIERO'S PASTRY** | E Vill
4.7 **VILLABATE ALBA** | Bensonhurst

DINER

4.1 **BAZ BAGEL** | L Italy
4.1 **BONNIE'S GRILL** | Park Slope
4.1 **BROOKLYN FARMACY** | Carroll Gdns
4.3 **COPPELIA** | Chelsea
4.5 **DINER** | W'burg
4.6 **GENUINE SUPERETTE** | L Italy
— **HAIL MARY** | Greenpt NEW
3.8 **JUNIOR'S** | Multi
4.1 **LITTLE POLAND** | E Vill
4.1 **SANFORD'S** | Astoria

DONUTS

4.2 **DONUT PUB** | Chelsea
4.4 **DOUGH** | Multi
4.3 **DOUGHNUT PLANT** | Multi
4.3 **DUN-WELL DOUGHNUTS** | Multi
4.5 **PETER PAN** | Greenpt

DOMINICAN

4.2 **MALECON** | Multi
3.9 **MAMAN** | Multi

EASTERN EUROPEAN

4.4 **BABA'S PIEROGIES** | Gowanus
4.4 **KAFANA** | E Vill
4.0 **SAMMY'S ROUMANIAN** | LES

ECLECTIC

3.9 **BERG'N** | Crown Hts
4.5 **CAROL'S CAFE** | Todt Hill
4.4 **CECIL** | Harlem
4.0 **CORKBUZZ** | Multi

3.8 **DEAR IRVING** | Gramercy
4.3 **DUCKS EATERY** | E Vill
3.8 **ELI'S ESSENTIALS** | Multi
4.4 **GOOD FORK** | Red Hook
— **NORM** | Prospect Hts NEW
4.3 **PUBLIC** | NoLita
4.6 **TRAIF** | W'burg
4.3 **VANDAL** | LES NEW

ETHIOPIAN

4.3 **AWASH** | Multi
4.3 **QUEEN OF SHEBA** | W 40s

EUROPEAN

4.3 **BAKERI** | Multi
4.5 **BÂTARD** | TriBeCa
— **GUNTER SEEGER** | Meatpacking NEW
4.6 **NOMAD** | NoMad
4.3 **SADELLE'S** | SoHo
4.4 **SPOTTED PIG** | W Vill

FILIPINO

3.9 **JEEPNEY** | E Vill
4.3 **KUMA INN** | LES
4.3 **MAHARLIKA** | E Vill
— **2ND CITY** | W Vill NEW

FONDUE

4.2 **ARTISANAL** | Murray Hill
4.4 **CHOCOLATE ROOM** | Multi
4.3 **KASHKAVAL** | W 50s
4.4 **MURRAY'S CHEESE** | W Vill

FRENCH

4.2 **ACME** | NoHo
4.0 **ALDO SOHM** | W 50s
4.5 **ALMONDINE BAKERY** | Dumbo
4.5 **ARCADE BAKERY** | TriBeCa
4.4 **AUTRE KYO YA** | E Vill
4.1 **AU ZA'ATAR** | E Vill
4.0 **BAGATELLE** | Meatpacking
4.3 **BOBO** | W Vill
4.3 **BOUCHON BAKERY** | Multi
4.9 **BOULEY** | TriBeCa
4.4 **BUVETTE** | W Vill
4.7 **CAFÉ BOULUD** | E 70s
4.1 **CAFE CENTRO** | E 40s
4.0 **CAFE GITANE** | Multi

4.0 **CAFÉ HENRI** | LIC

4.2 **CARLYLE** | E 70s

4.8 **CHEF'S/BROOKLYN FARE** | Downtown Bklyn

4.8 **DANIEL** | E 60s

4.2 **DBGB** | E Vill

4.6 **DEGUSTATION** | E Vill

4.1 **DIRTY FRENCH** | LES

4.5 **DOMINIQUE ANSEL BAKERY** | SoHo

4.4 **DOMINIQUE ANSEL KIT.** | W Vill

4.2 **ÉPICERIE BOULUD** | Multi

4.3 **FRANÇOIS PAYARD** | Multi

4.4 **FRENCH LOUIE** | Boerum Hill

4.8 **GABRIEL KREUTHER** | W 40s

4.3 **INDOCHINE** | G Vill

4.8 **JEAN-GEORGES** | W 60s

4.7 **JEAN-GEORGES' NOUG.** | W 60s

4.8 **KINGSLEY** | E Vill NEW

4.3 **LA BARAKA** | Douglaston

4.3 **LA BERGAMOTE** | Multi

4.1 **LA BOÎTE EN BOIS** | W 60s

4.3 **LADURÉE** | Multi

4.3 **LAFAYETTE** | NoHo

4.7 **LA GRENOUILLE** | E 50s

4.3 **LA MANGEOIRE** | E 50s

4.9 **LE BERNARDIN** | W 50s

4.4 **LE CIRQUE** | E 50s

4.2 **LE COLONIAL** | E 50s

4.4 **LE COQ RICO** | Flatiron NEW

— **LE COUCOU** | SoHo NEW

4.5 **LE GIGOT** | W Vill

4.2 **LE MARAIS** | W 40s

4.5 **LE PERIGORD** | E 50s

4.1 **LE RIVAGE** | W 40s

4.1 **LE TURTLE** | LES NEW

4.2 **MAISON KAYSER** | Multi

4.1 **MARGAUX** | G Vill

4.0 **MARSEILLE** | W 40s

4.2 **MERCER KITCHEN** | SoHo

— **MIMI** | G Vill NEW

4.4 **MINETTA TAV.** | G Vill

4.6 **MODERN** | W 50s

4.0 **MONTE CARLO** | E 70s

4.0 **NIZZA** | W 40s

4.0 **ODEON** | TriBeCa

4.2 **PASCALOU** | E 90s

4.6 **PER SE** | W 50s

4.4 **PETROSSIAN** | W 50s

4.2 **PONTY BISTRO** | Multi

4.3 **RACINES** | TriBeCa

4.3 **REBELLE** | NoLita

4.1 **ROTISSERIE GEORGETTE** | E 60s

4.6 **SIMONE** | E 80s

4.8 **TOCQUEVILLE** | Flatiron

4.3 **TRIOMPHE** | W 40s

4.6 **WALLFLOWER** | W Vill

FRENCH (BISTRO)

3.9 **ALMOND** | Multi

4.1 **A.O.C.** | W Vill

4.1 **BACCHUS** | Downtown Bklyn

4.3 **BAR BOULUD** | W 60s

4.1 **BAR TABAC** | Cobble Hill

3.9 **BEAUBOURG** | BPC

4.2 **BENOIT** | W 50s

4.0 **BISTRO CHAT NOIR** | E 60s

4.2 **CAFE CLUNY** | W Vill

3.9 **CAFE LOUP** | W Vill

4.2 **CAFE LULUC** | Cobble Hill

4.2 **CAFE LUXEMBOURG** | W 70s

4.2 **CHERCHE MIDI** | NoLita

4.0 **CHEZ JACQUELINE** | G Vill

4.1 **CHEZ JOSEPHINE** | W 40s

4.1 **CHEZ LUCIENNE** | Harlem

4.1 **CHEZ NAPOLÉON** | W 50s

4.0 **CHEZ OSKAR** | Ft Greene

4.2 **CLAUDETTE** | G Vill

3.8 **CORNELIA ST.** | W Vill

4.4 **DB BISTRO MODERNE** | W 40s

4.1 **DEUX AMIS** | E 50s

4.4 **JOJO** | E 60s

4.1 **JUBILEE** | E 50s

3.9 **LA BONNE SOUPE** | W 50s

3.9 **LANDMARC** | Multi

4.4 **LA SIRÈNE** | Hudson Sq

4.4 **LE BARRICOU** | W'burg

4.1 **LE BILBOQUET** | E 60s

4.2 **LE PARISIEN** | Murray Hill

3.8 **LE VEAU D'OR** | E 60s

3.9 **L'EXPRESS** | Gramercy

4.3 **LUCIEN** | E Vill

3.8 **LUCKY STRIKE** | SoHo

4.1 **MADISON BISTRO** | Murray Hill

4.0 **MAISON HARLEM** | Manhattanville

4.0 **MON PETIT CAFE** | F 60s

4.5 **MOUNTAIN BIRD** | E Harlem

3.9 **NICE MATIN** | W 70s

4.3 **PARDON MY FRENCH** | E Vill

4.2 **QUATORZE BIS** | E 70s

4.5 **RAOUL'S** | SoHo

4.1 **SAJU BISTRO** | W 40s

4.4 **TABLE D'HÔTE** | E 90s

4.2 **TARTINE** | W Vill

4.3 **TOURNESOL** | LIC

FRENCH (BRASSERIE)

4.2 **ARTISANAL** | Murray Hill

4.4 **BALTHAZAR** | SoHo

3.9 **BRASSERIE COGNAC** | Multi

4.2 **BRASSERIE 8½** | W 50s

3.9 **BRASS. RUHLMANN** | W 50s

4.1 **CAFÉ D'ALSACE** | E 80s

4.0 **ÇA VA** | W 40s

3.9 **JACQUES** | Multi

4.2 **LA GAMELLE** | LES

4.1 **LE DISTRICT** | BPC

4.1 **LE RELAIS** | E 50s

4.0 **LES HALLES** | Multi

4.0 **MAISON HUGO** | E 60s

4.0 **MARSEILLE** | W 40s

3.9 **ORSAY** | E 70s

3.9 **RUE 57** | W 50s

4.4 **VAUCLUSE** | E 60s

GASTROPUB

4.0 **BOULTON & WATT** | E Vill

4.4 **CANNIBAL** | Multi

4.2 **DBGB** | E Vill

4.1 **PENROSE** | E 80s

4.4 **SPOTTED PIG** | W Vill

4.2 **WASSAIL** | LES

GEORGIAN

4.3 **ODA HOUSE** | E Vill

4.2 **OLD TBILISI GDN.** | G Vill

4.4 **RED COMPASS** | LES NEW

GERMAN

4.3 **BLAUE GANS** | TriBeCa

4.2 **HEIDELBERG** | E 80s

4.2 **NURNBERGER BIERHAUS** | Randall Manor

3.5 **ROLF'S** | Gramercy

3.7 **STANDARD BIERGARTEN** | Meatpacking

4.2 **ZUM SCHNEIDER** | E Vill

4.5 **ZUM STAMMTISCH** | Glendale

GREEK

4.3 **AGNANTI** | Astoria

3.9 **AGORA TAV.** | Forest Hills

4.2 **AMMOS** | E 40s

4.1 **ANASSA TAVERNA** | E 60s

4.6 **AVRA** | Multi

4.4 **BAHARI ESTIATORIO** | Astoria

3.9 **DAFNI** | W 40s

4.5 **ELIÁ** | Bay Ridge

4.5 **ELIAS CORNER** | Astoria

4.2 **ETHOS** | Multi

4.2 **FISHTAG** | W 70s

3.9 **GREEK KITCHEN** | W 50s

4.2 **ITHAKA** | E 80s

4.1 **KEFI** | W 80s

4.2 **KELLARI TAVERNA** | W 40s

4.5 **KIKI'S** | LES

4.4 **LOI ESTIATORIO** | W 50s

4.5 **LOUKOUMI** | Astoria

4.7 **MILOS** | W 50s

4.3 **MOLYVOS** | W 50s

4.3 **MP TAVERNA** | Multi

4.4 **NERAI** | E 50s

4.2 **OVELIA** | Astoria

4.4 **PERIYALI** | Flatiron

4.5 **PYLOS** | E Vill

4.3 **SNACK** | Multi

4.2 **STAMATIS** | Astoria

4.5 **TAVERNA KYCLADES** | Multi

4.4 **TELLY'S TAVERNA** | Astoria

4.5 **THALASSA** | TriBeCa

4.0 **UNCLE NICK'S** | Multi

4.3 **YEFSI ESTIATORIO** | E 70s

HAWAIIAN

— **CHIKARASHI** | L Italy NEW

4.2 **NOREETUH** | E Vill

4.4 **SONS/THUNDER** | Murray Hill

4.1 **WISEFISH** | Chelsea NEW

HEALTH FOOD

(See also Vegetarian)

4.3 **BY CHLOE** | Multi

4.2 **CHOBANI** | SoHo

4.1 **COMMUNITY** | Morningside Hts

4.3 **DIMES** | LES

4.1 **HU KITCHEN** | Multi

4.0 **LITTLE BEET** | Multi

4.0 **MULBERRY & VINE** | Multi

4.4 **SWEETGREEN** | Multi

HOT DOGS

4.4 **CANNIBAL** | Multi

4.1 **CRIF DOGS** | Multi

4.0 **GRAY'S PAPAYA** | W 70s

4.5 **KATZ'S DELI** | LES

4.2 **MILE END** | Multi

4.1 **PAPAYA KING** | Multi

4.0 **SHAKE SHACK** | Multi

4.1 **SMOKE JOINT** | Ft Greene

4.1 **WESTVILLE** | Multi

ICE CREAM

4.4 **AMORINO** | Multi

4.7 **AMPLE HILLS** | Multi

4.4 **BIAGI GELATO** | NoLita

4.2 **BIG GAY ICE CREAM** | Multi

4.1 **BROOKLYN FARMACY** | Carroll Gdns

4.4 **BROOKLYN ICE CREAM** | Multi

4.5 **CONES** | W Vill

4.5 **DAVEY'S ICE CREAM** | Multi

4.5 **EDDIE'S SWEET SHOP** | Forest Hills

4.5 **GROM** | Multi

4.5 **ICE & VICE** | LES

4.6 **IL LABORATORIO** | LES

4.3 **KHE-YO** | TriBeCa

4.4 **L' ALBERO DEI GELATI** | Park Slope

4.4 **L&B SPUMONI** | Gravesend

4.6 **LEMON ICE KING** | Corona

4.3 **MANDUCATIS RUSTICA** | LIC

4.4 **MORGENSTERN'S** | LES

4.4 **ODDFELLOWS** | Multi

4.4 **ORIGINAL CHINATOWN ICE CREAM** | Chinatown

4.4 **RALPH'S FAMOUS** | Multi

4.0 **SERENDIPITY 3** | E 60s

4.1 **STELLA 34** | W 30S

4.5 **SUNDAES & CONES** | G Vill

4.4 **VAN LEEUWEN** | Multi

INDIAN

4.7 **AMMA** | E 50s

4.3 **AWADH** | W 90s

4.5 **BABU JI** | E Vill

4.0 **BENARES** | Multi

4.1 **BRICK LN. CURRY** | Multi

4.3 **BUKHARA GRILL** | E 40s

4.6 **CHAIWALI** | Harlem

4.3 **CHOLA** | E 50s

4.1 **DARBAR** | Multi

4.4 **DAWAT** | E 50s

4.3 **DHABA** | Murray Hill

— **GRAFFITI EARTH** | TriBeCa NEW

4.1 **HAMPTON CHUTNEY** | Multi

4.3 **HAVELI** | E Vill

4.3 **INDAY** | Flatiron

4.7 **INDIAN ACCENT** | W 50s NEW

3.9 **JACKSON DINER** | Multi

4.3 **JUNOON** | Flatiron

4.2 **KATI ROLL** | Multi

4.3 **MANHATTAN VALLEY** | W 90s

4.3 **MOTI MAHAL** | E 60s

— **PAOWALLA** | SoHo NEW

4.4 **PIPPALI** | Murray Hill

— **PONDICHERI** | NoMad NEW

4.1 **SAPPHIRE INDIAN** | W 60s

4.4 **SARAVANAA BHAVAN** | Multi

4.4 **SEVA INDIAN** | Astoria

— **TAPESTRY** | W Vill NEW

4.7 **TAMARIND** | TriBeCa

4.4 **THELEWALA** | G Vill

4.4 **TULSI** | E 40s

4.0 **UTSAV** | W 40s

4.4 **VATAN** | Murray Hill

ISRAELI

4.4 **AZURI CAFE** | W 50s

4.5 **BAR BOLONAT** | W Vill

— **DIZENGOFF** | Chelsea NEW

4.2 **HUMMUS PL.** | Multi

4.1 **MIRIAM** | Park Slope

4.6 **TAÏM** | Multi

ITALIAN

4.2 **83.5** | E 80s

4.4 **ACAPPELLA** | TriBeCa

4.2 **ACME** | NoHo

4.1 **ACQUA AT PECK SLIP** | Seaport

4.4 **ADORO LEI** | Hudson Sq

4.6 **AI FIORI** | W 30s

4.3 **AITA** | Multi

4.3 **ALBERTO** | Forest Hills

4.6 **AL DI LA** | Park Slope

4.0 **ALFREDO 100** | E 50s

4.7 **ALIDORO** | Multi

4.1 **ALTESI RIST.** | E 60s

4.1 **AMARONE** | W 40s

4.3 **AMORINA** | Prospect Hts

4.1 **ANGELINA'S** | Tottenville

4.4 **ANGELO'S/MULBERRY** | L Italy

4.1 **ANNABEL** | W 50s

3.8 **ANN & TONY'S** | Arthur Ave./ Belmont

4.6 **ANTICA PESA** | W'burg

4.4 **ANTONUCCI** | E 80s

4.4 **AREO** | Bay Ridge

4.3 **ARMANI RIST.** | E 50s

4.2 **ARNO** | W 30s

4.2 **ARTURO'S** | G Vill

4.4 **AURORA** | Multi

4.6 **BABBO** | G Vill

4.2 **BACARO** | LES

4.3 **BACI & ABBRACCI** | W'burg

4.3 **BAMONTE'S** | W'burg

— **BARANO** | W'burg NEW

4.1 **BARBETTA** | W 40s

4.6 **BARBUTO** | W Vill

4.4 **BAR CORVO** | Prospect Hts

4.2 **BAR EOLO** | Chelsea

4.2 **BAROSA** | Rego Pk

4.4 **BAR PITTI** | G Vill

4.4 **BAR PRIMI** | E Vill

4.3 **BAR TANO** | Gowanus

4.1 **BASSO56** | W 50s

4.2 **BASTA PASTA** | Flatiron

4.2 **BECCO** | W 40s

4.3 **BECCOFINO** | Riverdale

4.1 **BELLA BLU** | E 70s

3.8 **BELLA VIA** | LIC

4.4 **BEST PIZZA** | W'burg

4.2 **BIRRERIA** | Flatiron

4.0 **BISTANGO** | Multi

4.4 **BOCCA** | Flatiron

4.5 **BOCELLI** | Old Town

4.0 **BOTTEGA** | E 70s

4.0 **BRICCO** | W 50s

4.4 **BRIOSO** | New Dorp

4.5 **BRUNO PIZZA** | E Vill

4.2 **CACIO E PEPE** | E Vill

4.4 **CAFÉ ALTRO** | Hudson Sq NEW

4.0 **CAFE FIORELLO** | W 60s

4.2 **CAFFE E VINO** | Ft Greene

3.9 **CAFFE STORICO** | W 70s

4.4 **CAMPAGNOLA** | E 70s

4.3 **CAPRI** | L Italy NEW

3.9 **CARA MIA** | W 40s

4.4 **CARAVAGGIO** | E 70s

4.5 **CARBONE** | G Vill

4.1 **CARMINE'S** | Multi

— **CASA APICII** | G Vill NEW

4.4 **CASA LEVER** | E 50s

4.3 **CASA NONNA** | W 30s

4.4 **CELESTE** | W 80s

4.2 **CELLINI** | E 50s

4.2 **'CESCA** | W 70s

4.2 **CHAZZ PALMINTERI** | E 40s

4.3 **CIPRIANI** | Multi

4.1 **COTTA** | W 80s

4.5 **COURT PASTRY SHOP** | Clinton Hill

4.3 **CRISPO** | W Vill

4.3 **DA ANDREA** | G Vill

4.1 **DA NICO** | Multi

4.2 **DA NOI** | Multi

4.5 **DANTE** | G Vill

4.2 **DA SILVANO** | G Vill

4.0 **DA TOMMASO** | W 50s

4.5 **DA UMBERTO** | Chelsea

4.5 **DEFONTE'S** | Multi

4.4 **DEGREZIA** | E 50s

4.5 **DELL'ANIMA** | W Vill

4.7 **DEL POSTO** | Chelsea

— **DINNERTABLE** | E Vill NEW

4.4 **D.O.C. WINE BAR** | W'burg

4.4 **DOMINICK'S** | Arthur Ave./ Belmont

4.5 **DON ANTONIO** | W 50s

4.7 **DON PEPPE** | S Ozone Pk

4.1 **DUE** | E 70s

4.3 **EATALY** | Multi

4.1 **ECCO** | TriBeCa

4.5 **ELIO'S** | E 80s

4.2 **EMILIA'S** | Arthur Ave./ Belmont

4.6 **EMILIO'S BALLATO** | NoLita	4.5 **IL POSTINO** | E 40s
4.4 **ENOTECA MARIA** | St. George	4.2 **IL RICCIO** | E 70s
4.4 **ENZO'S** | Multi	4.4 **IL TINELLO** | W 50s
4.4 **ERMINIA** | F 80s	4.4 **IL VALENTINO OSTERIA** | E 50s
4.4 **ESCA** | W 40s	4.2 **IMPERO CAFFÈ** | Chelsea NEW
4.2 **ETC. ETC.** | W 40s	4.1 **ISLE/CAPRI** | E 60s
4.3 **F & J PINE** | Van Nest	4.6 **I SODI** | W Vill
4.4 **FARO** | Bushwick	4.3 **I TRULLI** | Murray Hill
— **FAUN** | Prospect Hts NEW	4.4 **JOE & PAT'S** | Castelton Cnrs
4.2 **FELICE** | Multi	4.1 **JOHN'S/12TH ST.** | E Vill
4.6 **FELIDIA** | E 50s	3.9 **LA LANTERNA** | G Vill
4.1 **FIRENZE** | E 80s	4.4 **LA MASSERIA** | Multi
4.1 **FLORIAN** | Gramercy	3.8 **LA MELA** | L Italy
4.4 **FORNINO** | Multi	4.4 **L'AMICO** | Chelsea
4.3 **FORTUNATO BROTHERS** | W'burg	4.4 **L&B SPUMONI** | Gravesend
4.4 **FRAGOLE** | Carroll Gdns	4.4 **LA PECORA BIANCA** | Flatiron
4.4 **FRANK** | E Vill	4.4 **L'APICIO** | E Vill
4.4 **FRANKIES** | Multi	4.4 **LA PIZZA FRESCA** | Flatiron
4.3 **FRANNY'S** | Park Slope	4.7 **L'ARTUSI** | W Vill
4.2 **FRED'S AT BARNEYS** | Multi	4.2 **LA SIRENA** | Chelsea NEW
4.3 **FRESCO** | E 50s	4.3 **LATTANZI** | W 40s
4.3 **GABRIEL'S** | W 60s	4.4 **LAVAGNA** | E Vill
4.2 **GARGIULO'S** | Coney Is	4.4 **LA VIGNA** | Forest Hills
4.3 **GEMMA** | E VIII	4.1 **LA VILLA PIZZERIA** | Multi
4.5 **GENNARO** | W 90s	3.9 **LAVO** | E 50s
4.1 **GIGINO** | Multi	4.3 **LEOPARD/DES ARTISTES** | W 60s
4.4 **GINO'S** | Bay Ridge	4.6 **LEO'S LATTICINI/CORONA** | Multi
4.3 **GIORGIO'S** | Flatiron	4.1 **LE ZIE** | Chelsea
4.3 **GIOVANNI** | E 80s	4.1 **LIDO** | Harlem
4.3 **GIOVANNI RANA** | Chelsea	4.3 **LIL' FRANKIE** | E Vill
4.3 **GNOCCO** | E Vill	4.6 **LILIA** | W'burg NEW
4.4 **GRADISCA** | W Vill	4.5 **LINCOLN** | W 60s
4.0 **GRAZIE** | E 80s	4.5 **LOCANDA VERDE** | TriBeCa
4.4 **GRIFONE** | E 40s	4.4 **LOCANDA VINI** | Clinton Hill
4.3 **HARRY CIPRIANI** | E 50s	4.1 **LORENZO'S** | Bloomfield
4.1 **HARRY'S ITALIAN** | Multi	4.3 **LUIGI'S** | Glen Oaks
4.4 **HEARTH** | E Vill	4.6 **LUPA** | G Vill
3.8 **HUGO & SONS** | Park Slope	4.4 **LUSARDI'S** | E 70s
4.5 **IL BAMBINO** | Multi	4.5 **LUZZO'S** | Multi
4.5 **IL BUCO** | NoHo	4.3 **MACHIAVELLI** | W 80s
4.5 **IL BUCO ALIMENTARI** | NoHo	4.6 **MAIALINO** | Gramercy
4.4 **IL CANTINORI** | G Vill	4.5 **MAIELLA** | LIC
4.3 **IL CORTILE** | L. Italy	4.3 **MALAPARTE** | W Vill
4.4 **IL FALCO** | LIC	4.3 **MALATESTA** | W Vill
4.4 **IL GATTOPARDO** | W 50s	4.3 **MAMO** | SoHo
4.6 **IL MULINO** | Multi	4.4 **MANETTA'S** | LIC
4.3 **IL MULINO PRIME** | SoHo	4.5 **MANZO** | Flatiron

CUISINES

4.5 **MARCONY** | Murray Hill	4.1 **PAUL & JIMMY'S** | Gramercy
4.2 **MARCO POLO** | Carroll Gdns	4.5 **PEASANT** | NoLita
4.7 **MAREA** | W 50s	4.4 **PELLEGRINO'S** | L Italy
4.0 **MARIA PIA** | W 50s	4.5 **PEPOLINO** | TriBeCa
4.1 **MARIO'S** | Arthur Ave./Belmont	4.3 **PERLA CAFE** | W Vill
4.4 **MARTA** | NoMad	3.6 **PETE'S TAV.** | Gramercy
4.2 **MARUZZELLA** | E 70s	4.6 **PICCOLA VENEZIA** | Astoria
4.3 **MERCATO** | W 30s	4.4 **PICCOLO ANGOLO** | W Vill
4.3 **MOMOFUKU NISHI** | Chelsea **NEW**	4.2 **PICCOLO CAFE** | Multi
4.3 **MONTEBELLO** | E 50s	4.5 **PIETRO'S** | E 40s
4.2 **MORANDI** | W Vill	4.4 **PISTICCI** | Morningside Hts
4.4 **MORSO** | E 50s	4.2 **PIZZARTE** | W 50s
4.1 **MULINO A VINO** | Chelsea	4.5 **PÓ** | W Vill
4.5 **NAKED DOG** | Greenpt	4.2 **POMODORO ROSSO** | W 70s
3.7 **NELLO** | E 60s	4.4 **PORCHETTA** | E Vill
4.0 **NICK & TONI** | W 60s	4.4 **PORSENA** | E Vill
4.3 **NICOLA'S** | E 80s	4.4 **PRIMOLA** | E 60s
3.9 **NICOLETTA** | E Vill	4.4 **QUALITY ITALIAN** | W 50s
4.0 **NINO'S** | Multi	4.3 **QUEEN** | Bklyn Hts
4.0 **NIZZA** | W 40s	4.5 **RAFELE** | W Vill
4.1 **NOCELLO** | W 50s	4.3 **RAO'S** | E Harlem
4.4 **NOODLE PUDDING** | Bklyn Hts	4.2 **REMI** | W 50s
4.5 **NOVITÁ** | Gramercy	4.5 **RIBALTA** | G Vill
4.1 **NUCCI'S** | Multi	4.4 **RISOTTERIA MELOTTI** | E Vill
4.3 **NUMERO 28** | Multi	4.4 **RIST. MORINI** | E 80s
4.1 **OBICÀ MOZZARELLA** | Multi	4.6 **ROBERTA'S** | Bushwick
4.2 **ORIGINAL CRAB** | City Is	4.5 **ROBERTO** | Arthur Ave./Belmont
4.3 **ORSO** | W 40s	4.1 **ROC** | TriBeCa
4.1 **OSTERIA AL DOGE** | W 40s	4.4 **ROMAN'S** | Ft Greene
— **OSTERIA DELLA PACE** | FiDi **NEW**	4.3 **ROSEMARY'S** | W Vill
4.1 **OSTERIA LAGUNA** | E 40s	4.4 **ROSSINI'S** | Murray Hill
4.5 **OSTERIA MORINI** | SoHo	4.5 **RUBIROSA** | NoLita
4.3 **OTTO** | G Vill	4.4 **RUCOLA** | Boerum Hill
4.5 **PALMA** | W Vill	4.4 **SALUMERIA ROSI PARMACOTTO** | W 70s
4.5 **PANEANTICO** | Bay Ridge	4.3 **SANDRO'S** | E 80s
4.3 **PAOLA'S** | E 90s	4.6 **SAN MATTEO** | E 90s
4.1 **PAPPARDELLA** | W 70s	4.5 **SAN PIETRO** | E 50s
4.5 **PARK SIDE** | Corona	4.4 **SANT AMBROEUS** | Multi
3.8 **PARM** | Multi	4.2 **SANTINA** | Meatpacking
4.1 **PARMA** | E 70s	4.0 **SAUCE** | LES
4.5 **PASQUALE JONES** | NoLita **NEW**	4.1 **SCALETTA** | W 70s
4.0 **PASQUALE RIGOLETTO** | Arthur Ave./Belmont	4.4 **SCALINATELLA** | E 60s
4.3 **PATRICIA'S** | Morris Pk	4.7 **SCALINI FEDELI** | TriBeCa
4.1 **PATSY'S PIZZERIA** | Multi	4.3 **SCALINO** | Multi
4.2 **PATSY'S** | W 50s	3.9 **SCARLATTO** | W 40s
	4.5 **SCARPETTA** | Chelsea
	4.1 **SCOTTADITO** | Park Slope

4.2 **SESSANTA** | SoHo

3.8 **SERAFINA** | Multi

4.2 **SESSANTA** | SoHo

4.4 **SETTE MEZZO** | E 70s

4.4 **SFOGLIA** | E 90s

4.4 **SISTINA** | E 80s

4.2 **SOTTO 13** | W Vill

4.5 **SPEEDY ROMEO** | Multi

4.2 **SPIGA** | W 80s

4.1 **STELLA 34** | W 30S

4.3 **SUPPER** | E Vill

4.3 **TAVOLA** | W 30s

4.4 **TIELLA** | E 60s

4.5 **TOMMASO** | Bath Bch

4.0 **TONY'S DI NAPOLI** | Multi

4.3 **TRA DI NOI** | Arthur Ave./ Belmont

4.3 **TRATTORIA DELL'ARTE** | W 50s

4.7 **TRATT. IL MULINO** | Flatiron

4.7 **TRATT. L'INCONTRO** | Astoria

4.6 **TRATT. ROMANA** | Dongan Hills

4.2 **TRATTORIA TRECOLORI** | W 40s

4.5 **TUSCANY GRILL** | Bay Ridge

4.3 **TUTTO IL GIORNO** | TriBeCa

— **ULIVO** | NoMad `NEW`

3.9 **UMBERTOS CLAM HSE.** | L Italy

4.2 **UVA** | E 70s

4.5 **VALBELLA** | Multi

4.4 **VENIERO'S PASTRY** | E Vill

4.4 **VESTA** | Astoria

4.2 **VESUVIO** | Bay Ridge

4.4 **VEZZO** | Murray Hill

4.6 **VIA CAROTA** | W Vill

4.2 **VIA EMILIA** | Flatiron

4.1 **VIA QUADRONNO** | Multi

4.3 **VICEVERSA** | W 50s

4.2 **VIC'S** | NoHo

4.7 **VILLABATE ALBA** | Bensonhurst

4.4 **VILLA BERULIA** | Murray Hill

4.2 **VILLA MOSCONI** | G Vill

4.0 **VIVOLO** | E 70s

4.3 **ZERO OTTO** | Multi

4.3 **ZIO** | Flatiron

JAMAICAN

4.1 **MISS LILY'S** | Multi

4.3 **NEGRIL** | G Vill

JAPANESE

(* sushi specialist)

4.5 **ABURIYA KINNOSUKE** | E 40s

4.4 **AUTRE KYO YA** | E Vill

4.4 **BAR GOTO** | LES

4.2 **BLUE FIN*** | W 40s

4.5 **BLUE RIBBON SUSHI*** | Multi

4.5 **BLUE RIBBON SUSHI*** | Multi

4.6 **BOHEMIAN** | NoHo

4.5 **BOND ST*** | NoHo

4.6 **BRUSHSTROKE/ICHIMURA** | TriBeCa

4.2 **CHA AN** | E Vill

4.8 **CHEF'S/BROOKLYN FARE** | Downtown Bklyn

— **CHERRY*** | Greenpt

4.3 **CHUKO** | Prospect Hts

4.3 **COCORON** | Multi

4.4 **EN JAPANESE** | W Vill

4.6 **15 EAST*** | Union Sq

4.2 **FUSHIMI*** | Multi

4.4 **GANSO** | Downtown Bklyn

4.3 **GANSO YAKI** | Downtown Bklyn

4.6 **GARI*** | Multi

3.9 **GYU-KAKU** | Multi

4.5 **HAKATA TONTON** | W Vill

4.0 **HARU*** | Multi

4.5 **HATSUHANA*** | E 40s

4.6 **HIBINO*** | Multi

4.4 **HIDE-CHAN** | E 50s

4.0 **INAKAYA** | W 40s

4.5 **IPPUDO** | Multi

4.1 **IVAN RAMEN** | Multi

— **IZI*** | W 40s `NEW`

4.4 **JAPONICA*** | G Vill

4.4 **JEWEL BAKO*** | E Vill

4.3 **JIN RAMEN** | Multi

4.6 **KAJITSU** | Murray Hill

4.6 **KANOYAMA*** | E Vill

4.3 **KAPPO MASA*** | E 70s

— **KARASU** | Ft Greene `NEW`

4.0 **KATSU-HAMA** | Multi

4.5 **KI SUSHI*** | Cobble Hill

4.4 **KOI*** | Multi

4.6 **KOSAKA*** | W Vill `NEW`

4.1 **KO SUSHI*** | Multi

4.1 **KOUZAN*** | W 90s

4.6 **KURUMAZUSHI*** | E 40s

4.7 **KYO YA** | E Vill

4.6 **LADY M** | Multi

4.5 **MASA*** | W 50s

4.2 **MEIJIN RAMEN** | E 80s

4.3 **MINCA** | E Vill

4.6 **MOMO SUSHI SHACK*** | Bushwick

4.4 **MOMOYA*** | Multi

4.6 **MORIMOTO** | Chelsea

4.5 **MU RAMEN** | LIC

4.1 **NATSUMI*** | W 50s

4.5 **NETA*** | G Vill

— **NEW YORK SUSHI KO*** | LES

4.4 **NIPPON*** | E 50s

4.7 **NOBU** | Multi

4.4 **OKONOMI** | W'burg

4.5 **1 OR 8*** | W'burg

4.3 **OOTOYA** | Multi

4.6 **O YA*** | Murray Hill

4.5 **POKE*** | E 80s

4.3 **RAMEN LAB** | NoLita

4.5 **SAKAGURA*** | E 40s

4.1 **SAKE BAR HAGI** | W 40s

4.6 **SASABUNE*** | E 70s

4.5 **SHALOM JAPAN** | W'burg

4.6 **SHUKO*** | G Vill

4.3 **SOBA NIPPON*** | W 50s

4.5 **SOBA TOTTO** | E 40s

4.3 **SOBA-YA** | E Vill

4.7 **SOTO*** | W Vill

4.3 **SUSHIDEN*** | E 40s

4.4 **SUSHI DOJO*** | Multi

— **SUSHI GANSO*** | Downtown Bklyn NEW

— **SUSHI GINZA*** | E 40s NEW

4.7 **SUSHI NAKAZAWA*** | W Vill

4.6 **SUSHI OF GARI*** | Multi

4.1 **SUSHISAMBA** | W Vill

4.6 **SUSHI SEKI*** | Multi

4.4 **SUSHI SEN-NIN*** | Murray Hill

4.8 **SUSHI YASUDA*** | E 40s

— **SUSHI ZO*** | G Vill NEW

4.4 **TAKAHACHI*** | Multi

4.6 **TAKASHI** | W Vill

4.6 **TANOSHI** | E 70s

— **TEISUI*** | NoMad NEW

4.6 **TEMPURA MATSUI** | Murray Hill

4.1 **TENZAN*** | Multi

4.5 **TOMOE SUSHI*** | G Vill

4.5 **TORISHIN** | W 50s

4.4 **TOTTO RAMEN** | Multi

— **TSURUTONTAN** | Union Sq NEW

4.5 **USHIWAKAMARU*** | Chelsea

4.3 **WASAN** | Multi

4.4 **YAKITORI TOTTO** | W 50s

4.4 **YAMA*** | Multi

4.2 **YUKA*** | E 80s

4.6 **ZENKICHI** | W'burg

4.3 **ZUMA*** | Murray Hill

JEWISH

4.3 **B & H DAIRY** | E Vill

4.5 **BARNEY GREENGRASS** | W 80s

4.1 **BAZ BAGEL** | L Italy

4.3 **BEN'S BEST** | Rego Pk

4.0 **BEN'S KOSHER** | Multi

4.3 **CARNEGIE DELI** | W 50s

— **FRANKEL'S DELI** | Greenpt NEW

4.5 **KATZ'S DELI** | LES

4.3 **LATTANZI** | W 40s

4.3 **LIEBMAN'S** | Riverdale

4.2 **MILE END** | Multi

4.3 **MILL BASIN DELI** | Flatlands

4.7 **RUSS & DAUGHTERS** | LES

4.5 **RUSS/DAUGHTERS CAFE** | Multi

4.5 **SABLE'S SMOKED FISH** | E 70s

4.3 **SADELLE'S** | SoHo

4.0 **SAMMY'S ROUMANIAN** | LES

4.5 **SHALOM JAPAN** | W'burg

4.5 **SHELSKY'S OF BROOKLYN** | Clinton Hill

4.3 **YONAH SCHIMMEL** | LES

KOREAN

(* barbecue specialist)

— **ATOBOY** | NoMad NEW

4.2 **BANN** | W 50s

4.1 **BARN JOO** | Multi

4.2 **BCD TOFU** | Multi

4.2 **BONCHON** | Multi

4.5 **DANJI** | W 50s

4.2 **DO HWA*** | W Vill

4.4 **DON'S BOGAM BBQ*** | Murray Hill

4.4 **FRANCHIA** | Murray Hill

4.1 **GAONNURI*** | W 30s

4.5 **HANGAWI** | Murray Hill

4.4 **HANJAN** | Flatiron

4.5 **HER NAME IS HAN** | Murray Hill NEW

4.3 **INSA*** | Gowanus NEW

4.7 **JUNGSIK** | TriBeCa

4.4 **KANG HO DONG*** | Murray Hill

3.9 **KANG SUH** | W 30S

4.3 **KRISTALBELLI*** | W 30s

4.2 **KUM GANG SAN*** | Multi

4.2 **KUNJIP*** | W 30s

4.0 **KYOCHON** | Multi

4.5 **MAPO KOREAN** | Flushing

4.0 **MISS KOREA*** | W 30s

4.3 **NEW WONJO*** | W 30s

4.1 **99 FAVOR TASTE*** | Multi

4.5 **OIJI** | E Vill

— **TYGERSHARK** | Prospect Hts NEW

4.1 **WHITE TIGER** | Prospect Hts

KOSHER/KOSHER-STYLE

4.0 **ABIGAEL'S** | W 30s

4.4 **AZURI CAFE** | W 50s

4.3 **BEN'S BEST** | Rego Pk

4.0 **BEN'S KOSHER** | Multi

4.2 **HUMMUS PL.** | Multi

4.2 **LE MARAIS** | W 40s

4.3 **LIEBMAN'S** | Riverdale

4.3 **MILL BASIN DELI** | Flatlands

4.5 **ORWASHER'S** | Multi

4.2 **PASTRAMI QUEEN** | E 70s

4.0 **PEACEFOOD CAFÉ** | Multi

4.1 **PRIME GRILL** | W 50s

4.3 **RESERVE CUT** | Financial

4.5 **RUSS & DAUGHTERS CAFE** | E 90s

4.3 **SACRED CHOW** | G Vill

4.2 **2ND AVE DELI** | Multi

LAOTIAN

4.3 **KHE-YO** | TriBeCa

LATIN AMERICAN

4.2 **BROKEN SPOKE** | Murray Hill

LEBANESE

4.2 **AL BUSTAN** | E 50s

4.4 **ALMAYASS** | Flatiron

4.2 **BALADE** | E Vill

4.5 **ILILI** | NoMad

4.4 **MANOUSHEH** | G Vill

4.2 **NAYA** | Multi

MALAYSIAN

— **AL SEABU** | Park Slope

4.2 **LAUT** | Union Sq

4.3 **NYONYA** | Multi

MEDITERRANEAN

4.5 **ALDEA** | Flatiron

4.4 **ALTA** | G Vill

4.3 **AMALI** | E 60s

4.2 **AMARANTH** | E 60s

4.4 **BALABOOSTA** | NoLita

4.1 **BARBOUNIA** | Flatiron

4.2 **BODRUM** | W 80s

4.5 **BOULUD SUD** | W 60s

4.3 **BUSTAN** | W 80s

4.1 **CAFE CENTRO** | E 40s

— **CAFÉ MEDI** | LES NEW

4.2 **CHOBANI** | SoHo

4.6 **CONVIV. OSTERIA** | Park Slope

4.4 **COVINA** | Murray Hill NEW

4.3 **DEE'S** | Forest Hills

4.6 **ESTELA** | NoLita

4.2 **EXTRA VIRGIN** | W Vill

4.2 **FIG & OLIVE** | Multi

4.5 **GATO** | NoHo

4.6 **GLASSERIE** | Greenpt

4.5 **IL BUCO** | NoHo

4.5 **IL BUCO ALIMENTARI** | NoHo

4.0 **ISABELLA'S** | W 70s

4.3 **KASHKAVAL** | W 50s

4.1 **KAT & THEO** | Flatiron

— **KING** | Hudson Sq NEW

4.4 **LIMANI** | W 50s

4.5 **LITTLE OWL** | W Vill

4.1 **MARGAUX** | G Vill

4.0 **MARSEILLE** | W 40s

4.4 **MÉMÉ** | Multi

4.1 **MIRIAM** | Park Slope

3.9 **NICE MATIN** | W 70s

4.0 **NICK & TONI** | W 60s

4.5 **OLEA** | Ft Greene

3.7 **PARK** | Chelsea

4.0 **PERA** | Multi
4.3 **RED CAT** | Chelsea
— **SCHILLING** | Financial `NEW`
4.3 **SMILE** | Multi
4.5 **TABOON** | Multi
4.7 **TANOREEN** | Bay Ridge
4.3 **TESSA** | W 70s
4.4 **TIMNA** | E Vill
4.2 **VIC'S** | NoHo

MEXICAN

4.0 **ALMA** | Columbia St.
3.9 **AÑEJO** | Multi
4.3 **BARRIO CHINO** | LES
4.0 **BLACK ANT** | E Vill
4.1 **BODEGA NEGRA** | Chelsea
4.1 **CAFÉ HABANA** | Multi
4.2 **CALEXICO** | Multi
4.5 **CASA ENRIQUE** | LIC
4.1 **CASCABEL TAQUERIA** | Multi
4.3 **CHAVELA'S** | Crown Hts
4.5 **COSME** | Flatiron
3.9 **DOS CAMINOS** | Multi
4.3 **EL ATORADERO** | Prospect Hts `NEW`
4.0 **EL CENTRO** | W 50s
4.3 **EL LUCHADOR** | Multi
4.2 **EL PARADOR** | Murray Hill
4.2 **EL PASO** | Multi
4.2 **EL TORO BLANCO** | W Vill
3.8 **EL VEZ** | Battery Pk
3.9 **EMPELLÓN/PASTOR** | E Vill
4.5 **EMPELLÓN COCINA** | E Vill
4.3 **FONDA** | Multi
4.3 **GRAN ELECTRICA** | Dumbo
4.1 **HECHO EN DUMBO** | NoHo
4.0 **HELL'S KITCHEN** | W 50s
4.4 **LA CONTENTA** | LES
4.3 **LA ESQUINA** | Multi
4.3 **LA PALAPA** | E Vill
4.7 **LOS TACOS** | Chelsea
4.2 **EMPELLÓN TAQ.** | W Vill
4.1 **MAYA** | E 60s
4.1 **MAZ MEZCAL** | E 80s
4.4 **MESA COYOACAN** | W'burg
3.9 **MEXICO LINDO** | Murray Hill
4.2 **MEZZALUNA** | E 70s
3.7 **MISSION CANTINA** | LES
4.1 **OFRENDA** | W Vill

3.9 **OTTO'S TACOS** | Multi
4.0 **PACHANGA PATTERSON** | Astoria
4.4 **PAMPANO** | E 40s
4.2 **ROCKING HORSE** | Chelsea
4.1 **ROSA MEXICANO** | Multi
4.0 **ROSIE'S** | E Vill
3.8 **SALVATION TACO** | Murray Hill
4.0 **SINIGUAL** | E 40s
4.1 **TACOMBI** | Multi
4.3 **TACUBA** | Multi
4.4 **TOLOACHE** | Multi
4.5 **TORTILLERIA NIXTAMAL** | Corona
4.6 **XIXA** | W'burg
4.2 **ZONA ROSA** | W'burg

MIDDLE EASTERN

4.1 **AU ZA'ATAR** | E Vill
4.4 **BALABOOSTA** | NoLita
4.5 **BAR BOLONAT** | W Vill
4.1 **GAZALA'S** | Multi
3.9 **HALAL GUYS** | Multi
4.4 **MAMOUN'S** | Multi
4.3 **MIMI'S HUMMUS** | Multi
4.2 **MOUSTACHE** | Multi
4.5 **TABOON** | Multi
4.7 **TANOREEN** | Bay Ridge
4.3 **12 CHAIRS** | Multi
4.1 **ZAYTOONS** | Multi

MOROCCAN

4.0 **CAFE GITANE** | Multi
4.3 **CAFE MOGADOR** | Multi
4.4 **MÉMÉ** | Multi

NEW ENGLAND

4.1 **LITTLENECK** | Multi
4.4 **LOBSTER JOINT** | Multi
4.3 **LUKE'S LOBSTER** | Multi
4.2 **MERMAID** | Multi
4.4 **MARY'S FISH** | W Vill
4.6 **PEARL OYSTER** | W Vill

NEW ZEALAND

4.5 **MUSKET ROOM** | NoLita

NOODLE SHOPS

4.3 **CHUKO** | Prospect Hts
4.4 **GANSO** | Downtown Bklyn

4.3 **GREAT NY NOODLE** | Chinatown

4.4 **HIDE-CHAN** | E 50s

4.5 **IPPUDO** | Multi

4.1 **IVAN RAMEN** | Multi

4.3 **JIN RAMEN** | Multi

4.4 **JUN-MEN** | Chelsea

4.4 **KUNG FU RAMEN** | W 40s

4.2 **MEIJIN RAMEN** | E 80s

4.3 **MINCA** | E Vill

4.5 **MOMOFUKU NOODLE** | E Vill

4.6 **MOMOSAN** | Murray Hill NEW

4.5 **MU RAMEN** | LIC

4.3 **NAKAMURA** | LES NEW

4.2 **NISHIDA SHOTEN** | E 40s

4.3 **OOTOYA** | Multi

4.1 **PHO BANG** | Multi

4.3 **RAMEN LAB** | NoLita

3.8 **REPUBLIC** | Union Sq

4.3 **SOBA NIPPON** | W 50s

4.5 **SOBA TOTTO** | E 40s

4.3 **SOBA-YA** | E Vill

4.3 **TASTY HAND-PULLED** | Chinatown

4.4 **TOTTO RAMEN** | Multi

— **TSURUTONTAN** | Union Sq NEW

4.2 **XI'AN** | Multi

NUEVO LATINO

4.2 **CABANA** | Multi

4.1 **CALLE OCHO** | W 80s

4.3 **COPPELIA** | Chelsea

3.9 **MAMAN** | Multi

PAN-LATIN

4.4 **ABC COCINA** | Flatiron

4.2 **BOGOTA** | Park Slope

4.3 **COPPELIA** | Chelsea

4.3 **YERBA BUENA** | Multi

4.1 **YUCA BAR** | E Vill

4.0 **ZENGO** | E 40s

PERSIAN

— **GRAFFITI EARTH** | TriBeCa NEW

4.1 **PERSEPOLIS** | E 70s

4.3 **RAVAGH** | Multi

PERUVIAN

4.0 **COCO ROCO** | Multi

4.1 **FLOR/MAYO** | Multi

4.5 **LLAMA INN** | W'burg NEW

4.3 **PIO PIO** | Multi

4.3 **RAYMI** | Flatiron

PIZZA

4.4 **ADRIENNE'S** | Financial

4.0 **AL FORNO** | E 70s

4.3 **AMORINA** | Prospect Hts

4.1 **ANNABEL** | W 50s

4.1 **ARTICHOKE BASILLE** | Multi

4.2 **ARTURO'S** | G Vill

4.1 **BELLA BLU** | E 70s

3.8 **BELLA VIA** | LIC

4.4 **BEST PIZZA** | W'burg

4.0 **BRICCO** | W 50s

4.2 **CO.** | Chelsea

4.3 **DEE'S** | Forest Hills

4.5 **DENINO'S** | Multi

4.5 **DON ANTONIO** | W 50s

4.1 **00 & CO** | E Vill NEW

4.7 **EMILY** | Clinton Hill

— **EMMY SQUARED** | W'burg NEW

4.4 **FORNINO** | Multi

4.3 **FRANNY'S** | Park Slope

4.3 **GG'S** | E Vill

4.1 **GIGINO** | Multi

4.1 **GRIMALDI'S** | Multi

4.1 **HARRY'S ITALIAN** | Multi

4.5 **HOUDINI KIT.** | Ridgewood

4.4 **JOE & PAT'S** | Castelton Cnrs

4.5 **JOE'S PIZZA** | Multi

4.1 **JOHN'S/12TH ST.** | E Vill

4.3 **JOHN'S PIZZERIA** | Multi

4.7 **JULIANA'S** | Dumbo

4.4 **KESTE PIZZA** | W Vill

4.4 **L&B SPUMONI** | Gravesend

4.4 **LA PIZZA FRESCA** | Flatiron

4.4 **L'ASSO** | NoLita

4.1 **LA VILLA PIZZERIA** | Multi

4.3 **LIL' FRANKIE** | E Vill

4.5 **LOMBARDI'S** | NoLita

4.7 **LUCALI** | Carroll Gdns

4.5 **LUZZO'S** | Multi

4.3 **MANDUCATIS RUSTICA** | LIC

4.4 **MARTA** | NoMad

CUISINES

4.5 **MILKFLOWER** | Astoria
4.3 **MOTORINO** | Multi
4.5 **NICK'S** | Multi
3.9 **NICOLETTA** | E Vill
4.0 **NINO'S** | Multi
4.3 **NUMERO 28** | Multi
4.3 **OTTO** | G Vill
4.4 **OVEST** | Chelsea
4.2 **PATSY'S** | W 50s
4.6 **PAULIE GEE'S** | Greenpt
4.6 **PIZZA MOTO** | Red Hook
4.2 **PIZZARTE** | W 50s
4.3 **PIZZERIA SIRENETTA** | W 80s NEW
4.4 **PIZZETTERIA BRUNETTI** | W Vill
4.5 **POSTO** | Gramercy
4.6 **ROBERTA'S** | Bushwick
4.5 **RUBIROSA** | NoLita
4.6 **SAN MATTEO** | E 90s
4.4 **SARAGHINA** | Bed-Stuy
4.5 **SPEEDY ROMEO** | Multi
4.3 **SPUNTO** | W Vill
4.5 **TOTONNO'S** | Coney Is
4.4 **VESTA** | Astoria
4.2 **VESUVIO** | Bay Ridge
4.4 **VEZZO** | Murray Hill
4.5 **WHEATED** | Ditmas Pk
4.3 **ZERO OTTO** | Multi

POLISH
4.1 **LITTLE POLAND** | E Vill

PORTUGUESE
4.3 **LUPULO** | Chelsea
4.0 **MACAO TRADING** | TriBeCa

PUB FOOD
4.2 **DEAD RABBIT** | Financial
4.1 **DONOVAN'S** | Multi
3.9 **FRAUNCES TAV.** | Financial
4.0 **HENRY PUBLIC** | Cobble Hill
4.2 **JEFFREY CRAFT BEER** | E 60s
4.1 **J.G. MELON** | Multi
3.9 **LANDMARK TAV.** | W 40s
4.3 **MOLLY'S** | Gramercy
3.9 **NEARY'S** | E 50s
3.8 **P.J. CLARKE'S** | Multi
3.9 **WALKER'S** | TriBeCa

PUERTO RICAN
4.3 **SAZON** | TriBeCa

QUÉBÉCOIS
4.1 **M. WELLS DINETTE** | LIC

RUSSIAN
4.2 **MARI VANNA** | Flatiron
3.8 **RUSSIAN TEA** | W 50s

SANDWICHES
(See also Delis)
4.7 **ALIDORO** | Multi
4.3 **BANH MI SAIGON** | L Italy
4.4 **BEST PIZZA** | W'burg
4.1 **BONNIE'S GRILL** | Park Slope
4.3 **BRENNAN** | Sheepshead
4.5 **DEFONTE'S** | Multi
4.0 **E.A.T.** | E 80s
4.0 **EISENBERG'S** | Flatiron
4.2 **FRIEDMAN'S** | Multi
4.2 **FUKU** | Multi
4.0 **HANCO'S** | Multi
4.5 **IL BAMBINO** | Multi
4.5 **LAMAZOU** | Murray Hill
4.6 **LEO'S LATTICINI/CORONA** | Multi
3.9 **MEATBALL SHOP** | Multi
4.2 **MILE END** | Multi
4.1 **NO. 7 SUB** | Multi
4.2 **NUM PANG** | Multi
3.8 **PARM** | Multi
4.4 **PORCHETTA** | E Vill
4.3 **PRESS 195** | Bayside
4.0 **QUEENS KICKSHAW** | Astoria
4.0 **ROLL-N-ROASTER** | Sheepshead
4.6 **SAN MATTEO** | E 90s
4.1 **SARGE'S DELI** | Murray Hill
4.3 **SMILE** | Multi
4.5 **TABOON** | Multi
4.6 **UNTAMED SANDWICHES** | W 30S
4.1 **VIA QUADRONNO** | Multi
4.1 **YURA ON MADISON** | E 90s

SCANDINAVIAN
— **AGERN** | E 40s NEW
4.5 **AQUAVIT** | E 50s
— **ASKA** | W'burg NEW

4.1 **SMORGAS CHEF** | Multi

SEAFOOD

4.2 **AMMOS** | E 40s
4.7 **AQUAGRILL** | SoHo
4.4 **ARTIE'S** | City Is
4.3 **ATLANTIC GRILL** | Multi
4.6 **AVRA** | Multi
4.2 **BLUE FIN** | W 40s
4.3 **BLUE WATER** | Union Sq
4.3 **BLU** | E 60s NEW
4.5 **BOCELLI** | Old Town
4.5 **BOIL** | LES
4.0 **BROOKLYN CRAB** | Red Hook
4.3 **CATCH** | Meatpacking
— **CHIKARASHI** | L Italy NEW
4.1 **CITY IS. LOBSTER** | City Is
3.9 **CITY LOBSTER/STEAK** | W 40s
4.4 **CLAM** | W Vill
4.3 **CRAVE FISHBAR** | Multi
4.6 **CULL & PISTOL** | Chelsea
4.0 **DOCKS OYSTER** | E 40s
4.0 **ED'S CHOWDER** | W 60s
4.3 **ED'S LOBSTER BAR** | SoHo
4.5 **ELIAS CORNER** | Astoria
4.2 **EL TORO BLANCO** | W Vill
4.4 **ESCA** | W 40s
4.2 **ETHOS** | Multi
4.2 **EXTRA FANCY** | W'burg
4.2 **FISH** | W Vill
4.2 **FISHTAG** | W 70s
4.4 **FLEX MUSSELS** | Multi
4.4 **FRANCISCO'S** | Chelsea
3.9 **GRAND ARMY** | Downtown Bklyn
4.2 **GRAND CENTRAL OYSTER** | E 40s
4.4 **GREENPOINT FISH** | Greenpt
4.2 **ITHAKA** | E 80s
4.2 **JOHN DORY** | NoMad
4.2 **JORDANS LOBSTER** | Sheepshead
4.1 **JUBILEE** | E 50s
4.2 **KELLARI TAVERNA** | W 40s
4.9 **LE BERNARDIN** | W 50s
4.1 **LITTLENECK** | Multi
4.4 **LOBSTER JOINT** | Multi
4.5 **LOBSTER PLACE** | Chelsea

4.3 **LONDON LENNIE'S** | Middle Vill
4.3 **LUKE'S LOBSTER** | Multi
4.4 **LURE FISHBAR** | SoHo
4.5 **MAISON PREMIERE** | W'burg
4.7 **MAREA** | W 50s
4.4 **MARY'S FISH** | W Vill
4.2 **MERMAID** | Multi
— **METROPOLIS** | Union Sq NEW
4.7 **MILOS** | W 50s
4.5 **NORTH END GRILL** | Battery Pk
4.5 **OCEANA** | W 40s
4.4 **OCEAN PRIME** | W 50s
4.3 **ORIENTAL GDN.** | Chinatown
4.2 **ORIGINAL CRAB** | City Is
4.4 **PAMPANO** | E 40s
4.6 **PEARL OYSTER** | W Vill
4.1 **PEARL ROOM** | Bay Ridge
4.4 **PERIYALI** | Flatiron
4.0 **PING'S SEAFOOD** | Multi
4.2 **RANDAZZO'S** | Sheepshead
4.0 **REDEYE GRILL** | W 50s
4.3 **RED HOOK LOBSTER** | Multi
4.2 **SAMMY'S FISHBOX** | City Is
4.2 **SAMMY'S SHRIMP** | City Is
4.6 **SEA FIRE GRILL** | E 40s
4.4 **SEA GRILL** | W 40s
4.1 **SEAMORE'S** | L Italy
4.0 **SEA SHORE** | City Is
4.4 **SONS/THUNDER** | Murray Hill
4.4 **STRIP HOUSE** | Multi
4.5 **TAVERNA KYCLADES** | Multi
4.4 **TELLY'S TAVERNA** | Astoria
4.5 **THALASSA** | TriBeCa
4.5 **UPSTATE** | E Vill
4.1 **WISEFISH** | Chelsea NEW
— **ZADIE'S OYSTER RM.** | E Vill NEW
4.5 **ZZ'S CLAM BAR** | G Vill

SINGAPOREAN

4.0 **CHOMP CHOMP** | W Vill

SMALL PLATES

(See also Spanish tapas specialist)
4.4 **ALMAYASS** | Flatiron
3.9 **AÑEJO** | Multi
4.4 **ALTA** | G Vill
— **ASKA** | W'burg NEW
4.5 **AVANT GARDEN** | E Vill

3.9 **BAR CENTRALE** | W 40s

4.4 **BAR PRIMI** | E Vill

4.2 **BEAUTY & ESSEX** | LES

4.2 **BEYOGLU** | E 80s

4.3 **BLU** | E 60s NEW

4.5 **BRUNO PIZZA** | E Vill

4.4 **BUVETTE** | W Vill

3.9 **CAFFE STORICO** | W 70s

4.4 **CANNIBAL** | Multi

4.5 **DANJI** | W 50s

4.5 **DANTE** | G Vill

4.2 **DAVID BURKE FAB.** | W 30s

4.6 **DEGUSTATION** | E Vill

4.4 **EL REY** | LES

4.5 **EMPELLÓN COCINA** | E Vill

4.4 **EN JAPANESE** | W Vill

4.6 **ESTELA** | NoLita

4.2 **FELICE** | Multi

4.6 **GRAFFITI** | E Vill

4.4 **HANJAN** | Flatiron

4.2 **EMPELLÓN TAQ.** | W Vill

4.3 **KASHKAVAL** | W 50s

4.2 **KOA** | Flatiron

4.3 **MÁ PÊCHE** | W 50s

4.5 **MILKFLOWER** | Astoria

4.5 **OIJI** | E Vill

4.3 **PIZZERIA SIRENETTA** | W 80s NEW

— **RIDER** | W'burg NEW

4.5 **SAKAGURA** | E 40s

4.3 **SALT & FAT** | Sunnyside

4.1 **SOJOURN** | E 70s

— **SUSHI GANSO*** | Downtown Bklyn NEW

4.6 **TEMPURA MATSUI** | Murray Hill

4.5 **TØRST** | Greenpt

4.6 **TRAIF** | W'burg

4.2 **UVA** | E 70s

4.3 **WASAN** | Multi

4.6 **ZENKICHI** | W'burg

SOUL FOOD

4.4 **AMY RUTH'S** | Harlem

4.3 **CHERYL'S GLOBAL** | Prospect Hts

4.3 **MISS MAMIE'S** | W 100s

3.9 **SYLVIA'S** | Harlem

SOUTH AFRICAN

4.2 **MADIBA** | Multi

SOUTH AMERICAN

4.6 **AREPA LADY** | Elmhurst

4.4 **DESNUDA** | Multi

4.4 **K RICO** | W 50s

SOUTHERN

4.4 **AMY RUTH'S** | Harlem

4.3 **BEEHIVE** | W'burg

4.2 **BIRDS & BUBBLES** | LES

4.3 **BOBWHITE** | Multi

4.4 **BROOKLYN STAR** | W'burg

— **CARLA HALL'S** | Columbia St. NEW

4.2 **COMMODORE** | W'burg

4.3 **EGG** | W'burg

4.1 **HILL COUNTRY CHICKEN** | Multi

4.2 **JACOB'S PICKLES** | W 80s

4.0 **KITCHENETTE** | Morningside Hts

4.3 **MARIETTA** | Clinton Hill

4.3 **MELBA'S** | Harlem

4.5 **MONTANA'S TRAIL HSE.** | Bushwick

4.3 **PEACHES** | Bed-Stuy

4.3 **PIES-N-THIGHS** | W'burg

4.2 **QUEENS COMFORT** | Astoria

4.1 **REDHEAD** | E Vill

4.4 **ROOT & BONE** | E Vill

4.3 **SWEET CHICK** | Multi

3.9 **SYLVIA'S** | Harlem

3.9 **TIPSY PARSON** | Chelsea

4.2 **WILMA JEAN** | Carroll Gdns

SPANISH

(* tapas specialist)

4.1 **ALCALA REST.*** | E 40s

— **AMADA*** | BPC NEW

4.1 **ANDANADA 141*** | W 60s

4.5 **BAR JAMÔN*** | Gramercy

4.6 **BESO** | St. George

4.3 **BOQUERIA*** | Multi

4.1 **CAFE ESPANOL** | Multi

4.6 **CASA MONO*** | Gramercy

4.3 **CATA** | LES

4.6 **DEGUSTATION** | E Vill

4.2 **EL PORRÓN*** | E 60s

4.2 **EL POTE** | Murray Hill
4.1 **EL QUIJOTE** | Chelsea
4.5 **EL QUINTO PINO*** | Chelsea
4.4 **FRANCISCO'S** | Chelsea
4.5 **HUERTAS*** | E Vill
4.1 **LA FONDA/SOL** | E 40s
4.7 **LA VARA*** | Cobble Hill
4.2 **REAL MADRID** | Mariners Harbor
4.2 **SALA ONE NINE*** | Flatiron
4.5 **SALINAS*** | Chelsea
4.4 **SEVILLA** | W Vill
4.2 **SOCARRAT*** | Multi
4.2 **TERTULIA*** | W Vill
4.4 **TÍA POL*** | Chelsea
4.5 **TORO*** | Chelsea
4.4 **TXIKITO*** | Chelsea

STEAKHOUSES
4.4 **AMERICAN CUT** | Multi
4.4 **ANGUS CLUB** | E 50s
4.1 **ARLINGTON CLUB** | E 70s
4.4 **ARTIE'S** | City Is
4.4 **BEN & JACK'S** | NoMad
4.2 **BENCHMARK** | Park Slope
4.6 **BENJAMIN STEAK** | E 40s
4.5 **BLT PRIME** | Gramercy
4.5 **BLT STEAK** | E 50s
4.3 **BLU** | E 60s NEW
4.2 **BOBBY VAN'S** | Multi
4.4 **BOWERY MEAT CO.** | E Vill
4.4 **BUENOS AIRES** | E Vill
4.3 **BULL & BEAR** | E 40s
4.4 **CAPITAL GRILLE** | Multi
4.4 **CHARLIE PALMER** | E 50s
4.4 **CHIMICHURRI GRILL** | W 40s
4.4 **CHRISTOS** | Astoria
4.4 **CHURRASCARIA** | W 40s
3.9 **CITY LOBSTER/STEAK** | W 40s
4.5 **CLUB A STEAK** | E 50s
4.5 **DEL FRISCO'S** | Multi
4.4 **DELMONICO'S** | Multi
4.3 **E&E GRILL HSE.** | W 40s
4.3 **EMPIRE STEAK** | Multi
4.2 **FRANKIE/JOHNNIE'S** | Multi
4.4 **GALLAGHERS** | W 50s
4.3 **HARRY'S CAFE** | Financial
4.2 **HUNT & FISH** | W 40s
4.3 **IL MULINO PRIME** | SoHo

4.3 **JAKE'S STEAKHSE.** | Fieldston
4.5 **KEENS** | W 30s
4.4 **K RICO** | W 50s
4.2 **LE MARAIS** | W 40s
4.1 **LE RELAIS** | E 50s
4.0 **LES HALLES** | Multi
4.3 **LINCOLN SQ. STEAK** | W 70s
4.5 **MALONEY & PORCELLI** | E 50s
4.5 **MANZO** | Flatiron
4.3 **MARKJOSEPH** | Seaport
4.4 **MASTRO'S STEAK** | W 50s
3.9 **MICHAEL JORDAN** | E 40s
4.4 **MORTON'S** | Multi
4.3 **M. WELLS STEAKHSE.** | LIC
4.2 **NICK & STEF'S** | W 30s
4.0 **NINO'S** | Multi
4.3 **NYY STEAK** | Multi
4.4 **OCEAN PRIME** | W 50s
4.5 **OLD HOMESTEAD** | Chelsea
4.4 **PALM** | Multi
4.1 **PARLOR STEAKHSE.** | E 80s
4.8 **PETER LUGER** | W'burg
4.5 **PIETRO'S** | E 40s
4.6 **PORTER HOUSE** | W 50s
4.1 **PRIME GRILL** | W 50s
4.3 **PRIME MEATS** | Carroll Gdns
4.5 **QUALITY EATS** | W Vill NEW
4.4 **QUALITY ITALIAN** | W 50s
4.5 **QUALITY MEATS** | W 50s
4.3 **RESERVE CUT** | Financial
4.4 **RICARDO** | E Harlem
4.3 **ROCCO STEAKHSE.** | NoMad
4.4 **RUTH'S CHRIS** | W 50s
4.4 **SMITH/WOLLENSKY** | E 40s
4.5 **SPARKS** | E 40s
4.5 **ST. ANSELM** | W'burg
4.2 **STK** | Multi
4.4 **STRIP HOUSE** | Multi
4.1 **T-BAR STEAK** | E 70s
4.3 **UNCLE JACK'S** | Multi
4.5 **WOLFGANG'S** | Multi
4.4 **WOLLENSKY'S** | E 40s

SWISS
4.0 **TRESTLE ON 10TH** | Chelsea

TAIWANESE
4.1 **BAOHAUS** | E Vill
4.3 **MIMI CHENG'S** | E Vill

CUISINES

— **WIN SON** | W'burg `NEW`

TEAHOUSE

3.9 **ALICE'S TEA** | Multi
4.1 **BOSIE TEA PARLOR** | W Vill
4.2 **CHA AN** | E Vill
4.0 **LADY MENDL'S** | Gramercy
4.1 **RADIANCE TEA** | Multi
4.2 **TEA & SYMPATHY** | W Vill

THAI

4.5 **AYADA** | Elmhurst
4.3 **ERAWAN** | Bayside
4.2 **JAIYA** | Multi
4.2 **JOYA** | Cobble Hill
4.2 **KAO SOY** | Red Hook
4.3 **KUMA INN** | LES
4.2 **LAND THAI** | W 80s
4.4 **LARB UBOL** | W 30S
4.2 **LAUT** | Union Sq
4.3 **NGAM** | E Vill
4.1 **PAM REAL THAI** | W 40s
— **PLANT LOVE** | Prospect Hts `NEW`
4.4 **POK POK NY** | Columbia St.
4.3 **POK POK PHAT** | Columbia St.
4.5 **PURE THAI** | W 50s
4.1 **QI** | Multi
4.3 **ROOM SERVICE** | W 40s
4.0 **SEA** | W'burg
4.3 **SOMTUM DER** | E Vill
4.1 **SONG** | Park Slope
4.6 **SRIPRAPHAI** | Woodside
4.3 **THAI MARKET** | W 100s
4.2 **TOPAZ** | W 50s
4.5 **UNCLE BOONS** | NoLita
4.1 **WONDEE SIAM** | Multi
4.1 **ZABB ELEE** | Multi

TURKISH

4.0 **AKDENIZ** | W 40s
4.0 **A LA TURKA** | E 70s
4.0 **ALI BABA** | E 40s
4.2 **BEYOGLU** | E 80s
4.2 **BODRUM** | W 80s
4.0 **PASHA** | W 70s
4.0 **PERA** | Multi
4.0 **SAHARA** | Sheepshead
4.3 **SIP SAK** | E 40s
4.6 **TACI'S BEYTI** | Sheepshead
4.3 **TURKISH KIT.** | Murray Hill
4.1 **TURKUAZ** | W 90s
4.2 **USKUDAR** | E 70s

UKRAINIAN

4.1 **VESELKA** | E Vill

VEGETARIAN

(* vegan)
4.2 **ANGELICA KIT.*** | E Vill
4.5 **AVANT GARDEN*** | E Vill
4.3 **B & H DAIRY** | E Vill
4.2 **BLOSSOM*** | Multi
4.2 **BUTCHER'S DAUGHTER*** | Multi
4.3 **BY CHLOE*** | Multi
4.3 **CANDLE CAFE*** | Multi
4.4 **CANDLE 79*** | E 70s
4.3 **DIRT CANDY** | LES
4.1 **00 & CO*** | E Vill `NEW`
4.3 **DUN-WELL DOUGHNUTS*** | Multi
4.5 **HANGAWI** | Murray Hill
4.2 **HUMMUS PL.** | Multi
4.6 **KAJITSU** | Murray Hill
— **LADYBIRD** | G Vill `NEW`
4.5 **NIX** | G Vill `NEW`
4.0 **PEACEFOOD CAFÉ*** | Multi
4.0 **QUEENS KICKSHAW** | Astoria
4.3 **SACRED CHOW** | G Vill
4.4 **SARAVANAA BHAVAN** | Multi
4.4 **SUPERIORITY BURGER** | E Vill
4.6 **TAÏM** | Multi
4.4 **VATAN** | Murray Hill

VENEZUELAN

4.3 **AREPAS** | Astoria
4.4 **CARACAS** | Multi

VIETNAMESE

4.3 **BANH MI SAIGON** | L Italy
4.4 **BRICOLAGE** | Park Slope
4.5 **BUNKER VIET.** | Ridgewood
4.0 **HANCO'S** | Multi
4.3 **INDOCHINE** | G Vill
4.2 **LE COLONIAL** | E 50s
4.2 **NHA TRANG** | Chinatown
4.2 **OMAI** | Chelsea
4.1 **PHO BANG** | Multi
4.2 **VIETNAAM** | E 80s

LOCATIONS

Includes names, cuisines and Food ratings.

MANHATTAN

BATTERY PARK CITY

(Chambers St. to Battery Pl., west of West St.)

— **AMADA** | Spanish **NEW**
3.9 **BEAUBOURG** | French
4.1 **BLACK SEED** | Bagels
— **BLACKTAIL** | Amer. **NEW**
4.5 **BLUE RIBBON SUSHI** | Japanese
4.1 **BLUE SMOKE** | BBQ
3.8 **EL VEZ** | Mex.
4.3 **FRANÇOIS PAYARD** | Dessert/ French
4.1 **GIGINO** | Italian
4.1 **HARRY'S ITALIAN** | Italian
4.1 **HUDSON EATS** | Food Hall
4.1 **LE DISTRICT** | Food Hall/French
4.3 **MIGHTY QUINN'S** | BBQ
4.5 **NORTH END GRILL** | Amer./ Seafood
4.2 **NUM PANG** | Cam./Sandwiches
3.8 **PARM** | Italian/Sandwiches
3.8 **PIER A** | Amer.
3.8 **P.J. CLARKE'S** | Pub
4.0 **SHAKE SHACK** | Burgers
4.0 **UMAMI BURGER** | Burgers

CENTRAL PARK

3.9 **BOATHOUSE** | Amer.
3.6 **TAVERN/GREEN** | Amer.

CHELSEA

(30th to 34th Sts., west of 9th Ave.; 14th to 30th Sts., west of 7th Ave.)

4.4 **AMORINO** | Ice Cream
4.4 **AMY'S BREAD** | Bakery
4.1 **ARTICHOKE BASILLE** | Pizza
3.9 **BAREBURGER** | Burgers
4.2 **BAR EOLO** | Italian
4.3 **BILLY'S BAKERY** | Bakery
4.4 **BLACK IRON BURGER** | Burgers
4.2 **BLOSSOM** | Vegan/Veg.
4.2 **BLUE BOTTLE** | Coffee
4.1 **BODEGA NEGRA** | Mex.

4.4 **BUDDAKAN** | Asian
3.9 **CAFETERIA** | Amer.
4.2 **CO.** | Pizza
4.3 **COOKSHOP** | Amer.
4.3 **COPPELIA** | Diner/Pan-Latin
4.0 **CORKBUZZ** | Eclectic
4.6 **CULL & PISTOL** | Seafood
4.5 **DA UMBERTO** | Italian
4.7 **DEL POSTO** | Italian
— **DIZENGOFF** | Israeli **NEW**
4.2 **DONUT PUB** | Dessert
4.3 **DOUGHNUT PLANT** | Dessert
4.1 **EL QUIJOTE** | Spanish
4.5 **EL QUINTO PINO** | Spanish
4.3 **FONDA** | Mex.
4.1 **FORAGERS CITY TABLE** | Amer.
4.4 **FRANCISCO'S** | Seafood/ Spanish
4.2 **FRED'S AT BARNEYS** | Amer./ Italian
4.2 **FRIEDMAN'S** | Amer.
4.3 **GIOVANNI RANA** | Italian
4.0 **GRAND SICHUAN** | Chinese
4.0 **GREY DOG** | Amer.
4.0 **HARU** | Japanese
4.2 **IMPERO CAFFÈ** | Italian **NEW**
4.1 **JOE** | Coffee
4.4 **JUN-MEN** | Noodles
4.3 **LA BERGAMOTE** | Bakery/ French
4.4 **LA COLOMBE** | Coffee
4.4 **L'AMICO** | Italian
4.2 **LA SIRENA** | Italian **NEW**
4.1 **LE ZIE** | Italian
4.5 **LOBSTER PLACE** | Seafood
4.7 **LOS TACOS** | Mex.
4.3 **LUPULO** | Portug.
3.9 **MEATBALL SHOP** | Sandwiches
4.1 **MILK BAR** | Dessert
4.3 **MOMOFUKU NISHI** | Asian/ Italian **NEW**
4.4 **MOMOYA** | Japanese

4.6 **MORIMOTO** | Japanese

4.1 **MULINO A VINO** | Italian

4.3 **MURRAY'S BAGELS** | Bagels

4.3 **NINTH ST ESPRESSO** | Coffee

4.2 **NUM PANG** | Cam./Sandwiches

4.5 **OLD HOMESTEAD** | Steak

4.2 **OMAI** | Viet.

4.4 **OVEST** | Pizza

3.7 **PARK** | Med.

4.1 **RARE B&G** | Burgers

4.3 **RED CAT** | Amer./Med.

4.2 **ROCKING HORSE** | Mex.

4.5 **SALINAS** | Spanish

4.0 **SARABETH'S** | Amer.

4.5 **SCARPETTA** | Italian

4.2 **SOCARRAT** | Spanish

4.5 **SULLIVAN ST.** | Bakery

4.6 **SUSHI SEKI** | Japanese

4.3 **TAO** | Asian

4.4 **TÍA POL** | Spanish

3.9 **TIPSY PARSON** | Southern

4.5 **TORO** | Spanish

4.0 **TRESTLE ON 10TH** | Amer.

4.4 **TXIKITO** | Spanish

4.0 **UNCLE NICK'S** | Greek

4.5 **USHIWAKAMARU** | Japanese

4.1 **WESTVILLE** | Amer.

4.1 **WISEFISH** | Hawaiian/ Seafood NEW

CHINATOWN
(Canal to Pearl Sts., east of B'way)

4.1 **AMAZING 66** | Chinese

4.2 **BIG WONG** | Chinese

4.2 **DELUXE GREEN BO** | Chinese

4.1 **DIM SUM GO GO** | Chinese

4.0 **EXCELLENT DUMPLING** | Chinese

4.1 **456 SHANGHAI** | Chinese

4.1 **GOLDEN UNICORN** | Chinese

4.3 **GREAT NY NOODLE** | Noodles

4.1 **HOP KEE** | Chinese

4.1 **JING FONG** | Chinese

4.1 **JOE'S GINGER** | Chinese

4.2 **JOE'S SHANGHAI** | Chinese

4.2 **NHA TRANG** | Viet.

4.1 **NOM WAH** | Chinese

4.3 **ORIENTAL GDN.** | Chinese/ Seafood

4.4 **ORIGINAL CHINATOWN ICE CREAM** | Ice Cream

4.3 **PEKING DUCK** | Chinese

4.0 **PING'S SEAFOOD** | Chinese/ Seafood

4.3 **TASTY HAND-PULLED** | Noodles

4.1 **WO HOP** | Chinese

4.2 **XI'AN** | Chinese/Noodles

EAST 40S

4.5 **ABURIYA KINNOSUKE** | Japanese

— **AGERN** | Scan. NEW

4.1 **ALCALA REST.** | Spanish

4.0 **ALI BABA** | Turkish

4.2 **AMMOS** | Greek/Seafood

4.3 **ARETSKY'S PATROON** | Amer.

4.6 **AVRA** | Greek/Seafood

4.1 **BEDFORD & CO.** | Amer. NEW

4.6 **BENJAMIN STEAK** | Steak

4.2 **BOBBY VAN'S** | Steak

4.3 **BUKHARA GRILL** | Indian

4.3 **BULL & BEAR** | Steak

4.1 **CAFE CENTRO** | French/Med.

4.4 **CAPITAL GRILLE** | Steak

4.2 **CHAZZ PALMINTERI** | Italian

4.3 **CIPRIANI** | Italian

4.2 **DA NOI** | Italian

4.1 **DARBAR** | Indian

4.0 **DOCKS OYSTER** | Seafood

4.4 **DOUGH** | Dessert

4.2 **GRAND CENTRAL OYSTER** | Seafood

— **GREAT NORTHERN FOOD HALL** | Food Hall NEW

4.4 **GRIFONE** | Italian

3.9 **GYU-KAKU** | Japanese

4.5 **HATSUHANA** | Japanese

4.5 **IL POSTINO** | Italian

4.1 **JOE** | Coffee

4.0 **KATSU-HAMA** | Japanese

4.6 **KURUMAZUSHI** | Japanese

4.4 **LA CHINE** | Chinese

4.1 **LA FONDA/SOL** | Spanish

4.3 **LUKE'S LOBSTER** | Seafood

3.9 **MICHAEL JORDAN** | Steak

4.4 **MORTON'S** | Steak

4.2 **NAYA** | Lebanese

4.2 **NISHIDA SHOTEN** | Noodles

4.2 **NUM PANG** | Cam./ Sandwiches

4.1 **OSTERIA LAGUNA** | Italian

4.4 **PALM** | Steak

4.4 **PAMPANO** | Mex.

4.1 **PATSY'S PIZZERIA** | Pizza

4.0 **PERA** | Med.

4.2 **PHOENIX GDN.** | Chinese

4.5 **PIETRO'S** | Italian/Steak

4.1 **RADIANCE TEA** | Teahse.

4.5 **SAKAGURA** | Japanese

4.6 **SEA FIRE GRILL** | Seafood

4.0 **SHAKE SHACK** | Burgers

4.0 **SINIGUAL** | Mex.

4.3 **SIP SAK** | Turkish

4.4 **SMITH/WOLLENSKY** | Steak

4.5 **SOBA TOTTO** | Japanese/ Noodles

4.5 **SPARKS** | Steak

4.3 **SUSHIDEN** | Japanese

— **SUSHI GINZA** | Japanese NEW

4.8 **SUSHI YASUDA** | Japanese

4.4 **TULSI** | Indian

4.2 **URBANSPACE VANDERBILT** | Food Hall

4.4 **VITAE** | Amer.

4.5 **WOLFGANG'S** | Steak

4.4 **WOLLENSKY'S** | Steak

4.4 **YAMA** | Japanese

4.0 **ZENGO** | Pan-Latin

4.2 **ZUCKER'S BAGELS** | Bagels

EAST 50S

4.2 **AL BUSTAN** | Lebanese

4.0 **ALFREDO 100** | Italian

4.4 **AMERICAN CUT** | Steak

4.7 **AMMA** | Indian

4.4 **ANGUS CLUB** | Steak

4.5 **AQUAVIT** | Scan.

4.3 **ARMANI RIST.** | Italian

4.0 **BISTANGO** | multi.

4.5 **BLT STEAK** | Steak

4.2 **BOBBY VAN'S** | Steak

4.3 **BOTTLE & BINE** | Amer. NEW

4.1 **BRICK LN. CURRY** | Indian

4.4 **CASA LEVER** | Italian

4.5 **CAVIAR RUSSE** | Amer.

4.2 **CELLINI** | Italian

4.4 **CHARLIE PALMER** | Steak

4.3 **CHOLA** | Indian

4.5 **CLUB A STEAK** | Steak

4.3 **CRAVE FISHBAR** | Seafood

4.1 **DARBAR** | Indian

4.4 **DAWAT** | Indian

4.4 **DEGREZIA** | Italian

4.1 **DEUX AMIS** | French

3.9 **DOS CAMINOS** | Mex.

4.3 **EMPIRE STEAK** | Steak

4.4 **ESS-A-BAGEL** | Bagels

4.2 **ETHOS** | Greek/Seafood

4.6 **FELIDIA** | Italian

4.2 **FIG & OLIVE** | Med.

4.3 **FRESCO** | Italian

4.0 **GRAND SICHUAN** | Chinese

4.3 **HARRY CIPRIANI** | Italian

4.4 **HIDE-CHAN** | Japanese/ Noodles

4.2 **HILLSTONE** | Amer.

4.4 **IL VALENTINO OSTERIA** | Italian

4.1 **JUBILEE** | French

4.2 **KATI ROLL** | Indian

4.7 **LA GRENOUILLE** | French

4.3 **LA MANGEOIRE** | French

3.9 **LAVO** | Italian

4.4 **LE CIRQUE** | French

4.2 **LE COLONIAL** | French/Viet.

4.5 **LE PERIGORD** | French

4.1 **LE RELAIS** | French/Steak

4.0 **LYCHEE HOUSE** | Chinese

4.5 **MALONEY & PORCELLI** | Steak

4.5 **MIKE'S BISTRO** | Amer.

4.0 **MONKEY BAR** | Amer.

4.3 **MONTEBELLO** | Italian

4.4 **MORSO** | Italian

4.3 **MR. CHOW** | Chinese

3.8 **NATIONAL** | Amer.

4.2 **NAYA** | Lebanese

3.9 **NEARY'S** | Pub

4.4 **NERAI** | Greek

4.3 **NINTH ST ESPRESSO** | Coffee

4.4 **NIPPON** | Japanese

4.1 **OBAO** | Asian

4.1 **OBICÀ MOZZARELLA** | Italian

4.3 **PEKING DUCK** | Chinese

3.8 **P.J. CLARKE'S** | Pub

4.1 **POLO BAR** | Amer.

4.1 **PRIME GRILL** | Kosher/Steak

LOCATIONS

4.1 **ROSA MEXICANO** | Mex.

4.1 **SALVATION BURGER** | Burgers

4.5 **SAN PIETRO** | Italian

3.8 **SERAFINA** | Italian

4.4 **SHUN LEE PALACE** | Chinese

3.9 **SMITH** | Amer.

4.2 **SOCARRAT** | Spanish

4.3 **TAO** | Asian

4.1 **TENZAN** | Japanese

4.4 **TOTTO RAMEN** | Japanese/ Noodles

4.2 **212 STEAKHSE.** | Japanese

4.5 **VALBELLA** | Italian

4.5 **WOLFGANG'S** | Steak

EAST 60S

3.9 **ALICE'S TEA** | Teahse.

4.1 **ALTESI RIST.** | Italian

4.3 **AMALI** | Med.

4.2 **AMARANTH** | Med.

4.1 **ANASSA TAVERNA** | Greek

4.6 **AVRA** | Greek/Seafood

4.3 **BAGELWORKS** | Bagels

4.1 **BIRCH COFFEE** | Coffee

4.0 **BISTRO CHAT NOIR** | French

4.3 **BLU** | Seafood/Steak NEW

4.2 **CABANA** | Nuevo Latino

4.8 **DANIEL** | French

4.1 **EAST POLE** | Amer./British

4.2 **EL PORRÓN** | Spanish

4.0 **FATTY FISH** | Asian

4.2 **FELICE** | Italian

4.2 **FIG & OLIVE** | Med.

4.0 **5 NAPKIN BURGER** | Burgers

4.2 **FRED'S AT BARNEYS** | Amer./Italian

4.6 **IL MULINO** | Italian

4.1 **ISLE/CAPRI** | Italian

4.2 **JEFFREY CRAFT BEER** | Pub

4.4 **JOJO** | French

4.1 **LE BILBOQUET** | French

3.8 **LE VEAU D'OR** | French

4.0 **MAISON HUGO** | French

4.1 **MAYA** | Mex.

4.0 **MON PETIT CAFE** | French

4.3 **MOTI MAHAL** | Indian

3.7 **NELLO** | Italian

4.1 **PATSY'S PIZZERIA** | Pizza

4.3 **PHILIPPE** | Chinese

4.4 **PRIMOLA** | Italian

4.3 **RAVAGH** | Persian

4.0 **REGENCY B&G** | Amer.

4.1 **ROTISSERIE GEORGETTE** | French

4.4 **SCALINATELLA** | Italian

3.8 **SERAFINA** | Italian

4.0 **SERENDIPITY 3** | Dessert

4.6 **SUSHI SEKI** | Japanese

4.4 **TIELLA** | Italian

4.0 **TONY'S DI NAPOLI** | Italian

4.4 **VAUCLUSE** | French

EAST 70S

4.0 **A LA TURKA** | Turkish

4.0 **AL FORNO** | Pizza

4.1 **ARLINGTON CLUB** | Steak

4.3 **ATLANTIC GRILL** | Seafood

3.9 **BAREBURGER** | Burgers

4.2 **BAR PLEIADES** | Amer.

4.1 **BELLA BLU** | Italian

4.3 **BOQUERIA** | Spanish

4.0 **BOTTEGA** | Italian

3.9 **BRASSERIE COGNAC** | French

4.7 **CAFÉ BOULUD** | French

4.0 **CAFE EVERGREEN** | Chinese

4.4 **CAMPAGNOLA** | Italian

4.3 **CANDLE CAFE** | Vegan/Veg.

4.4 **CANDLE 79** | Vegan/Veg.

4.4 **CARAVAGGIO** | Italian

4.2 **CARLYLE** | French

4.1 **COPPER KETTLE** | Amer. NEW

4.1 **DUE** | Italian

3.8 **ELI'S ESSENTIALS** | Eclectic

4.0 **HARU** | Japanese

4.2 **IL RICCIO** | Italian

4.1 **J.G. MELON** | Pub

4.1 **JOE** | Coffee

4.1 **JONES WOOD** | British

4.3 **KAPPO MASA** | Japanese

4.1 **KO SUSHI** | Japanese

4.3 **LADURÉE** | Bakery/French

4.6 **LADY M** | Dessert/Japanese

4.4 **LUSARDI'S** | Italian

4.3 **MARK** | Amer.

4.2 **MARUZZELLA** | Italian

3.9 **MEATBALL SHOP** | Sandwiches

4.2 **MEZZALUNA** | Mex.

4.3 **MIGHTY QUINN'S** | BBQ

4.0 **MONTE CARLO** | French

4.0 **NINO'S** | Italian

4.3 **NUMERO 28** | Pizza

3.9 **ORSAY** | French

4.5 **ORWASHER'S** | Bakery/Kosher

4.1 **PARMA** | Italian

4.2 **PASTRAMI QUEEN** | Deli/Kosher

4.1 **PERSEPOLIS** | Persian

4.2 **QUATORZE BIS** | French

4.5 **SABLE'S SMOKED FISH** | Deli/Jewish

4.4 **SANT AMBROEUS** | Italian

4.6 **SASABUNE** | Japanese

4.2 **2ND AVE DELI** | Deli/Kosher

3.8 **SERAFINA** | Italian

4.4 **SETTE MEZZO** | Italian

4.1 **SOJOURN** | Amer.

4.6 **SUSHI OF GARI** | Japanese

4.2 **SZECHUAN GOURMET** | Chinese

4.6 **TANOSHI** | Japanese

4.1 **T-BAR STEAK** | Steak

4.2 **USKUDAR** | Turkish

4.2 **UVA** | Italian

4.1 **VIA QUADRONNO** | Italian

4.0 **VIVOLO** | Italian

4.2 **XI'AN** | Chinese/Noodles

4.3 **YEFSI ESTIATORIO** | Greek

EAST 80S

3.9 **ALICE'S TEA** | Teahse.

4.4 **ANTONUCCI** | Italian

3.9 **BAREBURGER** | Burgers

4.2 **BEYOGLU** | Turkish

4.1 **CASCABEL TAQUERIA** | Mex.

4.1 **CAFÉ D'ALSACE** | French

4.2 **CAFÉ SABARSKY/FLEDERMAUS** | Austrian

4.3 **CHEF HO'S** | Chinese

4.0 **E.A.T.** | Amer.

4.2 **83.5** | Italian

4.5 **ELIO'S** | Italian

3.8 **ELI'S ESSENTIALS** | Eclectic

4.3 **ELI'S TABLE** | Amer.

4.4 **ERMINIA** | Italian

4.2 **FELICE** | Italian

4.1 **FIRENZE** | Italian

4.4 **FLEX MUSSELS** | Seafood

4.3 **GIOVANNI** | Italian

4.0 **GRAZIE** | Italian

3.9 **GRÜNAUER BISTRO** | Austrian NEW

4.2 **HEIDELBERG** | German

4.1 **HU KITCHEN** | Health

4.2 **ITHAKA** | Greek/Seafood

3.9 **JACQUES** | French

4.2 **JAIYA** | Thai

4.3 **KINGS' CARRIAGE** | Amer.

4.1 **KO SUSHI** | Japanese

4.3 **LUKE'S LOBSTER** | Seafood

4.2 **MAISON KAYSER** | Bakery/French

4.1 **MAZ MEZCAL** | Mex.

4.2 **MEIJIN RAMEN** | Japanese/Noodles

4.3 **NICOLA'S** | Italian

4.1 **PAPAYA KING** | Hot Dogs

4.1 **PARLOR STEAKHSE.** | Steak

4.1 **PENROSE** | Amer.

4.1 **PIG HEAVEN** | Chinese

4.5 **POKE** | Japanese

4.4 **RIST. MORINI** | Italian

4.3 **SANDRO'S** | Italian

4.0 **SHAKE SHACK** | Burgers

4.6 **SIMONE** | French

4.4 **SISTINA** | Italian

4.1 **TENZAN** | Japanese

4.4 **TOLOACHE** | Mex.

4.6 **TWO LITTLE RED** | Dessert

4.1 **VIA QUADRONNO** | Italian

4.2 **VIETNAAM** | Viet.

4.3 **WA JEAL** | Chinese

3.9 **WRITING ROOM** | Amer.

4.2 **YUKA** | Japanese

EAST 90S

3.9 **ABV** | Amer.

4.3 **BLUESTONE LANE** | Australian/Coffee

4.3 **EARL'S BEER/CHEESE** | Amer.

3.8 **ELI'S ESSENTIALS** | Eclectic

4.2 **EL PASO** | Mex.

4.5 **NICK'S** | Pizza

4.3 **PAOLA'S** | Italian

4.2 **PASCALOU** | French

4.3 **PIO PIO** | Chicken/Peruvian

4.5 **RUSS/DAUGHTERS CAFE** | Jewish

LOCATIONS

4.6 **SAN MATTEO** | Italian/Pizza

4.0 **SARABETH'S** | Amer.

4.4 **SFOGLIA** | Italian

4.4 **TABLE D'HÔTE** | Amer./French

4.1 **YURA ON MADISON** |
Sandwiches

EAST HARLEM
(100th to 135th Sts., east of 5th Ave.)

4.3 **AMOR CUBANO** | Cuban

4.2 **EL PASO** | Mex.

3.9 **HARLEM SHAKE** | Burgers

4.5 **MOUNTAIN BIRD** | French

4.2 **MOUSTACHE** | Mideast.

4.1 **PATSY'S PIZZERIA** | Pizza

4.3 **RAO'S** | Italian

4.4 **RICARDO** | Steak

EAST VILLAGE
(14th to Houston Sts., east of
3rd Ave.)

4.6 **ABRAÇO ESPRESSO** | Coffee

4.2 **ANGELICA KIT.** | Vegan/Veg.

4.1 **ARTICHOKE BASILLE** | Pizza

4.4 **AUTRE KYO YA** | French/
Japanese

4.1 **AU ZA'ATAR** | French/Mideast.

4.5 **AVANT GARDEN** | Vegan

4.3 **AWASH** | Ethiopian

4.5 **BABU JI** | Indian

4.2 **BALADE** | Lebanese

4.3 **B & H DAIRY** | Deli/Veg.

4.2 **BAO** | Chinese

4.1 **BAOHAUS** | Taiwanese

3.9 **BAREBURGER** | Burgers

4.4 **BAR PRIMI** | Italian

4.2 **BIG GAY ICE CREAM** |
Ice Cream

4.0 **BLACK ANT** | Mex.

4.4 **BLACK IRON BURGER** |
Burgers

4.1 **BLACK SEED** | Bagels

4.1 **BLUE RIBBON FRIED** | Chicken

4.3 **BOBWHITE** | Southern

4.0 **BOULTON & WATT** | Amer.

4.4 **BOWERY MEAT CO.** | Steak

4.1 **BRICK LN. CURRY** | Indian

4.2 **BRINDLE ROOM** | Amer.

4.5 **BRUNO PIZZA** | Italian

4.4 **BUENOS AIRES** | Argent./Steak

4.2 **CACIO E PEPE** | Italian

4.3 **CAFE MOGADOR** | Moroccan

4.2 **CAFE ORLIN** | Amer.

4.4 **CARACAS** | Venez.

4.2 **CHA AN** | Japanese/Teahse.

4.5 **CHIKALICIOUS** | Dessert

4.1 **CRIF DOGS** | Hot Dogs

4.5 **DAVEY'S** | Ice Cream

4.2 **DBGB** | French

4.6 **DEGUSTATION** | French/
Spanish

4.4 **DESNUDA** | S Amer.

— **DINNERTABLE** | Amer./
Italian NEW

4.1 **00 & CO** | Pizza/Vegan NEW

4.3 **DUCKS EATERY** | Eclectic

4.2 **DUMPLING MAN** | Chinese

4.3 **DUN-WELL DOUGHNUTS** |
Dessert/Vegan

4.5 **EDDY** | Amer.

4.2 **EDI & THE WOLF** | Austrian

3.9 **EMPELLÓN/PASTOR** | Mex.

4.5 **EMPELLÓN COCINA** | Mex.

4.3 **FLINDERS LANE** | Australian

4.3 **FONDA** | Mex.

4.4 **FRANK** | Italian

4.2 **FUKU** | Chicken/Sandwiches

4.3 **GEMMA** | Italian

4.3 **GG'S** | Amer./Pizza

4.3 **GNOCCO** | Italian

4.6 **GRAFFITI** | Eclectic

4.0 **GRAND SICHUAN** | Chinese

4.4 **HARRY & IDA'S** | Deli

4.3 **HAVELI** | Indian

4.4 **HEARTH** | Amer./Italian

4.5 **HUERTAS** | Spanish

3.9 **JEEPNEY** | Filipino

4.4 **JEWEL BAKO** | Japanese

4.1 **JOHN'S/12TH ST.** | Italian

4.4 **KAFANA** | E Euro.

4.6 **KANOYAMA** | Japanese

4.8 **KINGSLEY** | Amer./
French NEW

4.7 **KYO YA** | Japanese

4.3 **LA PALAPA** | Mex.

4.4 **L'APICIO** | Italian

4.4 **LAVAGNA** | Italian

4.3 **LIL' FRANKIE** | Italian/Pizza

4.1 **LITTLE POLAND** | Diner/
Polish

4.3 **LUCIEN** | French

4.3 **LUKE'S LOBSTER** | Seafood

4.5 **LUZZO'S** | Pizza

4.3 **MAHARLIKA** | Filipino

4.4 **MAMOUN'S** | Mideast.

4.2 **MERMAID** | Seafood

4.3 **MIGHTY QUINN'S** | BBQ

4.1 **MILK BAR** | Dessert

4.3 **MIMI CHENG'S** | Taiwanese

4.3 **MINCA** | Japanese/Noodles

4.1 **MISS LILY'S** | Jamaican

4.7 **MOMOFUKU KO** | Amer.

4.5 **MOMOFUKU NOODLE** | Amer.

4.5 **MOMOFUKU SSÄM** | Amer.

4.3 **MOTORINO** | Pizza

4.2 **MOUSTACHE** | Mideast.

4.5 **NARCISSA** | Amer.

4.3 **NGAM** | Thai

3.9 **NICOLETTA** | Italian/Pizza

4.3 **NINTH ST ESPRESSO** | Coffee

4.2 **NOREETUH** | Hawaiian

4.3 **NUMERO 28** | Pizza

4.3 **ODA HOUSE** | Georgian

4.4 **ODDFELLOWS** | Ice Cream

4.5 **OIJI** | Korean

3.9 **OTTO'S TACOS** | Mex.

4.1 **PAPAYA KING** | Hot Dogs

4.3 **PARDON MY FRENCH** | French

4.4 **PORCHETTA** | Italian/
Sandwiches

4.4 **PORSENA** | Italian

4.6 **PRUNE** | Amer.

4.5 **PYLOS** | Greek

4.3 **RAVAGH** | Persian

4.1 **REDHEAD** | Southern

4.3 **RED HOOK LOBSTER** | Seafood

4.4 **RISOTTERIA MELOTTI** | Italian

4.4 **ROOT & BONE** | Southern

4.0 **ROSIE'S** | Mex.

3.9 **SMITH** | Amer.

4.3 **SOBA-YA** | Japanese/Noodles

4.3 **SOMTUM DER** | Thai

4.4 **SUPERIORITY BURGER** |
Burgers

4.3 **SUPPER** | Italian

4.4 **SUSHI DOJO** | Japanese

4.4 **TAKAHACHI** | Japanese

4.5 **TAVERNA KYCLADES** | Greek/
Seafood

4.3 **THIRD RAIL COFFEE** | Coffee

4.4 **TIMNA** | Med.

4.4 **TOMPKINS SQUARE BAGELS** |
Bagels

4.5 **TUOME** | Amer.

4.5 **UPSTATE** | Seafood

4.0 **VANESSA'S DUMPLING** |
Seafood

4.4 **VAN LEEUWEN** | Ice Cream

4.4 **VENIERO'S PASTRY** | Dessert/
Italian

4.1 **VESELKA** | Ukrainian

4.4 **VIRGINIA'S** | Amer.

4.3 **WASAN** | Japanese

4.1 **WESTVILLE** | Amer.

4.2 **XI'AN** | Chinese/Noodles

4.3 **YERBA BUENA** | Pan-Latin

4.1 **YUCA BAR** | Pan-Latin

4.1 **ZABB ELEE** | Thai

— **ZADIE'S OYSTER RM.** |
Seafood NEW

4.2 **ZUM SCHNEIDER** | German

FINANCIAL DISTRICT
(South of Civic Center, excluding
South St. Seaport)

4.4 **ADRIENNE'S** | Pizza

3.9 **BAREBURGER** | Burgers

4.0 **BATTERY GDNS.** | Amer./Cont.

4.1 **BIRCH COFFEE** | Coffee

4.3 **BLUESTONE LANE** | Australian/
Coffee

4.2 **BOBBY VAN'S** | Steak

4.2 **BONCHON** | Chicken

4.4 **CAPITAL GRILLE** | Steak

4.3 **CIPRIANI** | Italian

4.2 **DEAD RABBIT** | Pub

4.4 **DELMONICO'S** | Steak

4.3 **EATALY** | Food Hall/Italian

4.3 **EL LUCHADOR** | Mex.

4.2 **FELICE** | Italian

3.9 **FRAUNCES TAV.** | Pub

4.3 **HARRY'S CAFE** | Steak

4.1 **HARRY'S ITALIAN** | Italian

4.0 **HARU** | Japanese

4.4 **LA COLOMBE** | Coffee

4.3 **LEO'S BAGELS** | Bagels

4.0 **LES HALLES** | French/Steak

4.3 **LUKE'S LOBSTER** | Seafood

4.4 **MORTON'S** | Steak

LOCATIONS

4.2 **NAYA** | Lebanese

4.2 **NUM PANG** | Cam./Sandwiches

4.1 **OBAO** | Asian

— **OSTERIA DELLA PACE** | Italian NEW

4.3 **RESERVE CUT** | Kosher/Steak

— **SCHILLING** | Austrian/ Med. NEW

4.0 **SHAKE SHACK** | Burgers

4.1 **SMORGAS CHEF** | Scan.

4.1 **ZAITZEFF** | Burgers

FLATIRON

(14th to 30th Sts., 7th Ave. to Park Ave. So., excluding Union Sq.)

4.4 **ABC COCINA** | Pan-Latin

4.5 **ABC KITCHEN** | Amer.

4.5 **ALDEA** | Med.

4.4 **ALMAYASS** | Armenian/ Lebanese

3.9 **ALMOND** | French

4.3 **A VOCE** | Italian

4.1 **BARBOUNIA** | Med.

4.1 **BARN JOO** | Korean

4.2 **BASTA PASTA** | Italian

4.2 **BIRRERIA** | Italian

4.4 **BOCCA** | Italian

4.3 **BOQUERIA** | Spanish

4.1 **BURGER & LOBSTER** | Amer.

4.3 **BY CHLOE** | Vegan

4.2 **CITY BAKERY** | Bakery

4.3 **CLOCKTOWER** | Amer.

4.5 **COSME** | Mex.

4.5 **CRAFT** | Amer.

4.2 **CRAFTBAR** | Amer.

4.4 **DOUGH** | Dessert

4.3 **EATALY** | Food Hall/Italian

4.0 **EISENBERG'S** | Sandwiches

4.7 **ELEVEN MADISON** | Amer.

4.1 **GANDER** | Amer.

4.3 **GIORGIO'S** | Amer./Italian

4.8 **GRAMERCY TAV.** | Amer.

4.4 **HANJAN** | Korean

4.2 **HILL COUNTRY** | BBQ

4.1 **HILL COUNTRY CHICKEN** | Chicken/Southern

4.3 **INDAY** | Indian

4.1 **JUE LAN CLUB** | Chinese NEW

4.3 **JUNOON** | Indian

4.1 **KAT & THEO** | Amer./Med.

4.2 **KOA** | Asian

4.4 **LA PECORA BIANCA** | Italian

4.4 **LA PIZZA FRESCA** | Italian/ Pizza

4.4 **LE COQ RICO** | French NEW

4.2 **MAISON KAYSER** | Bakery/ French

4.5 **MANZO** | Italian/Steak

4.2 **MARI VANNA** | Russian

4.2 **NUM PANG** | Cam./Sandwiches

4.1 **OBICÀ MOZZARELLA** | Italian

4.3 **OOTOYA** | Japanese/Noodles

4.4 **PARK AVENUE** | Amer.

4.4 **PERIYALI** | Greek

4.3 **RAYMI** | Peruvian

4.1 **ROSA MEXICANO** | Mex.

4.2 **SALA ONE NINE** | Spanish

4.0 **SHAKE SHACK** | Burgers

4.4 **SWEETGREEN** | Health

4.1 **TACOMBI** | Mex.

4.1 **TOBY'S ESTATE** | Coffee

4.8 **TOCQUEVILLE** | Amer./French

4.3 **TRATT. IL MULINO** | Italian

— **UNION FARE** | Amer. NEW

4.2 **VIA EMILIA** | Italian

4.3 **ZERO OTTO** | Italian/Pizza

4.3 **ZIO** | Italian

GRAMERCY PARK

(14th to 23rd Sts., 1st Ave. to Park Ave. So., excluding Union Sq.)

4.5 **BAR JAMÔN** | Spanish

4.5 **BLT PRIME** | Steak

4.6 **CASA MONO** | Spanish

3.8 **DEAR IRVING** | Eclectic

4.4 **ESS-A-BAGEL** | Bagels

4.1 **FLORIAN** | Italian

4.0 **FRIEND/FARMER** | Amer.

3.9 **HALAL GUYS** | Mideast.

4.0 **HOUSE** | Amer.

4.0 **LADY MENDL'S** | Teahse.

3.9 **L'EXPRESS** | French

4.6 **MAIALINO** | Italian

4.3 **MIMI'S HUMMUS** | Mideast.

4.3 **MOLLY'S** | Pub

4.5 **NOVITÁ** | Italian

4.1 **PAUL & JIMMY'S** | Italian

3.6 **PETE'S TAV.** | Amer./Italian

4.2 **PICCOLO CAFE** | Coffee/ Italian

4.2 **PONTY BISTRO** | African/ French

4.5 **POSTO** | Pizza

3.5 **ROLF'S** | German

4.4 **YAMA** | Japanese

GREENWICH VILLAGE

(Houston to 14th Sts., 3rd to 6th Aves., excluding NoHo)

4.4 **ALTA** | Med.

4.4 **AMORINO** | Ice Cream

4.1 **ARTICHOKE BASILLE** | Pizza

4.2 **ARTURO'S** | Pizza

4.4 **ASIA DE CUBA** | Asian/Cuban

4.6 **BABBO** | Italian

3.9 **BAREBURGER** | Burgers

4.4 **BAR PITTI** | Italian

4.7 **BLUE HILL** | Amer.

4.3 **BLUESTONE LANE** | Australian/ Coffee

4.4 **BURGER JOINT** | Burgers

4.3 **BY CHLOE** | Multi

4.1 **CAFE ESPANOL** | Spanish

4.5 **CARBONE** | Italian

— **CASA APICII** | Italian NEW

4.0 **CHEZ JACQUELINE** | French

4.2 **CLAUDETTE** | French

— **COCO & CRU** | Australian NEW

4.0 **CORKBUZZ** | Eclectic

4.3 **CUBA** | Cuban

4.3 **DA ANDREA** | Italian

4.5 **DANTE** | Italian

4.2 **DA SILVANO** | Italian

4.5 **DENINO'S** | Pizza

4.2 **FEAST** | Amer.

4.0 **5 NAPKIN BURGER** | Burgers

4.3 **FRANÇOIS PAYARD** | Dessert/ French

4.3 **FREUD** | Austrian NEW

4.8 **GOTHAM B&G** | Amer.

4.0 **GREY DOG** | Amer.

3.9 **GYU-KAKU** | Japanese

4.2 **HAN DYNASTY** | Chinese

4.1 **HU KITCHEN** | Health

4.5 **IL BAMBINO** | Italian

4.4 **IL CANTINORI** | Italian

4.6 **IL MULINO** | Italian

4.3 **INDOCHINE** | French/Viet.

4.5 **IPPUDO** | Japanese/Noodles

4.2 **JANE** | Amer.

4.4 **JAPONICA** | Japanese

4.1 **J.G. MELON** | Pub

4.1 **JOE** | Coffee

4.1 **JOE** | Coffee

4.5 **JOE'S PIZZA** | Pizza

4.2 **KATI ROLL** | Indian

4.1 **KNICKERBOCKER** | Amer.

4.4 **LA COLOMBE** | Coffee

— **LADYBIRD** | Veg. NEW

3.9 **LA LANTERNA** | Italian

3.8 **LIBRARY/PUBLIC** | Amer.

4.6 **LUPA** | Italian

4.4 **MAMOUN'S** | Mideast.

4.4 **MANOUSHEH** | Lebanese

4.1 **MARGAUX** | French/Med.

4.2 **MERMAID** | Seafood

— **MIMI** | French NEW

4.4 **MINETTA TAV.** | French

4.1 **MISS LILY'S** | Jamaican

4.3 **MURRAY'S BAGELS** | Bagels

4.3 **NEGRIL** | Carib./Jamaican

4.5 **NETA** | Japanese

4.5 **NIX** | Veg. NEW

4.3 **NORTH SQ.** | Amer.

4.2 **NUM PANG** | Cam./Sandwiches

4.2 **OLD TBILISI GDN.** | Georgian

4.3 **OOTOYA** | Japanese/Noodles

4.3 **OTTO** | Italian/Pizza

4.1 **PATSY'S PIZZERIA** | Pizza

4.0 **PEACEFOOD CAFÉ** | Kosher/ Vegan/Veg.

4.5 **RIBALTA** | Italian

4.3 **SACRED CHOW** | Kosher/ Vegan/Veg.

4.6 **SHUKO** | Japanese

4.4 **STRIP HOUSE** | Steak

4.0 **STUMPTOWN** | Coffee

4.5 **SUNDAES & CONES** | Ice Cream

— **SUSHI ZO** | Japanese NEW

4.4 **SWEETGREEN** | Health

4.4 **THELEWALA** | Indian

4.3 **THIRD RAIL COFFEE** | Coffee

4.4 **TOLOACHE** | Mex.

4.5 **TOMOE SUSHI** | Japanese

4.0 **UMAMI BURGER** | Burgers

4.2 **VILLA MOSCONI** | Italian

4.5 **ZZ'S CLAM BAR** | Seafood

LOCATIONS

HARLEM

(110th to 155th Sts., 5th to St. Nicholas Aves.)

4.4 **AMY RUTH'S** | Soul Food

4.1 **BLUJEEN** | Amer.

4.4 **CECIL** | Amer./Eclectic

4.6 **CHAIWALI** | Indian

4.1 **CHEZ LUCIENNE** | French

3.9 **HARLEM SHAKE** | Burgers

4.7 **LEVAIN BAKERY** | Bakery

4.1 **LIDO** | Italian

4.3 **LOLO'S SEAFOOD** | Caribb./ Seafood

4.3 **MELBA'S** | Amer./Southern

4.2 **PONTY BISTRO** | African/ French

4.2 **RED ROOSTER** | Amer.

3.8 **STREETBIRD** | Chicken

3.9 **SYLVIA'S** | Soul Food/Southern

HUDSON SQUARE

(Canal to Houston Sts., west of 6th Ave.)

4.4 **ADORO LEI** | Italian

4.4 **CAFÉ ALTRO** | Italian NEW

4.2 **HOUSEMAN** | Amer.

4.6 **JACQUES TORRES** | Dessert

— **KING** | Med. NEW

4.4 **KOI** | Japanese

4.4 **LA COLOMBE** | Coffee

4.4 **LA SIRÈNE** | French

4.1 **WESTVILLE** | Amer.

LITTLE ITALY

(Broome to Canal Sts., Bowery to Centre St.)

4.4 **ANGELO'S/MULBERRY** | Italian

4.3 **BANH MI SAIGON** | Sandwiches/Viet.

4.1 **BAZ BAGEL** | Bakery/Jewish

4.3 **CAPRI** | Italian NEW

— **CHIKARASHI** | Hawaiian/ Seafood NEW

4.1 **DA NICO** | Italian

4.3 **FERRARA** | Bakery

4.6 **GENUINE SUPERETTE** | Calif./ Diner

4.2 **HOMETOWN HOTPOT & BBQ** | Chinese

4.3 **IL CORTILE** | Italian

3.8 **LA MELA** | Italian

3.9 **MAMAN** | Dominican/ Nuevo Latino

4.3 **NYONYA** | Malaysian

4.4 **PELLEGRINO'S** | Italian

4.1 **PHO BANG** | Noodles/Viet.

4.1 **SEAMORE'S** | Seafood

4.3 **SHANGHAI CAFE** | Chinese

4.3 **TWO HANDS** | Australian

3.9 **UMBERTOS CLAM HSE.** | Italian

LOWER EAST SIDE

(South of Houston St., east of Bowery & Pike St.)

4.2 **BACARO** | Italian

4.5 **BALVANERA** | Argent.

4.4 **BAR GOTO** | Japanese

4.3 **BARRIO CHINO** | Mex.

4.2 **BEAUTY & ESSEX** | Amer.

4.2 **BIRDS & BUBBLES** | Southern

4.3 **BLACK TREE** | Amer.

4.5 **BLUE RIBBON SUSHI** | Japanese

4.5 **BOIL** | Seafood

4.4 **CAFE KATJA** | Austrian

— **CAFÉ MEDI** | Med. NEW

4.3 **CATA** | Spanish

4.4 **CECI-CELA** | Bakery

4.5 **CLINTON ST. BAKING** | Amer.

4.3 **COCORON** | Japanese

4.0 **CONGEE** | Chinese

4.6 **CONTRA** | Amer.

4.3 **DIMES** | Amer.

4.3 **DIRT CANDY** | Veg.

4.1 **DIRTY FRENCH** | French

4.3 **DOUGHNUT PLANT** | Dessert

4.2 **DUDLEY'S** | Amer./Australian

4.3 **EL LUCHADOR** | Mex.

4.4 **EL REY** | Amer.

4.4 **EMPANADA MAMA** | Colombian

4.1 **FAT RADISH** | Amer.

4.1 **FREEMANS** | Amer.

4.3 **FUNG TU** | Amer./Chinese

4.5 **ICE & VICE** | Ice Cream

4.6 **IL LABORATORIO** | Ice Cream

4.1 **IVAN RAMEN** | Japanese/ Noodles

4.5 **KATZ'S DELI** | Deli

4.5 **KIKI'S** | Greek

4.3 **KOSSAR'S BAGELS** | Bagels `NEW`

4.3 **KUMA INN** | Filipino/Thai

4.4 **LA CONTENTA** | Mex.

4.2 **LA GAMELLE** | French

4.3 **LAM ZHOU** | Chinese

4.1 **LE TURTLE** | French `NEW`

— **LUCKY BEE** | SE Asian `NEW`

3.9 **MEATBALL SHOP** | Sandwiches

— **METROGRAPH COMMISSARY** | Amer. `NEW`

3.7 **MISSION CANTINA** | Mex.

4.3 **MISSION CHINESE** | Chinese

4.4 **MORGENSTERN'S** | Ice Cream

4.3 **NAKAMURA** | Noodles `NEW`

— **NEW YORK SUSHI KO** | Japanese

4.1 **99 FAVOR TASTE** | Chinese/Korean

4.3 **PIG AND KHAO** | SE Asian

4.4 **RED COMPASS** | Georgian `NEW`

4.7 **RUSS/DAUGHTERS** | Jewish

4.5 **RUSS/DAUGHTERS CAFE** | Jewish

4.0 **SAMMY'S ROUMANIAN** | Jewish

4.0 **SAUCE** | Italian

3.8 **SCHILLER'S** | Cont.

3.9 **SONS OF ESSEX** | Amer.

4.5 **SPEEDY ROMEO** | Italian/Pizza

4.5 **STANTON SOCIAL** | Eclectic

4.3 **SWEET CHICK** | Southern

4.3 **VANDAL** | Eclectic `NEW`

4.0 **VANESSA'S DUMPLING** | Seafood

4.2 **WASSAIL** | Amer.

4.4 **WILDAIR** | Amer.

4.3 **YONAH SCHIMMEL** | Jewish

MANHATTANVILLE

4.0 **MAISON HARLEM** | French

— **SOLOMON & KUFF** | Caribb. `NEW`

MEATPACKING DISTRICT
(14th to Horatio Sts., west of Hudson St.)

4.0 **BAGATELLE** | French

4.0 **BUBBY'S** | Amer.

4.3 **CATCH** | Seafood

3.9 **DOS CAMINOS** | Mex.

4.2 **FIG & OLIVE** | Med.

— **GUNTER SEEGER** | Euro. `NEW`

4.5 **HIGH STREET/HUDSON** | Amer./Bakery `NEW`

4.2 **SANTINA** | Italian

3.8 **SERAFINA** | Italian

3.7 **STANDARD BIERGARTEN** | German

4.1 **STANDARD GRILL** | Amer.

4.2 **STK** | Steak

4.4 **SWEETGREEN** | Health

4.4 **UNTITLED** | Amer.

4.5 **VALBELLA** | Italian

MORNINGSIDE HEIGHTS

4.1 **COMMUNITY** | Amer.

4.2 **DINOSAUR BBQ** | BBQ

4.2 **FRIEDMAN'S** | Amer.

4.3 **JIN RAMEN** | Japanese/Noodles

4.1 **JOE** | Coffee

4.0 **KITCHENETTE** | Southern

4.4 **PISTICCI** | Italian

3.8 **SERAFINA** | Italian

MURRAY HILL
(34th to 42nd Sts., east of Park Ave.)

4.7 **ALIDORO** | Sandwiches

4.2 **ARTISANAL** | French

3.9 **BAREBURGER** | Burgers

4.1 **BIRCH COFFEE** | Coffee

4.0 **BISTANGO** | multi.

4.1 **BLUE SMOKE** | BBQ

4.2 **BONCHON** | Chicken

4.2 **BROKEN SPOKE** | Latin Amer.

4.4 **CAFE CHINA** | Chinese

4.4 **CANNIBAL** | Belgian

4.3 **CIPRIANI** | Italian

4.4 **COVINA** | Amer./Med. `NEW`

4.3 **DHABA** | Indian

4.4 **DON'S BOGAM BBQ** | Korean

3.9 **DOS CAMINOS** | Mex.

4.2 **EL PARADOR** | Mex.

4.2 **EL POTE** | Spanish

4.2 **ETHOS** | Greek/Seafood

4.4 **FRANCHIA** | Korean

4.5 **HANGAWI** | Korean/Veg.

LOCATIONS

4.5 **HER NAME IS HAN** | Korean NEW

4.3 **I TRULLI** | Italian

4.2 **JAIYA** | Thai

4.6 **KAJITSU** | Japanese/Veg.

4.4 **KANG HO DONG** | Korean

4.0 **KYOCHON** | Chicken

4.5 **LAMAZOU** | Sandwiches

4.2 **LE PARISIEN** | French

4.2 **LITTLE BEET** | Amer.

4.1 **MADISON BISTRO** | French

4.5 **MARCONY** | Italian

3.9 **MEXICO LINDO** | Mex.

4.6 **MOMOSAN** | Noodles NEW

3.9 **MORGAN DINING RM.** | Amer.

4.5 **NICK'S** | Pizza

4.6 **O YA** | Japanese

4.0 **PENELOPE** | Amer.

4.2 **PICCOLO CAFE** | Coffee/Italian

4.3 **PIO PIO** | Chicken/Peruvian

4.4 **PIPPALI** | Indian

4.1 **RARE B&G** | Burgers

4.5 **RIVERPARK** | Amer.

4.4 **ROSSINI'S** | Italian

4.4 **RUBY'S CAFE** | Australian

3.8 **SALVATION TACO** | Mex.

4.0 **SARABETH'S** | Amer.

4.4 **SARAVANAA BHAVAN** | Indian/Veg.

4.1 **SARGE'S DELI** | Deli/Sandwiches

4.2 **2ND AVE DELI** | Deli/Kosher

4.0 **SHAKE SHACK** | Burgers

4.1 **SMORGAS CHEF** | Scan.

4.4 **SONS/THUNDER** | Hawaiian/Seafood

4.4 **SUSHI SEN-NIN** | Japanese

4.6 **TEMPURA MATSUI** | Japanese

4.3 **TURKISH KIT.** | Turkish

4.4 **UPLAND** | Cal.

4.4 **VATAN** | Indian/Veg.

4.4 **VEZZO** | Pizza

4.4 **VILLA BERULIA** | Italian

4.3 **WATER CLUB** | Amer.

4.5 **WOLFGANG'S** | Steak

4.2 **XI'AN** | Chinese/Noodles

4.3 **ZUMA** | Japanese

NOHO

(Houston to 4th Sts., Bowery to B'way)

4.2 **ACME** | Italian

4.7 **ALIDORO** | Sandwiches

4.6 **BOHEMIAN** | Japanese

4.5 **BOND ST** | Japanese

— **BOWERY MARKET** | Food Hall NEW

4.5 **GATO** | Med.

4.1 **HECHO EN DUMBO** | Mex.

4.5 **IL BUCO** | Italian/Med.

4.5 **IL BUCO ALIMENTARI** | Italian/Med.

4.3 **LAFAYETTE** | French

4.2 **MILE END** | Deli/Sandwiches

3.9 **NOHO STAR** | Amer./Asian

4.3 **SAXON & PAROLE** | Amer.

4.3 **SMILE** | Med.

4.2 **VIC'S** | Italian/Med.

NOLITA

(Houston to Kenmare Sts., Bowery to Lafayette St.)

4.4 **BALABOOSTA** | Med./Mideast.

4.1 **BLACK SEED** | Bagels

4.2 **BUTCHER'S DAUGHTER** | Vegan

4.0 **CAFE GITANE** | French/Moroccan

4.1 **CAFÉ HABANA** | Cuban/Mex.

4.4 **CECI-CELA** | Bakery

4.5 **CHEFS CLUB** | Amer.

4.2 **CHERCHE MIDI** | French

4.3 **COCORON** | Japanese

4.1 **DELICATESSEN** | Amer.

4.1 **EGG SHOP** | Amer.

4.6 **EMILIO'S BALLATO** | Italian

4.6 **ESTELA** | Amer./Med.

4.0 **GREY DOG** | Amer.

3.9 **JACQUES** | French

4.4 **L'ASSO** | Pizza

4.5 **LOMBARDI'S** | Pizza

3.9 **MAMAN** | Dominican/Nuevo Latino

— **MR. DONAHUE'S** | Amer. NEW

4.5 **MUSKET ROOM** | New Zealand

3.8 **PARM** | Italian/Sandwiches

4.5 **PASQUALE JONES** | Italian NEW

4.3 **PEARL & ASH** | Amer.

4.5 **PEASANT** | Italian

4.3 **PUBLIC** | Eclectic

4.3 **RAMEN LAB** | Japanese/Noodles

4.3 **REBELLE** | French

4.4 **RICE TO RICHES** | Dessert

4.5 **RUBIROSA** | Italian/Pizza

4.4 **RUBY'S CAFE** | Australian

4.4 **SANT AMBROEUS** | Italian

4.2 **SOCARRAT** | Spanish

4.1 **SPRINGNATURAL** | Health

4.4 **SWEETGREEN** | Health

4.1 **TACOMBI** | Mex.

4.6 **TAÏM** | Israeli/Veg.

4.5 **UNCLE BOONS** | Thai

NOMAD

— **ATOBOY** | Korean NEW

4.4 **BEN & JACK'S** | Steak

4.1 **BIRCH COFFEE** | Coffee

4.1 **BLACK BARN** | Amer.

4.3 **BRESLIN** | British

4.2 **HILLSTONE** | Amer.

4.5 **ILILI** | Lebanese

4.2 **JOHN DORY** | Seafood

4.0 **LITTLE BEET** | Amer.

4.4 **MARTA** | Italian/Pizza

4.2 **MAYSVILLE** | Amer.

4.0 **MULBERRY & VINE** | Amer.

4.6 **NOMAD** | Amer./Euro.

4.4 **NOMAD BAR** | Amer.

4.1 **NO. 7 SUB** | Sandwiches

— **PONDICHERI** | Indian NEW

4.3 **ROCCO STEAKHSE.** | Steak

3.9 **SMITH** | Amer.

4.0 **STUMPTOWN** | Coffee

4.4 **SWEETGREEN** | Health

— **TEISUI** | Japanese NEW

— **ULIVO** | Italian NEW

SOHO

(Canal to Houston Sts., 6th Ave. to Lafayette St.)

4.7 **ALIDORO** | Sandwiches

4.7 **AQUAGRILL** | Seafood

4.4 **AURORA** | Italian

4.4 **BALTHAZAR** | French

4.3 **BISTRO LES AMIS** | French

4.2 **BLACK TAP** | Burgers

4.4 **BLUE RIBBON** | Amer.

4.5 **BLUE RIBBON SUSHI** | Japanese

4.3 **BOQUERIA** | Spanish

4.2 **BURGER & BARREL** | Pub

4.2 **CHALK POINT** | Amer.

4.2 **CHARLIE BIRD** | Amer.

4.2 **CHOBANI** | Med.

4.3 **CIPRIANI** | Italian

4.3 **CÓMODO** | Latin Amer.

4.4 **DAVID BURKE KIT.** | Amer.

4.5 **DOMINIQUE ANSEL BAKERY** | Bakery/French

3.9 **DOS CAMINOS** | Mex.

4.2 **DUTCH** | Amer.

4.3 **ED'S LOBSTER BAR** | Seafood

4.1 **HAMPTON CHUTNEY** | Indian

4.2 **HUNDRED ACRES** | Amer.

4.3 **IL MULINO PRIME** | Italian/Steak

4.2 **JACK'S WIFE FREDA** | Amer.

4.4 **LA COLOMBE** | Coffee

4.3 **LADURÉE** | Bakery/French

4.3 **LA ESQUINA** | Mex.

— **LE COUCOU** | French NEW

3.8 **LUCKY STRIKE** | French

4.4 **LURE FISHBAR** | Seafood

4.3 **MAMO** | Italian

4.2 **MERCER KITCHEN** | Amer./French

4.5 **OSTERIA MORINI** | Italian

4.0 **PERA** | Med.

— **PAOWALLA** | Indian NEW

4.5 **RAOUL'S** | French

4.3 **SADELLE'S** | Euro./Jewish

4.2 **SESSANTA** | Italian

4.3 **12 CHAIRS** | Amer./Mideast.

SOUTH STREET SEAPORT

4.1 **ACQUA AT PECK SLIP** | Italian

4.2 **JACK'S STIR BREW** | Coffee

4.3 **MARKJOSEPH** | Steak

4.3 **SMORGASBURG** | Food Hall

TRIBECA

(Barclay to Canal Sts., west of B'way)

4.4 **ACAPPELLA** | Italian

4.4 **AMERICAN CUT** | Steak

LOCATIONS

3.9 **AÑEJO** | Mex.

4.5 **ARCADE BAKERY** | Bakery/French

4.6 **ATERA** | Amer.

4.4 **BAKED** | Bakery

4.5 **BÂTARD** | Amer./Euro.

4.0 **BENARES** | Indian

4.3 **BILLY'S BAKERY** | Bakery

4.3 **BLAUE GANS** | Austrian/German

4.9 **BOULEY** | French

4.6 **BRUSHSTROKE/ICHIMURA** | Japanese

4.0 **BUBBY'S** | Amer.

4.1 **CHINA BLUE** | Chinese

4.1 **ECCO** | Italian

4.1 **GIGINO** | Italian

— **GRAFFITI EARTH** | Indian/Persian NEW

4.2 **JACK'S STIR BREW** | Coffee

4.7 **JUNGSIK** | Korean

4.3 **KHE-YO** | Laotian

4.4 **LA COLOMBE** | Coffee

3.9 **LANDMARC** | French

4.4 **LITTLE PARK** | Amer.

4.5 **LOCANDA VERDE** | Italian

4.0 **MACAO TRADING** | Chinese/Portug.

4.2 **MAISON KAYSER** | Bakery/French

3.9 **MAMAN** | Dominican/Nuevo Latino

4.6 **MARC FORGIONE** | Amer.

4.3 **MR. CHOW** | Chinese

4.0 **MULBERRY & VINE** | Amer.

4.7 **NOBU** | Japanese

4.0 **ODEON** | Amer./French

4.4 **PALM** | Steak

4.5 **PEPOLINO** | Italian

4.3 **RACINES** | French

4.1 **ROC** | Italian

4.1 **ROSA MEXICANO** | Mex.

4.0 **SARABETH'S** | Amer.

4.3 **SAZON** | Puerto Rican

4.7 **SCALINI FEDELI** | Italian

4.6 **SUSHI OF GARI** | Japanese

4.4 **SWEETGREEN** | Health

4.4 **TAKAHACHI** | Japanese

4.7 **TAMARIND** | Indian

4.5 **THALASSA** | Greek/Seafood

4.1 **TINY'S** | Amer.

4.3 **TRIBECA GRILL** | Amer.

4.3 **TUTTO IL GIORNO** | Italian

4.3 **TWO HANDS** | Australian

3.9 **WALKER'S** | Pub

4.1 **WHITE STREET** | Amer.

4.5 **WOLFGANG'S** | Steak

4.2 **ZUCKER'S BAGELS** | Bagels

UNION SQUARE
(14th to 18th Sts., 5th Ave. to Irving Pl.)

4.3 **BLUE WATER** | Seafood

4.6 **BREADS BAKERY** | Bakery

3.6 **COFFEE SHOP** | Amer./Brazilian

4.6 **15 EAST** | Japanese

4.0 **HARU** | Japanese

4.2 **LAUT** | Malaysian/Thai

— **METROPOLIS** | Seafood NEW

3.8 **REPUBLIC** | Asian

— **TSURUTONTAN** | Japanese/Noodles NEW

WASHINGTON HEIGHTS

4.2 **MALECON** | Dominican

WEST 30S

4.0 **ABIGAEL'S** | Eclectic/Kosher

4.6 **AI FIORI** | Italian

4.2 **ARNO** | Italian

4.1 **BARN JOO** | Korean

4.2 **BCD TOFU** | Korean

4.0 **BEN'S KOSHER** | Deli/Kosher

4.4 **BLACK IRON BURGER** | Burgers

4.2 **BONCHON** | Chicken

4.3 **CASA NONNA** | Italian

4.4 **CULTURE ESPRESSO** | Coffee

4.2 **DAVID BURKE FAB.** | Amer.

4.4 **DELMONICO'S** | Steak

4.2 **FRANKIE/JOHNNIE'S** | Steak

4.2 **FRIEDMAN'S** | Amer.

4.1 **GAONNURI** | Korean

3.9 **KANG SUH** | Korean

4.2 **KATI ROLL** | Indian

4.5 **KEENS** | Steak

4.3 **KRISTALBELLI** | Korean

4.2 **KUNJIP** | Korean

4.4 **LARB UBOL** | Thai

4.3 **MERCATO** | Italian

4.0 **MISS KOREA** | Korean
4.3 **NEW WONJO** | Korean
4.2 **NICK & STEF'S** | Steak
4.0 **PARKER & QUINN** | Amer.
3.9 **PENNSY** | Food Hall `NEW`
4.0 **SARABETH'S** | Amer.
4.0 **SHAKE SHACK** | Burgers
4.3 **SNACK** | Greek
4.1 **STELLA 34** | Italian
4.2 **SZECHUAN GOURMET** | Chinese
4.3 **TAVOLA** | Italian
4.3 **UNCLE JACK'S** | Steak
4.6 **UNTAMED SANDWICHES** | Sandwiches

WEST 40S

4.0 **AKDENIZ** | Turkish
4.1 **AMARONE** | Italian
4.4 **AMORINO** | Ice Cream
4.7 **AMPLE HILLS** | Ice Cream
4.4 **AMY'S BREAD** | Bakery
3.9 **AÑEJO** | Mex.
4.6 **AUREOLE** | Amer.
4.1 **BARBETTA** | Italian
3.0 **DAR CENTRALE** | Eclectic
3.9 **BAREBURGER** | Burgers
4.2 **BECCO** | Italian
4.2 **BLOSSOM** | Vegan/Veg.
4.2 **BLUE BOTTLE** | Coffee
4.2 **BLUE FIN** | Seafood
4.2 **BOBBY VAN'S** | Steak
4.3 **BOUCHON BAKERY** | Amer./French
3.9 **BRYANT PK GRILL** | Amer.
4.1 **BUTTER** | Amer.
4.4 **CANNIBAL** | Belgian
3.9 **CARA MIA** | Italian
4.1 **CARMINE'S** | Italian
4.0 **ÇA VA** | French
4.2 **CHARLIE PALMER/KNICK** | Amer.
4.1 **CHEZ JOSEPHINE** | French
4.4 **CHIMICHURRI GRILL** | Argent./Steak
4.4 **CHURRASCARIA** | Brazilian/Steak
4.0 **CITY KITCHEN** | Food Hall
3.9 **CITY LOBSTER/STEAK** | Seafood/Steak

3.9 **DAFNI** | Greek
4.1 **DAISY MAY'S** | BBQ
4.4 **DB BISTRO MODERNE** | French
4.5 **DEL FRISCO'S** | Steak
3.9 **DOS CAMINOS** | Mex.
4.4 **DOUGH** | Dessert
4.3 **E&E GRILL HSE.** | Steak
4.4 **ESCA** | Italian/Seafood
4.2 **ETC. ETC.** | Italian
4.0 **5 NAPKIN BURGER** | Burgers
4.2 **44 & X/44½** | Amer.
4.2 **FRANKIE/JOHNNIE'S** | Steak
4.8 **GABRIEL KREUTHER** | French
4.1 **GAZALA'S** | Mideast.
3.9 **GLASS HOUSE** | Amer.
4.1 **GOTHAM WEST** | Food Hall
4.0 **GRAND SICHUAN** | Chinese
3.9 **GYU-KAKU** | Japanese
4.4 **HAKKASAN** | Chinese
4.0 **HARU** | Japanese
4.0 **HAVANA CENTRAL** | Cuban
4.2 **HUNT & FISH** | Steak
4.0 **INAKAYA** | Japanese
4.1 **IVAN RAMEN** | Japanese/Noodles
— **IZI** | Japanese `NEW`
3.9 **JOE ALLEN** | Amer.
4.3 **JOHN'S PIZZERIA** | Pizza
3.8 **JUNIOR'S** | Diner
4.2 **KELLARI TAVERNA** | Greek/Seafood
4.4 **KOI** | Japanese
4.4 **KUNG FU RAMEN** | Noodles
4.6 **LADY M** | Dessert/Japanese
4.4 **LA MASSERIA** | Italian
4.3 **LAMBS CLUB** | Amer.
3.9 **LANDMARK TAV.** | Pub
4.3 **LATTANZI** | Italian
4.2 **LE MARAIS** | French/Kosher/Steak
4.1 **LE RIVAGE** | French
4.3 **LUKE'S LOBSTER** | Seafood
4.2 **MAISON KAYSER** | Bakery/French
4.0 **MARSEILLE** | French/Med.
4.3 **MARSHAL** | Amer.
4.4 **MÉMÉ** | Med./Moroccan
4.0 **NIZZA** | Italian
4.2 **NUM PANG** | Cam./Sandwiches

4.1 **OBAO** | Asian
4.5 **OCEANA** | Amer./Seafood
4.3 **OOTOYA** | Japanese/Noodles
4.3 **ORSO** | Italian
4.1 **OSTERIA AL DOGE** | Italian
3.9 **OTTO'S TACOS** | Mex.
4.1 **PAM REAL THAI** | Thai
4.2 **PICCOLO CAFE** | Coffee/Italian
4.3 **PIO PIO** | Chicken/Peruvian
4.5 **PRINT** | Amer.
4.1 **QI** | Asian/Thai
4.3 **QUEEN OF SHEBA** | Ethiopian
4.3 **RAINBOW RM.** | Amer.
4.3 **ROOM SERVICE** | Thai
4.1 **SAJU BISTRO** | French
4.1 **SAKE BAR HAGI** | Japanese
— **SAMMY'S HSE.** | BBQ NEW
3.7 **SARDI'S** | Cont.
3.9 **SCARLATTO** | Italian
4.4 **SEA GRILL** | Seafood
3.8 **SERAFINA** | Italian
4.0 **SHAKE SHACK** | Burgers
4.2 **STK** | Steak
4.4 **STRIP HOUSE** | Steak
4.5 **SULLIVAN ST.** | Bakery
4.3 **SUSHIDEN** | Japanese
4.6 **SUSHI OF GARI** | Japanese
4.6 **SUSHI SEKI** | Japanese
4.0 **THALIA** | Amer.
4.0 **TONY'S DI NAPOLI** | Italian
4.2 **TRATTORIA TRECOLORI** | Italian
4.3 **TRIOMPHE** | French
4.0 **UTSAV** | Indian
3.7 **VIEW** | Amer.
4.0 **VIRGIL'S** | BBQ
4.5 **WOLFGANG'S** | Steak
4.5 **WU LIANG YE** | Chinese
4.2 **XI'AN** | *Chinese/Noodles*

WEST 50S
4.0 **ALDO SOHM** | French
4.1 **ANNABEL** | Italian/Pizza
4.6 **ASIATE** | Amer./Asian
4.4 **AZURI CAFE** | Israeli/Kosher
4.2 **BANN** | Korean
4.3 **BAR AMERICAIN** | Amer.
3.9 **BAREBURGER** | Burgers
4.1 **BASSO56** | Italian

3.9 **BEAUTIQUE** | Amer./French
4.0 **BENARES** | Indian
4.2 **BENOIT** | French
4.5 **BETONY** | Amer.
4.3 **BILLY'S BAKERY** | Bakery
4.5 **BLUE RIBBON SUSHI** | Japanese
4.2 **BOBBY VAN'S** | Steak
4.3 **BOUCHON BAKERY** | Amer./French
3.9 **BRASSERIE COGNAC** | French
4.2 **BRASSERIE 8½** | French
3.9 **BRASS. RUHLMANN** | French
4.0 **BRICCO** | Italian
4.4 **BURGER JOINT** | Burgers
4.4 **CAPITAL GRILLE** | Steak
4.3 **CARNEGIE DELI** | Deli
4.4 **CASELLULA** | Amer.
4.1 **CHEZ NAPOLÉON** | French
4.2 **CHINA GRILL** | Asian
4.6 **CLEMENT REST.** | Amer.
4.5 **DANJI** | Korean
4.0 **DA TOMMASO** | Italian
4.5 **DEL FRISCO'S** | Steak
4.5 **DON ANTONIO** | Pizza
4.0 **EL CENTRO** | Mex.
4.3 **EMPIRE STEAK** | Steak
4.2 **ÉPICERIE BOULUD** | French
4.2 **FOGO DE CHÃO** | Brazilian
4.3 **FRANÇOIS PAYARD** | Dessert/French
4.2 **FUKU** | Chicken/Sandwiches
4.4 **GALLAGHERS** | Steak
3.9 **GREEK KITCHEN** | Greek
4.5 **GROM** | Ice Cream
4.1 **HARRY'S ITALIAN** | Italian
4.0 **HELL'S KITCHEN** | Mex.
4.4 **IL GATTOPARDO** | Italian
4.4 **IL TINELLO** | Italian
4.7 **INDIAN ACCENT** | Indian NEW
4.5 **IPPUDO** | Japanese/Noodles
3.8 **JAMS** | Calif.
4.2 **JOE'S SHANGHAI** | Chinese
4.3 **KASHKAVAL** | Med.
4.0 **KATSU-HAMA** | Japanese
4.4 **K RICO** | S Amer./Steak
4.3 **LA BERGAMOTE** | Bakery/French
3.9 **LA BONNE SOUPE** | French

4.6 **LADY M** | Dessert/Japanese

4.4 **LA MASSERIA** | Italian

3.9 **LANDMARC** | French

4.9 **LE BERNARDIN** | French/ Seafood

4.4 **LIMANI** | Med.

4.0 **LITTLE BEET** | Amer.

4.4 **LOI ESTIATORIO** | Greek

4.3 **LUKE'S LOBSTER** | Seafood

4.2 **MAISON KAYSER** | Bakery/ French

4.3 **MÁ PÊCHE** | Amer.

4.7 **MAREA** | Italian/Seafood

4.0 **MARIA PIA** | Italian

4.5 **MASA** | Japanese

4.4 **MASTRO'S STEAK** | Steak

4.3 **MICHAEL'S** | Cal.

4.1 **MILK BAR** | Dessert

4.7 **MILOS** | Greek/Seafood

4.6 **MODERN** | Amer./French

4.3 **MOLYVOS** | Greek

4.1 **NATSUMI** | Japanese

4.2 **NAYA** | Lebanese

4.0 **NINO'S** | Italian

4.7 **NOBU** | Japanese

4.1 **NOCELLO** | Italian

4.4 **NORMA'S** | Amer.

4.1 **NO. 7 SUB** | Sandwiches

4.3 **NYY STEAK** | Steak

4.4 **OCEAN PRIME** | Seafood/Steak

4.4 **PALM** | Steak

4.2 **PALM COURT** | Amer

4.2 **PATSY'S** | Italian

4.6 **PER SE** | Amer./French

4.4 **PETROSSIAN** | Cont./French

4.2 **PIZZARTE** | Pizza

4.1 **PLAZA FOOD HALL** | Food Hall

4.6 **PORTER HOUSE** | Steak

4.5 **PURE THAI** | Thai

4.4 **QUALITY ITALIAN** | Italian/ Steak

4.5 **QUALITY MEATS** | Amer./Steak

4.1 **RADIANCE TEA** | Teahse.

4.0 **REDEYE GRILL** | Amer./Seafood

4.2 **REMI** | Italian

4.1 **ROBERT** | Amer.

3.9 **RUE 57** | French

3.8 **RUSSIAN TEA** | Cont./Russian

4.4 **RUTH'S CHRIS** | Steak

4.0 **SARABETH'S** | Amer.

3.8 **SERAFINA** | Italian

4.3 **SOBA NIPPON** | Japanese/ Noodles

4.2 **SZECHUAN GOURMET** | Chinese

4.5 **TABOON** | Med./Mideast.

4.3 **TACUBA** | Mex.

4.2 **TANG PAVILION** | Chinese

4.4 **TOLOACHE** | Mex.

4.2 **TOPAZ** | Thai

4.5 **TORISHIN** | Japanese

4.4 **TOTTO RAMEN** | Japanese/ Noodles

4.3 **TRATTORIA DELL'ARTE** | Italian

— **TURNSTYLE** | Food Hall NEW

4.3 **21 CLUB** | Amer.

4.3 **UNCLE JACK'S** | Steak

4.0 **UNCLE NICK'S** | Greek

4.3 **VICEVERSA** | Italian

4.3 **VICTOR'S CAFE** | Cuban

4.1 **WONDEE SIAM** | Thai

4.4 **YAKITORI TOTTO** | Japanese

WEST 60S

4.1 **ANDANADA 141** | Spanish

4.3 **ATLANTIC GRILL** | Seafood

4.3 **BAR BOULUD** | French

4.5 **BOULUD SUD** | Med.

4.6 **BREADS BAKERY** | Bakery

4.0 **CAFE FIORELLO** | Italian

4.0 **ED'S CHOWDER** | Seafood

4.2 **ÉPICERIE BOULUD** | French

4.3 **GABRIEL'S** | Italian

4.1 **GRAND TIER** | Amer.

4.8 **JEAN-GEORGES** | French

4.7 **JEAN-GEORGES' NOUG. FRENCH**

4.1 **JOE** | Coffee

4.1 **LA BOÎTE EN BOIS** | French

4.3 **LEOPARD/DES ARTISTES** | Italian

4.5 **LINCOLN** | Italian

4.0 **NICK & TONI** | Med.

3.8 **P.J. CLARKE'S** | Pub

4.1 **ROSA MEXICANO** | Mex.

4.1 **SAPPHIRE INDIAN** | Indian

4.1 **SHUN LEE WEST** | Chinese

3.9 **SMITH** | Amer.

LOCATIONS

WEST 70S

3.9 **ALICE'S TEA** | Teahse.
4.4 **AMORINO** | Ice Cream
4.3 **BURKE & WILLS** | Australian
4.2 **CAFE LUXEMBOURG** | French
3.9 **CAFFE STORICO** | Italian
4.2 **'CESCA** | Italian
4.6 **DOVETAIL** | Amer.
4.2 **FISHTAG** | Greek/Seafood
4.0 **GRAND SICHUAN** | Chinese
4.0 **GRAY'S PAPAYA** | Hot Dogs
4.2 **HUMMUS PL.** | Israeli/Kosher/Veg.
4.0 **ISABELLA'S** | Amer./Med.
4.7 **LEVAIN BAKERY** | Bakery
4.3 **LINCOLN SQ. STEAK** | Steak
4.2 **MAISON KAYSER** | Bakery/French
3.9 **NICE MATIN** | French/Med.
4.1 **PAPPARDELLA** | Italian
3.8 **PARM** | Italian/Sandwiches
4.0 **PASHA** | Turkish
4.1 **PATSY'S PIZZERIA** | Pizza
4.2 **PICCOLO CAFE** | Coffee/Italian
4.2 **POMODORO ROSSO** | Italian
4.4 **REDFARM** | Chinese
4.0 **RIBBON** | Amer.
4.4 **SALUMERIA ROSI PARMACOTTO** | Italian
4.4 **SARAVANAA BHAVAN** | Indian/Veg.
4.1 **SCALETTA** | Italian
3.8 **SERAFINA** | Italian
4.0 **SHAKE SHACK** | Burgers
4.6 **SUSHI OF GARI** | Japanese
4.1 **TENZAN** | Japanese
4.3 **TESSA** | Med.
3.4 **W. 79TH ST. BOAT BASIN** | Amer.

WEST 80S

4.5 **BARNEY GREENGRASS** | Deli
4.2 **BLOSSOM** | Vegan/Veg.
4.2 **BODRUM** | Med./Turkish
4.3 **BUSTAN** | Med.
4.0 **CAFE LALO** | Coffee/Dessert
4.1 **CALLE OCHO** | Nuevo Latino
4.3 **CANDLE CAFE** | Vegan/Veg.
4.4 **CELESTE** | Italian
4.1 **COTTA** | Italian

4.3 **CRAVE FISHBAR** | Seafood
4.0 **5 NAPKIN BURGER** | Burgers
3.9 **GOOD ENOUGH/EAT** | Amer.
4.1 **HAMPTON CHUTNEY** | Indian
4.2 **HAN DYNASTY** | Chinese
4.0 **HARU** | Japanese
4.2 **JACOB'S PICKLES** | Southern
4.3 **JIN RAMEN** | Japanese/Noodles
4.1 **JOE** | Coffee
4.1 **KEFI** | Greek
4.2 **LAND THAI** | Thai
4.3 **LUKE'S LOBSTER** | Seafood
4.3 **MACHIAVELLI** | Italian
3.9 **MEATBALL SHOP** | Sandwiches
4.2 **MERMAID** | Seafood
4.1 **MILK BAR** | Dessert
4.3 **MILLING RM.** | Amer.
4.4 **MOMOYA** | Japanese
4.3 **MOTORINO** | Pizza
4.5 **ORWASHER'S** | Bakery/Kosher
4.0 **PEACEFOOD CAFÉ** | Kosher/Vegan/Veg.
4.3 **PIZZERIA SIRENETTA** | Pizza NEW
4.0 **SARABETH'S** | Amer.
4.2 **SPIGA** | Italian
4.1 **SPRINGNATURAL** | Health

WEST 90S

4.3 **AMSTERDAM BURGER CO.** | Burgers
4.3 **AWADH** | Indian
3.9 **BAREBURGER** | Burgers
4.1 **BIRCH COFFEE** | Coffee
4.1 **CARMINE'S** | Italian
4.5 **GENNARO** | Italian
3.9 **HALAL GUYS** | Mideast.
4.1 **KOUZAN** | Japanese
4.2 **MALECON** | Dominican
4.3 **MANHATTAN VALLEY** | Indian
4.3 **NUMERO 28** | Pizza
4.3 **PIO PIO** | Chicken/Peruvian

WEST 100S
(See also Harlem/East Harlem)
4.6 **ABSOLUTE BAGELS** | Bagels
4.3 **AWASH** | Ethiopian
4.1 **CASCABEL TAQUERIA** | Mex.
4.1 **FLOR/MAYO** | Chinese/Peruvian

4.3 **MISS MAMIE'S** | Soul

4.2 **SZECHUAN GOURMET** | Chinese

4.3 **THAI MARKET** | Thai

4.1 **TURKUAZ** | Turkish

4.2 **XI'AN** | Chinese/Noodles

WEST VILLAGE
(14th to Houston Sts., west of 6th Ave., excluding Meatpacking)

4.4 **AMY'S BREAD** | Bakery

4.7 **ANNISA** | Amer.

4.1 **A.O.C.** | French

4.2 **A SALT & BATTERY** | British

4.5 **BAR BOLONAT** | Israeli/Mideast.

4.6 **BARBUTO** | Italian

4.3 **BAR SARDINE** | Amer.

4.1 **BEATRICE INN** | Amer.

4.2 **BIG GAY ICE CREAM** | Ice Cream

4.1 **BIRCH COFFEE** | Coffee

4.2 **BLACK TAP** | Burgers

4.0 **BLENHEIM** | Amer.

4.2 **BLOSSOM** | Vegan/Veg.

4.4 **BLUE RIBBON** | Amer.

4.3 **BLUESTONE LANE** | Australian/Coffee

4.3 **BOBO** | French

4.3 **BOBWHITE** | Southern

4.1 **BOSIE TEA PARLOR** | Teahse.

4.2 **BUTCHER'S DAUGHTER** | Vegan

4.4 **BUVETTE** | French

4.1 **CAFE CLOVER** | Amer.

4.2 **CAFE CLUNY** | Amer./French

4.0 **CAFE GITANE** | French/Moroccan

3.9 **CAFE LOUP** | French

4.0 **CHOMP CHOMP** | Singapor.

4.4 **CLAM** | Seafood

4.5 **CONES** | Ice Cream

3.8 **CORNELIA ST.** | Amer.

4.2 **CORNER BISTRO** | Burgers

4.3 **CRISPO** | Italian

4.7 **DECOY** | Chinese

4.5 **DELL'ANIMA** | Italian

4.2 **DO HWA** | Korean

4.4 **DOMINIQUE ANSEL KIT.** | Bakery/French

4.2 **EL TORO BLANCO** | Mex./Seafood

4.2 **EMPELLÓN TAQ.** | Mex.

4.4 **EN JAPANESE** | Japanese

4.2 **EXTRA VIRGIN** | Med.

4.3 **FEDORA** | Amer./French

4.2 **FISH** | Seafood

4.4 **FLEX MUSSELS** | Seafood

4.4 **FRANKIES** | Italian

4.1 **GOOD** | Amer.

4.4 **GRADISCA** | Italian

4.0 **GRAND SICHUAN** | Chinese

4.0 **GREY DOG** | Amer.

4.5 **GROM** | Ice Cream

4.5 **HAKATA TONTON** | Japanese

— **HAO NOODLE** | Chinese NEW

4.1 **HUDSON CLEARWATER** | Amer.

4.2 **HUMMUS PL.** | Israeli/Kosher/Veg.

4.6 **I SODI** | Italian

4.2 **JACK'S STIR BREW** | Coffee

4.2 **JACK'S WIFE FREDA** | Amer.

4.4 **JEFFREY'S GROCERY** | Amer.

4.1 **JOE** | Coffee

4.5 **JOE'S PIZZA** | Pizza

4.3 **JOHN'S PIZZERIA** | Pizza

4.3 **JOSEPH LEONARD** | Amer.

4.4 **KESTE PIZZA** | Pizza

4.6 **KOSAKA** | Japanese NEW

4.7 **L'ARTUSI** | Italian

4.3 **LEFT BANK** | Amer.

4.5 **LE GIGOT** | French

4.5 **LITTLE OWL** | Amer./Med.

4.2 **MAISON KAYSER** | Bakery/French

4.3 **MALAPARTE** | Italian

4.3 **MALATESTA** | Italian

4.4 **MARKET TABLE** | Amer.

4.4 **MARY'S FISH** | Seafood

4.7 **MAS** | Amer.

3.9 **MEATBALL SHOP** | Sandwiches

4.4 **MÉMÉ** | Med./Moroccan

4.3 **MIGHTY QUINN'S** | BBQ

4.2 **MONUMENT LANE** | Amer.

4.2 **MORANDI** | Italian

4.2 **MOUSTACHE** | Mideast.

4.4 **MURRAY'S CHEESE** | Amer.

4.3 **NUMERO 28** | Pizza

4.1 **OFRENDA** | Mex.

4.4 **ONE IF BY LAND** | Amer.

LOCATIONS

3.9 **OTTO'S TACOS** | Mex.

4.5 **PALMA** | Italian

4.6 **PEARL OYSTER** | New Eng./ Seafood

4.3 **PERLA CAFE** | Italian

4.6 **PERRY ST.** | Amer.

4.4 **PICCOLO ANGOLO** | Italian

4.6 **PIORA** | Amer.

4.4 **PIZZETTERIA BRUNETTI** | Pizza

4.5 **PÓ** | Italian

4.5 **QUALITY EATS** | Steak `NEW`

4.5 **RAFELE** | Italian

4.4 **REDFARM** | Chinese

4.3 **ROSEMARY'S** | Italian

4.4 **SANT AMBROEUS** | Italian

— **2ND CITY** | Filipino `NEW`

4.4 **SEVILLA** | Spanish

4.3 **SNACK** | Greek

4.7 **SOTO** | Japanese

4.2 **SOTTO 13** | Italian

4.4 **SPOTTED PIG** | Euro.

4.3 **SPUNTO** | Pizza

4.7 **SUSHI NAKAZAWA** | Japanese

4.1 **SUSHISAMBA** | Brazilian/ Japanese

4.1 **TACOMBI** | Mex.

4.6 **TAÏM** | Israeli/Veg.

4.6 **TAKASHI** | Japanese

— **TAPESTRY** | Indian `NEW`

4.2 **TARTINE** | French

4.2 **TEA & SYMPATHY** | Teahse.

4.2 **TERTULIA** | Spanish

4.1 **TOBY'S ESTATE** | Coffee

4.7 **UPHOLSTERY STORE** | Amer.

4.4 **VAN LEEUWEN** | Ice Cream

4.6 **VIA CAROTA** | Italian

4.6 **WALLFLOWER** | French

4.6 **WALLSÉ** | Austrian

— **WARREN** | Amer. `NEW`

4.2 **WAVERLY INN** | Amer.

4.1 **WESTVILLE** | Amer.

4.3 **YERBA BUENA** | Pan-Latin

BRONX

ARTHUR AVENUE/BELMONT

3.8 **ANN & TONY'S** | Italian
4.4 **DOMINICK'S** | Italian
4.2 **EMILIA'S** | Italian
4.4 **ENZO'S** | Italian
4.5 **MADONIA BROS. BAKERY** | Bakery
4.1 **MARIO'S** | Italian
4.0 **PASQUALE RIGOLETTO** | Italian
4.5 **ROBERTO** | Italian
4.3 **TRA DI NOI** | Italian
4.3 **ZERO OTTO** | Italian/Pizza

BRONX PARK

4.2 **HUDSON GARDEN** | Amer.

CITY ISLAND

4.4 **ARTIE'S** | Seafood/Steak
4.0 **BLACK WHALE** | Amer.
4.1 **CITY IS. LOBSTER** | Seafood
4.2 **ORIGINAL CRAB** | Italian/Seafood
4.2 **SAMMY'S FISHBOX** | Seafood
4.2 **SAMMY'S SHRIMP** | Seafood
4.0 **SEA SHORE** | Seafood

CONCOURSE/DOWNTOWN

4.3 **NYY STEAK** | Steak

FIELDSTON

4.3 **JAKE'S STEAKHSE.** | Steak

KINGSBRIDGE

4.2 **MALECON** | Dominican

MORRIS PARK

4.4 **ENZO'S** | Italian
4.3 **PATRICIA'S** | Italian

MOTT HAVEN

4.3 **PIO PIO** | Chicken/Peruvian

RIVERDALE

4.3 **BECCOFINO** | Italian
4.3 **LIEBMAN'S** | Deli/Kosher

VAN NEST

4.3 **F & J PINE** | Italian

WAKEFIELD

4.4 **ALI'S ROTI** | Carib.

BROOKLYN

BATH BEACH
4.3 **NYONYA** | Malaysian
4.5 **TOMMASO** | Italian

BAY RIDGE
4.4 **AREO** | Italian
4.2 **CEBU** | Cont.
4.4 **CHADWICK'S** | Amer.
4.3 **DAVID'S BRISKET** | Deli
4.5 **ELIÁ** | Greek
4.2 **FUSHIMI** | Japanese
4.4 **GINO'S** | Italian
4.5 **PANEANTICO** | Bakery/Italian
4.1 **PEARL ROOM** | Seafood
4.7 **TANOREEN** | Med./Mideast.
4.5 **TUSCANY GRILL** | Italian
4.2 **VESUVIO** | Italian

BEDFORD-STUYVESANT
4.4 **ALI'S ROTI** | Carib.
4.0 **CHEZ OSKAR** | French
4.3 **DAVID'S BRISKET** | Deli
4.4 **DOUGH** | Dessert
4.3 **PEACHES** | Southern
4.4 **SARAGHINA** | Pizza

BENSONHURST
4.1 **TENZAN** | Japanese
4.7 **VILLABATE ALBA** |
Dessert/Italian

BOERUM HILL
4.6 **BATTERSBY** | Amer.
4.2 **BLUE BOTTLE** | Coffee
4.4 **FRENCH LOUIE** | Amer./French
4.2 **MILE END** | Deli/Sandwiches
4.4 **RUCOLA** | Italian
4.4 **VAN LEEUWEN** | Ice Cream

BROOKLYN HEIGHTS
— **BEASTS/BOTTLES** |
Chicken NEW
4.0 **CHIPSHOP** | British
4.5 **COLONIE** | Amer.
4.4 **FORNINO** | Pizza
4.0 **FRIEND/FARMER** | Amer.
4.0 **HANCO'S** | Viet.
4.5 **HENRY'S END** | Amer.
4.2 **JACK THE HORSE** | Amer.
4.5 **LUZZO'S** | Pizza

4.4 **NOODLE PUDDING** | Italian
4.3 **QUEEN** | Italian

BUSHWICK
4.7 **BLANCA** | Amer.
4.4 **FARO** | Italian
4.6 **MOMO SUSHI SHACK** |
Japanese
4.5 **MONTANA'S TRAIL HSE.** |
Southern
4.6 **ROBERTA'S** | Italian/Pizza
— **SUPERCROWN** | Coffee NEW
— **SYNDICATED** | Amer. NEW
— **TWIN SUNS** | Deli NEW

CARROLL GARDENS
4.1 **BROOKLYN FARMACY** |
Ice Cream
4.6 **BUTTERMILK** | Amer.
4.5 **DOVER** | Amer.
4.4 **FRAGOLE** | Italian
4.4 **FRANKIES** | Italian
4.7 **LUCALI** | Pizza
4.2 **MARCO POLO** | Italian
4.1 **MILK BAR** | Dessert
4.3 **PRIME MEATS** | Amer./Steak
— **TAKE ROOT** | Amer.
4.2 **WILMA JEAN** | Southern
4.1 **ZAYTOONS** | Mideast.

CLINTON HILL
4.3 **AITA** | Italian
4.7 **EMILY** | Pizza
4.6 **FINCH** | Amer.
4.4 **LOCANDA VINI** | Italian
4.3 **MARIETTA** | Southern
4.5 **SPEEDY ROMEO** | Italian/Pizza
4.4 **TILDA ALL DAY** | Coffee
4.1 **ZAYTOONS** | Mideast.

COBBLE HILL
4.3 **AWASH** | Ethiopian
3.9 **BAREBURGER** | Burgers
4.1 **BAR TABAC** | French
4.2 **CAFE LULUC** | French
4.4 **CHOCOLATE ROOM** | Dessert
4.5 **COURT PASTRY SHOP** |
Dessert/Italian
4.0 **HANCO'S** | Viet.

4.0 **HENRY PUBLIC** | Pub

4.6 **HIBINO** | Japanese

4.2 **JOYA** | Thai

4.5 **KI SUSHI** | Japanese

4.7 **LA VARA** | Spanish

4.3 **NUMERO 28** | Pizza

4.5 **SHELSKY'S OF BROOKLYN** | Deli/Jewish

— **TEKOÁ** | Coffee NEW

COLUMBIA STREET WATERFRONT DISTRICT

4.0 **ALMA** | Mex.

4.2 **CALEXICO** | Mex.

— **CARLA HALL'S** | Southern NEW

4.4 **POK POK NY** | Thai

4.3 **POK POK PHAT** | Thai

CONEY ISLAND

4.2 **GARGIULO'S** | Italian

4.1 **GRIMALDI'S** | Pizza

4.5 **TOTONNO'S** | Pizza

CROWN HEIGHTS

4.3 **AITA** | Italian

4.4 **ALI'S ROTI** | Carib.

3.9 **BERG'N** | Food Hall

— **BKW** | Amer. NEW

4.3 **CHAVELA'S** | Mex.

4.3 **GLADY'S** | Carib.

4.2 **MAYFIELD** | Amer.

4.3 **MIGHTY QUINN'S** | BBQ

DITMAS PARK

4.2 **FARM/ADDERLEY** | Amer.

4.3 **MIMI'S HUMMUS** | Mideast.

4.3 **PURPLE YAM** | Asian

4.5 **WHEATED** | Pizza

DOWNTOWN BROOKLYN

4.1 **BACCHUS** | French

4.8 **CHEF'S/BROOKLYN FARE** | French

4.4 **GANSO** | Japanese/Noodles

4.3 **GANSO YAKI** | Japanese

3.9 **GRAND ARMY** | Seafood

4.2 **HILL COUNTRY** | BBQ

4.1 **HILL COUNTRY CHICKEN** | Chicken/Southern

3.8 **JUNIOR'S** | Diner

— **SUSHI GANSO** | Japanese NEW

DUMBO

4.5 **ALMONDINE BAKERY** | French

4.0 **ATRIUM DUMBO** | French

4.3 **BLUESTONE LANE** | Australian/Coffee

4.4 **BROOKLYN ICE CREAM** | Ice Cream

4.3 **GRAN ELECTRICA** | Mex.

4.1 **GRIMALDI'S** | Pizza

4.7 **JULIANA'S** | Pizza

4.3 **LUKE'S LOBSTER** | Seafood

4.1 **NO. 7 SUB** | Sandwiches

4.6 **RIVER CAFÉ** | Amer.

4.0 **SHAKE SHACK** | Burgers

FLATLANDS

4.3 **MILL BASIN DELI** | *Deli/Kosher*

FORT GREENE

4.1 **CAFÉ HABANA** | Cuban/Mex.

4.2 **CAFFE E VINO** | Italian

— **KARASU** | Japanese NEW

4.2 **MADIBA** | S African

4.1 **NO. 7 SUB** | Amer.

4.5 **OLEA** | Med.

4.4 **ROMAN'S** | Italian

4.1 **SMOKE JOINT** | BBQ

4.1 **WALTER** | Amer.

GOWANUS

4.7 **AMPLE HILLS** | Ice Cream

4.4 **BABA'S PIEROGIES** | E Euro.

4.3 **BAR TANO** | Italian

4.2 **DINOSAUR BBQ** | BBQ

4.1 **FLETCHER'S** | BBQ

4.5 **FOUR & TWENTY** | Bakery

— **FREEK'S MILL** | Amer. NEW

4.3 **INSA** | Korean NEW

4.1 **LITTLENECK** | Seafood

4.3 **NINTH ST ESPRESSO** | Coffee

4.4 **PINES** | Amer.

4.4 **RUNNER & STONE** | Amer./Bakery

GRAVESEND

4.4 **L&B SPUMONI** | Ice Cream/Pizza

4.3 **PIO PIO** | Chinese/Seafood

GREENPOINT

4.3 **BAKERI** | Bakery/Euro.

4.4 **BROOKLYN ICE CREAM** | Ice Cream

4.2 **CALEXICO** | Mex.

— **CHERRY POINT** | Amer. NEW

4.4 **ESME** | Amer.

4.3 **FIVE LEAVES** | Amer.

4.4 **FORNINO** | Pizza

— **FRANKEL'S DELI** | Deli/Jewish NEW

4.6 **GLASSERIE** | Med.

4.4 **GREENPOINT FISH** | Seafood

— **HAIL MARY** | Diner NEW

4.1 **LITTLENECK** | Seafood

4.4 **LOBSTER JOINT** | New Eng./Seafood

4.5 **LUKSUS** | Amer.

3.9 **MAMAN** | Dominican/Nuevo Latino

4.5 **NAKED DOG** | Italian

4.6 **PAULIE GEE'S** | Pizza

4.5 **PETER PAN** | Dessert

— **SAUVAGE** | Amer. NEW

4.3 **SCALINO** | Italian

4.5 **TØRST** | Danish

4.4 **VAN LEEUWEN** | Ice Cream

4.2 **XI'AN** | Chinese/Noodles

MIDWOOD

4.6 **DI FARA** | Pizza

— **DI FARA DOLCE** | Dessert/Italian

MILL BASIN

4.1 **LA VILLA PIZZERIA** | Pizza

PARK SLOPE

4.6 **AL DI LA** | Italian

— **AL SEABU** | Malaysian

4.1 **ARTICHOKE BASILLE** | Pizza

3.9 **BAREBURGER** | Burgers

4.2 **BENCHMARK** | Amer./Steak

4.4 **BLUE RIBBON** | Amer.

4.2 **BOGOTA** | Pan-Latin

4.1 **BONNIE'S GRILL** | Burgers

4.4 **BRICOLAGE** | Viet.

4.2 **CALEXICO** | Mex.

4.4 **CHOCOLATE ROOM** | Dessert

4.0 **COCO ROCO** | Chicken/Peruvian

4.6 **CONVIV. OSTERIA** | Med.

4.0 **FLATBUSH FARM** | Amer.

4.3 **FONDA** | Mex.

4.3 **FRANNY'S** | Italian/Pizza

4.0 **HANCO'S** | Viet.

3.8 **HUGO & SONS** | Italian

4.4 **L' ALBERO DEI GELATI** | Ice Cream

4.1 **LA VILLA PIZZERIA** | Pizza

4.3 **LUKE'S LOBSTER** | Seafood

4.1 **MIRIAM** | Israeli/Med.

4.3 **NUMERO 28** | Pizza

4.1 **PATSY'S PIZZERIA** | Pizza

4.6 **ROSE WATER** | Amer.

4.3 **SCALINO** | Italian

4.1 **SCOTTADITO** | Italian

4.0 **SHAKE SHACK** | Burgers

4.1 **SONG** | Thai

4.5 **STONE PARK** | Amer.

4.4 **TALDE** | Asian

4.0 **12TH ST. B&G** | Amer.

4.3 **WASAN** | Japanese

PROSPECT HEIGHTS

4.3 **AMORINA** | Italian/Pizza

4.7 **AMPLE HILLS** | Ice Cream

4.4 **BAR CORVO** | Italian

4.3 **CHERYL'S GLOBAL** | Soul

4.3 **CHUKO** | Japanese/Noodles

4.3 **DOUGHNUT PLANT** | Dessert

4.3 **EL ATORADERO** | Mex. NEW

4.5 **FOUR & TWENTY** | Bakery

— **FAUN** | Italian NEW

4.4 **JAMES** | Amer.

4.1 **MORGANS BBQ** | BBQ

— **NORM** | Eclectic NEW

— **OLMSTED** | Amer. NEW

— **PLANT LOVE** | Thai NEW

4.2 **ROSE'S** | Amer.

— **TYGERSHARK** | Korean NEW

4.1 **WHITE TIGER** | Korean

4.1 **ZAYTOONS** | Mideast.

PROSPECT PARK

4.3 **SMORGASBURG** | Food Hall

RED HOOK

4.4 **BAKED** | Bakery

4.0 **BROOKLYN CRAB** | Seafood

4.5 **DEFONTE'S** | Sandwiches

4.2 **FORT DEFIANCE** | Amer.

4.4 **GOOD FORK** | Eclectic

4.6 **HOMETOWN** | BBQ
4.2 **KAO SOY** | Thai
4.6 **PIZZA MOTO** | Pizza
4.3 **RED HOOK LOBSTER** | Seafood

SHEEPSHEAD BAY

4.3 **BRENNAN** | Sandwiches
4.2 **JORDANS LOBSTER** | Seafood
4.2 **RANDAZZO'S** | Seafood
4.0 **ROLL-N-ROASTER** |
Sandwiches
4.0 **SAHARA** | Turkish
4.6 **TACI'S BEYTI** | Turkish

SUNSET PARK

4.1 **99 FAVOR TASTE** | Chinese/
Korean
4.3 **NYONYA** | Malaysian
4.5 **PACIFICANA** | Chinese

VINEGAR HILL

4.4 **VINEGAR HILL HSE.** | Amer.

WILLIAMSBURG

4.1 **ALLSWELL** | Amer.
4.6 **ANTICA PESA** | Italian
— **ASKA** | Scan. NEW
4.4 **AURORA** | Italian
4.3 **BACI & ABBRACCI** | Italian
4.3 **BAKERI** | Bakery/Euro.
4.3 **BAMONTE'S** | Italian
— **BARANO** | Italian NEW
4.3 **BEEHIVE** | Southern
4.4 **BEST PIZZA** | Pizza
4.3 **BLACK TREE** | Amer.
4.2 **BLUE BOTTLE** | Coffee
4.4 **BLUE RIBBON** | Amer.
— **BRASSERIE WITLOF** | Belgian
4.3 **BRISKETTOWN** | BBQ
4.4 **BROOKLYN STAR** | Southern
4.3 **CAFE MOGADOR** | Moroccan
4.4 **CARACAS** | Venez.
4.2 **COMMODORE** | Southern
4.1 **CRIF DOGS** | Hot Dogs
4.5 **DAVEY'S** | Ice Cream
4.5 **DELAWARE/HUDSON** | Amer.
4.4 **DESNUDA** | S Amer.
4.5 **DINER** | Amer.
4.4 **D.O.C. WINE BAR** | Italian
4.3 **DUMONT BURGER** | Burgers

4.3 **DUN-WELL DOUGHNUTS** |
Dessert/Vegan
4.3 **EGG** | Southern
— **EMMY SQUARED** | Pizza NEW
4.2 **EXTRA FANCY** | Seafood
4.5 **FETTE SAU** | BBQ
4.4 **FORNINO** | Pizza
4.3 **FORTUNATO BROTHERS** |
Bakery/Italian
4.5 **FOUR HORSEMEN** | Amer.
4.2 **FUSHIMI** | Japanese
4.5 **JOE'S PIZZA** | Pizza
4.4 **KINGS COUNTY IMPERIAL** |
Chinese
4.3 **LA ESQUINA** | Mex.
4.4 **LE BARRICOU** | French
4.6 **LILIA** | Italian NEW
4.5 **LLAMA INN** | Peruvian NEW
4.5 **MAISON PREMIERE** | Seafood
4.4 **MARLOW/SONS** | Amer.
4.7 **MEADOWSWEET** | Amer./Med.
3.9 **MEATBALL SHOP** | Sandwiches
4.4 **MESA COYOACAN** | Mex.
— **MEYERS BAGERI** | Bakery NEW
4.1 **MILK BAR** | Dessert
4.3 **MOTORINO** | Pizza
4.3 **MP TAVERNA** | Greek
4.4 **ODDFELLOWS** | Ice Cream
4.4 **OKONOMI** | Japanese
— **OLEANDERS** | Amer.
4.5 **1 OR 8** | Japanese
3.8 **PARM** | Italian/Sandwiches
4.8 **PETER LUGER** | Steak
4.3 **PIES-N-THIGHS** | Southern
4.1 **QI** | Asian/Thai
4.4 **REYNARD** | Amer.
— **RIDER** | Amer. NEW
4.4 **RYE** | Amer.
4.0 **SEA** | Thai
4.6 **SEMILLA** | Amer.
4.5 **SHALOM JAPAN** | Japanese/
Jewish
4.3 **SMORGASBURG** | Food Hall
4.5 **ST. ANSELM** | Amer./Steak
4.3 **SWEET CHICK** | Southern
4.4 **SWEETGREEN** | Health
4.1 **TOBY'S ESTATE** | Coffee
4.6 **TRAIF** | Eclectic
4.3 **12 CHAIRS** | Amer./Mideast.

LOCATIONS

4.0 **UMAMI BURGER** | Burgers

4.0 **VANESSA'S DUMPLING** |
Seafood

4.4 **VAN LEEUWEN** | Ice Cream

4.1 **WALTER** | Amer.

— **WIN SON** |
Amer./Taiwanese NEW

4.6 **XIXA** | Mex.

4.6 **ZENKICHI** | Japanese

4.2 **ZONA ROSA** | Mex.

WINDSOR TERRACE

4.2 **KRUPA** | Amer.

QUEENS

ASTORIA

4.3 **AGNANTI** | Greek
4.3 **AREPAS** | Venez.
4.3 **AREPAS** | Venez.
4.1 **ARTICHOKE BASILLE** | Pizza
3.9 **ASTOR ROOM** | Amer.
4.4 **BAHARI ESTIATORIO** | Greek
3.9 **BAREBURGER** | Burgers
4.2 **BONCHON** | Chicken
4.3 **BUTCHER BAR** | BBQ
4.4 **CHRISTOS** | Steak
4.5 **ELIAS CORNER** | Greek/ Seafood
4.5 **IL BAMBINO** | Italian
4.5 **LOUKOUMI** | Greek
4.5 **MILKFLOWER** | Pizza
4.3 **MP TAVERNA** | Greek
4.2 **OVELIA** | Greek
4.0 **PACHANGA PATTERSON** | Mex.
4.6 **PICCOLA VENEZIA** | Italian
4.2 **QUEENS COMFORT** | Southern
4.0 **QUEENS KICKSHAW** | Coffee/ Sandwiches
4.1 **SANFORD'S** | Amer.
4.4 **SEVA INDIAN** | Indian
4.2 **STAMATIS** | Greek
4.1 **STRAND SMOKEHSE.** | BBQ
4.1 **SUGAR FREAK** | Cajun/Creole
4.3 **TACUBA** | Mex.
4.5 **TAVERNA KYCLADES** | Greek/ Seafood
4.4 **TELLY'S TAVERNA** | Greek/ Seafood
4.7 **TRATT. L'INCONTRO** | Italian
4.4 **VESTA** | Italian

BAYSIDE

4.2 **BCD TOFU** | Korean
4.0 **BEN'S KOSHER** | Deli/Kosher
4.2 **BONCHON** | Chicken
4.1 **DONOVAN'S** | Amer.
4.3 **ERAWAN** | Thai
4.3 **PRESS 195** | Sandwiches
4.4 **RALPH'S FAMOUS** | Ice Cream
4.3 **UNCLE JACK'S** | Steak

BELLEROSE

3.9 **JACKSON DINER** | *Indian*

CORONA

4.6 **LEMON ICE KING** | Ice Cream
4.6 **LEO'S LATTICINI/CORONA** | Italian/Sandwiches
4.5 **PARK SIDE** | Italian
4.5 **TORTILLERIA NIXTAMAL** | Mex.

DOUGLASTON

4.1 **GRIMALDI'S** | Pizza
4.3 **LA BARAKA** | French

ELMHURST

4.6 **AREPA LADY** | S Amer.
4.5 **AYADA** | Thai
4.1 **PHO BANG** | Noodles/Viet.
4.0 **PING'S SEAFOOD** | Chinese/ Seafood
4.1 **ZABB ELEE** | Thai

FLUSHING

4.1 **DUMPLING GALAXY** | Chinese
4.4 **GOLDEN SHOPPING MALL** | Chinese
4.2 **JOE'S SHANGHAI** | Chinese
4.2 **KUM GANG SAN** | Korean
4.0 **KYOCHON** | Chicken
4.5 **MAPO KOREAN** | Korean
4.1 **NEW WORLD MALL** | Food Hall
4.1 **PHO BANG** | Noodles/Viet.
4.4 **SPICY & TASTY** | Chinese
4.2 **SZECHUAN GOURMET** | Chinese
4.4 **WHITE BEAR** | Chinese
4.2 **XI'AN** | Chinese/Noodles

FOREST HILLS

3.9 **AGORA TAV.** | Greek
4.3 **ALBERTO** | Italian
4.2 **CABANA** | Nuevo Latino
4.3 **DEE'S** | Pizza
4.5 **EDDIE'S SWEET SHOP** | Ice Cream
4.0 **GRAND SICHUAN** | Chinese
4.4 **LA VIGNA** | Italian
4.5 **NICK'S** | Pizza

GLENDALE
4.5 **ZUM STAMMTISCH** | German

GLEN OAKS
4.3 **LUIGI'S** | Italian
4.4 **RALPH'S FAMOUS** | Ice Cream

HOWARD BEACH
4.1 **LA VILLA PIZZERIA** | Pizza

JACKSON HEIGHTS
3.9 **JACKSON DINER** | Indian
4.3 **PIO PIO** | Chicken/Peruvian

JFK AIRPORT
4.1 **BLUE SMOKE** | BBQ
4.2 **BOBBY VAN'S** | Steak

LONG ISLAND CITY
3.9 **ALOBAR** | Amer.
3.9 **BAREBURGER** | Burgers
3.8 **BELLA VIA** | Italian
4.1 **BIRCH COFFEE** | Coffee
4.0 **CAFÉ HENRI** | French
4.5 **CASA ENRIQUE** | Mex.
4.2 **CORNER BISTRO** | Burgers
4.6 **HIBINO** | Japanese
4.4 **IL FALCO** | Italian
4.3 **JOHN BROWN** | BBQ
4.3 **LIC MARKET** | Amer.
4.5 **MAIELLA** | Italian
4.3 **MANDUCATIS RUSTICA** | Italian
4.4 **MANETTA'S** | Italian
4.5 **MU RAMEN** | Japanese/Noodles
4.1 **M. WELLS DINETTE** | Québécois

4.3 **M. WELLS STEAKHSE.** | Steak
4.1 **SHI** | Asian
4.3 **TOURNESOL** | French

MIDDLE VILLAGE
4.3 **LONDON LENNIE'S** | Seafood
4.3 **PIO PIO** | Chicken/Peruvian
4.4 **RALPH'S FAMOUS** | Ice Cream

REGO PARK
4.2 **BAROSA** | Italian
4.3 **BEN'S BEST** | Deli/Kosher

RIDGEWOOD
4.5 **BUNKER VIET.** | Viet.
4.5 **HOUDINI KIT.** | Pizza

ROCKAWAY BEACH
4.4 **CARACAS** | Venez.

SOUTH OZONE PARK
4.7 **DON PEPPE** | Italian

SUNNYSIDE
4.4 **AMY'S BREAD** | Bakery
4.3 **DOUGHNUT PLANT** | Dessert
4.3 **SALT & FAT** | Amer./Asian

WHITESTONE
4.4 **RALPH'S FAMOUS** | Ice Cream

WILLETS POINT
4.2 **FUKU** | Chicken/Sandwiches
4.6 **LEO'S LATTICINI/CORONA** | Italian/Sandwiches

WOODSIDE
4.1 **DONOVAN'S** | Amer.
4.6 **SRIPRAPHAI** | Thai

STATEN ISLAND

ARDEN HEIGHTS
4.4 RALPH'S FAMOUS |
Ice Cream

BLOOMFIELD
4.1 LORENZO'S | *Italian*

CASTLETON CORNERS
4.4 JOE & PAT'S | *Italian/Pizza*

DONGAN HILLS
4.6 TRATT. ROMANA | *Italian*

ELM PARK
4.5 DENINO'S | *Pizza*
4.4 RALPH'S FAMOUS | *Ice Cream*

GRANT CITY
4.2 FUSHIMI | *Japanese*

MARINERS HARBOR
4.2 REAL MADRID | *Spanish*

NEW DORP
4.4 BRIOSO | *Italian*
4.4 RALPH'S FAMOUS | *Ice Cream*

OLD TOWN
4.5 BOCELLI | *Italian/Seafood*

PRINCE'S BAY
4.4 RALPH'S FAMOUS | *Ice Cream*

RANDALL MANOR
4.2 NURNBERGER BIERHAUS |
German

ROSEBANK
4.3 BAYOU | *Cajun*

SHORE ACRES
4.2 DA NOI | *Italian*

ST. GEORGE
4.6 BESO | *Spanish*
4.4 ENOTECA MARIA | *Italian*

STAPLETON
4.5 DEFONTE'S | *Sandwiches*

TODT HILL
4.5 CAROL'S CAFE | *Eclectic*

TOTTENVILLE
4.1 ANGELINA'S | *Italian*
4.1 DA NICO | *Italian*
4.1 NUCCI'S | *Italian*

TRAVIS-CHELSEA
4.2 DA NOI | *Italian*

WEST BRIGHTON
4.1 NUCCI'S | *Italian*